Learning and Cognition

FIFTH EDITION

Learning and Cognition

Thomas Hardy Leahey
Virginia Commonwealth University

Richard Jackson Harris
Kansas State University

Prentice
Hall

Upper Saddle River, New Jersey 07458

Library of Congress Cataloging-in-Publication Data:

Leahey, Thomas Hardy.
   Learning and cognition / Thomas Hardy Leahey, Richard Jackson Harris.—5th ed.
     p.   cm.
   Includes bibliographical references and index.
   ISBN 0-13-040199-4
   1. Learning, Psychology of.   2. Cognition.   3. Human information processing.   I. Harris,
Richard Jackson.   II. Title.
BF318 .L37 2000
153.1—dc21

                                                        00-055766

VP, Editorial Director: Laura Pearson
Acquisitions Editor: Jayme Heffler
Editorial Assistant: April Dawn Klemm
Managing Editor: Mary Rottino
Production Liaison: Fran Russello
Project Manager: Publications Development Company of Texas
Prepress and Manufacturing Buyer: Tricia Kenny
Cover Art Director: Jayne Conte
Cover Designer: Bruce Kenselaar
Marketing Manager: Sharon Cosgrove

This book was set in 10/12 Times Roman by Publications Development Company of Texas
and was printed and bound by R. R. Donnelly & Sons Company.
The cover was printed by Phoenix Color Corporation.

 © 2001, 1997, 1992, 1987, 1980 by Prentice-Hall, Inc.
A Division of Pearson Education
Upper Saddle River, New Jersey 07458

Printed in the United States of America

10 9 8 7 6 5 4 3 2

ISBN 0-13-040199-4

Prentice-Hall International (UK) Limited, *London*
Prentice-Hall of Australia Pty. Limited, *Sydney*
Prentice-Hall Canada Inc., *Toronto*
Prentice-Hall Hispanoamericana, S.A., *Mexico*
Prentice-Hall of India Private Limited, *New Delhi*
Prentice-Hall of Japan, Inc., *Tokyo*
Pearson Education Asia Pte. Ltd., *Singapore*
Editora Prentice-Hall do Brasil, Ltda., *Rio de Janeiro*

Contents

Preface

The great systematic controversies that used to shape the field of learning and cognition are over. With the exception of the small community of radical behaviorists, the study of learning and cognition belongs to cognitive science and the computer model of mind, whether symbol-system based or connectionist. Our book has been reorganized to reflect this fact. The prior emphasis on metatheoretical disputes is greatly reduced, and the text is now organized to move from the simple aspects of learning and cognition to the more complex. Part I provides a general overview of the field, first through history and philosophy (Chapter 1) and then through discussion of the architectures of cognition that guide today's cognitive scientists (Chapter 2, Chapter 10 in the fourth edition). This chapter also now contains a treatment of evolutionary theory and human evolution, including the evolution of intelligence. Part II is a two-chapter version of the previous three chapters on behaviorist theories of conditioning and learning, focusing now on the simpler processes of cognition as studied primarily in animal models. Discussions of Hull, Tolman, and Skinner remain (Chapter 4), but the space devoted to them has been reduced, and their treatment now is organized around a few general empirical issues in the study of conditioning. Part III moves into the realm of information processing (Chapter 5) and memory (Chapter 6). Part IV treats the higher mental processes of language (Chapter 7), comprehension and discourse (Chapter 8), and thinking (Chapter 9). These chapters include dozens of new references from the 1990s to reflect the many advances in the field since the fourth edition. Part V is concerned with the development of cognition (Chapter 10) and language (Chapter 11).

In general, the biggest change in the new edition reflects the increasing importance of cognitive neuroscience, which is given its own section (Part VI). Although this book is not a text in cognitive neuroscience, it is becoming increasingly difficult to talk about cognition without talking about events occurring in the brain. For example, the number of studies of cognitive processing through using techniques of brain imaging (CT, PET, fMRI) has been exploding recently and has produced a window into the neurological basis of cognition never before available. Chapter 12, on the neurophysiology of learning and cognition, has been expanded from its old emphasis on learning and memory to broader treatment of cognitive neuroscience in most of its aspects. There is a new chapter on emotion (Chapter 13), one of the hottest and most significant areas in cognitive science and neuroscience today. Findings from cognitive neurosciences are also included throughout the text. Evolutionary psychology, of course, remains, as a key aspect of understanding the human mind, though parts have been moved to Chapter 2, as noted.

We have reorganized some of the chapters to reflect the latest thinking in the field. For example, Chapter 8 (Comprehension) is now organized around the framework of the different levels of representation in discourse processing offered by Graesser, et al. (1997), including the surface code, propositional textbase, and situation model levels. Finally, we have added some new boxes discussing interesting applications and areas of new research. Some of these include change blindness (Chapter 5); remembering your child's immunizations (Chapter 6); gender and language in the workplace (Chapter 7); mistaking rhyming for accuracy (Chapter 7); bialphabetic writing in the former Yugoslavia (Chapter 7); argumentation as a cultural attribute (Chapter 9); emotional control, and emotional letting-go and health (Chapter 13).

As always, we would like to hear any comments that students, professors, and readers may have about this new edition of *Learning and Cognition*. THL was the primary author of Chapters 1–4 and 10–14. RJH was the primary author of Chapters 5–9.

THOMAS HARDY LEAHEY
tleahey@vcu.edu

RICHARD JACKSON HARRIS
rjharris@ksu.edu

PART I

INTRODUCTION

1   History and Issues

LEARNING, COGNITION, AND PHILOSOPHY

How people learn and know (*cognize* means know) is a question much older than organized psychology. Philosophers and biologists have wondered and investigated how people perceive, know, and learn since the time of the ancient Greeks. Their ideas shaped and continue to shape how psychologists study learning and the theories they have constructed to explain learning and cognition.

Like all sciences, psychology was originally part of philosophy and inherited many of its problems and proposed solutions from the parent discipline. With regard to learning and cognition, two philosophical issues are most important—the problem of how we know, and the mind-body problem.

Knowing the World

One subdiscipline of philosophy is *epistemology,* concerned with the nature of human knowledge. The epistemologist wants to know what knowledge is, how to distinguish knowledge from opinion and falsehood, how people acquire knowledge, and how they use it. The study of cognition is part of epistemology, and the psychology of learning and cognition has inherited from epistemology a set of orientations to knowledge and its acquisition.

Perhaps the oldest theory of knowledge is the *copy theory* of cognition originally proposed by the Greek philosophers Alcmaeon, Empedocles, and Democritus in the fourth and fifth centuries B.C. According to copy theory, we perceive an object, and the act of perception creates a mental copy of the object in our minds. We know only the copy, because it exists in our minds and we are directly acquainted with it; we know about the object only indirectly, via the copy. Because epistemology is about knowledge, it might seem, then, that knowledge—what we are certain of—concerns the copies of objects in our heads, not objects themselves.

Unfortunately, this leaves us in a disquieting situation, one that made many philosophers search for a better epistemology. Copy theory created the problem of *skepticism:* Is it possible to know the world at all? Our mental copies might never correspond to reality. If so, knowledge would not be worth much, being only about sensations in our heads, and never about anything outside of us.

From the standpoint of the psychology of learning and cognition, three aspects of the skeptical problem are important: *realism, idealism,* and *pragmatism.*

The skeptical problem lies in questioning the resemblance of the mental copy of the real object. The skeptic points out that the representation may not resemble the object, and since we only know the copy, there is no way to verify if the copy is accurate. One answer to the skeptic is to reject the copy theory in favor of *realism*. Realism restores knowledge of the real world by eliminating the copy. According to the realist we know objects directly, without the intervention of any mental representation. It was first proposed by the eighteenth-century Scottish philosopher Thomas Reid. According to Reid, the realist view is the one ordinary people believe without philosophical tutoring—the Scottish commonsense school. The philosophical problem with realism has always been the problem of error. If, as the realist says, we know the world directly, how is it that we make mistakes, thinking that what we see is a ladybug when it is really a spot of paint?

Returning to the skeptical challenge, we can see another, perhaps more drastic, way of answering the skeptic, first suggested by the Greek philosopher Plato, then developed by a number of philosophers in the eighteenth and nineteenth centuries. The skeptical problem is the possible lack of correspondence between object and representation; the *realist* solves the problem by eliminating the representation: The *idealist* solves the problem by eliminating the object! If ideas—representations—are all that exist, then there is no skeptical problem, because our knowledge is of ideas, not things. The audacious proposal of the idealist can be supported by serious arguments, but doing so would take us too far afield.

The realist and the idealist accept the skeptical challenge and abandon the copy theory for theories of cognition that do not rely on copies. The *pragmatist* sticks with the copy theory and attacks the skeptic. The force of the skeptic's argument depends on an absolute conception of knowledge. If we assume that knowledge must be perfectly and absolutely true now and forever, the skeptic's point is disquieting: If we can be wrong about one thing—the ladybug or the spot of paint—then we can be wrong about everything. The pragmatist simply replies that being wrong about one thing does not mean that we are wrong about everything; most of the time our beliefs work out.

Each of these views will find a place among the psychological theorists discussed in this book. The copy theory will be found in the later theory of E. C. Tolman, one of the two greatest learning theorists of the behaviorist era. It is also found in the representational theory of knowledge of the symbol system hypothesis in contemporary cognitive science. Cognitive science draws a strong parallel between the workings of a computer and the workings of the human mind. Computers represent the world internally and perform computations on the representations. Thus, holds the cognitive scientist, people form representations of the world and think with them.

Realism will be found in the radical behaviorism founded by B. F. Skinner. Skinner denounced the copy theory of knowledge as part of his general denunciation of mentalistic theorizing in psychology. Instead, Skinner believed that the environment controls us directly, without any intervention of mental processes. If there are no representations, then there are no mental processes to operate on them, and we may safely delete reference to them from scientific psychology.

There are no outright idealists in psychology today, but idealism's influence is real nevertheless. The great contribution of idealism to epistemology was pointing out that the environment does not simply impose itself on us. The tendency of both copy theorists and realists is to think that objects make impressions on the mind the way a signet ring leaves an impression in soft wax. The idealist, however, rejects this passive view of human perception, holding that every perception is an act of interpretation. A view accepting the constructive nature of perception—the idealist lesson—is incorporated in the constructivist view of perception and memory in cognitive psychology, and in Jean Piaget's genetic epistemology.

Finally, pragmatism is the working philosophy of most psychologists. The philosophy of pragmatism was propounded and developed by three of the founders of American psychology, Charles S. Peirce, William James, and John Dewey. The working psychologist may ignore the ultimate philosophical import of his theories. If the copy theory is a correct account of human cognition, then that is what the psychologist must be concerned with, no matter the consequences for absolute truth. The psychologist is, then, a natural pragmatist, concerned with how people in fact learn. At the same time, a philosopher might decide that epistemology must rest on the best psychological account of real human thinking. In modern cognitive science, the pragmatist-psychologist and some philosophers have come together to pursue naturalized epistemology, an account of knowledge resting upon psychological research instead of on philosophical speculation.

The Mind-Body Problem

The conceptual foundations of cognitive science lie in the history of philosophers' and psychologists' struggles with the mind-body problem. Philosophy of mind bequeathed to cognitive science both its central problem—how mind and body are related—and a set of strategies for dealing with it. While the puzzle over mind and body is ancient, the French philosopher, psychologist, and scientist René Descartes (1596–1650) created its modern formulation and the problems that came with it.

Dualism

By introspectively reflecting on his own mind, Descartes arrived at an answer to the mind-body problem called *dualism*. Descartes proposed that every human being is a bipartite creature, composed of a material body and an immaterial soul. Soul and body interacted, Descartes thought, via the pineal gland, a small organ at the base of the brain whose exact functions remain obscure. At first glance, Descartes' proposal seems consistent with religious conceptions of the soul. Most religions, including Christianity, Islam, and Hinduism, hold dualistic conceptions of human beings. According to religious dualism, the soul is the essence of a person and survives bodily death, so that when a soul is separated from its host body—as in heaven for Christians and Muslims—it remembers its life on earth and possesses all the normal functions of an embodied human mind.

Descartes, however, took a much narrower view of the functions of the soul. Like Christian and Muslim theologians, Descartes held that only human beings have souls. But as a scientific observer of nature, Descartes realized that animals share many psychological functions with human beings. For example, dogs learn to obey commands, and cats can remember where they have caught mice. Therefore, the brain alone, without the presence of a soul, can carry out the supposedly mental functions of learning and memory. The only psychological function unique to the soul, according to Descartes, was thinking, and its vehicle, language, was a capacity restricted to the human species. For a strict Cartesian, the soul that survives bodily death is an impersonal one, shorn of memory and personal identity, as in some Buddhist conceptions.

Descartes' answer to the mind-body problem was awkward and ultimately self-destructive. On the one hand, Descartes' dualism honored human intuition by radically separating thought and brain. At the same time, as a leading scientist of the Scientific Revolution, Descartes knew that much of what ancient generations had deemed mysterious and spiritual—the angelic revolution of the heavenly spheres, for example—could be explained as the result of material, natural processes alone. Descartes felt the attraction of the central dogma of science, naturalism, the idea that all events (however spiritual they may seem) have material, natural causes. His dualism is, as a result, a compromise between religion and intuition on the one hand, and the imperative of scientific explanation on the other. Where it seemed plausible, Descartes deferred to naturalistic science, and explained mental—previously soulful—functions in physiological terms. For example, Descartes was the first psychologist to describe the reflex and propose its physiological basis. Where it seemed beyond the reach of matter, as in thinking and self-consciousness, Descartes remained with the dualistic, religious view.

The Challenges of Consciousness

Descartes identified thinking and thus the soul with consciousness, or more precisely with self-consciousness. He believed animals are aware, but they are not self-aware. We do many things, such as driving a car over familiar roads, without reflection at all, with our minds elsewhere. We see and respond to traffic lights, but we do not think about them, and so are not really aware of them. Descartes thought that animal consciousness is always like that, and that because they do not have souls, it is never like the consciousness we have when we are actively thinking about something (Gaukroger, 1995). Descartes' conclusions made consciousness a seemingly intractable problem that has bedeviled psychologists, philosophers, biologists, and physicists from his day to ours (Crick, 1994; Dennett, 1991; Flanagan, 1993; Leahey, 1994; Searle, 1993). Before Descartes, the word *consciousness* was hardly used, even by Socrates, Plato, or Aristotle, despite their concern with human life and the human mind. After Descartes, consciousness became a standing affront to science and remains perhaps the deepest mystery that has yet to "fall to science" (Dennett, 1991).

The first blow for materialism—the belief that there is no soul at all, that people are simply complex animals—was struck by J.-O. La Mettrie (1709–1751), a physician and psychologist, in his 1748 book, *L'Homme Machine.* While admiring Descartes for incorporating so much of the traditional Christian soul into naturalistic science, La Mettrie argued that Descartes had shied away from the logical conclusion of his arguments, that all the functions of the so-called "soul," including thought and language, were functions of the brain. Writing from his experience as a physician, La Mettrie pointed out that thought processes were affected by states of the body. Thinking is different when a person is ill than when healthy, when drunk than when sober. It was plausible to believe, La Mettrie proposed, that thinking was just as much a bodily function as any other. In the ensuing decades, La Mettrie's materialism—the view that the soul is as mythical as the gods—became accepted by more and more people until in one form or another it was the common belief among psychologists of the twentieth century (Leahey, 2000).

Although it was controversial in 1748, by the mid-nineteenth century scientific psychologists followed La Mettrie in subtracting the soul from Descartes' metaphysics, leaving behind only consciousness. The soul eludes science by definition. If souls exist, they are supernatural and have no place in science. Descartes had not, as he asserted, proved the existence of the soul. What Descartes had apparently established instead was the reality of a private inner world, consciousness. We do not apprehend our souls, but we do apprehend our experience. Human beings are self-aware in ways no animal, perhaps, can be. Subtracting the soul from Cartesianism, however, creates a scientific problem. If consciousness is real, and not a manifestation of a supernatural soul, then how is it connected to the body? Certainly consciousness does not seem to be a bodily process; when we look inward, we do not find neural firings, only thoughts and feelings. We experience red, joy, sweet, hot, and anger, not brain processes. The mystery of the soul was replaced by the mystery of consciousness.

Descartes' dualism is double: It is first a dualism of soul versus body, and it is also a dualism of subjective conscious experience versus objective external reality. Consciousness was not a problem for ancients and medievals, because for them all of experience was objectively "out there," in the physical world. For Descartes and other scientists, only a very few aspects of experience were objectively "out there," most were subjective, locked up in the private consciousness of the mind.

The ancient copy theory created the problem of skepticism. To this, Cartesian dualism added the problem of consciousness. Where did the subjective world come from? Moreover, the problem of consciousness was threatening. Scientists and philosophers strove heroically to provide a complete and objective account of the world, yet right in their own heads was another world, the world of consciousness whose subjectivity defied objective, naturalistic science (Searle, 1992). So great was the threat that consciousness was banished from psychology altogether. Behaviorists and cognitive scientists said little about consciousness, but it has recently returned as an important topic of research and controversy. What place, if any, should consciousness have in the scientific architecture of cognition? Does consciousness play a role in causing behavior, or is it a helpless observer of the world and its body's responses to it?

The Challenge of Evolution: Why Are We Conscious?

In the middle of the nineteenth century the problem of consciousness acquired a new dimension raised by the theory of evolution: What is consciousness good for in the struggle for survival? William James took up the evolutionary function of consciousness in earnest in his great work *Principles of Psychology* (1890).

James began by attacking the *automaton theory* advocated by some natural scientists. By denying them souls and consciousness, Descartes had proposed that the behavior of animals was entirely caused by the mechanical operations of their nervous systems. No thought was needed. Soon after, naturalistically inclined thinkers proposed that human beings, too, were mere machines, and this line of scientistic thought had reached its apogee in the nineteenth century. Darwin's great popularizer, Thomas Henry Huxley wrote:

> The consciousness of brutes [animals] would appear to be related to the mechanism of their body simply as a collateral by product of its working, and to be completely without any power of modifying that working as the steam-whistle which accompanies the work of a locomotive engine is without influence on its machinery. . . . The soul stands to the body as the bell of a clockwork to the works, and consciousness answers to the sound which the bell gives out when it is struck. . . . [Moreover] the argumentation which applies to brutes holds equally good of men. . . . [O]ur mental conditions are simply the

symbols in consciousness of the changes which takes place in the organism. . . . We are conscious automata. (Quoted by James, 1890, Vol. 1, p. 131)

According to this view, consciousness is not good for anything, it serves no purpose in evolution, contributing nothing to survival, or even responsible behavior. Every automobile must have some color, but an auto's color contributes nothing to its operation. Similarly, according to the automaton theory, brains have consciousness, but consciousness contributes nothing to causing behavior. Huxley once said that he would be happy to be a machine if only he could be wound up so as to behave properly.

James, however, rejected the automaton hypothesis as "an impertinence," and marshaled impressive arguments that consciousness has a vital evolutionary function. James argued that "consciousness is at all times primarily *a selecting agency*," (Vol. 1, p. 139) and that without such an agency survival would not occur.

A mere machine, James urged, behaves blindly and therefore not adaptively. When she was little, my daughter had a plastic Snoopy-the-dog doll. Wound up, it would walk on its hind legs. The problem with mechanical behavior, as James pointed out, is that it is blind to challenges and changes in the environment. Snoopy would walk over the edge of a table or forever into a wall unless someone prevented it. A creature like Snoopy would not last very long in the evolutionary struggle for existence. Endow Snoopy with consciousness, however, and it gains choice and increases its chances of survival. Without consciousness, Snoopy doesn't care if he lives or dies; with consciousness, things change. Consciousness is a "fighter for ends" which decrees that "Survival shall occur, and therefore organs must so work" (James, 1890, Vol. 1, p. 141).

James' assertion that the evolutionary function of consciousness is selection—choice—has three closely related facets.

1. Conscious choice makes learning—adapting to changed conditions—possible. The psychological equivalent of Snoopy-like behavior is habit. We perform familiar routines without thought, habitually running off behaviors that have worked in the past. Only when habit fails us—an auto accident blocks our usual drive to work—do we become conscious, carefully choosing new behaviors to cope with a changed environment. James' linkage of consciousness to learning helped make it the central topic of psychology for Thorndike and later theorists, although eventually they studied adaptive behavior without reference to mental processes.

2. Not only does consciousness enable us to choose new, more adaptive behaviors, it allows us to shape our very experience. In many situations, we find ourselves bombarded by more information than we can handle, and we have the ability, studied as focal attention, to track some stimuli at the expense of others. Many information-processing psychologists follow James in identifying consciousness with focal attention.

3. Central to attention and learning is the most basic function of consciousness from James' point of view, giving its bearer interests. Mere machines have no interests; they do not care if they live or die, if they adapt or become extinct. It is consciousness that endows organisms with a will to live. As the philosopher Wilfred Sellars said to another philosopher, Daniel Dennett, over a bottle of fine wine: "But Dan, qualia [conscious sensations] are what make life worth living" (Dennett, 1991, p. 383). This aspect of consciousness will be taken up in Chapter 13.

Without consciousness, James concluded, animals and human beings would not survive. Consciousness gives each organism a reason to live and the means to live, the ability to attend to what's important in the environment and ignore what's not, and to adaptively cope to changed circumstances. We cannot be automata accidentally endowed with consciousness.

Despite James' plea that consciousness be taken seriously because without it animals and humans could not adapt to a changing world, consciousness faded from psychology because its very existence remained the mystery Descartes had made it. In fact, advances in understanding the nervous system made consciousness ever more puzzling. When we respond to a stimulus, there must be a complete neural path from the sensory receptors that register the stimulus to the motor neurons that cause our response. For example, if we see a friend on the street and say "Hi!" we could in principle trace a complete neural path from the light receptors on the retina into the brain and out again to the muscles controlling our vocal system. There seems no place for consciousness to play a role in affecting our response. As James' handpicked successor at Harvard, Hugo Münsterberg, said, from the standpoint of the organism's survival, it is irrelevant if a response is accompanied by consciousness. The material, neural machinery of the body, seems to be all that is needed.

For decades after James, psychologists dealt with consciousness in two ways. A few psychologists hoped to find the neurological seat of consciousness in the brain, but they were hampered by the lack of sophisticated and safe ways of observing the brain at work, and by limitations in understanding the detailed operation of the brain and nervous system. Most psychologists chose to ignore consciousness altogether. Because consciousness is private—only I have access to my thoughts and only you have access to yours—they decided that consciousness was simply not a fit object for scientific study. Science demands public data, facts that all scientists can observe, and so psychologists came to check their consciousness, as they already had their souls, at the door of their laboratories. As Dennett (1991) says, most psychologists have been "zombists," pretending that their subjects were zombies, possessing no conscious experience at all.

However, the current Decade of the Brain has revived a more radical interest in consciousness, a desire to do away with it the way chemistry did away with phlogiston. Dennett (1991) writes, "Human consciousness is about the last surviving mystery" (p. 21). Moreover, he looks forward to the "postconscious period" when consciousness "falls to science" (p. 24). The phrase "postconscious period" suggests a third challenge of consciousness: "Does consciousness exist?" If Descartes invented the concept of consciousness instead of discovering it, perhaps we can discard it as a bad idea.

Does Consciousness Exist?

A sophisticated and powerful theory of consciousness, the *multiple drafts model,* has been proposed (Dennett, 1991; Dennett & Kinsbourne, 1992). Dennett believes that while psychologists and philosophers no longer believe in the soul, they nevertheless remain unwittingly in the grip Descartes' picture of consciousness. Descartes said that the soul was the single place where all the manifold features of human experience—diverse sensations, thoughts, and feelings—came together in a single, private, privileged stream of consciousness. He also proposed that there was a single place in the brain, the pineal gland, where soul interacted with body. The senses projected a moving image of the world onto the smooth surface of the pineal gland, and the soul pushed the pineal gland around, controlling the impulses to the motor nerves of the body (Gaukroger, 1995). Although the soul is now excluded from science, Dennett believes the Cartesian image of a single place like the pineal gland where "it all comes together" persists. He dubs this place the *Cartesian Theater,* and the implicit theory it embodies, *Cartesian materialism.* The Cartesian Theater, Dennett argues, does not exist, because Cartesian materialism is false.

Dennett describes some strange phenomena of experience to undermine belief in the Cartesian Theater. One surprising finding involves a color version of an old and well-known experiment called the *phi-phenomenon,* the starting place for the Gestalt movement in psychology. Max Wertheimer discovered that if people are shown two alternately flashing lights a few inches apart, they do not see two lights blinking in turn but see a single light moving smoothly from point to point. At the suggestion of a philosopher, Nelson Goodman, Kolers, and von Grunau (1976) changed the experiment so the two lights were of different colors, perhaps red and blue. The key observation concerns what happens on the first trial, before the subject becomes aware that there are two colored lights. Two resulting experiences seem intuitively likely. Adding the colors might undermine the *phi* experience, so that subjects would see what's really there, alternately blinking lights. On the other hand, the illusion of movement might be preserved so that a single red light moves to the left and suddenly becomes blue when it reaches the blue light's position.

Kolers and von Grunau found something quite surprising. Even on the first trial, subjects reported seeing a red light move left and become blue in the middle of the apparent movement. Since the blue light had not yet come on when the red light changed to blue, the experience of color *phi* was extraordinary, even shocking.

Ruling out precognition—psychically knowing that the blue light was there and would come on—defenders of the Cartesian Theater must offer one of two explanations of color *phi,* called by Dennett the *Orwellian* and *Stalinesque* theories of consciousness. In his novel *1984,* George Orwell describes an unhappy human future ruled by a tyrant, Big Brother, who commands an insidious and manipulative bureaucracy. Big Brother's minions write history books full of made-up history, describing events that never happened or occurred differently than they are described in Big Brother's falsified histories. Applied to consciousness, the Orwellian model says that sensory input and immediate raw experience is heavily edited, so that what becomes conscious in the Cartesian Theater may not be true. For example, one may have initially seen the red dot become blue only at the end of its motion, but this initial experience is erased and replaced by the experience of red becoming blue halfway across. Like citizens ruled by Big Brother, consciousness in the Cartesian Theater may be systematically deceived.

When he ruled the Soviet Union, the tyrant Joseph Stalin put on show trials of his political enemies. The trappings of real trials were present—lawyers, judges, defendants, and juries—and courtroom events took place—there were questions and answers, motions by lawyers, rulings from the judges, defendants' confessions—but what happened was theater, not justice. The confessions had been wrung out of the accused by torture and threats before the trials took place. The show trials were put on to intimidate Stalin's foes and fool credulous Westerners about the nature of the Soviet system. Applied to consciousness, the Stalinesque model places the editing room between sensory input and the Cartesian Theater. The experience of color *phi* is created in the editing room and projected into the Cartesian Theater. Like the Orwellian version of the Cartesian Theater, consciousness is deceiving but it is deceptive from the beginning rather than through later editing.

Having laid out the Orwellian and Stalinesque theories of the Cartesian Theater of consciousness, Dennett points out that there is no way to tell which is correct. Each theory accounts for color *phi,* or for any strange or deceptive experience. If a viewpoint leads to a situation in which rival theories cannot be successfully compared, something is wrong with the viewpoint. Therefore, because we cannot determine which theory about the Cartesian Theater is correct, Dennett argues that there must be something wrong with the picture of the theater itself, and the Cartesian materialism of which it is a part. The key flaw of Cartesian materialism, he believes, is the unexamined assumption that there must be a single place where all information comes together in a definitive moment of consciousness: The Cartesian Theater.

Dennett uses two analogies to motivate his alternative theory of consciousness, or, more precisely, of experience. In 1814, British and American armies fought the last battle of the War of 1812, the Battle of New Orleans. Ironically, however, the last battle was fought after the war had ended, because unknown to the generals, a treaty between Britain and the United States had been signed several weeks before. Like color *phi,* the Battle of New Orleans was anomalous, being part of a war that was over. More precisely, Dennett asks, "When did the British Empire become notified of the signing of the Treaty of London?" This appears to be a meaningful question because the British Empire seems to be a single entity, but in fact it is not an easy question to answer. It seems unreasonable to say the Empire was notified at the moment of the signing. The King, the Prime Minister, and other diplomats present may have known it, but it was unknown to every other Briton, including the soldiers who fought and died at New Orleans. On the other hand, it seems unreasonable to say the Empire was not notified until every official of the Empire learned of the treaty. It might take months, perhaps in the case of remote officials, a year, for everyone to be told about the treaty. The difficulty of answering the question suggests that it was, in fact, meaningless from the start. The British Empire was not a single thing, but a far-flung, worldwide collection of people and institutions through which information flowed at a slow pace. There was no single place where all information came together to constitute the definitive notification of the Empire. Perhaps the Cartesian Theater, even consciousness itself, is, like the British Empire, a name that corresponds to no one thing.

Dennett's second metaphor leads to his theory of experience, the multiple drafts model. Papers by scientists, philosophers, and other scholars are published in learned journals, and these would seem to be the definitive texts of the papers that affect the scholars' colleagues. Decades ago, this was in fact the case, but it is no longer. Today, papers go through many drafts, each circulated to changing constellations of colleagues. They are affected by the drafts, and affect the production of new drafts. Thus the drafts are what have an impact on a field, the published paper being archival, of value only to historians, not the researchers in the field. Dennett points out that deciding which is the definitive is impossible. Circulated drafts affected the field, while others were discarded before being sent out. No version, not even the published one, is uniquely privileged as the true article.

Consciousness, Dennett concludes, resembles the production, editing, and circulation of multiple drafts of a scholarly paper. Information processes in different parts of the brain produce varying drafts of experience, often at the same time, and interacting in diverse ways. Some drafts affect others, while some vanish without a trace. A few drafts become conscious when they are probed; most do not. A probed draft causes what philosophers call "content fixation," the writing down of an experience in memory, and it is this writing down that is criterial for consciousness in the multiple drafts model. Some drafts have no effects at all, some may have effects but not get written down, and so do not become conscious. No draft is definitive. There is no place where "it all comes together"; there is no Cartesian Theater. Dennett summarizes:

> Where does it all come together? The answer is: Nowhere. Some of these distributed contentful states [the drafts] soon die out, leaving no further traces. Others do leave traces, on subsequent verbal reports and memory, on "semantic readiness" and other varieties of perceptual set [see Chapter 5], on emotional state, behavioral proclivities, and so forth. Some of these effects—for instance, influences on subsequent verbal reports—are at least symptomatic of consciousness. But there is no one place in the brain [Descartes' pineal gland] through which all these causal trains must pass in order to deposit their content "in consciousness." (1991, p. 135)

That information can affect us without passing through consciousness may be illustrated by some striking effects that occur when the brain is damaged in certain ways. One example is *blindsight*. Damage to certain parts of the visual information processing system of the brain may cause one half of a person's normal visual field to go dark. Although patients report they can't see anything in the dark half of their visual field, they can make simple discriminations about objects in their blind side, for example, between one or two fingers held up by the doctor (Shimamura, 1995; Weiskrantz, 1986).

Our own experience, too, supports the idea that there are "drafts" of experience that only sometimes make it to consciousness. You have probably gone to bed occasionally with a pain, gone to sleep, and then later been awakened by the pain. Was there pain while you were asleep, or did the pain only exist while you were awake and conscious of it? The former alternative seems more plausible. If the pain literally ceased to exist when you were asleep—were not conscious of it—it could not have caused you to wake up (Searle, 1990). In Dennett's terminology, the pain continued to exist as a draft of consciousness. An increase in the pain caused it to be "written down," waking you up.

Intentionality

Nevertheless, the intuition that consciousness was not just a brain process remains powerful, and various thinkers have tried to reformulate the mind-body distinction in a way that did not involve dualism (Leahey, 2000). From the standpoint of cognitive science, the most important attempt to redraw the line between mind and brain was Franz Brentano's (1838–1917) concept of intentionality. In its own time, Brentano's idea went almost unnoticed, but, as we will learn, it haunts cognitive science like the ghost of the soul. Brentano proposed that there was a property—intentionality—possessed by mental states alone. As used by Brentano, intentionality is a difficult and elusive concept, but Dennett (1978) helpfully defines it as *aboutness*. Skinner wrestled with the problem in his concept of the *tact:* How do ideas refer to their object? Consider, for example, the picture on the front of a $1 bill. Clearly, it designates—or, as Brentano would have said, its intentional object is—George Washington. But when we ask how the picture refers to George Washington, things become more mysterious. One might think that the picture refers to George Washington because it looks like him. However, suppose we learned from an autopsy that George

Washington in fact looked very different from any of his portraits: We would not then conclude that the $1 bill picture does not and never did refer to George Washington. Or suppose your best friend happened to look just like the image on the $1 bill: We would not think that the picture referred to your friend.

What these arguments suggest is that the way in which the $1 bill picture refers to George Washington does not depend on any physical attribute of the picture. *A fortiori,* then, whatever set of cells in my brain refers to George Washington when I think about him refers to him not by virtue of any physical property possessed by my neurons, but by something else. Brentano's idea was that mental states such as beliefs or feelings are always directed toward—intend or refer to—some object (such as George Washington) and that this property of reference was fundamental and unexplainable by physiology. The directedness of thought does not depend on any particular physical property possessed by the brain state that underlies the belief or feeling. So, for example, although one might by inspection of a person's bodily state infer that he or she was in love, no examination of the nervous system—however minute—could disclose the name of the beloved.

Brentano's intentionality thesis offers a powerful challenge to any materialist, naturalistic science of mind. The central thesis of naturalistic psychology is that ultimately all so-called mental processes may be explained as physical processes, whether they be S-R connections or environment-behavior relationships. But if Brentano is right, then at least one aspect of mental states—their crucial ability to refer to objects—must elude scientific psychology. Intentionality is especially bedeviling to scientific psychology because, while it separates mind (the realm of the intentional) from body (the realm of the physical), it is not dualistic, since intentionality is a relationship between a thought and its object, not a state in a spiritual soul. Thus, even without faith in a soul, the mind-body knot seemed as tangled as ever by the mid-twentieth century.

The Problem of Other Minds

Another difficulty created by Descartes' formulation of the mind-body problem is the problem of other minds. According to Descartes, each of us is directly aware of our own consciousness, that is, our own mind. We do not have direct access to anyone else's mind. Therefore, the question arises: How do I know anyone other than myself has a mind? Obviously, we do attribute mentality to other people, but on what basis do we do so?

Descartes argued that the behavioral sign from which we may infer the existence of mind in another creature is language. Descartes believed that the one distinct function of the mind is thinking. Thinking produces thoughts. Language expresses thoughts. Therefore, language use implies thinking, which in turn implies a mind that thinks. It is important to separate two aspects of Descartes' argument. First, he asserted that postulation of mind in another is an inference from behavior; then he proposed a particular—and very strict—behavioral criterion for the attribution of mind, use of language.

At first glance, Descartes' worry seems like a pointless philosopher's puzzle, but it bears on profoundly important issues with deep moral ramifications. Consider, for example, the question of whether or not to discontinue life support for a comatose patient. Our concern is to avoid destroying a human mind, and we look for signs that a mind is present in the patient's body. Similar considerations may arise in controversies over abortion: At what point in fetal development is a mind present? In cases of insanity, we similarly look for signs of mind in deciding how to treat, or perhaps forcibly institutionalize, someone who may be "mindless."

The problem of other minds has thrice proved important to the psychology of learning and cognition. Descartes' criterion clearly denies that animals have minds, for they do not possess language. In the nineteenth century, acceptance of evolution undermined Descartes' radical separation of human and animal. Because humans evolved gradually from the lower animals, it began to seem implausible that animals have no minds at all, and psychologists began to work on the problem of how to attribute mind to animals. This problem directly led to the importance of learning to scientific psychology, and we will discuss it in more detail later. Animals are also involved in the second way the problem of other minds has affected psychology of learning and cognition. In 1748 another French philosopher, Julien Offroy de La Mettrie, challenged Descartes' denial that animals have minds by proposing teaching apes the language of the deaf; if they could acquire language, La Mettrie said, they would become "perfect little gentlemen," the equal of humans. La Mettrie never undertook his project, but in the 1960s, prompted by a revival of Cartesian thinking, psychologists did, and their findings have proved most controversial, as we shall see in Chapter 11. Finally, today's high-tech computer raises the problem of other minds in yet another way. We call computers "electronic brains": Do they—can they—have minds? Contemporary cognitive science is built on the premise of a close similarity between human and computer intelligence, and this belief rests on the assumption that computers have minds, rightly defined.

Consciousness and Self

One of the oldest and unresolved, yet important, issues in psychology is the degree to which we can look inside our own minds to find out how we think. Some philosophers such as John Locke thought we could reflect on the operations of our minds, while others such as Immanual Kant thought that the operations of the mind were impenetrable by introspection. If we could simply observe our own minds the way we observe the world outside, deciding between rival theories in cognitive science would be easy. The founding psychologists of consciousness bitterly divided on the question of introspective access to thinking, and some of behaviorism's appeal was that it promised to set such conflicts aside. Because unlike behaviorists cognitive psychologists posit the existence of inner information processes, they have returned to asking to what degree we can know and control our thought processes. There is now evidence that personal access to our own information processes is limited, suggesting to some psychologists that behaviorists were right in claiming that consciousness may be safely ignored in building models of mind and behavior. Much of this data has been collected by social psychologists.

How Do We Know Ourselves?

From the Cartesian perspective, knowledge of our own minds is radically different from, and superior to, our knowledge of the minds of others, because it is based on direct introspective access to our mental processes. Social psychologists, however, have questioned this claim, arguing that how we know ourselves in not very different from how we know others, and that we have little, if any, access to our mental processes.

For example, developing the Skinnerian perspective of realism and radical behaviorism (see Chapter 4), Darryl Bem (1967) argues that we know ourselves exactly as we know others, from observation of behavior. For the realist, there is no private mental world, and therefore there can be no introspective access to it. According to Bem's *self-perception theory,* therefore, we know about ourselves by observing ourselves. Social psychologists have long studied the process of attribution, the process by which people use folk psychology to explain other's behavior by attributing to them mental states such as beliefs and desires. We also engage in self-attribution, explaining our own behavior by citing beliefs and desires. In Bem's scheme, there is no difference between self and other attribution. In both cases, we observe behavior and come up with a little theory to explain it. We have no special access to the causes of our own behavior that we do not have with respect to others beyond the fact that we've had lots more chance to observe ourselves behave in many situations and can therefore predict our behavior better than that of strangers, and maybe no better than that of a spouse or child with whom we have long lived.

Nisbett and Wilson (1977) have reached an almost identical conclusion within the information-processing perspective. Cognitive scientists believe that most information processing is done outside of consciousness, and Nisbett and Wilson asked what access, if any, we have to nonconscious cognitive processes, and what degree of control, if any, consciousness exerts over information processing and decision making. Nisbett and Wilson propose that people have virtually no access to their mental processes, and that our explanations of our own behavior are based solely on erroneous theories in folk psychology rather than any special access we have to the causes of behavior.

To support their claim, Nisbett and Wilson adduce a number of experimental results in which subjects are asked to explain an action or decision, and in which the subjects' explanation seems to be at odds with the real causes of their behavior. One of the simplest and most discussed experiments involved subjects' evaluation of four pairs of pantyhose. The experimenters set up a booth at a drycleaners and asked customers to come over and examine some pantyhose that might be placed on the market. Unknown to the subjects, all four pairs of pantyhose were identical. Nevertheless, subjects strongly tended to choose one pair—the fourth, or rightmost pair—as the best, citing virtues such as superior color or smooth texture. Because the pantyhose were identical, the reasons given by the subjects cannot have been the real ones. Instead, say Nisbett and Wilson, it was the position of the fourth pair that caused subjects to rate it as best. However, no one said to the experimenters, "I think this pair is best because it's the rightmost pair," leading Nisbett and Wilson to conclude that their subjects had no access to the real cause of their behavior. Instead, they made up plausible stories to satisfy themselves and their interrogators. More generally, Nisbett and Wilson propose that we are aware only of the results of the processes taking place unconsciously, not the processes themselves.

At first glance, the ideas of Bem and of Nisbett and Wilson appear alarming. They suggest that we don't know ourselves any better than we know a lifelong friend, and that we seldom, if ever, know what's going on in our own minds. However, more careful reflection should temper this reaction.

When Dwight D. Eisenhower gave the order for the invasion of Europe (D-Day) on June 6, 1944, he put into motion a plan familiar to him only at its topmost level. He and his staff established the grand strategy for the retaking of Europe from the Nazis, but they did not plan the detailed assault on the beaches and bridges of Normandy. Lower level strategic and momentary tactical decisions were left to a considerable hierarchy of officers and enlisted men. The structure of our minds is similar (Morris, 1981). At the top, corresponding to General Eisenhower, we have the largely conscious BOSS system, which forms intentions and sets goals. Strategic orders such as "Get up and turn on the television" are formulated and passed off to myriad EMPLOYEE systems, corresponding to the officers and enlisted men who actually landed on the beaches of Normandy. These EMPLOYEE systems carry out the execution of behavior in detail, and they are nonconscious. William James' conception of consciousness is similar to Morris'. When we are learning a complex task, the BOSS is involved, and we have to think through every step. As we master the task, nonconscious EMPLOYEES are created or come into control, and we no longer need think about the task consciously. Therefore, we should not find it frightening that much of our information processing is not conscious, because it is done by EMPLOYEES, not BOSS. General Eisenhower did not expect to be apprised of every detail of the fighting in Normandy, only the results.

There are other constraints on the sweeping conclusions of Bem and Nisbett and Wilson about our supposedly impoverished self-consciousness. While clearly some of our self-knowledge comes from observation of our own behavior, just as clearly not all of it does. We may infer, for example, that we are shy by observing that we don't go to parties, just as we may infer that a friend is shy by observing that she doesn't go to parties. However, although we infer that someone has a toothache by observing them hold their hand over their cheek, we do not infer that we are in pain from observing our hand on our cheek. We pity someone for having a toothache, not for putting hand to cheek (Luckhardt, 1983). There is an important difference between third-person knowledge of others and first-person knowledge of ourselves.

Finally, we should bear in mind that psychological experiments typically introduce artificial elements into social behavior that may distort subjects' behavior and self-reports. For example, in the pantyhose study, the subjects had every reason to think that the pairs of pantyhose were not identical—why would market researchers ask for opinions otherwise?—and were under pressure to choose one as best. Even if they sensed no difference between the pairs, they probably felt obliged to say something, and picking the last pair, the one in their hands at the moment, was no doubt easiest.

Should We Always Be Self-Aware?

It has been an axiom of Western life since the time of Socrates that it is better to base one's actions on thought-out reasons than on intuition (Leahey, 2000). However, sometimes self-knowledge can be destructive. This is most clearly the case with regard to skilled actions, which are best done intuitively. There is the well-known story of the centipede that had no trouble walking on 100 legs until asked how he did it. More generally, experts tend to think less about problems in their domain of expertise than do novices, because they have learned to act intuitively (see Chapters 2 and 9).

Recently, social psychologists have collected data suggesting that introspective self-awareness is sometimes undesirable. Timothy Wilson and his colleagues (Wilson, Dunn, Kraft, & Lisle, 1989) have conducted a number of experiments showing that thinking about the reasons for an attitude can disrupt the attitude and sometimes lead to bad decisions. Social psychologists believe that *attitudes* have two components, cognitive and affective. For example, you probably have a favorite musical group or performer. Your feeling of liking for the group is the affective component of your attitude, and the facts you know about the group are the cognitive component. Furthermore, there may be an imbalance between the two components. If you are a serious fan of a musical group, you may have accumulated a large body of knowledge about the band and be able to explain exactly why you like them. On the other hand, you may hear a song on the radio for the first time and love it, without knowing anything about its writer or performer, or even being able to say why you like it. The first attitude has strong cognitive and affective components; the second attitude is simply affective.

Wilson has found that when an attitude is primarily affective, thinking about our reasons for holding it is disruptive and may lead to self-defeating behavior. In one study, subjects were asked to rate their liking for five posters of the type students hang in their rooms. Two of the posters were "art" posters, reproductions of Impressionist paintings. Three were "pop" posters, such as a drawing of a cute cat with a clever saying. Half of the subjects were asked to think carefully about their ratings, and to write down their reasons for liking or disliking each poster, while the other half simply did the rating. All subjects were allowed to take a poster home as a reward for participating in the study. Wilson expected that the initial affective response to the art posters would be greater than for the pop posters, and his expectation was confirmed by the fact that the simple rating group rated the Impressionists much higher than the pop posters, and they almost uniformly chose one of the Impressionists to take home. However, the group asked to think about and report the reasons for their ratings tended to rate the pop posters more highly, and were more likely to take a pop poster home. Follow-up inquiries showed that the simple rating group was still happy with their Impressionist posters, but the reasons group had become disenchanted with their pop choices. Finally, subjects in the reasons group who were knowledgeable about art rated the Impressionists more highly than the pop posters, and took an Impressionist home.

Wilson believes that the unknowledgeable subjects in the reasons group felt an initial, affective pull toward the Impressionists, just as the subjects in the simple rating group did. However, they were not allowed to express their affective preference, but were forced to give cognitive reasons for their ratings. Knowing little about art, they could not find any way to express their liking for the Impressionist posters, but were able to find reasons for liking the simpler pop posters. The knowledgeable subjects could give reasons for their preference for the Impressionists, and were immune to the reasons manipulation. Being forced to give reasons for their attitudes temporarily overcame the unknowledgeable subjects' feelings. With the passage of time, affect reasserted itself and the subjects who had chosen the pop posters became unhappy with them.

Thus too much thought may disrupt attitudes that are mostly affective. Wilson et al. describe the case of the South American writer Mario Vargas Llosa who was asked to be a judge at a Berlin film festival. He tried to be very conscientious, taking note cards to each screening and carefully recording his reactions. "The result, of course, was that the movies ceased to be fun and turned into problems. . . . I was so worried about evaluating every aspect of every film that my entire system of values went into shock, and I quickly realized I could no longer tell what I liked or didn't, or why" (p. 288). Wilson concluded that when it comes to things whose pleasures are purely affective—the art we hang on the wall, the jam we put on our bread, the songs we like—it may be a bad idea to think too much about our likes and dislikes. In many cases thought is useful, even imperative—what car to buy, what candidate to vote for—

but too much thought may be a curse. Wilson quotes the poet Theodore Roethke: "Self-contemplation is a curse/That makes an old confusion worse" (p. 288).

Mental Control

While we may feel we know our consciousness intimately—although we have seen psychologists challenge Descartes' claim—it is remarkable how hard it can be to control consciousness. I remember in high school being challenged by a friend to *not* think of a bear in a snowstorm. Trying not to think of something is difficult, and I found the bear returning unbidden to my thoughts even as I tried to banish it. Frequently our efforts to achieve things boomerang and bring us exactly what we wish to avoid. We try to fall asleep but cannot; we try to impress a date but stammer and stumble; we try to wish a pain away but it gets worse; the nervous Superbowl quarterback tries to throw to his receiver but hits a defender. These are all examples of ironic failures of mental control (Wegner, 1994). Mental control has become a major topic in social psychology (Wegner & Pennebaker, 1993). We will look at our fascinating tendency to get what we don't want. It turns out that not only are there times when we should not examine our feelings too closely, but there are times when the best way to get what we want is to consciously try to do the opposite.

Wegner (1994) draws on the information-processing approach to psychology to explain ironic failures of mental control. Any control system, whether it's our mind or a machine, must contain two components, an operating system and an error detection system. A thermostat is an example of a control system, because its job is to control the temperature of a room or building. The operating system is the circuitry that turns heating and air conditioning on and off. The error detection system is the circuitry that checks to see if the building's air temperature departs from the desired set temperature. Similarly, Wegner proposes, mental control involves a system that tries to bring about a desired result and an error control system that looks for deviations between what is being achieved and the desired goal. Information-processing psychologists distinguish between *effortful information processing*—the processing of the conscious processor—and *automatic processing*—processing that proceeds without awareness. Effortful processing is sensitive to *mental load*. That is, we can usually do only one effortful thing at a time, and effortful processes are easily distracted. Automatic processes proceed by themselves and are much less sensitive to mental load. For example, while driving I cannot listen to the news and my wife at the same time, but I can listen to the news (or my wife) and drive at the same time. Attentive listening is an effortful process; driving is (now) automatic. Wegner believes that the mental operating system is an effortful process, likely to break down under mental load, while the error detection system is automatic. Ironic processes occur when mental load disturbs the operating system, leaving the error detecting system to bring failures of control to consciousness.

Various experiments support Wegner's hypothesis. Trying to sleep often keeps us awake, and research has shown that telling insomniacs to try to stay awake actually helps them go to sleep. Wegner suggests that insomniacs worry about sleep loss, placing mental load on the operating system that is trying to bring about sleep, making it less effective. At the same time, trying to go to sleep activates the error monitoring system so that every distraction—the drip of a faucet, a wrinkle in the blanket—comes to consciousness, keeping the insomniac awake. Trying to stay awake, on the other hand, directs the monitoring process to signs of sleepiness, bringing them to the fore and inducing sleep. To test his idea, Wegner conducted an experiment in which subjects listened to a tape as they lay in bed upon retiring. At the beginning of the tape, a narrator engaged the mental operating system by telling half of the subjects to go to sleep "as fast as you can," and the other half to go to sleep "whenever you want." Mental load was varied by the music following the narrator's instructions. Half of each group, the low-load subjects, heard 45 minutes of soothing "New Age" music, while the other half, the high load subjects, heard 45 minutes of John Phillips Sousa marches.

Under conditions of low load, the operating system was effective. Subjects trying to go to sleep while listening to New Age music got to sleep the fastest, taking 15 minutes to achieve slumber. Subjects listening to New Age music who were told to fall asleep whenever they wanted, took longer, requiring 28 minutes to get to sleep. Therefore, it was not the soothing (or boring) New Age music that effected sleep in the first group. In fact, the subjects not trying to get to sleep while listening to Sousa marches actually got to sleep faster than those listening to New Age music (24 minutes). The group that took the longest to get to sleep were the subjects trying to get to sleep while listening to the Sousa marches, at 32 minutes. Wegner argues that this group experienced a classic ironic effect. The mental load of the Sousa marches disrupted the effortful process of trying to go to sleep, but did not disrupt the automatic error detecting process of finding and reporting signs of wakefulness. Like insomniacs, this group's efforts to sleep boomeranged into not sleeping.

In another study, subjects watched an infomercial extolling the virtues of amino acid dietary supplements. Half the subjects simply watched the infomercial (no mental load condition), while the other half watched and had to count the number of plural nouns said by the pitchman (load condition). Within each load condition there were three mental control conditions. One-third of the subjects were told to believe the pitchman, one-third were told to disbelieve him, and one-third, the control subjects, were given no instructions. In the no-load condition, the mental control operating process was effective. Subjects told to believe the infomercial believed it more than control subjects, and subjects told to disbelieve believed less than the control subjects. The outcome was dramatically reversed in the load condition, under which ironic effects occurred as predicted. Under load, subjects told to disbelieve were the most credulous of all subjects, while subjects told to believe were the most skeptical.

Wegner offers several pieces of advice for avoiding ironic effects. One is to try to avoid mental load and control stress. If we can do this, the mental operating system can achieve our goals. Another is to try to rescind mental control. The oldest finding of ironic processes goes back to 1833. Spiritualist mediums would try to demonstrate the power of unseen forces by having a person hold an object on a string perfectly still. They could not, and the medium claimed this showed the power of a spirit over the subject. However, the effect disappears when the subject is blindfolded. It was not a spirit that made the pendulum move, but small muscle movements caused by the attempt to hold the pendulum still. In the movie *The Empire Strikes Back,* the Jedi sage Yoda tells Luke Skywalker, who has failed to lift his starfighter out of a swamp by mental effort, that there is no trying, only doing or not doing. This Zen-like advice dampens the mental operating system, making ironic effects less likely. Finally, Wegner suggests trying to make the mental control an automatic rather than an effortful process, rendering it less susceptible to being damaged by mental load. This process is most apparent in skilled motor performances such as athletics or music. The quarterback who concentrates on hitting his receivers will do less well than the quarterback who simply throws to them. Perhaps, Wegner suggests, we can apply this lesson in other areas such as thought suppression or positive mood induction.

LEARNING AND COGNITION IN EARLY PSYCHOLOGY

The European founders of psychology, such as Wilhelm Wundt, who established the first recognized laboratory of psychology, conceived of psychology as the science concerned with conscious experience. Not surprisingly, early psychology focused on the areas of sensation, attention, and perception. Although learning, memory, and thought were not ignored, they were not psychology's central concern. Exceptions to this were the research on human memory of Hermann Ebbinghaus, who founded one important means of studying human learning, verbal learning, and the research on thinking carried out at the University of Würzburg under the leadership of Oswald Külpe from 1901 to 1909. The Würzburg School attempted to introspect their thought processes, but their results were inconclusive and controversial, helping lead to the behaviorists' rejection of introspection altogether (Leahey, 1992).

Verbal Learning

Empirical studies of learning arose in the late nineteenth century in two quite different areas. The study of human learning began with Hermann Ebbinghaus' study of memory (1850–1909), and the study of animal learning grew out of the impact of evolution on psychology. In 1879, Ebbinghaus began to use himself as the only subject in the first experimental investigations of learning and memory. Although he did not say so explicitly, it is clear that Ebbinghaus' research program was built on *associationism.* By the nineteenth century, most philosophical psychologists thought of the mind as a sort of tinkertoy arrangement. Your mind is full of ideas: "Horse," "boy," "telephone," "Ebbinghaus," and so on. Associationists believe that these ideas are connected to one another by a kind of mental thread—Ebbinghaus' term—that is, an *association.*

You may have heard of *free-association tests:* "Say the first word that comes to your mind when I say _____ ." Likely free associates would be boy-girl, horse-rider, telephone-call, Ebbinghaus-memory. According to the associationists, when you learn something, you learn an idea and tie it, or associate it, to other ideas you already have. Thus, you learn to associate, for a multiple-choice test perhaps, "associationism" with "Ebbinghaus" and "mental thread." Pushing this theory as far as it can go, associationists argue that mind and behavior are just collections of ideas or responses linked by association, and that the basic problem of the psychology of learning is finding out how people learn to associate ideas.

Ebbinghaus was the first person to use experiments to find out how ideas and associations are learned. His most important achievement was thinking of an experimental procedure to substitute for philosophical speculation. Ebbinghaus saw that in starting out in a new field, as memory then was, he would have to simplify the problem to be solved. Most of our learning is both complex and haphazard.

To simplify the material, Ebbinghaus invented the *nonsense syllable,* constructed by placing a vowel between two consonants: TOB, SAB, GEN, and so on. They were easy to make up and produced a large amount of learnable material. Being meaningless, they simplified the process of learning to sheer memorization, ruling out such factors as motivation, interest, and relevance to what has already been learned. Ebbinghaus believed they would reveal the processes of learning, retention, and forgetting, unclouded by any other mental processes. They also resemble the associationists' *simple ideas,* the basic copies in the mind.

To impose experimental control, Ebbinghaus would compose lists of syllables to be presented to himself at a constant rate of speed, and at consistent times of the day. The whole procedure was easily quantifiable: Ebbinghaus could measure how long it took him to learn or relearn lists of syllables as he changed independent variables. He hoped to discover scientific laws that govern the process of learning and, thus, to transform at least part of psychology from a branch of philosophy into a branch of experimental science.

One of the most obvious facts about memory is that the longer ago we learned something, the harder it is to remember. On the basis of personal experience, we can say no more than that—hardly a scientific statement. But Ebbinghaus' experimental approach made it possible to frame the question more precisely and receive a quantitative answer. In a series of experiments, Ebbinghaus learned by heart eight lists of 13 nonsense syllables each; later, after differing amounts of time (20 minutes, 1 hour, 8.8 hours, 1 day, 2 days, 6 days, or 31 days), he learned them by heart again. Consequently, Ebbinghaus could ask precisely, in terms of difficulty of relearning: How much of a list of nonsense syllables is forgotten at a given time?

Figure 1.1 illustrates the results of Ebbinghaus' experiments; it shows the percent of material forgotten as a function of hours after initial learning. Most forgetting takes place quickly. Only an hour after learning, more than 55 percent of the nonsense syllables have been forgotten, while the additional loss past 8.8 hours is only 14 percent after 31 days. Ebbinghaus showed exactly how forgetting takes place, rapidly at first and then more slowly; moreover, he managed to quantify the rate of forgetting.

FIGURE 1.1 Ebbinghaus' curve of forgetting. (Based on Ebbinghaus, *On Memory,* 1885.)

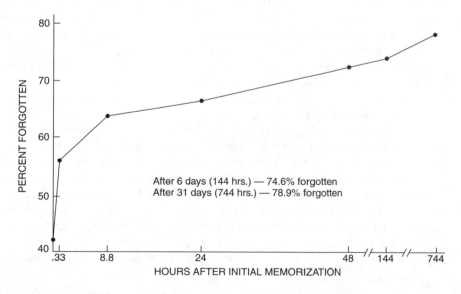

After 6 days (144 hrs.) — 74.6% forgotten
After 31 days (744 hrs.) — 78.9% forgotten

PERCENT FORGOTTEN

HOURS AFTER INITIAL MEMORIZATION

Ebbinghaus' nonsense syllable learning experiment also enabled him to investigate precisely other commonsense hypotheses. He asked, What is the effect of amount of material on learning? He quantified amount as nonsense syllable list-length, and obtained quantitative results showing (not surprisingly) that the longer the list, the longer it takes to learn. He compared learning a list of nonsense syllables to learning a stanza of poetry from Byron's *Don Juan,* and found that learning the poem was easier, notwithstanding the fact that the poem contained many more syllables than the lists. This demonstrates that the more organized material is, the easier it is to learn. Nonsense syllables are meaningless and the list has no structure; poetry is made of meaningful words put together with controlled structure of grammar, meter, and rhyme. Ebbinghaus' discovery, and his finding that the number of syllables he could hold in his mind at one time was seven, are important to memory researchers today. Ebbinghaus also showed that the more a list is repeated, the better it is remembered after one day.

Ebbinghaus could also use his experimental method to scientifically answer questions raised by philosophical associationists. So, for example, philosophers had argued over whether, if three ideas a, b, and c are presented in a series one at a time, will a and c be associated, or if only a and b and b and c will be associated. Ebbinghaus experimented on this heretofore speculative question. He learned lists, scrambled them in various ways, and then relearned them. He found relearning was always easier despite the scrambling. He concluded from this that syllables do get associated not only with their immediate successors but also with their remoter fellow list members, although the farther apart two syllables are, the weaker the association is. His conclusion follows, because if only adjacent pairs were associated, then learning a, b, c, d, e, and f will not make it easier a day later to learn a, c, e, d, b, f, since none of the new pairs is the same.

Animal Learning

Despite Ebbinghaus' study of memory, learning did not become a central problem for psychology until evolution began to be integrated into psychology in Great Britain and the United States. Evolution revived the problem of other minds and made it central to psychology. Descartes, by making language the mark of a mind, had drawn a sharp line between humans and animals; Descartes' line coincided neatly with the old religious-creationist view that men and women have souls but animals do not. Evolution, however, erased Descartes' line, and it made drawing a new line between mind and mechanism more difficult than ever before.

Descartes had said that animals were mere machines, physiological devices without thought or feeling. Humans were machines inhabited by conscious souls, revealing thought through language. But evolution taught that humans were evolved from simpler animals, implying either that people were machines or that animals possessed minds. In the nineteenth century and for several decades of the twentieth, it seemed easier to claim that animals had minds. For people of the nineteenth century, the prototypical machines were the watch and the steam engine. What is characteristic about the behavior of such machines is their blindness to the environment. A watch runs until it runs down, relentlessly and unchangingly telling the time, keeping the seconds, minutes, and hours. Left unattended by an engineer, a steam engine could overheat and blow up. It is apt to call a watch or a steam engine a "mindless machine." People, by contrast, adjusted their behavior to the environment, responding to changes in circumstances with changes in behavior. Moreover, inspection of the animal world suggested that many animals adjusted their behavior to the environment, although perhaps not as well as humans.

Thus, the early comparative psychologists of the nineteenth century set out in search of an animal mind, confident that animals were not mere machines. Generally, they agreed that the mark of the mind was not language, as Descartes had maintained, but learning, the ability of creatures to change their behavior to adapt to the environment. Having erased Descartes' old line between mind and machine, evolution suggested the new one of learning. Just as species adapt physically to the environment by evolving over generations, so organisms adapt psychologically to the environment by learning over time. Learning became the central problem of psychology. Learning was the outward sign of mind—and psychology is the study of the mind—and learning was an important biological process, being no less than the means by which individuals (the subjects of psychological research) adapted to their environments.

However, the continuity of humans and animals proved to be a two-edged sword. The early comparative psychologists happily inferred mind from behavior, but they did not actually see mind. As their researches progressed, moreover, they found signs of adaptive behavior in some very simple organisms. Cockroaches, for example, can locate food and then return to it night after night. While a watch can't match this simple feat, we might be hard-pressed to justify attributing mentality to a cockroach, and if we refuse to attribute mentality to the cockroach who is capable of learning, what becomes of learning as the mark of mind? The early comparative psychologists thus wrestled with the problem of other minds, caught—to change metaphor—on the slippery slope of phylogenetic continuity. Continuity could be used to argue that both humans and animals have minds, with the animal mind a simpler version of the human. On the other hand, continuity might be used to argue that humans and animals are both machines, with the human machine a more complex version of the animal. In the end, as we shall see later in the text, the latter view won out, as psychologists became convinced that machines could learn.

One might have expected that just as evolution revived and reshaped the problem of other minds, it would have revived and reshaped the nature/nurture question. However, it did not, because of the overriding influence of associationism.

The man who first applied evolution to psychology was Herbert Spencer in his book *Principles of Psychology,* written five years before Darwin published his *Origin of Species* in 1859. Spencer was a follower of the French evolutionary theorist J. B. Lamarck, who, among other things, believed that physical characteristics acquired by parents during their own lifetime could be passed on to their offspring. To Lamarck, Spencer added associationism. Like other associationists, Spencer believed that the mind registered sensations and that learning consisted of building up associations between them. Associationism implied an extremely strong form of phylogenetic continuity: Human minds were not merely continuous with animal minds; they were virtually identical to animal minds. According to associationism, the sole difference between human and animal minds lays in the number of associations they can make; otherwise they are the same. Associationism, greatly simplified the nature/nurture issue. The only possible things that might be innate were certain associations, or reflexes, possessed at birth and perhaps differing between species. Spencer, following Lamarck, believed that some associations highly learned in one generation might become heritable in subsequent generations.

Spencer's views were important to the first generations of psychologists of learning, the *behaviorists*. Spencer's paradigm makes learning the master process in all psychology. Everything that a person becomes is created by associative learning, either in one's own lifetime of learning or in one's ancestors' lifetimes of learning. Species differences are trivial and may be ignored, because learning is the same in all species—association-formation—and what innate properties any species possesses can be no more than a few prelearned associations. Finally, these conclusions suggest an attractive research strategy. Because learning is the same in all species, including human beings, and differences between species are unimportant, then we can discover the principles of learning by studying one convenient animal—the rat, as things turned out—knowing that the principles would be the same throughout the animal kingdom. The difficulties of experimentally studying learning in humans could be bypassed. Thus Spencer at once laid the foundation for behaviorism and buried the nature/nurture problem.

OVERVIEW: ISSUES IN THE STUDY OF LEARNING AND COGNITION

We have chosen to organize our text around key topics in the study of learning and cognition.

Mind Design (Chapter 2)

Central to modern cognitive psychology is its participation in a larger, interdisciplinary enterprise called *cognitive science*. Cognitive science brings together cognitive psychologists, linguists, philosophers of mind, workers in artificial intelligence, and neuroscientists. The field of artificial intelligence is devoted to creating intelligent computer programs and robots. It engages, therefore, in the artificial design of minds. Cognitive psychology is devoted to understanding the human mind, which was designed by evolution. Trying to design minds from the ground up has shed light on the human mind, and the attempt to understand how intelligence has evolved and functions today, sheds light on the problems of designing artificial minds. In the next chapter we will look at the architecture of cognition—ways of building intelligence—and at human evolution, to see how our own minds were designed by the struggle for existence and reproduction.

Behavior (Part II)

In the next three sections, we move from simplest behavioral processes to the higher mental processes. Part II deals with the most basic processes of learning and behavior, focusing on the behavioral tradition in psychology that dominated the study of learning for the first part of the twentieth century. Behaviorists shunned the study of mental processes because there seemed to be no way to observe them directly or to make rigorous, testable inferences about their workings. Radical behaviorists such as B. F. Skinner (Chapter 4) admitted consciousness into psychology because at least one person—the person having them—observes conscious events, but they refused to theorize about nonconscious mental processes that no one could see. Methodological behaviorists such as Clark Hull and E. C. Tolman (Chapter 4) excluded consciousness from science because conscious events, though real, are private and therefore not capable of being independently verified in the way we can verify the public events of science such as physics or chemistry. They did, however, theorize about nonconscious processes, but defined them in terms of behavior, refraining from calling them "mental." All the behaviorists adopted the Spencerian strategy of studying simple forms of learning, assuming they could later bootstrap their animal-based theories into accounts of human behavior.

Information Processing (Part III)

The advent of the computer model of the mind (Chapter 2) changed the theoretical situation in psychology. Computers process information in precise ways specified by their programming. This offered a way of theorizing about the human mind, regarding it as a computational program running in the "wetware" of the brain. Thus, psychologists could formulate precise theories about how the human mental program operated and make testable predictions about the behavior that should result. In Part III we will look at the basics of human information processing, attention, pattern recognition, and various stages and forms of memory.

The Higher Mental Processes (Part IV)

Parts II and III concerned behavioral and information processes that to a large degree we share with the other animals. In Part IV we move on to the higher mental processes that Descartes would have said were unique features of the human mind, setting us off sharply from the lower animals. Although no one today endorses Descartes absolute separation of animal and human cognition, the higher mental processes of language, discourse, comprehension, and thinking—the topics of Part IV—are certainly more developed in Homo *sapiens sapiens* than even in our closest relatives, the chimpanzees.

Development (Part V)

The chapters in Part V take up the study of the development of cognition (Chapter 10) and language (Chapter 11). The guiding theme of both chapters will be the degree to which the long-term development of the human mind from infancy to adulthood can be explained as the result of changes in the behavioral and cognitive processes we studied in Parts II to IV. Some psychologists think they can, while other psychologists believe that important aspects of human cognition—especially language—are innate, and others believe that cognitive development is the unfolding of a series of stages of cognitive development. Roughly speaking, the first camp sees cognitive development as the gradual programming of the human mind by the environment, while the latter camp sees it as like the inner-directed process by which an acorn becomes an oak.

Cognitive Neuroscience (Part VI)

The 1990s were the decade of the brain, and it witnessed a rich harvest of findings and theories about learning and cognition as they are actually implemented by the wetware of the human nervous system. The brain is perhaps the final frontier in humans' quest for self-understanding, and the years to come promise exciting developments in understanding the biological bases of learning and cognition. Chapter 12 is a quick overview of cognitive neuroscience, surveying the topics of Parts II through V at the level of the brain. Chapter 13 is an extended study of one of the most important areas of cognitive neuroscience, emotion. Recent work on emotion shows that rather than being a distraction to the computations of pure reason, it is a key to the operation of reason in the real world. We end with Chapter 14, which looks at the evolution of learning and cognition, focusing on how the constraints of Darwin's struggle for existence shaped the formation of the human mind as revealed by modern psychology.

SUGGESTED READING

For more information on the place of learning in the history of psychology, see Thomas H. Leahey, *A History of Psychology: Main Currents in Psychological Thought,* 5th ed. (Upper Saddle River, NJ: Prentice-Hall, 2000).

2   Mind Design

Perhaps the most perplexing question in psychology is the mind-body problem. Intuitively, consciousness and self-awareness seem altogether distinct from our bodies, so it is not surprising that philosophers, psychologists, and biologists have debated the nature of the mind-body knot for millennia. In the context of the study of learning and cognition, the mind-body problem can be more precisely stated as discovering how learning and thought are carried out by the nervous system. This question was by and large avoided by psychologists for most of the twentieth century, but advances in our ability to study the brain and nervous system have made possible serious insights about the biological bases of learning and cognition.

A parallel scientific development—the invention of the computer—also promised to throw new light on the mind-body problem. Computers are sometimes called "thinking machines," implying an exciting (but to some frightening) possibility, constructing artificial minds. Moreover, advocates of artificial intelligence (AI) believe that building artificial intelligences will create insights into our own. Out of this belief has arisen a new field of scientific endeavor, cognitive science, based on the idea that there is a deep similarity between the computer and its controlling program and the brain and its controlling mind.

DESIGNING MINDS: THE ARCHITECTURE OF COGNITION

Two main architectures of cognition have been proposed, the symbol-system hypothesis and connectionism. Before discussing them, however, we need to establish some frameworks to guide our inquiries into mind design. They are the late David Marr's analysis of cognitive architecture as a set of computational levels, and Paul Smolensky's distinction between the conscious information processor and the intuitive information processor, and Daniel Dennett's analysis of explanatory stances.

Levels of Computation

Marr (1982) proposed that the analysis of intelligent action takes place at three hierarchically arranged levels. In the case of artificial intelligence, the levels define the job of making a mind, while in the case of psychology—which studies an already evolved intelligence—they define three levels of psychological theory. The levels are most readily described from the standpoint of artificial intelligence:

1. The cognitive level specifies the task the AI system is to perform.
2. The algorithm level specifies the computer programming that effects the task.

3. The implementation level specifies how the hardware device is to carry out the program instructions.

To flesh out Marr's analysis, let us consider a simple arithmetical example. At the cognitive level, the task is to add any two numbers together. At the algorithm level, we write a simple program in the BASIC language that can carry out the addition, as follows:

```
10 INPUT X
20 INPUT Y
30 LET Z = X + Y
40 PRINT Z
50 END
```

Line 10 presents a prompt on the computer screen requesting input, which it then stores as a variable called X. Line 20 repeats the process for the second number, the variable Y. Line 30 defines a variable Z, the sum of X and Y. Line 40 displays the value of Z on the screen. Line 50 says that the end of the program has been reached. If we want to repeat the process many times, we could add a new line between 40 and 50:

```
45 GOTO 10
```

that returns the program to its starting point. Loading the program into a computer and running it brings us to the implementation level. The computer takes the BASIC program and translates—the computer term is compiles—it into the binary language that actually controls the movement of electrons through wires and silicon chips.

Having reached the implementation level, we come to a point that is extremely important to the debate between the symbol-system hypothesis and connectionism. At the cognitive level we proceeded without considering the device that performs the addition: It could be a computer, a slide rule, a pocket calculator, or a fourth-grade child. At the algorithm level, we specified a set of rules that could also be performed by various devices, including a computer or a child, but not by a pocket calculator that cannot be programmed. Pocket calculators perform addition electronically, without being programmed with rules. However, when we reach the implementation level, the nature of the hardware (or wetware) becomes crucial, because the implementation consists in actually carrying the calculation out with a real machine or real person, and different computers implement the same cognitive task in different ways.

Even the same algorithms are carried out differently by different machines. We could enter the BASIC program on any machine that understands BASIC. However, the binary machine code and the electronic processes that run the program vary from computer to computer. I could run the program on my ancient Texas Instruments TI-1000, my antique Apple IIe, my CompuAdd 386/20, the one I originally wrote this sentence on, a CompuAdd 325TX notebook, or the one I'm now editing on, a Gateway PII 300. In every case, the electronic processes that implement the program will be different. For example, my CompuAdd 386/20 computed with an Intel 80386 microprocessor, while the 325TX uses an Advanced Micro Devices AMD 386SXL chip. Thus at the implementation level two very similar computers run the same programs differently. One of the two main issues that separates the symbol-system architecture of cognition from its connectionism concerns whether or not psychological theories of learning and cognition need be concerned with the implementation level. According to the symbol-system view, the implementation of programs in a brain or a computer may be safely ignored at the cognitive and algorithm levels, while, according to the connectionist view, theorizing at higher levels must be constrained by the nature of the machine that will carry out the computations.

The second main difference concerns the algorithmic level of intelligence. William James (1890) first addressed this fundamental problem. James observed that, when we first learn a skill, we must consciously think about what to do; as we become more experienced, consciousness deserts the task and we carry it out automatically, without conscious thought. For example, consider learning to fly (Dreyfus & Dreyfus, 1990), specifically what at Marr's cognitive level may be described as "how to take off in a small plane." Novice pilots talk themselves through the process of taking off by following memorized rules resembling a set of computational algorithms:

1. "Taxi to the flight line."
2. "Set the accelerator to 100 percent."
3. "Taxi down the runway until take-off speed is reached."
4. "Pull the stick back halfway until the wheels are off the ground."
5. "Retract the landing gear."

However, as the novice pilot becomes an expert pilot, taking off becomes automatic, no longer requiring step-by-step thinking. What had formerly required conscious thought becomes intuitive, and an important question concerns what happened to the rules followed consciously by the novice pilot. What psychological change takes place when such expertise is acquired and consciousness is no longer needed for appropriate behavior to occur?

The Conscious and Intuitive Processors

To help answer this question, Paul Smolensky (1988) analyzes the architecture of cognition from the perspective of how thoughtful processes become intuitive actions. Smolensky's framework distinguishes two levels, the conscious processor and the intuitive processor. The conscious processor is engaged when we consciously think about a task or problem, as the novice pilot does. However, as a skill becomes mastered, it moves into the intuitive processor; we just "do it" without conscious thought. Thus experienced pilots become one with their planes and fly without conscious thought (Dreyfus & Dreyfus, 1990). Similarly, driving an automobile over a familiar route requires little if any conscious attention, which we turn over to listening to the radio or a cassette, or having a conversation with a passenger. Not everything the intuitive processor performs was once conscious. Many of the functions of the intuitive processor are innate, such as recognizing faces or simple patterns, while some abilities can be learned without ever becoming conscious. For example, chicken sexers can identify the sex of the chick within an egg by holding it up before a light. However, they do not know how they do it, and one learns to be a chicken sexer by sitting next to a master and watching him work.

When it becomes automatic, a skill such as flying or driving is performed by the intuitive processor, but what happens during the transition from conscious thought to intuition is a difficult issue to resolve. To see why, we must distinguish between rule-following and rule-governed behavior.

Physical systems illustrate how rule-governed behavior need not be rule-following behavior. The earth revolves around the sun in an elliptical path governed by Newton's laws of motion and gravity. However, the earth does not *follow* these laws in the sense that it computes them and adjusts its course to comply with them. The computer guiding a spacecraft does follow Newton's laws, as they are written into its programs, but the motions of natural objects are governed by physical laws without following them by internal processing.

The following example suggests that the same distinction may apply to human behavior. Imagine seeing a cartoon drawing of an unfamiliar animal called a "wug." If I show you two of them, you will say "There are two wugs." Shown two pictures of a creature called "wuk," you will say "There are two wuks." In saying the plural, your behavior is governed by the rule of English morphology that to make a noun plural, you add an -*s*. Although you probably did not apply the rule consciously, it is not implausible to believe that you did as a child. However, your behavior was also governed by a rule of English phonology that an -*s* following a voiced consonant (e.g., /g/) is also voiced—*wugz*—while an -*s* following an unvoiced consonant (such as /k/) is also unvoiced—wuks. Like the chicken sexer, it is unlikely you ever consciously knew this rule at all.

Having developed the distinction between rule-governed and rule-following behaviors, we can state the algorithm level distinction between the symbol-system architecture and the connectionist architecture. All psychologists accept the idea that human behavior is rule governed, because if it were not there could be no science of human behavior. The issue separating the symbol-system hypothesis from connectionism concerns whether and when human behavior is rule following. According to the symbol system view, both the conscious processor and the intuitive processor are rule-following and rule-governed systems. When we think or decide consciously, we formulate rules and follow them in behaving. Intuitive thinking is likewise rule following. In the case of behaviors that were once consciously followed, the procedures of the intuitive processor are the same as the procedures once followed in consciousness, but with awareness subtracted. In the case of behaviors such as chicken sexing, the process is truncated, with rules being formulated and followed directly by the intuitive processor. Connectionists hold that human behavior is rule following only at the conscious level. In the intuitive processor, radically different processes are taking place (Smolensky, 1988). Advocates of the symbol-system view are somewhat like Tolman, who believed that unconscious rats use cognitive maps like conscious lost humans. Connectionists are like Hull or even Guthrie, who believed that molar rule-governed behavior is at a lower level, the strengthening and weakening of input-output connections. After all, Thorndike called his theory connectionism 80 years ago.

The intuitive processor lies between the conscious mind—the conscious processor—and the brain that implements human intelligence. According to the symbol-system account, the intuitive processor carries out step-by-step unconscious thinking that is essentially identical to the step-by-step conscious thinking of the conscious processor, and so Clark (1989) calls the symbol-system account the mind's-eye view of learning and cognition. According to connectionism, the intuitive processor carries out nonsymbolic parallel processing similar to the neural parallel processing of the brain, and Clark calls it the brain's-eye view of learning and cognition. Indeed, some computer scientists are building brainlike computers.

Explanatory Stances

The philosopher Daniel Dennett (1989) proposed that intelligent behavior can be explained by taking any of three not mutually exclusive *stances*. Unlike Marr's and Smolensky's levels of explanation, Dennett's stances do not form a hierarchy because they are ways we have to explain and understand things and events for our own purposes. As we will see, a stance does not have to be literally true in order to be useful:

1. *Design stance* is similar to Marr's cognitive level. When we take the design stance, we specify what a given device or process is for, specifying the function it serves. In the case of an engineered device, the design stance tells us what the device was built to do. For example, a thermostat regulates the temperature in a building. In the case of an evolved bodily organ or physiological function, the design stance tells us what natural selection evolved the organ or function to do. For example, the heart (more specifically the beating of the heart) circulates the blood.

2. *Hardware stance* specifies the actual physical process that carries out the design function. For example, the typical house thermostat contains within it a strip (usually wound in a spiral) made of two different metals sandwiched together. The two metals have different coefficients of expansion and contraction, so that as the temperature changes, the strip changes shape, and this movement can be used to activate electrical relays which turn off and on the house's heat pump. In some "smart" buildings, however, there are sensors in each room which relay temperature information to a central computer that controls the flow and temperature of the building's air. Note that the same design goals can be met by very different physical mechanisms. This is a critical idea in artificial intelligence, because it suggests that the same mental functions that are hosted by human brains could be implemented in a computer. An artificial heart could fill the same function as an organic heart.

3. *Intentional stance* is the most important for psychology because it is the stance of folk psychology. When we take the intentional stance, we attribute to a device or person beliefs and desires, treating them as rational agents making choices based on their knowledge and motives. Thus when I play chess, I believe that my opponent wants to win, and, being a rational agent, will choose the best move available on any turn. This helps me anticipate what he or she will do and thus plan my own strategy. Observe that a thermostat can be explained taking the intentional stance. One might tell a child that the thermostat *wants* to keep the house at a comfortable temperature, that it *knows* when it's too hot or too cold, and *decides* to turn on the heat pump. In the case of a human chess opponent, the intentional stance seems natural and right. In the case of the thermostat, it seems suitable only for children, an "as if" form of psychological explanation. Between these two cases lies the interesting case of playing chess against an artificial intelligence, a computer chess program. I will attribute to it the same motives and cleverness I attribute to a human opponent. But does the computer really want to win and believe it can do so by making a given move? Does the computer possess only "as if" intentionality? If it possesses real intentionality, why doesn't the thermostat? If it doesn't possess real intentionality, do people? These are knotty questions (Dahlbohm, 1995; Searle, 1994, 1997).

The importance for us of Dennett's stances is that there can be different yet compatible ways of explaining the same things. Which stance we take depends on the purpose at hand as much as it does the physical nature of the system we are trying to explain. Even if computer programs possess only "as if" intentionality, it may nevertheless be useful for our purposes to treat them as rational, intelligent agents; one could never beat a computer chess player by trying to learn the computer code it's written in. Dennett's design stance also reinforces the importance of considering what a given human mental ability or function evolved to do. Knowing what survival problems the human mind was designed by natural selection to solve should throw great light on the design of our own minds and thus help us explain it and design new minds.

TWO ARCHITECTURES OF COGNITION

Because introspection cannot make the mind transparent to itself, cognitive psychologists construct their theories of the mind by making inferences about mental processes from behavior. Radical behaviorists, of course, view such inference making as a grave error, but they are in the minority today (see Chapter 4). Two architectures of cognition guide cognitive science today, the more traditional symbol-system hypothesis and the newer architecture of connectionism. Each approach has its strengths and weaknesses and tends to be suitable for explaining different cognitive domains. In general, symbol-system models are more suitable for explaining cognitive processes that involve consciousness, such as problem solving and language, while connectionist models are more suitable for intuitive tasks such as perception and learning.

The Mind's Eye View: The Symbol-System Hypothesis

According to the symbol-system hypothesis (Newell & Simon, 1976/1990) intelligence, whether natural or artificial, consists of the manipulation of symbols by computational rules. An organism or computer stores within it representations of the world—symbols—which it manipulates to construct new representations. The simple addition program on page 28 illustrates the essence of the symbol-system view of cognition. We provide as input two numbers that are then symbolically stored inside the computer as the values of the variables X and Y. The computer then "thinks," manipulating X and Y by applying to them the algorithm of addition, generating a new symbol, the value of the variable Z. Finally, the computer "behaves" by displaying Z on its screen. Applied to living organisms, the symbol-system view says that creatures accept input via the senses, represent the inputs internally as symbols, and think by manipulating the symbols following programlike rules. The goal of cognitive scientists who adopt the symbol-system hypothesis is to merge the study of information processing in living organisms and computers into a single rigorous enterprise that explains artificial and natural intelligence as produced by symbol manipulation.

Functionalism

Their hope is based on an answer to the mind-body problem called *functionalism*. The basic thesis of functionalism is that mind is to body as program is to computer. A program is a collection of rules that operate on stored information and control the behavior of its computer. Similarly, a mind may be treated as a set of rules—such as the rules of logic—that manipulate information stored in working memory and LTM, and that control the behavior of its body. Functionalism was the inspiration that created the field of cognitive science, because if functionalism is true then organisms and computers are fundamentally the same. Humans and computers are both informavores (Pylyshyn, 1984)—consumers of information—processing encoded information by following programs. According to functionalism, the only difference between humans and computers is that we are made of wetware and they are made of hardware, and psychologists are computer programmers faced with the task of inferring the program of the human mind the way programmers might if faced with an alien computer.

Central to functionalism is the fact that the same program can be run on physically different machines. The algorithms of symbolic information processing create intelligence and because the same algorithms can be implemented by different hardwares, they should be implementable by neural wetware too. The details of "mere implementation" form no part of the theory of intelligence, according to functionalism, and may be left to computer engineers and physiologists. Although functionalism does not posit the existence of a spiritual human soul, it is to a degree dualistic (Searle, 1980/1990; 1990a, 1991), because it sharply separates the processes of intelligence from their physical implementation. A computer program is not spiritual, but it is quite distinct from silicon or tissue. Indeed, a kind of immortality is offered by functionalism, since if one's mind could be written as a program it could be downloaded into a computer and survive the death of the body (Dennett, 1978). The symbol-system hypothesis thus takes the intentional stance to both human beings and computers.

On the functionalist view, psychology should be pursued by writing programs that simulate the processes of thought. Doing so requires distinguishing pure AI from computer simulation. At the cognitive level, no distinction need be made between physical embodiments of intelligence, because specifying the task to be performed says nothing about the device that is to perform it. However, at the algorithm level, there is usually more than one set of computations capable of achieving the same result. For example, consider the cognitive-level task "playing good chess." Currently, the best computer chess program is called *Deep Blue,* and it has even defeated Gary Kasparov, the reigning human world champion. However, the way *Deep Blue* plays chess is unlike the way any human, even Kasparov, plays chess. Given a chess problem, the human grandmaster considers just a few promising lines of attack and the opponent's likely replies. One grandmaster was asked how many moves ahead he thought, and replied, "Just one, but it's the right one."

Kasparov acknowledges that *Deep Blue* possesses real chess intelligence, but says it's weird. In contrast to the human master, *Deep Blue,* like almost all computer chess programs, uses a brute force approach. Given a problem, *Deep Blue* considers every possible move and countermove, however stupid, computing thousands of moves and countermoves. When it runs out of time—the number of possible chess situations is perhaps equal to half the number of molecules in the universe—it chooses the best position from among the millions it has calculated, and moves back to find the current move most likely to arrive at that superior position. Human consciousness and thought are incapable of calculating on such a gargantuan scale.

Deep Blue is an example of pure AI: It accomplishes the cognitive level task of playing good chess, but it does so by following procedures quite different from that of any human. On the other hand, one might try to write a program that approaches chess as a human grandmaster does, as do a few, such as the first serious chess program, *Belle* (developed at the AT&T Bell Telephone Labs). *Belle* is thus an example of computer simulation, achieving a cognitive level task by following the same program steps as human minds. The pioneers in computer simulation of human thinking and the creators of the symbol-system hypothesis are Herbert Simon and Allen Newell (1976/1990). They divide human intelligence into two realms: general purpose problem solving and intuitive expertise (Simon, 1991).

Problem Solving: Representation and Search

Beginning in the 1950s, Newell and Simon worked on a program called the *General Problem Solver.* Their goal was to create a program able to solve problems regardless of content, as do humans. Two processes were central to problem solving as they conceived it. The first was *representation,* precisely defining a problem and its solution, and *search,* looking for the path leading from the current problematic situation to its solution.

Representation.   As an example, take the extensively studied *Tower of Hanoi* problem. The *Tower of Hanoi* is a children's game involving three different-sized washers stacked pyramid-like on the leftmost of three poles.

This position constitutes the initial state of the *Tower of Hanoi* game. The goal state consists of the same pyramid-like arrangement of the washers on the rightmost pole. The rules of the game state that one can move only one piece at a time, and may never place a larger washer on a smaller washer, defining the sole operator in *Tower of Hanoi.* Applying the operator to the initial state (e.g., moving the small washer to the middle pole) generates a new state of the game. Applying the operator over and over, we could list every possible state of the game—that is, every possible legal arrangement of washers on poles—one of which would be the initial state and one of which would be the goal state. A complete illustration of all the possible states arranged to show how each is generated by the operator would constitute the complete state space, problem space, or search space of the *Tower of Hanoi* game. Any problem can be represented as a state space containing the initial state, the goal state, and all the possible intervening states. This generalized search space is shown in Figure 2.1.

Search.   Once a problem has been represented as a problem space, solving the problem involves searching for a path—optimally, the shortest path—between the initial and goal states. With an extremely simple problem such as the *Tower of Hanoi* or *Tic-Tac-Toe,* it is possible to carry out an exhaustive search, representing all possible states of the game, so that finding the shortest path is quite easy. However, in more difficult problems such as chess, it is impossible to generate and represent the complete problem space. In such cases, the problem solver, whether human or machine, can look ahead only a few moves, applying the operator or operators to the current state and generating new states, hoping to move closer to the goal.

The simplest way to proceed is to generate all the possible new states from the current state, a process called blind search. *Deep Blue* uses a type of blind search to play chess, since it generates all possible moves from a given situation without regard for how good they are. Blind search can be conducted as breadth-first search or depth-first search. In breadth-first search, all possible moves from a given position are computed; then all the possible moves from each of the new positions; then all the possible moves from the third set of positions, and so on. In depth-first search, one move is generated, then one move from that one, then one move from that one, and so on. In

FIGURE 2.1 Representation and search.

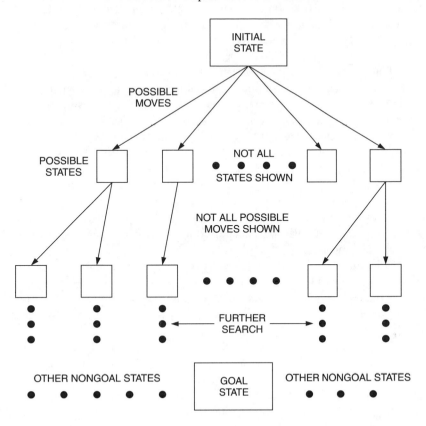

breadth-first search, the search space grows like a broad bush, filling out all moves at a given level before moving on to the next, while depth-first search moves through the search space like a single tree branch. In general, breadth-first search is conservative, while depth-first search has the potential to suddenly find the solution—show insight—although it may explore many blind alleys.

Search can be forward-chaining or backward-chaining. In forward-chaining search, also known as data-driven search, search begins at the initial state and works forward toward the goal. Backward-chaining, or goal-directed, search begins at the defined goal state and moves backward toward the goal. Mixed search strategies, combining forward- and backward-chaining, are also possible, in which the system conducts both kinds of searches looking for an intersection of the two.

The problems of blind search illustrate the challenges of *bounded rationality,* a central concern of Simon's since his days as an economist. As we have seen, human beings are cognitively incapable of thinking about all aspects of complex problems. We are not optimally rational because our thought processes are constrained, or bounded, by cognitive limitations such as the restricted size of working term memory (Chapter 5) and outside constraints such as time. Dealing with bounded rationality is a key aspect of the study of thinking (Chapter 9), the evolution of mind (see following and Chapter 14); emotion has a role to play in helping us act effectively (Chapter 13).

Even a computer is constrained by time and computational power, and can rarely carry out an exhaustive search. But without a complete representation of the problem space, blind search is groping in the dark hoping to stumble on the solution to the problem. Search can be improved if guided by an evaluation function capable of deciding which of various generated moves is the most promising.

For example, since it cannot generate the complete search space for chess, *Deep Blue* searches ahead for a limited period of time, generating as many move and countermove possibilities as possible in the time allotted. Then it evaluates the positions it has generated, and chooses to move toward the one that seems most favorable to it. Over the years, chess masters have developed ways of evaluating positions, and these can be embodied in chess programs. One simple evaluation function concerns material balance. Chess players assign point values to different chess pieces, for example, assigning 1 point to pawns, 3 to knights and bishops, 5 to rooks (castles), and 9 to the queen. It is thus possible to evaluate a chess position in terms of the point values of the pieces captured by each side. So, for example, if White has captured a knight and a bishop (6 points), and Black has captured a rook and two pawns (7 points), Black has the material advantage.

Computer chess programs can easily incorporate a material balance algorithm as an evaluation function, and use it to choose the most favorable position from among those generated by the search process. Use of evaluation functions improves blind search by allowing the system to prune unpromising lines of search from the search space tree.

The great contribution of Newell and Simon to artificial intelligence was the concept of *heuristic search*. Since rationality in both human and machine is bounded, search can be improved by the adoption of imperfect rules of thumb. Heuristics are to be contrasted with algorithms. In logic and mathematics, an algorithm is an effective decision procedure, that is, a procedure that, if followed correctly, guarantees an answer to a problem. The normative rules of logic discussed in Chapter 9 or the rules of arithmetic are examples of algorithms, because, when followed correctly, they guarantee that an argument is logically valid. The BASIC program for addition is an algorithm; unless the computer is defective, the value of Z will always be the sum of X and Y. Exhaustive search is algorithmic, since if the complete search space is known, the path to the goal becomes obvious. Use of algorithms guarantees optimal solutions.

However, bounded rationality means that optimal solutions can rarely be found. Constrained resources mean that complete search spaces can rarely be generated, and problem space searches need to be guided by satisfying heuristics, cognitive shortcuts that provide satisfactory solutions to problems, rather than optimizing algorithms that would, if we had world enough and time, provide the best possible solution to any problem. Evaluation functions are one way to guide search in the absence of complete information; heuristics (which can include evaluation functions) are another. Heuristics are search procedures or evaluation functions that guide search toward a solution but do not ensure that the goal will be reached.

Because chess is so difficult, it challenges human (and computer) bounded rationality, and chess masters have proposed many rules that are helpful but that cannot assure victory. Although players who follow these rules will not win every game, they will win more games than those who do not follow them.

In their attempt to build a general problem solver (GPS), Newell and Simon wanted heuristics that were not limited to the domain of chess or to any other specific task. They believed that human intelligence was truly general, applicable to any sort of situation, and that differences between problem solvers reflected differences in general problem-solving ability. In this respect, Newell and Simon agreed with constructors of intelligence tests and with Piaget, who regard intelligence as a content-independent ability to reason. They formulated a number of heuristics that they believed underlie intelligent problem solving in any situation, such as means-ends analysis and subgoaling (see Chapter 9).

Intuition: Expertise and the Importance of Knowledge

Ultimately, Newell and Simon's general problem solver proved chimerical. They discovered that intelligent behavior only rarely depends on having a general purpose high-IQ tool kit. Instead, intelligent action requires deep knowledge about the problem domain. A study by Chase and Simon (1973) of chess players drove the point home. Novice and expert chess players were briefly shown chess positions that they were then to reproduce on an empty board. Some of the positions were made by randomly placing pieces on the board, while others were drawn from actual chess matches. Novices and masters did not differ in their ability to reproduce random positions, but masters were nearly perfect at remembering real games. Masters had an intuitive ability to see without conscious thought the move and countermove tensions in the real games, which were lacking in the random positions. Thus the difference between masters and novices was caused not by domain-independent abilities to hold items in working memory, but by domain-specific knowledge, possessed by the former but not the latter.

The insight that intelligent action demands domain-specific knowledge, not simply a few domain-independent heuristics, wrought a sea change in artificial intelligence. Traditional computer programming languages implicitly assumed that thinking was domain independent, and cleanly separated program steps (thinking) from data (knowledge). The simple BASIC program for addition, for example, is empty of knowledge, since the values of X, Y, and Z are not specified. Building computer systems with humanlike expertise (expert systems) required new programming languages intermingling program steps and data, thought and knowledge. One of the most influential programming languages for expert systems is the *production system* (Newell, 1973), which has been widely used in AI and computational modeling since its introduction (see Figure 2.2).

At the heart of any production system are the *production rules* stored in long-term memory. Productions are program rules cast as "if . . . then" statements consisting of a condition and an action. Let us take as an example an expert system for appraising the value of yachts (Minasi, 1990). We would interview an expert yacht appraiser and extract from him the rules he follows when setting the price of his wares, a process called knowledge engineering. For example, shown a picture of a yacht, the appraiser might say it's worth $700,000, explaining that "It's a 35-foot yawl with teak above deck" (p. 13). In our computer expert system, we could represent this knowledge with the production:

10 *If* a yacht is a yawl,
    and it is 35 feet long,
    and it has teak above deck,
    then it is worth $700,000.

FIGURE 2.2 Structure of a Typical Production System.

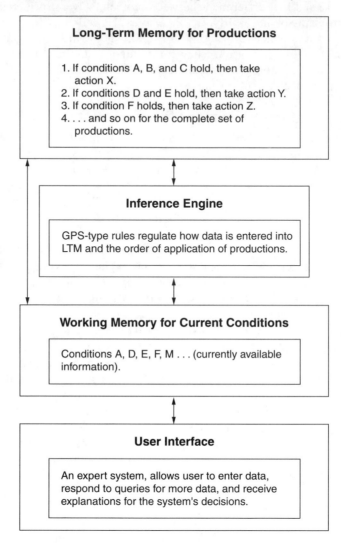

The condition describes the item, and the action sets its value. Another production might read:

20 *If* a yacht is a yawl,

    and it is 35 feet long,

    then it is worth $500,000.

This rule sets the value of yachts whose above deck wood is not teak or is unknown. Making the conditions more precise can make productions be more knowledgeable. For example, we show the appraiser a picture of a yacht that looks just like the first one, but are told it's worth $800,000. Inquiring why, we're told "No, that's a Horton Special. They only made 70 of them. Quite in demand. That's not just any yawl" (p. 13). We would then write a new production:

30 *If* a yacht is a yawl,

    and it is 35 feet long,

    and it has teak above deck,

    and it is a Horton Special,

    then it is worth $800,000.

Notice that unlike the content-free rules of the GPS, production rules commingle data (knowledge) and program procedures (rules of thought). Thus production systems can model the expert knowledge typically needed for intelligent behavior in the real world as opposed to the artificial world of abstract and unfamiliar problems such as the Tower of Hanoi.

In operation, production systems operate by first loading information into working memory. The inference engine determines which information in working memory matches a production, and that production's action is carried out. For example, if we loaded into working memory the information that a yacht was a 35-foot yawl with teak above deck, we would be told that its value was $700,000. In a sophisticated expert system (see Box 2.1), the program also asks questions to elicit further information, and may carry out actions that place new data in working memory, triggering further productions before carrying out any actual behavior.

In Chapter 3, we look at a production system model for explaining Pavlovian conditioning.

The Brain's-Eye View: Connectionism

For many years, the symbol-system view of learning and cognition dominated the field of cognitive science. As Jerry Fodor, one of its creators, said, it was the only game in town. Much of the appeal of the symbol-system view came from its contention that thinking is following rules. When we think consciously, we often follow rules, as we saw previously, and the idea that rational behavior is rule-following behavior has an ancient and persuasive lineage. In the mid-1980s, however, cognitive science was unsettled by the appearance of a new cognitive architecture, connectionism, that capitalized on discontent with the symbol-system hypothesis. The basic thesis of connectionism is that psychological theory ought to be modeled on the human brain, not on the unhuman computer (Rumelhart et al., 1986). Because connectionism says the intuitive processor operates like the brain rather than like the conscious processor, Clark (1989) calls it the brain's-eye view of learning and cognition.

Critique of the Symbol-System Hypothesis

For a few years after its dramatic appearance in the mid-1980s, cognitive scientists seemed to have to choose between the symbol-system hypothesis *or* connectionism as the right way to model the mind (Fodor & Pylyshyn, 1988; Hintzman, 1990; McCloskey, 1991; Penrose, 1989; Pinker & Prince, 1988). Although the two architectures are now seen as complementary, a good place to begin to understand the value of the connectionist approach to psychology is to return to the criticisms its

■ Box 2.1 ■

CYC: The Ultimate Expert System?

"Mary saw a bicycle in the store window. She wanted it." How do we know—as we do immediately and without thought—that Mary wants the bicycle, not the store and not the window? Newspaper headline: "British Left Waffles on Falklands." How do we know the headline means that British left-wing politicians were unsure what policy to adopt when the Argentineans seized the Falkland Islands, not that waffles were left behind by British visitors?

In both cases, the answer is that in reading and understanding these sentences we bring to bear enormous amounts of knowledge over and above the syntax of the sentences and the dictionary meanings of the words. We know, without having ever been told, and without the fact being written down in any encyclopedia or dictionary, that girls or boys covet what the window contains, a bicycle, not the window itself or the shop to which it belongs. Our understanding of the sentence would change, or at least become equivocal, if the sentence read, "Mary, whose velocipede shop had been destroyed in the earthquake, saw a bicycle in the store window. She wanted it." The vast store of knowledge that we habitually use to interpret experience is common sense.

Computer programs, however, lack common sense. Ultimately, GPS failed because it lacked common sense; it had no knowledge at all, just a few general purpose problem-solving heuristics quite incapable of understanding simple sentences or headlines. Knowledge engineering—the construction of expert systems—represents an attempt to create computers with common sense in a specific knowledge domain. Expert systems possess knowledge in addition to reasoning heuristics. Yet expert systems' commonsense intelligence is (at best) limited to a single topic. Douglas Lenat thinks that ordinary common sense is everyday expertise, and can be duplicated by a computer program.

Lenat is working to create a computer program—CYC, for encyclopedia, but probably also for psychology—which will contain the commonsense expertise of the ordinary person. It is a daunting task that Lenat has been working on, aided by a team of programmers, for several years, and which he hopes to complete by 1999. Lenat's team reads encyclopedias, dictionaries, books, magazines, how-to manuals in an effort to figure out what humans need to know to let them understand language and act adaptively in the world, and then build it into frame schemata in CYC's memory. The work often reveals that what people know they did not know they knew. Have you ever thought about the fact that toast-like breakfast breads and dithering are designated by the same word, "waffles"? Even the simplest statements depend on huge amounts of prior understanding. It required two months of work programming in information about life, death, and emotions to get CYC to compute the sentence "Napoleon died in 1821; Wellington was saddened."

Even some partisans of AI doubt if Lenat will succeed. His former student Rodney Brooks—creator of the animat approach to AI—thinks that CYC is the last gasp of GOFAI. His project has already demonstrated that even simple behavior requires awesome amounts of knowledge. Lenat thinks that one day every computer will contain CYC as a universal database that we will be able to talk to like a person. Can human intelligence be held on tape? By 2000, CYC still had not achieved parity with human common sense, but Lenat had founded CYCORP to sell CYC as an intelligent search engine for the Internet (www.cycorp.com).

See David H. Freedman, "Common Sense and the Computer," *Discover,* August 1990, pp. 65–71. If you go to www.cycorp.com, various articles about Lenat and his projects are posted.

founders made of the older approach, sometimes called Good Old Fashioned Artificial Intelligence (GOFAI).

Computers are powerful and capable of many impressive feats, such as playing championship chess. However, there are good reasons for rejecting GOFAI as the only acceptable architecture of cognition (Rumelhart et al., 1986). We will mention just three complaints that were especially important in making connectionism attractive to cognitive scientists. The first is the obvious fact that the brain is not a step-by-step serial-processing device. Unlike conventional computers with a single powerful CPU through which all data flows one step at a time, brains are composed of thousands of simple computing units (neurons) all working at the same time and massively interconnected.

This dissimilarity between computer and brain leads to the second reason for doubting the validity of the symbol-system conception of human intelligence. Computer CPUs are incredibly fast, able to compute several hundred thousand program steps per second. Neurons, however, are relatively slow, depending on chemical processes to both carry impulses along axons and propagate signals across synaptic clefts. If brains had to think by carrying out only one step at a time, they would be hard pressed to salivate for food, much less play basketball. Since human brains can think and react quickly, it seems necessary that they do so by processing in parallel, carrying out many computational steps at the same time. This point is especially important for thinking about an evolved intelligence such as our own. Surviving to reproduce—the key problem of evolution—means not just finding the right solution to a problem, but finding the solution in time. Shakespeare's Hamlet was "sicklied o'er by the pale cast of thought," unable to act effectively, as computer scientists say, "in real time," and by the end of the play has brought death not only to himself but to those he loved and ruin for the kingdom of Denmark. Faced by a bear in the woods, Hamlet might be eaten while thinking what to do. Parallel processing systems, capable of several thoughts at a time, should be better at solving problems in real time than serial systems (see Chapter 13).

The third shortcoming of traditional artificial intelligence is empirical and fascinating and was the main source of excitement about connectionism in AI. Computer programs now exist that do things humans admire because they find them extremely difficult. For example, *Deep Blue* is a world-class chess player, and most people look in awe on human grand masters as geniuses. However, no computer can as yet perform the wide variety of tasks that even animals and toddlers carry out without thought: moving around in a room full of objects, reading handwriting, recognizing a friend's face.

In an interview, Michael Jordan once described one of his most famous shots. After relating what he was thinking during the few seconds involved, Jordan observed that he really hadn't had those thoughts at all, but simply made his moves. Reflective, step-by-step construction of his actions—the "thoughts" he described to the reporter—came later. The failure of traditional artificial intelligence to simulate the simplest human skills, despite years of work and increasing computational power, has made many psychologists suspect that the symbol-system, serial processing model of the human mind needs to be supplemented by theories better suited to explain intuitive, nonconscious behavior, and that, instead of looking to the computer for our model of mind, we should look to the brain.

Connectionist Cognitive Architecture: Units and Neural Nets

In one sense, the connectionist architecture is much simpler than the symbol-system architecture. The symbol-system view distinguishes various memory systems and executive processes responsible for different cognitive processes. Connectionism makes no distinction between types of memory or memory versus thinking. Instead, its architecture of cognition consists of many simple neuron-like computing units multiply interconnected into a brain-like network. Each unit is identical to every other unit, and learning, memory, and thought are all changing patterns of activity in the network as a whole.

Figure 2.3 shows a typical connectionist computing unit. The conceptual inspiration for these units is the neuron, so that connectionist systems are sometimes called *neural networks*. Neurons receive multiple dendritic connections from many other neurons in the nervous system; in connectionist units, this becomes a fan-in of connections from other units. In neurons, synaptic connections from one neuron to another can be excitatory (if the presynaptic neuron fires, it increases the chance that the postsynaptic neuron will fire), or inhibitory (if the presynaptic neuron fires, it reduces the chance that the postsynaptic neuron will fire). In connectionist units, connections may likewise be excitatory or inhibitory. In real neurons, synaptic strengths vary from zero (firing of the presynaptic neuron has no effect on the activity of the postsynaptic neuron) to very great. Similarly, connectionist units' connections are weighted, typically from zero (no strength) to 1.00 (full strength). Weights can also be used to represent whether a connection is inhibitory or excitatory, taking values ranging from −1.00 through 0 to + 11.00. Neurons fire action potentials down an axon that is connected to many other neurons. In connectionist units, this is represented by a fan-out of connections from one unit to others. Finally, neurons react to the sum of all the inputs it is receiving from its input dendritic connections, and if the overall level of excitation is at the input synapses, the neuron will fire an axon potential, sending an electrochemical

FIGURE 2.3   Typical unit in connectionist "neural network."

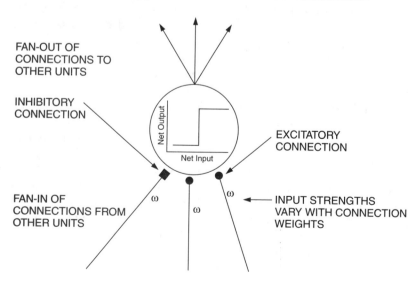

impulse to other units with which it is connected. Connectionist units also sum the net input they receive, and send some output to other units in consequence. The figure shows a unit that, like most neurons, computes a step function: Like neurons, it computes to total input, inhibitory and excitatory, and if the overall level of excitation (net input) reaches a threshold value, it sends a full strength message to the units to which it is connected. A connectionist unit may compute any mathematical function. For example, the output may be graded instead of all-or-none: the greater the level of input, the greater the output strength. If graded, the output may be a linear function of input or a nonlinear function. Different connectionist networks use different rules, depending on the task at hand and the tastes of the network designer.

Connectionist neuron-like units are then assembled into working models, or neural networks. Many possible neural network types are possible. Figure 2.4 shows a very simple, hypothetical three-layer neural network of the "feedback" type.

Any neural network has to have at least two layers, one to represent stimuli from the environment (the input layer) and another to represent behavioral responses to the stimuli (the output layer). Two-layer networks of these types were proposed in the 1950s, but their inability to simulate complex behaviors led to the dominance in AI and cognitive science of the symbol-system architecture. Modern developments in mathematics and computing have made possible creation of networks that have hidden layers intervening between input and output. It is possible to design networks with many hidden layers, but the network in Figure 2.4 has just one. It is also a feedforward network because connections between units proceed layer by layer from input to output. Networks can also have connections between units within a layer and from later layers to earlier layers (feedbackward).

Symbol-system models of cognition are programmed: the designer builds in the rules that govern the system or, in the case of a production system, encodes the system's knowledge. Neural networks learn instead, making them attractive to cognitive

FIGURE 2.4   Hypothetical feedback neural network.

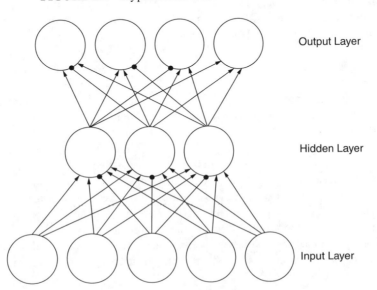

scientists interested in learning rather than problem solving or expertise. A designer simply sets up a network like the one in the figure and then assigns random weights to the connections between units. He or she then trains it to behave correctly. As with conditioning an animal, the designer presents stimuli to the input layer and observes the "behavior" of the output layer. If the response is correct, the connection weights are left alone. If the response is incorrect, the connection weights are tweaked to move the response in the correct direction. This procedure is then iterated until the network has learned the required responses to the different stimuli. In Chapter 3 we will look in more detail at this process in the case of Pavlovian conditioning.

Hybrid Models and the Mind-Body Problem

Connectionist models have a number of features that have excited psychologists of learning and cognition. The first is their plausibility as first-approximation models of brain function. Another concerns learning. While some symbol-manipulation models, such as SOAR, are capable of learning, most are not; they represent knowledge and can make decisions. Few symbolic models can adjust their own programs. Neural networks learn spontaneously, however, in roughly the same way animals and people do, by trial, error, and feedback. Neural networks, like living creatures, are thus spontaneously self-organizing, needing no explicit programming.

A third advantage of connectionist systems is that neural networks, unlike traditional symbol-system models, are fault-tolerant. Symbol systems are notoriously "brittle" in two respects. First, presented with situations other than those in which they have been programmed, their behavior breaks down completely because they have not been encoded with the information they need to act. Neural networks, however, act more like people. Presented with new stimuli that resemble but are not identical with those on which they were trained, they can make good guesses as to the pattern or concept. Thus, neural networks are much better at pattern recognition, one of the apparently simple human abilities that traditional artificial intelligences lacked.

The second respect in which traditional serial processing systems are brittle is familiar to any computer user: If even one small thing goes wrong with a program or with hardware, the entire system crashes. In this respect, serial computers are unlike human beings, who can suffer brain damage, yet continue to function, albeit less well. For example, former President Reagan's Press Secretary Jim Brady was shot in the head during John Hinckley's attempted assassination of Reagan, yet, despite massive cortical damage, Brady's personality and intelligence are reasonably intact. Like humans, neural networks show this same graceful degradation. They can be damaged by hypothetical lesions and still function at reduced levels of efficiency. The fault-tolerance of neural networks has attracted considerable commercial attention, since computer users would prefer systems that continue to work despite being damaged.

Connectionist theory suffers from some drawbacks. An important one stems from its promise to substitute realistic brain-style theories of the mind for unrealistic computer-style theories. Although the inspiration for connectionist units and neural nets lies in biological neurons and brain circuits, there are important differences between them. For example, real brains operate in a biochemical soup whose contents modify neural operations. Neurons communicate by sending chemical messages through chemically complex synapses, processes that are completely foreign to connectionist networks. In connectionist networks, all units are the same, while in real brains there are many kinds of neurons. Standard back-propagation procedures for changing connection weights assume that error information can be sent back along the connections from response units to sensory units. Real neurons can transmit information in only one direction. In short, while in a gross way connectionist units and networks model the structure of biological nervous systems, their mode of operation does not. Neural units, connections, and connection weights are mathematical fictions, not real things even inside the computers that run their programs, with the exception of a small number of machines like the Connection Machine.

Another problem with connectionist networks is that, since they learn instead of being programmed, the inner workings of neural nets is as mysterious as the inner workings of the brain, and therefore connectionism is unhelpful as an explanation of human behavior. Attempts to specify what neural networks learn is an object of much research (e.g., Hanson & Burr, 1990). Substituting an artificial mystery for a natural mystery is a limited advance for psychology, though it may be acceptable in pure AI.

Finally, artificial neural nets have a hard time learning to do more than one thing. When we learn a new task, our ability to learn it may be hindered by earlier learning. For example, Americans learn to drive on the left side of the road, so that mastering driving in Britain—on the right side of the road—poses a special challenge. Also, learning a new task may interfere with the ability to perform an already learned one. If you drive in Britain long enough, it may take a while to reacclimatize to driving on the left when you leave. These are example of *interference,* occasions when learning one task makes learning or retrieving another more difficult (see Part III). Frequently, learning one task has no influence on another. Thus, learning to speak French does not interfere with our ability to drive. Connectionist networks, however, suffer from *catastrophic* interference (French, 1999). We might train a network to predict the winners of horse races from the past performance of the horses, and then train it to diagnose mental disorders from the results of mental tests. If a human learned both tasks, we would not expect mastering one job to interfere with the other. The neural network, on the other hand, would have forgotten all it knew about handicapping horse races by being taught psychological diagnosis. Solving the problem of catastrophic interference in artificial neural networks has proved daunting, and has moved some connectionists to give up some of their more radical ideas. For example, connectionists originally rejected the traditional psychological distinction between short-term (or working) memory and long-term memory (see Part III), but now see accepting it as the only way to solve the problem of catastrophic interference (French, 1999).

Because each kind of architecture is best at different kinds of tasks, they can be reconciled as psychological theories by regarding the human mind as a hybrid of the two (Bechtel & Abrahamsen, 1991; Clark, 1989). At the neural level, learning and cognition must be carried out by connectionist-type processes, since the brain is a collection of simple but massively interconnected units. Yet as we have learned, physically different computational systems may implement the same programs. Therefore it is possible that, although the brain is a massively parallel computer like the Connection Machine, the human mind in its conscious aspects is a serial processor of representations. The more automatic and unconscious (intuitive) aspects of the human mind are connectionist in nature. Connectionist theories thus have a valuable role to play in being the vital interface between symbol-system models of rational, rule-following thought, and intuitive, nonlinear, nonsymbolic thought.*

Dennett's multiple drafts model of consciousness (Chapter 1) relies on the idea of the mind as a hybrid of serial and parallel processing. Specifically, Dennett proposes that consciousness—Smolensky's conscious processor—is a serial virtual machine implemented in the brain's parallel architecture—Smolensky's intuitive processor. Many computer environments contain virtual calculators. If you activate a calculator, an image appears on the computer screen of a real calculator. On the image, one can place the mouse's cursor on a key, click the left mouse button, and the virtual calculator will carry out the operation just like the real calculator.

Real calculators carry out their functions by virtue of how they are wired. The calculators in computers carry out their functions by virtue of programs written to imitate real calculators. Computers are general purpose devices that can be programmed to imitate any special purpose device. The virtual calculators seem to work just like the real calculators they mimic, but the electronic work done behind the scenes is completely different. Broadly speaking, every program running on a computer implements a different *virtual machine*. The calculator programs create a virtual calculator; a flight simulator creates a virtual airplane, a chess program creates a virtual chessboard and a virtual opponent.

Dennett argues that consciousness is a virtual machine installed by socialization on the brain's parallel processor. Most importantly, socialization gives us language, and in language we think and speak one thought at a time, creating our serial-processing conscious processors. Human beings are remarkably flexible creatures, able to adapt to every environment on earth and aspiring to living in space and on distant planets. Animals are like real calculators, possessing hardwired responses that fit each one to the particular environments in which its species evolved. People are like general purpose computers, adapting to the world not by changing their physical natures but by changing their programs. The programs are cultures that adapt to changing places and changing times. Learning a culture creates consciousness, and consciousness is adaptive because it bestows the ability to think about one's actions, to mull over alternatives, to plan ahead, to acquire general knowledge, and to be a member of one's society. It is through social interaction—not through solitary hunting, foraging, and reproduction—that individual humans and cultures survive and flourish.

May we in this way solve the mind-body problem? Can the mind be regarded as a two tier—one serial and rule-following, the other parallel and mathematical—cognitive system implemented in a neural, parallel processing computer? The question is a vexed and controversial one (Churchland & Churchland, 1990; Searle, 1990) focusing on intentionality. Brentano said the hallmark of the mental is intentionality, and

---

*Two other approaches to artificial intelligence deserve mention, artificial life and *animats*. Artificial life (Levy, 1993) researchers use mathematical complexity theory to study how organized, apparently intelligent behavior can arise spontaneously out of essentially random combinations of simpler, less intelligent rules. The situated cognition (Mataric, 1998) or animat approach (Brooks, 1995, Dean, 1998) to AI rejects the GOFAI approach of building large and complex systems meant to capture intelligence from the top down. Instead, advocates of the animats build much simpler AI devices that mimic simple intelligent behaviors such as those of insects, hence the name animat. They hope then to work from the bottom up to high-level intelligence. AI-life and animats share two important features, working from simplicity to complexity and being based squarely on evolution. However, at least at present they are primarily forms of pure AI, and while they provide important warnings about GOFAI, they have not exerted strong influence on cognitive psychology.

we may ask if computer systems of either type possess intentionality. John Searle thinks not. Because computers are not actively connected to the outside world, their representations, whether coded as symbols or connections, are arbitrary and, to the computer, meaningless. For example, when I consult my word processor's thesaurus, it gives me a set of words that mean roughly the same as my target word. Let's try it now for artificial. The first five alternatives it listed were dummy, ersatz, false, imitation, and mock. Superficially my computer can do what a human can do, come up with words of similar meaning. However, my computer does not understand the meaning of the word artificial. To it, artificial is just a pattern of 0s and 1s in its random access memory, and when I highlight artificial on my screen and invoke the thesaurus, the program simply compares the highlighted RAM pattern with patterns found in a particular area of my computer's hard disk, retrieves associated patterns of 0s and 1s, and displays them on my screen as a pattern of dots that I interpret as words of similar meaning.

Thus, although I have intentionality—I know the meanings of artificial, dummy, ersatz, false, imitation, and mock—my computer and my word processor do not. Therefore, if intentionality is the criterion of the mental, my computer does not have a mind. At present, the validity of this argument is controversial. Perhaps intentionality is not the criterion for possessing a mind (Dennett, 1992). Perhaps current computers' lack of intentionality is merely a limit imposed by today's technology, and computers of the future will have minds (Searle, 1991). Perhaps although serial, symbolic processing computers do not and cannot have intentionality, future parallel machines will possess intentionality because they will interact with the environment and spontaneously self-organize instead of being programmed (Dreyfus & Dreyfus, 1990). These considerations take us into philosophical fields far removed from learning and cognition (Leahey, 1992). In the field of artificial intelligence, cognitive scientists are building something mind-like with both symbol manipulation and connectionist architectures. Whether mind-like becomes mind-identical remains to be seen.

Important to examining this question is the fact that humans design artificial intelligences, but our own intelligence is natural, designed over many generations by evolution.

NATURAL MIND DESIGN: EVOLUTION

Artificial intelligence is an attempt by scientists to design minds that work effectively in the real world. However, there are minds—animal and human minds—that already work effectively in the real world, and these minds were designed by natural selection (Dawkins, 1996; Deacon, 1998; Dennett, 1996). In the last few years, an important new movement in psychology has begun, called *evolutionary psychology* (Barkow, Cosmides, & Tooby, 1994), that studies how the human mind evolved. Evolutionary psychologists reject the reigning Standard Social Science Model (SSSM) of human mind and behavior (Barkow et al., 1994; Pinker, 1994). The SSSM holds that people are entirely molded by their environment—by learning—and that our genes—the vehicles that carry our evolutionary inheritance—play no important role in determining how we think, feel, and act. In contrast, evolutionary psychologists believe that how we think, feel, and act is powerfully constrained and directed by our ancestors' success in evolution. Specifically, they reject the idea associated with the general problem solver that human intelligence is a general-purpose problem-solving device. Instead, they argue that the human mind is a collection of separate modules that evolved to solve particular evolutionary problems (Cosmides & Tooby, 1997; Mithen, 1996; Pinker, 1999). Thus, there is a specialized module for language, a specialized module for social intelligence, a specialized module for attributing thoughts and beliefs to other people (see Box 2.2), and so on. In AI terms, some aspects of human expertise are innate rather than learned.

In this last section we will examine the process of natural selection, trace what is known about the course of human evolution, and examine how *Homo sapiens*' most important adaptive trait—intelligence—may have evolved. Chapter 9 will include discussion of the evolution of specific cognitive abilities and Chapter 14 will take up the evolutionary psychology of human social behavior.

Principles of Evolution

Although everyone has heard of Darwin and Darwin's theory, it is so misunderstood that a review of its basics is called for. The first thing we associate with Darwin is something he did not discover, and which was well on its way to acceptance before Darwin published his *Origin of Species* in 1859. It is the idea of descent—the notion that present living forms are the altered descendants of long-extinct predecessors down millions of years of change. What Darwin contributed was a workable mechanism for explaining why species should change; why some should go extinct, some remain stable for millennia, and still others undergo alteration toward their present form. Integrated with Mendelian genetics, this Neo-Darwinian theory is the most widely accepted account of the mechanism of evolutionary change, and forms the foundation of evolutionary psychology.

Darwinian Natural Selection

The basic Darwinian concept is simple: species become extinct if they fail in the struggle for existence. They will survive unchanged if they are perfectly suited to their environments. They change (evolve) when some of their members struggle more effectively than others and are therefore able to pass on their genes to more offspring that live longer, while the weak die young and childless and their genes with them. There is no obvious reason to exclude social behavior from the process of natural selection. The ability to find, choose, and keep a mate and to rear offspring with it are abilities needed for the struggle for existence, and so will be subject to selection. When group living confers selective advantage, it will evolve; when the ability to learn quickly and react flexibly to new challenges confers selective advantage, it will evolve.

Natural selection can shape behavior in subtle ways. It is often thought that all evolution does is to promote bloody aggression between individuals. Although evolution may favor aggression, it also constrains it. Moreover, the competition of natural selection may take place in wholly nonviolent ways, bringing many behaviors under evolutionary control. All that really counts in evolution is having offspring that live to maturity. Any trait or behavior that serves that end, or, more precisely, that aids one in having more successful offspring than anyone else, confers selective advantage.

For example, Bird A competes with bird B not (necessarily) by attacking it or killing it or depriving it of resources, but in other, more subtle ways. The female (A) may attract a stronger, fitter mate, who is better able to help protect and raise her (and his) offspring. A may be able to lay more eggs than B, have more clutches than

Mindblindness: An Anthropologist on Mars

Autism is a puzzling mental disorder that appears in earliest infancy. Autistic infants strike their mothers as strange, responding to being held by stiffening up, for example. Some autistic children withdraw totally into themselves, failing to learn to talk and sitting alone, clutching themselves and rocking compulsively, and the worst of these live out their lives in institutions. However, many autistics cope well enough to live on their own, and some, high-functioning autistics, excel.

It was for some time believed that autism was a childhood form of schizophrenia but it is now seen as a separate disorder. Some psychologists view autistics as suffering from "mindblindness." As discussed in the text in this chapter and elsewhere, all human beings possess a theory of the mind called "folk psychology" that is the basis for the process social psychologists call attribution. We readily explain other peoples' behavior as the outcome of their beliefs and desires, and we explain our own behavior by citing our own beliefs and desires. We are all natural psychologists before we ever study psychology. In a sense, we are mind readers who can immediately sense the motives and thoughts of others, although we do it by inference from how people act rather than by any paranormal power.

We are often wrong in our attributions precisely because we do not really read minds. What is most revealing about our mind-reading ability is how intuitive and automatic it is. Only rarely do we have to think hard about what people think and feel. Indeed it is impossible for us to refrain from attributing mental states to just about everything, including recalcitrant machines that "hate us." Attribution is as natural to us as breathing. Abilities that are intuitive are likely to be innate, wired into the brain rather than being products of conscious, serial, thought. Baron-Cohen (1995) suggests normal humans have an innate "Theory of Mind Module," but that autistics are born without one. They do not "see" motives and thoughts in behavior the way other people do.

Normal and autistic children behave very differently in experiments that require them to be natural psychologists. For example, imagine watching a child, Sally, place a marble in a basket on a table and leave the room. Another child, Anne, enters and places the marble in a box. Anne leaves, and Sally comes back. Where will she look for her marble? By age 3 to 4, normal children and children with Down syndrome know that Sally will look in the basket. They attribute to her the belief that the marble is still in the basket, and will look there because she does not know Anne moved it to the box. However, all but a few autistic children, even those some years older than the normal subjects, expected Sally to look in the box where the marble actually was. They do not ascribe a false belief to Sally. In another test, with British subjects, children were shown a familiar Smarties box that they expected to contain a popular type of candy. The box was opened revealing pencils instead of candy. The children were then asked what they had thought the box contained before it was opened, and what the next child would expect to find in the box. Normal children answered "Smarties" to both questions, remembering their own false belief and attributing the same false belief to the next subject. However, most autistic children answered "pencils" to both questions, unable to understand their own earlier false belief or the probable false belief of another, naive, child (Baron-Cohen, 1995).

(continued)

Perhaps the most remarkable high-functioning autistic is Temple Grandin, who survived childhood autism to become a famous professor of agricultural engineering, specializing in designing farms and factories for production and slaughtering of cattle, pigs, and sheep, but for whose welfare she is a ferocious advocate. She has learned to cope with other people through sheer computational—her word—intelligence and hard work. The mission of cognitive science has been thrust upon her by fate. She is unable to understand what minds are. She describes her own mind as a parallel-processing computer, and it has features the rest of us find strange. For example, she has memories that are perceptual in their clarity, almost hallucinatory, that she describes as like running a scene laid down on videotape. Moreover, once a memory has begun to play, it must be completed; she has no mental fast-forward button.

Grandin describes herself as being like "an anthropologist on Mars" surrounded by mysterious creatures whom she cannot understand and with whom she can cope only by dint of hard work. When she was young, she noted how children seemed to be able to read each others' minds, and thought they must be telepathic. Like most autistics, she was the butt of jokes and was often taken advantage of. Because she cannot ascribe motives and thoughts to others, she could not perceive that sometimes people have bad motives and lie to cover them. When acting as a consultant to a company whose machinery was experiencing abnormal rates of breakdown, she figured out that a particular employee was sabotaging the equipment by correlating his presence with broken machinery. "I had to learn to be suspicious, I had to learn it cognitively. I could put two and two together but I couldn't see the jealous look on his face" (Sacks, 1995, p. 260).

While Grandin and other high-functioning autistics know they lack things others have—Grandin does not know what falling in love is and takes no pleasure in a glorious sunset and finds no grandeur in the mountain ranges she is surrounded by in Colorado—she feels there are compensations, that being autistic is not so much being ill as being different. There is a tremendous ability to focus all one's mental energy on a single task, feeling none of the personal distractions that disrupt the thought of ordinary people. Autistics have powerful visual imagery. Grandin watched an engineer draw a building and found she could immediately do likewise without any training whatever. As she puts it, she has a powerful graphics computer workstation in her head. She can mentally design a building in the finest detail, and then walk through it, rotate it, zoom in, zoom out, locate problems, and then fix them. Drawing the plans is uncreative afterbirth. Autistics have a kind of moral purity. They lack all guile and deceit and do not see it in others. Grandin says, "If I could snap my fingers and be nonautistic, I would not because then I wouldn't be me." She warns against plans to eliminate genes for autism and other syndromes that make people "different": "It is possible that people with bits of these traits are more creative, or possibly even geniuses . . . science eliminated these genes, maybe the whole world would be taken over by accountants" (Sacks, 1995, pp. 291–292).

See T. Grandin and M. Scariano (1986), *Emergence: Labeled Autistic* (Novato, CA: Arena Press); S. Baron-Cohen (1995), *Mindblindness* (Cambridge, MA: MIT Press); and O. Sacks (1995), *An Anthropologist on Mars: Seven Paradoxical Tales* (New York: Knopf).

B, secure a better nest site than B. These behaviors need not involve direct competition between A and B, but they do confer a selective advantage on A. She will have more of her genes present in the next generation, and that is what evolution is all about—the changing frequencies of genes in the total gene pool.

The Concept of Fitness

The concept of fitness refers to how successful an individual is in passing his or her genes on to the next generation. Traditionally, the measure of fitness has been the number of offspring, since this is the most obvious and direct way of transmitting one's genes. More recently, however, gene thinking has expanded the older concept of fitness. In gene thinking we realize that (to speak metaphorically) it is each gene that seeks to replicate itself, and to increase its frequency in the next generation. Because an individual is genetically related to many people besides his children, a gene can increase its frequency in the population by changing his behavior toward his relatives as a whole. If a gene causes a person to act so as to enhance his or her relatives' fitness, that gene—which is very likely to be present in those relatives—will increase its numbers in the next generation.

Evolutionary theorists distinguish the concepts of *individual fitness* and *inclusive fitness*. Individual fitness refers to my genes' level of success in the struggle for existence as measured through my own individual offspring; the more offspring, the higher is the level of individual fitness. Inclusive fitness adds to this a proportion of my fitness measured through my effects on my relatives. To the extent that my genes lead me to help my relatives survive and raise their offspring, I will increase my inclusive fitness. Inclusive fitness includes individual fitness, being the measure of my gene's total fitness in the struggle for existence.

Another way of defining inclusive fitness has been suggested by Brown and Brown (1982). We may distinguish between **direct** and **indirect fitness pathways.** An individual receives fitness directly from his or her parent and contributes it directly to his or her children. An individual receives fitness indirectly from others, either from kin-selected behaviors or from reciprocity, and contributes it to others, whether relations (kin selection) or nonrelative (reciprocity). The terms direct and indirect fitness help us see that inclusive fitness includes effects that may not be based on genetic relatedness, but embrace aid or harm done to nonrelatives as well. So inclusive fitness includes the fitness we inherit from relatives (individual fitness and kin-selected fitness) and the fitness we accrue from interactions with nonrelatives.

The concept of inclusive fitness leads to the idea of **kin selection,** already inherent in our discussion so far. A gene whose strategy is to enhance only individual fitness, perhaps by causing an individual to want and raise many offspring, is subject to **individual selection:** Whether it succeeds or fails depends on the life and death of its host survival-machine. A gene whose strategy is to cause me to help my relatives—and thereby to help itself replicate through them—is subject to *kin selection:* Whether it succeeds or fails depends less on my own life or death than on the degree to which my sacrifices aid my kin. The logic of kin selection is central to the evolutionary psychological analysis of altruism.

Levels of Selection

Evolution consists, then, of survival of the fittest, but an important question is: Survival of the fittest what? More formally, scientists and philosophers ask what unit is selected by evolution. Evolution may proceed at three levels, the level of the group, of the individual, and of the gene.

The idea of group selection is that, because individuals come and go whereas the species endures for generations, evolution acts primarily to preserve the group. Individuals are supposed to behave for the good of the species, sacrificing themselves if necessary so that others may survive. The degree to which group selection occurs in nature is currently controversial (see Wilson & Sober, 1995, plus following commentary). There is no question that group selection can occur, but much disagreement on how much takes place. One camp argues vigorously that group selection is extremely rare in evolution, precisely because it is the individual who lives or dies. It is the individual organism who either reproduces or does not, not the species, and individuals act to preserve themselves and their relatives, not strangers who happen to be of the same species. The other camp likes to see groups (not species, but groups competing within a social species) as themselves being like organisms, whose success or failure as a group in the struggle for existence determines which genes are passed on and which are not. Which group of theorists will survive this intellectual struggle for existence is unclear.

Individual selection is the second level at which evolution may occur. After all, it is individuals who actually carry genes within them and who actually live and die or mate and reproduce or fail to reproduce. In this view, the struggle for existence is primarily a struggle between individual organisms, sometimes even a struggle with members of ones own group. Individuals jockey for power, rank, and reproductive success within social groups, and the outcomes of such competition affect reproductive success. Social animals often cooperate, but not all members of a group are equally fit. In solitary animals individual survival is the whole story.

There is, however, a third level of selection, at the level of the gene, which lies behind the gene thinking we have already discussed. The concept of gene selection is that evolution really operates on an individual's traits and behaviors, rather than the individual itself. Hence, genes that produce favorable traits or favorable behaviors will increase in frequency, whereas those that produce unfavorable traits or behaviors will decrease in frequency. Someone once tried to poke fun at Darwinian evolution by saying that, according to Darwin, a chicken is just an egg's way of making more eggs. Gene thinkers accept the characterization, viewing individuals primarily as vehicles by which genes struggle to survive.

For our purposes, we need only accept the idea that natural selection can operate at every level, and examine hypotheses proposed from each point of view. Most workers in evolutionary psychology tend to think at the individual or gene level, but we will meet at least one compelling idea about human evolution at the group level.

HUMAN EVOLUTION

In practicing evolutionary psychology, it is vital always to remember that environmental conditions during the period in which human beings evolved—the Era of Evolutionary Adaptation (EEA)—were radically different than those prevailing today (Barkow, Cosmides, & Tooby, 1994; Tooby & Cosmides, 1990). You, like millions of people around the world, live in a complex, urban, technologically sophisticated culture utterly unlike the world of 100,000 years or more ago. In a sense, from an evolutionary perspective, our minds are living fossils. Our patterns of thought and feeling were selected by a world very different from the one we now live in. Thus, in order to understand what our basic human nature was like, we need to look to selection pressures of the past, not the present.

As a result of exciting finds in paleoanthropology, the overall picture of human evolution has become clearer, although the exact steps from the first hominids to anatomically modern *Homo sapiens* remain hard to trace. Paleoanthropologists face important difficulties in interpreting the fossil record. Unlike experimental scientists, paleoanthropologists cannot produce new findings to settle theoretical disputes. They have only the fossils they discover, and these are always fragmentary. Moreover, they must wrestle with the natural physical variations that occur among the members of any species. When a new fossil is found, it will both resemble and differ from other remains of similar antiquity. Thus, the difficulty arises of deciding whether the new find is a member of an already established ancestral species or whether it is a new species or even a new genus. Imagine that archeologists discover the fossils of a pro football lineman and a female Olympic gymnast; they might be forgiven for thinking that the skeletons belonged to related but different species, one large and big-boned, the other short and small-boned. In archeology, there is a perennial tension between "lumpers" and "splitters." Lumpers prefer to assimilate new finds to existing categories while splitters prefer to create new species out of new finds, and these styles tend to take turns dominating paleoanthropology. Twenty years ago lumpers held sway, while today splitters do (Lewin, 1998), although the pendulum may be swinging back toward lumping.

A final methodological difficulty for both paleoanthropologists and evolutionary psychologists is that behavior does not fossilize. If we knew the behavioral patterns of extinct hominids it would be easier to categorize them into meaningful species. When we come to us, *Homo sapiens,* distinctive behaviors such as language and problem solving become defining traits, but before writing began, we have no record of either. All we can do is try to interpret evidence of intelligence or symbolic capacities from patterns of stone tool manufacture and use, wear patterns on teeth (which can reveal ancient diets), and early art.

Nevertheless, paleoanthropologists tend to agree on the following general picture of the broad steps in human evolution:

- *The Australopithecines.* The cradle of the hominid line is east central Africa. The first hominids—the first of our ancestors to (generally) walk upright—were the Australopithecines ("southern apes"). The oldest known is *Australopithecus ramidus,* known from a 4.5 million-year-old site in Ethiopia. How many species of Australopithecines there were is a major bone of contention between the lumpers and splitters. Typically, paleoanthropologists list 4 early species, A. *ramidus,* A. *anamensis,* A. *bahrelghazali,* and A. *afarensis* (Lewin, 1997), although some splitters place raise *ramidus* to its own genus, *Ardipethecus ramidus* (Wood, 1996). Australopithecines survived for many years, dividing into further species, of which two, A. *africanus* and A. *robustus,* are widely recognized, with splitters again dividing these into subtypes (Lewin, 1997). Some Australopithecus species evolved into our genus, Homo. Most theories propose *afarensis* as the source of Homo, but whether *afarensis* gave rise directly to Homo, or whether other Australopithecines such as A. *africanus* link *afarensis* to Homo is a matter of dispute. At any rate, later forms of Australopithecines and early Homo coexisted. One of the most remarkable features of hominid evolution is that all forms other than *Homo sapiens* became extinct (Lewin, 1998).

- *Homo habilis.* The human genus—Homo—begins with *Homo habilis* ("handy man"), dated to about 2.6 millions years ago. *Habilis* is assigned to the Homo genus because of association with the earliest stone tools, and toolmaking is widely regarded as a uniquely human behavior.

- *Homo erectus.* The first hominid fossils found outside Africa are members of the next grade of human evolution, *Homo erectus,* so named because until the discovery of the Australopithecines *H. erectus* was thought to be the first bipedal hominid. *Homo erectus* arose in Africa about 2 million years ago and left Africa perhaps as early as 1.8 million years ago (Gabunia & Vekas, 1995; Swisher et al., 1994), spreading across Asia into China and Indonesia, but not into Europe or the New World. Some paleoanthropologists now separate *Homo erectus* into an early form known only in Africa, *Homo ergaster* ("work man"), and the later, more widespread form, *Homo erectus* proper (Lewin, 1998). Erectus was the first hominid to regularly use fire. It was a very stable hominid type whose form and simple tool assembly lasted almost unchanged for 2 million years. The latter point is important, because a mark of *Homo sapiens* is constant technological innovation (Lewin, 1998).

- *Neandertals.* Perhaps the most famous—and certainly the most controversy-generating (Stringer & Gamble, 1992; Trinkaus & Shipman, 1993)—of the ancient hominids was Neandertal man. Erectus never lived in Europe, but Neandertal finds are extensive in Europe and the Near East. Their skulls housed a brain a little bit bigger than ours, but its shape is more ape-like. Their tools represent an advance on those of *H. erectus,* but do not rival those of *H. sapiens.* They *may* have buried their dead and had religious ritual, but these claims are speculative and contentious, as are claims that they had language. As a result of these characteristics, since their discovery in the nineteenth century, Neandertals have been alternately seen as in and then out of the evolution of *Homo sapiens.* The question may have been settled by DNA analysis (Krings et al., 1997). Neandertal mitochondrial DNA is outside the range of modern human variation, indicating that they are a separate species, *Homo neandertalensis,* a species specially adapted to cold European weather (Lewin, 1998; Stringer & Gamble, 1992), which did not mate with or give rise to anatomically modern Homo sapiens.

- *Homo sapiens.* There are two main theories about the origin of *Homo sapiens.* The first is the multiregional hypothesis. It holds that *H. erectus* evolved into *Homo sapiens* separately but at the same time in different parts of the world, with Neandertals being seen as transitional between *H. erectus* and *sapiens* in Europe. The second hypothesis is called the Out of Africa (Stringer & McKee, 1996) or Garden of Eden (Lewin, 1998) hypothesis. It holds that *Homo sapiens* evolved in Africa out of *H. erectus* or possibly *H. ergaster,* and then moved to colonize the whole of the world, including Europe and the New World, probably causing the extinction of erectus and Neandertal. The origin of humans may have taken place as recently as 100,000 years ago, a mere eye-blink in evolutionary time. It also appears to have been sudden, with the appearance of many new tool types and even symbolic art. Competition between advocates of the multiregional and Out of Africa hypotheses has been intense, but the latter hypothesis is gaining impressive support from analyses of fossil skulls (de Castro et al., 1997; Kappelman, 1996; Turbon, Perez-Perez, & Stringer, 1997), post-cranial skeletons (Holliday, 1997), and DNA (Foley, 1998; Lewin, 1998; Stringer & McKee, 1996; Waddle, 1994).

Homo sapiens sapiens' most unique traits are intelligence and language. No other creature possesses science, technology, art, religion, or culture generally (see Box 2.3). No other creature's means of communication approaches human language in power and subtlety. There is also good reason to believe that in the final evolution of *Homo sapiens sapiens* intelligence and language are closely intertwined.

■ Box 2.3 ■

Self-Awareness in Animals?

Introspectively considered, humankinds' most striking trait is probably our self-awareness. Indeed, the seventeenth-century philosopher René Descartes made self-awareness (Cogito, ergo sum, "I think, therefore I am") the cornerstone of modern rationalism. Psychologists themselves have debated the importance of human self-awareness. The radical behaviorist B. F. Skinner sees it as no more than a collection of socially learned labels for internal sensations and observations of one's own behavior, while humanistic psychologists, such as Carl Rogers and Abraham Maslow, follow Descartes in seeing self-awareness as the sine qua non of the human condition.

It is interesting to ask if any other animals possess self-awareness. Descartes thought not; he viewed animals as mere deterministic machines, lacking reflection and consciousness. Gordon Gallup (1977) has used mirrors to investigate the question empirically. Monkeys and apes are known to enjoy looking at mirrors and can even use them as tools to solve visual problems. However, like all animals, they typically respond to a reflection of themselves as an image of a conspecific—they do not perceive themselves in the mirror. But since similar self-perception is learned by humans (it does not appear until age two, may never appear in severely retarded persons, and is sometimes lost in schizophrenia) Gallup wondered if perhaps apes and monkeys could learn self-perception.

His first experiment was to place a ten-foot mirror in a cage with wild-born chimpanzees. Initially, they responded to the image as to a conspecific, but after two days their behavior indicated self-recognition. For examples, they groomed parts of the body they could not normally see, they picked their teeth, and they made faces at the mirror. To further test them, Gallup anesthetized the chimps and applied a bright red, odorless, nonsensitive dye over their foreheads. When they awoke, each chimpanzee clearly showed that it knew the dye was on its own face: They examined the spot in the mirror and touched it repeatedly. When the same procedure was performed with chimpanzees who had never experienced mirrors before, they showed no sign of recognizing the red spot as belonging to themselves. Gallup and others have tried these and similar experiments with virtually all species of monkeys and apes, and they have found that only the great apes—our closest living relations—learn self-perception. Despite hundreds of hours of exposure to mirrors, monkeys and the lesser apes (for example, gibbons) continue to see mirror images as just another conspecific.

If we may take self-perception as a reasonable indicator of self-awareness, then, while awareness is not unique to human beings as Descartes supposed, it is limited to a few highest primate species. It also appears that while the great apes may develop self-awareness, they do not do so routinely as humans do. Finally, Gallup's research suggests that as with so much of our nature, the origin of self-awareness is a social phenomenon. Chimpanzees raised in social isolation never learned to perceive themselves in the mirror and never passed the painted forehead test. It seems we must live with others before we can learn to see ourselves.

Evolution of Intelligence and Language

There are three closely interrelated adaptations that define *Homo sapiens* as a biological species: bipedalism, intelligence, and language. The lone naked ape is not a very fearsome creature. Instead of claws we have fingernails; instead of fangs we have teeth; instead of fur we have bare skin; instead of four legs we have two; we have no wings. We cannot see as well as hawks, hear as well as owls, or navigate by sound like bats, or by the stars like migrating birds. Instead, we have great cunning—intelligence. Bipedalism made intelligent tool use possible, and language expresses thoughts and facilitates social cooperation, an adaptive trait we share with other animals but improve through speech. Tools amplify our weak inherent abilities. For claws and fangs, we invent knives, spears, arrows, and guns. For fur we invent clothes and armor. Lacking four legs, we tame horses and then invent cars. Lacking wings we invent airplanes and then rockets to take us where no bird can go. We emulate the hawk with telescopes, the owl with microphones, the bat with sonar, and migrating birds with compasses and sextants. We exceed them all with radar, spacecraft, and satellites. In addition to intelligence, social cooperation allows us to work together and accomplish what we cannot alone. A single hunter was no match for a woolly mammoth, but a group of hunters together could kill it or dive it off a cliff. Traveling to the moon required the close cooperation of thousands of people. Traditional theories of the evolution of intelligence emphasized tool use, but modern theories tend to emphasize the importance of social interaction. In this section we will survey what evolutionary psychologists believe about the evolution of our key adaptive traits.

Bipedalism

It has always been clear that tool use, and thus human intelligence, is linked to bipedalism. Unlike all other mammals, we walk upright on two feet, leaving the hands free to use tools. But for a long time, which came first—intelligence or bipedalism—seemed to be a chicken-and-egg question. Did our ancestors first evolve an intelligence that demanded upright posture to use tools, or did they first walk upright, and then evolve an intelligence to exploit their free hands? The discovery of Lucy, *Australopithecus afarensis,* decisively settled the matter in favor of the second hypothesis. Lucy was either fully bipedal (or nearly so; Lewin, 1998), but had a brain not much larger than a chimpanzee's.

Why bipedalism evolved remains a matter of speculation. There has been a general drift in the evolution of all apes toward bipedal posture (Lewin, 1998). Moreover, because there was a considerable gap between the appearance of upright posture with the *Australopithecines* and the appearance of the first tools with *Homo habilis,* it seems clear that bipedalism did not evolve *in order to* make tool use possible. It arose for some other reason or reasons, and was later exploited by human intelligence.

Owen Lovejoy (1981) advanced the first comprehensive theory of the origin of bipedalism. Lovejoy's theory links bipedalism to a dramatic reorganization in early hominid social life. The point of departure for Lovejoy's theory is the danger of extinction faced by species practicing *K*-selection. Most species of animals are *r*-selected, producing huge numbers of offspring who are not cared for by their parents. Only a few survive to adulthood, but these are enough to continue the parental line. *K*-selected species, however, produce fewer young, but they are cared for after birth and all or most will survive to adulthood. Human beings are undoubtedly *K*-selected. The infant human, born typically one at a time, is physically helpless for years after birth, and must be carefully tended if it is to survive, and it is difficult to effectively care for more than one infant at a time. Unfortunately, it is possible to become too *K*-selected, so that a species' rate of reproduction falls below the number needed to replace those who die. For example, gorilla females reproduce at such wide intervals that the gorilla species may have been heading to extinction before the destruction of its habitats by humans.

Lovejoy proposed that the selection pressures operating on early hominids were driving them more and more to the extreme of *K*-selection: The need for parental care of children during an extended childhood, which required increased intelligence and brain development, hence a reduced number of large-headed offspring who could only survive within a protective group held together by complex social behaviors, which required intelligence, and so on. Each adaptation was causally linked to each other, being mutually reinforcing, and made ancient hominids increasingly vulnerable to extreme *K*-selection. Because we are here, our ancestors must have somehow increased their rate of reproduction enough to avoid extinction.

According to Lovejoy, bipedalism was our ancestors' way out of the *K*-selection trap, for it allowed them to avoid the extreme childbearing spacing of gorillas. If females walked upright, they could carry and protect one infant while being pregnant with another. Thus, they could bear one child every 12 to 18 months, ensuring enough offspring for the ancestral line to survive. Lovejoy assumes that prior to development of bipedalism, our ancient ancestors' way of life was that of most mammals today. Male and female come together only to mate, and the female feeds and protects their young. Adopting bipedalism, therefore, created a problem, because hominid females would be forced to move around less and thus be able to exploit a smaller resource area.

Bipedal survival, therefore, required that the females receive help from the sex not encumbered with children, males. Males could hunt and bring back meat, which requires bipedalism to carry the meat, and share their food with females. Lovejoy proposed that early males and females formed pair-bonds, alliances between a single female and a single male. The male would hunt and return with food, which he would share with the female in exchange for sex. Pair-bonding would also reduce the fighting over females characteristic of species without pair-bonds. In these species, males spend a great deal of time fighting for access to females or to protect a harem of females. Reducing such aggression would promote the social cooperation important to the survival of naked apes.

Rival theories on the adaptive value of bipedalism have been put forward (Lewin 1998). One sees its origin in the need to control aggressive interactions in a species for which social cooperation is imperative. Male chimpanzees and gorillas make "threat displays" toward each other, threatening violence if not appeased in some way, and the male gorilla imperiously pounding his chest is an accurate part of their popular image. Chimpanzees establish themselves in male hierarchies through success at similar displays. However, threat displays are not always successful, and the resulting fights are a major cause of death among the apes, and are sources of social strain. As the chest pounding gorilla suggests, ape threat displays are made while standing (briefly) erect, and Jablonski and Chaplin (1993) theorize that human bipedalism is simply the threat display made permanent. At the same time, bipedalism facilitates making gestures of appeasement, and lessens the risk that threats will degenerate into fights. This in turn reduces deaths and group tension and facilitates cooperation in the hominid troop. Other theories emphasize the benefits of bipedalism for the exploitation of food resources (Lewin, 1998). Although bipedal locomotion is less efficient than quadrupedal locomotion at high speeds—we can't outrun cheetahs—it is more efficient at slower (i.e., walking) speeds. Humans can move around more efficiently than knuckle-walking apes, enabling our forbears to gather food over much wider areas. Thus they could live in areas of dispersed resources all around the world. These theories are not mutually exclusive, suggesting that once it began, bipedalism served several adaptive functions. Ultimately, bipedalism made possible—though it did not cause—the evolution of human intelligence.

Intelligence

Unfortunately, tracing the evolution of intelligence is difficult because behavior and language leave no fossils. The archeological record consists of the remains of our hominid ancestors, becoming more and more fragmentary as we look farther and farther back in time, and of stone tools, which are the products of some of our ancestors' thinking, not thought itself. By the time art, and, later, writing appear, our ancestors were fully human, having completed the change from *Australopithecus afarensis* to *Homo sapiens sapiens.*

Paleoanthropologists and evolutionary psychologists have therefore used brain size as a sort of a stand-in for direct evidence of human mental powers. Because much of any animal's brain is dedicated to directing and monitoring bodily functions, students of the evolution of the brain try to determine how much of an animal's or fossil's brain was "leftover" for higher cognitive functioning, including intelligence and language. The most widely cited measure of leftover brain capacity is **encephalization,** proposed by Jerison (1991; Killackey, 1995). Paleoanthropologists and evolutionary psychologists assume that the more a species' brain is encephalized—possessing neural computing power not dedicated to running the body—the greater is its intelligence. Lucy, *Australopithecus afarensis,* is no more encephalized than modern primates. Encephalization increases with *Homo habilis* and then with *Homo erectus,* peaking in the primate line with *Homo sapiens.* Our brains are three times larger than would be expected in a primate of our body size; or, put the other way, if we possessed the low level of encephalization of the other primates, we would stand 3.1 m (10 feet) tall and weigh 454 kg (1,000 pounds)! However, increases in brain size over the course of human evolution may not have been continuous. Each form lasted unchanged for long periods of time, with rapid jumps from one fossil species to the next (Bickerton, 1990). However, given the fragmentary nature of the fossil record, the brain size might have evolved gradually.

Interpreting the evolutionary growth of the human brain is complicated by the fact that our brains did not simply grow quantitatively over time, but must have changed in qualitative ways, too. Unfortunately, trying to infer the structure of ancient brains from fossil skulls is risky and extremely controversial, with different scientists coming to radically different conclusions about the same skulls (Falk, 1992). A new approach to the problem is to compare primate and human brains in more detail than simple size (Deacon, 1992). With regard to general structural divisions, human and primate brains are similar, making it possible to compare the relative sizes of different functional areas of the brain. One can imagine a primate brain enlarged to human size, and then determine which areas are relatively large and which are relatively small in humans compared to the hypothetical primate. When we do this, we find that with the exception of hearing, our senses are weaker (in terms of brainpower) than other primates', as is our motor control. On the other hand, our prefrontal cortex, traditionally thought to be the site of thinking (Benson, 1993), is more than twice as large as that to be expected from the primate model. Over the course of evolution it appears we have traded increased intellectual powers for weakened sensorimotor ones.

Early theories of human evolution saw tool use as the driving force. However, this scenario has fallen out of favor. Tool use was made possible by upright posture, but neither tool use nor large brains quickly follow bipedalism in the fossil record. Early grades of Homo used tools, but they did not become sophisticated until the appearance of *Homo sapiens*. If tool use drove the evolution of intelligence, they should get more sophisticated at the same pace as brain size. The fossil record indicates that tool use arose with *Homo habilis* but remained relatively unchanged through the long years of *Homo erectus*. Then suddenly, with the appearance of *Homo sapiens*, tool types proliferate as new means of making tools were invented (Mithen, 1996).

Current theories about the evolution of intelligence in *Homo sapiens*, therefore, look elsewhere for the driving force behind intelligence, specifically to managing the complexities of social life. This new approach has pointedly come to be called the **Machiavellian Hypothesis** of the evolution of human intelligence (Byrne & Whiten, 1988; Cummins, 1998; Ridley, 1993; Tomasello, 1999; Whiten & Byrne, 1988). The central thesis of the Machiavellian Hypothesis was stated long ago by George Eliot in her novel *Felix Holt, the Radical:*

> Fancy what a game of chess would be if all the chessmen had passions and intellects, more or less small and cunning; if you were not only uncertain about your adversary's men, but a little uncertain also about your own. . . . You would be especially likely to be beaten, if you depended arrogantly on your mathematical imagination, and regarded your passionate pieces with contempt. Yet this imaginary chess is easy compared with a game a man has to play against his fellowmen with other fellowmen for instruments. (quoted by Ridley, 1993, p. 333)

Getting ahead in a social species, moving up the social hierarchy while keeping rivals from doing so (Cummins, 1998), wooing and keeping a mate, cooperating with others yet achieving one's own goals, requires cleverness. However, as evolutionary time passes everyone else becomes clever, too, so getting ahead requires yet more cleverness. The result is a Red-Queen style (see Chapter 12) "cognitive arms race" (Pinker, 1994) in which each person has to become as clever as possible just to keep up, so that as generation succeeds generation only the smartest are selected, and intelligence grows.

Note, however, that as Eliot's quote suggests, it is not abstract, logical, "mathematical" intelligence which is selected, but social—that is, Machiavellian—intelligence. One theme of this book is the intertwining of cognition, evolution, and social life, and nowhere is their connection stronger than here. *Homo sapiens* survived and evolved not because we were good logicians, but because we were good psychologists (Ridley, 1993), able to anticipate and outwit others in the social gamepersonship of group life. Sexual selection, too, may have played a role in the evolution of social intelligence. Women look—and presumably always have looked—for witty men, signs of

Machiavellian guile. And women would keep their desirably intelligent mates by being intelligent, too, like Scheherazade spinning out a thousand and one entrancing—and survival making—tales. Wit and tale telling take us to the evolution of language.

Language

Language sets human intelligence qualitatively apart from animal intelligence (Dennett, 1994). Therefore, how, when, and why human intelligence and language arose in the course of evolution are important questions.

The evolution of language is a venerable field of human speculation (Aarsleff, 1976) that has again become active (Corballis, 1991; Foley, 1991; Harnad, Steklis, & Lancaster, 1976; McCrone, 1991; Noble & Davidson, 1991; Pinker & Bloom, 1990). Chomsky's nativist thesis, the ape-language projects, improved knowledge of the human evolutionary tree (Johanson & Edey, 1981), including studies in paleoneurology, and evolutionary psychology have all come together to revive theories of language origins. We must remember as we proceed, however, that informed speculation is the best we can achieve. Behavior does not fossilize: All we can do is to infer cognitive and linguistic capacities from fossil skeletons, remains of tools, campsites, and art, seasoned with judicious cross-species comparisons. Because language is the vehicle of symbolic meaning, language not only creates human culture, but is to a degree identical with culture (Milo & Quiatt, 1993).

An intriguing scenario for the evolution of language has been propounded by Dunbar (1993). As the Machiavellian hypothesis suggests, group living requires intelligence, and presumably larger groups require larger intelligence. The larger the group is, the greater the number of social relationships of which each individual must keep track. Among the Old World primates, there is a positive correlation between the size of the neocortex—the part of the brain associated with intelligence—and the size of the groups in which they lived. If we apply that correlation to humans, it predicts a group size of about 150 people. While in both traditional and modern societies people operate in groups both smaller and larger than 150, there is evidence that 150 people constitutes a natural ideal. Among traditional societies, overnight camps are formed of about two dozen or so people, while tribes may number well over a thousand. However, villages—the stable units in which people dwell—average about 150. The highly traditionalist religious sect, the Hutterites, who are communal farmers in North Dakota and Canada, live in villages of 150 people, and form new villages when they get much bigger. They have found that when villages become too big, maintaining social order becomes difficult without a police force. A final clue indicating that the natural human group size is 150 comes from the military. Dating back to Roman times, the basic fighting unit of armies has been the company, which has numbered between 100 and 200 men.

For a group to work together smoothly and effectively, there must be friendly yet structured ties among its members. Among the Old World primates, the oil of social commerce is grooming. Grooming promotes health (it's the only reason New World primates groom) but it also allows for sociable, nonaggressive interaction among a troop of primates, and who grooms whom indicates and maintains social status. However, as group size increases, the amount of time spent in grooming increases, coming to compete with important activities such as foraging, eating, sleeping, and mating. Along with cortical size, grooming time thus sets a constraint on maximum group size. Among living primates, at most 20 percent of individuals' time can be allotted to grooming. Applying the primate model to a human group size of 150 would mean humans would have to devote from 28 percent to 66 percent—on average 42 percent—of their time grooming.

Dunbar believes that language arose originally in human evolution as a more efficient means of promoting social bonding among members of early human groups. Along with toolmaking, social cooperation—especially during the big-game hunting stage—was the key to the survival of the naked ape, and intelligence subserves both. Language made it possible for our ancestors to do two things at once. They could use their hands to make or hold tools, to gather foodstuffs, or to carve up meat, while at the same time talking together, cementing social bonds. Moreover, talking is more efficient at social bonding than is grooming. You can groom only in pairs, but you can converse in a group. Dunbar's hypothesis might be called "Man the schmoozer" (Dean, 1993). Our love of gossip supports Dunbar's assertion that we talk about social relationships, but scientific studies of conversational content do, too. For example, Dunbar conducted an investigation of university professors—who might be expected to talk about more weighty things—and found that about 60 percent of their lunchroom conversations dealt with personal experiences or personal relationships.

In Dunbar's view, language evolved in three stages. First, Australopithecines possessed a primate vocalization system akin to those discussed earlier in the section on Apes and Language. At this stage of hominid evolution, there was little encephalized intelligence and presumably no form of language. With *Homo erectus,* encephalization increased, and Dunbar believes that part of the evolution from Australopithecines to *Homo erectus* involved a transformation of the former's vocal calls into a simple kind of language suitable for social bonding. Finally, with the appearance of anatomically modern *Homo sapiens* about 50,000 to 35,000 years ago, fully symbolic modern language emerged. Language then became uncoupled from its social origins and became a conceptual tool of abstract thinking and information communication.

Other paleoanthropologists and evolutionary psychologists agree that language first appeared in a limited form with *Homo erectus,* but only became fully symbolic with anatomically modern *Homo sapiens*. However, they disagree with Dunbar on the details of the transformation. Some believe that erectus' protolanguage was a vocal system rather like the earliest two-word sentences of modern children or the limited signing capacities of the trained apes (Bickerton, 1990, 1995). Others believe that instead of erectus using a vocal protolanguage, they had a simple language of gestures (Milo & Quiatt, 1993), while Burling (1993) thinks they had a compound gesture-call system that still exists in us today, which was—and is—ideally suited to communicate emotions. Burling observes that people are reluctant to discuss emotion-laden topics on the telephone, suggesting that we still rely on the ancient gesture-call system to share socially important, hard to verbalize, messages. Scientists also debate whether *Homo sapiens'* symbolic language evolved from erectus' protolanguage, or whether it appeared suddenly in an evolutionary leap. Bickerton, for example, thinks that modern language appeared all at once in a single genetic mutation in a single person. Jackendoff (1998), on the other hand, proposes that language evolved slowly through nine incremental steps. Finally, whether language evolved primarily as a means of communication (Bloom, 1998; Pinker, 1997; Pinker & Bloom, 1990) or as a vehicle for internal thought (Bickerton, 1995; Burling, 1993; Jerison, 1991) remains debated.

CONCLUSION

We have now established some guiding principles for our foray into cognitive science. We have seen that designing a working mind is a formidable task that has so far daunted bright minds with well-funded research projects. Nevertheless, we have learned that the mindless process of evolution by natural selection has already succeeded in designing one very successful mind, the mind of *Homo sapiens*.

SUGGESTED READINGS

There is no shortage of good books on cognitive science and artificial intelligence, whether symbol-system or connectionist. A witty introduction to AI and cognitive science is provided by Haugeland (1985) and its companion prequel reader (less witty), Haugeland (1981). Two fine surveys of cognitive science from the symbol-system view are Gilhooly (1989) and Stillings et al. (1987), from which I drew my accounts of the representation and search approach to AI. For the more technically oriented reader, there is the handbook of AI, Barr, Feigenbaum, and Cohen (1982–1989). Turning to connectionism, in some respects the bible of the movement remains Rumelhart et al. (1986). An outstanding introduction to connectionism is Bechtel and Abrahamsen (1991), who combine psychology, AI, and philosophy into a single volume. More philosophically oriented and idiosyncratic is Clark (1990). Boden (1990) is in some respects an updated version of Haugeland's reader, covering classical AI, connectionism, and the controversy between them. Finally, two science journalists have written about the connectionist revolution, William F. Allman, *Apprentices of Wonder: Inside the Neural Network Revolution* (New York: Bantam Books, 1989), and Jeremy Cambell, *The Improbable Machine: What New Discoveries in Artificial Intelligence Reveal About the Mind* (New York: Touchstone, 1989), whose coverage is broader. For human evolution, see Lewin, 1998, Mithen, 1996. For evolutionary psychology, see Buss, *Evolutionary Psychology: The New Science of the Mind* (Boston: Allyn & Bacon, 1998); Barkow, Cosmides, and Tooby, 1994; C. Crawford and D. Krebs, *Handbook of Evolutionary Psychology* (Hillsdale, NJ: LEA, 1997); Henry Plotkin, *Evolution in Mind* (Cambridge, MA: Harvard University Press, 1998).

PART II

BEHAVIOR

3 Fundamentals of Conditioning

LEARNING, COGNITION, AND CONDITIONING: BEHAVIOR THEORY

Behaviorists built their theories of learning primarily on studies of animal behavior, which they assumed, or hoped, would throw light on human learning, too. They believed that the traditional "higher mental processes" studied by philosophers and early psychologists were really just complex assemblages of simple behaviors found in animals. They therefore devoted themselves to the careful study of learning in animals, believing that their findings could eventually be extended to human beings. Their goal was the formulation of a *general process learning theory* that would include at least all mammals, and which would posit no special mental processes found only in humans. In this chapter, we will discuss the two main forms of learning distinguished by most behaviorists, Pavlovian, or classical or respondent, conditioning, and instrumental, or operant, conditioning. In the next chapter, we will look at three of the general process-learning theories proposed by behaviorists during the Golden Age of Theory.

Kinds of Conditioning

We intuitively distinguish involuntary reflexes and voluntary acts. A reflex is an immediate response over which we have little control. We possess many reflexes, many of which we never even think about: Our pupils enlarge in the dark, get smaller in sunlight; if someone brushes a finger against our bare feet, our toes contract (in babies they spread out); if wind suddenly blows in our face, we blink. Emotional responses are reflexive: In grade school, when the local bully hit us we felt afraid; going to the dentist makes us feel queasy; erotic stimuli arouse us. Although we may stand up to the bully, see the dentist, and not attend pornographic films, we still feel the emotions associated with each setting, showing them to be deeply rooted reflexes.

Opposing reflexes, we have voluntary behavior: We choose to fight (or run away from) the bully; we choose to see (or avoid seeing) the dentist; we choose to attend (or not attend) pornographic films. These two kinds of behavior are quite different. Reflexes have to do with extremely simple muscle responses and gut feelings, while voluntary behavior concerns how we choose to live our lives. We make different kinds of moral and legal judgments about reflexes and voluntary acts. We do not blame soldiers for being afraid of battle, but we punish them severely for running away. We may exonerate the criminal whom we judge insane—He "had to do it." He "couldn't help himself."

Although the distinction has sometimes been challenged, psychologists who study learning have usually maintained a parallel distinction, speaking of two types of conditioning, Pavlovian conditioning of "reflexes" and instrumental conditioning of "voluntary" behavior. Historically, two widely separated scientists brought the two forms of learning into the laboratory at the close of the nineteenth century. But the basic strategy behind each research program was the same: Isolate a simple form of learning that is subject to experimental control and map out its parameters and limits in animal subjects. We will begin by looking at the work of these pioneers, Ivan Pavlov and Edward Lee Thorndike. Then we will look at some of the controversies involving conditioning, including recent findings and alternative theories.

CLASSICAL FINDINGS

The scientific study of reflexes began in Russia with a serendipitous discovery by Ivan Petrovich Pavlov (1849–1936). Pavlov was a brilliant physiologist whose study of the digestive system won him a Nobel Prize in 1904. In the course of that work, part of which involved surgically bringing the opening of the salivary gland to the outside of a dog's skin and watching the secretion of saliva when food was presented, Pavlov noticed a curious thing. After being used as a subject for some time, a dog would not only salivate when food was presented, but would also salivate to previously neutral stimuli—the sight of the experimenter who fed it, for example. Pavlov saw that not only are there innate reflexes (put food in a dog's mouth and it salivates) but there are also learned reflexes (the dog salivates at the sight of food or at the sight of the experimenter). The learned reflexes Pavlov originally called *psychical* (as opposed to biological) reflexes, and he soon came to focus his research on them, abandoning the term psychical and bringing both unlearned and learned reflexes into the province of physiology.

Pavlovian Conditioning

Pavlov's basic conceptions came from the founder of Russian physiology, I. M. Sechenov (1829–1905), mixed with associationism. Sechenov (1863) espoused an extreme form of the sensorimotor conception of the nervous system, believing that all behaviors are reflexes caused by some external stimulus. The sensori-motor view of the brain meshes conveniently with associationism, because learning can be thought of as acquiring new reflexes by association of stimulus and response.

Pavlov's achievement was harnessing associationism and the reflex theory to a particular experimental setting, as Ebbinghaus did for the study of memory. Pavlov saw that his "psychical secretions" were the outcome of associative learning; the food, which already elicited salivation became associated with the experimenter, who then elicited salivation. As an experimental physiologist, Pavlov knew how to put careful controls on his happenstance discovery, creating a rigorous experimental paradigm. Pavlov went to great lengths to control the experimental conditions, building a special laboratory which, to ensure exclusion of uncontrolled stimuli, had thick glass windows, specially separated rooms, a foundation embedded in sand, and a straw-filled moat! The dogs were kept in a harness, and from another room the experimenter could control stimulus presentations and count the drops of saliva produced in the dog's mouth. When Pavlov's experimental setup allowed complete control of the animal's environment and produced an objective quantitative measure of learning, his brilliant research program could begin.

Before considering these experiments, however, we must define some Pavlovian terms. A stimulus that biologically elicits a reflex (food placed in the mouth, a puff of air at the eye) does so reliably and unconditionally, and so is called an **unconditional stimulus** (US). The biologically elicited reflex is, therefore, an **unconditional response** (UR). A stimulus that through pairing with a US comes to elicit a response usually almost identical with the UR is called a **conditional stimulus** (CS) for its ability to elicit the UR is conditional on pairing with the US and other conditions elucidated by Pavlov. The reflex elicited by a CS is a **conditional response** (CR). Finally, the US is often called a **reinforcer,** since its pairing with the CS strengthens (reinforces) the power of the CS to elicit the CR.

Basic Phenomena of Pavlovian Conditioning

One of the primary laws of association is **contiguity,** which says that two ideas will get associated if they occur in the mind at the same time. Translated into Pavlov's hypothetical brain theory, the theory says that stimuli set up centers of activity in the cerebrum, and that centers regularly activated together will become linked, so that when one center is activated, the other will be, too. Given Pavlov's experimental paradigm, the law of contiguity may be readily investigated by controlling when we present CS and US in relation to each other. Pavlov employed two USs— food, which elicited salivation as part of digestion, and mild acid, which elicited salivation as a defensive reflex. He used many CSs—the clicking of a metronome, musical tones, odors, the sound of bubbling water—though he did not use the famous bell. We will here assume the US is food (appetitive conditioning) and the CS is a musical note or tone. Figure 3.1 shows the various possible temporal relationships between the US and the CS.

From the law of contiguity, we might expect exact simultaneous presentation of US and CS to be most effective. Oddly, such pairings produced weak conditioning, as also happens when the US is presented, however briefly, before the CS begins (backward conditioning). Instead, the CS must begin slightly before the US and overlap with it. If the CS begins and ends before the US, it is called **trace conditioning,** which is extremely difficult to establish. The fact that CS and US must overlap to create a CR supports the law of contiguity, but the finding that the onset of the CS must precede the US suggests that CSs become effective only if they act as signals to the organism (Pavlov, 1927).

One other kind of CS-US arrangement was investigated by Pavlov. Suppose the CS starts well before the US is presented, perhaps 30 seconds before, and overlaps US onset. This is called **delay conditioning;** it is like the standard procedure except that the CS begins far before the US. In this case a CR gets established, but it changes as CS-US pairings proceed. At first, the dog begins to salivate as soon as the CS begins, but as trials continue, the salivation does not begin until a little before the US is scheduled to arrive. This finding suggested to Pavlov (1927) that time itself could act as a CS. The tone alone no longer was the CS eliciting the salivation CR, but it was the compound stimulus of tone plus a certain passage of time.

Other compound stimuli were investigated by Pavlov. He found one could condition two or more CSs at the same time, for example, pairing a light and a tone with

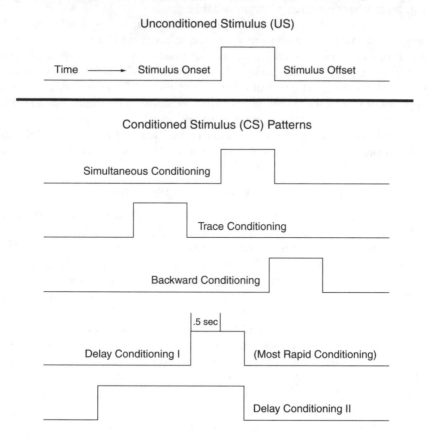

FIGURE 3.1 Temporal patterns in Pavlovian conditioning.

Unconditioned Stimulus (US)

Time ——→ Stimulus Onset   Stimulus Offset

Conditioned Stimulus (CS) Patterns

Simultaneous Conditioning

Trace Conditioning

Backward Conditioning

.5 sec

Delay Conditioning I   (Most Rapid Conditioning)

Delay Conditioning II

food. An old law of association was vividness: A given idea will get mostly associated with concurrent vivid ideas, rather than with weak ones. Pavlov's work bore this out. If the two CSs were about equal in intensity, and if they were presented alone, after conditioning, each would elicit the CR. But if one were stronger than the other, a bright light and a dim tone, for instance, only the more vivid stimulus became a CS. This phenomenon, when one CS of a compound is much more powerful than the others, is called **overshadowing.**

The conditioning of a distinct positive response, such as salivation, Pavlov (1927) called **conditioning of excitation.** The US naturally excites the brain center controlling the UR, and, after several pairings, so does the CS. Pavlov also believed that the action of CRs could be inhibited as well as excited.

If we return to delay conditioning we see **inhibition** in action. After many CS-US pairings, the CR occurred only near the end of the CS interval, near the anticipated time of the US. Why then did the earlier CRs to the start of the CS disappear? Was the first part of the tone simply disconnected, disassociated from the CR? Pavlov thought not. He believed that the early part of the tone actively inhibited the CR from taking place. As evidence, Pavlov pointed to disinhibition: If, during the early stages of the CS, before any CR would occur, a wholly new stimulus is introduced, such as a light flash, the CR would occur. Now if the CR had simply been disconnected from the early CS, the light would not cause salivation, any more than it would outside the laboratory. But the unexpected appearance of salivation when the light flashed during the CS indicated to Pavlov that the light interfered with the cortical process, specifically, inhibition, thus releasing the suppressed CR to the tone.

Pavlov (1927) distinguished several kinds of **inhibition,** the most important of which is **extinction.** What happens if we present an established CS alone, without further reinforcement? The CR occurs for a while, slowly weakens, and finally falls to zero: No saliva appears when the tone is sounded. It seems plausible to say here that the CS has been disassociated from the CR, even that the CS is no longer a CS but a neutral stimulus, and there is no CR—the reflex has literally extinguished.

But further investigation reveals that the CS-CR association is still present, only inhibited by the extinction procedure. If we simply put the animal aside for some time, even as little as 20 minutes, and present the CS again, salivation appears. The conditional reflex has spontaneously recovered. This indicates that the reflex was not unlearned by extinction, but was actively inhibited; it also indicates that inhibition is a temporary state, abating with time.

Another kind of evidence also supports Pavlov's argument. Suppose we continue extinction well beyond the point at which zero salivation occurs, presenting the CS over and over. If extinction were simply unlearning the conditional reflex, additional unreinforced pairings would have no effect: Once a CS has become a neutral stimulus, it makes no sense to say it has become more neutral still. Instead, Pavlov found that the longer extinction continued past zero, the longer it took for the CR to spontaneously recover, indicating that additional reinforced pairings deepened and so prolonged the inhibition of the CR.

Higher Order Conditioning. What happens when we take an established CS (CS_1) and pair it with a new, neutral stimulus? Will the new stimulus become a CS eliciting a CR of salivation? Pavlov found that in the right conditions it could, and called it secondary conditional reflex; the building of a new CS on old CSs is called **higher order conditioning.** If CS_2 is presented before, and not overlapping with CS_1, then CS_2 will come to elicit a CR. On the other hand, if CS_1 and CS_2 overlap, conditional inhibition occurs. The dog will salivate to CS_1 alone, but will not salivate to CS_1 and CS_2. CS_1 has been reinforced, and so a CR remains until extinction occurs, but the compound stimulus $CS_1 + CS_2$ has never been reinforced, and so the CS_1-CR reflex is inhibited by the presence of CS_2.

How far can higher order conditioning be pushed? Can we build CS_3 on CS_2 and CS_4 on CS_3? Pavlov found that in alimentary conditioning he could go no further than secondary conditioning, and with defensive conditioning, he could go no further than third-order conditioning. Pavlov's finding has not been overturned.

Another law of association is similarity: Similar ideas are easily associated. Pavlov found that CRs occur not just to the trained CS, but to similar stimuli, too. Suppose we have trained a dog to salivate to a tone of 1,000 cycles per second, and then present tones near or far from 1,000 cycles, either above or below. We find that the CR occurs to the related tones, and that the closer the new tone is to the original CS, the greater the CR; the farther away, the less the CR. The extension of a CR to stimuli similar to the CS is called **generalization,** and the gradual weakening of the CR as the test stimuli increasingly differ from the CS is called the generalization gradient. Pavlov experimented with many different kinds of CSs and replicated the same finding over many stimulus dimensions.

On the other hand, we can set excitation and inhibition against one another to produce **stimulus discrimination.** Suppose we condition salivation to a CS (CS+) of a luminous circle presented on a screen before the dog's eyes (Pavlov, 1927). If we then present ellipses varying from near-circular to extremely elliptical, we find a generalization gradient. However, right after presenting the CS, we repeatedly present an extreme ellipse alone and never reinforce it. Inhibition will build up to the ellipse (CS−). We have created stimulus discrimination. The animal responds to CS+, and does not respond to CS−.

Knowing about generalization, we can now ask the following question: What happens if we continue the discrimination procedure while making successive CS−'s more and more circular? The generalization gradients of excitation and inhibition will begin to clash: CS−, being like a circle, will to some degree elicit salivation, while as an ellipse it will elicit inhibition; CS+, being similar to an ellipse, will to some degree elicit inhibition, while as a circle it will elicit salivation. As CS− increasingly resembles CS+, the antagonistic tendencies will agonizingly clash. Pushed far enough, Pavlov's dog "presented all the symptoms of acute neurosis." It squealed, it wiggled, it tore at the apparatus and barked violently. All conditioning vanished and had to be started over (Pavlov, 1927, p. 291). These results indicated to Pavlov that psychopathology is learned by conditioning and should be "undoable" by new conditioning.

Pavlovian Conditioning of Humans

Behaviorists eagerly adopted Pavlov's objective method—here was sound experimental procedure yielding quantitative results with no nonsense about consciousness and introspection. But the behaviorists' interests were altogether different from Pavlov's. They were interested in finding regularity in behavior, and Pavlov's method let them do that. But they did not care at all about supposed brain functions. They were behavior theorists, not physiologists, questing after knowledge of adaptive behavior, not after the inferred secrets of brain function. They therefore took Pavlovian conditioning as a fact and Pavlov's technique as a proven method, and went on from there, for which Pavlov himself (Pavlov, 1941) reproved them.

The behaviorists, even when they experimented on animals, really aimed at explaining human behavior. It is no surprise, therefore, that it was American psychologists, not Pavlov, who applied his method to human beings. The most famous application of Pavlov's method to a human being was carried out by the founder of behaviorism himself, John B. Watson (1878–1958), with Rosalie Rayner, his lover who was soon to be his second wife (Watson & Rayner, 1920). Watson wanted to discover what he thought were the basic human emotions and how by conditioning they were elaborated into the complex feelings of adults.

Watson (1930) believed that all human behavior was reflexive, and his studies with Rayner were designed to support his thesis. Watson and Rayner stated that in newborns there are a few emotional URs (fear, rage, and love) elicited by a few USs (noise, frustration, patting, and rocking). The complex emotional patterns of the adult or older child, such as fearing the IRS, raging at Saddam Hussein, loving one's spouse, had to be learned, specifically through Pavlovian conditioning—they were CRs and CSs. Emotional CRs Watson and Rayner called **conditioned emotional reactions** (CERs).

To try to support their hypothesis, Watson and Rayner used a nine-month-old baby, "Albert B.," as a subject, and investigated the CER of fear. First, they determined for a wide range of stimuli that Albert was not afraid of them, that is, that they elicited no fear UR or CER. Then they found a reliable elicitor (US) of fear, striking a hammer on a steel bar. Albert would check his breathing, start, and finally cry.

At 11 months, Albert was presented with a tame white rat he was known to approach. This time, when he touched the rat, the US was applied—the bar was struck. After a total of seven pairings (spaced over a week), the rat was presented alone and proved to be a CS: "The instant the rat was shown the baby began to cry. Almost instantly he turned sharply to the left, fell over on the left side, raised himself on all fours and began to crawl away . . . rapidly . . ." (Watson & Rayner, 1920, p. 5, italics deleted). A CER had been established.

Five days later, Albert's CER was tested for generalization. Albert still showed fear to the rat, considerable fear to a rabbit and a fur coat, less to a dog, Watson's hair, a Santa Claus mask, and cotton balls, and none at all to his blocks. So generalization of the CER was shown. Watson did, however, have to keep "freshening up" the CR with new reinforcement. Even without freshening, the CER lasted at least a month, when Albert was removed from the hospital where his mother worked, and the tests ended.

Contrary to popular belief (B. Harris, 1979), Watson and Rayner never undid their conditioning. It is to be hoped that the CER weakened completely. Watson and Rayner had intended to "cure" Albert, however, and they list three of the later important techniques of behavior modification they would have used: implosion (extinction), counter-conditioning (pair the CS with a pleasant US), and modeling.

Instrumental Conditioning

Just a few years before Pavlov discovered his "psychical reflexes," an American psychologist named Edward Lee Thorndike (1874–1949) began his own experimental researches into what he called **trial-and-error learning.** Today, this other kind of learning is usually called instrumental or operant learning, because instead of being completely passive, like Pavlov's harnessed dogs, organisms in this kind of experiment learn to operate on the environment in some way to get rewarded.

While Thorndike also was influenced by associationism, his research program was quite different from Pavlov's. To begin with, Thorndike was a psychologist, not a physiologist, and was consequently interested in behavior change itself instead of in the light thrown by learning on cerebral functioning. Moreover, the intellectual tradition out of which Thorndike came was American functional psychology, not physiology. The functionalists were interested in the individual Darwinian question: How does an organism's mind serve to adapt it to the demands of its environment? Finally, the specific context in which Thorndike worked was Anglo-American comparative or, as it was called then, animal psychology.

Animal psychologists wanted to be able to establish the relative mental abilities of different animal species. The work began with Darwin's friend George Romanes (1848–1894) and his 1882 book *Animal Intelligence*. Romanes employed what has come to be called the anecdotal method. He collected stories (anecdotes) about the behavior of animals, often pets, in different situations. He then sifted through the stories and attempted to reconstruct the mental processes of the animals involved, aiming at a relative assessment of the intelligence of each species.

But Thorndike (1911) was highly critical of the anecdotal method. It tended, he believed, to overestimate the abilities of animals. One tends to notice only when animals are being clever, not when they are being ordinary or even stupid; in the case of pets, the tendency to see only the best will be especially strong. Worse, the anecdotal method, with its attendant reconstruction of the animal's thought processes, was easily given to anthropomorphism. If we watch an animal solving a problem, we tend to put ourselves in its place and project onto the animal the thoughts we would have while doing the same thing. Thorndike observed, as had Pavlov, that experimentation was needed to gather conservative, objective scientific data about this area of psychology.

But Pavlov was a physiologist studying the reflexes of the brain, and Thorndike was a functionalist psychologist studying the adaptation of individual organisms to their environment. Thus, their methodologies diverged sharply. Pavlov's research exemplar was admirably suited to studying nervous reflexes: Start with a US that already elicits a reflex and pair it with a CS to create a new, learned reflex. What Thorndike needed was an environment, more controlled than a pet-owner's backyard, that could present a set problem to an animal. In short, he needed to invent a controlled but challenging environment to which a subject would have to adapt. He hit on a solution with his famous puzzle boxes.

Less well-established than the famous Pavlov, Thorndike, a graduate student at Harvard, set up his laboratory in William James' basement. However, he did most of his work at Columbia University, where he gained a job even before graduating. Thorndike constructed a number of puzzle boxes in which he placed one of his subjects, a kitten or a dog (he also experimented with chicks placed in a maze). The puzzle box is a sort of cage so constructed that the door can be opened by the animal from the inside, providing it learns to make a correct response. Thorndike designed many variations of his boxes, but most required the animal to operate a string dangling in the box, which in turn ran over a pulley and opened the door, releasing the animal, who was then fed before being placed back in the box. Thorndike wanted to know exactly how the subject learns the correct response. He described what happens in a box in which the cat must pull a loop or button on the end of the string:

> The cat that is clawing all over the box in her impulsive struggle will probably claw the string or loop or button so as to open the door. And gradually all the other nonsuccessful impulses will be stamped out and the particular impulse leading to the successful act will be stamped in by the resulting pleasure, until, after many trials, the cat will, when put in the box, immediately claw the button or loop in a definite way. (Thorndike, 1911, p. 36)

Thorndike conceived his study as one of association-formation, and interpreted his animals' behaviors in terms of associationism:

> Starting, then, with its store of instinctive impulses, the cat hits upon the successful movement, and gradually associates it with the sense-impression of the interior of the box until the connection is perfect, so that it performs the act as soon as confronted with the sense-impression. (Thorndike, 1911, p. 38)

The phrase *trial-and-error,* or perhaps more exactly trial-and-success, learning aptly describes what these animals did in the puzzle boxes. Placed inside, they try out

LEARNING AND COGNITION

(or, as Skinner called it later, emit) a variety of familiar behaviors. In cats, it was likely to try squeezing through the bars, clawing at the cage, sticking its paws between the bars. Eventually, the cat is likely to scratch at the loop of string and so pull on it, finding its efforts rewarded: The door opens and it escapes, only to be caught by Thorndike and placed back in the box. As these events are repeated, the useless behaviors die away, or extinguish, and the correct behavior is done soon after entering the cage; the cat has learned the correct response needed to escape.

Thorndike's description of his cats' struggles meshes with our own intuitions of how we ourselves learn nonreflexive, voluntary behaviors. Confronted by a new situation, we try out a number of reactions. Eventually, we hit on a behavior that works (unless we give up). Later, when we meet the situation again, or one like it, we know what to do. In short, both Thorndike's cats and people slowly adapt to the environment. This kind of learning is not reflexive. Pavlov could initially make his dogs salivate by presenting the US, but there is no stimulus that Thorndike could have presented that would have forced the cats, zombie-like, to walk over to and pull the dangling cord leading to escape. In a sense, a US forces a subject to make the correct, reinforced response; the dog salivates and is fed. In trial-and-error learning, however, we must await for the correct response to occur, and then pounce on it with reinforcement.

The specifics of Thorndike's shared exemplar, the puzzle box, had limited influence. Although the puzzle box exerted more experimental control than the natural environment of the anecdotal psychologists, it really did not give the experimenter much to manipulate besides the intricacy of the release mechanism. Therefore, later behaviorists used other specific experimental arrangements, first the maze and then, the triumphant exemplar of operant learning, the Skinner box. Despite their differences, the spirit of each device remains Thorndikian—provide a controlled environment in which an animal is rewarded for the specific response you want the animal to learn.

THE ASSOCIATIVE TRADITION: CLASSICAL THEORIES

Until recently, most theories of Pavlovian and instrumental conditioning were developed within the associationist tradition that also guided Ebbinghaus. Physiologists such as Pavlov thought of association in terms of brain processes, behaviorists thought of association in terms of connections between stimulus and response, and cognitive psychologists thought of associations in the traditional philosophical way as associations of internal representations of stimuli and responses, that is, association of ideas. In this and the next section we will look at the long history of associative thinking about conditioning, turning in the final section to more complex alternatives based on the architectures of cognition discussed in Chapter 2.

Pavlovian Conditioning

Pavlov explained conditioning in terms of a speculative theory of brain function, in which CSs and USs set up centers of activity in the brain that became linked in either an excitatory or inhibitory way. More psychologically, his regarding of the CS as a signal suggests that CSs tell the organism that a US is about to occur, triggering behavior adapted to that US anticipating current theories of Pavlovian conditioning as an adaptive process based on information processing of US and CS.

Stimulus Substitution Theory

However, within the behaviorist tradition, the dominant theory of Pavlovian conditioning was the **stimulus substitution** or **reflex transfer account** (Holland, 1984). According to this theory, control of the unconditioned reflex got transferred to the CS as it was paired with the US, so that in the future the CS could be substituted for the US, as it had the same effect of the animal. The reflex transfer theory may be diagrammed as in Figure 3.2 with the assumption that the UR and the CR are identical or nearly identical responses, as in salivary conditioning. In terms of associationism, the stimulus substitution view held that, although US and CS are paired, an association is formed not between them, but between the CS and the UR, with the UR renamed "CR." Or, in terms of S-R learning theory, Pavlovian conditioning involves S-R learning between CS and CR, not S-S learning between CS and US.

The stimulus substitution theory of Pavlovian conditioning made five basic claims:

1. *Nature of the association:* Stimulus substitution theory holds that the association acquired during conditioning is between the CS and the CR it evokes.

2. *Cause of the association:* The sole cause of the association between CS and CR is the close contiguity between CS and CR.

3. *Specificity of the CS:* The cue that evokes the CR is the CS alone.

4. *CR-UR equivalence:* The CR is essentially the same as the UR, differing at most only in quantity, not behavioral form.

5. *Equipotentiality:* The nature of the CS is irrelevant to learning; any stimulus the animal can perceive can become a CS through pairing with any US.

Research has challenged all five of these claims in recent years, and contemporary associationist theories have modified or abandoned them (see discussion following).

Instrumental Conditioning: Thorndike's Laws of Learning

Thorndike began his research program seeking to understand how the mind adapts an organism to its environment. He ended up, however, seeing learning as a far simpler affair, probably not involving mind at all. He seemed to find that animals, or at least cats, dogs, and chicks, do not learn by imitation, nor do they reason and have memory. Instead, he found himself driven to the conclusion that although association is real enough, what is associated is not ideas at all, but simply situations and responses. Learning, Thorndike concluded, consisted only in changing the degree of control a certain stimulus exerts over a given response, by either rewarding or punishing the

FIGURE 3.2 Traditional S-R stimulus substitution theory of Pavlovian conditioning.

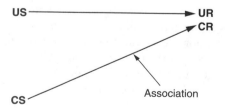

connection, which was also the basic idea of Clark Hull's more elaborate theory of learning (see next chapter). Thorndike proposed three laws of learning. One was the **Law of Exercise** that states that use of a response strengthens its connection to the stimuli controlling it, while disuse weakens them. Another was the **Law of Readiness,** having to do with the physiological basis of the Law of Effect. Thorndike proposed that if the neurons connected to a given action are prepared to fire (and cause the action) their neural firing will be experienced as pleasure, but that if they are inhibited from firing, displeasure will be felt.

The most famous and debated of Thorndike's laws was the **Law of Effect:**

> The Law of Effect is that: Of several responses made to the same situation, those which are accompanied or closely followed by satisfaction to the animal will, other things being equal, be more firmly connected with the situation, so that, when it recurs, they will be more likely to recur; those which are accompanied or closely followed by discomfort to the animal will, other things being equal, have their connections with that situation weakened, so that, when it recurs, they will be less likely to occur. The greater the satisfaction or discomfort, the greater the strengthening or weakening of the bond. (Thorndike, 1911, p. 244)

Thorndike seems to state a truism not in need of scientific elaboration, that organisms learn how to get pleasurable things and learn how to avoid painful things. However, as we will see, problems surround the Law of Effect. We will look at three of the problems in this and the next chapter. First, is reward *necessary* for learning? Reward and punishment surely affect behavior, but must they be present for learning to occur, as many psychologists thought? Second, exactly what about a reward or punishment makes it change behavior? Is it the pleasure and pain they bring, as Thorndike said, or the fact that they inform us that we have just done the right or wrong action? Finally, does punishment really cause a response to be "unlearned," or does it affect only when a learned behavior is performed or expressed?

Similar questions can be asked about Pavlovian conditioning. Observe that USs are stimuli that if deployed in instrumental conditioning would be rewards, such as food, or punishers, such as shock. In fact, some theorists call a US a "reinforcer." Therefore, we might ask if associations can be formed between a CS and a CR in the absence of a US. We may also ask exactly how USs affect behavior, by their affective or their informational qualities. And we might ask if a painful US such as shock causes associations to be weakened, or if they simply control their expression. Finally, the issue of equipotentiality arises in the study of instrumental conditioning as well as the study of Pavlovian conditioning. If instrumental learning is no more than connecting stimuli with responses, as Thorndike said, then one might expect that any instrumental behavior of which an animal is capable can be associated with any stimulus it can perceive.

THE ASSOCIATIVE TRADITION: BASIC THEORETICAL ISSUES

Pavlov and Thorndike stand as the pioneers of experimental research on conditioning. Each contributed an important experimental paradigm for studying the two types of learning, Pavlovian and instrumental. Each offered a theory of learning that endured for decades, albeit while being controversial. We have traced developments in their theoretical orientations down to the present, finding that, while in some respects the associative theory of learning and the law of effect have perhaps become out of date, psychological scientists have built steadily on—while revising—Pavlov's and Thorndike's foundational work. No scientist could wish for more.

As later psychologists further investigated conditioning and offered rival theories to explain how learning takes place, a number of issues recurred again and again. Theorists disagreed about the nature of learning and about the causes of learning.

The Nature of Learning

How Many Kinds of Learning Are There?

Although we have found the distinction between Pavlovian and instrumental conditioning to be intuitively appealing, reflecting folk psychology's separation of reflex response from voluntary behavior, many psychologists have pointed out that the two kinds of conditioning are more similar than we thought.

We can most easily approach the problem through a simple thought experiment. Suppose I subject you to a typical conditioning procedure involving the eye-blink reflex. Holding your head fixed in a stand, I sound a tone and mechanically puff air into your face. If I do this a few times, I find that when I sound the tone you blink your eye. We can analyze this as an experiment in Pavlovian conditioning. We start with an unconditional reflex between a US (puff of air) and a UR (eye blink), and pair the US with a neutral CS (the tone), finding that you acquire a CR (eye blink). At first glance, eyeblink conditioning seems to be a straightforward Pavlovian procedure.

But is it? Suppose instead of the actually pairing tone and air puff I had told you, "When the tone sounds, you'll shortly find your eye puffed at with air." In all likelihood, to avoid the unpleasant puff of air in your eye, you would blink voluntarily when you heard the tone. The US would not elicit the reflex, the eye already being closed. So there need be no US-CS pairing at all for "conditioning" to occur, since eye blinks are voluntary as well as reflexive behaviors.

If we return to the original experiment, then, we find it can be analyzed as instrumental conditioning. You find the air puff aversive and close your eye for the reward of ending your pain. The law of effect seems to operate—you learn to blink your eye for the satisfaction of ending the uncomfortable blast of air. Even such a simple experiment as this one blurs the apparently clear distinction between Pavlovian and instrumental conditioning.

While a number of criteria have been advanced to separate Pavlovian and instrumental learning (see Hearst, 1975, for a review), two of these, one substantive and one procedural, have been most frequently defended. Substantively, it has been proposed that different kinds of responses, mediated by different nervous systems, are conditionable only by one kind of procedure or the other. Thus, Pavlovian conditioning applies only to the glandular and smooth muscle responses of the autonomic nervous system, instrumental conditioning applies only to the striated muscle, and skeletal responses of the somatic nervous system.

But eyelid movement is a skeletal response, and it is easily conditioned by Pavlovian procedures. Instrumental control of autonomic processes has proved possible, and indeed has become famous as *biofeedback*. People have learned to modulate their heart rate, blood pressure, and brain alpha waves simply by being hooked up to devices that tell them if their heart rate is high or low, blood pressure high or low, or alpha wave production high or low. People do not necessarily learn direct control over

ʌver, using instead little tricks that lead to the re-
ʰt alter one's heart rate by indulging in sexual
ᵗhese cases, an instrumental behavior has
ˑ Pavlovian response. Consequently,
ıl skeletal activity, and then have
ıty.

ɹumental and Pavlovian learning on
leaves us with the procedural distinc-
ınter presents US and CS together, quite
ˌponse occurs. In instrumental condition-
ʌs and, more importantly, is contingent on
ıy when the desired response occurs (the cat

ˌ, even this simple procedural distinction is often
ˌd what he calls "superstitious behavior." Food is
ˌpigeon walking around in a chamber. What happens
the behavior occurring when it's delivered, and after
ˌehaving very oddly indeed, trying to do all the behav-
for. However, the food delivery did not actually depend
ˌy more than food delivery depended on what Pavlov's dog
ɹr regarded superstitious behavior as an example of operant,
ˌing. Is he right?

ˌ waters have become is shown by considering that instrumental
ˌitioning always go on at the same time. After pressing a bar to get
ˌɔox, the animal eats food (US) in the box (CS) and so we should not
ˌind that the animal begins to salivate when we put the creature in the
ˌʃay of training. Similarly, a dog, Pavlovianly conditioned to salivate to
ˌa metronome, would, if simply released in the room, run to the machine,
ˌit, and wag its tail—all operant behaviors (Hearst, 1975).

ˌ interaction of Pavlovian and instrumental conditioning is powerfully
ˌɹrated by autoshaping (Brown & Jenkins, 1968). Here, a pigeon is put in a
ˌr box with a key that can be lighted up. Then we simply put food in the cup and
ˌ the key at the same time. We find that after some pairings of US (food) and CS
ˌght), the pigeon will peck the key when it's lighted even though it does not have to
ˌn order to get fed. The behavior of pigeons during autoshaping is just like that of pigeons being taught to peck a key in order to be rewarded with food. So, we find operant behavior controlled by simple, "Pavlovian" US-CS pairings. Autoshaped
key-pecks even violate the law of effect, as a variation on this experiment shows. If
the pigeon's pecking at the key is made to block delivery of food, while not pecking
would produce food, the pigeon pecks the key anyway! This is called auto-
maintenance. Autoshaping is now regarded as a form of Pavlovian conditioning. Food
is a US that elicits a UR of pecking. The lighting of the response key is a CS that is
paired with the US, and eventually elicits pecking—now a CR—by itself.

Should the distinction of Pavlovian and instrumental conditioning be abandoned? As the psychophysicist S.S. Stevens remarked, just because the exact border-
line between night and day may be hard to pinpoint does not mean we should not
distinguish them. Similarly the distinction between Pavlovian and instrumental conditioning may be defended as useful if a little fuzzy.

How Does Learning Proceed?

One of the most enduring issues in the study of learni
takes place gradually or suddenly. In the context of the asso
been treating so far, this becomes the question of whether assoc
gle trial or whether they must be built up over numerous trials.
rists—including Pavlov, Thorndike, Hull, Skinner, and modern a
(see below) have preferred the **continuity** view, holding that lear
ian or instrumental response is a gradual affair. However, a few t
ferred the **discontinuity** or **insight** view, holding that associations a
be, acquired all at once.

Two advocates of one trial learning or insight raised issues that
yond the field of learning to the nature of psychology as an experi
Science seeks universal laws that govern natural events at all times an
chologists, then, seek laws that govern the behavior of animals and peop
and places. Psychologists of learning seek laws that govern learning in
places, such as Thorndike's proposed Law of Effect. Such laws of learnin
are derived from observations made in psychological laboratories, and a
sumed to be true everywhere else. A law of learning that was valid only in
academic laboratories would be of little scientific interest or practical value

When Thorndike studied cats learning to escape from his puzzle b
saw them learning gradually, by trial and error. This was one reason he co
that animals form connections only between stimulus and response rather t
tween ideas. If animals had ideas in their minds, they could think about the
reason their way to solutions of their problems. Because they showed no sign o
soning—insight—Thorndike concluded they had no ideas to think with or a
However, in an important critique of Thorndike's theory, the Gestalt psycholo
Wolfgang Köhler (1887–1967) argued that Thorndike's findings were determi
by his experimental setting—the puzzle box—rather than by limitations on anim
thinking (Köhler, 1925).

In his work with apes, Köhler (1925) repeatedly found that they were capable o
sudden insight into the problems he set them. Perhaps the most famous of Köhler's
studies was the box-and-banana problem. An ape would be brought into a room in
which a banana would be hanging from the ceiling, frustratingly just out of reach. In
the room also was a wooden box. Köhler found that even without being rewarded in
any way, apes often noticed the box, dragged it under the banana, and stood on the
box to reach the desired fruit. His star ape, Sultan, even stacked up several boxes
when one was insufficient. Unfortunately, Sultan was a poor architect, stacking the
boxes irregularly, so when he clambered to the top of his pile he swayed back and
forth in precarious balance as he grabbed the banana. In his critique of Thorndike,
Köhler pointed out that his apes found themselves in a very different situation from
Thorndike's cats. Köhler's subjects could see everything relevant to the solution of
their problem, the banana and the box. All they needed to do was bring them into the
right relationship. Thorndike's subjects, on the other hand, could not see the connection between the manipulandum in the puzzle box. Because they were denied this
critical information, they could not solve the problem by thinking, but had to resort to
simple trial and error. Köhler argued that Thorndike's conclusion that all learning
takes place by trial and error was an artifact of the puzzle boxes, not a discovery

about the limits of animal cognition. What was true about puzzle-box learning need not be true in all times and places. Thorndike's experiment was not a genuine replica of the world at large.

Work deriving from the Golden Age learning theorist E. R. Guthrie (1886–1959) raises a related issue about the generalizability of experimental findings outside the laboratory. Guthrie (1939) agreed with Thorndike and Pavlov that learning was due to association of stimulus and response, but unlike them he believed that associations were formed immediately on a single trial. Guthrie's position often seemed outrageously absurd. Anyone who has learned to hit a golf ball, pitch a baseball, or drive a car knows that it took a long time—often unbearably long—to master. It appears ridiculous to say we learned these things all at once.

But Guthrie would reply that these are complex activities. Swinging a golf cub or driving a car are assemblages of simpler behaviors. Each component piece was learned on a single trial, Guthrie held, but it takes many trials to assemble the movements into the complex act. In Guthrie's theory, then, it is not an act that gets conditioned to stimuli but whatever movements are happening in their presence. Objecting that it takes a long time to learn to drive a golf ball did not disprove his theory, because it was about learning simple movements. In Guthrie's scheme of things, essentially, we learn particular muscle responses on one trial, but it may take many trials to learn and coordinate all the muscle responses that assemble together into a complex act.

To empirically support Guthrie's theory, it is obvious the researcher cannot study a complex act. Guthrie himself tried to study elementary muscle-movements in his own puzzle box studies (Guthrie, 1952). Instead of a complex manipulandum, his cats needed only to rub against a pole in the center of the box to open the door. He and his colleagues photographed cats at the moment they activated the pole and escaped. They found that a cat's subsequent responses varied only a little from trial to trial, indicating that it had learned, and retained, the first trial's movements. But Virginia Voeks (1954) carried out an even more precise study using human eyeblink conditioning. Specifically, Voeks compared Guthrie's theory to that of Hull, who held the continuity view (mathematically expressed) that learning a habit, however simple, is a gradual affair, each reinforcement adding a little bit to the strength of the habit. Previous studies had supported Hull. If 20 subjects are put through a conditioned eyeblink experiment and we plot trial-by-trial the total number of eyeblinks given to the CS on each trial, we find that total rises slowly and finally levels off.

Adopting Guthrie's molecular strategy, however, Voeks argued that group data are misleading. Suppose one-trial learning does occur. Then, on each trial a given subject either learns or does not learn. One subject may learn on the first trial, another on the third; three may learn on the fourth trial and so on. Adding their responses together we would see "evidence" of gradual learning: trial 1, 1 blink; trial 2, 1 blink; trial 3, 2 blinks; trial 4, 5 blinks, and so on. Each subject would learn to blink on a given trial, and blink on every subsequent trial (all or none learning). However, since as we go from trial to trial more subjects condition (and blink ever after), the total number of blinks rises slowly and gradually, seeming to show gradual learning. Voeks looked at the behavior of each subject in her study and found that for most of them, once the blink CR occurred, it occurred on every trial thereafter, just as Guthrie's theory predicted. But when she pooled the data, "gradual learning" appeared, an illusion created by adding up everyone's responses.

Today, the continuity versus insight issue is not prominent. Psychologists agree that learning sometimes requires time, but that insight also occurs, and they investigate the details of both processes. But the arguments of Köhler and Voeks are important nonetheless. They remind us of the difficulties of formulating general theories of behavior that are, necessarily, based on laboratory experiments. Köhler reminds us that we must be careful to make our experiments as true to life as possible, and be wary of making sweeping generalizations from a few studies, however rigorous. Voeks reminds us that psychologists are supposed to be interested in individual behavior, in how learning and cognition operate in individual people. However, for methodological reasons we aggregate the data from many subjects in any single study. We must be wary of confusing group averages with individual processes.

What Is Learned?

Stimulus substitution theory is an S-R learning theory, maintaining that what is learned in Pavlovian conditioning is an eliciting association between the CS and the UR, which becomes a CR when it comes under the stimulus control of the CS. However, it is possible that a different association is learned, between an internal representation of the CS and a representation of the US, as in the philosophical association of ideas tradition (Rescorla, 1988). In this conception, a learned CS presented alone evokes the CR indirectly by causing retrieval of the US with which it was associated, which in turn activates the response. (See Figure 3.3.) In this alternative conception, learning is the formation of S-S associations rather than S-R associations. One phenomenon that demonstrates the formation of S-S associations is sensory preconditioning. If two stimuli, such as a tone and a light flash, are presented together several times, and one is later paired with a US, such as shock, the other one will also evoke fear responses even if it is never paired with shock itself. Clearly, the two stimuli had become associated by occurring together.

Indeed, as Tolman would emphasize (see Chapter 4), organisms learn about the environment, not simply how to respond to it, and even in rats such learning can be quite sophisticated. An important phenomenon in Pavlovian conditioning is **latent inhibition.** If a stimulus is presented alone without any consequence, and is later used in conditioning, it will take longer to become an effective CS than a wholly

FIGURE 3.3   S-S cognitive theory of Pavlovian conditioning.

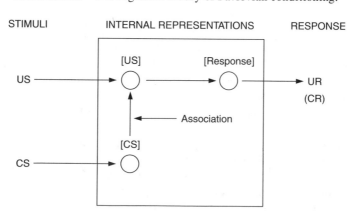

LEARNING AND COGNITION

novel stimulus, suggesting that the stimulus has become resistant to learning. However, this conclusion is too simple, as shown by an experiment (Hall & Honey, 1989) in which rats became familiar with two objects placed in their home cages before being used as CSs in conditioning procedures. Paired alone with a US, the objects showed latent inhibition, but when paired together in a discrimination learning paradigm in which one was CS+ and the other was CS−, especially rapid learning occurred. If the objects had simply become hard to condition, learning should have been retarded in both settings, but instead we see that the objects had become **perceptually differentiated** by simple exposure, and thus became easy to discriminate.

The existence of S-S associations does not imply, of course, that S-R associations are never formed, but they do show the limitations of the S-R, stimulus substitution, theory of conditioning. Traditional S-R psychology depicted animals—including humans—as reactive machines whose behaviors are reflexes set off by innate and learned stimuli. Modern students of conditioning view animals and humans as active information seekers who build internal representations of significant environmental regularities, and who consult those representations when behaving (Rescorla, 1988). Moreover, N. J. Mackintosh (1985) has put the S-S versus S-R controversy in a broader context borrowed from philosophy via human cognitive psychology. Philosophers have long distinguished *knowing how* from *knowing that.* Most of us can ride a bicycle, but few of us could explain the physical and physiological principles involved: We *know how* to ride a bike, but we do not *know* the principles *that* we use to do so. On the other hand, a physicist might know very well the physical principles involved in making a 20-foot jump shot in basketball but be unable to make such a shot. Cognitive psychologists refer to "knowing how" as **procedural learning,** and "knowing that" as **declarative learning.** These new terms help us see that arguing about whether learning is S-S or S-R is a mistake, for both occur and both are important, so they both deserve study.

Specificity of the CS: The Importance of Context.
While the experimenter knows what stimulus an animal ought to be learning about—the CS—from the animal's point of view the bell or tone or light flash is one of many stimuli that might be significant in anticipating food or shock. Recent research has shown that background stimuli—the conditioning **context**—play an important role in associative learning. The role of experimental context has been investigated as it pertains to many Pavlovian phenomena, but we will review some of its effects on what appears at first glance to seem the simplest of all aspects of Pavlovian conditioning: extinction.

Bouton (1991) argues that an extinguished CS is like an ambiguous word. The word **loafer** is ambiguous, since it may mean "someone who goofs off" or "type of shoe without laces." A conditioned CS is unambiguous: For Pavlov's dog the bell came to mean "food's coming." Subjected to extinction, however, the bell becomes ambiguous—it could mean "food's coming" or "food's not coming." With words, we try to use context to disambiguate meanings: "Sarge chewed out the loafers" means one thing, "Sarge was given loafers for Christmas" means another, while "Sarge hates loafers" remains ambiguous. Similarly, Bouton (1991) argues, animals try to use the available context to decode the meaning of a CS. Organisms do not "unlearn" CS-US associations during extinction, but learn certain CS-context relationships that modify their responding. Thus, according to Bouton, extinction involves performance, or expression, rather than learning.

The phenomena of reinstatement and renewal illustrate the role of context in responding to extinguished CSs. Reinstatement refers to the fact that following extinction, simple reexposure to the US by itself causes CRs to reoccur to the "extinguished" CS even if the CS is not repaired with the US. However, the reinstatement effect is context sensitive. If the US is represented in the context in which the CS is later tested, reinstatement occurs; if the CS is tested in a different setting, reinstatement does not occur. Thus the context helps disambiguate the meaning of the CS: in the same context in which the US was represented, the context helps the CS mean "US is coming," while in a different context the CS still means "US is not coming." Renewal is more complicated. If a CS is conditioned with a US in one experimental context, and then extinguished in another context, but tested in the first (original conditioning) context, it provokes a CR. Weaker renewal occurs when the extinguished CS is tested in a third, novel context. Again, the testing context and its similarity to the conditioning context help determine the meaning of the CS. Pavlov's spontaneous recovery may be interpreted as an instance of renewal in which the critical contextual variable is time (Bouton, 1991).

Context may also affect learning as well as extinction. An example concerns the US preexposure effect. In latent inhibition, preexposure to the CS retards learning. Similarly, preexposure to a US also retards later Pavlovian conditioning involving that US. However, the US preexposure effect is context specific: If CS-US pairing takes place in a context different from that in which US preexposure occurred, no retardation of learning is observed (Durlach, 1989). The US-preexposure effect may thus be interpreted as a form of blocking, in which the context associated with the US is sufficient to predict it, so that when a CS is introduced into the setting, its ability to be associated with the context-familiar US is impeded (Durlach, 1989).

Context effects show that the effective stimulus controlling an animal's response in Pavlovian conditioning is not the CS alone, but a complex and changing amalgam of the CS relative to the conditioning, extinction, and testing contexts.

THE CAUSES OF LEARNING: CONTIGUITY OR CONTIGENCY?

Pavlovian Conditioning

The phenomena of sensory preconditioning, latent inhibition, and perceptual differentiation show that associations can be formed between stimuli that are simply experienced together, that is, are contiguous in space and time. Stimulus substitution theory of classical conditioning maintained the stronger position that simple contiguity of CS and US is the *sole* cause of association formation in Pavlovian conditioning, leading researchers for decades to focus almost exclusively on the CS-US interstimulus interval as the key factor in Pavlovian conditioning (Furedy & Riley, 1987). However, even from the beginning, some phenomena suggested that CS-US contiguity was not the sole cause of Pavlovian conditioning. For example, one of the most robust findings in learning of all types is the superiority of **spaced** over **distributed practice.** Suppose you wanted to become good at making foul shots in basketball. You might decide to practice foul shots for several hours at a time (massed practice), when in fact short practice intervals separated by rests (spaced practice) would be more effective (Woodworth, 1954). Similarly, Pavlovian conditioning is slower with massed CS-US pairings than with the same number of pairings separated by rest spaces (Durlach, 1989). If contiguity were the only factor governing the formation of conditioned responses, there should be no effect of spacing. Moreover, in some Pavlovian preparations, the CS-US interstimulus interval is unimportant for determining whether conditioning occurs (Furedy & Riley, 1987). The conventional wisdom that conditioning occurs most rapidly when CS precedes US by just under 0.5 sec was based on studies of conditioning of the human eye-blink response. However, in other forms of conditioning—most notably conditioned fear and conditioned taste aversion (see discussion following)—the CS may precede the US by intervals of up to hours. Contiguity alone cannot be the sole cause of conditioning.

Most recent research has focused on a predictive contingency between CS and US as the basis for Pavlovian conditioning. Pavlovian conditioning is now viewed as involving much more than simple association-formation: It involves organisms detecting predictive relationships between important environmental events and signals that anticipate them (Rescorla, 1988).

The most dramatic evidence that contiguity alone is insufficient for association-formation is the phenomenon of **blocking** (Kamin, 1968, 1969). In a blocking experiment, we first create a Pavlovian response in the usual way, say by pairing a tone (CS) with footshock (US) in rats. The tone itself becomes a fear-producing stimulus, as demonstrated by conditioned suppression: The rat is taught to bar-press for food, and after it has learned this response we occasionally present the conditioned tone CS. Because the tone now elicits fear, the bar-pressing is briefly suppressed following its presentation. Suppose now we return to Pavlovian conditioning and further pair the tone CS with shock, only now we add another CS presented with the tone, for example, a light flash. Observe that the light flash and the shock are contiguous, just as the tone and the shock always have been. If contiguity theory is correct, presentation of the light-flash with the shock should make the light flash a fear-producing CS. But it does not: Previous and continued pairing of the first CS blocks the formation of any association with the light-flash.

Examination of **unblocking** experiments will help us see what is going on here (Schwartz, 1984). An unblocking experiment proceeds just as a blocking experiment until the introduction of the second CS, when the US is changed. To continue our example, after the fear conditioning of the rat to the tone is complete, we begin to pair the tone with a light flash and with two shocks at a time. In this case blocking does not occur, and the light flash becomes fear producing. In a related experiment, rats were first conditioned with the tone to pairs of shocks, and then when the second CS was introduced, both were paired with just one shock. In this case, too, blocking did not occur.

The current view among animal-learning theorists is that stimuli become CSs only to the extent that they predict the US (Rescorla, 1968, 1975, 1978, 1985, 1988; Rescorla & Holland, 1982; Rescorla & Wagner, 1972). In the blocking experiment, the light flash does not condition and become a CS because despite perfect contiguity between it and the US, it does not help the animal predict the US, because it is perfectly predicted already by the original tone CS. Another way to state this is to say the animal learns to ignore the light flash because it does nothing to help the animal cope with shock (Mackintosh, 1978; Wagner, 1978). If a stimulus is going to become a CS, there must be a unique predictive contingency between it and the US; contiguity alone is insufficient. The importance of contingency is underscored by the unblocking experiments. In them, the second CS does predict something new, a change in the nature of the US. The contingency between the new CS and the change in the US is helpful to the animal in preparing for shock, so the contingency is noted and unblocking occurs. Pavlovian conditioning is not the mechanically automatic process associationism suggests it should be, but it is a more complex process involving the animal computing contingencies between environmental events, and learning to behave accordingly.

What is not entirely clear at present is whether predictive CS-US contingencies determine the learning of Pavlovian CS-US associations or their expression. One of the most difficult issues in the study of learning and cognition is teasing apart the conditions that affect the acquisition of a behavior or memory—learning—from those that determine when and how learning is expressed—performance. Intuitively, the distinction is simple enough; for example, each of us has learned how to add and subtract, but under conditions of stress we make mistakes with our checkbooks. Separating performance, or the expression of learning, from learning itself has proven one of the most difficult issues in learning and cognitive psychology. Learning is not always reflected in performance, as the phenomena of sensory preconditioning, latent inhibition, and sensory differentiation make clear: In each case, initial exposure to one or more stimuli had no immediate observable effect on behavior, but affected the later acquisition of CRs; these are all examples of hidden, or latent, learning, brought out in performance after the learning occurred.

The problem of expression arises in interpretation of the effects of contingency on learning, too. The dominant model of Pavlovian conditioning, the Rescorla-Wagner model (Rescorla, 1988; Rescorla & Wagner, 1972), holds that contingencies affect learning, specifically that CS-US associations cannot form unless the CS predicts the US. However, an alternative interpretation is possible in terms of latent learning. Since clearly S-S associations can form from simple contiguity, animals in blocking and unblocking experiments might have formed latent CS-US associations not directly manifested in performance. Specifically, recent **comparator theories** of Pavlovian conditioning (Baker & Mercier, 1989; Martin & Levey, 1987; Miller & Matzel, 1989) argue that organisms always learn CS-US associations even in blocking experiments, but compare the (learned) ability of the CS to signal the US with the experimental contexts (learned) ability to signal the US. In ordinary Pavlovian conditioning, the ability of the CS to reliably signal a US is greater than the context's, as food or shock is delivered only when preceded by the CS, and the animal expresses this knowledge by responding with a CR. In blocking experiments, however, comparator theory holds that the animal learns that the CS sometimes predicts the US (as opposed to the Rescorla-Wagner view, which says no learning occurs at all), but since the CS predicts no better than the experimental context—which is always present when the US is delivered—the animal fails to express its learned CS-US association with a CR. Which of these two views is correct remains unclear (Durlach, 1989), and since one theory deals with learning and the other with expression of learning, their viewpoints may be complementary rather than competitive (Miller & Matzel, 1989). The rise of comparator theories has led to increased interest in the effect played by context in Pavlovian conditioning.

Instrumental Learning: Learned Helplessness

We have just learned how Pavlovian conditioning depends on a predictive contingency between CS and US. The same issue arises in the study of instrumental conditioning. Do rewards and punishments affect learning simply by occurring closely in time to the relevant response (the contiguity view) or because there is an actual contingency between the behavior and its consequence.

One of the most dramatic findings to emerge from the controversy between the contiguity and contingency accounts of reinforcement was the phenomenon of **learned helplessness** (Maier, 1989; Maier & Seligman, 1976; Seligman, 1975). Two dogs are placed in harnesses and subjected to identical periodic electrical shocks. One dog can terminate the shock by pressing a lever in front of its nose; the other dog, his yoked companion, has no control over the shock. When the first dog receives a shock, the second one does too. When the first dog stops the shock by pressing the lever, the shock stops for the second dog too. Both dogs receive identical patterns of shock and nonshock. The only difference is that the first dog can control its shocks, and naturally learns to do so, while the second dog is a helpless victim—what does the animal learn?

What the second dog learns is revealed in the second phase of the experiment when each animal must learn to jump a barrier to avoid receiving a shock. The first canine, like any normal dog that had never before been exposed to shock, quickly learns to jump the hurdle and avoids being shocked. The second dog, however, who was helpless during the first phase of the experiment, remains helpless even now when action could relieve its suffering. The creature whines and yelps, but after a while it becomes totally passive, simply accepting the shocks without complaint or any attempt to avoid them. It has *learned* to be *helpless*. A pious observer might even say that the second dog has acquired the resignation to the will of God, or of the gods that most religions try to teach.

How does this finding reflect on the contiguity-contingency debate? Remember that the two dogs received exactly the *same* pattern of shock and nonshock in phase 1. A contiguity view of learning would say that the first dog learned to press the lever because it was followed by negative reinforcement while the second dog learned "superstitiously" to act passive in the face of shock. A contingency analysis would say that the first dog learned that what it did made a difference—that it could avoid shock through effective action, learning that appropriately transferred to the hurdle-jumping phase of the experiment. But the second dog learned literally to be helpless—that there was no connection between what it did and shock, that there was no point even in wasting its energy whining and yelping—and so remained helpless even in the new situation of phase 2.

To test these hypotheses Maier (1970) repeated the original experiment, except that this time the first dog learned to be master of its fate by standing rigidly still to terminate the shock. The creature's companion remained helpless as in the standard experiment. Now, if the first dog simply learned to stand still to avoid shock, we would expect it to stand still in the hurdle-jumping phase of the experiment. But these dogs did not act passively—they learned to jump the hurdle—while the yoked dogs were again rendered helpless. So it appears that reinforcement works because of contingency between action and reward, not just because reward happens to follow a behavior. Organisms can tell when their activities affect their lives and when they do not.

The learned-helplessness phenomenon has had considerable impact on the theory and treatment of human depression and on social psychological theories on peoples' perception of control. It has been theorized that perhaps human depressives have had experiences similar to the learned-helplessness dogs, and have similarly concluded that nothing they do will be effective in getting what they want, falling into the misery and stupor of depression. Normal people, on the other hand, believe in their mastery of the world, behave effectively, and are reasonably happy. The flip side of learned helplessness is the *illusion of control.* If it is possible to falsely believe one is not in control of one's life—learned helplessness—then it must also be possible to falsely believe that one is in control of one's life—illusion of control.

Research on learned helplessness and illusion of control has revealed an interesting pattern of results (Thompson, 1999). In some now classic experiments, Alloy and Abramson (1979, 1982) compared depressed to nondepressed subjects in an experiment designed to measure the degree to which subjects felt in control of a simple outcome. Subjects tried to get a green light to come on by pushing a button. There was, in fact, no relationship between their pushing the button and the light coming on. In one condition, the light randomly came on after the button push 75 percent of the time (high reinforcement condition); in the other it randomly followed 25 percent of the time (low reinforcement). In the low reinforcement condition, all subjects correctly perceived that they had little, if any control of the situation. In the high reinforcement condition, however, only depressives realized they could not control the green light, while normal subjects experienced an illusion of control, falsely thinking their button-pushing made the light come on. Depressed mood alone seems to dissipate the illusion of control, because subjects who are not chronic depressives but are made depressed by an experimental manipulation act like depressives in these experiments (Thompson, 1999). It is interesting to observe that being happy seems to depend on an illusion and that chronic depressives have more accurate perceptions of control than normal people. It appears that being normally happy depends, as one depressive has said, on being a foolish cockeyed optimist. Depressives know better. They would agree with the cartoon character who told his psychiatrist, "I don't mind being in touch with reality, but I don't want to live there."

In both Pavlovian and instrumental learning, learning and performance depend on contingency, not contiguity. Hence, CSs must uniquely predict USs for Pavlovian conditioning to happen, and reinforcement must be truly contingent on behavior for instrumental learning to occur. Contiguity is still important as a variable affecting the strength of conditioning (Rescorla, 1985)—it still helps for CS and US to be near one another—but we now know it is not the major cause of conditioning; contingency is.

What Is the Role of Reward?

Ever since Thorndike proposed it, the Law of Effect has been controversial. To the most hard-headed behaviorists, Thorndike's reference to the animal's "satisfaction" was unscientifically mentalistic. To others (such as Guthrie) the Law of Effect violated the basic principle of causality by which causes much precede effects, because according to Thorndike, the reward strengthens the S-R bond that preceded it. Hull and Tolman differed over how reinforcement worked, Hull maintaining that reward strengthened behavior by reducing a biological drive, while Tolman emphasized the informational value of rewards and punishments. Years of research left the status of the Law of Effect unclear, but a novel and promising line of inquiry was opened up by David Premack (1959, 1962, 1965a). Premack described reward not as a discrete thing or even an event, but as a relationship between behavior frequencies. His idea is called **relativity of reinforcers,** or more informally, the **Premack principle.**

The basic idea is simple. A person or other animal engages in many activities and does some more frequently than others. So activity A is more frequent than activity B, which is more frequent than C, and so on: A.B.C.D. Premack says simply that any activity higher on the scale can be used to reinforce any activity lower on the scale. Eating is more common than lever-pressing in a naive rat, and so we can use the opportunity to eat to reinforce bar-pressing. A child may prefer playing baseball to reading, and so we can use access to baseball as a reinforcer for reading.

Premack's suggestion is useful in two ways. First, it reminds us of individual differences. At least in people, what is reinforcing for one person may not be reinforcing for another. A shy, introverted child may read more than play baseball, and a teacher concerned with the child's loneliness may make access to books contingent on playing with other children.

Second, the Premack principle offers concrete guidance to the behavior modifier. It points out that for any given low-level behavior you wish to strengthen, there must be many potential reinforcers, and it tells how to locate and use them.

Despite its utility, the Premack principle breaks down in interesting ways. Suppose (the following figures are illustrative only, based on Allison, 1989) we observe that out of every hour a rat spends 8 minutes licking at its water spout and 4 minutes running in its activity wheel, so that the baseline frequency of licking (behavior A) is greater than the baseline frequency of running (behavior B; A>B). Thus according to the Premack principle, we should be able to increase the frequency of B (running) by making access to A (licking) contingent on running. So we institute a requirement, called a **schedule of reinforcement,** such that the rat has to run for 1 minute to get 2 minutes of licking. Since A is now contingent on B, B should be reinforced, and increase in frequency. Such is not the case, however: Running is still performed about 4 minutes of every hour. We can see why B's frequency did not increase by looking at the schedule of reinforcement more closely. If the rat ran at its baseline rate (4 minutes per hour), it would achieve its baseline rate of licking. Thus there is no reason for the rat to run any more than before, despite running's apparent "reinforcement" by licking.

James Allison (1989) has proposed replacing the principle of relativity of reinforcers with his **response deprivation hypothesis.** The basic idea of the response deprivation hypothesis may be seen by a simple change in the running-licking schedule that does increase running. If we require that the rat run for 4 minutes to get 2 minutes of licking, then to fulfill its baseline of licking the rat will have to run 16 minutes. That Allison's theory is not simply a refinement of Premack's is shown by the fact that we can establish a schedule of reinforcement by which a less frequent behavior may be used to reinforce a more frequent behavior, contrary to the Premack principle. Suppose that we make running contingent on licking, specifically that the rat will have to lick for 4 minutes in order to get 1 minute of access to its running wheel. Under this schedule, to fulfill its baseline running rate of 4 minutes per hour, the rat will have to lick for 16 minutes, and this is, in fact what occurs.

Just as comparator theories of Pavlovian conditioning interpret phenomena such as blocking in terms of performance rather than learning, Allison proposes that schedules of reinforcement are principles governing performance rather than learning, primarily affecting an organism's allocation of already learned behaviors. An animal engages in many activities and tries to divide its time on each so that each is performed at some optimum level, or as near to optimum as possible. Thus for any two behaviors there is a **bliss point** such that each can be performed at its ideal (free baseline) level. So for our imaginary rat, the running/licking bliss point was 4 minutes and 8 minutes. Schedules of reinforcement will change frequencies of responding only when they put the bliss point out of reach, as the animal strives to reach it. People often behave in accordance with bliss point theory, providing a simple example of behavioral economics (see Chapter 4). People work and people have leisure, and hardly anybody would want only one or the other. So there is presumably some "bliss point" of hours of work per week and hours of leisure per week that workers strive to achieve by balancing the amount of time spent on each (Allison, 1989).

More radically, Allison proposes abolishing the Law of Effect altogether as a chimera, "the fantastical One Ring that gives its user mastery of all creatures" (p. 36). Thorndike and the other behaviorists looked for a single tool—reinforcement—that would give them mastery over animal and human behavior. But both Premack's and Allison's work reinforce the conclusion of students of associative learning that organisms—human and animal—are not simply passive creatures shaped by the whim of psychologists. Humans and animals are active adapters, pursuing their own agendas of happiness within the constraints they find in the environment.

What Is the Role of Consciousness?

Asking whether humans condition may be surprising, since we have already discussed some studies of human conditioning, but William Brewer (1974) has suggested that the picture is not so simple. If we reward people for some activity, or pair USs and CSs, their behavior will change. But as scientists, we want to know why behavior changes, not just record that it does.

From the time of Thorndike, most behaviorists have believed in the automatic action of reinforcers. As Thorndike put it, reward and punishment simply stamp in or stamp out the responses they follow. A subject does not have to be aware of the connection between one's behavior and its consequences, or of the regular pairing of US and CS, for conditioning to occur. The action of reinforcers was held to be direct and automatic, unmediated by consciousness or thought (Postman & Sassenrath, 1961), which behaviorists were trying to throw out of psychology anyway. In the behaviorist view, then, the mental state of a person is simply irrelevant to behavior, which is instead the outcome of stimuli and reinforcers in one's environment.

On the other hand, cognitive psychologists like Brewer contend that when a subject learns something, or "conditions," what really happens is that the subject figures out what's going on in the experiment and then acts appropriately. In the cognitive view, then, what changes during a person's "conditioning" is his or her conscious mental state, with behavior changing because the subject has "solved" the experiment. Therefore, it should be possible to create and extinguish CR's and instrumental responses by directly manipulating subjects' mental states, without actually doing any conditioning. Or it should be possible to fool people about what's really going on in an experiment so that they do not condition desire manipulation of stimuli or reinforcers, or learn associations other than those of CS and US, or response and reward. In general, the cognitive hypothesis maintains that beliefs about the environment are more important in regulating behavior than the actual environment.

Brewer (1974) reviewed over 200 studies done by others that tested the automatic action of the reinforcers view against the cognitive view. To illustrate the findings on this dispute we will just look at the results from two traditional areas of learning, one Pavlovian, and the other instrumental.

As an example of Pavlovian conditioning of an autonomic response, we will consider conditioning the galvanic skin response (GSR). When you are frightened or aroused, you sweat, changing the ability of your skin to conduct electricity; lie detectors use this fact to detect the bodily arousal that should accompany the stress of lying. Electric shock produces the GSR response, and we can pair a tone (CS) with the shock (US) to condition a conditional GSR.

What if we simply tell subjects that when they hear the tone they will be shocked, without ever doing it? The result is that subjects acquire a conditional GSR. On the other hand, already conditioned subjects who are told the shocks will no longer follow the CS show immediate extinction, at least in those subjects who believe us; however, many don't. Studies that follow the usual conditioning procedures and then ask the subjects if they figured out the CS-US connection found that only those who had figured out the connection displayed any conditioning (Davey, 1987).

As an example of motor response learning, we will select finger-withdrawal conditioning. In this kind of experiment, subjects rest their fingers, palm down, on an electrode. A tone is sounded and the subject is shocked. Subjects soon learn to avoid the shock.

Subjects in finger-withdrawal conditioning have been fooled by instructions. After we condition subjects by ordinary means, suppose we turn their hand over and present the tone? Will they withdraw their finger, making the opposite motor response from what they had learned, or will they move their finger in the same way as before, pressing their finger into the electrode? About 75 percent of subjects make the new flexion response that gets their finger off the electrode, 5 percent press their fingers into the electrode, and 20 percent make no response.

With this established finding in mind, let us consider an experiment in which subjects' beliefs are manipulated. One group is put through the above procedure. Another group receives the same conditioning, but is told that what they are expected to learn is a particular muscle movement—withdrawing the finger up, with palm down. Finally, the last group is conditioned, but in the second half of the experiment they are lied to about the location of the electrode, so that in trying to avoid the shock they will actually be pressing their finger into the electrode. The first, or standard, group produced the usual results just described. In the group told they were learning a simple muscle reflex, only about one-third gave responses away from the electrode in the second part of the experiment when they turned their hands over. The third group gave all their responses into the electrode. What subjects think the experimenter wants them to do is generally more powerful than actually getting shocked.

From his review, Brewer concluded that there is no evidence for Pavlovian or instrumental conditioning in normal adult human beings, meaning conditioning without awareness. In some behaviorist circles, Brewer's conclusion evoked outrage (e.g., Maltzman, 1977, 1979, 1987), but subsequent research has supported his conclusions. The most thorough studies evaluating the role of consciousness in conditioning have been performed by Dawson and his colleagues (for a review see Dawson & Schell, 1987) on human autonomic conditioning. Dawson has extensively investigated the acquisition of skin conductance responses (SCRs; formerly known as galvanic skin responses, or GSRs) to electric shock USs in paradigms that mislead subjects about the significance of the CSs that signal the shock. For example, in one series of experiments subjects were told they were in an auditory perception experiment and would receive occasional electric shock to test its effects on perceptual accuracy. Subjects listened to an initial tone and then to a series of five randomly arranged tones varying in pitch from 800 to 1200 Hz, one of which matched the initial tone. The subjects were instructed to note and report which of the five tones matched the initial tone, and which was highest and which was lowest in pitch. Unknown to the subject, the highest tone in the series was always a CS;1 for electric shock. Since the 1200 Hz tone reliably signaled the shock US, it should have later triggered SCRs when presented alone. However, using careful postexperimental questionnaires, Dawson determined that only subjects who became conscious of the CS-US contingency showed signs of conditioning. At the same time, Dawson has shown that, once acquired, conditioned fear responses may be carried out without consciousness, for example, under conditions in which the CS is outside the focus of attention. Using the terminology of information-processing, acquisition of a CR is a controlled process while its execution is automatic (see also Furedy & Riley, 1987).

As we observed in Chapter 1, and will observe later, the nature of consciousness and its role in controlling behavior remain elusive and controversial. It has become clear that behavior can be changed without the involvement of consciousness. In Chapter 12, for example, we will find evidence from experimental and clinical neuropsychology that learning can take place in animals that cannot experience a stimulus and humans who are unable to form conscious memories. Moreover, it is adaptively important that such learning be possible. On the other hand, it is clear from the studies just reviewed that conscious experience is relevant to learning and behavior—we are not always conscious automatons. Scientific understanding of consciousness is in the forefront of cognitive science and neuroscience.

LEARNING AND ADAPTATION

CR-UR Equivalence: CR as Adaptation to Expected UR

In Pavlov's experiments, CR and UR were virtually indistinguishable. Both were salivary responses differing, if at all, only in the CR being quantitatively smaller than the UR. Similarly in Pavlovian fear conditioning, the CS comes to elicit fear just as the UR—usually shock—did. This makes sense if stimulus substitution is the mechanism of conditioning, since the CS comes to substitute for, and have the same effect as, the US. However, research has shown that CR and UR may be dramatically different—even opposite—leading to a different interpretation of the role of the CR. It is no longer seen merely as a reflex controlled by the CS, but as an adaptive response by which the organism prepares for the UR event.

Change in the CR from resemblance to the UR appears in extended fear conditioning. One effect of fear is acceleration of one's heart rate. If we pair a tone (CS) and shock (US), and measure heart rate (UR and CR), we find that, following initial conditioning, the tone elicits an increase in heart rate, as stimulus substitution theory leads us to expect. However, with more pairings the form of the CR changes from an increase in heart rate to a decrease in heart rate (Obrist, Sutterer, & Howard, 1972): Thus the CR becomes the opposite of the UR, contrary to stimulus substitution theory. This change in heart rate, however, can be explained if we think of conditioning not as a mechanical process by which CS and US get reflexively associated, but as a sophisticated adaptive process by which organisms learn to prepare themselves for biologically important events. If an organism knows that a shock will follow a tone, then the biologically adaptive thing to do is compensate for the coming shock, which will elevate heart rate, by lowering heart rate, so that the effect of the shock will be to elevate heart rate to roughly normal levels. Responding to the CS by continued elevation of heart rate, which would be elevated still further by the US, would be biologically maladaptive. Ordinary forms of Pavlovian conditioning also fit into this new view of conditioning as an adaptive process (Bolles, 1975; Turkkan, 1989); for example, the most adaptive way to prepare for the arrival of food is to salivate.

Compensatory conditional responses are especially common in preparations in which the US is a drug (Turkkan, 1989), and provide a possible way of explaining drug addiction as a Pavlovian conditioned response (Siegel, 1983). This hypothesis is based on the observation that in conditioning with a drug as the US, the acquired CR is the opposite of the UR. This makes adaptive sense, because the CS acts as a signal warning of imminent drug delivery (the US), and the body prepares itself by altering its physiology (the CR) in directions opposite to the effects of the drug (the UR). As a result, over trials, the actual effect of the drug becomes weaker and weaker.

Consider a person taking heroin. Initially, the drug creates a pleasurable high. However, certain stimuli regularly precede drug use—most immediately the sight of the hypodermic, but also the user's regular haunts and friends. These stimuli come to act as CSs, signaling drug delivery, and a preparatory CR appears and strengthens over time. So increasing doses are needed to experience any high at all, as the net drug effect diminishes; the addict—for he or she has become one—may overdose in time. Moreover, the CR is the opposite of the UR—the craving of the addict for more heroin, making life miserable without the drug.

If this hypothesis is correct, then certain implications for drug rehabilitation become apparent. For example, in animal studies, drug tolerance has been extinguished by presenting the cues (CSs) that formerly signaled drug delivery, without administering the drug (US). So perhaps the best way to treat drug addicts is in their home community, where familiar places and people may be experienced without heroin. Removing addicts to a remote treatment center may be ineffective, because their eventual return home will return them to CSs that will elicit an unextinguished CR, and a probable return to the heroin habit.

Pavlovian conditioning is more than blind, reflexive learning: Organisms learn about the world from their experience, and what they learn provides the basis for adaptive action.

Equipotentiality: Evolutionary Heritage Affects Associative Learning

Philosophical associationism, followed, until recently by behavioral theorists, assumed that associations, whether S-S or S-R, were essentially arbitrary. Put in the terminology of Pavlovian conditioning, this assumption of equipotentiality held that any stimulus an animal can perceive has equal potential with any other to become a CS when paired with any arbitrarily chosen US. The assumption of equipotentiality was important for behavior theorists because their goal was to construct a general process-learning theory, a theory of learning that would apply equally to all species under all conditions. Their research strategy was to perform rigorous experiments on arbitrarily chosen stimuli (like tones and shocks) in the belief that the laws of association they discovered in their simple animal experiments could be straightforwardly generalized to human and complex animal behavior. As B. F. Skinner put it (1961b, p. 118): "Pigeon, rat, monkey, which is which? It doesn't matter." However, it has now been shown that how animals form associations depends very much on different organisms' different evolutionary history as a species and the different ecological problems they have to solve to survive. The most dramatic and famous of the research findings that demonstrated the falsity of equipotentiality, and which thus threatens the goal of general associative learning theory, was the work of John Garcia and his associates on conditioned taste aversion.

Over the course of many experiments, Garcia and his colleagues studied aversion learning based on food. During the course of his research, Garcia discovered phenomena anomalous to the general-process program. Rats allowed to drink a novel-tasting fluid (saccharin-flavored water), and made sick hours later by drug injection or X-irradiation, learned to avoid drinking the flavored water. This violated the usual law of classical conditioning, which holds that the US-CS interval must be very short—about 0.5 second—for learning to occur. Moreover, the aversion was always to the most recent novel substance, since rats who drank saccharin water, then familiar tap water, and then got sick, avoided only the saccharin water.

The selectivity of the taste-sickness association is strengthened by further experiments. Rats would learn to avoid foods on the basis of its taste, not its appearance (Domjon, 1980). In an elegant two-factor experiment, Garcia, Clarke, and Hankins (1973) let rats drink saccharin water while they heard a click, were shocked, or were later made ill. The rats learned specifically to associate sweetness with illness and the click with shock. Sickened rats avoided only the food and did not try to run away from the click. Shocked rats tried to avoid the click but drank the sweet water. The obvious conclusion is that sick rats conclude, "It must have been something I ate," and attribute the cause of their distress to the newest food they ate rather than exterior cues or to familiar foods. That this process is genetic is supported by findings that the same phenomena occur in newborn rat pups.

These particular dispositions to learn are well adapted to the rat's ecology (Shettleworth, 1972). Wild rats are omnivores who sample small amounts of new foods and avoid those that make them ill. Long before Garcia's findings, rodent-control experts knew that rats easily become bait-shy, outwitting their hunters. Under these conditions, it would be an ill-adapted rat indeed who drank tainted water, later got ill under a bush and learned to avoid the bush (the immediate CS), while returning to drink the water. Evolution has produced rats who adaptively associate taste with illness and external cues with external threats.

Different ecologies produce different food aversions. Wild rats are nocturnal feeders with poor vision, so taste, not food appearance, is their best cue for avoiding poison. Quail, on the other hand, are diurnal (daytime) feeders with excellent vision, and they can easily and directly associate a new food's appearance with later illness (Wilcoxon, Dragoin, & Kral, 1972). Bluejays, like rats, are scavengers and learn as rats do, in a two-step process: Taste (CS) is averted by illness (US) and then visual cues (CS) are avoided by the aversive taste (US). Animals' ecological niches and consequent evolutionary pressures direct the ways animals learn even simple associations (Garcia, Quick, & White, 1984; Shettleworth, 1972; Wilson, 1975a).

Other phenomena further demonstrate the complex ways in which animal instinct shapes animal learning. An example is a sensory preconditioning experiment performed by Holland (1981). In the sensory preconditioning phase, Holland exposed rats to pairings of a tone with a flavor in their water. In the conditioning phase, he paired the same tone with chemically induced nausea. In tests, Holland found that the rats showed no aversion to the tone, but considerable aversion to the flavor. Besides supporting an S-S theory of Pavlovian conditioning (Rescorla, 1984), Holland's finding reveals the control of learning by instinct. Rats seem to know innately that an external stimulus like a tone cannot cause an internal effect like nausea, so they do not associate the tone with nausea even though it is directly paired with nausea; the tone does not, and it appears cannot, become a CS in such circumstances. It is likely that something eaten or drunk could cause nausea, so the aversion is directed to the flavor associated with the tone. It becomes the CS even though it has never been directly paired with nausea. Instinct tells the rat what kinds of associations to make and what kinds not to make.

In addition to assuming that all CS-US pairs are equally associable, the doctrine of equipotentiality assumed that the CS plays no role in determining the nature of the CR, since it is evoked originally by the US and the CS gets its power from pairing with the US. However, the CS can determine the form of the CR (Rescorla, 1975, 1988). For example, if we pair a tone or a light with foot shock, a rat will in the future freeze or run away from the CS. On the other hand, if we shock the rat with a prod, the rat will bury the prod rather than freeze or run away (Holland, 1984). Different CSs will have different effects even if paired with the same US, depending on the animal's inherited ability to cope with different kinds of stimuli. Sometimes, innate associations may override the usual principles of conditioning. As we have seen, backward conditioning is very difficult to bring about. This is natural, for if we regard CSs as signposts telling animals what to expect, then a sign that follows a turn in the road is not very useful (B. Schwartz, 1984). However, if we signal a foot shock with a tone, and right after the tone throw a rubber hedgehog in the rat's cage, the rat will later avoid the hedgehog rather than the tone, even with just one such trial (Staddon, 1985). Even though the hedgehog comes after the tone, its lifelike properties as a natural danger to rats make it a far more likely natural CS than a tone, and rats backward condition to it, ignoring the signaling tone CS.

When Pavlov first set out to investigate the psychical reflexes, he serendipitously had discovered, he thought—and generations of psychologists followed him in his belief—that Pavlovian conditioning represented an extremely simple and elementary form of associative learning. However, the picture of Pavlovian conditioning we hold today is very different. We now see Pavlovian conditioning as a complex adaptive process by which the organism seeks out and uses information about predictive stimulus-event relationships, and uses this information to choose responses that are biologically adaptive. Gone is the mechanistic stimulus substitution concept. In its place stand associative theories of animal learning revealing that "Pavlovian conditioning isn't what you think" (Rescorla, 1988).

LEARNING IN THE ARCHITECTURES OF COGNITION

While conditioning was originally studied by behaviorists, and the associative tradition of studying conditioning continues in theories such as the Rescorla-Wagner theory of Pavlovian conditioning, cognitive scientists have proposed theories of conditioning, too. As examples, we will look now at a symbol system model and a connectionist model of Pavlovian conditioning.

The Symbol System Hypothesis: Pavlovian Conditioning in a Production System

Production systems can represent knowledge, but if they are to provide a model of human intelligence they must be able to learn. Building production systems that learn is an object of extensive research (Newell, 1990). To provide a simple example of a familiar kind of learning in a production system, we will discuss the production system model of Pavlovian conditioning proposed by Holyoak, Koh, and Nisbett (1989).

The architecture of the Holyoak, Koh, and Nisbett model is basically the same as that discussed in Chapter 2, with three important differences. The first difference concerns memory systems. In most production systems, the only declarative memory is in working memory, where current information is stored; LTM, consisting solely of productions, is purely procedural. In the Holyoak, Koh, and Nisbett production system, there is both short-term and long-term declarative memory for events. LTM holds memory about past events, tagged for familiarity. STM consists of information about recent unusual events (familiar ones are ignored), and three messages. The first message contains information about events occurring on the previous trial (such as whether the US occurred or not); the second message contains predictions about what will happen on the current trial (e.g., whether the US will occur or not), placed there by production rules; and the third message is an observation about what is occurring on the present trial (e.g., whether the US is present or not).

The second new feature of the Holyoak, Koh, and Nisbett model concerns the form of the production rules in procedural LTM. Instead of rules taking the form "if condition X, then take action Z," Holyoak, Koh, and Nisbett's production rules have the form "if condition X, then expect Y and take action Z," or in a version suitable for conditioning, "if stimulus X occurs, then expect stimulus Y and make response Z." This revised production rule structure reflects the contemporary understanding that Pavlovian conditioning involves learning to predict important stimulus events from preceding stimuli. In the Holyoak, Koh, and Nisbett production system, attached to productions are strength values that reflect how well the production has predicted the occurrence of reinforcements (USs), representing the idea of associative strength. The third innovation of this model is elimination of the inference engine. Instead of being regulated by the inference engine, the productions compete with each other to be the one that fires on a given trial.

Learning occurs by two processes, rule generation and changing production strengths. Rules are generated in accord with an unusualness heuristic. STM contains information about recent unfamiliar stimuli, and if these seem to predict the occurrence of a US, rule generation occurs and a tentative production is established in procedural LTM. For example, if an unfamiliar 1000-Hz tone has preceded food on several trials, a production of the form "If a 1000-Hz tone occurs, then expect food and salivate" is set up. If on subsequent trials the production rule correctly predicts US occurrence, it gains strength. Strength becomes important when more than one rule might predict the US. For example, in blocking experiments, a new CS that predicts a US shows no conditioning if there is already a CS that does so. In the Holyoak, Koh, and Nisbett model, occurrence of the new CS may in fact become embodied in a production because it is unusual and predicts the US, but fails to control behavior because of the great preexisting strength of an already established production.

Other phenomena of Pavlovian conditioning can also be simulated by the Holyoak, Koh, and Nisbett production system. During extinction, an established, high-strength production will incorrectly predict US occurrence and lose strength thereby. New behaviors will emerge during extinction, as productions with lower strength emerge from under the shadow of a dominant production. Latent inhibition will occur because, if a stimulus is presented many times without consequence, it will enter declarative LTM tagged as familiar, will not be entered into STM, and will not become a candidate for production generation.

This presentation of the Holyoak, Koh, and Nisbett model of Pavlovian conditioning is simplified, but it illustrates the essential features of the symbol-system approach to learning and cognition. Declarative memory stores representations (symbols) of recent and current events, and these symbols are then operated on (manipulated) by productions (rules) contained in procedural LTM. The fundamental thesis of symbol-system architectures of cognition is that all thought, from Pavlovian conditioning to chess playing, consists of the manipulation of symbols by formal rules, whether or not the symbols and rules are conscious.

Connectionism: A Model of Pavlovian Conditioning

Figure 3.4 illustrates the connectionist approach to Pavlovian conditioning (Kehoe, 1988, 1989; Rumelhart, Hinton, & Williams, 1986). A simple two-layer, feed-forward network exhibits many of the phenomena of Pavlovian conditioning. It is a layered network, because units are organized into an input layer responsible for sensation and an output layer responsible for behavior. Networks can also be built without layers, units being arranged and interconnected almost at random, but most working networks are layered. It is a feed-forward network, because activation—impulses sent from one unit to the next—spreads in one direction, forward from the input layer to the output layer. Again, there are networks in which connections exist between units in the same layer, or in which there are feedback connections from later units to earlier units, but most working networks are feed-forward. Discussing only layered feed-forward networks simplifies our discussion.

The input layer contains three units, each of which represents a sensory input: two for the conditional stimuli and one for the unconditional stimulus. The output layer contains only one unit; if it fires, the UR or CR occurs; if it does not fire, no behavior occurs. Before learning, only one connection is active—that is, has a weight greater than 0—the US → UR/CR connection, which has a high excitatory weight. Taking salivary conditioning as our example, if food (US) is presented, the UR/CR unit is activated, and the organism salivates.

FIGURE 3.4 Simple two-layer neural net for basic phenomena of Pavlovian conditioning.

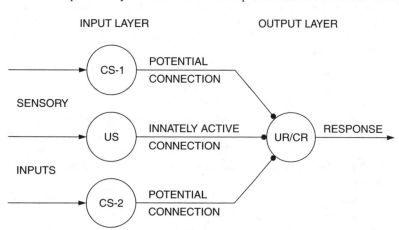

In connectionist models, learning consists of modifying the strength of connections between units. In Pavlovian conditioning, we present a US (which activates the UR/CR unit) together with a CS, and learning consists of activating the excitatory connection between the CS and the UR/CR units. This may be accomplished in several ways in neural nets, but the most important one is back-propagation. We train—not program—a neural net by presenting to the network a training set of input-output pairs that show the network what output it should produce given a certain input. In the case of Pavlovian conditioning with a single stimulus, the training set consists of a short list:

Presented Input	Presented Input (Reinforcement)	Desired Output
CS-1	US	UR/CR
ON	ON	ON
ON	OFF	ON
OFF	ON	ON
OFF	OFF	OFF

On each trial we present a member of the training set, a pattern of input stimuli and a reinforcing event that tells the network if it has produced the correct output. The back-propagation algorithm takes the reinforcement information concerning the correct response, and propagates it back down the net, so that the network adjusts its weights a little bit on each trial until the pattern of output activation it produces to a given stimulus pattern matches what is desired by the trainer. In our simple network this means that the initially inactive connection between CS-1 and the UR/CR unit (initial weight = 0) will gain in strength, until activation of the CS-1 unit by itself turns on the UR/CR output unit.

The network depicted in Figure 3.4 is also capable of simple discrimination learning between two stimuli, CS-1 (e.g., a tone), the reinforced stimulus and CS-2 (e.g., a light), the nonreinforced stimulus. In the training set, the US is presented only when CS-1 is present, and never when CS-2 is present. As we know from Pavlov's work, a CS- (in this case CS-2) becomes inhibitory, and so we will train the network until the CS-1 connection becomes strongly excitatory and the CS-2 connection becomes inhibitory. As in the first case, this is accomplished by gradual adjustment of the connection weights.

In addition to simple conditioning and discrimination, this little network also shows blocking. If we first train the network to respond to CS-1 presented alone, the CS-1 → UR/CR connection becomes strongly positive. If we then introduce a new CS, CS-2, perhaps a light, paired with the US, its connection strength never changes from 0, since every occurrence of the US is predicted by CS-1, and there is no gain to the network in altering the CS-2 → UR/CR connection strength. Because no improvement in output behavior can be obtained by altering the strength of the CS-2 → UR/CR connection weight, it will remain at 0.

The difference between the connectionist and symbol-system account of blocking resembles the debate between the associative and performance (comparator) theories of blocking discussed in Chapter 2. Connectionism and traditional associationism explain blocking by claiming that a connection between the new (blocked) CS and the response is not acquired. Comparator theories of conditioning and the production system model of Holyoak, Koh, and Nisbett (1989) assert that the organism learns that the new CS predicts the US, but does not express that knowledge in behavior.

Although our simple two-layer network can simulate the basic phenomena of Pavlovian conditioning, more sophisticated phenomena are beyond its reach. While sometimes Pavlovian learning involves responding to a single stimulus, frequently an organism must learn to respond adaptively to several stimuli, or to a stimulus considered in comparison to its context, as we learned earlier. Learning involving multiple and contextual stimuli is called **configurational learning,** because the organism must learn to respond to patterns (configurations) of stimuli. Perhaps the most sophisticated form of configurational learning is **negative patterning.**

In negative patterning, the reinforcer (the US) is paired with either of two CSs presented alone, but is withheld when both CSs are present at the same time. The two-layer network of Figure 3.4 cannot perform negative patterning. For the network to respond correctly with a CR to CS-1 alone or to CS-2 alone, the connection weights between CS-1 and the UR/CR unit and between the CS-2 and UR/CR unit must be positively excitatory. However, simultaneous presentation of both CSs makes the CR occur, so that the network does not exhibit negative patterning.

Historically, the early connectionist networks of the 1950s and 1960s were limited to two layers for technical mathematical reasons, and were therefore abandoned in favor of the symbol-system approach. In contemporary connectionist theory, however, it is possible to build networks having layers of hidden units intervening between input and output units. Figure 3.5 shows a very simple three-layer network with the same two input and output layers as before, but possessing a one-unit hidden layer, so-called because it is not directly connected to either perception or action.

Training a network with a hidden layer is more complicated than training one without, but the process is basically the same. We present the network with a training set specifying the various possible inputs and the outputs we want the network to make. As a consequence, the network gradually changes the connection strengths between its

FIGURE 3.5 Simple three-layer neural network for negative patterning in Pavlovian conditioning.

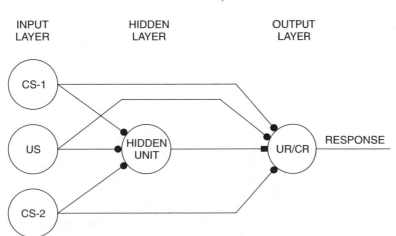

units until it produces the appropriate output. What the network of Figure 3.5 must learn is to establish moderate excitatory connections between the CSs and the hidden unit, and a strong inhibitory connection between the hidden unit and the UR/CR unit. When either CS is presented alone, its strong connection to the UR/CR unit (as in standard Pavlovian conditioning) activates it. The single CS's moderate excitatory connection with the hidden unit is below its threshold, and it does not fire. However, when both CSs are presented, their combined moderate connections to the hidden unit sum to above the hidden unit's threshold, and it fires, producing an inhibition at the UR/CR unit that subtracts from the positive input of the two CSs, causing the response unit not to fire. The network of Figure 3.5 thus shows negative patterning.

SUGGESTED READINGS

Broad views of the Golden Age of Theory may be had from T. Leahey, *A History of Modern Psychology,* 3rd ed. (Upper Saddle River, NJ: Prentice-Hall, 2001), and from Sigmund Koch (Ed.) *Psychology: A Study of a Science* (New York: McGraw-Hill, 1959). Volume 2 of Koch's work contains the theories presented here, plus others, and are reviewed by the participants themselves. The work of B. F. Skinner is presented in historical context in T. H. Leahey's, *A History of Psychology,* 4th ed. (Englewood Cliffs, NJ: Prentice-Hall, 1996). There is now a biography of Skinner, Daniel Bjork (1993) *B. F. Skinner: A Life* (New York: Basic Books). Howard Rachlin provides a fine introduction to *Modern Behaviorism,* 3rd ed. (New York: W. H. Freeman, 1991). For a sampling of work on the application of radical behaviorism to humans, see "Special Issue on the Experimental Analysis of Human Behavior," D. J. Navarick, D. J. Bernstein, and E. Fantino (Eds), *Journal of the Experimental Analysis of Behavior, 54:* 3. Useful surveys of research on animal cognition included Roitblat (1987) and Pearce (1987).

4 Behavioral Therories of Learning

Having reviewed the fundamental research that began the behavioral psychology of learning, we will now turn to the theoreticians who built their ideas on Pavlov's and Thorndike's works. Inspired by the apparent generality of the laws of learning propounded by Pavlov and Thorndike, several psychologists developed large-scale theories of learning that they hoped would scientifically explain virtually all behavior in all animals, including human beings. These efforts began in the 1930s and 1940s, an era known to historians of psychology as the "Golden Age of Theory." The first section of this chapter will describe the theories advanced by the two leading theorists of the Golden Age, Clark L. Hull (1884–1952), and Edward Chace Tolman (1886–1959). Their influence waned in the 1950s, but B. F. Skinner (1904–1990), whose radical behaviorism will be treated in the second section, carried on the quest for a general theory of learning and behavior.

The three theories discussed in this chapter have not survived in their original forms, but retain influence through students and by having made certain topics in the psychology of learning centrally important. We will therefore focus only on the general orientation of each theory.

THE GOLDEN AGE OF THEORY

Logical Behaviorism

Inspired by Isaac Newton, Clark Hull proposed a theory that he hoped would do for psychology what Newtonian theory had done for physics: make it a quantitative science able to predict and explain events in minutely precise detail. Just as a physicist can predict to the microsecond how long it will take an object in free fall to traverse a given distance, Hull wanted to be able to predict to the microsecond how long a rat with a given history of reinforcement and recent feedings would take to run a given distance to get food. Unsurprisingly, Hull's theory was fearsomely complex and systematically stated as a network of axioms, corollaries, and theorems expressed in mathematical and logical form.

For example, one of the fundamental postulates of Hull's system as set forth in Hull (1943) was:

$$_sE_R = {_sH_R} \times D$$

What this says is that the tendency to make a given response, **reaction potential** or $_sE_R$, is a function (=) of motivation, **drive** or D, multiplied by how well the response

99

has been learned, **habit strength** or $_sH_R$. Hull's proposed axiom is based on common sense, for it says you will only give a response if you have learned it as a habit ($_sH_R$ is positive) and are motivated to give the response (D is positive). Should you either not know what to do ($_sH_R$ is 0) or not be motivated (D is 0), you will not respond ($_sE_R$ is 0).

Testing the validity of the axiom is relatively straightforward, at least if we do not try to put exact numbers on the theoretical terms. As our response we might choose pressing a bar in a Skinner box to get food, and as our measure of the strength of the response ($_sE_R$) we can use how quickly the bar is pressed after our subject, a rat, is released into the box, assuming quite reasonably that the more quickly the bar is pressed the stronger is the response tendency; $_sE_R$ is our dependent variable, and we can manipulate our independent variables $_sH_R$ and D to see if they affect $_sE_R$ in the right way.

To manipulate D we simply compare well-fed animals (D is 0) to animals of moderate drive strength (e.g., 12 hours without food) and animals of high drive strength (24 hours without food). We cross the drive factor with $_sH_R$. Contrary to Guthrie, Hull believed that learning, the acquisition of habits, is a gradual affair, and he expressed this by saying that habit strength grows slowly to a limit as an organism's responses are reinforced. More precisely, $_sH_R$ is a positive function of the number of reinforced responses. So we manipulate $_sH_R$ by having some rats never learn the bar-press response ($_sH_R$ is 0), some learn it moderately well (50 reinforced presses) and some very well (100 reinforced presses).

We can infer from the equation that those animals who have no motivation (D is 0) will not respond no matter how well they have learned the bar press; neither will animals respond who have not learned the response ($_sH_R$ is 0) regardless of their drive state. Other groups will respond to the bar with varying degrees of swiftness, with the fastest response (highest $_sE_R$) coming from the group that combines the longest food deprivation with the best-learned habit. Experiments along these general lines were carried out (Hull, Felsinger, Gladstone, & Yamaguchi, 1947), although they were aimed at actually quantifying Hull's theoretical terms. Hull was not content with mere qualitative confirmation of his theory, however, but with precise and detailed prediction of behavior.

Hull's system was open to change. For example, it doesn't take research—though research was done—to see that other important factors should determine reaction strength besides drive and habit strength. Surely you, or any organism, will work harder for a large reward than for a small one, and will react more strongly to powerful than to weak stimuli. These considerations were duly incorporated into Hull's revised system (Hull, 1952) as **incentive motivation** (K), to reflect the effects of size of reward, and **stimulus-intensity dynamism** (V), to reflect effect of stimulus intensity. The revised equation constituting reaction potential became:

$$_sE_R = D \times V \times K \times {_sH_R}$$

Logical behaviorism evolved as a research program through the 1930s and 1940s as Hull modified his theory in the light of new data and theoretical reflection. Nevertheless certain ideas were central to Hull's program. To begin with, Hull's theory was an S-R theory. Following Thorndike, he believed there was only one kind of learning (Hull, 1937), in which responses are attached to controlling stimuli. For Hull, every response had its eliciting stimulus, however hard to find. When it was impossible to find an external stimulus for some response, Hull (1930b, 1931) argued there had to be internal, covert stimuli controlling it. An example concerns Hull's theory concerning how motivational states control behavior. Given that Hull responses are controlled only by physical stimuli, it is at first glance hard to explain how food deprivation, in which nothing actually happens to an organism, has any effect on behavior. Hull (1930b, 1931) proposed that food deprivation created internal stimuli (presumably something like hunger pangs), that could be associated with responses leading to reduction of the drive. In fact, Hull believed that all learning depended on drive reduction—that is, he accepted the Law of Effect. This belief led to controversies with Tolman's informational psychology, as we shall soon see.

Hull's deepest commitment as a scientist was somewhat obscured by his axiomatic theory and its widespread influence. Hull believed that living organisms—including human beings—were nothing but complicated machines, whose behavior patterns could be described with mathematical precision, hence his faith in quantified, axiomatic theory. Believing that organisms are machines also implied that it should be possible to build machines capable of behaving like animals and, ultimately, like human beings. Fascinated with machinery all his life—he originally wanted to be an engineer—Hull tried to build simple machines capable of replicating the basic phenomena of S-R learning. He occasionally published accounts of his machines (see Hull & Baernstein, 1929), and demonstrated one during his presidential address to the American Psychological Association (Hull, 1937). However, for personal reasons that remain obscure and because his axiom theory was so widely hailed as psychology's salvation, he did not pursue the construction of learning machines after 1936. Nevertheless, his belief that organisms are machines was basic to his construction of mathematical learning theories and continued to shape his theorizing for the rest of his life (L. J. Smith, 1986).

Hull's theory on the issues in the study of learning discussed in Chapter 3 may be characterized as follows:

The Nature of Learning

- *How many kinds of learning are there?* Hull's theory closely resembled Thorndike's connectionism, holding that there is only one form of learning, strengthening or weakening connections between stimulus and response.

- *How does learning proceed?* Hull proposed that habit strength increases a bit with each reinforced trial. Therefore, his theory was a continuity theory.

- *What is learned?* Hull held that fundamentally what is learned are stimulus-response connections. With Thorndike, he did not believe in old-fashioned philosophical association of ideas, and he explicitly rejected Tolman's positing of cognitive processes (see below). On the other hand, his theory was complex, and he recognized that many factors determine behavior other than habit strength. For example, his theory recognized the difference between learning and performance (or expression). Habit strength was the learning variable, representing what an animal had learned; reaction potential was the performance variable, affected by factors such as motivation (drive) and inhibition.

The Causes of Learning

- *Contiguity or contingency?* Hull's theory was mechanistic and rejected the existence of cognitive processes. Therefore, he endorsed the contingency view of learning. Contingency theories, as we have seen, see organisms as information-processors computing the predictive value of conditioned stimuli and causal connection between actions and their consequences.

■ *What is the role of reward?* Hull explicitly endorsed a drive-reduction theory of reward: Learning occurs only if it is followed by reward and the reward reduces a biological need such as hunger or thirst. As we have seen, however, Hull and Spence modified Hull's theory to recognize the incentive—pleasure-giving—aspects of rewards. Nevertheless, Hullian theory always held that learning depends crucially on being followed by a biologically significant consequence.

■ *What is the role of consciousness?* None. Hull stated in his APA Presidential Address that he did not include consciousness in his theory because he found no need for it. If his machines could learn without consciousness, then it followed that living organisms could, too. Hull clearly believed in the automaton theory rejected by James (Chapter 1).

Not long after Hull's death in 1952, his theory was subjected to severe criticism. It was argued that Hull's predictions could not really be logically derived from his theory (Cotton, 1955), that it could not account for certain maze-learning experiments with rats that suggested they could reason (Deutsch, 1956), and that Hull's theory was just too simple to explain human behavior (Ginsberg, 1954). The most scathing and influential critique was that of Koch (1954), who showed that Hull's formal system was a logical mess; that he did not practice what he preached, for example, ignoring contrary data available while writing his postulates; and that his quantificational program was ill-conceived and doomed from the start. For Koch, Hull's usefulness lay in his failure, demonstrating the impossibility of Hull's heroic, or foolhardy, system building.

The stream of influence from Hull's theory divided after World War II. Those of his students, colleagues, and admirers who wanted to study human learning largely abandoned the formal and quantificational aspects of logical behaviorism, while retaining a commitment to Hull's S-R theory. Their hypotheses were stated rather informally, and in this respect they merged into a mass of eclectic behaviorists dominating American psychology in the 1950s. They also augmented the S-R formula by elaborating the idea of central, covert mediating responses, S-r-s-R, to handle certain special problems of human learning. Both trends will be discussed later in this chapter.

Hull's most important student, Kenneth Spence, continued to study animal learning, and his influence has been long lasting. While moving away from Hull's excessive quantification, Spence remained a powerful spokesperson for formal theories (see Spence, 1944, 1956). Because our topic is human learning, we will pass over the important contributions of Spence and his students to animal learning. There is a good discussion of their work in Hilgard and Bower (1975). We will move on to Hull's formidable rival, a devilishly clever experimenter and charming writer named E. C. Tolman.

Purposive Behaviorism

Tolman (1959) said that both his system and his research were based on hunch and common sense. His research program was not guided by formal deductions from postulates like Hull's or by a single law of learning like Guthrie's. Rather, it appears that in designing an experiment Tolman asked himself what he would do in the rat's position as opposed to what a Hullian or Guthriean rat would do. Tolman was gratified to learn that rats were generally as commonsensical as he was. Especially in reading his occasional attempts to formalize his theory (see Tolman, 1932, 1938, 1959), you sense that technical formulae and a playful, occasionally bizarre vocabulary ("means-ends-readiness," "sign-gestalt-expectation") are being used to express straightforward common sense. Central to Tolman's theory are two ideas that, more than anyone else, he kept alive during the behaviorist era: **purpose** and **cognition.**

Tolman always maintained that behavior and learning are a "getting toward" or a "getting away." That is, behavior is purposive; it is oriented toward a goal, be it securing something good or avoiding something bad. In Tolman's view, no psychology could dispense with reference to purposes. Tolman's commitment to purpose as a basic feature of behavior grew out of his training in philosophical realism at Harvard. He said that purpose is not an inner mental state *inferred from* behavior, but is a *directly observable* feature *of* behavior. When you see a rat striving to get to the goal in a maze, Tolman argued, one sees purpose itself, not the mere behavioral manifestation of an inner purpose.

His commitment to purpose made Tolman the supreme **molar** theorist. Because behavior for Tolman was guided by goals, the proper level of analysis is of the acts that lead to the goal, not of the muscle movements that happen to be involved at the moment. Guthrie and Hull, on the other hand were **molecular** theorists, because they thought of learning as acquiring specific muscular responses to environmental stimuli. Tolman and his associates performed experiments designed to show that learning was more than acquiring muscle twitches.

So, for example, a rat that has learned to walk through a maze could also swim through it when it was filled with water, even though the muscle responses were different in each case (MacFarlane, 1930). Moreover, simply pulling a rat through a maze in a basket can result in learning, even though no R's have occurred to be reinforced and learned (McNamara, Long, & Wike, 1956). These results supported Tolman's contention that the proper study of psychologists is an organism's goals and the acts it can mobilize to reach them.

The molecular-mechanistic versus molar-purposive issue is profound and important, involving much more than interpreting rat maze-learning behavior. Consider a game of tennis. In a molecular-mechanistic account all that happens is a series of physical events: A ball is propelled through different trajectories because of the muscle movements two organisms use to strike the ball. The psychologist could only talk about the fluctuating strengths of $_sE_R$'s under changing stimulus conditions. The psychologist could not talk about strategies for winning, and could not even account for the end of the match except to say that when the ball fell on the outside of a certain line the behavior exchange ended. But of course we, and Tolman, reject such a view. Tolman would talk about a player's purpose—winning—and we could discuss a player's game as a set of meaningful acts aimed at the goal of winning. A purposive, molar account respects the human world of meaning and purpose; a molecular-mechanistic account reduces them to muscular twitches and glandular secretions. Nor is this issue dead with Guthrie, Tolman, and Hull. It is very much alive in debates over Skinner's theory, cognitive science, and evolutionary psychology.

The other notion central to Tolman's program was cognition. Tolman believed that an organism learns about its environment; it doesn't just learn to react to it. Tolman (1932, p. 330) wrote that a conditioned response will occur only if an organism "believes" that the old response-reinforcement contingencies hold. Subsequently, Seward and Levy (1948) demonstrated in animals the kind of "instant extinction" Tolman's theory predicted. Seward and Levy trained rats to run from a start box down an alleyway to a goal box containing food. Then they simply placed the rat in the goal box several times without feeding it. The rats, "knowing" that food was no longer in the goal box, now generally did not run down the alley when placed in the start box. As others had shown with humans, Seward and Levy showed that extinction in animals can occur even without the occurrence of nonreinforced R's. This is contrary to Hull's theory, in which $_sH_R$ must be lowered by nonreinforcement of a response, but is expected by Tolman's cognitive theory.

Nor were beliefs the only cognitive processes Tolman attributed to rats. His associate I. Krechevsky (later David Krech) showed that rats seemed to act on hypotheses. Krechevsky (1932) found that in certain kinds of mazes rats would systematically try different modes of behavior. Thus, a rat might try all right turns, then all left turns, then alternating left and right, as if it were formulating hypotheses and then trying them out, rather than engaging in a random trial-and-error process (see also Tolman, 1948).

Tolman's cognitive emphasis led him to reject the law of effect. S-R reinforcement theories like Thorndike's and Hull's say that what causes learning to occur, or be "stamped in," is pleasure or pain-avoidance. Rather, Tolman stressed the cognitive role of reinforcement as a signal to the organism.

Tolman, Hall, and Bretnall (1932) offered a disproof of the Law of Effect, in which introductory psychology students learned a punchboard maze. In front of them was placed a board with many sets of pairs of holes. The subjects inserted a mental stylus into one of each pair of holes, one of which was "correct," the other "incorrect," and they had to pass through the maze by repeatedly inserting the stylus in sequential pairs of holes until they did it once without choosing a "wrong" hole.

For our purposes, the important groups are as follows:

1. *Bell-right.* When the subject inserted the stylus into the correct hole of each pair, an electrical circuit closed and rang a bell.
2. *Bell-wrong.* When the subject inserted the stylus into the incorrect hole of each pair the bell rang.
3. *Bell-right-shock.* When the subject chose the correct hole, not only did the bell ring, but the subject also received a painful electric shock through the stylus.
4. *Bell-wrong-shock.* When the subject chose the incorrect hole, not only did the bell ring, but the subject was shocked.

The results were that the bell-right group made the fewest errors followed very closely by the bell-right-shock group. Many more errors were made by the bell-wrong group, and many more still by the bell-wrong-shock group.

Let us first discuss the effects of the bell. The bell is a supposedly neutral stimulus of no reinforcing value, yet it acted to "emphasize," in Tolman's words, whatever response it followed. So, regardless of shock, both bell-wrong groups learned more slowly than the bell-right groups. As Tolman put it, the bell exerted a "baleful fascination" on his subjects, who had some trouble learning to choose the hole that did not ring the bell.

Turning to the shock, we find that it acted contrary to the law of effect. Subjects in the bell-right-shock group were learning to receive shocks, not avoid them, as suggested by the law of effect. Indeed, their rate of learning was not significantly different from the bell-right group. On the other hand, the bell-wrong-shock group was learning to avoid shocks, since for them every error resulted in a shock. But the shock did not make them learn faster; in fact, they were the slowest of all the groups. The shock seemed to act as an emphasizer that impeded learning rather than helped it.

Tolman's research has here demonstrated an important phenomenon that could not be properly articulated until the later development of the concept of information. Every reinforcing event possesses two distinct dimensions, **affective** and **cognitive** (Estes, 1972). First, it is either pleasurable or painful; this is the affective dimension. Second, it provides information to the organism about the correctness or incorrectness of its behavior; this is the cognitive dimension. Most of the time, the two dimensions are redundant, because a pleasurable outcome to a response—a reward—means that one has made the correct response. A rat getting food for finding its way out of a maze or a child getting stars for good schoolwork is experiencing pleasure that tells it that it has done the right thing and that motivates it to continue to behave the same way. A rat shocked for pressing a lever or a child spanked for drawing on the wall is experiencing pain that tells it that it has done the wrong thing and that motivates it to behave differently in the future. However, Tolman's experiment separated the affective and cognitive values of the reinforcers he used. A bell has no affective value by itself; it changes behavior solely by telling the subject he or she had chosen the correct move in the pegboard maze. In the shock-right groups, the affective value of the reinforcer was brought in conflict with its cognitive value. While the shock was painful, it told the subject that he or she had chosen the correct move. Significantly, Tolman showed that the cognitive value of the reinforcer is more important than its affective value. Subjects learned to make the correct responses in the shock-wrong groups even though it caused them pain and should have motivated them to choose the incorrect moves through the maze. Information, it appears—at least in human beings—trumps feeling.

Although Tolman championed the scientific respectability of purpose and cognition throughout his career, his treatment of them changed. In his earliest writings, Tolman took a realistic approach to purpose and cognition, claiming that they were directly observable aspects of behavior. He contrasted his view with the traditional Cartesian belief that when one sees an animal striving for a goal one could infer an inner purpose behind the striving, and maintained instead that the striving simply was purpose, openly visible and not inferred. In the mid-1930s Tolman seemed briefly to abandon the reality of purposes and cognitions, and flirted with physiological reductionism. Finally, however, Tolman developed the representational view for which he was best known. He abandoned realism and accepted the copy theory, arguing that learning consists of building representations of the environment—**cognitive maps**—that are consulted by an organism when it behaves.

Tolman's Cognitive Maps versus Hull's Habit Family Hierarchy

Although Tolman was an unsystematic theorist, he was a wonderfully clever experimenter, and he loved to devise experiments to show that Hull's S-R theory of learning was simplistic, and that animals really did possess intentions and thoughts. Some of the most famous of these experiments concerned maze-learning. Hull said that when an animal learned a maze it learned a chain of S-R connections, learning which way to turn at each choice point. Tolman, in contrast, held that animals learn maps that they use to plan their route through the maze.

Hull's Habit-Family Hierarchy

Perhaps because it appeared in Hull's writing very early (Hull, 1930a) and so was not inextricable from the later axiomatic theory, Hull's habit-family hierarchy proved to be a flexible and durable concept of widespread application. While the formal system generated much animal research, the habit-family hierarchy has been a useful tool to behaviorists concerned with human learning.

The idea is really quite simple, and is inherent in any S-R psychology. Recall what a cat does when placed in a puzzle box by Thorndike. The situation calls forth many responses: The cat reaches through the slats, claws at the walls, pushes its head against the door, and eventually pulls the string and escapes. In trial-and-error learning a single stimulus situation calls forth a series of responses, one at a time, until the correct one is executed and reinforced. Adopting S-R terminology, we can say that the situation elicits several responses, but each S-R connection is of a different strength. We may note this and call it a **divergent habit-family hierarchy.** There is a family of habits diverging from a single stimulus arranged in a hierarchy of strengths:

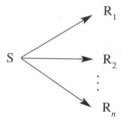

This is what happens in trial-and-error learning (Hull, 1930a, 1934). A situation calls forth a hierarchy of responses, and the one with the strongest $_SH_R$ occurs first. If the response is not reinforced, the S-R bond, that is, the habit strength, weakens. When it weakens enough, it becomes weaker than the next habit in the hierarchy, which now is tried out. If it fails, too, it will weaken until the third response takes over. The trial-and-error process continues until the incorrect responses are extinguished and the correct response occurs and is reinforced. Subsequent reinforcements strengthen the response until it is the strongest response in a remade habit-family hierarchy.

Just as one stimulus may elicit many responses, so many stimuli may tend to elicit the same response in a **convergent** hierarchy:

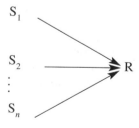

The phenomenon of stimulus generalization can be thought of as a convergent hierarchy: Many related stimuli evoke a CR with differing strengths. Learning involves changes in the S-R connection strengths of convergent and divergent hierarchies.

Tolman's Cognitive Maps

Tolman's theory was well summed up in his paper "Cognitive Maps in Rats and Men" (1948). In it, Tolman contrasted the S-R view, in which learning consists in establishing S-R connections by reward and breaking them by punishment, with his own view in which organisms selectively take in information from the environment and work it over into a map of their world. It is this cognitive map that controls behavior for Tolman, not blind reactions to external and internal stimuli.

The most famous kind of research that addresses this question, as well as the role of reinforcement in learning, is research on **latent learning** (see reviews by MacCorquodale & Meehl, 1954; Thistlethwaite, 1951). The classic experiments were Blodgett's (1929) and Tolman and Honzik's (1930). In these experiments, some rats learned to negotiate a maze for food reward in the goal box, while others simply wandered around the maze for several trials before food was introduced in the goal box. According to reinforcement theory, learning will not take place without reward—the first group of rats should learn because they are rewarded for learning, and the second group should not begin to learn until reinforcement begins. According to Tolman, even the rats just wandering the maze are learning about their environment—building up a cognitive map—even though that learning may not be apparent. Since the food box is not yet a goal, the wandering rats will not head right to it like the rewarded rats.

An S-R reinforcement theory predicts for this experiment that the always rewarded group will learn the maze in some number of trials, for example 12; the wandering group will only *begin* to learn when food is introduced, for example, on the eleventh try, and should take 12 trials beyond that to master the maze. Tolman's theory maintains that after ten trips through the maze even the nonrewarded rats will have learned its layout, and when food is introduced on trial 11 they will do just as well as the rewarded group, their "latent learning" being immediately transformed by purpose into goal-directed performance. Most of the many experiments designed to test latent learning supported Tolman's prediction.

After enough tinkering, Hull's theory was adjusted to "predict" latent learning, but such tinkering has the appearance of defensive rationalization. Tolman's theory is the simpler and more appealing, and he had other research designed to challenge the fundamental S-R idea of the habit-family hierarchy.

We have seen how Hull's habit-family hierarchy is able to give a plausible account of trial-and-error learning. Tolman, however, was able to design experiments in which the hierarchy leads to predictions contrary to intelligent common sense, and thus to Tolman's cognitive-map theory. One of the simpler experiments is shown in Figure 4.1, where a maze used by Tolman and Honzik (Tolman, 1933) is schematically shown.

By suitably placing the blockades, we can force rats to run from start through the different paths to the goal, where they are fed. The crucial choice-point is just down the path from the start box, where the rat must choose path 1, path 2, or path 3. According to Hull, after learning, the stimuli at the choice-point evoke a divergent hierarchy (shown in Figure 4.1) such that path 1 is preferred to path 2, which is preferred to path 3.

FIGURE 4.1   Tolman-Honzik maze.

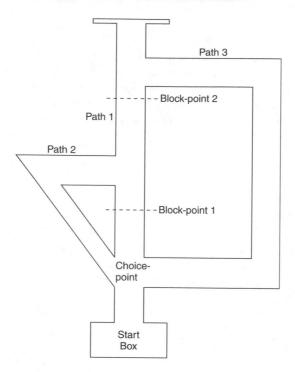

This is quite reasonable, since rats, like people, won't work any harder than they have to for a given reward. We can also justify it on more technical Hullian grounds because Hull's is an S-R chaining theory. Running down a maze path is, in Hull's theory, a chain of responses ultimately rewarded by the terminal reinforced response. The longer the behavior chain, the weaker is its first link. Therefore, since the chain of response links is longest along path 3, the initial turn-right response will be weaker than the turn-left or straight-ahead response. Similarly, the turn-left response will be weaker than the straight-ahead response.

After the rats have learned the three paths, we introduce a barrier at block-point 1. What will a Hullian rat do after bumping its nose on the barrier? It will retreat to the choice-point and execute the next habit in its hierarchy, running, successfully as it turns out, down path 2. Now suppose, instead of blocking at point 1, we block at point 2. The Hullian rat will retreat to the choice-point and again execute its second strongest habit, running down path 2, only to be thwarted again. S-R path 2 now being eliminated, it will return to the choice-point and finally and successfully run down path 3.

But a Tolman rat would behave differently. What it learned to begin with was a map of the environment, rather like Figure 4.1 itself. Now you, and the rat, can see on the diagram that if there is a barrier at choice-point 2, then there is no point in taking path 2, since only path 3 will get you to the goal box. Therefore, the Tolman rat will return to the choice-point and immediately choose path 3. Of course when the block is at point 1, the Tolman rat will choose the shorter path 2, being just as commonsensically lazy as the rest of us.

Unsurprisingly, Tolman's research found most rats to be Tolman rats, and so did most outside research. This kind of finding is powerful evidence that the S-R connection formula and its associated habit-family are hard put to account for all learning by animals or humans.

Positions on the Issues

Tolman's positions on the issues listed in Chapter 3 are quite different from Hull's:

The Nature of Learning

- *How many kinds of learning are there?* Because of his cognitive orientation, Tolman recognized the existence of many kinds of learning beyond even the Pavlovian-instrumental distinction.

- *How does learning proceed?* The "instant extinction" and Tolman-Honzik experiments show that Tolman believed in the possibility of insight; in fact he picked up the idea from the Gestalt psychologists. At the same time, Tolman recognized that learning a complex maze takes time.

- *What is learned?* This was the focus of the Hull-Tolman intellectual tennis match. Hull espoused simple S-R learning, while Tolman insisted on the reality of cognitive forms of learning.

The Causes of Learning

- *Contiguity or contingency?* Various of Tolman's experiments, for example the latent learning experiments, show that he believed that learning could take place by mere exposure to the environment, without there being any predictive S-S contingency or response-reward contingency. In a sense, then, he was a contiguity theorist. On the other hand, his emphases on purpose and cognition show that he regarded organisms as information-processers gathering useful facts by which to anticipate the future. Learning for Tolman was more than association formation whether S-S or S-R.

- *What is the role of reward?* This was the other great focus of the Hull-Tolman contest, and considering it will help clarify Tolman's position on the contiguity-contingency issue. Tolman and Bretnall's disproof of the Law of Effect shows that Tolman did not think that learning depended on receiving pleasure or pain after making a response in order to learn that response. The latent learning experiments show that Tolman did not regard drive-reduction as necessary for learning to occur.

- *What is the role of consciousness?* Tolman's position was necessarily awkward and ambiguous. As a methodological behaviorist, he excluded consciousness from scientific psychology, and so never assigned it a role in learning or behavior. Given when he was trained at Harvard, Tolman probably came to accept, as many psychologists did, that mind and consciousness were co-extensive (Chapter 1). Mentalists like James and behaviorists like Hull agreed that below consciousness lay only mechanistic brain processes. James thought that consciousness added something to the mechanisms of the brain; Hull thought that it did not. Neither thought of mind as information processing that might take place outside of consciousness: Mind was consciousness or nothing. Tolman was placed in an awkward position, however, because he believed in cognitive processes, but could not call them mental, because of the equation of consciousness and mind. Thus he said that the brain, not the mind, has a central control room. This is a rather awkward metaphor, suggesting that somewhere in the brain is a single structure where decisions are made. Of all the theorists of the Golden Age, Tolman would have been most receptive to the view of mind as computation.

The Legacy of the Golden Age

Tolman was a resourceful and clever experimenter, able to challenge effectively S-R psychologies with uncomfortable data. But his own theory was never set out in a systematic enough way for others to use it as well as he did. As he conceded in 1959, his research program was really guided by his own common sense and his own hunches, and these do not travel well to even one's closest associates. He seems to have had more fun than most psychologists of learning (Tolman, 1959), but his influence is hard to trace. When a psychologist, all too rarely, follows common sense, is he or she doing it on one's own or following Tolman? Tolman did not have the kind of neo-Tolmanians who followed him the way neo-Hullians followed Hull.

Nevertheless, Tolman did keep open a line of theorizing that without him would perhaps have vanished. He upheld a cognitive account of learning while most psychologists were S-R connectionists. So even though his direct influence on them has not been great, cognitively oriented psychologists such as today's human-information-processing psychologists pay homage to Tolman as their precursor.

Hull and Tolman influenced the psychology of learning. But the overall impact of the Golden Age of Theory is harder to make out. For our purposes, two influences are paramount. First, the grand battle of the theorists convinced one psychologist that theories were useless at best, positive burdens at worst. B. F. Skinner (1950) argued that psychology did not really need theories at all, and he proposed his atheoretical approach instead. His radical behaviorism has been so successful that today radical behaviorism is the only behaviorism.

On the other hand, many psychologists considered the grand theories to be dinosaurs, impressive but unwieldy, which should be replaced by newer ways of theorizing. Two new theories did evolve to replace the formal dinosaurs. Many psychologists simply reduced the scope of their theorizing, occupying themselves with relatively specific kinds of animal and human behavior. These mini-theorists, often called modelers, proposed small theories in their particular problem areas and refused to think about the laws of all mammalian behavior. This method of constructing theoretical models of specific behaviors has been characteristic both of much of learning theory in the 1950s and the information-processing psychology of the 1960s and 1970s. Other psychologists were reluctant to abandon the broad claims of the big learning theories, especially those psychologists concerned with social learning and clinical intervention. They wanted some scientific base for thinking about aggression, moral learning, and psychotherapy, but saw that the fine details of the grand theories, especially Hull's, were simply unworkable. So they "liberalized" the theory, which meant including new concepts to help deal with human learning, and giving up mathematical precision for informal theorizing about significant problems.

We will give a sample of the less formal, "liberalized" S-R theory next, and then treat Skinner's radical behaviorism.

HUMAN LEARNING IN THE GOLDEN AGE

Throughout the 1930s, 1940s, and 1950s, psychologists influenced by the major theorists—especially Hull—continued to experiment on human learning. Their approach was generally S-R in nature but unconstrained by Hull's mania for quantification and his system of axioms. We will look at two areas of human learning in this tradition: **mediation theory** and **verbal learning.**

Thinking as Mediation

S-R psychologists concerned with human behavior found that they had trouble accounting for human thought within Hull's system. People can symbolize their environment, and act on the symbols—think—before behaving. Although Hull did not exploit the idea, he suggested the concept of mediation that his followers used to explain human thinking. Two notions of Hull's suggested the idea of mediation. First was his concept of the pure stimulus act. If you ask a man how he ties his shoes, he will very likely make shoe-tying movements with his hands, and will simultaneously describe his movements. The purpose of the hand movements, Hull believed, was purely to provide a stimulus to verbal behavior, and so was a pure stimulus act.

A second source of the concept of mediation was Hull's discussion of anticipatory goal-response errors. As a rat approached the goal of a maze, Hull observed that it was increasingly likely to make a mistaken movement identical to the last movement into the goal box. So, for example, if the last movement was a turn to the right, rats were increasingly likely to turn mistakenly to the right the closer they were to the goal; this is an anticipatory goal-response error, for it anticipates the final correct turn. Hull proposed that such errors occur because of unobserved fractional anticipatory goal responses. In the goal box, various behaviors, such as salivation, get associated with the goal. As the rat gets closer to the goal on later trials, these covert responses occur and stimulate the terminal response to occur too soon. Using lowercase letters to designate the covert responses we can write this concept in S-R language: $S \rightarrow r \rightarrow s \rightarrow R$. The choice-point stimuli elicit the covert response (e.g., salivation) whose stimulus properties trigger the too-early goal turn.

Hull's treatment of these ideas was completely peripheralistic. That is, they were conceived as actual miniature behaviors which provide stimuli that trigger subsequent responses. However, it is easy to imagine both pure stimulus acts and r-s links as central mental or brain processes. So one might imagine in mental imagery tying one's shoe, and r-s connections might be internal copies of overt S-R links. If so, then the covert behaviors in the brain, the r-s processes, would *mediate* between external stimulus and overt response. Various of Hull's followers interested in human behavior developed exactly this view (Goss, 1961; Kjeldergaard, 1968). Such neobehaviorists accepted Hull's S-R framework, but elaborate on it by considering the existence and influence of covert, mediating s-r processes that take place in the brain and intervene between a received stimulus and an overt response. Mediational theory allowed behaviorists interested in human cognition to propose concrete models of human thinking. However, mediational theory was soon replaced by information processing (Leahey, 2001).

Verbal Learning

With his invention of the serial-learning method, Ebbinghaus founded a sturdy line of research into human learning and memory. New methods were added to Ebbinghaus' theory by later researchers. In 1894 Mary Calkins described the method of paired associate learning, in which instead of being presented with a serial list of items to be remembered, subjects are presented with pairs of items to be associated, learning to say the response word or nonsense syllable when presented later with the stimulus word or nonsense syllable. (In her pioneering study, Calkins used colors as stimulus items.) Remarkably, in the same year (1894) the third major method in verbal learning, free recall, was introduced by E. A. Kirkpatrick. In this technique, subjects are presented with a list of words all at once, and then are asked to recall as many as possible in any order. With some variation, serial learning, paired-associate learning, and free recall were the mainstays of verbal-learning research for 75 years (Kausler, 1974).

Theoretically, the early students of verbal learning continued Ebbinghaus' eclectic associationism, couching their investigations in the classical terms of vividness, recency, and contiguity. However, in the 1930s and 1940s, theories of verbal learning were increasingly dominated by the major behaviorist theories we have reviewed, especially Hull's, so that by the end of World War II the fields of animals and human learning had effectively merged (Horton & Turnage, 1976; McGeoch & Irion, 1952).

Verbal learning was very easy to interpret in S-R terms. Serial learning was treated as the creation of an S-R chain. Each item was both a response and the stimulus for producing the next item: $S \rightarrow R(S) \rightarrow R(S) \rightarrow (S) \ldots$ and so on until the end of the list. Because in serial learning the response and stimulus functions of each word or syllable are mixed up together, S-R theorists preferred the paired-associate paradigm, in which the stimulus and response are clearly separated. Each item in paired-associate learning can be thought of as an S-R pair; for example, in the item VOC-KAS, VOC is the stimulus to which the subject must learn to respond "KAS." Free recall was interpreted as forming responses to the context stimuli in the experimental situation. The idea was that as each word was presented to the subject, he or she would repeat it silently, building up an association between the saying of the word and the experiment room stimuli. The list as a whole would then be learned as a divergent habit-family hierarchy in which the central controlling S was the experimental context and the R's were the words in the list.

An enormous amount of research on verbal learning was done within the S-R framework from 1930 to 1970. To give some idea of it, we will look at one important phenomenon found in both serial and free-recall paradigms, the **serial-position effect.** In serial learning, Ebbinghaus and others found that the middle items of the list took longest to learn compared either to the earlier or later items, with the greatest difficulty being with the items just after the middle one. In free recall, it was found that people were most likely to recall the first items in a list (primary effect) and the last items in the list (recency effect). These findings received a great deal of interest among investigators of verbal learning, and they also have received explanations in terms of information-processing cognitive psychology, as we shall see later.

Serial Learning

Lepley (1934) and Hull himself (1935) provided the standard S-R analysis of the serial-position effect; although it was modified somewhat by Hull's student Hovland (1938a, 1938b) it remained unchallenged until the 1950s. Consider a list consisting of nine items: a-b-c-d-e-f-g-h-i. The excitatory stimulus for the production of response a is the experimental situation. The excitatory stimulus for response b is the stimulus properties of saying a. The excitatory stimulus for c is a compound stimulus consisting of the stimulus properties of b plus the trace of a. The excitatory stimulus for d is the convergent compound of traces of a, b, and saying c, and so on until i. Observe, however, that traces of earlier responses are linked to several later items, not just the correct one. So, the compound stimulus for e is made up of excitatory traces from items a through d, but these same traces are also linked to response f as well. In order to correctly learn the list, one must inhibit the incorrect excitatory S-R links. Thus, the S-R link of a to b is correct, but the link of a to c is not, and must be inhibited. It now follows that the middle of the list will be hardest to learn. An early item like b will have no excitatory incorrect links to it, and increasingly weak stimulus links to c, d, e, f, g, h, and i to be inhibited. An end item like i will have no inappropriate stimulus links at all, and increasingly inappropriate triggering links from a, b, c, d, e, f, and h. A middle item like d will have relatively strong links to items on both sides of it to be inhibited, and will therefore be hardest to learn. In sum, the most inhibition will have to be learned at the exact middle of the list, with increasingly less necessary inhibition at either end of the list, and the serial position effect is the result.

Although the Lepley-Hull-Hovland theory provides a general explanation of the serial-position curve, it runs into certain difficulties. For example, it fails to explain why the serial-position effect is asymmetrical, with the hardest to learn item being not the middle one but one shortly after it. As a result, alternative S-R explanations were proposed. To pick just one, Ribback and Underwood (1950) proposed that association formation is anchored at the first item in a list and at the last item, and proceeds as subjects establish associative chains working inward from each anchor. Because backward associations are weaker than forward ones, the chain anchored by the end item builds up more slowly, so that when the chains meet and the list is learned, the meeting point is not the middle item but one shortly after it. By 1970, when information-processing theories of learning supplanted S-R ones, there were several S-R theories of the serial-position effect, none of them entirely satisfactory.

Free Recall

The serial-position effect in free recall was given an S-R explanation by Postman and Keppel (1968). The recency effect was explained by noting that the early items in a list are likely to be rehearsed more than later items. Thus, they are paired more frequently with the experimental context, so that the S-R bonds between them and the contextual S will be stronger than for later items. The recency effect was explained in rather Guthrean terms. The terms at the end of the list are followed by few (and in the case of the last item, no) later items. Thus, there is little or no new learning to interfere with the S-R connections between the context S and the last items. Lack of interference also helps explain the primacy effect, since the early items do not have to compete with already-being-rehearsed items, the way later items do. As we shall see, this Guthrean notion of interference plays an important role in information-processing explanations of the serial-position effect in free recall.

RADICAL BEHAVIORISM

The thinkers of the Golden Age of Theory wore themselves out disputing the field of learning. Then a new voice arose calling for an end to theories. B. F. Skinner (1950) argued that theories, while they might be fun, got in the way of the real job of the psychology of learning—collecting hard facts about behavior change. Skinner would heartily agree with the character in many detective stories who challenges the sleuth by saying, "But this is mere theory. What we need are facts."

Radical Behaviorism as a Philosophy

Skinner (1974) distinguished his research program, the experimental analysis of behavior, from the philosophy of mind and science that justify and are justified by his empirical findings. Skinner's philosophy is **radical behaviorism.** Like the behaviorism of Hull or Tolman, radical behaviorism takes behavior as psychology's subject matter. However, it goes much further than formal behaviorism in the implications it draws from this idea. In fact, Skinner's central idea is so simple, yet so challenging to common sense, that it is difficult to grasp.

Every day, each of us tries to explain the behavior of people we know or of public figures. We ask, "Why did Bill break up with Susan?" "Why did that Congressman kite checks?" We generally try to explain these things by appealing to causes inside the person. So we might say that Bill "felt threatened" by Susan's academic excellence; or that the Congressman is "greedy." We do not see Bill's insecurity or the Congressman's greed, but we infer it from their behavior and then use it to explain their actions.

In a more sophisticated way, most psychologists, including the formal behaviorists, do the same thing. Tolman did not see little maps in the rats' brains. Rather, he inferred them from their maze-running behavior, and then explained their maze running as based on having acquired maps. Hull, similarly, did not see little $_sH_R$'s and Ds in rats; he inferred them from what he did to the rats—reinforcements for $_sH_R$ and food deprivation for D—and then explained their behavior as an outcome of the joint action of $_sH_R$ and D, namely $_sE_R = {_sH_R} \times D$. Within both common sense and the scientific study of learning, people try to explain behavior in terms of internal causes or purposes.

It is precisely this making of inferences about mental states thought to cause behavior that Skinner's radical behaviorism repudiates. According to Skinner, "greed," "cognitive map," and "$_sH_R$" are equally unscientific and mythical and can be replaced by descriptions of behavior. Skinner insists on sticking to what we can observe, describing behavior precisely and scientifically, and refraining from unnecessary inferences. Why do we say, "Congressman X is greedy?" Because we see him or her take bribes. Skinner says we should forget about "greed"—a mythical mental concept—and just say, "Congressman X tends to kite checks," which precisely describes such behavior and makes no inference past the facts. Similarly, a Hullian would say, "$_sH_R$ is high" because a rat has received 500 reinforcements. Skinner says that inventing $_sH_R$ is needless—just say, "This rat has a cognitive map," because the rodent chose the smart route in the Tolman-Honzik maze. Skinner says that inventing the cognitive map is needless. Just say, "This rat chose route 3 over route 2 in the Tolman-Honzik maze."

Skinner's philosophy of radical behaviorism holds that the causes of behavior and learning lie entirely in an organism's environment—including the environment of consciousness within the organism—rather than in the organism itself. Observable behavior is a lawful function of environmental changes, and the job of the psychologist is to understand that function without inventing mental or other hypothetical entities to intervene between environment and behavior. Skinner hopes to do for psychology what Newton did for physics. Before Newton, many people believed angels pushed the planets around their orbits; Newton's laws of motion showed the angels to be unnecessary and therefore probably mythical. Before Skinner, people believed the mind controls behavior; Skinner hopes to show the mind to be a myth.

Radical behaviorism says that behavior is a lawful function of environmental variables. This belief dictates a research program aimed at discovering such functional relationships or natural laws. That program is the experimental analysis of behavior.

The Experimental Analysis of Behavior

Prior to Skinner's initial work (Skinner, 1938) the most popular experimental setting in learning research was the maze, whether a simple straight alley or a replica of the royal Hampton Court maze in England. Skinner, however, believed that maze learning was not a representative behavior. Most notably, maze learning requires the imposition of separate learning trials: The rat is placed in the start box, navigates the maze, is picked up, and replaced in the start box. But real-life behavior—which is what psychologists of learning ultimately want to understand—is not chopped up into discrete and separate trials. One bit of action leads immediately to another as long as we are awake. So Skinner looked for an experimental arrangement that would keep the virtues of experimenting—control and precise manipulability of the environment—without artificially segmenting the free flow of behavior.

In his desire to achieve the most general account of behavior possible, Skinner made another important decision, namely, to study the acquisition of an arbitrary behavior. Skinner feared that many of the responses studied by other psychologists, such as Pavlov's salivation or Watson's conditioned fear, raised the possibility that whatever laws emerged from research on these or similar responses would be valid only for such responses and could not be generalized to other behaviors. Skinner believed that if he studied an arbitrary behavior, one not tied to a specific reinforcer or eliciting circumstance, any discovered regularities in its acquisition would be of general validity.

Putting these requirements together we see that Skinner desired a methodology that would be rigorously experimental, that would produce results of wide generality, without interfering with the natural flow of behavior. What he hit upon has become famous as the "Skinner box," although he preferred to call it "an experimental space," and it quickly eclipsed all competitors as the favored methodology in animal learning research, even among psychologists who are not radical behaviorists.

There are two main kinds of Skinner boxes, one for rats, Skinner's original subjects, and one for pigeons, his favorite subjects in later years. Both boxes are usually made of clear plastic on three walls, some with a shock grid on the floor, and are just large enough to hold the subject comfortably and allow it to move around. The fourth wall contains a magazine that can dispense food or water to a feeding cup, a speaker, a light or lights for discriminative stimuli, and the manipulandum that the subject must operate to get food or water. The manipulandum for the rat is a horizontal lever sticking out of the wall; for pigeons it is a lighted key or keys set into the wall. Operation of the manipulandum activates recording devices and the food or water magazine. Figure 4.2 shows the chamber for a rat (Figure 4.2a) and for a pigeon (Figure 4.2b).

With one exception, these boxes meet Skinner's requirements. Once placed in the box, animals move about freely and need not be handled until an experiment is over, so that separate trials are not imposed. For the rat, bar-pressing is an arbitrary behavior unlikely to occur in the wild and, therefore, unlikely to be closely tied with a special set of circumstances. In the case of the pigeon, pecking a lighted key appears to be an arbitrary behavior, but it really is not, because pecking is how wild pigeons get their

FIGURE 4.2 The Skinner box. (Reproduced from *Psychology of Learning and Behavior* by Barry Schwartz, by permission of W. W. Norton & Company, Inc., Copyright © 1984 by W. W. Norton & Company, Inc.)

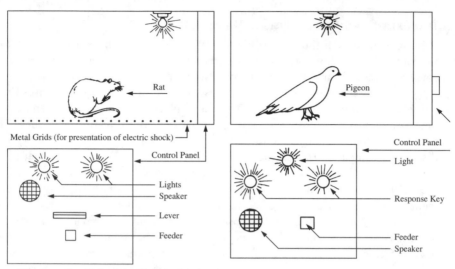

a. The Rat-Conditioning Chamber. Diagram of a standard conditioning chamber for rats (a) and a rat's-eye view of the control panel housed in the chamber (b).

food and drink. But just as Guthrie's difficulties with the cat's greeting response, this short-coming of the key-peck did not become apparent for more than 20 years, when autoshaping was discovered.

In addition to meeting Skinner's theoretical requirements, Skinner boxes have practical virtues. Bar-presses and key-pecks are easily defined and counted, allowing precise quantification of behavioral laws. A good dependent variable—response rate—is easily calculated and graphed, directly revealing the impact of experimental manipulations. Finally, data collection can be automated, removing much of the drudgery from research. Because there are no experimental trials, the experimenter need not be present after putting the animal in the box. The control panel can be linked to simple computers that record and plot each response and control discriminative stimuli and reinforcement delivery. Skinner's shared exemplar has also provided the inspiration for various human applications ranging from teaching machines to token economies in mental hospitals and schools to behavior therapy.

The Contingencies of Reinforcement

Skinner believed that in order to describe scientifically the acquisition, retention, or loss of a piece of behavior, one should specify three things: the response itself, the setting in which the response is most likely to occur, and the reinforcer responsible for acquisition and maintenance of the response. These three things Skinner (1969) called the **contingencies of reinforcement.**

The Response

Skinner was always one of the most influential advocates of the view that there are two kinds of learning corresponding to two kinds of responses, **respondents** and **operants.** Respondent behavior was studied by Pavlov. A respondent is a response that is unconditionally elicited by some particular stimulus, a US. Operant behavior was studied by Thorndike. An operant is a response that simply occurs for no observable reason; as Skinner explained, an operant is a response that is simply emitted, not re-flexively elicited. An operant *operates on* the environment, and the result of the opera-tion—reinforcement, punishment, or nothing—determines whether the response will become more or less likely to occur.

Because behavior is observable, it seems at first glance easy to define a particu-lar operant behavior. But this ease is altogether illusory, and Skinner was careful to avoid the pitfalls into which other behaviorists stumbled.

The major pitfall of behaviorism has been defining responses as particular movements, as Hull did. It is tempting to define the operant a rat learns in a Skinner box as a paw push of the lever, that is, as a particular movement made by the rat. But doing this leads to serious difficulties that may be best illustrated with respect to language, an important topic to Skinner. In the first place, the same physical re-sponse can have different meanings. For example, the response "Fire!" means very different things when shouted by a patron in a theater and when shouted by the cap-tain of a firing squad. In the second place, several physically different responses may mean the same thing. For example, "George Washington," "The first President of the US," "The father of his country," and "The man on the one-dollar bill" all designate the same person.

One of the important criticisms of behaviorism has always been that in reducing action to mere physical movement, the meaning and significance of behavior is lost. Tolman tried to get around this difficulty by leaving purpose in animals, ascribing the significance of behavior to the purpose behind it, be that purpose avoiding a finger shock in Wickens' (1938) experiment, or getting fed at the end of a maze. But Skinner thought purposes too mentalistic because we cannot see them or describe them di-rectly. So in his characteristic way Skinner moved the meaning and significance of be-havior out of the organism's invisible mind and into its visible environment. To a large degree, Skinner's conception of purpose resembles Tolman's early neo-realist formu-lation of behaviorism, because like the early Tolman, Skinner says purpose is a rela-tional property of behavior itself, not of an inner mind. Specifically, Skinner, defines an operant as a relation between a piece of behavior and the environment—the setting and the reinforcer that control it.

We can illustrate this relational definition first with the Skinner box and then apply it to human language. We could teach a hungry and thirsty rat to press one bar for water and another for food. While the movements involved in pressing each bar might be identical, Skinner would identify two different operants, each controlled by its consequence, or reinforcer, because each bar press stands in a different relation to its reinforcer. This is a laboratory analogue to the case of "Fire!" For the firing squad or the audience the shout creates different reactions and different consequences for the speaker, and so, despite the similarity of the vocal movements and sounds, we may identify two different operants. In our human example, of course, the operants are distinguished by setting as well as by consequences.

On the other hand, in a standard Skinner box the rat could press the lever in many ways—with the right paw, left paw, both paws; with the nose, by biting it and pushing down, and so on. But all these movements achieve the same end, namely, depressing the lever and closing an electrical switch that delivers food. Therefore, since the setting and the consequence of all these movements are the same, we identify only one operant, lever-pressing, or even switch-closure. As Schwartz (1984) points out, an operant exists only for the experimenter, not for the learner. The learner may do many things, but the Skinnerian counts only one thing—switch-closure, because the same relation obtains between the bar-presses and the food that reinforces the different ways of pressing the bar. Applying this example to language, Skinner would identify only one operant in the various phrases that designate George Washington. Each phrase is different, but the discriminative stimulus for each is the same.

I (THL) used to joke in class that if rats had psychokinetic abilities and could push levers by mere thought, it would count as a member of the bar-pressing operant. A remarkable recent experiment (Chapin et al., 1999) has brought my joke to reality. Rats were trained to control a robot arm that brought them spoonfuls of water by pressing a bar. As they did so, electrodes made recordings of the brain processes involved in pressing the lever. Using mathematical and neural net methods, the signals from the electrodes were combined into a single signal that controlled the robot arm itself, so that in this "neurorobotic mode" each rat's brain activity could deliver water without any actual lever-pressing. Four of the six rats in fact learned to control the robot arm by "thought" alone, giving up lever-pressing, creating an operant behavior in which there is no behavior! The authors' goal, however, was practical rather than theoretical. They hope that their work may make it possible in the future for paralyzed humans to be able to act on the world by thought—brain activity—alone.

Skinner, then, defines an operant not as a single behavior, but rather as a *class of behaviors,* all controlled by the same setting and consequences, that is, by the same relational contingencies of reinforcement.

Precisely because operants are emitted and not elicited, there is no way we can make them occur. If we put a naive rat in a Skinner box we might have to wait days before it pressed the lever and got reinforced. Similarly, if parents waited until their child said, "Mother, I am thirsty and would like some juice," before responding, they would have a long and fuss-filled wait. Both experimenters and parents, therefore, resort to shaping, to leading the organism to make the correct response.

The basic idea behind shaping is the law of effect—an animal will be more likely to do that for which it has just been rewarded. We place our naive rat in the Skinner box. It wanders around the cage, and when it goes into the end near the bar we press a button and food is delivered in the tray. As a result, the rat will spend more time near the control panel. Next we require a little more. At some point while hanging around the control panel the rat will align itself facing the bar. We reinforce it. Soon the rat is facing the bar most of the time. So we require a little more, that the rat touch the bar before we reinforce it. Now that we have gotten it to touch the bar, the rat is likely to press it sometime, and the terminal response of bar-pressing will have been acquired.

Shaping, therefore, is the gradual molding of diffuse behavior into a well-defined operant. Just as the sculptor shapes clay, so the experimenter shapes the behavior of animals into the form he or she wants it to take. Similarly, parents respond to imperfect "ma-ma's" and badly pronounced "juice's" when their children are two, but successively require better responses as the children get older. Thus, the parent, albeit not always successfully, tries to shape a fussing baby into a civilized adult.

The Setting

Both common sense and psychologists of learning agree that behavior is controlled by its setting. We act very differently with friends, with parents, with professors or deans, in the gym, in bed, or in the army. Beginning with Pavlov, psychologists have studied the controlling effect of the situation as the **stimulus control of behavior.** We have already studied how Pavlov discovered and elaborated on stimulus generalization—the tendency of a response learned in one setting to occur in similar ones—and stimulus discrimination—the capacity of an organism to respond to one stimulus but not to another.

These processes also apply to operant behaviors. An operant trained to one discriminative stimulus, for example a 1000-Hz tone, will generalize to tones close to 1000 Hz, the rate of response declining as new tones depart from 1000 Hz. We can create a **discriminated operant** by reinforcing a lever-press in the presence of a 1000-Hz tone, but withholding reinforcement to a 2000-Hz tone. Soon the animal will use the lever only when the 1000-Hz tone is sounding.

The fact that generalization and discrimination apply to the wider field of instrumental behavior, as well as to classical responses, gives radical behaviorists the hope that even complex behaviors, not obviously under stimulus control, can be explained if only the search is conducted thoroughly enough. So, for example, much of child development might be explained as the outcome of generalization and discrimination. Children must learn to act appropriately in certain settings (parents are fond of saying things like, "This is the dining room, not a gymnasium!") and this is discrimination learning. At the same time children must apply what they learn in school to new situations—being able to add not just 2 + 2 but also 432 + 182—and this is generalization.

In discussing Pavlov's study of discrimination learning we spoke of discrimination as setting the processes of inhibition and generalization against one another. So a nonreinforced CS becomes an active inhibitor of the response, while the reinforced CS becomes an elicitor. This is also normally the case in operant conditioning. A discriminative stimulus that signals reinforcement (S+) increases response rate, while a nonreinforced discriminative stimulus (S−) reduces the rate.

However, it has proved possible in operant conditioning to create discriminations in which the subject almost never responds to S−, so that it never acquires negative, inhibitory properties, remaining a truly neutral stimulus. This technique is called **fading** (Terrace, 1963a, 1963b).

Terrace first trained pigeons to peck a red key to obtain reinforcement; the red key became a S+. Then he turned the light on the key off for 1 second. Pigeons generally do not peck dark keys, so they resumed responding when the light came back on. Then Terrace gradually increased the duration of the dark interval to 30 seconds. The change was so gradual that the pigeons rarely pecked the darkened key. Thus, an errorless discrimination was established between the red S+ and the dark S−. Then Terrace faded in a new S− by very dimly illuminating the key during its darkened interval with a green light. Because the key was still mostly dark, it remained an S−, not being pecked. Very gradually Terrace again increased the green illumination until it was just as bright as the red S+. Nevertheless, the green key became an S−, and a new discrimination was established between green and red, with few if any errors being made.

In his second experiment, Terrace showed that the fading procedure was much more efficient than the usual method of discrimination learning, which may involve hundreds or even thousands of keypecks to S− and various emotional reactions of rage and frustration.

It is through the process of discrimination and generalization, in the radical behaviorists' view, that the setting comes to exert control over behavior. Learning involves not only the acquisition of a new response, but also learning when that response will be reinforced and when it will not be—discrimination—and learning to transfer the new response to similar situations—generalization.

The Reinforcer

A **reinforcer** is anything that strengthens the behavior that leads to it. More technically, a reinforcement is any event that increases the probability, that is, raises the response rate, of the operant upon which it is contingent. Between them, the setting and the reinforcer determine what behavior will occur when.

There are two types of reinforcement, **positive reinforcement** and **negative reinforcement.** Positive reinforcement corresponds to what common sense calls reward. Positive reinforcement is an event that, when it follows an operant response, increases the likelihood that the response will recur.

Negative reinforcement is an event whose termination, when it occurs following an operant response, increases the likelihood that the response will recur. A negative reinforcer is typically a noxious stimulus that an animal will learn to avoid. So, for example, if a rat is placed in a box divided into two compartments by a low wall and is shocked in one compartment, and jumps the wall into the safe compartment, we can say that the jump was negatively reinforced by the termination of shock. Obviously, the rat will quickly learn to jump the barrier whenever placed in the electrified compartment. An example of everyday negative reinforcement is nagging—your mother nags at you to clean up your room until you do so, and then she stops her nagging, hoping you will keep your room clean. Torture may also be regarded as negative reinforcement: "Tell us what we want to know and then we will stop!"

One of the two most common confusions in all psychology (the other two being confusing schizophrenia with multiple personality disorder and using "feedback" to mean reinforcement) is to identify negative reinforcement with punishment. This happens because "negative reinforcement" sounds like the opposite of "positive reinforcement," as punishment is the opposite of reward, and because the stimuli used to engender negative reinforcement are frequently the same used in punishment.

But punishment is not a reinforcer at all, since its aim is the reduction of the frequency of some behavior. Punishment may be defined as an event, following an operant response, that reduces (or attempts to reduce) the likelihood of that response being repeated. The difference between negative reinforcement and punishment may be painfully illustrated by the Inquisition (Le Roy Ladurie, 1978). If a heretic is put on the rack as a consequence of being a heretic, this is punishment, for the pain follows the offensive behavior and aims to reduce it. If, on the other hand, the heretic is put on the rack to obtain the names of other heretics, this is negative reinforcement. For the pain will cease when the desired behavior occurs, and the Inquisitor hopes it will lead to further confessions.

To our list of behavior controllers—positive reinforcement, negative reinforcement, and punishment—we may add extinction. Extinction (already familiar from Pavlov's research) like punishment aims at the reduction of some response rate, but it does this by withdrawing previously available reinforcement.

Which means of controlling behavior works best is controversial, even among behaviorists. Punishment is the traditional favorite among governments and parents alike. Typically, the citizen or child is allowed to emit behaviors except for a few that are punished. Negative reinforcement is also popular, whether as parental nagging or as government harassment.

Positive reinforcement mostly occurs in praise, raises, and government contracts, but in a day when most raises depend on union threats and the cost of living, it is unclear if they are really rewards for any individual's behavior. Extinction—simply ignoring an unpleasant behavior until it goes away—is probably the least-used technique.

Skinner himself has been a consistent opponent of punishment as a behavior controller. In the first place, Skinner maintains that punishment is generally ineffective. It does not really "unlearn" behavior; it just temporarily suppresses it. The high recidivism rates of American convicts may support his view. In the second place (and this shortcoming applies to negative reinforcement as well), aversive stimuli create unfortunate emotional side effects. Punishment or its threat produces anger, hostility, anxiety, and aggression even in animals. Since happiness consists in getting what you want, Skinner advocates thoroughgoing and careful use of positive reinforcement by parents and by society. People can be shaped into acceptable behaviors by proper application of rewards, and, as a direct consequence, they will be made happy by receiving rewards.

However, there have always been those who dispute Skinner's claim that punishment is necessarily ineffective (e.g., Solomon, 1964). They argue that punishment can be effective, but fails because it is not used properly. For instance, it is well established that delaying the consequences of an act, whether reward or punishment, attenuates the reinforcing or punishing effects and does little to strengthen or weaken the behavior. But in most human cases punishment is long delayed, as when a mother waits for father to get home to spank his naughty boy. And, of course, criminals do not go to jail until months, even years, after their crimes were committed.

Likewise, to be effective, punishment must be reasonably severe—which rarely happens to children. Punishment must also be inescapable, for if the organism can avoid punishment, it obviously will have no effect. Finally, punishment is most effective if alternative, rewarded behaviors are available, but all too often neither children nor criminals are taught such alternatives.

Ultimately, the choice of whether or not parents and society should use punishment depends on ethics as much as on science. Can we in good conscience eliminate the legal system that creates the delay between crime and incarceration? If imprisonment is too weak to be an effective punishment do we return to whips, to the severing of noses and ears? Capital "punishment" is, of course, not punishment at all because it does not reduce the strength of the operant that led to the crime, except in the sense that it reduces all operant strengths to zero.

Similarly, we must ask how much pain are we willing to inflict on a child to get it to behave?

In Chapter 3 we discussed higher order classical conditioning, in which an established CS can be paired with a neutral CS until the new CS elicits the same response as the established CS. The same phenomenon occurs in operant conditioning, where it creates a secondary, or conditioned, reinforcer.

A primary reinforcer, like a US, is a reinforcer whose reinforcement value is biologically established. Food is a US in classical conditioning and a primary reinforcer in operant conditioning. We can create new reinforcers by pairing a neutral stimulus with a primary reinforcer, whether as a CS in classical conditioning or as an S+ in operant conditioning. The new stimulus then acquires reinforcing powers. We can use it to reward and establish some new behavior. Of course, primary reinforcement must sometimes be forthcoming, otherwise the secondary reinforcer would lose its value through extinction.

Most human behavior is neither taught nor maintained by primary reinforcement, therefore, the concept of secondary reinforcement is of special importance in accounting for human learning. Parents, teachers, and employers do not run around popping food into the mouths of those who please them, but they do dispense praise, gold stars, and bonuses.

Patterns of Reinforcement

Because he (Skinner, 1959) wanted to economize on the costs of feeding his experimental subjects, Skinner (1938) made an interesting discovery, one that was made independently by Humphreys (1939). Instead of reinforcing every bar-press his subject made, Skinner reinforced only some of the responses. In the developed jargon of learning psychology, Skinner shifted from continuous reinforcement, in which every response is reinforced; to **partial reinforcement,** in which only some of the responses are reinforced on one schedule or another.

Skinner found that when an animal was on a partial reinforcement schedule it took longer for a learned bar-press response to extinguish than if it had been on a continuous reinforcement schedule. Particularly in the light of Hullian theory, this finding appeared paradoxical. Suppose we compare two hypothetical rats, both of which have made 500 bar-presses, but one rat has been continuously reinforced while the other has been only partially reinforced, receiving one reinforcement every ten presses. Because habit strength grows with the number of reinforcements, we would expect the continually reinforced rat, who has received 500 reinforcers, to have a stronger, more resistant habit than the partially reinforced rat, who has received only 50 reinforcements. The opposite, however, is the case.

This greater resistance of partially reinforced responses is called the **partial reinforcement effect,** and it is a reliable and robust phenomenon. Practically, it has proved to be of great value to behavior modifiers, because it provides a reliable means of strengthening a behavior and preparing it for the real world, where people get less attention than in an institution, be it a school, a prison, or a mental hospital. The partial reinforcement effect indicates that positive learned behaviors should transfer to the real world if they are at least occasionally reinforced.

The effect has its drawbacks. If a child learns to whine and fuss to get things from its parents, and the parents decide to ignore the behavior to get it to go away, then they will have to possess great fortitude and resistance to aversive stimuli. For, if they give in occasionally, they put their child on a partial reinforcement schedule and will wind up with more persistent whining than if they simply indulged the child for a while when it was an infant and then stopped cold.

Theoretically, the partial reinforcement effect has proven controversial. Two main theories have been offered to explain it. The first one, the discrimination theory, Capaldi (1966, 1971), says that it is easy for a continuously reinforced animal to tell when extinction begins, because the shift from continuous reinforcement to no reinforcement is abrupt and obvious. But to a partially reinforced animal the onset of extinction is much less obvious, and so, instead of quickly giving up responding, it keeps pressing the bar for no reward.

The second theory, the expectancy theory (Amsel, 1958, 1962, 1967), says that when an animal expects a reinforcement but it does not occur, this event is frustrating and aversive. In a sense, failure to get an expected reward is punishing. Now the partially reinforced animal has learned to live with this kind of frustration, but the continuously reinforced animal, having never experienced nonreward, has not. Consequently, when extinction begins, the punishing effect of nonreward is much greater for the continuously reinforced animal, and it quickly stops responding, while the partially reinforced animal, feeling less punished, will continue the response longer.

Schedules of Reinforcement

Once the idea of partial reinforcement was in hand, it opened up a new research program. It became possible to manipulate systematically the schedule on which reinforcement was delivered to the learning organism and to the effect of each schedule on the response rate. Such a program occasioned Skinner's most massive empirical work (Ferster & Skinner, 1957) and has remained a prime focus of research among radical behaviorists ever since. While the number of schedules investigated by Ferster and Skinner is quite large, and new ones have been invented since, four basic schedules of reinforcement—**fixed ratio, variable ratio, fixed interval,** and **variable interval**—illustrate how behavior is changed by altering its reinforcing consequences:

- *Fixed ratio.* In a ratio schedule, delivery of reinforcement depends on the number of times the learner makes the response. In a fixed ratio (FR) schedule, there is a fixed number of responses that must be made before the reward will be forthcoming. Continuous reinforcement is an FR1 schedule, because there is a fixed ratio of one reinforcer per response. In an FR5 schedule only every fifth response is reinforced, whereas in FR8 every eighth response is reinforced, and so on.

- *Variable ratio.* In a variable ratio schedule, it is still the number of responses that determines delivery of reinforcement, but in this case the ratio changes from reinforcement to reinforcement. So, for example, reinforcement might be delivered after the fifth response, then the second, then the tenth, twelfth, third, and so on. In some cases the ratios may go through a regular cycle; for example, reinforcing the third response, then the tenth, then the fifth, then the seventh, and then back to the third, the tenth, and so forth.

- *Fixed interval.* In an interval schedule, delivery of reinforcement depends on the passage of time. After a reinforced response, some interval of time passes during which reinforcement is unavailable; after the interval is over, the next response is reinforced which begins the nonreinforcement interval again. In a fixed interval schedule, the nonreinforcement period is the same every time. For example, an FI3″0 schedule would impose a 30-second interval of nonreinforcement, while an FI′2 schedule would impose a 2-minute wait, and so on.

■ *Variable interval.* By now you should be able to guess what this is. A variable interval schedule is an interval schedule in which the period of nonreinforcement is different after each reinforced response.

Ratio schedules typically produce higher rates of responding than interval schedules. Variable schedules produce a steadier rate of response than fixed schedules. This is because fixed schedules produce what is called the **post-reinforcement pause:** After reinforcement the animal does not respond at all for a while, then begins to respond slowly, and finally more quickly. Such acceleration is especially pronounced in FI schedules, when the animal may be responding quite frantically at the time of reinforcement.

When we think of applying schedules of reinforcement to interpreting human behavior there are only two obvious examples. Workers who are paid on a piece-work basis, in which the amount of pay depends on the number of items built, may be on a fixed-ratio schedule—a certain number of pieces yields a fixed return. Slot machines are a more obvious analogue, right down to the response of lever-pressing. These machines pay off at random, on a variable schedule, and produce steady, persistent responding that is highly resistant to extinction.

Other interpretations of natural human schedules are more dubious. Is a person who gets paid every Friday on a fixed-interval schedule, as appears at first glance? Probably not. In the case of animals, the reinforcement, on whatever schedule, reinforces the immediately preceding response. This would make the paycheck reinforce the behavior of going to the payroll office and picking up the check. If people behaved exactly like animals, we would hang around the payroll office all Friday, periodically asking if the check had arrived, and never go to work.

Conclusion

For Skinner, analysis of the contingencies of reinforcement completely exhausts what a psychologist may scientifically say about a piece of behavior. Skinner sometimes calls this approach **functional analysis,** because it aims at uncovering lawful functional relationships that hold between behavior and its environmental determinants.

The response itself is the **dependent variable,** usually quantified by measuring the rate of response. The things in the environment the experimenter manipulates—discriminative stimuli: kind, quality, and quantity of reinforcer; schedule of reinforcement; and hours of reinforcer deprivation—are the **independent variables** of which the dependent variable is a function. The research program dictated by Skinner's framework is clear: Exert total control over the learner's environment by controlling all the independent variables, and then systematically manipulate the independent variables, observing the consequent changes in behavior, the dependent variable. Properly done, functional and causal laws linking the dependent variable to its antecedent independent variables will emerge.

In the perspective of radical behaviorism, the organism, animal or human, is a locus of variables (Skinner, 1969), a place where independent variables come together and interact to determine the dependent variable—behavior. Some of these variables lie inside the organism, in bodily, private stimuli such as headaches that help control behavior. What Skinner rejects are internal mental causes of behavior, whether they are habit strengths, cognitive maps, ids, or beliefs. Radical behaviorists also ignore physiological causes of behavior. They know, of course, that all behavior has physiological causes, but they believe that the laws of behavior linking independent and dependent variables can be discovered without worrying about the underlying physiological story.

Another important way of looking at radical behaviorism and the experimental analysis of behavior is by comparing them to Darwin's theory of natural selection, as Skinner often does (Skinner, 1969). Darwinian theory states that species' offspring are variations of their parents—new combinations of genes and mutations of genes— each quite different from the other. Out of this variation nature selects some favorable traits and rejects harmful ones; animals with the good traits live while those with the bad traits die. Finally, the successful variants grow up and pass their successful traits on to their offspring. Variation, selection, and retention are the three processes of evolution, and, for Skinner, of learning.

An organism emits many different behaviors (variation). Some of these are reinforced; others are not reinforced or are even punished (selection). Reinforced behaviors are learned (retention). Darwin's theory of natural selection eliminated the need for God or any other supernatural principle to give direction and purpose to evolution, by reducing evolution to blind variation, natural selection, and genetic retention. In the same way, Skinner hopes to eliminate the need for a mind or inner purpose to account for learning, by reducing learning to blind emission of operant behaviors, selection by reinforcement, and retention of learned behaviors. Let's look at Skinner's position on the issues discussed earlier:

The Nature of Learning

- *How many kinds of learning are there?* As we have seen, Skinner was the leading exponent of the distinction between operant (instrumental) and respondent (Pavlovian) conditioning.

- *How does learning proceed?* Skinner clearly viewed learning as a gradual process by which environmental outcomes "shape" behavior. On the other hand, in some of his last experiments (Epstein, 1991), Skinner studied "insight" in pigeons confronted with Köhler's banana-box problem. Pigeons were trained to peck at a plastic banana. Some pigeons were also trained to peck at a little plastic box until it was at a certain point in the floor of their cage. Then, all were placed in a situation in which a plastic banana was hanging from above too high for them to peck (experimental pigeons' wings are clipped) in a chamber that also had a small plastic box in the corner. Pigeons who had been trained to peck the box to a spot showed "insight," pecking the box under the plastic banana so they could peck it and be rewarded. Thus, Skinner recognized that insight might occur, but saw it as the outcome of previous bits of learned behavior being assembled into a new sequence, rather than as the result of mental processes.

- *What is learned?* On this point, Skinner was unique. As we have seen, he was not an S-R theorist, because stimuli do not elicit operant responses, they simply set their occasion. Because he defined operants in terms of their setting and consequences rather than in terms of the movements involved, Skinner was not a molecular theorist along the lines of Guthrie or Hull. At the same time, Skinner was not really a molar theorist, either, because he believed that complex behaviors were assemblages of simpler behavioral units; he just defined these units functionally rather than physically. And, of course, Skinner consistently rejected the postulation of cognitive processes. The best general characterization of radical behaviorism on the "what is learned" issue was that he remained true to the realist philosophy he learned at Harvard. Tolman retreated from it, positing the existing of inner representations—cognitive maps—in his theory. Skinner rejected any such compromise with cognitive psychology, and stood by realism to the end. Thus, for

Skinner what is learned is a set of relationships between an organism's behavior and the environment in which it takes place. Looking in the organism for "what is learned" was a mistake, Skinner said.

In an important sense the question of what causes learning is the question Skinner wished above all to avoid posing. One section of "Are theories of learning necessary?" (Skinner, 1950) is headed "Why learning occurs," but Skinner rejected existing theories. With regard to Hullian theoretical entities such as habit strength and drive, Skinner saw that they are unnecessary. Each of Hull's terms has an operational definition: habit was defined as number of reinforced responses, and drive was defined as hours of food privation. However, Skinner pointed out we can simply drop the theoretical terms and simply say that learning is a function of number of reinforcements and hours without food. The terms habit strength and drive add nothing to the more direct and descriptive explanation of behavior and the observable variables of which it is a function. Skinner rejected Tolman's more mentalistic notions, because "they refer to processes in another dimensional system" (Skinner, 1950, p. 210), and Skinner offered behavioral reformulations of terms such as *choose* (see behavioral economics, below). Nevertheless, we can sketch Skinnerian answers to our questions.

The Causes of Learning

- *Contiguity or contingency?* Skinner called his theory the "contingencies of reinforcement," indicating that he viewed learning as dependent on actual contingencies between response and consequence. However, as we saw in Chapter 3, his treatment of "superstitious behavior" suggests that sometimes Skinner saw response-consequence contiguity as sufficient to cause learning.

- *What is the role of reward?* Clearly, Skinner believed that learning was a matter of modifying responses because of their consequences. Reinforcement increases the frequency of the behaviors it follows; nonreinforcement and punishment decrease the frequency of the behaviors they follow. Skinner refused to inquire into why reinforcement worked, because "when we try to say *why* reinforcement has this effect, theories arise" (Skinner, 1950, p. 200). When asked why gravity worked, Isaac Newton refused to offer any hypothesis, saying that his mathematical description of its effects was sufficient for science, allowing one to predict and control the movements of physical bodies. Similarly, Skinner said that the precision of his descriptions of animal behavior under the control of reinforcement was sufficient to predict and control behavior. Asking for more was, for Skinner as for Newton, to abandon science for metaphysics.

- *What is the role of consciousness?* As a realist, Skinner believed that consciousness does not exist as a thing separate from the body and the environment. He consistently rejected the copy theory of perception and its postulation of mental "ideas." What people ordinarily treat as consciousness Skinner handled in alternate ways. For example, mental imagery is a behavior, seeing, with no actual object seen. Experiences such as pains or itches he treated as *private stimuli*. They arise from physiological processes within the body, and are therefore no different in principle from visual or auditory experiences that arise from physiological processes in the brain. The only difference is that private stimuli are experienced by only one person, while other stimuli are public (see next section). Note that on this point Skinner breaks with methodological behaviorism, which ruled private stimuli out of science. Skinner attempted to explain experience while methodological behaviorists avoided it.

Extension to Humans

Since World War II, Skinner's major preoccupation was extending the results of his animal research and his philosophy of radical behaviorism to human behavior. Two problems in particular occupied him: understanding language and scientifically designing cultures.

Verbal Behavior

As a would-be writer (Skinner, 1976), Skinner had a keen interest in language. He worked for years on the problem of language, and his operant analysis was finally published in 1957 as *Verbal Behavior.* He treated language as a complex set of operant responses shaped by a child's parents, teachers, and peers, being brought under the control of stimulus and reinforcement. This is in strong contrast to the traditional Cartesian account of language as a unique human possession that sets people—who have free souls—apart from merely mechanical animals. Skinner's book is lengthy, complex, and full of novel terminology. We will briefly consider one operant class distinguished by Skinner, the tact, which has nothing to do with polite public behavior.

What Skinner calls a tact we might intuitively call a naming response; it deals with the ancient philosophical problem of universal concept terms (see Leahey, 2000). The problem is this: How does a child learn to categorize correctly the objects in its world as cats, dogs, toys, cars, and so forth? As every parent knows, it takes a long time for children to label correctly what they see. One child known to the author had a pet gerbil, and at the age of two the youngster called all furry animals, even big dogs, "Gerbil!"

Skinner views such class names—or universal terms as opposed to the individuals that make up the class—as **discriminated operants.** Applying contingencies analysis, let us select one operant, the class-name, or tact, "cat." The discriminative stimulus controlling emission of "cat" is, of course, some cat the child sees. Stimulus generalization comes into play, for since all cats resemble each other, learning to label a few cats "Cat!" will generalize to new cats. The reinforcement control is through praise for correct responses of "cat" to cats, and corrections of incorrect responses of "cat" to other animals. In this way, shaping takes place, and soon the child will say "cat" only to cats.

This is Skinner's whole analysis; being a realist, he does not bring in mental images of cats, or "the idea of the cat," or "the concept of the cat," or any other unobservable mental entity. For Skinner, a class-label, a tact, is no more than a type of verbal operant that refers to its controlling stimulus. It makes contact with the environment, hence its name.

While Skinner's analysis of class names, or tacts, is unusual, it has some plausibility. Its difficulties emerge when we try "tacting" our own behavior. Skinner faced up to the difficulty of accounting for utterances such as, "I am looking for my glasses." This utterance has elements of the tact about it for it names the object of my search. But the object is not present to control my speech, and Skinner could not allow that I have an image of my glasses to which I am referring. Instead Skinner (1957) maintained that the stimulus control of the verbal operant "I am looking for my glasses" is the observation of my searching behavior. The meaning of the statement does not derive from any idea in my mind, but instead means, "When I have behaved in this way in the past, I have found my glasses and have then stopped behaving this way." Simply put, according to Skinner when you ask me what I am doing, I observe my own behavior, see myself rummaging around in my desk, and am moved to say as a result of my observations, "I am looking for my glasses."

As an otherwise sympathetic observer (Malcolm, 1964) has observed, Skinner's description of such sentences is "weird." If you asked me what I am doing and I uttered the real meaning of "I am looking for my glasses," namely, "Well, since I'm rummaging around in my desk, I must be looking for my glasses," you would think that I was either joking or behaving like a radical behaviorist who takes his theory too seriously—or perhaps an alien who had read only Skinner's works as preparation for visiting Earth.

On the empirical front, difficulties have arisen in showing that speech is under operant control. Beginning in the mid-1950s, various researchers (Greenspoon, 1955; Verplanck, 1955) tried to show that verbal behavior follows the laws of reinforcement and extinction. In Verplanck's study, for example, undergraduate student experimenters modified subjects' opinion-giving statements. The experimenters talked to subjects and were only to agree, disagree, or keep silent when opinions were given, refraining from nodding, smiling, asking questions, and so forth. They talked to their subjects for 30 minutes, which was divided into learning phrases, when they agreed with opinions, and extinction phases, when they kept silent (in some groups) or disagreed (in other groups). The results were that the frequency of emission of opinions rose when they were reinforced and fell when they were extinguished.

However, Azrin, Holz, Ulrich, and Goldiamond (1961) showed that Verplanck's data were suspect. In the course of replicating Verplanck's study (as a class exercise), they discovered that many of the experimenters had violated the procedures; for example, by participating in the conversation through nods, smiles, and questions, or had been unable to finish the study because the subjects quit during extinction.

Using undergraduate classes, they replicated Verplanck again, except that one class was told what Verplanck told his student-experimenters—that agreement increases verbal operant rate and disagreement depresses it—while the other class was told just the opposite. Each class reported data confirming what it was told to expect. Covert questioning by a student who the class members did not know was working for Azrin and colleagues showed that most of the students had simply made up their data, while nearly all the rest cheated during the experimental sessions.

Finally, four professional experimenters, well-drilled in animal behavior shaping and scientifically aware of the importance of negative results (one suspects they were Azrin, Holz, Ulrich, and Goldiamond themselves), tried to condition 12 subjects. None could complete an experimental session of 30 minutes because each of the 12 subjects got up and left the room before ten minutes were up. As we discovered before, we again find great difficulties in extending the theories and methods of behaviorism to human beings.

Scientific Design of Cultures

During World War II, Skinner (1960) worked on a bizarre project, building a pigeon-guided missile! He designed a missile that contained pigeons in the warhead; their pecking at an image of their target operated flaps on the missile and guided it home. While the kamikaze pigeons performed well in dry runs, the Navy found the project a bit laughable, and Skinner lost his funding. It is ironic that the same military problem—

guiding weapons to their targets—helped produce computers and the information-processing psychology that is radical behaviorism's main rival today. But at the time Skinner was most impressed by the degree of behavioral control he had established over the pigeons. In the aftermath of his project's failure he wrote a novel, *Walden II* (1948b), which reveals his postwar obsession, the idea of constructing a scientifically managed society. *Walden II* describes Skinner's fictional utopia, whereas other works (e.g., Skinner, 1972) argue that this utopia can actually be attained through behavioral technology.

Through these works the same ideas run like distinct threads. Skinner maintains that existing societies are badly managed, mainly because we believe in myths such as free will. People are no freer than pigeons, Skinner asserts, and to deny that our behavior is controlled is to deny scientific truth. Instead, Skinner asks us to accept that we are just as controlled by our environments as pigeons and rats, and apply the established laws of learning to ourselves. If we do this, Skinner concludes, society will be much better managed, and everyone will be happy under the control of positive reinforcement.

Walden II and Skinner's vision of a remade Western culture are the fruits of his psychology of learning; he maintains that what we have learned in the laboratory of behavior should be applied to the problems of society in the same way that we apply what we have learned from physics and chemistry. While no one has seriously tried to remake Western society along Skinnerian lines, applying behavior modification to social and individual problems has been tried in many settings.

Behavioral Economics

Perhaps the most widely studied schedule of reinforcement today is the **concurrent schedule.** In a concurrent schedule of reinforcement, two responses are available to the organism, such as two levers to press or two keys to peck, and each response is controlled by a different schedule of reinforcement or a different reinforcer. Thus, one lever might be running a VI 5 schedule of food, and the other might be running a VI 10 schedule; or one lever might yield food while another might yield water; or one might yield large food pellets and the other small food pellets. One can readily see that many concurrent schedules might be set up, but what they have in common is that they offer the experimental subject a choice of behaviors, and psychologists can then study the circumstances that lead to different patterns of choice.

The leading student of choice behavior under concurrent schedules of reinforcement has been Richard Herrnstein (1970), whose **matching law** governing choice is one of the most important principles of modern behaviorism. The general idea of the matching law is that organisms' behaviors will come to mirror the contingencies of reinforcement in the environment (Rachlin, 1989). More precisely, in the case of concurrent VI schedules of reinforcement, the number of responses a rat or pigeon makes to each key will reflect the ratio of reinforcement available on each. The matching law may be expressed as an equation expressing the ratio of time spent making each of two responses, A or B, as equal to the ratio of the availability of reinforcement on A and B:

$$\frac{\text{Responses on A}}{\text{Responses on B}} = \frac{\text{Reinforcement on A}}{\text{Reinforcement on B}}$$

or equivalently,

$$\frac{\text{Rs on A}}{\text{Rs on A} + \text{Rs on B}} = \frac{\text{Rf on A}}{\text{Rf on A} + \text{Rf on B}}$$

So, in our hypothetical example, out of every hour, 12 reinforcers are available on lever A and 6 reinforcers are available on lever B, thus: Rs on A/Rs on A + Rs on B = $^{12}/_{12}$ + 6 = $^{12}/_{18}$ = $^2/_3$. Thus, a rat will spend two-thirds of its time pressing lever A and one-third pressing lever B. The matching law has been shown to hold true not only for the frequency of reinforcement on VI schedules, but also for variables such as magnitude of reinforcement and delay of reinforcement. Thus, for example, if key A yields 5 pellets of food and key B yields 1 pellet (and response ratios are held constant), animals will press A $^5/_6$ of the time and key B $^1/_6$ of the time. Or, if key A requires a 2-second delay for food and key B a 4-second delay, animals will peck A $^2/_3$ of the time and B $^1/_3$ of the time. The matching law also holds across species and a wide variety of operant responses (Rachlin, 1989; Schwartz & Reisberg, 1991).

The study of choice opened up the possibility of merging economics—the study of how people choose goods—and behavior theory, creating the rapidly growing field of **behavioral economics.** Interesting parallels emerge between economists' study of human economic behavior and behaviorist's studies of animal choice behavior. To illustrate some of the parallels, we will examine two economic concepts in behavioral form, the concept of **demand-price elasticity,** and the difference between **open** and **closed economic systems.**

Some goods are very sensitive to changes in prices. Suppose you like to buy mystery novels. If you are like most people, you prefer to buy the $2.95 paperback to the $19.95 hardback version, even if it means waiting a few months; moreover, if the price of paperback mysteries suddenly trebled to $8.95, you'd buy fewer of them. On the other hand, if the price of bread trebled from $.99 to $2.99, you'd probably buy about as much bread as before. To the degree that sales of a good are sensitive to its price, demand for it is said to be elastic; in general, luxury goods have elastic demand (when the U.S. government put stiff taxes on luxury goods such as yachts, sales plummeted), while necessities are inelastic.

The concept of elasticity may be applied to reinforcers as well. Food or water is a good for which animals in Skinner boxes must "pay" by making bar-presses or key-pecks. Food and water are necessities, and animals are willing to work very hard—tolerate long ratio or interval schedules—to get them. But let us consider electrical stimulation of the brain. There are certain sites in the brain—so-called "pleasure centers"—whose stimulation by an implanted electrode is very reinforcing. But is brain stimulation a luxury or a necessity?

Experiments by Hursh and Natelson (1981) and Hursh and Bauman (1987), described by Schwartz and Reisberg (1991), compared the effects on responding of concurrent schedules of food and electrical stimulation of the brain (ESB) at differing fixed ratios of response. First, rats could choose between levers delivering food and ESB on FR 2 schedules. Under these conditions, rats earned much more ESB than food—about 9 times as much—and application of the matching law suggests that rats like ESB nine times as much as food pellets. Then, the animals were switched to FR 8 schedules. The amount of food produced per hour stayed about the same, meaning rats were paying 4 times as much in bar-presses to get each food pellet and maintaining their eating at a steady rate. At the same time, the amount of ESB produced dropped so much that at the FR 8 schedule the rats were producing more food pellets than ESB jolts. Thus, demand for ESB is elastic—it's a luxury—while demand for food is inelastic—it's a necessity. Interestingly, demand for ethanol is relatively inelastic (Heyman & Oldfather, 1992).

Another example of behavioral economics involves the distinction of open and closed economies. Schwartz and Reisberg (1991) use the following example to illustrate the difference between open and closed economies. Given that you have a fixed income, you must choose between an array of goods, and money spent on one good makes money unavailable for another. So if the price of bread skyrockets, you keep buying it anyway (it's an inelastic necessity) and stop buying mystery novels, even if the price remains constant (it's an elastic luxury). Suppose, however, you have an indulgent uncle in the book business who can get you any book you want for free if only you wait a week. Under these happy circumstances, you can get as many mysteries as you wish without regard to price. In the first circumstance, bread and food are both parts of a closed economy in which goods must be bought at a price. In the second, mystery novels constitute an open economy in which goods are freely available. At first glance it may seem that in real life there are no free goods—no open economies—but in fact some goods are free or, more dangerously, appear to be. We do not pay for the air we breathe, for example, and some economists believe that because air is free, no one has a stake in keeping it clean, since no one profits by its "sale." Perhaps if we paid for air we would be more careful about its quality. Similarly, wildlife conservation is often most fervently supported by hunters and fishermen who have to pay fees for access to the woods and fields.

One of the most interesting applications of the concept of open versus closed economic systems reveals the importance of seemingly innocuous, even unconscious, assumptions in the experimental study of behavior (Schwartz & Reisberg, 1991). One standard feature of animal experimentation that is taken for granted as given—such conditions of research are called *ceteris paribus* (all other things being equal) conditions—is that animals are kept at a certain fraction of their free-feeding weight, typically 80 to 85 percent. If they do not consume enough food during an experimental session to maintain that weight, subjects are allowed free access to food at the end of the session until they are at the target weight. However, such an experimental regime constitutes an open economic system, since the experimenter is like your indulgent uncle; the rat or pigeon does not actually have to pay for food with responses at all, since it can wait for the experimental session to end.

Schwartz and Reisberg (1991) assembled data from a number of experiments to show that responding during experimental sessions is affected by whether the organism is in an open or closed economy. In an open economy—the standard laboratory situation—animals' response rates decline severely as ratio or interval schedules are lengthened, while in a closed economy when there is no free feeding period, long schedules produce high rates of responding. For example, in an open economy at FR 160, response rate is barely above 0, while in a closed economy animals make about 2,250 responses per hour at FR 160. Closed versus open economic regimes also affect standard assumptions about the effect of reinforcement size on learning (Collier, Johnson, & Morgan, 1992).

In addition to illustrating the promise of behavioral economics to integrate behavior theory and economics (Rachlin, 1989), these findings, like those of Voeks reviewed in the last chapter, should encourage us to look skeptically at the *soi-disant* laws of behavior that emerge from laboratory research. All experiments rest on assumptions, some of which we may think are unimportant or which we overlook altogether. However, principles of behavior that hold true under one set of conditions may not hold true in all, making more elusive the search for a general science psychology.

The Legacy of Radical Behaviorism

A thinker as radical and aggressive as B. F. Skinner has naturally been heavily criticized on a number of fronts. His analysis of language has been termed folk psychology masquerading as science (Chomsky, 1959). His attacks on mentalism have been found confusing and overdrawn (Dennett, 1978). His theoretical approach to science has been reproached as simplistic, narrow, and restrictive (Shimp, 1984). Although radical behaviorism continues without Skinner (Pierce & Epling, 1999), its influence on psychology is limited. Radical behaviorists have their own division in the American Psychological Association (Division 25, Behavior Analysis) and their own societies, such as the Association for Applied Behavior Analysis. However, outside these functional ghettoes, radical behaviorism is not a serious force. Other psychologists sometimes adopt Skinnerian methods—for example, operant methods are crucial to fields such as behavioral pharmacology—but Skinner's nontheory theory has been swamped by cognitive science and cognitive neuroscience.

COGNITIVE PROCESSES IN ANIMALS

Research and theory on animal learning has continued since the Golden Age of Theory and outside the experimental analysis of behavior. In general, two important trends today dominate the field of animal learning theory: a trend toward biology and a trend toward the study of animal cognition. We will look at biologically oriented animal research in Part V, Cognitive Neuroscience.

Animal Memory

As an example of the cognitive trend in the study of animal learning and cognition, we will discuss the study of memory in pigeons and rats. The paradigm used to study short-term memory in pigeons is called delayed matching to sample, on which several variations are possible; we will discuss just two. Imagine a pigeon Skinner box with a row of four possible keys to peck. In a delayed-matching-to-sample procedure we light one of the keys, say with a green light; this is the sample. Then there is a variable memory interval when no keys are lighted. When the memory interval is over we present a pair of test stimuli by lighting two of the keys, one with the same color as before—green in our example—and one with another color, say red. The animal is reinforced for pecking the same color key as presented in the sample. The position of the correct key in the test phase is chosen at random, so the pigeon cannot simply learn always to press one of the keys on the basis of position.

Pigeons can perform this task, although their ability to do so declines (as does human short-term memory in analogous tasks) as the memory interval increases. It appears that pigeons can remember the sample for a period of time and can base their test response on memory. However, interesting questions now arise. For example, why does the pigeon's performance decline as the memory interval gets longer? Borrowing from theorizing about human memory, two possibilities present themselves: **decay** and **interference.** First, the memory of the sample might simply decay, so that the longer the memory interval, the weaker the trace and the poorer the performance. On the other hand, new experiences in the box might interfere with the stored memory, making it harder to retrieve the memory of the sample. That the latter occurs in pigeons is suggested by the finding that when we turn off the room lights during the memory interval, test performance is intact over very long times (B. Schwartz, 1984).

Another question about pigeon short-term memory is to ask exactly what is stored during the memory interval. One might think it is just a visual image trace of the sample stimulus, so that in the test phase the pigeon simply pecks the same colored light as its image. However, delayed symbolic or conditional matching undermines this simple hypothesis. In symbolic, or conditional, matching to sample, the test stimuli are different from the sample stimuli. For example, the test pair might be horizontal and vertical lines, with the pigeon reinforced for pecking the vertical lines when the sample was green, horizontal lines when the sample was red. Although a trace might still be involved, clearly there is more involved in delayed symbolic matching to sample than merely matching up a trace with a new stimulus. Some sort of rule must be learned of the sort, "If sample is green, peck the vertical lines."

This conclusion is underscored by the results of a clever experiment by Stonebreaker (1981, described by Honig & Thompson, 1982). In this experiment, the memory interval was followed by either the standard matching test stimuli or by a conditional test pair. The pigeon was told which to expect by a signal given just after the sample; a circle meant a standard test, and a triangle signaled a conditional test. Occasionally, a **probe test** was given, in which the test was the opposite of the one that had been signaled. Performance was good on trials when the test matched the signal, but was dismal on probe trials. The finding strongly suggests that when the signal was given the animal decided on what the correct response would be at test, and stored this information in memory. Thus, on probe trials the pigeon was not ready with the correct response and performed poorly. If the pigeon simply held a trace of the sample stimulus and used it at the time of the test to choose the correct response, the probe trials should have given it no trouble. Pigeons also seem able to control their short-term stores, as evidence by directed forgetting experiments in which a sample is sometimes followed by a signal to forget it. Tests after forgetting signals produce very poor results, suggesting that the animal did dump memory of the sample when signaled.

Short-term memory in rats is studied in the multiarm radial maze (Roitblat, 1987; Pearce, 1987). A radial maze consists of a central platform from which radiates numerous arms, each of which is baited with food. The best thing for a rat to do is visit each arm once. It might adopt two memory strategies for accomplishing this task. On the one hand, it might use retrospective coding, trying to remember which arms it had already visited, and not visit those arms. In this case, the list of visited arms held in memory would increase through the experiment, and the number of mistakes would thereby increase. On the other hand, the rat might use prospective coding, initially putting in memory a list of arms not yet visited, and only visit arms on that list, deleting arms as it visited them. In this case, the list to be remembered would get shorter during the experiment, and mistakes should decrease. Rats—pigeons and monkeys in such tasks—use both retrospective and prospective coding, depending on conditions

(Brown, 1992; Wright, 1989; Zentall, Urcuioli, Jackson-Smith, & Steirn, 1991), though whether they also use a cognitive map, as Tolman expected, remains controversial (Brown, 1992).

SUGGESTED READINGS

Broad views of the Golden Age of Theory may be had from T. Leahey, *A History of Psychology,* 5th ed. (Upper Saddle River, NJ: Prentice-Hall, 2000), and from Sigmund Koch (Ed.) *Psychology: A Study of a Science* (New York: McGraw-Hill, 1959). Volume 2 of Koch's work contains the theories presented here, plus others, and are presented by the participants themselves.

PART III

INFORMATION PROCESSING

5 Early Information Processing: Recognition, Attention, and Working Memory

As the computer age began in earnest after World War II ended in 1945, psychologists found in computers and computer programming a new conceptual basis for psychology. Computers accept information, store and process that information, make decisions, and generate output. Perhaps computers could even think! It became popular to view both humans and computers as information-processing devices studied by psychologists on the one hand and computer scientists on the other. Cognitive psychology's courtship of computer science and behavioral neuroscience has culminated in a new field called **cognitive science,** the study of computational devices both of silicon and steel and of nerve and tissue (Kosslyn & Koenig, 1995; O'Nuallain, 1995; Quinlan, 1991; Stillings et al., 1995). Although cognitive neuroscience is further explored later in this book, the next several chapters examine cognitive psychology.

Although cognitive and S-R psychology are sometimes sharply contrasted, the reality may not be quite so simple. Cognitive psychology and radical behaviorism are quite different, since Skinner did not tolerate the postulation of any interal psychological entities, whether it be Freud's ego or the cognitive psychologist's long-term memory. However, behaviorists such as Tolman and Hull postulated inferred entities that controlled behavior, for example, cognitive maps and mediating responses. Neobehaviorists routinely enbraced cognitive concepts in studying human development (see Chapter 4), and many animal behaviorists talk in cognitive terms. Many of the basic questions of cognitive psychology are the same as those in learning. Although the specific answers that cognitive psychologists offer frequently differ from behaviorists' answers, their quest is the same. Much of the behavior of interest to cognitive psychologists, however, is internal and not directly observable.

In this section of the book, we will present the cognitive view of learning beginning with the relatively earlier, perceptually based processes, then moving to the later, more cognitive ones. This chapter begins by discussing the initial stages of information processing: what happens to stimuli (input) as they are initially recognized, attended to, and prepared for encoding into memory. In Chapter 6, the subject is long-term memory, the processes and representations involved in storing, maintaining, and retrieving learned information. Chapter 7 takes up the topic of language, perhaps humans' most important cognitive tool. Chapter 8 examines comprehension of language, discourse, and complex nonlinguistic information. Finally, Chapter 9 surveys the topics of reasoning, problem solving, decision making, and scientific thinking.

Most human experiences, whether studying for a test, sizing up a new acquaintance at a party, coping with an experience of abuse, or watching a television commercial, involve the processing of information. It is difficult to separate perception, memory, comprehension, language, problem solving, and decision making. Thus, our discussion of each problem will necessarily have frequent allusion to other topics. Throughout these chapters, both applications in our daily lives and theoretical conceptual principles will be addressed.

AN OVERVIEW OF THE INFORMATION-PROCESSING SYSTEM

Before examining the various processes that occur when we take in and interpret information, it is useful to have some general understanding of the overall information-processing system. Figure 5.1 schematically illustrates a general conceptual view of the most characteristic way that most cognitive psychologists of the past few decades have understood the information-processing system. Much of this conceptualization is traceable to Atkinson and Shiffrin (1968), who developed an extensive description of such a model. What is presented in Figure 5.1 is very much in the tradition of Atkinson and Shiffrin, without necessarily adhering to all the details and assumptions of their theory. For a good review of the influence of this model on the study of memory, see Izawa (1999).

Generally, with some important exceptions to be discussed later, processing proceeds from left to right in Figure 5.1. Environmental input comes into sensory memory, which holds information for a very short time (about 0.5 to 1.0 seconds in the visual system), just long enough for us to select what to attend to and process further.

Attention and pattern recognition occur to help identify and select information for further processing.

Material in working memory includes everything we are thinking about at the moment. This material comes from two sources: the external environment (new sensory information) and previously learned information retrieved from long-term memory. Both types of information interact in working memory.

Material may be retained in working memory only a very short time (some experiments suggest 15 to 30 seconds), unless it continues to be processed in some way. This could occur by repeating (rehearsing) the material over to yourself, as when you look up a phone number and repeat it to yourself while you dial the phone. It could also

FIGURE 5.1   Overview of information-processing system.

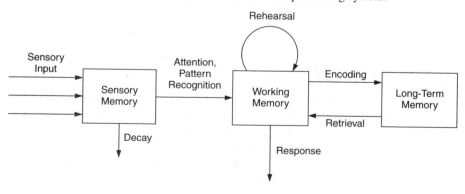

be retained in working memory indefinitely by continuing to think about it for some reason, as when solving a problem. If we make a response (verbal or behavioral), it must be from working memory, not sensory memory, which is too short-lived and unprocessed, and not long-term memory, which is not in immediate consciousness.

If we want to remember something for the future, we seek to somehow encode it into long-term memory. If it is encoded successfully, we can forget about it for the moment, knowing we can retrieve it later when we need it. If it is not encoded and we do not continue to process it in working memory, it is quickly and probably permanently forgotten. If material is encoded well, it can more likely be successfully retrieved. On the other hand, if it is not encoded inaccurately or not at all, even the best retrieval strategies may be doomed to failure. Encoding and its sister set of processes, retrieval, are both places where memory can go wrong.

A consistent and recurring issue in information processing is the juxtaposition of **top-down** (conceptually driven) and **bottom-up** (data-driven) processes. Bottom-up processes refer to the processing of the actual environmental stimuli, with processing determined only by the nature of those stimuli (data) themselves. Although such pure processing is perhaps the typical layperson's view of how we perceive and comprehend information, it almost never occurs in pure form in either the real world or the laboratory. Typically, top-down and bottom-up processing occur simultaneously. Top-down processing involves expectations about what the data will hold, based on our past experiences and knowledge in long-term memory. Such expectations inevitably color our interpretation of those data and prevent us from doing purely data-driven processing. Sometimes top-down processing can make us surprisingly "blind" to what is right in front of us; see Box 5.1 for a striking example.

Another important distinction in discussing cognitive processes is differentiating **serial** and **parallel** processes. Serial processes are performed *sequentially,* one after the other, while parallel processes are performed *simultaneously,* at least partially overlapping in time. For example, if you scan a list of words to see if the letter *T* occurs anywhere and then scan the list again to see if the letter *P* occurs, you are performing the two scanning processes serially. If you scan the list once, looking for *either* a *T* or a *P,* you perform the two operations in parallel.

At this point we begin examining each of the separate memory stores and sets of processes that occur as we comprehend and remember information.

SENSORY MEMORY

The most immediately perceptual store of memory is **sensory memory,** also sometimes called the sensory register or sensory information store. Its function is to hold information just long enough for it to be selectively attended to and marked for further processing in working memory. Material in sensory memory has usually been thought to be completely unorganized, basically a perceptual copy of objects and events in the world. Material decays very rapidly from sensory memory (about 1 second or less for vision and 3 to 4 seconds for hearing), unless it is selected for further processing. Although you generally are not conscious of information in sensory memory, you can informally demonstrate its existence by quickly waving your arm from side to side in front of your face. You continue to see a very faint copy or shadow of your arm for a fraction of a second after it has sped by. This is the **icon,** the visual sensory memory representation. Another example of the icon is the ribbon of light that you see in a dark

Box 5.1

Change Blindness, or How Top-Down Processing Helps Us Watch Movies by Seeing What Isn't There

Because movies are usually not filmed in the order appearing in the final version of the movie, film editors must be very careful that background scene details do not change from one shot to the next as they cut and paste shots filmed on different days. In fact, they almost never totally succeed in this endeavor. For example, in *Ace Ventura: When Nature Calls* pieces on a chessboard disappear from one scene to the next, and a child in *Goodfellas* plays with blocks that appear and disappear across shots of the "same scene" (Levin & Simons, 1997; Simons & Levin, 1997).

In an experiment testing change blindness, Simons and Levin (1997) found that people watching a film clip of a man sitting at a desk and then getting up to answer the phone did not notice that the man answering the phone was a different person! Even more surprisingly, in a naturalistic experiment, an experimenter began talking to someone on the sidewalk and was interrupted by two workers carrying a door between the two conversants. Unbeknownst to the second conversant (the "real" research participant), the experimenter switched places with someone else while the door stood between them. Less than half of the participants noticed that they were not talking to the same person after the door was removed (Simons & Levin, 1998)!

Why do we do this? Simons and Levin conclude that we are likely to miss changes that do not affect the overall meaning of the scene. Top-down processing carries the day.

---

room immediately after waving a flashlight. What we experience as a lightning flash is actually a sequence of several short bolts in sequence.

Although information in sensory memory is not generally open to introspection, its existence was convincingly demonstrated many years ago in a clever experiment by George Sperling (1960). When an array of 12 letters (three rows of four each) was flashed on a screen for 50 milliseconds (one-twentieth of a second), participants were barely aware of its presence yet could consistently report three or four letters accurately. Although this result was first assumed to reflect the actual processing capacity, Sperling demonstrated that many more letters had in fact entered sensory memory. To demonstrate this, Sperling used a high-, middle-, or low-pitched tone to request reporting only the top, middle, or bottom line of the array. Using this **partial-report** method, about 75 percent of the letters were reported correctly, about twice as many as when the **whole-report** ("repeat all the letters") method was used. This finding suggests that the limits of sensory memory are temporal, not visual, and that considerable information is there, but decays very rapidly, faster than the time it takes to report it. In the case of the visual system, decay from sensory memory is essentially complete in one second or less. If the tone signaling which line to recall was delayed as much as a second, the number of letters recalled was down to the equivalent of four out of twelve, the number reported under the whole-report procedure.

Sperling's effect was replicated in a study using the auditory system, with one important difference (Darwin, Turvey, & Crowder, 1972). The auditory sensory memory, or **echo,** can last for several seconds, with recall under partial report superior to that under whole report for up to four seconds. Recent neuromagnetic research suggests it may sometimes last as long as ten seconds (Samms, Hari, Rif, & Knuutila, 1993). The auditory sensory memory is critical for understanding speech. Sounds early in a word must remain in sensory memory long enough to be mentally combined with the later sounds. Just how much time this requires remains in some dispute (Massaro & Loftus, 1996).

The fact that information decays so rapidly from sensory memory is actually an adaptive feature of our information-processing system. We might experience double images in the visual system or confusing echoes in the auditory system if everything we had perceived in the last few seconds remained in our sensory memory. Rapid delay removes the clutter.

Not everyone, however, accepts that sensory memory necessarily passively copies all incoming stimulus information with no interpretation whatsoever. For example, Merikle (1980) argued that different aspects of stimuli (for example, location or identity) are encoded at different rates and do not require the postulation of a separate sensory memory. He replicated Sperling's study using mixed arrays of numbers and letters. Cuing by category ("recall the numbers") was just as effective as cuing by position ("recall the top line"). If sensory memory is entirely precategorical (that is, information is not yet organized into categories), such categorical cuing should not have been effective. Evidence such as this has been used to question the postulation of a qualitatively separate sensory memory of pure and unanalyzed sensory information.

A different sort of critique argues against Sperling's work and the general idea of sensory memory on the grounds that the whole notion of the icon is an artifact of a highly artificial laboratory task. For example, Haber (1983, 1985) says that visual perception in the real world, unlike in Sperling's task, is dynamic, not static. In actual vision, attentional processes and eye fixations routinely connect what would otherwise be static icons. Thus, Haber argued that the laboratory identification of the entity called the icon is largely irrelevant to perception as it occurs in real life.

The purpose of sensory memory is to hold information just long enough for some of it to be selected for further processing in working memory. For this to occur, it must be *attended* to and we must start to *recognize patterns*. It is to these processes that we now turn, in examining how material is selected from sensory memory for further processing. We begin by examining attention.

ATTENTION

Attention is one of those psychological constructs that everyone has intuitions about, but few know exactly how to precisely define. Although discussed by William James (1890) and even earlier by the German introspectionists, it was long ignored in the behaviorist era as being too mentalistic and unobservable to be worthy of study in scientific psychology. In the 1950s and 1960s, however, there arose a resurgence of interest in studying attention, primarily by several British researchers, notably Donald Broadbent (1958), Anne Treisman (1964), and Colin Cherry (1953). Since then, the problem has received intense study, though many unanswered questions remain.

One of the most fundamental issues in attention research involves a recurring paradox in information processing. While attention seems to be an early process in the sequence of processing information (that is, we must attend to something before it can be processed too deeply), the factors affecting how we choose what to attend to suggest some extensive processing before that early decision could be made. How to resolve this tension between the top-down and bottom-up processes is a continuing theme in this research.

For example, suppose that you are at a party and suddenly turn your head to begin attending to a new conversation because you've just heard your name spoken in that conversation. Even though you were not consciously attending to it, you must have been unconsciously processing meaningful elements of that unattended conversation to some degree, in order to be able to recognize your own name. The top-down process of drawing on knowledge from long-term memory (knowledge of your name) has interacted with the bottom-up processes of understanding the words spoken by the other people in the conversation.

Selective Attention

How we select activities to attend to and how we determine how many stimuli we can process simultaneously depend on a variety of factors. First of all, the number of sources is important. It is harder to pay attention to five people talking than it is to one. Second, the similarity of sources is important. For example, some people find that they can study well with instrumental music in the background, but not with vocal music. The latter, being linguistic, is similar enough to reading to interfere, while purely instrumental music is not. However, if you are solving algebra problems rather than reading, you may be able to work with vocal music in the background, because there is only one linguistic stimulus.

The complexity of sources or tasks is another important variable. It is much easier to pay attention to several simple stimuli or simultaneously perform more than one simple task than it is if the stimuli or tasks are complex. For example, you may be able to read *TV Guide,* watch television, and talk to a friend simultaneously, but watching a complex television documentary or reading this textbook would each require all your attention for that single activity. Some people, especially children, have trouble selecting a single source to attend to. See Box 5.2 for a discussion of a disorder of selective attention.

Unpredictable sources tend to capture our attention, whereas highly predictable ones do not. Sometimes very predictable stimuli are not really noticed until they stop; for example, a whirring heater or air conditioner or a continuing conversation goes unnoticed until it stops, at which time attention immediately is drawn to it. In this case, the cessation of the stimulus is the unpredictable attention-capturing, event. Gradual habituation occurs to continual, highly predictable stimuli; that is, we gradually allocate less and less attention to it until we may not even be consciously aware of its presence.

Automaticity

Perhaps the most important variable in determining the allocation of attention is the degree of **automaticity.** Shiffrin and Schneider (1977) and others have made the distinction between automatic and controlled (or deliberate) processes. **Automatic** processes do not require much allocation of attention and can be executed in parallel with other cognitive processes or activities. For example, we can often drive and carry on a conversation simultaneously because little if any attention must be allocated to driving. If, however, unusually demanding conditions arise while driving (heavy traffic, bad weather), we may have to cease the conversation

Attention Deficit Hyperactivity Disorder

Over 5 percent of preadolescent children in the United States, 90 percent of them boys, suffer from Attention Deficit Hyperactivity Disorder (ADHD), a condition that makes selective attention very difficult because the child is unable to "tune out" the irrelevant messages (Armstrong, 1995). This condition may or may not occur with associated hyperactivity and/or deficient social skills (Frederick & Olmi, 1994). Although it is not correlated with intelligence, such children often perform poorly in school, because they are easily distracted and do not listen well, due to their inability to focus their attention on one activity to the exclusion of others. Recently, the frequency of diagnosing ADHD has increased sharply. Some critics point to societal causes such as decreasing opportunities for rough-and-tumble play, which is required by the brain for normal growth (Panksepp, 1998). Drug therapy has been shown to help 70 to 80 percent of ADHD children, probably by stimulating part of the brain involved in controlling attention; in addition, behavior therapy, sometimes in combination with drug therapy, may be useful (Gomez & Cole, 1991). Finally, it is very helpful to provide education about the disorder to those who have it, as well as to their parents and teachers. Although children often outgrow the condition, about one-third of the cases persist into early adulthood (Lie, 1992). For an in-depth look at ADHD, see Barkley (1990, 1997); for a book directed at parents of ADHD children, see Barkley (1995).

to devote full attention to the driving activity, which now becomes a controlled, no longer automatic, process. **Controlled** processes must be executed serially because they require so much attention, while automatic processes may be executed in parallel. Sometimes it is very difficult to "turn off" a highly practiced automatic process, even when we do not need it (see Box 5.3).

As a controlled task becomes habitual and greatly overlearned, it eventually may become automatic. Musicians may recall the first thrill of realizing that their hands moved to the right piano keys or guitar frets without conscious attention to the finger movement. A skilled basketball player is not consciously concerned about placement of the feet at most times, whereas a beginner might be very preoccupied with such considerations and not be able to devote much attention to more global concerns like overall game strategy. Much of the process of learning skills like sports or musical performance may be seen as increasing the automaticity of more and more of the specific motor and cognitive skills involved.

A useful distinction may be made between **declarative** and **procedural** knowledge (J. R. Anderson, 1983, 1990). Declarative knowledge ("knowing *that*") consists of information that typically can be communicated verbally. Most studies of memory and cognition over the years have examined declarative knowledge. On the other hand, procedural knowledge ("knowing *how*") is a skill. It is often, though not necessarily, motor in character: typing, riding a bicycle, driving a car, dribbling a basketball, or playing a piano. Procedural knowledge, especially that which is involved in motor skills, is not readily expressible verbally. If you don't find yourself convinced of this, try to write a description of how to ride a bicycle.

Procedural knowledge may also be entirely internal, such as our knowledge of how to apply linguistic rules in speaking or our knowledge of how to use certain

Why Is It So Hard to See Red If It Is Written in Blue?

Sometimes it may be exceedingly difficult to "turn off" an automatic process that is highly overlearned, even when it is unnecessary or interfering in a particular situation. A vivid illustration is the Stroop effect, first demonstrated in the doctoral dissertation of J. R. Stroop (1935). In this task names of colors are written in colors inconsistent with the color (e.g., the word "BLUE" written in red ink). Reading the words takes no longer than reading a list of color names all written in black. However, naming the colors of the words takes almost twice as long. Reading is so highly overlearned that it is difficult to **not** read in response to seeing words. In the case of the Stroop task, the performance of this automatic, but in this case undesired, behavior is distinctly interfering with the target behavior of naming the colors. In a review of the half-century of research on the Stroop effect, MacLeod (1991) reports that over 700 studies have examined this effect or used it to study some other problem. Many have made substantial contributions to our understanding of different areas of cognitive psychology. Few other psychologists can claim to have generated so much research from their doctoral thesis!

strategies in decision making or problem solving. We often apply such knowledge implicitly without being able to verbalize the rule we are using.

The limits of how much controlled tasks can become automatic may be less than we think. In a dramatic demonstration, Spelke, Hirst, and Neisser (1976) trained two participants for 85 sessions over several weeks in the formidable job of taking dictation and reading an unrelated story aloud simultaneously. Although both of these tasks are normally highly controlled, after several weeks of intensive practice these two people acquired a high enough degree of automaticity to do both tasks simultaneously with little apparent interference. This suggests that attentional limits in the area of automaticity may be due more to limited practice than to inherent cognitive processing limits. Our minds may be capable of a lot more than we suspect, given sufficient practice of the right kind.

Models of Attention

The earliest contemporary psychological model of attention was Broadbent's (1958) filter model. Broadbent proposed that there are different information channels coming through our senses into our information-processing system. The filter selects one of these channels for further processing and largely blocks the others out. The basis for this selection was thought to be perceptual, often based on gross physical characteristics, such as overall voice quality or loudness. Only these characteristics should be noticed from the unattended message.

While this model has much intuitive appeal (we speak of "tuning someone out"), there is numerous anecdotal and experimental evidence showing that we do perceive some, even if very limited, information from the unattended channels. For example, we start attending to another conversation at a party when we hear our name or some other very salient stimulus spoken. This suggests that we must be monitoring the unattended source at some level rather than totally filtering it out. To account for such cases, Anne

Treisman (1964) modified Broadbent's filter model. Instead of a filter, she proposed an **attenuator** that "turns down" the unattended channels, somewhat as we would turn down the volume on a television set to the point that we would perceive something especially interesting but otherwise would not attend to it. This still leaves unexplained what determines when something is important enough to be perceived from an unattended channel.

Beginning with Kahneman (1973), some researchers began to think of attention as a limited set of processes or resources to be allocated. These **capacity** models focus on describing the processing differences between these two types of processes. Contemporary theories of attention in this tradition fall into two global categories, theories that view attention as a causal mechanism and those that see attention as consequences of other processes (Johnston & Dark, 1986). Those in the former category generally distinguish between automatic and controlled processes (Hirst & Kalmar, 1987; Marcel, 1983; Schneider, Dumais, & Shiffrin, 1984; Schneider & Shiffrin, 1997; Treisman & Gelade, 1980). The particular theories of this type differ primarily in terms of how automatic and controlled processing interact.

The second major class of capacity theories sees attention as a consequence of priming activities of some other processing. For example, attention is directed one way rather than another by the presence of some stimulus (somebody shouts "fire" in a classroom and our attention is turned from the teacher to the shouter). This view was discussed by William James (1890) and much later by Hochberg (1978) and Neisser (1976). Reviews of theories of attention may be found in Broadbent (1982), Enns (1990), LaBerge (1995), Pashler (1998), and Shiffrin (1985). As well as the basic research of building theories of attention, there is great relevance for a variety of applied problems. See Box 5.4 for an application to watching television.

Neuropsychology of Attention

The parietal lobe, as well as certain areas of the frontal lobe, are known to be associated with attention (Banich, 1997). Patients with parietal lobe damage will have trouble attending to information in the opposite visual field. For example, a person with right parietal lobe damage who is copying a simple drawing may omit part of the left side (Posner & Raichle, 1994). Furthermore, they seem to be unaware of the omission.

Brain correlates of attention are no simple matter, however. By one measure (LaBerge, 1995), 32 different areas of the brain become active in visual processing. The critical networks or connections among the areas associated with different tasks appear to be important (Posner & Raichle, 1994). Posner (1995) and Posner and Dehaene (1994) have identified an anterior attentional system in the frontal lobe and a posterior attentional system in the parietal lobe. The anterior system is activated in tasks requiring awareness, while the posterior system is activated in tasks of visuospatial searching and attention-shifting.

Also, event-related potentials (ERPs), averages of EEG potentials recorded at various intervals after presentation of a stimulus, differ for attended and unattended stimuli. Beginning at about 80 milliseconds after presentation, the amplitude of the waveforms for attended stimuli is greater than for unattended stimuli (Pashler, 1998). ERPs provide a very sensitive measure of attentional responses of the brain over time (Näätänen, 1992).

How Much Attention Are We Paying to Television?

Although the average person in the United States watches 3 to 4 hours of television per day and the average set is on over 7 hours a day, it is still unclear how much attention is being paid to the turned-on TV set during those hours. By examining the extent of people's visual fixation on the TV screen, as well as other measures, psychologist Daniel Anderson and his colleagues have begun to answer that question (D. Anderson & Burns, 1991; D. Anderson & Field, 1991). Children at age three attend to television about 55 percent of the time it is on; this figure rises to 70 percent by age five and remains there throughout childhood. Attention is highest to sports and children's television (e.g., cartoons) and to material that challenges but does not cognitively overwhelm the viewer. Young children do not attend well to adult programs far beyond their level; similarly, adults watching highly predictable genres, such as sitcoms, need not devote full attention in order to comprehend most of the material. Anderson and his colleagues have identified a phenomenon they call attentional inertia, which basically says people presently attending are more likely to keep attending, while those not attending are more likely to continue not attending. Thus programming designed to attract viewers' attention becomes more necessary, from the producer's or advertiser's point of view, than programming designed to keep viewers' attention.

PATTERN RECOGNITION

The process of pattern recognition is one of the central problems in human information processing. It involves the question of how we recognize environmental stimuli as exemplars of concepts already in memory. This is part of the more general set of processes of attaching meaning to information that we process. Like attention, pattern recognition must occur if information is to reach working memory for further processing. Pattern recognition is a very general phenomenon, cutting across all sensory modalities, including everything from how we recognize a certain letter we read as a *T* or understand someone's speech as containing the sound /p/ to how we recognize Rover as a dog or recognize a certain social interchange as one of that class of events of "getting dumped" in a dating relationship. There are three general classes of models of pattern recognition: **template matching, prototypes,** and **feature analysis.**

Template Matching

In many ways, **template matching** is the most straightforward and intuitively appealing type of model. We store mental copies of environmental stimuli in our memory; pattern recognition then proceeds by matching up the external stimuli with these stored mental copies called templates. This model postulates something like police fingerprint or DNA files, where a suspect's fingerprints or DNA are checked with a computer file of other prints or DNA until a match is recognized. Another example of a template-matching system is the Universal Product Code (black and white lines) symbol on consumer products scanned by retailer checkout registers. In these cases, the stored template is an *exact* match with the stimulus.

In spite of the practicality of such a system for forensic identification and grocery checkout, template matching fails as a model of human pattern recognition. For one reason, we would need an enormously large number of templates to match up with every possible stimulus, including all the possible variations on a basic theme. Figure 5.2 shows several possible variations of even a trivially simple stimulus like the letter *X*. An *X* that was slightly larger, smaller, tilted, elongated, flattened, or stylized would not match one's stored template of an *X*. Even modifying the theory to include some preprocessing operations to reduce, enlarge, or rotate the retinal image before comparing it to the stored template cannot adequately deal with the variety of stimuli that are still recognized as members of the same class. For example, how do we recognize as members of the class "dog" such breeds as German shepherds, chihuahuas, fox terriers, collies, and any other number of canines, while at the same time recognizing that physically similar wolves, coyotes, and cats belong to other categories?

Frequently it is very small features that distinguish the different categories, while much grosser physical differences occur across members of the same category. For example, only a tiny mark differentiates an *O* from a *Q*, while a cursive *Q* (*Q*), though also a *Q*, looks much less like a *Q* than an *O* does.

Moreover, sometimes we recognize an instance of a category even when we have never seen that particular stimulus before; for example, the neighbor's mutt is still recognized as a dog even if we've never seen that particular type of dog before. Clearly, some more abstract type of model than template matching is required to account for pattern recognition.

Prototypes

The **prototype** model of pattern recognition says that what is stored is not an exact copy of each stimulus, but rather an abstracted general instance. This prototype represents no actual object or exemplar in that class, but contains key features present in all or most instances. The pattern-recognition process recognizes a match if enough of the properties of the stimulus match the properties of the prototype. Memory about particular instances of subclasses may be stored as the prototype plus information about variations and special features; this is a more parsimonious and economical system than storing separate templates for each example.

A prototype theory has intuitive appeal and support in that we often seem to have truly general ideas about what a dog, a criminal, or a party is like, without necessarily storing information about any particular instance. Still, defining exactly what is and is not contained in the prototype is difficult, although schema theory (see Chapter 8) may offer some insights.

Feature Analysis

The third class of theories of pattern recognition is **feature analysis,** or feature detection. In this case, the input is analyzed into specific attributes called features. After such analysis, the resultant list of features is examined for a possible match to the concept, which is identified by that particular list of features.

FIGURE 5.2   Examples of stimuli all recognized as "X."

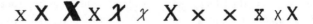

Such a model has both intuitive and experimental support. Many concepts and classes of stimuli are defined, at least in part, by distinctive features. For example, a break in a certain place in the circle distinguishes a *C* from an *O,* vibration in the throat differentiates the */s/* and the */z/* sounds, and such features as warm-bloodedness and the presence of feathers distinguish birds from reptiles. Because features may be combined in so many possible ways, feature-analysis models get around the problem of the template-matching model having to store such a large number of templates. Although feature-analysis models are sometimes criticized for not clearly specifying exactly what a feature is and how they are organized and structured, there are obviously many possibilities for combination. Furthermore, features have the advantage of greater specificity than prototypes.

There is also evidence from physiological studies to support feature analysis, going back to the pioneering studies of single-cell recording of neurons in the eye and visual cortex of cats and monkeys (Hubel & Wiesel, 1962, 1968). Cells at various places in the visual pathways and in several layers of the visual cortex in the occipital lobe of the brain fire in response to very specific types of stimuli that are well characterized by features. One cell might fire in response to a vertical line, another only to a moving vertical line, and another to a moving small, dark, round object. Certain combinations of features are the triggering stimuli for certain neurons to fire. The brain's analysis of the firing patterns of all these neurons then recognizes the object.

Whatever emerges as an eventual definitive model of pattern recognition must somehow incorporate both holistic top-down principles, as well as very fine-tuned bottom-up analytical processes like feature analysis.

SPEECH PERCEPTION

Now that we have examined the basic problem of pattern recognition, we turn in more detail to one of the most important but also most complex problems in pattern recognition: how we understand speech. Before beginning, we must first have a little background knowledge of the nature of speech sounds. Then we will examine how these sounds are perceived. Finally, we will examine the rules specifying how speech sounds are to be combined and the role of cues like intonation and stress in the speech-perception process.

Phonemes

On an intuitive level any spoken word or sentence may be analyzed into a chain of discrete sounds called **phonemes,** the smallest acoustic units of language that can make a meaningful psychological difference in that language. For example, the word "bit" is made up of three phonemes. By substituting the first phoneme */p/* for */b/,* the meaning of the resulting sequence of three phonemes is changed; "bit" becomes "pit." (*Note:* Letters between slashes represent the phonemes, not the written letters.) Incidentally, there is not always exactly one phoneme in the pronunciation for each letter in the spelling. For example, the word **date** only has three phonemes, and the sounds spelled **th** or **sh** in English typically are in fact only one phoneme each. It is the phonemes, not the letters, that we must consider in examining speech perception. Every language uses a subset of the over 200 possible phonemes. Most dialects of English use between 40 and 46 phonemes, although other languages range from as few as 12 to as many as 140 phonemes.

Although you can identify the sequence of phonemes in any sample of coherent speech, there is, perhaps surprisingly, no machine that can do this nearly so well. This is because the same phoneme is not always perceived for a given sequence of acoustic sounds. For example, the physical sound is not identical for every sound we understand as the phoneme /b/. If such were the case, it would be a relatively simple matter for the brain to perceive the sound and record the information, which it would then immediately identify as the particular phoneme /b/, perhaps using a template-matching model. A sequence of sounds like this could thus be identified and eventually be put together into words.

There are several reasons why speech perception cannot possibly occur in this way, however. One reason is that the acoustic speech stimulus changes depending on the pitch, intensity, and voice quality of the speaker. A 4-year-old girl, a gravelly voiced old man, and an operatic soprano are not emitting the same physical stimulus for the sound that anyone hearing it interprets as the phoneme /t/. For that matter, no single person says any given sound exactly the same way every time he or she says it.

Similarly, we can usually understand different dialects quite readily even though the actual sequence of phonemes may be quite different. For example, in standard American English the word "water" is pronounced [WAH-der], whereas in standard British English it is more like [WAU-tuh]. Even with three out of the four phonemes different, these sounds are still clearly identifiable by most people on either side of the Atlantic as the word "water," especially if it occurs in an appropriate meaningful context.

Although computer scientists have had great difficulty programming a machine to reliably analyze and interpret a wide range of phonemes from real speech, human listeners can do so quickly and easily. Spoken speech can be followed as fast as 400 words per minute, about 30 phonemes per second. This is quicker than the fastest rate that we can pick out individual sounds in any other sequence of sounds; thirty separate sounds per second of most anything except natural language is perceived only as white noise, like a buzz or static on the radio.

Other evidence also indicates that the sequence of phonemes heard in a word or syllable is not a succession of physically separate sounds. Single phonemes can be spliced from spoken speech by cutting a tape where the boundaries between the phonemes appear to be. Such detached phonemes are only identified about 80 percent as accurately as the same phonemes in either normal spoken language or in a group of phonemes that are pronounceable but do not make an identifiable word (*bup, jiz*). This suggests that part of how we identify the phoneme /p/ comes not only from the part of sound clearly identified as the phoneme /p/, but also from the surrounding vowels and especially from the transitions between consonants and vowels.

Another series of speech-splicing experiments produced even more surprising and compelling evidence. Take the syllable /pee/ and cut the tape into parts containing the /p/ and that containing the /ee/. If the /p/ part of the tape is then spliced to a recording of the vowel /oo/, the resulting string is understood as /poo/. So far, so good. However, if the same cutting /p/ from /pee/ is spliced to /ah/, the resulting syllable is consistently heard as /kah/ (Schatz, 1954). Even more surprising are results indicating that nothing may be perceived as something! For example, the word *slit* was recorded and then 75 milliseconds of time, less than a tenth of a second, spliced in between the /s/ and the /l/ phoneme. The resulting word perceived was *split,* that is, the pause was heard as /p/ (Liberman, Harris, Eimas, Lisker, & Bastian, 1961)! Normally, however, cutting recorded speech into pieces and splicing the phonemes back together in a different but meaningful order does not produce intelligible speech but only gibberish or, at best, misperceived phonemes such as the *split*-for-*slit* example above.

One often overlooked way that spoken language is more complex than written language is that there are no consistent physical boundaries between words or phrases comparable to the spaces between words or sentences in writing. Although there are sometimes clear pauses between phonemes, such pauses do not necessarily occur at word boundaries any more often than at other places in normal rapid speech. Consider listening to someone speaking a language you do not understand. Can you pick out the word boundaries?

In comprehension, there are segmentation ambiguities that occur precisely because such acoustic cues of spacing are absent; these ambiguities may be bases for humor. Consider the following symbol:

This is a "round tuit" that you give to someone who always says he or she will do such-and-such "as soon as I get a round tuit!" Other segmentation ambiguities are seen in young children's misperceptions of rote-memorized material such as song lyrics or Bible verses. For example, one little girl named her cross-eyed teddy bear "Gladly" after the animal they sang about in church: "Gladly, the cross-eyed bear."

Sometimes whole sets of sounds may be present in one language but absent in another. For example, French, Polish, and Portuguese have nasal vowels that do not occur in English, German, Spanish, or Italian. German, Dutch, Welsh, Polish, and some Scottish dialects of English have one or more consonants spoken far back in the throat (e.g., the last phoneme of Scottish-English *loch* or the German composer *Bach*). Arabic, Cockney English, and many Native American languages contain consonants that involve stopping or constricting the air stream very far back in the throat.

Phonological Rules

Besides the knowledge of phonemes themselves, we also have knowledge of the phonological rules of our language; these are the implicit instructions that tell how to combine phonemes into possible words in that particular language. Sometimes certain phonemes are permitted, but only in certain places and under certain conditions. For example, the final consonant in *sing* (which is not /n/ or /g/ or a combination of them but rather a totally separate sound) is very common in English at the end of a word but never occurs at the beginning; in fact, it is very difficult for an English-speaker to pronounce it at the beginning, though some languages allow it; for example, *Nguyen* is a common Vietnamese family name. Similarly, the sound spelled by *s* in *measure* and *ge* in *rouge* cannot begin a word in English, except possibly for loan words from other languages, though it very commonly begins French words. Moreover, English contains a constraint that the schwa (/ə/) sound, the vowel spelled by *e* in women, *ai* in curtain, *o* in lemon, and so forth, may occur only in unstressed syllables. Some languages (Arabic or French, for example) allow it in stressed syllables, and the resulting sequence, even if it contains only phonemes which occur in English, sounds very unlike English, simply because of the stressed schwa vowel. Still another example involves consonant blends. English allows only certain consonants to follow /s/. Thus /st/, /sk/, and /sp/ are allowed but /sd/, /sg/, and /sb/ are not, although the latter three are pronounceable and in fact occur frequently at the beginning of Italian words.

Suprasegmental Cues

Besides phonemes and phonological rules for combining them, there is a whole class of additional important sound cues in language, the **suprasegmental** (prosodic) factors such as **stress, pitch,** and **intonation.** The most important suprasegmental cue in English is **stress,** which often can make the meaningful difference between two words. For example, IN-sult and PER-mit are nouns, while in-SULT and per-MIT are verbs; the phonemes are the same, but each member of the pair stresses a different syllable. Differential stress in a sentence can also distinguish an adjective-noun combination and a proper name. Consider the spoken sentence, HE LIVES IN THE WHITE HOUSE. If *HOUSE* is heavily stressed (as nouns normally are in adjective-noun combinations), it may be the dwelling next door, while if *WHITE* is stressed, it is more likely 1600 Pennsylvania Avenue in Washington, DC, and "he" refers to the President of the United States.

Compared to many languages, English has a high degree of differential stress. Where these stresses occur is determined by some fairly regular, though highly complex, rules. This is a very difficult aspect of English for speakers of languages such as French, Turkish, or Japanese, where differential stress is much less marked. Similarly, it is a reason that makes song lyrics, which depend heavily on differential stress, difficult to translate from a heavily stressed language to a lightly stressed one, or vice versa. It also is one reason that an otherwise fluent speaker of a second language may appear to have an accent if, for example, a Parisian speaks English with the comparatively even stress of French.

In addition, any word may receive particularly heavy stress as a means of emphasizing it in some way. Such emphasis can radically alter the meaning of the sentence. Stressing different words implies different sorts of contrasts. For example, "Drive to the *park*" stresses the destination (not downtown!), while "*Drive* to the park" stresses the means of travel (don't walk!).

Another suprasegmental cue is **pitch,** or **tone.** Although in English and most other modern European languages it makes no difference within a given syllable what pitch is used, in many **tonal** languages such as Chinese, Vietnamese, and some Native American languages, pitch can distinguish one word from another! For example, in Mandarin Chinese there are four distinct tones, that is, four distinct pitch patterns with which a syllable may be spoken (flat, rising, falling-rising, and falling). The syllable "he" /hə/ can mean "to drink" (flat tone), "river" or "and" (rising tone), "box" (falling-rising tone), or "congratulations" (falling tone), depending on the pitch with which it is spoken.

Pitch is important in English, however, insofar as it combines with stress to produce characteristic **intonation** patterns, which are used to indicate whether an utterance is a statement, question, or exclamation. For example, statements in English typically have an intonation pattern of the highest pitch near the end of the sentence, but then falling at the very end. On the other hand, yes-no questions end with a rising intonation, with the highest pitch at the end. Intonation patterns carry such strong information that even a declarative sentence becomes a question if spoken in a certain way, such as speaking *This is a good job?* with rising intonation.

To fully appreciate the contributions of suprasegmental cues to the understanding of language, consider an example of how an appropriate intonation pattern can suggest meaning even when the phonemes are incorrect. If Box 5.5 is read as what it appears to be, that is, a list of unrelated words, it will make no sense. However, if read, or better, sung, with a certain intonation pattern, it is recognized as three familiar songs.

Any adequate theory of spoken language comprehension will have to explain how we perceive phonemes and suprasegmental cues in speech. Speech perception has long been one of the most complicated puzzles facing psychologists (Mattingly & Studdert-Kennedy, 1990; Pisoni, 1978). It has also proven to be the most difficult task to program computers to perform. Although there has at last been some significant progress in recent years, programming computers to understand speech has failed to bring them even close to the ability of a two- or three-year-old child!

■ **Box 5.5** ■

Graze Seem Use Sick

"Omen Do Wrench"
Oak if meow womb
Were dew buff hello roman
Do tyranny ankle hope lay,
Wears hell dumb absurd
Add as courage inward
And does geyser knock loud he halt hay.

"Gin Gulp Else"
Gin gulp else, gin gulp else,
Gin gulp wall dew hay,
Owe it phone add hiss tour eye
Done new runner soap punks lay.

"Hiss Slanders Yule Lamb"
Hiss slanders Yule lamb,
Hiss slanders mile lamb,
Thumb gal leaf horn yeah
Tooth anew yore guile inn.
Farm thumb rid wooed far wrist,
Tutor gulls dream what terse,
Hiss slanders mate fur ruin mean.

The fact that these chains of unrelated words can sound like meaningful song lyrics, even when the phonemes are not quite "correct," suggests the powerful contribution of suprasegmental cues, specifically intonation, in speech perception.

As if comprehending speech spoken forwards were not complex enough, some have wondered about the impact of speech spoken backward, especially as allegedly placed in rock music recordings! (See Box 5.6.)

Now that we have completed our look at attention and pattern recognition, those processes that select information in sensory memory for further processing, we turn to working memory, where some further processing occurs.

■ Box 5.6 ■

── Backward Messages in Rock Music: Do They Affect Us? ──

In spite of the complexity of normal speech perception, sometimes we hear the claim that we may also be adversely affected by rock music containing embedded messages recorded backwards. Although no one claims such messages can be consciously perceived easily when played forward, concern has been expressed that there may be some unconscious effect unbeknownst to the listener. Some have been concerned that such messages may be satanic and have at times introduced legislation in various places calling for warning labels about such messages to appear on CD inserts.

In response to a request by a radio announcer for information about this phenomenon, Canadian psychologists John Vokey and Don Read of the University of Lethbridge conducted a series of studies testing the effects of such messages (Vokey & Read, 1985). They first noted that the **presence** of embedded messages does not necessarily imply any **effect** of such messages on the listener. Evidence presented by concerned members of the public is usually highly anecdotal and often debatable but nearly always speaks to the presence question, not the effects question. Too often a simple anecdotal demonstration of a message's existence is assumed to demonstrate its effectiveness as well, a connection that Vokey and Read point out as completely unwarranted.

These psychologists conducted a careful series of studies on the effects of such messages, even assuming for the moment that they exist (an assumption not at all established, but we'll leave that for now). When verbal messages were played backwards, listeners showed no understanding of the meaning; identifying the sex of the speaker was about all they could perceive. Next, they tested for unconscious effects by giving a spelling test where some of the words were homophones (read, reed). A biasing context sentence (a saxophone is a reed instrument) was played backwards but subjects were no more likely than a control group to write "reed" instead of "read." When backward messages were played and participants merely asked to assign the statement to one of the categories Christian, satanic, pornographic, or advertising, based on its content, they could not do so at greater than chance level. The only time that people ever perceived and reported anything at greater than chance level was when the experimenter picked out words in advance and asked people to listen for them. Only under conditions of such strong suggestibility could participants perceive anything from the backward messages.

Vokey and Read's studies clearly demonstrate that, even if backward messages do exist in rock music, it is highly unlikely they could be having any effect on the hearers. This conclusion is all the more striking considering that, in their studies there was no competing forward message like the music in real CDs. In at least a couple of cases, proposed record-labeling legislation was withdrawn based on results of Vokey and Read's research. Maybe some people in the "real world" do believe that cognitive psychology has something important to say!

After some material has been selected for further processing, it comes to the memory store that has been variously called "short-term memory," "short-term store," "working memory," "immediate memory," "active memory," or "primary memory." Each of these labels highlights a different aspect of this limited-capacity memory store. It contains all that we are thinking about and working on right now; hence the term *working memory*. In this sense, it is our current consciousness, where information is held just enough to make a decision about further processing, especially for encoding into long-term memory. All of the information that we are thinking about right now includes both information activated from long-term memory and new stimulus information entering through our senses to sensory memory; hence the term *active memory*.

Material in working memory does not stay in this state of activation very long unless it is continually being used in some way; hence the term *short-term memory* (or *store*), which emphasizes this transient character. If material is actively attended to, rehearsed, or otherwise thought about, it can remain in working memory indefinitely. For example, if you look up a number in the phone book and hold it in your working memory by repeating it to yourself while you walk across the room to dial the phone, you can hold the numbers there.

Working memory has three major components (Baddeley, 1990, 1992; Gathercole & Baddeley, 1993). The **central executive** regulates information flow through working memory and oversees storage and retrieval of information from long-term memory. As the seat of conscious processing, it coordinates attentional resource allocation. The **phonological loop** (sometimes called the "articulatory loop") stores material in a short-lived verbal code and is thus very important in the reading process (see Chapter 7). The phonological loop need not be acoustic, however; in the case of deaf signers, there is evidence that this loop is based on manual handshape instead of speech (Wilson & Emmorey, 1997, 1998). The **visuo-spatial sketchpad** processes and stores visual and spatial information, including material encoded as visual imagery (Logie, 1995). These components work together under the supervision of the central executive, but the phonological loop and the visuo-spatial sketchpad operate largely independently of each other.

In our discussion that follows, we examine working memory through looking at several of its most salient characteristics. The three components of working memory are all involved in these operations.

Limited Capacity and Rapid Decay

One of the most important aspects of working memory is its **limited capacity.** There is only so much that we can think about at one time. Measuring exactly what this amount is, however, is more difficult than you might expect. As we have already seen, there are clear attentional limits on what we can process. George Miller (1956) showed many years ago that the so-called memory span was between 5 and 9 numbers in a digit-span task ("the magical number 7 plus or minus 2"). This means that, when you hear a list of numbers read and immediately afterward must repeat them, you can do so effectively with about seven digits. It is no coincidence that local phone numbers in much of the world are exactly seven digits long; anything more would be much more difficult to remember without encoding into long-term memory.

The metaphor of a series of slots (called the **rehearsal buffer**) in working memory has been useful. As the central executive processes new incoming material and/or old material retrieved from long-term memory, these slots are filled one-by-one until there is no remaining space in the rehearsal buffer. Once this happens, in order for new material to be added to working memory, something currently there must be bumped out of immediate consciousness, either through forgetting or encoding and transfer to long-term memory. This slot metaphor reflects the intuitive feeling we often have that our mind is so full that there is no room for even one more piece of information without something already there being pushed out.

If information is not attended to or processed in some way, it decays from working memory in 15 to 30 seconds, as first demonstrated by Brown (1958) and Peterson and Peterson (1959), in their landmark working memory studies. Participants saw a consonant trigram, such as NBX, followed by a retention interval of between 3 and 18 seconds, after which they were to recall the letters. While this task is trivially easy if rehearsal is allowed during this interval, these participants spent the retention interval counting backwards by threes from a given three-digit number. This task was intended to prevent rehearsal of the letters, thus measuring the curve of "pure decay" in working memory. Results showed that, while recall was about 80 percent correct at a 3-second delay, the decay function of material in working memory fell very sharply over time. Although it might at first sound unfortunate, this rapid-decay property is actually very adaptive; it keeps our mind from becoming cluttered with unnecessary information we have already finished using.

Although Miller's so-called magical number of 7 plus or minus 2 bits of information has been demonstrated as the memory span for a wide variety of materials, there is a tremendous amount of variation of what can be put into each of those seven bits. For example, we can hold seven numbers in our working memory, but also seven words, seven pictures, or sometimes even seven sentences. In fact, the bits may be made considerably larger through the processes of **chunking,** by which we combine pieces of information together in a form which takes up less space in working memory. For example, you might chunk the words *rabbit, hat,* and *hamburger* from three bits into one by encoding them as one coherent image of a rabbit wearing a baseball cap and chomping on a Big Mac. Similarly, you might chunk the 19 letters CNNUSAUNAIDSOPECSOB into the six units CNN, USA, UN, AIDS, OPEC, and SOB, which represent six meaningful concepts. The issue of chunking is examined further in the discussion of mnemonics in Chapter 6.

Rehearsal

Another important process that occurs in working memory is **rehearsal,** the temporary activation or recycling of information by the phonological loop. Rehearsal may be either **maintenance** or **elaborative. Maintenance rehearsal** merely holds information in working memory long enough for it to be acted upon in some way. For instance, when you look up a phone number, it may serve your needs adequately to repeat it over to yourself while you dial the phone; you make no effort to encode it into long-term memory. Often in such cases a brief maintenance in working memory is all that is required.

Maintenance rehearsal has been used to explain the **primacy** effect of the so-called **serial position** curve (Figure 5.3), that is, relatively good memory for the first few items in a list. Early items in the list have received more rehearsal, both because there has been more time to practice them and because when they were presented there was less information competing for the limited resources available for

FIGURE 5.3 Serial position curve.

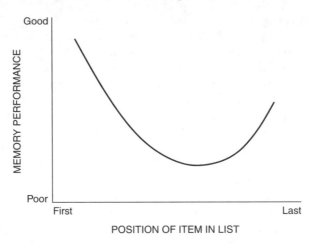

rehearsal. The **recency** part of the serial position curve (relatively good memory for the last few items in the list) is explained by the fact that the last items are still in working memory because they have not yet had time to decay. Very often, studies examining long-term memory have a brief interfering task (e.g., counting backwards by threes) immediately after presentation of the to-be-remembered material and before the response task. The purpose of the counting is to tie up enough attentional resources to ensure that none of the material remains in working memory and thus that anything retained must have been encoded into long-term memory and been retrieved from there during recall.

In contrast to maintenance rehearsal, **elaborative rehearsal** encodes and transfers information to long-term memory. Rather than merely repeat the to-be-remembered information, elaborative rehearsal relates it to other concepts already in long-term memory and develops new associations among those concepts. An example would be learning the concept of reinforcement by relating it to concepts already learned (e.g., response, contingency, operant conditioning, punishment, behavior) and by generating examples of its application, such as animal training or child-rearing. Elaborative rehearsal is very helpful in learning class material for exams. It is also helpful for your teachers, as illustrated in Box 5.7, which discusses learning the names of students in a class.

There is another way to think of rehearsal, as an ongoing review of events in our lives. Whenever we think about something that has happened to us, we are rehearsing that event. If the event was interesting, the rehearsal will be frequent and spread over time. Each time we rehearse the event, we refresh, or reinstate, the memory for that event. Because the rehearsal is spread over time, that rehearsal should slow the rate of forgetting for that event. Such slowing of forgetting through frequent rehearsal has been demonstrated in studies of memory for naturally occurring events (Thompson, 1982). The inability to do such rehearsal of events in one's life before the age of three or four may be a major reason why most adults have no reliable memories of events in their lives occurring before that age (Nelson, 1993).

■ Box 5.7 ■

Learning Names of Students in a Class

Every semester a teacher is faced with the task of learning the names of the new students. Employing maintenance and elaborative rehearsal and other techniques from memory research, I (RJH) am now able to learn the names of almost all the students in my classes (up to 50 or so per class) during the first three or four class meetings. Below are some "secrets" of the trade:

1. Collect information on each student the first day (address, phone, e-mail, major, year in school, interests, hometown, career goals, background experience relevant to that course).

2. Rehearse names frequently, at least once before and after each class. This ensures familiarity with the names and starts associating the names with the other information, which serves to elaborate the memory network around that name.

3. Call the roll the first few classes until names are learned. Go through slowly to concentrate on associating the name and the face.

4. During the first few classes, maintain good eye contact and think about making the faces familiar. Once the faces and the names are both familiar independently, associating the two is much easier. Take advantage of individual contacts such as students talking to you individually after class and watch the names as students hand in papers.

5. Elaborate the concept of each student by associating the name or face with information collected the first day or actions observed in class.

   a. Notice the place where the student generally sits in the room.

   b. Notice the general physical appearance, especially very salient physical characteristics or those that strongly remind you of someone else.

   c. Take note of unusual names or cases where a student uses a middle name or nickname. Such information can serve to distinguish that student from others.

   d. Remember comments made in class, especially insofar as they relate to information given on the first day; for example, mentioning a young child in class discussion and writing "learning how to toilet train a child" as an interest.

   e. Look for similarities of the students to people you know; try to remember possible prior contacts with the student. ("I remember seeing her in the animal lab last semester.")

   f. Use mnemonic techniques to associate the face with the name or other information, for example, "Lefty Hefty" for a southpaw named John Hefty.

   g. Once a network of information about the student is learned, in addition to observing a couple of class periods, it is fairly easy to make the connection between the names and the faces.

Encoding

Although material in working memory has not been as extensively processed as has most encoded material in long-term memory, it has been partially analyzed and interpreted. Acoustic or phonetic encoding is very common in working memory (involving the phonological loop), and for a long time psychologists thought that was the only (or at least the predominant) method of encoding. While we now know this is not completely true, acoustic encoding is nonetheless a very important form of memory representation in working memory. Evidence of its importance is documented by studies that show, for example, that the similar-sounding letters *C* and *T* are more likely to be confused in working memory than the similar-appearing *C* and *O,* even when the letters are presented visually (Conrad, 1964; Wickelgren, 1965). Such results suggest that people recode the visual symbols to acoustic representations.

In spite of the great importance of acoustic encoding, there is ample evidence of visual and semantic encoding in working memory as well. For example, the Stroop effect (see Box 5.3) shows that it is difficult *not* to encode the meaning of the color words in working memory, even when we consciously try to ignore that information as totally irrelevant to the task of naming the colors. Another example of semantic encoding in working memory is shown in the way we semantically cluster words in a free-recall task; for example, remembering all the animal words together, the clothing words together, and the food words together, when animal, clothing, and food words had been mixed together in the acquisition list.

Working memory is important in ways far beyond the instances of simple learning and memory we have discussed so far. Box 5.8 presents an extended application of working memory to musical performance.

Forgetting

The explanations offered for forgetting from working memory typically identify two general processes. On the one hand, forgetting is said to occur due to the **decay** of the memory over time, much as a radioactive isotope decays over its half life. This explanation uses the notion of memory strength. In this view, a strong memory is more likely to be retrieved than a weak memory. Thus, forgetting occurs as a result of the weakening of a memory over time. This type of explanation would be very appealing if we were to find that the underlying physiological correlate of working memory is some sort of transient change whereby a neuron or set of neurons is temporarily altered in some way and then takes some time to restore to its initial state. However, the picture of brain involvement in working memory is much more complex. Many different areas, both cortical and subcortical, are involved in various aspects of working memory processing (Desimone, 1992; Schacter, 1996; Shimura, 1995; Smith & Jonides, 1997).

The other class of explanations for forgetting uses the notion of **interference.** Material is forgotten because other material that is similar in some way interfered by replacing or distorting it. Interference may be **retroactive,** which means it occurs after the original learning. In **proactive** interference, the interfering material comes first and hinders the learning of something else later. There is much experimental evidence that both types of interference occur.

There is probably some truth to both the decay and interference explanations. While interference can be demonstrated fairly easily, it is difficult in principle to design an experiment to once and for all competitively test the two predictions. Any test of decay necessarily involves allowing time for the decay to occur. However, it is difficult to be sure that no interfering activity is occurring during that time. No matter what you ask someone to think about, there is no assurance that whatever is going through his or her mind is not in some way interfering with the material to be tested.

Working Memory and Musical Sight-Reading

Sight-reading is the act of reading music and immediately performing it. Like oral reading, this skill makes heavy use of working memory, since the notes of music must be held in working memory for a few seconds before they are played on the piano (or on the flute, or sung, or whatever). This is a very different use of memory from that of the musician who memorizes a whole piece and performs from rote memory. Professional pianists are generally either excellent sight readers or excellent memorizers, but seldom highly skilled at both (Wolf, 1976). Either technique could lead to excellent performance, but for entirely different reasons: Either the working or long-term memory store (but not both) is highly developed.

Several factors are involved in sight-reading ability. During sight-reading the information on the written music is chunked into units in working memory. The skilled musician can draw on knowledge of music theory as well as performance experience to chunk those visual stimuli into larger and more useful units; for example, coding all the notes in both clefs for a whole measure as one chunk, whereas the less accomplished musician might have to encode every note, every key signature, and every tempo indicator as a separate chunk.

This offers a scientific argument for the importance of studying music theory, at least for its usefulness in sight-reading. Musicians report that there were vast differences in difficulty of sight-reading different types of music. For example, baroque chamber music is quite easy, because there is so much similarity in the different parts of a given piece. The constraints on composition at that time were so great that the predictability is much greater than, say, atonal twentieth-century music, which follows many fewer "rules." Thus, the latter is far more difficult to sight-read because the chunks of information in working memory must be much smaller. There is also a lot less redundancy in the modern music.

Wolf illustrates this point with a compelling anecdote about the discovery of a misprinted note in a Brahms capriccio (opus 76, no. 2). A student, upon arriving at a certain C# major chord, played a G instead of the G# that would normally occur in a C# major triad. When her startled teacher stopped her, the student replied that that was what was written on the page. In later checking other editions of the piece, they all had the same "misprint," assuming Brahms must have really meant a G# rather than a G in that C# major chord. Apparently few, if indeed anyone, had ever caught his error before, since everyone had apparently been playing the chord with the predictable G# instead of the written G-natural. This suggests that in sight-reading, we don't really read everything, but rather read some of the input and construct the rest drawing on knowledge from long-term memory (see Chapter 6).

Memory Scanning

Many operations may be performed in working memory, including those where we are not consciously aware of all the subprocesses. Such operations were nicely illustrated in a series of experiments by Saul Sternberg (1966, 1975). Sternberg decided to study working memory by using reaction time instead of the more traditional memory measures. The time measured was then used to infer the nonobservable processes that must have occurred.

The task chosen by Sternberg was a very simple one. Participants learned some materials arbitrarily included in a set to be learned, for example, the numbers 74926.

After this *positive set* had been learned, participants were presented with another item and asked to indicate yes or no to show whether or not the new item was in the positive set. With practice, they could generally do many trials of this task quite rapidly with an error rate under 5 percent. Using digits as stimuli, Sternberg varied the size of the positive set and found that the mean reaction time (RT) increased linearly with set size, as if each additional item that must be searched added a constant amount of extra time (38 milliseconds, to be exact) to scan in working memory.

Furthermore, the slope (rate of increase) was the same for positive ("yes") and negative ("no") responses. This is somewhat counterintuitive, because negative responses require searching the entire set, to check all members before being sure there is no match. With the positive responses, however, one ought to be able to stop scanning, on the average, halfway through the list (the position of the test digit was systematically varied across all positions). One should not need to keep searching after a match has been found, yet that appears to be exactly what happened in this task. Based on these data, Sternberg posited a **serial exhaustive search** model, which says that we check each member of the positive set in turn through *the entire set,* even if we have already found a match. This speed of search is very rapid, at a rate of 25 to 30 items per second and is thus not open to introspection.

Sternberg has replicated this basic finding of equal slopes for positive and negative responses with a wide variety of stimuli (letters, words, shapes, colors, numerals), though the slopes vary depending on the complexity of the stimulus. Other researchers have confirmed his basic findings but with some qualifications. It may be that people use different search models in different situations. For a discussion of alternative models and interpretations, see Glass (1984).

Although this research may appear to have no apparent application in the real world, it has had many applications probably not initially envisioned by Sternberg. For example, some processing deficits in special populations may be more precisely identified. Schizophrenics, alcoholics, and those high on marijuana show higher y-intercepts but the same slopes as normal people. This shows that the memory deficit from the drug or pathology is due to increased encoding or response time but not increased search time. On the other hand, some elderly and brain-damaged retarded people show steeper slopes, indicating a longer search time. This ability to identify memory deficits more precisely than a general memory deficit vastly improves diagnosis of problems. Tasks like Sternberg's are increasingly being tested and incorporated into intelligence testing as well (e.g., E. Hunt, 1983).

Working Memory and Language Comprehension

One active area of recent research on working memory has focused on its role in language comprehension. For example, the phonological loop maintains acoustic information by subvocalization and converts visually presented information to a phonological code (Baddeley, 1992). Language stimuli, even if irrelevant to the task at hand, seem to interfere with its operation. The phonological loop seems to be particularly important in the acquisition of vocabulary in one's first or second language, especially in the processing of unfamiliar sound patterns of novel speech input (Badeley, Gathercole, & Papagno, 1998).

Carpenter and Just and their colleagues argue that individual differences in working memory capacity directly affect reading ability. Specifically, the effect is on the processing of syntax (Carpenter & Just, 1989; Just & Carpenter, 1992; King &

Just, 1991). For example, readers with larger working memory capacities maintained both interpretations of a syntactically ambiguous garden-path sentence briefly in memory, while readers with smaller working memory capacities maintained only the most likely interpretation (MacDonald, Just, & Carpenter, 1992). If one hears a sentence beginning "The soldiers warned about the dangers . . .", "soldiers" might be

■ Box 5.9 ■

Learning Disabilities

Learning disabilities (LD) stem from a problem with the nervous system and affects the way that as many as 5 percent to 10 percent of children, as well as some adults, perceive different stimuli. People with LD are not mentally retarded or emotionally disturbed. They have normal or above average intelligence, a fact which actually helps them to find ways to compensate for their disabilities. Perceptual problems develop by early childhood but may remain undiagnosed until adulthood. Sometimes a diagnosis of LD can answer many questions for an adult or teen who has long been searching for an explanation for their difficulties in processing information brought into their senses inaccurately.

Learning disabilities are diagnosed through extensive evaluation by an appropriate professional who sees large discrepancies between a person's intelligence and normal test performance and behavior. Some symptoms of LD include short attention span, restlessness, and distractability; it is difficult to ignore irrelevant sounds and visual stimuli. Sometimes those with LD also show impulsivity and poor motor coordination, as well as perseveration—tending to do or say things over and over. Their handwriting, spelling, and copying abilities are often poor. Individuals with LD may have much more trouble expressing themselves in writing than in speaking, although they often misunderstand what someone else says.

Individuals with LD may show problems organizing time and pacing their performance. They may show decrements in depth perception or spacing pieces of an assignment on a page. Their thoughts may appear to wander and they may experience difficulty sequencing ideas or even smaller sequences (e.g., hearing, seeing, or writing "aminal" for "animal" or "frist" for "first"). They may also show difficulty in recall.

Some people with LD appear moody or quick-tempered, perhaps due to frustration stemming from the cognitive disabilities. They may misread nonverbal cues like facial expressions or gestures and may have difficulty or discomfort looking others directly in the eyes while talking. In terms of speed of work, they may be either very slow but very accurate or very fast with many errors and omitted items.

Many persons with LD learn to cope by devising compensatory strategies and creative new techniques for study and problem solving. However, there is also educational support, counseling, and medication available. Schools and colleges offer accommodations in test taking and study, such as extra time on exams in a quiet room and textbooks on audio tape. There are also some programs moving toward using more personalization and a greater variety of testing methods in schools, allowing children to demonstrate their own strengths (Black, 1994). Some excellent resources are available for families with children with LD, such as Smith (1991) and Fisher and Cummings (1990), the latter of which is on a fifth-grade reading level and designed for parents and children to learn together about learning disabilities. (This box co-authored by Karen S. Looney.)

the subject of "warned," or the whole phrase might be a complex subject of the sentence, that is, "The soldiers (who were) warned . . ." Readers with larger working memory capacities might be able to keep both interpretations activated until further words disambiguated the two meanings.

CONCLUSION

We have now completed our examination of the perceptual and working memory aspects of information processing. In the next chapter we shall turn to long-term memory, and the encoding and retrieval processes involved with it.

Even though long-term memory is probably the sort of memory that you primarily think of when someone talks about remembering, it is not the only important component of information processing. Material must pass through sensory memory and working memory, and attentional and pattern recognition processes must occur, before material is ever encoded in long-term memory, much less retrieved from there. If it survives all these hurdles, it may enter more permanent memory. For a discussion of a common problem whereby some of these hurdles are more difficult than for most people, see Box 5.9 on page 161.

Conceptualizing working memory and long-term memory as qualitatively separate memory stores, as represented in Figure 5.1 and Atkinson and Shiffrin (1968), is not the only possible framework for conceptualizing memory, however. After we have examined long-term memory in the next chapter, we shall return to the examination of some alternative theoretical frameworks.

SUGGESTED READINGS

The topics in this chapter are covered in more detail in several excellent cognitive psychology texts. Particularly recommended are Ashcraft (1994), Best (1999), Payne and Wenger (1998), Solso (1998), and Sternberg (1999). For a book with a somewhat more applied approach, see Galotti (1999). For an overview of cognitive psychology directed at the nonpsychologist cognitive scientist, see Barsalou (1992); Kosslyn and Koenig (1995) present a reasonably accessible introduction to cognitive neuroscience. Pinker (1997) offers a highly readable introduction to cognitive science and the brain in a fact-filled yet extremely engaging style. The most extensive discussion of working memory, especially its relation to language and reading, is found in Gathercole and Baddeley (1993).

6 Long-Term Memory

In discussing working memory, we necessarily addressed aspects of long-term memory as well, especially in processes of encoding material for storage. In this chapter, however, we examine in depth this more permanent store of memory. We consider encoding and retrieval processes relating long-term to working memory, the structure of information in long-term memory, and processes for searching through that information structure. Later we will look at alternative conceptualizations of the whole information processing sytem. Finally, we will focus in more detail on two controversial applications of memory principles to societal problems, namely, eyewitness identification and the recovery of repressed memories in psychotherapy. These are but two of the most striking ways that memory can go wrong. In fact, there are many ways that memory can get us into trouble. See Box 6.1 for a list of the "seven sins" of memory.

In the examination of long-term (permanent) memory, the dichotomy of **episodic** versus **semantic** memory systems (Tulving, 1972, 1983, 1989) has been particularly useful. While **semantic** memory is all the general information that we have in our long-term memories, **episodic** memory is our storehouse of more personal memories associated with the particular time and place that we learned that information. For example, remembering that people frequently have cereal for breakfast is part of semantic memory. Remembering that you ate oatmeal for breakfast this morning while you crammed for your Abnormal Psychology exam is episodic memory. Remembering that Bismarck is the capital of North Dakota is semantic memory; remembering that you first learned this fact on a cold, snowy December day when your fifth-grade teacher made you stay after school and write "Bismarck is the capital of North Dakota" fifty times is episodic memory.

Episodic and semantic memories may be connected to each other. For example, one result of traveling is to accumulate episodic memories which build on previously learned semantic memories. For example, before ever visiting Brazil, you may know that Rio de Janeiro is a large coastal city in a beautiful setting where rugged mountains meet the Atlantic Ocean. Perhaps you have even heard of popular tourist spots there such as Copacabana Beach, the cable car up Mount Sugarloaf, and the Christ statue on Mount Corcovado. After a visit to Rio, however, your semantic memory is supplemented by episodic information of the wave that knocked you in the surf at Copacabana, the lunch with friends at the halfway stop on Sugarloaf, and the cold wind blowing at the top of Corcovado as you savored the magnificent view of Rio on an early spring afternoon.

Tulving (1972) argued that most memory research up to that time tested episodic memory, that is, specific information learned at a particular time, such as in a memory experiment ("Was this word on the list or wasn't it?"). Equally important,

The "Seven Sins" of Memory

Psychologist Daniel Schacter (1999) has nicely captured the essence of the fallibility of memory in a description of seven ways that memory can fail us:

1. **Transience.** This is the gradual forgetting over time. Older memories are less vivid than recent ones.
2. **Absent-mindedness.** Failure to fully attend during encoding often is a cause of memory failure. For example, we witness a car accident but do not pay attention to the car's color.
3. **Blocking.** This occurs when a memory is present but inaccessible, perhaps due to an inadequate or misleading cue, as when we fail to remember someone's name we know.
4. **Misattribution.** In this case the memory is present but is attributed to the incorrect source. For example, we remember we heard that Dan and Amy broke up but we forget who told us.
5. **Suggestibility.** Here incorrect information is unknowingly incorporated into the memory representation. Such information might be introduced, for example, by a leading question in the courtroom or the implanting of a false belief about an event in one's life.
6. **Bias.** In this case memory is distorted by one's prior knowledge that becomes mingled with the specific memory. For example, someone who believes members of a certain ethnic group are lazy or criminal will be more likely to interpret and remember ambiguous behaviors of a member of that group in a negative way.
7. **Persistence.** Here the problem is a memory that is highly intrusive or obsessive. For example, victims of trauma often relive the memories in unwelcome and frightening flashbacks, and depressed people continually think of the most negative interpretations of events.

Schacter reviews the psychological and neuroscience support for each type of memory failure. In this chapter we shall see examples of each of these as we examine memory.

Tulving said, was semantic memory, all the knowledge that we have and can retrieve at will, even though we may not remember exactly when and where we learned it. Starting in the 1970s, cognitive psychologists increasingly turned to studying semantic memory. Although episodic memory is also still widely researched, it is studied in some very different ways than it had been before 1972.

There is neuropsychological evidence supporting the episodic-semantic distinction. For example, Schacter (1996) reported case studies of amnesia where a person loses either episodic or semantic memory but not the other. For example, one man suffered extensive damage to his frontal and temporal lobes and left hippocampus in a motorcycle accident. Afterwards he could not recall any past events from his life but still retained extensive semantic memory. On the other hand, another patient, who had encephalitis, remembered specific events from her life but little general information.

THE QUESTION OF REPRESENTATION

One of the central issues in the study of long-term memory is **representation;** that is, what is the form of information in memory? Although this very basic question was long debated by philosophers before the emergence of scientific psychology, we concentrate here on some forms of representation that have been proposed and studied in recent years. While the question of representation involves the development of some highly complex theoretical models, we shall also see that the form of information encoded in memory is a highly practical issue.

The form of information stored in long-term memory may be either **analogue** or **analytic** (abstract) in nature. An **analogue** representation physically resembles what it represents in some important way. The similarities may be very extensive and detailed or may be limited to only one or two superficial similarities. One example of an analogue representation is a map, which physically resembles the territory it represents in the relative locations of places, while remaining very different in other ways, such as size, color, and amount of detail. Other examples of analogue representations include physical models, graphs, drawings, and thermometers.

In contrast to analogue representations are **analytic** representations, which are totally abstract and arbitrary and bear no physical resemblance to their referent. The most complex and pervasive analytic representational system is language, which is entirely analytic, with the trivial exception of onomatopoeic words like "meow" and "ding dong." A dog has no more intrinsic relation to the word "dog," "chien," "perro," or "Hund" than to "truck" or "idea." Other examples of analytic codes include mathematics, formal logic, musical notation, computer languages, and propositions. Language will be discussed in more detail in the next chapter and will not be further considered here. Rather, we turn now to examining one of the most important types of analogue mental representations, namely imagery.

Imagery

Imagery has been discussed by philosophers for centuries and was a major area of inquiry among the nineteenth-century German introspectionists (see Chapter 1), the earliest experimental psychologists. However, because of its mentalistic character, imagery fell out of favor during the behaviorist era, only to be rediscovered in the 1960s. It has been an active area of research ever since (see Barlow, Blakemore, & Weston-Smith, 1990; Finke, 1989; Kosslyn, 1994; Logie & Denis, 1991; Marschark, Richman, Yuille, & Hunt, 1987; Shepard, 1984).

Although imagery is most often discussed in terms of visual examples, it is not necessarily a visual phenomenon. Imagery, in fact, occurs in all sensory modalities. **Auditory** imagery is clearly illustrated by one's mental response to the request "think of the sound a cow makes" or "think of the first few notes of Beethoven's *Fifth Symphony*." In fact, a melody can be a powerful memory cue (Wallace, 1994; Wallace & Rubin, 1991), which is why advertising jingles are so effective. **Olfactory** imagery occurs when we image the smell of a turkey cooking in the oven; this may be followed by **gustatory** (taste) imagery imagining how it would subsequently taste (Schab & Crowder, 1995). When we imagine how velvet would feel on the skin or imagine the touch of a loved one in a sexual encounter, we use **tactile** imagery. **Kinesthetic** imagery is involved in some forms of relaxation training, where people are taught to put their bodies in a relaxed state and become sensitive to kinesthetic feedback from muscles that may be tense or relaxed ("Imagine how your body feels as you breathe all the tension from your stomach to your lungs and then exhale it from your body").

Imagery is often discussed in terms of the metaphor "pictures in the head." Such a metaphor is useful in certain ways but may be misleading in others, even within the visual modality. Unlike pictures, imagery is very dynamic and constructive with a high degree of plasticity. We can image moving objects, changing events, and things and situations we have never actually seen or experienced. We use imagery to help understand vivid metaphors like "He is an octopus on a date" or "Her hair is brush fire" (Gibbs & Bogdonovitch, 1999). The mental imagery of our minds has a richer store of special effects than directors will ever create in their motion pictures.

Some sort of imagery code is almost certainly at the base of the earliest instances of memory in children. When an infant moves an arm to indicate "bye-bye" to an adult, the child's mind must contain some mental representation of an adult making such a motion to indicate a departure from the scene. Indeed, a child's conception of time must rely on imagery in conceptualizing the past and future, as well as to imagine hypothetical present events. Perhaps the earliest concrete evidence of this is the demonstration of the attainment of object permanence by an infant during the second six months of life. If a baby sees a toy covered up with a blanket and immediately removes the blanket to reach the toy, he or she must have had some mental representation, perhaps an image, of that toy after it had been covered. Otherwise, the child would have stopped looking for the toy or, indeed, doing any other behavior that reflected a memory of the missing toy. This is, in fact, the way that infants six months old or younger behave.

Imagery can be used in problem solving as a means of assessing and testing out possible solutions and restructuring a problem (see Chapter 9). This occurs in ill-defined real-world problems such as figuring out how to rearrange the furniture in your living room to increase the available seating. It is certainly easier to rearrange the furniture through visual imagery first before doing so in reality. Similarly, it is easier to decide what meal to prepare for a dinner party if you have visually imagined the appearance of the dish, and used the senses of taste and smell to imagine those properties.

Imagery may be useful in problem solving in ways beyond such purposive imagining. Shepard (1978) reported several examples of scientific and literary discoveries made through the use of visual imagery. For example, the German chemist Kekulé used the visual imagery of dancing atoms linking together to form molecules. In one such reverie the atoms united to form a ring, which Kekulé immediately recognized as the long elusive structure of the benzene molecule, a discovery that became central to all organic chemistry.

Imagery can be used to perform different types of operations. One of the most studied operations is the mental rotation of figures such as letters and three-dimensional block designs (Bethel-Fox & Shepard, 1988; Paquet, 1991; Shepard & Feng, 1972; Shepard & Metzler, 1971). In one study participants saw a picture of some sort of three-dimensional block pattern and judged if another pattern was a rotation of the first pattern (Shepard & Metzler, 1971). The time it took to correctly identify a match was a linear function of the number of degrees of rotation separating the two figures. Researchers argued from this result that people were mentally rotating the first figure until they produced a match with the second figure.

Imagery is frequently used to encode information for transfer to long-term memory. Some types of information are more amenable to imagery encoding than others. Allan Paivio (1986, 1991; Paivio & Begg, 1981) proposed the **dual-coding theory** to account for why concrete information is typically remembered better than abstract information. For example, in a serial-learning task, subjects remember words like *chicken, piano,* or *truck* better than equally frequent but abstract words like *liberty, idea,* or *happiness.* The same effect has been demonstrated with sentences (Begg & Paivio, 1969). Paivio postulated that concrete words have a readily available imagery code that abstract words lack. Therefore, abstract words must be encoded as the words themselves, or perhaps as abstract propositions (see Chapter 7). Concrete words may be encoded in these ways as well, but they also have an additional very useful memory code available through visual imagery. This accounts for their greater memorability. Although abstract words could conceivably be encoded by visual imagery, and no doubt are on occasion, it is a considerably less efficient code for abstract than for concrete words.

Cognitive Maps

One way that we all use imagery is in **cognitive maps** (mental maps). We have imagery representations of familiar places and use these to find our way around or give someone else directions. However, these cognitive maps are not merely internalized aerial photographs.

The general axes of orientation are important in cognitive maps. Although the most common type of axis is a grid system (city blocks, NSEW directions, and so forth), some geographical areas, especially coastal and mountainous regions, use different axes. For example, in areas near large bodies of water, people often figure mental maps in terms of distance away from the shore. This may be confusing if that body of water has an unexpected local orientation in that area. For instance, the normally north-south Pacific coast runs roughly east-west between Santa Barbara and Los Angeles. In mountainous areas, a perpendicular grid system is useless, because the paths are constantly curving. Someone moving from hilly Boston or Pittsburgh to the flat and perpendicular midwestern United States at first may have a difficult time thinking and speaking in terms like north, south, east, and west. Similarly, a Midwesterner has difficulty understanding directions like, "Follow the highway for three miles, then bear to the right and follow the road a ways down the hollow, till you get to a little past the red barn, where you veer to the left. . . ."

Another important characteristic of cognitive maps is their mobile quality; they are not purely static images. When Linde and Labov (1975) asked students to describe the layout of their apartments, 97 percent of them gave a **tour,** including the information in the form of mobile vectors such as, "you keep walking straight ahead, turn right at the kitchen," or "go from the bathroom into the bedroom." Very few used a static aerial view cognitive map.

Like most memory representations, cognitive maps include **inferred** and **constructed** information as well as information mentally reproduced. We draw on stored knowledge about what typical rooms, cities, or countrysides are like. This knowledge may occasionally be misleading if the **local** relations are not consistent with the **global** ones. For example, although the Pacific Ocean is west of the Atlantic Ocean, the Pacific end of the Panama Canal is actually east of the Atlantic end. Although California is generally west of Nevada, Los Angeles is east of Reno, Nevada. One travels south, not north, to go from Detroit, Michigan, USA, to Windsor, Ontario, Canada. Although most people's mental map of the Americas may place South America directly south of North America, it is in fact southeast, with Miami, Florida actually being west of Lima, Peru, on the west coast of South America. Traveling due south from the western

Aleutian Islands of southwestern Alaska (USA), the first landmass encountered, other than tiny islands, is New Zealand, all the way in the Eastern hemisphere!

We may acquire our initial cognitive map information from either maps or navigation (Schneider & Taylor, 1999; Taylor & Tversky, 1996; Thorndyke & Hayes-Roth, 1982). Information acquired from maps is **survey** knowledge and is very similar to the map itself, including shapes, locations of objects, and easily estimated straight-line distances. In contrast, knowledge acquired from **navigation,** that is, actual experience traveling through the environment, is more procedural (see Chapter 5). We remember specific routes with associated landmarks, but the information is organized around the routes we travel. In many ways, knowledge from navigation is probably stronger and more useful than knowledge from maps, but it takes much longer to acquire. Sometimes this procedural navigational knowledge is not very amenable to put into words; remember when someone could not *tell* you how to get somewhere but they asked you to follow them on the route!

Network Models of Semantic Memory

Although imagery is one major type of memory representation, much of the recent research on the representation issue has been on developing global structural models that describe how information is coded and organized in semantic memory, using more analytic forms than imagery. The general aim of all semantic memory models is to specify (a) the structure and organization of information in long-term memory, and (b) the processes operating on these structures. The major general class of such models is the network model (Anderson, 1976, 1983, 1996; Anderson & Bower, 1973; Collins & Loftus, 1975; Collins & Quillian, 1969). All network models assume knowledge to be represented as a set of nodes, representing concepts, and relations connecting the nodes. Retrieval involves some sort of process of searching through this network.

The earliest network models were hierarchical in nature, that is, every node has exactly one mandatory superset relation. For example, the node DOG has one superset relation and only one, to ANIMAL (see Figure 6.1). The earliest and best-known hierarchical network model (Collins & Quillian, 1969) posited a branching network of subordinate and superordinate nodes (concepts) in a hierarchical arrangement. Information about the various nodes is stored as attributes at each node. Each attribute applies to that node but also to all nodes below it in the hierarchy. For example "has feathers" is stored at the node *bird* and thus does not need to be stored at each of the many specific bird nodes subordinate to *bird.* This is the principle of **cognitive economy,** whereby each feature need only be stored at one node but is accessible from all subordinate nodes, to which it necessarily applies. More recent network models have focused on specifying the character of the relationships between the various nodes and have also explored different types of organization other than hierarchical.

One advantage of network models, or indeed of most models of semantic memory, is that they allow for individual differences. Each person's hierarchy of knowledge may be slightly, or perhaps substantially, different from everyone else's. For example, the typical urban dweller may divide the superordinate class *farm animals* into subordinate classes like *horses, cows, pigs, sheep,* and *chickens,* with no further differentiation within each subordinate class. On the other hand, the farmer or rancher

FIGURE 6.1 Sample hierarchical network model. (Type of Collins & Quillian, 1969.)

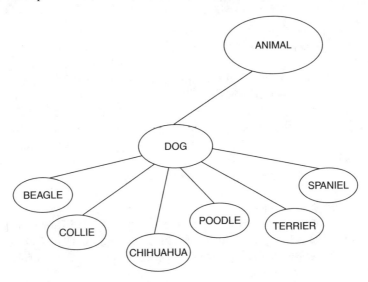

would require further subdivision; a class *livestock* could be divided into *dairy* and *beef cattle*. *Beef cattle* could be divided into *Angus, Herefords, Charolais,* and *Simmentals,* subclasses that would have little meaning or use to the city apartment dweller.

The failure to subcategorize concepts within one's semantic memory can have some important social and political consequences when certain types of semantic memory organizations are characteristic of whole cultures. For example, North Americans' failure to distinguish subordinate classes of Muslims, such as Sunni and Shi'ite, made it difficult to fully understand the dynamics behind Middle Eastern conflicts such as the 1975–1990 civil war in Lebanon, the Iran-Iraq War of the 1980s, the 1991 Persian Gulf War, or the 1979 Islamic Revolution in Iran.

Feature Comparison Model of Semantic Memory

An alternative conception of the structure of semantic memory was proposed by Smith, Shoben, and Rips (1974; see also E. E. Smith, 1978). Instead of claiming that concepts were stored in hierarchical networks, Smith et al. (1974) proposed that each concept contains lists of features, corresponding to its common attributes (e.g., a bird has feathers, can fly, has two legs, is warm-blooded). These features are of two types: **defining** and **characteristic. Defining** features are those that absolutely must be present for the example to be a member of that concept. For example, a bird must have feathers; otherwise it isn't a bird. **Characteristic** features, on the other hand, are attributes that are typically, but not necessarily, present. For instance, birds typically can fly, but there are exceptions (penguins, ostriches). In fact, characteristic features are much more numerous than defining features when considering real-world concepts. (See discussion of fuzzy sets in Chapter 7.)

Smith et al. (1974) proposed different sorts of processes that occur in verifying the truth of a sentence. They proposed a two-stage process, as illustrated in slightly simplified form in Figure 6.2. Consider the following example:

1. A canary is a bird.
2. A chicken is a bird.
3. A bat is a bird.
4. A table is a bird.

A person sees (1), for example, and retrieves the concepts "canary" and "bird" and begins comparing both the defining and characteristic features of each to determine if there is a sufficient match to respond "true." In this case a match would quickly be found, leading to an immediate reply of "true." Similarly, for (4), there is such a clear mismatch between the features of "table" and "bird" that one could quickly respond "false."

The other two cases are more complex, however. With either (2) or (3) one might find an intermediate degree of matching on defining and characteristic features. In such cases, a second stage of processing must be initiated, namely, a comparison on the basis of the defining features only. Thus, one would compare only on the attributes that a bird *must have*. Even though "bat" and "bird" share many characteristic features (can fly, are small), when compared on defining features only, the

FIGURE 6.2 Overview of feature comparison model. (Adapted from Smith, Rips, & Shoben, 1974.)

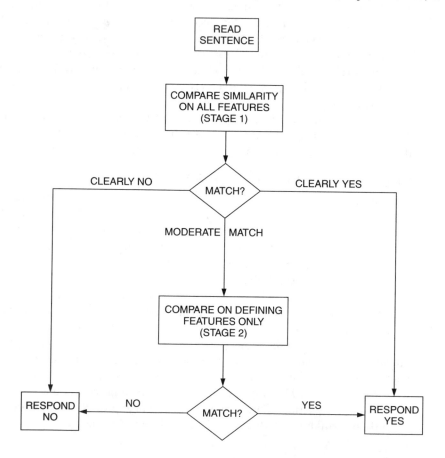

match is poor. After this second stage of comparison, (2) could be answered "true" and (3) could be answered "false." The model proposed by Smith et al. (1974) nicely explains the so-called **typicality effect,** where it takes longer to verify the truth of category membership of less typical instances ("chicken" or "turkey" as opposed to "canary" or "robin"). This robust and consistent finding had always posed problems for the simple network model.

The feature-comparison model also has its drawbacks, however, most notably the criticism that it does not deal seriously enough with how all the features are organized. Positing collections of features throughout semantic memory could be very uneconomical if they are not organized in some way. See E. E. Smith, Johnson-Laird, Herrmann, & Chaffin (1984), and Chang (1986) for reviews and critiques of semantic memory models.

One important aspect of meaning that has not been considered adequately by any of these models is meaning's flexibility. Though "piano" generally has but one meaning, different aspects of its meaning are more salient in some situations than others. For example, a comment like "Help me move the piano" highlights its heavy furniture aspect, whereas "You play the piano beautifully" highlights its musical aspect (Barclay, Bransford, Franks, McCarrell, & Nitsch, 1974). While both features are present in both contexts, each is present to a different degree. Schoen (1988) explored this aspect of semantic flexibility more thoroughly and argued that all models of semantic memory must eventually deal with the phenomenon. They have not been particularly successful in doing so.

Now we turn from examining the representation of information in memory to the processes involved in using that information. Most memory operations fall into the two general classes of encoding and retrieval processes.

ENCODING AND RETRIEVAL PROCESSES

Ways of Measuring Memory

How do we measure memory? What kinds of dependent variables can be used to make inferences about structure and process in long-term memory? When we test someone's memory, we may use either **explicit** or **implicit** measures. **Explicit** measures, which are clearly and overtly intended to measure memory, have been the primary measures of episodic memory over the last century. These include the general categories of **recall** and **recognition. Implicit** measures, on the other hand, measure memory only indirectly, while they more directly measure something else. We will discuss each of these types in turn. Finally, we look briefly at **brain-scanning** measures, one of the newest ways to study memory.

Recall

Both recall and recognition have several variations, but the basic difference is that, in recall, one must both *generate* the response and *recognize* that it is correct, while in recognition memory the response is already generated and we are merely asked to judge whether or not it is the correct response.

Recall may either be **free recall** or some form of **cued recall.** In total **free recall** there are no cues or hints to help us remember the desired information. An extreme form of this might be a test question "Tell all that you know about reinforcement" or an attorney's questioning of a witness "Tell me what you remember about the night of April 27." Because there are no potentially biasing cues present, free recall data are less subject to distortion than are more structured memory tasks. Unfortunately, there is a tradeoff, in that there is also less total accurate information remembered. Thus, quality is high but quantity is low (Lipton, 1977).

In contrast, **cued recall** is generally easier, since there is some sort of cue present to aid retrieval, but that cue may bias the reconstruction of the response. Cued recall has been studied extensively in the psychological literature using paired-associate learning tasks and various forms of completion tasks. An actor learning lines for a play is also practicing a cued recall task, where each preceding line acts as the cue for the next line. When you take a fill-in-the-blanks test, you are performing cued recall.

Recognition

In contrast to recall measures, **recognition** memory presents some pregenerated stimulus which must be judged as accurate or not. Like recall, there are two general kinds of recognition. The first kind, often called **yes-no** or **old-new** recognition, presents some item and asks you to indicate, "Yes, I remember that" or "No, I don't remember it." There are two important factors involved in this type of recognition memory. First, there is the **strength** parameter, that is, how strong the memory trace of the information is. Generally, a strong memory is going to be recognized more accurately than a weaker memory.

However, strength is not the only relevant parameter. There is also a **criterion,** that is, how sure you have to be in order to say, "Yes, that's it." Upon examining a recognition-memory item and your own memory trace of that information, a decision must be made. If there is a strong and obvious match or mismatch, the decision is easy, but how about the intermediate case? For example, if you are looking at a mugshot photo and must indicate whether or not this was the man who mugged you, how sure do you have to be before you say "yes," given that your fragmentary memories *somewhat* match the characteristics of the suspect in front of you? If a yes decision means sending a suspect to prison, you might set a more stringent criterion than you would in a more trivial situation with a memory of equivalent strength and match to the recognition-memory item.

Besides yes-no recognition, we also have **forced-choice** recognition memory, perhaps best exemplified by the multiple-choice test, where you must choose one answer from among several but where one, and only one, is correct. The difficulty of forced-choice recognition memory may vary greatly depending on the nature of the distractors in which the correct item is embedded. Consider the relative difficulty of the following two multiple-choice test items:

5. The capital of Burkina Faso is

   a. Los Angeles,   b. Mexico City,   c. Tokyo,   d. Ouagadougou,   e. All of the above.

6. The capital of Mali is

   a. Timbuktu,   b. Bamako,   c. Niamey,   d. Abidjan,   e. Conakry.

One could easily answer the first question correctly with no knowledge whatsoever of Burkina Faso, while the second could be difficult even for someone fairly knowledgeable about West Africa. (Incidentally, the answers to (5) and (6) are d. and b., respectively.)

Savings

Although it has been used far less often than recall or recognition, there is a third type of explicit memory measure, one which has a long history. Ebbinghaus (1885/1964), in his classic treatise on memory, used the **savings score** method to measure his own memory over time. This consisted of measuring the difference in the number of trials to learn some material at one time minus the number of trials to learn the same material at some later time. Although the savings method explicitly measures memory, sometime it measures memory for material we thought we had long forgotten (e.g., facility of relearning a long unused motor skill or foreign language). This method has not been widely used in the century since Ebbinghaus but may have some applicability, especially to situations where our phenomenological perception is that we have totally forgotten the material.

Implicit Memory

While the three explicit types of memory measures discussed previously typically require conscious recollection of remembered material, other measures may test memory more indirectly by measuring performance on some task that may indirectly or **implicitly** reveal the effects of memory.

One example of an implicit memory measure is **word-fragment completion,** a method widely used in recent research. For example, suppose you are asked to identify the word in the fragment D____L____H____N; performance on this task is greatly affected by an earlier **priming** task like seeing the word "porpoise" (Graf & Schacter, 1985; Roediger & Blaxton, 1987; Tulving, Schacter, & Stark, 1982; Weldon & Roediger, 1987). Such prior exposure (priming) improves performance on the word-fragment-completion task, compared to a control group with no priming task, even if the person has no conscious memory for the priming information.

Implicit memory tasks may be sensitive to differences not picked up by recall and recognition tasks, sometimes demonstrating the presence of memories in cases where all explicit memory tests show a complete loss of memory. Perhaps the most dramatic case is that of **amnesia,** by definition a complete loss of explicit memory. Yet the use of a repetition priming task has demonstrated that amnesics do show the facilitation (priming) effect of prior information that had been apparently completely forgotten (Paller et al., 1992; Shimamura & Squire, 1989).

Another dramatic example of implicit memory in a case where it would not be expected is in patients under general anesthesia. For example, surgery patients were later more likely to generate particular words of a given category if they had heard earlier those words while under anesthesia (Millar, 1987). Also, they were more likely to touch their ears during a post-operative conversation if that suggestion had been given to them while under general anesthesia (Bennett, Davis, & Giannini, 1985; Goldmann, Shah, & Hebden, 1987). In neither case was there any explicit conscious memory for the information heard under anesthesia. Surgeons should be forewarned not to make derogatory comments about the patient while operating!

Another application of implicit memory comes in the area of advertising. When participants saw a set of fifty magazine ads and later were tested on recognition memory and attitude, Perfect and Askew (1994) found that people liked the ads they had seen before better than new ads, *even when they did not recognize that they had seen them previously!* This is exactly what advertisers hope for: A positive attitude toward the product is inculcated without people having to remember that they saw the ad.

In an excellent review of historical and contemporary uses of implicit memory measures, Schacter (1987) argued that, because implicit memory measures have yielded quite different results than those obtained from more traditional explicit measures, models of memory must take such data into account and explain why implicit memory measures often show the existence of memories not detected by the traditional explicit memory measures. See Roediger (1990) and Schacter (1995) for reviews of implicit memory research, Parkin, Reid, and Russo (1990) for an experimental comparison of implicit and explicit memory measures, and Graf and Masson (1993) or Lewandowsky, Dunn, and Kirsner (1989) for collections of papers further exploring various aspects of implicit memory.

Brain Scanning

The use of brain-scanning techniques (PET, CAT, MRI, fMRI imaging) to study cognitive processing has only been available the last decade or so but is already greatly adding to our knowledge of memory. Brain scans allow a noninvasive peek into the brain in ways never before possible.

For example, using the HERA (hemispheric encoding/retrieval asymmetry model), it has been reliably shown that encoding processes preferentially activate certain left frontal lobe regions, while retrieval processes activate right frontal regions (see Buckner, 1996; Cabeza & Nyberg, 1997; Nyberg, Cabeza, & Tulving, 1996; Tulving, 1998, for reviews). However, this is further qualified by whether the information is related to the self or not; the encoding of self-related material also activates some areas of the right frontal lobe in PET scan studies (Craik et al., 1999). One new theory of episodic memory uses PET scans, as well as other types of data, to argue that portions of the prefrontal cortex are critical in the memory for experiences in your life (Wheeler, Stuss, & Tulving, 1997). Still another promising new technique uses event-related fMRI (D'Esposito, Zarahn, & Aguirre, 1999; Gabrieli, 1998).

Now that we have examined some ways of measuring memory, let us turn to examining encoding and retrieval more directly, beginning with the memory strategies called **mnemonics.**

Mnemonics

Probably the most promising way to work on improving your memory is by improving your encoding strategies. One, though by no means the only, way to do this is to use **mnemonics,** strategies for more efficient encoding. Mnemonics are the products of conscious decisions to organize and chunk information into larger and more meaningful units for the purpose of remembering it better.

Let us examine some types of mnemonics to better understand what they do and how they work. Sometimes they may add an additional memory code to the original code, allowing two, instead of one, possible avenues of retrieval. For example, if you make up a little song to help you remember something, this gives you two potential ways to retrieve that information later: Either remember the words, or remember the melody and use that to retrieve or reconstruct the words. This is why advertising jingles are so durable in memory. See Yalch (1991) for a test of the conditions where music facilitates memory for advertising slogans.

Mnemonics are perhaps at their most useful when they impose meaning on a rote series of items that otherwise would have little or no meaning. For instance, it may seem arbitrary whether to set the clocks ahead or behind in the spring and fall, but if you remember that maxim "Spring ahead and fall behind," the direction seems less capricious because it has been linked meaningfully (through the use of the second meanings of "spring" and "fall") to the season to which it belongs. Mnemonics may also be used to remember spelling of those few troublesome words that continually elude us ("The Double-C Double-M Motel gives good accommodations" to remind us that the word "accommodation" has two *C*'s, two *M*'s and an *O* after the *M*'s). In constructing a mnemonic, try to make it as meaningful as possible and as closely related as possible to all aspects of the to-be-remembered information.

There are more elaborate mnemonic systems. The **method of loci** has been around since ancient times, reported in Cicero's *De Oratore* to have been used by the Greek poet Simonides (Yates, 1966). This involves learning a list of items by associating them in sequence with different positions in some very familiar spatial network. For example, you might use visual imagery to remember a shopping list by associating milk with your front door (a milk carton hanging on the doorknob); eggs with the sidewalk (eggs rolling up the walk toward your house); coffee with the street corner (coffee flowing into the sewer at the intersection), and so on. To retrieve the information, simply retrace your familiar route and pick up the mental images left there earlier.

The **pegword** system involves learning a system of associations in advance and then using these to peg items to be learned on. One popular system involves the associations 1 = bun, 2 = shoe, 3 = tree, 4 = door, 5 = hive, 6 = sticks, 7 = heaven, 8 = gate, 9 = line, 10 = hen. Notice that these are made easier to learn initially because of the auxiliary code of rhyme. To use the pegword system, associate the first item to be learned with a bun, the second with a shoe, and so on. To retrieve, simply count through the numbers and retrieve the associated images. The initial pegword associations, once learned, may be reused any number of times.

A highly developed use of mnemonics can have valuable practical benefits and is not limited to people with exceptional ability. A Colorado waiter, John Conrad, developed his own elaborate mnemonic system for remembering customers' dinner orders, associating the entree with the person's face and afterward associating the side dishes and salads they had ordered (Ericsson & Polson, 1988a, 1988b). He perfected this system up to the point where he could take orders from a party of 20 without writing anything down and without making any errors. His extraordinary skill captured the attention of his customers and helped him win lucrative tips. His coworkers were so impressed that they asked him to teach them his system, as did University of Colorado psychologists interested in studying memory. These studies revealed Conrad to be highly organized and systematic although he was probably only of average intellect overall. Some even more extraordinary memory feats are discussed in Box 6.2.

Why Do Mnemonics Work?

On the surface, mnemonics might appear to make learning more difficult, since some additional information must be learned beyond what one is trying to master (the pegword associations, the slogan encoding how to spell a word). However, if done

Amazing Feats of Memory

While most research on memory has been done on "normal" people, usually college students, there are occasional reports of outstanding memory feats by other individuals (Neisser & Hyman, 1999). While it is often difficult to draw general conclusions from such case studies, the tantalizing fact remains that these astounding memory feats are possible, at least by some people in some circumstances.

While many professional musicians have exceptional memories, astounding even among these was Arturo Toscanini (Marek, 1975). Toscanini apparently had rote-memorized every note of every instrumental part for around 250 symphonic works and about 100 operas. He could apply this knowledge in a most impressive fashion. One anecdote reports a bassoonist discovering just before a performance that the lowest note on his instrument was broken. Upon hearing this, Toscanini thought for a moment and replied that there was no problem, since that note did not occur anywhere in the bassoon repertoire of that evening's concert! He could also, at will, sit down and correctly write from memory any instrumental part from a huge collection of works.

Sometimes the exceptional memory is highly specific. For example, the memorist Rajan Mahadevan memorized the digits of the value of Π to 31,811 decimal places, placing himself in the *Guinness Book of World Records*. How he did so was examined in depth by Thompson, Cowan, and Frieman (1993). Rajan had an amazing ability to memorize numbers, which he did largely by rote memory without the use of mnemonics or visual imagery. However, this ability did not transfer well to other information, on which his memory was only average or somewhat above (Biederman, Cooper, & Fox, 1992).

Some preliterate societies have oral traditions that often place a high value on an extensive memory for past history of the community or the nation. This can be seen, for example, in the griots, the oral historians of West African societies (D'Azevedo, 1962; Haley, 1976). With our easy access to reading and recorded written history, it is hard to imagine the high value placed on such oral memory; thus, the memory feats of these oral historians seem entirely amazing (Rubin, 1995). With the motivation and circumstances of their situation, however, such feats may have been within the reach of many.

well, learning this extra information can actually make learning the target information easier, because it increases the meaningfulness of the information. The more meaning something has, the easier it is to remember. Mnemonics are not very helpful in learning material that is already meaningful, but they are quite useful in learning arbitrary, verbatim information where elements are not particularly associated with other elements or where a specific and arbitrary order must be learned.

Mnemonics take advantage of our natural information-processing tendency to impose structure and organization on material that we process. It is natural, not exceptional, to try to make meaningful something that does not have much meaning. The more links we can establish between the material we are trying to learn and information already in our long-term memory, the more potential avenues of retrieval we have available later. This same principle applies to your studies, in that it is easier to learn and remember information if you have made connections of that information with knowledge already in your memory. If you find it difficult to make such connections, that information will probably be very difficult to remember.

Many, though by no means all, mnemonics make use of visual imagery in one way or another. This draws on our large natural capacity for picture memory. Visual images tend to be among the easiest units of information to remember. They also have the advantage of allowing us to combine elements within an image. For example, the logo for a product to use on basement walls to seal out water once used a seal (animal) splashing in water under the label "Water Seal." This combines one aspect of the function of the product (water) with its specific function (sealing) plus an additional meaning (the animal seal) of the same sound. Such information-processing principles are known and used by advertisers (Alesandrini, 1983). Box 6.3 explores an application of imagery mnemonics to second-language vocabulary learning.

Contextual Variables in Encoding and Retrieval

Memory and cognition research has historically been curiously silent about contextual, especially social-personality, variables. However, in the last couple of decades this situation has rapidly changed; several recent books and papers have looked at encoding more broadly and even tried to integrate personality and social variables like attitude, empathy, and mood into existing theories of cognition (Bower, 1981; Christianson, 1992; Fiske & Taylor, 1990; Nisbett & Ross, 1980).

■ Box 6.3 ■

Application of Mnemonics to Second-Language Learning

Atkinson (1975; Atkinson & Raugh, 1975) developed a key-word method for second-language vocabulary learning, which is all-too-often a process of tedious rote memory for language students. The idea is to provide a key word relating the pronunciation of a word with its English translation. An image is then constructed using the key word and the English equivalent of the to-be-learned word. For example, to learn the Spanish word "pato" (duck), one might use the key word "pot" and image a duck with a pot on its head. Thus, one could remember "pato" by thinking of a duck, remembering the image, retrieving "pot" from the image, and associating "pot" with "pato." An experimental group using this method was shown to be superior to a control group in a vocabulary test six weeks after learning. In fact, it was so successful that it was implemented in Russian classes at Stanford University. Computers were programmed to present the word, its translation, and the key word. The student then formed his or her own image. The method has even been adapted to teach grammatical gender in German (Desrochers, Gelinas, & Wieland, 1989; Desrochers, Wieland, & Cote, 1991) and tones in Chinese (Schrag, 1996). There is, however, some debate in the literature about the strength of the positive *long-term* effects of the keyword method (Beaton, Gruneberg, & Ellis, 1995; Gruneberg, 1998; Thomas & Wang, 1996).

Encoding Specificity

One important basic construct identified some years ago by Thomson and Tulving (1970) and Tulving and Thomson (1973) is **encoding specificity.** This principle says that the probability of recall depends on the similarity of the context of encoding during initial learning to the context of retrieval at test time. To illustrate this, if you hear the list of words January, March, June, July, September, October, December, Mary, Alice, Joanne, Linda, Cathy, Ann and are then asked for the seven girls' names, you may find it difficult to find all seven. The word "June" at study appeared in the context of months and was probably encoded as a month, not as a girl's name, the context at retrieval. Similarly, Anderson and Ortony (1975) presented the sentence: *The container held the apples* or *The container held the cola.* They found that "basket" was an effective cue for the former but not for the latter, and "bottle" exactly the reverse. Unlike the "June" example, "container" does not have two separate meanings here, but it is vague as to the exact nature of the container. Certain types of containers tend to hold fruit and certain other types hold drinks.

State-Dependent Learning

Encoding specificity is related to the concept of **state-dependent learning,** which derives from the literature on the effects of drugs. Information learned in one state of mind (such as while intoxicated) is relatively less accessible for retrieval while one is in a different state. Thus, it may be easier to recognize someone when you are drunk if you originally met that person while in a similar state of inebriation, though this does not, of course, mean that memory is enhanced by alcohol. In fact, it is depressed overall; state-dependent learning merely suggests that it may not be as far depressed when intoxicated again as during subsequent sober moments (Goodwin, Powell, Bremer, Hoine, & Stern, 1969).

Perhaps the most dramatic demonstration of state-dependent memory occurred in a study where divers learned a list of words either on land or underwater. Words learned on land were recalled better on land and those learned underwater were recalled better underwater (Godden & Baddeley, 1975). Similar context-dependent memory effects have been found for music (Balch, Bowman, & Mohler, 1992; S. M. Smith, 1985), odors (Cann & Ross, 1989; Schab, 1990), and hypnotically induced states (Lewis & Williams, 1989).

The same logic is invoked in forensic hypnosis, when witnesses are hypnotized and put into a mental state more similar to that which they were in when they observed a critical crime. The hope is that, in this similar state, they will remember previously irretrievable information about the crime. However, comparable results have been obtained without hypnosis using a method called the **cognitive interview,** whereby the witness is interviewed in such a way as to try to re-create the context at the original encoding of the to-be-remembered event (Fisher & Geiselman, 1988; Geiselman, 1988; Geiselman, Fisher, MacKinnon, & Holland, 1985, 1986; Kohnken, Thorer, & Zoberbier, 1994; Mantwill, Kohnken, & Aschermann, 1995). The four general retrieval principles of the cognitive interview are (1) mentally reinstate the environmental and personal context present at the crime, (2) report every remembered detail, no matter how minor or irrelevant it appears, (3) recount the incident in different orders (e.g., backwards and forwards) and (4) recount the incident from a range of different perspectives (e.g., victim, assailant, witnesses). These principles are increasingly used by police and others in actual forensic investigations. See Bekerian and Dennett (1993) for discussion of the theoretical issues in regard to the cognitive interview.

FORGETTING

Through our examination of encoding and retrieval, we have implicitly considered **forgetting,** since the failure to either encode or to retrieve effectively will naturally lead to forgetting. Now, however, we focus more specifically on forgetting from long-term memory. There are several possible reasons why we may forget something that we had apparently learned previously.

Failure to Encode

One major reason for forgetting is that the material was never encoded properly to begin with. While we may have used the material in working memory, there was perhaps not enough elaborative rehearsal strategies to transfer it to long-term memory. This may occur, for example, when you fail to remember information on a test because you never encoded it when studying, that is, never learned it to begin with. You may forget what a physician told you because you did not understand what he or she said in the first place (see Box 6.4).

Retrieval Failure

Sometimes the forgetting is due not to failure to encode but rather from failure to access the material in long-term memory. A book that is in the library but on the wrong shelf is nearly impossible to find, unless one stumbles upon it serendipitously. So it is sometimes with lost memories.

The selection of an appropriate retrieval cue is critical to the retrieval process. What is an effective retrieval cue for one person might be ineffective to another person trying to retrieve the same information. For example, if you try to remember all the states of the United States and all the provinces of Canada that begin with the letter *N*, there are many possible retrieval cues you could use. If you have good visual memory and imagery ability, you might imagine a map of North America and start

■ Box 6.4 ■

─── Remembering Your Child's Immunizations ───

Sometimes it makes a big difference whether the reason for forgetting something was retrieval failure or not encoding it correctly in the first place. In a fascinating application of memory research to public health issues, Lee and coworkers (1999) asked parents at pediatric health clinics in Chicago and Oakland, CA, what vaccinations their children had had. Neither various memory aids nor different ways of testing (recall vs. recognition) helped improve memory several weeks later. The problem was that the information was never encoded correctly. Parents who were questioned immediately after their children's vaccinations answered only slightly above chance accuracy. A major confusion was distinguishing vaccines which required multiple versus single doses. These results suggest that this apparent memory problem is not memory failure as such but rather confusion by parents in understanding the vaccines to begin with.

scanning east to west for states and provinces starting with *N*. Another retrieval cue might be to imagine combinations of letters which may form official postal abbreviations (NA, NB, NC, etc.). Still another approach would be to retrieve a previously learned alphabetical list. Other possible strategies include retrieving by regions (New England, Rocky Mountains, Prairie provinces) or by different collegiate athletic conferences!

The Freudian defense mechanism of **repression** would explain retrieval failure by saying that some threatening event was unconsciously expelled from our consciousness because of its anxiety-evoking nature. We cannot access this memory because of the defensive barriers that have been erected to prevent it from becoming conscious. Therapy, especially in the psychoanalytic tradition, tries to break down the barriers to allow retrieval of the repressed memory, in order to start the healing process. A recent controversy about the possible recovery of such repressed memories is further discussed later in the chapter.

Decay and Interference

The decay-interference issue, discussed in the section on working memory in the last chapter, is also relevant to long-term memory. As with working memory, there is ample demonstration of forgetting due to **interference** (both proactive and retroactive), but it is far more difficult to unequivocally demonstrate the existence of **decay.** Clearly, we remember less with the passage of more time; whether this is due purely to decay is much less clear.

Over the last few decades one popular view has been that anything we have ever learned is still in our long-term memory somewhere and that forgetting occurs because of retrieval failure. Much of the evidence for this permanent memory has come from case studies from the brain stimulation neurosurgery of Wilder Penfield (1969; Penfield & Roberts, 1959). Penfield reported some very dramatic case studies of neurosurgical patients who, when under local anesthesia with their brains electrically stimulated during the course of neurosurgery, reported long-forgotten memories from early childhood. However, in an important paper reexamining Penfield's findings, along with other arguments from hypnosis and psychoanalysis, Loftus and Loftus (1980) concluded that this permanence hypothesis is a severe overinterpretation of some case-study data, which may in fact have been reflecting reconstruction, based on other memories, rather than actual retrieval.

Source Monitoring and Source Amnesia

Sometimes we remember some material but forget where we learned it; for example, we recall that Jane has started dating Jeff but we cannot remember who told us that. **Source monitoring** is the memory for the source of a memory. Source monitoring is subject to distortion under a variety of conditions (Goff & Roediger, 1998; Johnson, Hashtroudi, & Lindsay, 1993). Many times we remember an event relatively accurately but forget or misattribute the source of that information.

Source amnesia, the forgetting the source of the memory, has sometimes been attributed to the aging process. Craik and McIntyre (1986) presented young and old adults with 30 Canadian trivia questions either on overhead transparencies or spoken by the experimenter. A week later they were tested for this knowledge but also were asked whether the fact was presented visually or auditorily. In terms of the information, recall by young and old adults was about the same (on one measure even better in the older adults). However, in the source recall younger adults did much better than the older ones (89 percent versus 56 percent correct). A second study had young and older adults learn obscure "Fictitious Facts"; for example, that Jane Fonda's favorite color is blue. Participants were later tested after varying intervals. Again, older people showed considerable source amnesia, especially at the longer delays. Craik and McIntyre concluded that source amnesia is not true amnesia but rather is a natural part of the aging process.

AUTOBIOGRAPHICAL MEMORY

One of the most productive areas of recent research on memory has been the study of memory for events in one's own life. This was an area off limits to study during the time of behaviorism, and it was in fact very difficult to publish research on the topic in mainstream psychology journals as late as the early 1980s.

What are characteristics of autobiographical (personal) memories? First of all, they are typically experienced as having occurred at a unique time, although there are also some personal recurring events (e.g., those childhood summer trips to the beach). Second, they are remembered as having been experienced by the self, not merely reported by someone else. Third, they are remembered as a highly accurate record of the episode; whether they in fact are so accurate is less clear. Fourth, they seem to appear almost involuntarily, with little sense of conscious effort to retrieve. Fifth, they include much visual imagery and affect (emotion).

Because everyone's personal memories are different and usually are not subject to independent verification of accuracy, this area requires great inventiveness as to methodology. Some examples of methodologies that have been used are discussed following.

One of the earliest (and still very common) techniques was asking participants to keep daily diaries or records of events in their lives, for which they are later tested (Barclay, 1986, 1988; Burt, 1992; Harris, 1984; Linton, 1986; Thompson, 1982; Thompson, Skowronski, & Lee, 1988; Wagoner, 1986). As an example of what can be learned from such research, participants consistently rated recent events as having occurred longer ago than they in fact did (time expansion) and longer-past events as more recent (telescoping) (Thompson et al., 1988).

Other research has had participants record events at random, beeper-signaled intervals, to avoid the bias of selecting salient events (Brewer, 1988). Still others have analyzed verbal think-aloud protocols as participants retrieve personal memories (Reiser, Black, & Kalamarides, 1986), tested participants' ability to correctly order pictures of an experienced event (Burt, Watt, Mitchell, & Conway, 1998), studied the organization of personal events in memory (Brown & Schopflocher, 1998), examined how motives affect content and structure of emotional autobiographical memories (Woike, Gershkovich, Piorkowski, & Polo, 1999), determined how popular music elicits autobiographical memories (Schulkind, Hennis, & Rubin, 1999), or compared different people's memories for the same events (Ross, Buehler, & Karr, 1998).

Some studies have looked at how autobiographical memories change across the lifespan (Fitzgerald, 1986; Fitzgerald & Lawrence, 1984; Howe & Courage, 1993; Ornstein et al., 1998; Rubin, Wetzler, & Nebes, 1986). Still others have studied autobiographical memory for distressing events (Brewin, 1998; Chapman & Under-wood, 2000) or media experiences (Harrison & Cantor, 1999; Hoekstra, Harris, & Helmick, 1999). Occasionally the focus has been on the autobiographical memory of famous and influential persons (Blight, 1990; Neisser, 1981); for example, see Box 6.5 for a study of the 1970s Watergate scandal figure John Dean's memory. Social memories of a culture have even been examined (Middleton & Edwards, 1990).

Developmental of Autobiographical Memory

Deficiencies in the development of autobiographical memory may account for what is commonly called **infantile amnesia,** the highly reliable finding that adults are unable to recall events from their own lives that occurred before the age or three or four. Nelson (1993) suggests that experiences in early childhood are all taken into semantic, rather than episodic, memory and thus are not well marked as distinct events. Young children have a lesser sense than adults of what about an event is most important and what are peripheral details, and this interferes with encoding events in memorable form, although fragmentary memories may persist in some form, perhaps connected up with other events.

To some degree, autobiographical memory may be *socially constructed.* Social interaction and storytelling are critical in establishing events in autobiographical memory (Eacott, 1999; Fivush & Schwarzmueller, 1998; Hudson, Fivush, & Kuebli, 1992). By hearing parents tell stories and telling them themselves, children learn how to formulate their own memories as narratives, which provides some structure for encoding into memory. Talking about events as they occur and frequently retelling them will increase the chances of the children remembering those events later. Some research suggests that verbalizing an event *as it is being experienced* in young childhood is critical for subsequent retrieval of that memory (Fivush & Schwarzmueller, 1998).

■ Box 6.5 ■

John Dean's Watergate Memory

In an interesting and insightful application of memory research, Neisser (1981) studied former Nixon presidential counselor John Dean's memory for Watergate conversations of the early 1970s by comparing his courtroom testimony about these conversations with the actual transcripts of the conversations as covertly taped by President Nixon. This offered an unusual opportunity to test the accuracy of verbatim recall in a natural setting, in that there was a tape recording of the original conversation made without John Dean's knowledge. Neisser found that, as laboratory studies have shown, verbatim memory was very poor. However, he also found that "gist" memory was not all that good either. Neisser, however, argued that Dean's memory was in fact quite good at a still more abstract level, that he "captures the 'tenor,' though not the gist, of what went on" (Neisser, 1982, p. 150). Distortions tended to be in the direction of details and intrusions from other conversations. They also were somewhat distorted by "ego needs" of Dean himself; memory errors tended to somewhat enhance his own importance in the conversations. Nonetheless, Neisser concludes that overall Dean captured the "theme and spirit" of the Watergate conversations quite well.

Parents may encourage this by talking about family events as they occur and encouraging children to reminisce (discuss shared experiences) and recount (discuss unshared experiences) those events in the days, weeks, and even years following (Reese & Brown, 2000).

For an excellent historical and conceptual review of autobiographical memory, see Brewer (1995). For a good set of recent studies in the area, see the special issue of *Applied Cognitive Psychology* (Conway, Bruce, & Sehulster, 1998).

Flashbulb Memory

One particularly interesting type of autobiographical memory is the memory for the personal context of hearing the news of a major (usually tragic) public event, such as the assassination of a national leader. For example, most people over a certain age in the United States believe that they have a highly accurate memory for where they were and what they were doing when they heard the news of President John F. Kennedy's assassination in 1963. Using what is now an unfortunately anachronistic term, this has come to be called a **flashbulb memory** (Brown & Kulick, 1977). Memory has been impressive for these personal memories associated with certain public events (Pillemer, 1984, 1998; Winograd & Killinger, 1983), particularly if they involve intense affective experiences or if the person suffers from post-traumatic stress disorder (Conway, 1995).

However, there is also increasing evidence for reconstruction and less than perfect memories (Bohannon, 1988; Christianson, 1989; Finkenauer et al., 1998; McCloskey, Wible, & Cohen, 1988; Winograd & Neisser, 1992). For example, in a test of Swedes' flashbulb memories for hearing the news of the assassination of Prime Minister Olaf Palme in 1986, Christianson (1989) found considerable alteration and forgetting of memories between a few weeks after the events and one year later. Certain core information was remembered well, but many details were not.

It may be that unusually high levels of confidence in the accuracy of one's memory are the most distinctive characteristic of flashbulb memories. Weaver (1993) tested students' memories for an ordinary event occurring on January 16, 1991, and for the beginning of the bombing of Iraq to start the Persian Gulf War on that same day. Memories were equally accurate up to a year later, but the level of confidence in that accuracy was much higher for the public event (the start of the bombing). Other research has shown a decrement in flashbulb memories in an aging population (Cohen, Conway, & Maylor, 1994). Whether flashbulb memories are qualitatively different from other autobiographical memories remains unresolved. For a cognitive model of flashbulb memories, see Conway (1995).

ALTERNATIVE CONCEPTUALIZATIONS OF MEMORY

Although we have largely been assuming an Atkinson-Shiffrin type of multistore model, as described at the beginning of the last chapter (see Figure 5.1), there is considerable evidence that such a qualitative separation of working and long-term memory may not be warranted. While no other approach has been so completely developed or widely accepted, there are other frameworks for conceptualizing memory. We begin with levels-of-processing, to be followed by spreading activation, long-term working memory, and, finally, embodied cognition.

The Levels (Depth) Metaphor

Craik and Lockhart (1972; see also Craik & Tulving, 1975, and Lockhart & Craik, 1990) proposed an alternative metaphor as a framework for conceptualizing memory. Instead of discrete memory stores like working and long-term memory, they proposed that memory involves different **levels of processing,** with trace persistence being a function of how deeply the analysis has proceeded. For example, processing speech only to the point of understanding what language the speaker is using or how loud or soft the speech is would be a very shallow level of processing, while understanding the content thoroughly, including all its implications and nuances, would be a very deep level. Memory is thus viewed as the natural residue of both the transient products of sensory analyses and the much more durable traces of semantic (meaningful) processing.

Familiar memory phenomena may be reinterpreted using a levels-of-processing framework. For example, forgetting due to a failure to transfer from working to long-term memory occurs because the analysis during comprehension has not proceeded to a sufficiently deep level. Rehearsal or continued attention to the material is reconceptualized as recirculation of the material, which may occur at any level by continued attention to the analysis at that particular level.

The well-documented superiority of intentional over incidental learning (we remember something better if we try to remember it) is reinterpreted by saying that in intentional learning we have processed the material to a deeper level and it is this fact, rather than an intention to remember as such, that accounts for the better memory performance. If participants are induced to process material deeply, even though they are not expecting a memory test, incidental recall is much improved. This finding suggested that depth of processing, not the intention to remember, is the critical factor.

As insightful as it has been, there are criticisms of the levels-of-processing approach (Baddeley, 1978), many of them centering around the vagueness of its constructs. See Craik (1979) and Lockhart and Craik (1990) for summaries of this debate.

The most fundamental criticism is that there is no independent measure of depth of processing. In most studies using this framework, two tasks are chosen intuitively as differing in depth of processing. It is also sometimes defined by what is remembered better. Shallow processes are usually done faster than deeper ones, but there may be some exceptions; for example, deciding if the word "rabbit" fits the CVCCVC pattern by most definitions would be shallow processing, since it is totally nonsemantic, but it is not trivially easy. Lockhart and Craik (1978) admit this problem but defend the approach by saying that levels-of-processing was intended to be a framework, not a theory, and that it can still have heuristic (discovery) value even without an independent measure of depth.

A related concern is that, especially for semantic processing, there is no real consensus on what constitutes deep versus shallow processing. For example, people very readily draw inferences from all that they hear or read (Chapter 8). In one sense inference-drawing would seem like a relatively deep level of processing; however, to stop people from drawing inferences requires considerable effort to invoke a metalinguistic monitor to stop such natural processes from occurring. Is such a monitor relatively deep or shallow processing? The answer is not clear. Perhaps depth of processing is not a linear dimension.

Under some conditions we remember information from so-called shallow processing very well, such as the way people remember certain kinds of thematically irrelevant comments verbatim such as jokes, song lyrics, or offhand comments in a lecture or conversation (Hyman & Rubin, 1990; Keenan, MacWhinney, & Mayhew, 1977; Kintsch & Bates, 1977; MacWhinney, Keenan, & Reinke, 1982). Lockhart and Craik (1990) admit there is better memory for such shallowly processed information than they acknowledged in 1972, although they suggest it may be due to different sorts of processing, such as pictorial memory or memory for the modality of presentation.

In spite of its serious definitional and precision problems, the metaphor of levels of processing has been influential in offering an alternative way to think about memory and in generating considerable productive research.

Spreading Activation

A second useful metaphor for looking at memory has been the notion of **spreading activation** (J. R. Anderson, 1983; Collins & Loftus, 1975). Instead of speaking of two separate memory stores, with information retrieved from long-term to working memory, we may say that information we are using is **activated** or brought into a state of activation. The more consciously aware we are of some information, the higher level of activation it is in at the moment.

When we enter our memory, usually postulated to be some form of network, to search for information, activation spreads from the node of entry to related concepts stored close by. The more nodes that are in that area, the more diffuse the activation and probably the longer the time required to retrieve the information. When one concept (node) is primed, related nodes, relations, and property statements are primed as well. Such activation may or may not be conscious. The concept of spreading activation may eventually be useful in describing other areas in psychology. For example, psychoanalysis may be viewed as an attempt to activate previously dormant concepts and relations among those concepts in the patient's mind.

The concept of activation has important implications for structural aspects of memory discussed early in this chapter. How the activation spreads through the network from the entry point is determined in part by the structure of that particular individual's memory. Instead of positing separate working and long-term memory stores, activation theorists often argue that what we are thinking about at the moment are the highly activated concepts, while nonactivated concepts remain in memory until needed and activated.

The use of different models and metaphors to describe memory can each be helpful and lend insight in different ways, even if none of them is totally correct. Over the years memory has been described in terms of all sorts of metaphors; some others are discussed in Box 6.6.

Long-Term Working Memory

A very recent model proposed by Ericsson and Kintsch (1995) argues for the addition of a long-term working memory (LT-WM) to account for the apparent need of highly accessible but very extensive information during the on-line processing of text comprehension or expert skills. For example, when reading complex material, considerable knowledge is activated for use in understanding the new text. This knowledge remains

■ Box 6.6 ■

Memory Metaphors

The way we talk about something may actually affect the way we conceptualize it. Roediger (1980) offered a fascinating survey of the metaphors used to discuss memory. Like most basically abstract and unobservable concepts, memory is typically described in concrete, though metaphorical, terms. In examining these metaphors, Roediger (1980) concluded that the majority of them have been some sort of spatial metaphor, usually combined with some action of searching through this space. While the most popular and prevalent of these spatial search metaphors is probably the computer metaphor, there have been many others as well, including the wax tablet, rooms in a house, storehouse, switchboard, workbench, acid bath, dictionary, pushdown stack, conveyor belt, subway map, leaky bucket, and even a cow's stomach!

While the spatial-search metaphors predominate, they are not the only metaphors used to discuss memory. For example, all the network models of semantic memory use a more structural metaphor, and there are several more dynamic metaphors, such as construction, levels of processing, activation, and signal detection. The archaeology metaphor was central to Freud and the entire psychoanalytic tradition and still colors much popular thinking about memory. Memories are pieces of experience and knowledge to be excavated out of the dirt of the past. This notion of memory as self-contained things to be found in a matrix of irrelevant material is inconsistent with the thrust of most current research and thinking. Memory is inextricably a part of its context, not isolated bits of information as many earlier memory researchers conceptualized it (Larsen, 1987).

Although metaphors are certainly often insightful, perhaps even essential, to discuss such an abstract concept as memory, they can channel our thinking into excessively rigid modes of conceptualizing. Roediger warns against thinking of memory so much as spatial storage and search that we do not take seriously enough its other characteristics not included in this particular metaphor. Koriat and Goldsmith (1996) argue that what they call the storehouse metaphor of memory has favored laboratory over applied research, because thinking of memory as a repository for information and events naturally leads to counting and measuring this information. They suggest rather a correspondence metaphor, whereby memory is seen as a vehicle for interaction with the world, a view much more congenial with applied rather than laboratory research.

In a study of metaphors appearing in the journal *Psychological Review* between 1894 and 1975, Gentner and Grudin (1985) found that far fewer metaphors were used in the period 1925–1945 than in earlier (1894–1915) or later (1955–1975) periods. This middle period corresponded to the time of greatest dominance of Behaviorism. Do you see a connection?

in a highly activated state for some time without constant use and appears to suffer no loss of activation if the reading task is interrupted over 30 seconds. Another argument centers around the memory skills of experts (e.g., Ericsson & Polson, 1988a, 1988b; Thompson et al., 1993). A memory expert has learned to construct an amazing mnemonic framework or other amount of information for constant on-line referral when performing memory tasks such as remembering restaurant customer orders or reciting digits of pi. Ericsson and Kintsch argue that such prodigious information could not be retained in the very limited working memory as traditionally conceived. Their notion of LT-WM seems promising but has not yet been extensively tested.

Embodied Cognition

Another new but promising approach stresses the integrated nature of comprehension and action (Barsalou, 1999a, 1999b; Glenberg & Robertson, 1999, in press). Material is comprehended, and by extension remembered, through action. This has implications for learning strategies. For example, science principles are best taught through hands-on lab experiences (Roth, 1999), and theatrical dialogue is best learned through acting it out, motions and all (Scott, Harris, & Rothe, 2001). The physical enactment may contribute to comprehension and memory above and beyond its role in encouraging deeper processing.

To complete our discussion of long-term-memory, we turn now to a more detailed examination of two practical applications of many of the memory principles we have studied in the last two chapters: eyewitness memory and the recovery of repressed memories. Here the psychological study of memory is having some real impact on some serious social problems.

EYEWITNESS MEMORY

A popular view of eyewitness testimony is that it is nearly infallible. To say that there is an eyewitness to a crime is often considered practically the equivalent of saying the whole event was recorded on videotape. However, the scientific study of eyewitness memory presents quite a different picture. Although this problem was considered in psychology as far back as Hugo Münsterberg's (1908) book, *On the Witness Stand,* it has been studied intensively in the last 20 years (Deffenbacher, 1991; Doris, 1991; Greene, 1988; Kassin, Ellsworth, & Smith, 1989; Loftus, Donders, Hoffman, & Schooler, 1989; Loftus & Hoffman, 1989; Loftus & Ketcham, 1991; Wells, 1993; Wells et al., 1998).

Eyewitness identification may be considered a recognition memory signal-detection problem with four possible outcomes. Someone could be guilty and be correctly recognized as guilty (**hit**). Someone could be innocent and be correctly not recognized (**correct rejection**). As well as these two correct responses, there are two types of errors, analogous to the two types of errors in statistical inference, where one falsely rejects a true null hypothesis or fails to reject a false null hypothesis (Type I and Type II). Someone could be guilty but not be recognized (**miss**); therefore the guilty party might go free. On the other hand, the person could be innocent but falsely recognized as guilty (**false alarm**). Part of the philosophy of the legal system of many democratic countries is the intent to minimize the false alarm type of error, assuming that it is better to set an occasional guilty person free than to risk punishing someone who is innocent. Unfortunately, adjusting the criterion (see earlier discussion on recognition memory) to reduce false alarms necessarily increases the probability of misses.

One of the major concerns in determining the difficulty of eyewitness identification is the construction of the lineup. Some recent research has offered some concrete suggestions and evidence for how to measure lineup fairness and construct the most unbiased lineups (Lindsay, Smith, & Pryke, 1999; Malpass & Lindsay, 1999; Wells & Bradfield, 1999).

What Is Eyewitness Memory Like?

Many factors can affect eyewitness memory for an accident or criminal act. One major concern is the delay between the event and the identification. Frequently, an identification lineup occurs days, if not weeks or months, after the crime, allowing much opportunity for decay and retroactive interference to occur in memory. Second, many situational factors frequently contribute to the event's not being deeply processed at the time of occurrence. For example, most crimes that are observed happen very quickly, often in poor lighting, and are totally unexpected. There is little time to redirect one's attention; by the time one has done so, the event is often over.

Third, several factors about the observer contribute to less-than-perfect memory for eyewitness events. Often the observer is under extreme stress, especially if one feels in any personal danger, which is often the case when witnessing a crime in progress (Kassin, 1984; Loftus & Messo, 1987). Our own prejudices enter in the way we process information; we are more likely to recognize an assailant as a member of another racial group than our own. Many otherwise upstanding and conscientious citizens develop some strong motivation to be heroes, to prove themselves right, to ensure that someone is convicted, or to be important. Such motivations can affect our setting of the criterion and thus adversely affect information processing.

People place great faith in eyewitness testimony in spite of its demonstrated fallibility. Loftus (1974) presented the same evidence in a simulated robbery-murder case to three groups of participants. In two of the groups, some of the evidence was presented as having come from an eyewitness, though in one of those two groups additional evidence was presented discrediting the eyewitness by showing his vision was too poor to have possibly recognized anyone at that distance. Although in the control (no eyewitness) group, only 18 percent of the "jurors" voted to convict, 72 percent of the eyewitness group did. Most surprising, however, was the eyewitness-discredited group, where 68 percent voted to convict, suggesting that the mere presence of an eyewitness carried more weight than the expert testimony discrediting him.

Although eyewitnesses can often be discredited, either through specific cross-examination or through general expert testimony about the fallibility of such testimony, most eyewitnesses to crimes never enter a courtroom and are never cross-examined, because a large majority of criminal cases are settled by pre-trial plea bargaining. The mere presence of an eyewitness carries a lot of weight in arranging such pleas.

Introducing Misleading Information

In a careful study of several important variables in eyewitness memory, Lipton (1977) showed people a film of a robbery and shooting in a park and questioned them either immediately afterward or one week later. He was interested in the effects of time and type of question on both accuracy and quantity of information. Lipton used questions ranging from very open-ended to highly structured (multiple choice). The most open-ended questions yielded the most accurate information but the least information overall. Multiple-choice questions yielded more but less accurate information. Questions worded in a biased fashion produced information that was highly subject to reconstructive bias. In conclusion, the style of questioning has enormous impact on how much an eyewitness remembers and how accurate those memories are. Such effects are applicable even beyond the problem of eyewitness memory (see Box 6.7).

Elizabeth Loftus and her associates at the University of Washington conducted an important research program in eyewitness memory. Her typical method was to show participants a film of a crime or auto accident and then question them afterward about their recollection of the incident. She introduced misleading prostevent information through the wording of the question. For example, asking what happened when the car came to the *yield* sign when in fact it was a *stop* sign increased the number of people who later falsely remembered that there had been a yield sign (Loftus, Miller, & Burns, 1978; Schooler, Gerhard, & Loftus, 1986). In another case, people saw a film of an auto accident and were later questioned, "Did you see *the* broken headlight?" or "Did you see *a* broken headlight?" (Loftus & Palmer, 1974). Twice as many questioned with the first question responded "yes," even though no one saw a broken headlight.

Such biasing effects of questions can permanently alter the character of eyewitness memory. In the same set of studies, Loftus and Palmer questioned people with either "About how fast were the cars going when they smashed into each other?" or the same sentence with "smashed" replaced by "hit." The speed estimates were faster by those questioned with "smashed" than those questioned with "hit" (41 mph versus 34 mph), though both were overestimates. One week later, the same people were asked if they had seen any broken glass in the film (there was none); more "smashed" participants falsely reported that they had seen it than did "hit" participants. Apparently broken glass is very consistent with one's knowledge about what

■ Box 6.7 ■

Being an Eyewitness to Yourself

The subject of how the form of a question influences memory has ramifications beyond the eyewitness memory problem. The wording that a doctor or counselor would use to question a person about his or her physical or psychological condition could greatly affect their responses and even their self-perception. This may be an even greater problem than with eyewitness testimony, since what is being remembered is often very subjective and ambiguous to begin with, for example, one's feelings or reactions to others. Consider how differently you might answer each question in each of the following pairs:

1. Do you feel threatened by your boss? Don't you feel threatened by your boss?

2. Do you occasionally have sinus trouble? Do you frequently have sinus trouble?

3. Are you often very anxious when talking in front of a group? Are you often unable to cope when talking in front of a group?

Means and Loftus (1991) found that medical patients often underreported the number of visits to the doctor, especially in cases of several very similar visits, as for a chronic health condition. Using a structured interview, designed to encourage memory for otherwise forgotten doctor visits, greatly improved the memory for those events and the ability to accurately date them. Applied to a different problem, reporting of food-intolerant episodes of eating varied as a function of the type of information accessed (Knibb, Booth, Platts, Armstrong, Booth, & Macdonald, 1999).

happens when cars *smash* into each other. The wording of the question thus helps guide reconstruction through the activation and retrieval of relevant knowledge from long-term memory. Slightly different knowledge is activated to remember an accident of smashing than one of hitting.

Loftus' research on eyewitness memory was conducted using laboratory simulations. For obvious reasons, it is very difficult to do such a study in the real world, though a few such studies have been done (Brigham, Maas, Snyder, & Spaulding, 1982; Krafka & Penrod, 1985; Yuille & Cutshall, 1986). Participants in some of these studies showed more accurate memory than those in the laboratory studies and better resisted attempts to mislead them through the wording of the questions. Even in these more ecologically valid studies, however, some errors were made over time, especially for personal details such as age, height, weight, and color of clothing.

In interpreting her findings, Loftus argued that the underlying memory representation is **overwritten** or permanently altered by misleading postevent information and that warning of this possibility has at best a very limited effect. Others, however, have suggested that a more accurate representation may still exist in the form of a **parallel memory representation** and may still be retrievable, given the right conditions (Hammersley & Read, 1986; Schreiber & Sergent, 1998). Using various methodological arguments, Zaragoza and her colleagues claim that misleading postevent information does not distort memory for the original event to nearly the degree that Loftus claims, and that specific procedural differences greatly affect memory accuracy (Zaragoza & Koshmider, 1989; Zaragoza & Lane, 1994; Zaragoza & McCloskey, 1989; Zaragoza, McCloskey, & Jamis, 1987; Zaragoza & Mitchell, 1996). See Ayers and Reder (1998) for a review and theoretical integration of research on the misinformation effect.

What may we conclude from this examination of eyewitness memory? Even if laboratory studies somewhat exaggerate the fallibility of eyewitness memory, Loftus' work shows that under the right conditions, it can be so distorted. This alone is cause for concern, given that eyewitness testimony is often the central, and sometimes the only, evidence in a prosecution's case. However, all parties involved should bear in mind that eyewitness memory is highly subject to distortion by reconstructive errors, stemming both from a failure to encode the event accurately at the time it occurred or from the distortion introduced later by the wording of the questions. Courtroom procedural rules rather tightly prescribe the sort of questions that may or may not be asked of a witness on the stand, and many, though not all, of the blatantly biasing questions would be disallowed. Control of pretrial questioning, however, is much less regulated, and this is as far as most eyewitnesses ever get. Even those who do come to trial have already been through the potentially distorting influence of the pretrial questioning.

The many years of psychological research on eyewitness memory finally bore some considerable fruit in public policy in the late 1990s in the United States. The use of forensic DNA evidence, first allowed in court in 1989, led to the exoneration of several people falsely convicted of crimes based on eyewitness evidence. This confirmation of what psychologists had long been saying about the fallibility of eyewitness memory captured policymakers' attention and led U.S. Attorney General Janet Reno to convene a panel of police officers, prosecutors, defense attorneys, and psychologists to draw up the first ever national guidelines for the formation of lineups and the questioning of eyewitnesses. First released in September 1999, these guidelines drew heavily on the behavioral research discuss previously. For example, questioners are to make sure that the witness understands that the guilty party may not be in the lineup, in order to ensure a recognition criterion sufficiently high to avoid false recognitions. Also, lineups should be composed only of plausible distractors (nonsuspects). See Wells et al. (1998) for a thorough discussion of recommendations for procedural improvements, based on the body of research on eyewitness identification.

Now we will turn to an area of recent intense controversy where the nature of retrieval from memory is at the heart of a debate that is tearing apart many families, as well as the field of counseling psychology, threatening to destroy the credibility of sexual abuse survivors and their therapists.

RECOVERY OF REPRESSED MEMORIES: UNCOVERED LIFE EVENTS OR IMPLANTED FABRICATIONS?

Ever since the advent of Freud's psychoanalytic theory of personality nearly a century ago, psychologists have been interested in the phenomenon of **repression,** whereby threatening memories or experiences are said to be banished from consciousness. Much of the business of psychotherapy, particularly the therapeutic approach known as psychoanalysis, has been to uncover such repressed memories and urges, as a first step toward healing. Far beyond the profession of therapy, most of the general public tacitly accepts a sort of psychoanalytic model with its belief that unpleasant memories can be exiled from conscious awareness.

A current area of intense interest in regard to repression is how therapists deal with survivors of childhood sexual abuse. It has become clear that significant numbers of adults were sexually abused as children, and that reports of such abuse had, until fairly recently, often been ignored or discredited. We now know that such experiences often have serious and lifelong detrimental psychological effects. The controversy comes in the possibility that some of these "recovered" memories may be for events that never actually occurred but were unintentionally implanted by well-meaning therapists personally convinced that they were dealing with abuse survivors. How could this occur?

What Is the Nature of Unquestioned Abuse Memories?

Sexual abuse, especially when it happens repeatedly over a long period of time, is a painful traumatic experience. Most victims struggle not with the loss of such memories, but with their unwelcome recurrence; they cannot be rid of those memories. Like the survivor of battle or assault crimes like rape, the abuse survivor frequently is haunted by recurring obsessive memories of the abuse. The veracity of such abuse claims is not in question. More uncertain, however, is the case of the person who has *no memory* of being abused until this possibility is suggested by a therapist. While it is clear that we all do forget significant experiences of our past from time to time and later recall them in response to some prompting from others, whether we could forget an extended sequence of experiences like abuse is questioned by many (e.g., Loftus, 1993, 1997; Loftus & Ketcham, 1994). The fact is that there is very little, if any, scientific evidence for the construct of repression in a century of research (Holmes, 1990).

How Can False Memories Be Implanted by Suggestion?

The research on eyewitness memory clearly shows that misleading information can be introduced after an event and subsequently be incorporated into a memory representation and believed to be real. Can such distortion occur for significant traumatic events in one's life, however? In an ingenious simulation of such an event, Loftus and Pickrell (1995; see also Loftus & Ketcham, 1994) implanted a false memory in a teenager that he had been lost in a shopping mall at age five. This was accomplished over some time with the assistance of his older brother who "remembered" the bogus event and discussed it with his brother. Over time the boy increasingly remembered richer and richer details of this fictitious event.

Similar results were obtained by Hyman, Husband, and Billings (1995), in a study where fictitious childhood memories were successfully implanted in 25 percent of college students (with the prior cooperation of their parents in providing some background information!). Students falsely remembered childhood events like being hospitalized for an ear infection or accidentally releasing the hand brake when left in a car. In another study, introducing false information through the context of "dream interpretation" by an alleged trained therapist led to an increased belief that the critical false event, in this case being bullied by another child before the age of three, had actually occurred (Mazzoni, Loftus, Seitz, & Lynn, 1999). Even imagining a fictitious childhood event can increase the later confidence that the imagined nonevent actually occurred—the **imagination inflation effect** (Garry, Manning, Loftus, & Sherman, 1996; Heaps & Nash, 1999; Hyman & Pentland, 1996)!

What Techniques Are Used by Repressed Memory Recovery Therapists?

What greatly concerns memory researchers is that the techniques that have successfully implanted false memories in research are exactly the sort of techniques used by the recovered memory therapists. There are many popular books on recovering repressed memories (Bass & Davis, 1988; Blume, 1990; Frederickson, 1992). These books and many therapists assume that many common symptoms of psychological distress in women (e.g., low self-esteem, depression, anxiety, substance abuse, eating disorders, sexual dysfunction, relationship difficulties, intrusive thoughts) are most likely symptoms of childhood sexual abuse. Readers/clients are told that if they have these symptoms, they were probably abused. Even more troubling, if the client disputes this interpretation, she is viewed as *in denial*. Thus a diagnosis of abuse cannot easily be falsified by the client.

There have been several cases of therapy sessions covertly taped by journalists or former clients preparing legal action. These transcripts showed a frequent early diagnosis of abuse based only on the presentation of very nonspecific symptoms. Although no one knows how widespread this practice is, it appears to be not limited to only a few "bad apples" in the helping professions. Although the motivation of such zealous therapists stems from a genuine concern for the client and a desire to help victims of abuse, some counselors have come to see sexual abuse behind every mental health problem.

Lindsay and Read (1994) suggest several points about the psychology of eyewitness suggestibility that give cause for concern about the veracity of recovered repressed memories. Suggestibility increases with increasing delay between the event and the time it is remembered. It also increases with high perceived authority of the source of the misleading information and a high degree of perceived plausibility of the false information. The impact of misleading information also increases with repetition of the information. All three of these conditions typically hold strongly in the case of discussing repressed memory in the context of therapy.

Not all cognitive psychologists are completely convinced that most recovered memories are fabrications, however. Pezdek, Finger, and Hodge (1997) demonstrated that false memories of a religious ritual could be implanted in high school students, but only within certain boundaries. For example, a story of becoming separated from one's parents when going forward to receive communion was successfully implanted in some Catholic students but in almost no Jewish students.

Others argue that there is physiological evidence for a distinctive effect of stress from traumatic events on particular brain structures involved in memory (Nadel & Jacobs, 1998). For example, high levels of cortisol resulting from stress impair functioning of the hippocampus, which may lead to lesser coherence of the memories, which may still be there in terms of memory for the affect, although a coherent narrative weaving the affective fragments together may be lacking. Whether traumatic events are encoded qualitatively differently than mundane events continues to be debated.

We have not seen the last of this recovered memory issue. Families are being torn asunder by accusations of abuse, and some of them are fighting back through lawsuits against therapists, often with the support of the False Memory Syndrome Foundation, a group of family members (and sometimes recanting clients as well) who argued that therapist-implanted false memories of abuse have destroyed their lives. The critical and urgent question before us now is how to sort out and process the genuine cases of abuse without accepting the spurious ones. The research on memory gives us serious concern that some of the unverified allegations of abuse that emerge in therapy may never have, in fact, occurred. However, we still have no good way of determining whether a particular individual claim of abuse is valid or not. It would be truly tragic if the zealous excesses of some therapists would have the lasting effect of trivializing or calling into question even unquestioned verified cases of childhood sexual abuse. A better understanding of this type of memory is desperately needed. For good discussions of the cognitive issues involved in repressed memory, see Loftus and Ketcham (1994) and the special edition of the journal *Applied Cognitive Psychology* in 1994 devoted to this topic, especially the papers by Lindsay and Read and Ceci and Loftus. For a balanced review of the issue, more from the clinical perspective and including the historical origins in Freud, see Bowers and Farvolden (1996). For other collections of papers, some more critical of the memory recovery critics, see Pezdek and Banks (1996) and Williams and Banyard (1998).

MEMORY AS CONSTRUCTION AND RECONSTRUCTION

Throughout this chapter and the last, we have examined questions in the psychology of information processing. The major by-product of information processing is memory. Whenever we process any information more than extremely superficially, we are necessarily encoding it, though usually to a less-than-perfect degree. Encoding involves processes of **constructing** a memory representation, that is, we build something in our memory to represent that information that we have been thinking about. Such construction may be conscious and deliberate, as in the use of mnemonics, or it may be completely unconscious and accidental, as in the impression you take away of someone you meet in a social encounter when you are not even aware of forming a judgment. When you have cause to think about that information again, you retrieve the relevant information from long-term memory and set about to reconstruct the original input ("Let's see, what were the freedoms guaranteed in the Bill of Rights?" "What does Mary Jones look like and what did she tell me when I saw her last week?"). In this process of reconstruction, we have the remains, perhaps very fragmentary, of our original constructed memory representation, plus all the information that we have added to it through subsequent experiences and during the processes of reconstruction. Sometimes "memory fragments" give us a **feeling of knowing,** even when we cannot quite retrieve the exact information (Calogero & Nelson, 1992; Koriat, 1993; Lupker, Harbluk, & Patrick, 1991; Metcalfe, Schwartz, & Joaquim, 1993; Schwartz & Metcalfe, 1992).

One type of feeling-of-knowing where we can almost but not quite generate a particular word is called the **tip of the tongue (TOT)** phenomenon, first identified by Brown and McNeill (1966). This occurs when we are very sure that we have some knowledge, such as a word or someone's name, but we cannot quite access it. Sometimes we remember fragmentary information ("I know it starts with 's' and has two syllables"). In a review of empirical studies of TOT, A. Brown (1991) concluded that this work has produced several consistent findings, namely: (1) Almost everyone reports some TOT experiences, and the numbers increase with age. (2) Many types of cues can elicit a TOT state, including definitions, faces, line drawings, and odors. (3) TOTs are reported to occur in life about once a week. (4) TOTs are frequently elicited by proper names of personal acquaintances or famous people. (5) The first and last letters of the word and the number of syllables are frequently estimated correctly. In a later review, Schwarz (1999) argues for a high degree of universality of the "tongue" metaphor across many different languages and also argues for looking at TOT as a metacognitive phenomenon.

A very different type of feeling-of-knowing is **prospective memory,** the memory of an intention, the memory that one should do something (Einstein & McDaniel, 1996; Kvavilashvili,1998; McDaniel, 1995). This type of memory is not in the form of information, but it is less clear exactly what form it is in. For example, you remember that you are supposed to stop at the grocery store on the way home from school today, or remember you should call to make a hair appointment. Such intentions are in a heightened state of activation until they are performed or canceled (you change your plans and decide not to do it). After the intention is either canceled before being carried out, which happens about one-quarter of the time in real life, or the act is performed, the memory is inhibited (Marsh, Hicks, & Bryan, 1999; Marsh, Hicks, & Landau, 1998). Prospective memory has considerable marketing applications, in the study of how people remember and forget the intention to buy something (Shapiro & Krishnan, 1999).

This reconstructive character of memory was discussed at length by pioneering British psychologist Sir Frederick Bartlett (1932) in his book *Remembering,* but that approach was not taken seriously in American psychology before the late 1960s. Still, however, some old ways of thinking have persisted. F. Smith (1985) argues that over the years most of cognitive psychology has thought of information processing as a "shunting of information" between the real world and the brain. Rather, he suggests that the fundamental and ongoing activity of the brain is more helpfully conceptualized as the "creation of worlds." Thought involves constructing these worlds, and learning involves elaborating and modifying them. Rather than containing primarily information, the brain "contains nothing less than a theory of the world, . . . an interpreted summary of all past experience" (p. 199). The key is interpretation. The mind is not primarily a repository of information in long-term memory banks but rather is constantly interacting with the world. Learning, then, occurs not so much from the acquisition of new information into the mind but rather from the modification of the internalized theory of the world, which may only imperfectly correspond with that world itself. Smith argues that the traditional shunting-of-information view of memory is subtly reflected in educational systems that stress the acquisition of information rather than the construction of ideas and arguments. The idea of constructive memory has considerable support from research in neuroscience as well (Schacter, Norman, & Koutstaal, 1998).

The ideas of construction and reconstruction in memory have many actual and potential applications. Look at Box 6.8 for a brief account of the way an actor constructs a memory for a character being portrayed on the stage. See Box 6.9 for a study of how much students remembered from a course like this ten years later.

Before we can deal further with construction and reconstruction, we need to examine our most abstract and analytic representational system—language—in more detail. So much information comes to us in the form of language that we must understand something of its structure and character. This will be the focus of the next

■ Box 6.8 ■

Cognitive Psychology in the Theater

The study of memory has wide relevance to actors, but in ways more subtle than the memorization of lines. In fact, professional actors do not try that hard to memorize lines. Rather, they try to develop the character and use elaborative rehearsal strategies to do so (Noice, 1992; Noice & Noice, 1997). These strategies involve getting in touch with the character's feelings, intentions, and inner thoughts, as well as practicing the blocking (movements) that accompany the lines. In this sense the theatrical "rehearsal" is more like elaborative than maintenance rehearsal.

In so creating a mind of the character, not only can the actor learn the lines better and come across more convincingly in the role, but unforeseen circumstances can be handled much more adeptly. For example, if the roof of the theater suddenly starts leaking at center stage, an actor could respond in the character of the part she is playing by observing, "It looks like the kids let the tub run over again."

To a much lesser extent this principle of creating a character is useful to a teacher (Harris, 1977). A teacher can create a character that he or she believes would be the most effective teacher. This character would have a lot of characteristics of the person but probably some that were not characteristic at all. For example, a rather shy person might create a teacher character that was somewhat less shy, figuring that a high degree of shyness would diminish one's effectiveness as a teacher. Keeping this teacher persona in mind, the teacher could respond from the working memory of this created teacher character when talking to a student.

How Much of This Class Will You Remember in Ten Years?

Just in case you think you will have trouble remembering what you learn in this class past the next exam, considering the following study. Conway, Cohen, and Stanhope (1991) tracked down 373 former cognitive psychology students from The Open University in Milton Keynes, England and gave them five memory tests for material they learned in a cognitive psychology course between three months and ten years earlier. Memory for concepts and names of researchers declined for the first three years and stabilized thereafter at above-chance levels. Names of researchers were forgotten faster than concepts. Memory for general facts and research methods remained about the same (also above chance) across the ten years. Overall, students who had received higher grades remembered more information at all retention intervals than those receiving poor grades. Perhaps professors can take some comfort that considerable material from their courses is probably remembered years afterward! Comparably impressive findings were obtained in studies of very long-term memory for faces of people in one's high school graduating class and for Spanish vocabulary learned in school, with substantial retention after as long as fifty years (Bahrick, 1984; Bahrick, Bahrick, & Wittlinger, 1975; Bahrick & Phelps, 1987; Bruck, Cavanagh, & Ceci, 1991).

chapter, after which we will return to the questions of construction and reconstruction in the processes of comprehension (Chapter 8).

SUGGESTED READINGS

The topic of memory is covered extensively in all of the cognition texts cited at the end of Chapter 5. In addition, Baddeley (1990) gives a comprehensive and highly readable treatment of only memory. Searleman and Herrmann (1994) offer a very readable textbook on memory with a particular emphasis on applications often neglected by other texts. Collins, Gathercole, Conway, and Morris (1995) and Izawa (1999) offer collections of more technical chapters reviewing recent research and theory in different areas of memory. For an excellent review article on the fallibility of memory, see Schacter's (1999) article in the *American Psychologist*. For the most comprehensive review of research in different areas of memory, see the handbook edited by Tulving and Craik (2000).

Neisser and Hyman's (1999) *Memory Observed* is a fascinating and highly readable anthology of papers about memory in natural settings. For more rigorous research studies and conceptual papers on autobiographical memory, see Rubin (1986) and the August 1998 special thematic issue of *Applied Cognitive Psychology*. For engrossing case studies of exceptional individuals, see Luria (1968) and Thompson et al. (1993). For a readable and absorbing discussion of the recovery of repressed memories controversy, see Loftus and Ketcham (1994); for a more clinically-oriented review, see Bowers and Farvolden (1996). For a discussion of memory failures in everyday life, see Herrmann and Gruneberg (1999).

PART IV

THE HIGHER MENTAL PROCESSES

7 Language

Readers of this book *know* English (and perhaps other languages as well). When people *know* a language, what is it that they *know?* It is many types of information, including elements such as sounds, letters, words, meanings, sentences, and grammatical constituents, as well as rules for combining these elements. The information that we possess when we know a language may be grouped into four general categories, or components: the **phonological** (sound) component, the **semantic** (meaning) component, the **syntactic** (structural) component, and the **pragmatic** (contextual) component. Each of these components includes both elements of information and rules about how those elements may and may not be combined and used together. In this chapter we will look at these components and their ramifications for the processing of language. Finally, we will discuss the psychology of reading and writing.

PHONOLOGY

The phonological (sound) component of language includes (1) the perceived speech sounds, phonemes and suprasegmental cues, and (2) the implicit phonological rules for how these sounds may be combined. This component of language was discussed in Chapter 5, as an example of complex pattern recognition. Thus, we will not discuss it further here, except to note that any adequate theory of comprehension will have to include how we perceive phonemes and suprasegmental cues in speech and how we use phonological rules. However, the phonological component is only one of four components that any such comprehension theory must include. It is the other three that we will now examine.

SEMANTICS

A second component of language is meaning, or semantics. If there were no meaning to be communicated or understood, there would be little reason for any structure, sound, or context. Because it is so difficult to isolate and identify, however, meaning is in many ways the most difficult aspect of language to study. Just what is meaning anyway?

Lexical Meaning

The smallest unit of language that has meaning is called a **morpheme.** Many words are morphemes, and some smaller units are also morphemes. For example, prefixes and suffixes like *un-, dis-, -ness, or -ful* (*bound* morphemes) have meaning in and of themselves, even though they may not stand independently as words.

Here we focus primarily on the psychology of the **lexicon,** our collection of *word* meanings (Landauer, 1998; Miller, 1999; Schwanenflugel, 1991; Taft, 1991). What a word refers to in the real world is its **referent.** Every word carries the cues to at least one meaning. Many, if not most, words may have more than one completely distinct meaning (river *bank* versus money *bank*). In fact, however, ambiguity is more potential than real in the normal usage of language. For example, the context would typically make clear which sense of *bank* was intended. Occasionally, of course, genuine confusion does result because of the ambiguity of some word, and such ambiguity can be the source of humor. Often the punch line of a joke is the information that the earlier, and normally most likely, interpretation of some word or words was, in fact, incorrect, as:

1. The bells were peeling; in fact, the whole tower needed painting badly.

See Box 7.1 for some entertaining examples of lexical ambiguity in newspaper headlines.

Denotation and Connotation

One issue in the psychological study of semantics is whether our stored mental representations of word meanings are more like dictionary definitions or more like extensive information in an encyclopedia. The basic definitional information about a word is its **denotation;** the emotional or evaluative content is the **connotation.** Connotation is often very important psychologically. Consider the differences in connotation in American English between "black," "Negro," "African-American," "colored," and the highly inflammatory "N-word" as terms referring to American citizens of African descent. Most people would be flattered to be called "slender" or "slim" but offended to be called "skinny." Sometimes the connotation of a subject is considered so negative or uncomfortable that new, more positive works are coined to speak of that topic. See Box 7.2 for a discussion of **euphemisms,** words explicitly used to improve the connotation.

Presupposition

The semantics of even single words that are not ambiguous can nonetheless be quite complex. For instance, there are many verbs that carry as part of their meaning a **presupposition** about whether the speaker believes some other piece of information to be true (Green, 1989). A presupposition is something that the speaker assumes to be true; it is a necessary precondition to the overall statement being either true or false.

■ **Box 7.1** ■

──────── **Lexical Ambiguity in the Headlines** ────────

"Boy gets in line for liver"
"Preacher shocked at Senator's sex position"
"Politician stoned at rally"
"Hookers appeal to Mayor"
"Heavy TV watchers tend to be obese"

LEARNING AND COGNITION

Euphemisms: Always Benign or Sometimes Malignant?

Although most people are familiar with such relatively harmless euphemisms as "passed away" for "died," "make love" for "have sexual intercourse," or "restroom" for "bathroom," some euphemisms may actually be somewhat more misleading and even malicious. When does a euphemism go so far as to become "lying," and when is it only, as a U.S. government official once said, "massaging the truth"?

In the nineteenth century, a time of significant economic decline in the United States was called a "panic," as in the Panic of 1873 or Panic of 1893. After the severe economic collapse following the stock market crash of 1929, however, there was concern about avoiding panic and chaos: Thus the state was called by the gentler name "depression." Later, "depression" came to signify that particular time of extreme economic distress in the 1930s, and governmental leaders were loathe to invoke it again, for fear of eliciting those negative memories and associations. Thus more recent economic declines became "recessions." Even that word was too hard for some seeking public office to say, so it was called an "economic downturn."

Perhaps the most vicious euphemisms come in the kinder, gentler terms used to describe wartime atrocities. Civilians killed by "collateral damage" or one's own soldiers killed by the mistake of "friendly fire" are just as dead. The bombing and obliteration of Vietnamese villages in the Vietnam War of the 1960s was termed "pacification." Nazi Germany referred to its "Final solution" for its extermination of six million Jews. Widespread expulsion of Albanians from the Serbian province of Kosovo in 1999 was called "ethnic cleansing."

Consider example (2) following, which presupposes that the speaker of sentence (2) believes the information in the subordinate clause, namely, that Elaine had left, to be true. Indeed, if Elaine has not left, (2) would not be either true or false; it would just be strange. Consider the weirdness of (3) and (4). While both (3) and (4) suggest that Eric is a little weird for believing that unicorns were real, (3) suggests as well that the speaker is also a little weird and holds the same strange belief. (A possible exception would be if heavy unnatural stress were laid on "knew" to make it sound ironic, but that possibility will be ignored at present.)

2. Janice regretted that Elaine had left.
3. Eric knew the unicorns were real.
4. Eric was sure that unicorns were real.

Sometimes what a word asserts directly versus what it presupposes can be the basis of the difference of two contrasting words. For example, *accuse* presupposes that the act in question is considered bad by the speaker while it asserts that a particular person was responsible. In contrast, the otherwise similar verb *criticize* presupposes that a particular person is responsible and asserts that the act was bad (Fillmore, 1971). If a presupposition is violated, absurdity (as opposed to falsehood) results. While (5) presupposes that the act is bad, it seems odd that the speaker would think it bad to rescue a little girl; thus, a presupposition of *accuse* appears to be violated. In (6), the presupposition of responsibility appears to be violated, since Aunt

Jemima did not shoot Abraham Lincoln, and it seems highly unlikely anyone would believe she did.

5. Bill accused Jim of rescuing the little girl.
6. Bill criticized Aunt Jemima for shooting Abraham Lincoln.

Fuzzy Sets

When examined closely, even what at first appear to be very clearly defined semantic concepts or classes become *fuzzy,* or difficult to define precisely. A good example is *furniture.* What constitutes a piece of furniture? Most would agree that objects like beds, couches, chairs, tables, and dressers are furniture, but how about grandfather clocks, card tables, ping-pong tables, wastebaskets, rugs, footstools, floor lamps, table lamps, vases, pillows, flower pots, plant stands, built-in bookshelves, pianos, cellos, music stands, typewriters, coasters, trunks, and picture frames? Is the class "furniture" defined by size (e.g., a grandfather clock is a piece of furniture, but an alarm clock is not), by position (all things that sit on the floor are pieces of furniture while those that sit on tables or hang on walls are not), or by object class (plants and flower pots are not furniture, even if a six-foot plant sits in a two-foot diameter pot on the floor)? Everyone has his or her own conceptions of what is and is not furniture, and each definition may be slightly different from all the others. For this reason we say that furniture is a **fuzzy set.** Fuzzy sets are very common, being the rule rather than the exception for natural-language categories.

A similar example involves differentiating between a "glass," a "cup," and a "mug." People typically classify based on physical attributes, such as cups having handles and sitting on saucers (but then what about paper and styrofoam cups—why aren't they glasses?). If mugs also have handles but are thicker and don't take saucers, is there a certain thickness after which a cup becomes a mug? If a glass can be of many shapes (tumblers, wine glasses, shot glasses, juice glasses) but must have no handle and be made of either plastic or glass, then why is an object the same size, shape, and thickness but made of paper called a cup instead of a glass? One final complication: Does what we call a drinking vessel in part depend on what drink is in it? If a paper cup is filled with pop or beer, is it still a cup of pop or a cup of beer, or has it become a glass (or perhaps a glass of pop in a cup!)?

Clearly glasses, cups, and mugs, like furniture, are all fuzzy sets, but, perhaps surprisingly, we are usually able to comprehend and converse about them with little confusion. In fact, we can construct categories whenever we need them; such categories may sometimes contain objectively very disparate members; for example, a class of situations (party, class, club meeting) in which one might make new friends (Barsalou, 1983). There might be very few, if any, concrete attributes common to all instances of such a class, but yet we would be able to construct a category and use it, for example, in trying to structure one's life in such a way as to make new friends.

The fuzzy set issue is not a purely academic one but manifests itself in some serious social problems. For example, physicians and legal scholars are discovering that the concept death is a very fuzzy set. Such issues as euthanasia, organ transplants, and reviving someone after a brief heart stoppage underline the importance of defining death more precisely. Similarly, the abortion debate issue can be posed as: When does personhood begin? If a first-trimester fetus is in fact a person, then aborting it is murder; if it is not, then the abortion is merely a surgical procedure. "Person" is a fuzzy set in that an egg and sperm are not persons, but a baby at birth is; just where in between does the entity enter the class person?

Acquisition of Word Meaning

How do we acquire the meaning of so many words (6,000 or so by the time we enter school, perhaps 10 times that many by the time we start college)? We do not yet completely understand this amazing process, but one intriguing recent theory, Landauer's Latent Semantic Analysis model (Landauer, 1998, Landauer & Dumais, 1997; Landauer, Foltz, & Laham, 1998) suggests a link between every word we hear or read and the context of its use. Once many such links have been established, it becomes easier to figure out the meaning of new words we have *not* encountered before. This helps to explain how we acquire new word meanings faster than we could possibly study or be taught them explicitly. Every instance of a word we encounter is connected somehow with the material in which it occurs. Just how this happens is very complex, the subject of several computer simulations, and it is not yet fully tested.

Negation

One semantically interesting type of word is a **negation** (Horn, 1989). This may be expressed directly by a negative word, like *not, no one, never,* or *none,* by negative prefixes (*un-, dis-, im-, in-*), or even by certain words that have an inherent negation in their meaning (abolish, subtract, lose, pretend, forget, fail, prevent). Most psychological research has found that, other things being equal, a negative statement is typically more difficult to comprehend or remember than a corresponding affirmative one. However, this may depend considerably on the context. Negatives are often used to deny something and tend to be reasonable only if such a denial is plausible (Johnson-Laird & Tridgell, 1972; Wason, 1965). Thus, sentence (7) seems a reasonable negation because someone could easily think that a bat was a bird, but (8), although a true statement, is somewhat bizarre in that it is hard to imagine the need to ever assert it; who would ever think a table *was* a bird?

7. A bat is not a bird.
8. A table is not a bird.

Context

As already mentioned, the context of a word's use gives valuable clues to its meaning, and the ability to exploit that context is an important linguistic and cognitive ability (Miller, 1999). For certain words, the meaning is particularly heavily determined by surrounding words or by nonverbal context. One type of word for which this is particularly true are quantifiers, words like *all, many, few, some, several,* or *none.* For example, consider (9) and (10). How many people would have to have earned over $30,000 to make (9) true, and how many would have to have died in tornadoes to make (10) true? For most people, "many" killed by tornadoes is not nearly as many as "many" earning over $30,000. Thus, many has meaning only in relation to what it is modifying and what the person using it expects; it means "many" relative to what might be expected. Hence, something as "purely linguistic" as word meaning can, in fact, be defined in part by psychological factors.

9. Many people earned over $30,000 last year.

10. Many people were killed by tornadoes last year.

Another type of context-dependent word meaning involves **deictic** words, that is, words that take on their meaning only by relating to a context (Duchan, Bruder, & Hewitt, 1995). For example, demonstrative adjectives such as *this, that, these,* and *those* mean nothing more than *the* unless there is a near or far context to point to in order to discriminate, for example, "these" people from "those" people. Consider the silliness of sitting in an office and saying (11), unless there happened to be pictures of ostriches or real birds within sight. Other examples of deictic words include *here* and *there,* verb tense, and verbs like *come* and *go* and *bring* and *take.* People remember, or misremember, deictic words as having been spoken from the rememberer's own perspective (Brewer & Harris, 1974).

11. These ostriches are pretty.

Translation

Sometimes one language will have one word to cover two different ideas, while another language will have two separate words. In American English the word *rent* can refer either to what the landlord or the tenant does in a rental transaction, while in a sales transaction we distinguish between *buy* and *sell.* In German, however, there are two corresponding words for the two senses of *rent* (*mieten* and *vermieten*), a distinction which also exists in British, but not American, English (*let* versus *rent*). English has one word, *know,* which can mean either to know a piece of information or to be acquainted with someone. French, Spanish, Portuguese, and German have two separate verbs for these two senses of know (*savoir-connaître, saber-conocer, saber-conhecer,* and *wissen-kennen,* respectively). On the other hand, Romance languages have one verb (*faire, hacer, fazer*), which means both "make" and "do" in English.

Sometimes there is, within a given language, a concept that has no name in that language: This is called a **lexical gap.** For example, in English there is no single unambiguous word for the person one lives with sexually outside of marriage; such words as *friend, lover, fiancé(e), boy/girl friend,* or *significant other* can also refer to other people. There may be many concepts that seem to require a word in some languages and cultures more than others. For example, the Criolo language of Guinea-Bissau in West Africa has words for "to hide something in one's armpit," "to look away from something disgusting," and "to store something under one's bed" (Macauley, 1990). Sometimes a needed word may be borrowed from one language to another to fill a lexical gap (*Zeitgeist* from German, *taco* and *piñata* from Spanish, *dénouement* and *esprit de corps* from French, *fjord* from Norwegian, or *apartheid* from Afrikaans.)

The same word can mean something slightly, or considerably, different in another dialect of the same language. Consider, for example, the many differences between British and American English. For example, what Americans call *cookies* and *apartments* the English call *biscuits* and *flats.* If you talk about your *pants* in London, you may receive a few titters, since the word refers to underwear in Britain; *trousers* are what you wear over your underwear. *Chips* in Chicago are *crisps* in London, while *chips* in Britain are *french fries* in America. If a woman says "I'm easy," it means "I don't care" in Britain but "I'm sexually available" in America. Asking for *rubbers* in a British drugstore will get you pencil erasers, while in North America it will get you condoms. A high-class Indian ballpoint pen magazine ad once boldly proclaimed, "At last, pens that have the balls to promise you the earth"; that might convey quality and style in Indian English but in America is a vulgar expression loosely referring to testicles. Translation across languages, and even some dialects, can be fraught with peril. (See Box 7.3.)

Lest you think that ambiguous or unclear word meaning is an interesting but not terribly consequential issue, see Box 7.4 for an explanation of one of history's most devastating events arising from lexical ambiguity.

The cognitive processes involved in the translation of larger bodies of discourse from a source language to a target language offer a rich potential area to study language processing (Danks, Shreve, Fountain, & McBeath, 1997). Thus far there have been rather few cognitive studies of the translation process. Translation done by professional translators can be literary or simultaneous oral translation. Depending on the task, translation involves varying degrees of interpretation as well as direct translation. Much translation also occurs very informally, such as when children in immigrant or sojourner families translate between their teachers and their parents. The most common methodology to study translation processes has been using think-aloud protocols (e.g., Kiraly, 1997). Translation has also been studied using word or sentence units or by varying characteristics of the language input, such as signal-to-noise ratio or text structure (de Groot, 1997). For a cognitive model of the translation process, see Danks and Griffin (1997).

■ Box 7.3 ■

Embarrassments in International Marketing

General Motors did not understand for a while why its popular Chevrolet Nova was not selling in Puerto Rico. When someone finally pointed out that Nova in Spanish means "it doesn't go (run)," the name in that market was changed to "Caribe" and sales improved. For similar reasons, the AMC Matador did not do well in Latin America, but then an imported car named "Killer" or "Murderer" probably wouldn't sell too well in the United States!

The company that is now the Exxon Corporation made some preliminary plans several years ago to change the firm name to "Enco," short for "Energy Company." While this sounded very appropriate in English, in Japanese the word "enco" means "flat tire," hardly a good name for a company of service stations. Thus, that name was dropped too.

A certain brand of toothpaste did not sell in Buenos Aires, quite possibly because "Colgate" in Argentinian Spanish means "go hang yourself." A type of Brazilian bank account was marketed under its Portuguese acronym "PIS," which would not market well to North America, nor would Japanese Mypee Shampoo or Bluebird Drops candy, Iranian Barf detergent, or Mexican Bimbo bread. Some products actually marketed in the United States include Calpis (a Japanese soft drink pronounced "cow-piss"), Pfanni (a German dumpling mix), and Superglans (a Dutch carwax) (Aman, 1982). Slogans can also cause problems. The unfortunate translation of "Come alive, you're in the Pepsi generation" in Thai was "Pepsi brings your ancestors back from the dead."

Box 7.4
The Semantics of Hiroshima

Coughlin (1953) speculated that the mistranslation of the Japanese word *mokusatsu* may have been partly responsible for the atomic bombing of Hiroshima in 1945. The literal translation of *mokusatsu* is "to kill with silence." Denotatively, this can mean two things to a Japanese: (1) to ignore or (2) to withhold from comment. When Premier Suzuki confronted the press on July 28, 1945, in response to the Potsdam Declaration of the Allies, which demanded the unconditional surrender of the Japanese armed forces at the end of World War II, he announced that the Japanese cabinet was holding to a policy of *mokusatsu*. Testimony after the war from Japanese cabinet officials indicated that Suzuki's intended meaning was to withhold from comment until the Allies' ultimatum was communicated to the Japanese government through official channels. To do otherwise would have meant acting upon unofficial, perhaps erroneous information that was transmitted over radio. Japanese translators at the Domei News Agency, however, chose the "ignore" meaning. Thus, the Allies received the message, "The Japanese government ignores the demand to surrender." Not only was the denotative meaning erroneous, but the connotations associated with being ignored are usually quite negative. The atom bomb was dropped a week later on Hiroshima, killing approximately 70,000 people (Rothwell, 1982, p. 27).

Metaphor

Another important but often overlooked aspect of meaning is the **figurative** meaning, sometimes simply called **metaphor.** Metaphor discusses the actual **topic** of discussion *in terms of* something else, the **vehicle.** For example, in (12) following the topic is baseball and the vehicle is cooking. Very often language is intended nonliterally and is very clearly so. Metaphor is widely used in all types of language and is even a part of the way we think (Cacciari, 1998; Gibbs, 1994; Lakoff & Johnson, 1980; Turner, 1998). It is frequently present in sports (12), persuasive rhetoric (13), name-calling (14), literature (15), and counseling (16) (see sentences following). Any eventual theory of semantics will have to explain how we comprehend figurative as well as literal meaning (Gibbs, 1994, 1998; Glucksberg, 1991; Glucksberg & Keysar, 1990; Katz, 1998).

12. The Mets creamed the Phillies.
13. This Administration is bleeding the state dry.
14. Tim is a real pain in the butt.
15. ". . . suffer the slings and arrows of outrageous fortune . . ."
16. I know I keep my feelings all locked up inside.

How do we comprehend figurative meaning? Some argue that deep conceptual metaphors such as "ideas are food" or "theories are buildings" guide the comprehension of metaphors like "the lecture was a three-course meal" or "that theory is on shaky ground" (Lakoff, 1993; Murphy, 1996, 1997). Others claim that a metaphorical statement like "our marriage was a rollercoaster ride" asserts that the topic is a member of some attributed category exemplified by the vehicle, for example, stating that the marriage and a rollercoaster are both in a class of "exciting scary situations" (Glucksberg, 1991; Glucksberg, Manfredi, & McGlone, 1997; McGlone, 1996). See McGlone (in press) for a complete discussion of these issues.

So far we have considered the semantic aspect of language largely in regard to the meaning of single words. Another important aspect of the semantic component of language is the meaning of a sentence or utterance as a whole. This may be referred to as its propositional meaning, and it will be considered more carefully after a look at syntax.

SYNTAX

The third component of language is its **syntax,** or structure. Syntax involves rules for describing how words, or, more precisely, abstract grammatical constituents like subjects, predicates, noun phrases, and other elements, may be put together to form an acceptable sentence in a given language. Words cannot be put together in random order and be meaningful.

Syntax, as the linguist and psychologist deal with it, is descriptive; it attempts to identify rules actually used in real language. It is not intended to be normative or prescriptive, that is, telling us what we should do. Contrary to what might be your memories of eighth-grade English class, the interest in psychology is not in coercing people to say "isn't" instead of "ain't" or "brought" instead of "brung." The scientist studying language is interested in how people actually talk, not how some expert *thinks* they should talk (Pinker, 1994).

Surface and Deep Structure

Any sentence may be broken down into grammatical constituents, or structural units, such as subject, predicate, or prepositional phrase. Different words belong to functional classes most often called parts of speech (noun, verb, adjective, etc.). Such an analysis of a sentence is its **surface structure.** For example, the surface structure of both (17) and (18) following is noun-verb-adjective-infinitive. A very large number of different words could be plugged into each of these "slots," but they would have to conform to the type of word allowed there. For example, the word "the" could not be inserted in the verb position, nor the word "friendly" in the noun position. The sentence diagramming you learned back in junior high and the grammar drills you labored through studying a foreign language were basically surface structure exercises, training you to identify and use the surface syntactic constituents. Although syntactic knowledge is largely implicit by the time a child starts school, to bring it to a conscious level requires careful, even laborious, teaching.

17. Henry is easy to please.
18. Henry is eager to please.

Surface structure is not the only possible level of analysis, however. There is a deeper level, first pointed out by the linguist Noam Chomsky (1957, 1965a), called the **deep,** or sometimes the **underlying, structure.** Let's go back to (17) and make a companion to it (18). Both (17) and (18) have the same surface structure. They do, of course, contain one word different from the other, and that changes the meaning, but it is structure, not the meaning, which is of concern here. Although the two sentences have identical surface structures, there is something very different about them syntactically, specifically the relation of the noun *Henry* to the verb *please*. In (18) "Henry" is the deep-structure subject of "please," while in (17) "Henry" is the deep-structure object. In one case he is doing the pleasing; in the other he is being pleased. We might say that Henry is the agent or actor in (18) and the acted-upon in (17). Nowhere in the surface structure of noun-verb-adjective-infinitive is this important distinction captured.

Even though you may have never before thought about differences like the contrast between the syntax of (17) and (18), you must have in some sense "known" that knowledge in order to be able to speak and understand such sentences correctly, that is, to know whether Henry was doing the pleasing or being pleased. This also has ramifications for language acquisition in children. If part of what children must know about a language involves deep-structure relationships, there is no way they could learn that purely by imitating surface structures of parents. Language acquisition will be discussed further in Chapter 11.

The importance of deep-structure relationships can be further illustrated with an additional example (19), which has one surface structure (noun-verb-adjective-infinitive), but two possible deep structures, depending on whether the chicken is the deep-structure subject or object of *eat*.

19. The chicken is ready to eat.

On the other hand, there are cases where one deep structure may have different possible alternative surface structures, such as the active and passive versions of the same idea (20) and (21). Here the same deep structure can be realized into either of two surface structures.

20. Robin Hood rescued the princess.
21. The princess was rescued by Robin Hood.

See Box 7.5 for some humorous examples of how multiple surface or deep structures can lead to multiple meanings, some quite different from what was intended!

Parsing and the Given-New Contract

Although Chomsky and other linguists focused mainly on describing the structural knowledge we must have to know a language, syntax is also very important psychologically in helping us understand language we hear and read every day. Although syntax is not the same as meaning, it helps to signal the meaning and thus helps us interpret a given sentence. To take a simple example, articles like *a, an,* or *the* signal that a noun phrase is beginning and one can reasonably expect the next word to be either a noun or a modifying adjective preceding a noun.

When we comprehend language, we use strategies of **parsing,** identifying structural components of a sentence (Altmann, 1990). For example, we use a **canonical sentence strategy** to infer that a sequence of noun-verb-noun (a very common pattern) corresponds to subject-verb-object. This will yield a correct parsing in a majority of cases, though not in all. We also must learn to identify certain cues that indicate exceptions to the canonical sentence strategy. The relative frequency of occurrences of different syntactic structures in the language may also play a role in parsing (Mckoon & Ratcliff, 1998).

■ Box 7.5 ■

Syntactic Ambiguity

Surface Structure Ambiguity
>   Headlines: "Police Kill Man with Club"
>
>   "Professor Gives Talk on Mars"
>
>   "Criticisms about Council Members Growing Ugly"
>
>   Sign in gym: "I will be taking people out of lockers who haven't paid their rental fee."
>
>   Report in newspaper: "She saw sexual intercourse taking place between parked cars."

Deep Structure Ambiguity
>   Sign at bank: "Drive through window"
>
>   Signs: "SLOW MEN WORKING"
>
>   "SLOW CHILDREN CROSSING"
>
>   "FOR BATHROOM USE STAIRS"
>
>   Headlines: "Man Eating Fish Mistakenly Sold as Pet"
>
>   "Legislative Panel Eats, Discusses New Tax Plan"
>
>   "Potential Witness to Murder Drunk"
>
>   "UFO Talks at University"
>
>   "All Texas Condemned to Face Death"
>
>   "Deer Kill 100,000"

Syntax can also tell us what information the hearer already knows and what information is new in that sentence. For example, consider (22) and (23). Both contain the same information, even the same words, but somehow there is a difference. A particular piece of information (that the toad is ugly) is in a different syntactic structure in each sentence. As (22) would normally be used, the hearer and the speaker are both aware of some toad that is ugly (**given** information) and the speaker is telling the hearer that the toad is on the mushroom (**new** information). In (23), however, the speaker and hearer know that there is a toad on the mushroom and the new information says that it is ugly.

22. The ugly toad is on the mushroom.

23. The toad on the mushroom is ugly.

Part of the unwritten conventions of language is that we have an implicit agreement to put given information in certain syntactic structures of a sentence, for example, in adjectives or prepositional phrases modifying the subject of a sentence, and new information in other forms—in adjectives or phrases following the verb. This allows the listener to pick out what the new information is and link it up with given information already in our memory and repeated in the given part of the sentence (Clark, 1977; Clark & Haviland, 1977; Haviland & Clark, 1974). The given-new distinction may be further illustrated by looking at appropriate and inappropriate denials of (22) and (23). For example, (24) would be an appropriate denial of (23), but a very awkward and inappropriate response to (22), while the reverse is true for (25).

24. No, it's a pretty toad.

25. No, it's on the lily pad.

It has long been known that people often do not notice blatantly contradictory information, such as in the old children's riddle "How many pairs of animals did Moses take into the ark?" or "If a plane crashes on a national boundary, where do they bury the survivors?" (Bredart & Docquier, 1989; Bredart & Modolo, 1988; Erickson & Mattson, 1981; van Oostendorp & de Mul, 1990). Part of the reason such false information may be missed is due to its given-new status in the sentence. For example, Baker and Wagner (1987) had participants listen to sentences such as either (26) or (27) and respond true or false. They were told to respond false if any part of the sentence were false. Subjects like (26) were correctly identified as false more often than sentences like (27). A second study confirmed that this result occurred independent of the position of the information in the sentence. These findings suggest that one way to introduce misleading information is to place false information in subordinate clauses (given) rather than main clauses (new). People are less likely to notice the false information there. This is one way of introducing misleading postevent information, as discussed in the previous chapter.

26. Emerald City, the home of the Wizard of Oz, was named after the precious red stone.

27. Emerald City, named after the precious red stone, was the home of the Wizard of Oz.

When we communicate through language, we are always making assumptions about what our hearers know and what they do not know. Evidence exists that we often overimpute our own knowledge to others, assuming a greater shared body of knowledge than is in fact the case (Nickerson, 1999). Such assumptions can lead to miscommunication.

Language Production

Syntax is also very important in language production. For example, speech errors very often preserve the syntactic form, even at the expense of the meaning. Although the classic psychodynamic "Freudian slip" interpretation of the BBC broadcaster who once signed off for the "British Broadcorping Castration" speaks of unconscious sexual motivations, a more pedestrian (but almost surely more correct) explanation has to do with the preservation of the syntax and inversion of two syllables in the expression. Even when someone cannot recall a particular word, they can sometimes recall syntactic information such as grammatical gender or whether a noun is a mass or a count noun.

Style

Another manifestation of differences in syntax occurs in the matter of **style.** Certain placements of words and phrases indicate a more formal style than others. Subtle stylistic differences are some of the cues that tip off a teacher that a student paper is plagiarized, because its style is a little too formal to be a typical student composition. Moreover, in formal speaking and writing, people tend to use more complex syntax, involving a greater number of subordinate clauses. In more colloquial speech, shorter, choppier sentences are the rule, if indeed speech is composed of grammatically well-formed sentences at all, which it often is not.

As is true of all aspects of language, the syntax of style evolves and changes over time. For example, modern English transforms a declarative (28) into a yes-no question by the addition of a form of the verb *do* (29). However, in Elizabethan English one could simply invert the subject and verb (30), a form of question common in the time of Shakespeare (31), but no longer used. It is in part the many uses of unfamiliar syntax that makes Shakespeare and his contemporaries difficult for the modern reader. Unfortunately, sometimes contemporary language is also very difficult to understand because of its style. See Box 7.6 for a discussion of a judge's instructions to the jury.

■ Box 7.6 ■

Instructions to the Jury

One area of concern in forensic psychology is the language in the judge's instructions to the jury prior to deliberation (Elwork & Sales, 1985; Imwinkelried & Schwed, 1987; Kagehiro, 1990; Kassin & Wrightsman, 1985; Severance & Loftus, 1982; Tanford, Penrod, & Collins, 1985; Wiener, Habert, Shkodriani, & Staebler, 1991). The custom of the judge instructing the jury arose from the need to inform the jurors and help them apply the law to the case at hand. In the late nineteenth and early twentieth centuries, U.S. state statutes started requiring the courts to reduce all instructions by the judge to writing; this had the effect of formalizing the instructions being read verbatim at a trial. These verbatim instructions were used repeatedly because these were the instructions that had been upheld on appeal. Any judge who deviated and used another set of instructions ran the risk of having that decision later overturned on a technicality. Now most state and federal courts have those so-called pattern instructions for most crimes. Since they are used for all trials for a particular crime, they are, not surprisingly, broad and abstract and do not allow very well for integration of the specifics of the trial. The instructions seldom use examples, for fear of biasing the jury. While the use of pattern instructions makes excellent sense from a legal point of view, from a cognitive perspective it is considerably more questionable.

In a cognitive study of a judge's instructions to the jury, Charrow and Charrow (1979) asked prospective jurors to paraphrase 14 standard civil instructions from the California state judicial system. Their results showed that over 60 percent of the ideas in the instructions were either paraphrased inaccurately or completely forgotten. Certain types of syntactic constructions cause a lot of comprehension difficulty. These included passive constructions, certain prepositional phrases, especially those containing the stylistically awkward expression "as to," and sentences with two or more negations. Other difficult constructions included sentences with discontinuous constituents, such as "A proximate cause is a cause which in natural and continuous sequence produces an injury." The phrase "which . . . produces an injury" is broken up with an intervening phrase, thus making it more difficult to assign a subject of "produces." Charrow and Charrow did not find that jurors' difficulty with the instructions stemmed from the inherent difficulty of the legal concepts, but rather from the way the concepts were stated. Every concept was much more understandable if phrased in a way more consistent with our natural language comprehension strategies.

28. Anne likes broccoli.

29. Does Anne like broccoli?

30. Likes Anne broccoli?

31. Think you that the king is mad?

Propositional Structure

At a level more abstract (or deep, if you will) than even the deep structure is the structure of the ideas in the sentence. This is when the division between syntax and semantics becomes particularly murky. Most cognitive psychologists would agree that meaningful discourse is composed of semantic units called **propositions.** An example of how a sentence could be broken up into propositions would be (32). Sentence (32) contains five separate simple propositions; we might remember some of these and forget others some time after hearing the sentence.

32. Brave young Snoopy withstood the cat's sharp blows.

    (a) Snoopy was brave.

    (b) Snoopy was young.

    (c) The blows were sharp.

    (d) The blows came from the cat.

    (e) Snoopy withstood the blows.

As you can see, the propositional level of analysis really involves semantic factors (meaning), as well as syntactic ones. In fact, many psychologists and linguists question the usefulness of talking about a deep-structure level of syntax, preferring to consider the level more abstract than the surface structure as entirely semantic.

In describing propositions, they are first of all, not analogical, that is, they bear no physical relationship to the referent they represent. They are highly analytic and abstract, a fact worth keeping constantly in mind when using graphic or schematic representations of them, which necessarily must represent them as words (see Kintsch, 1974; van Dijk & Kintsch, 1983) or some combination of words and graphic representations (J. R. Anderson, 1983, 1996).

Second, propositions are primarily semantically based, that is, a representation of the meaning, although some variants of propositional theory do also contain some structure. Unlike language, they are not ambiguous and do not contain the surface structure at all. A proposition coding the idea of John kissing Mary could have had its stimulus source in any one of several spoken or written sentences ("John kissed Mary," "Mary was kissed by John") or in an observation of the event of John kissing Mary. Propositions are not dependent on the form of the input, nor are they typically good avenues to retrieving that exact surface information.

Propositions have some kind of internal organization and, as such, contain both units and relations. Units, like concepts or nodes in semantic network models, could be entities like *agent, object,* or *instrument,* while relations could be the identity relationship (A is B), possession, or relationships like *acts upon* or *object of.* The internal organization of propositions may be reflected in its different components. For example, an action *hit* may contain elements of agent, object, and instrument, any of which could appear as the surface structure object of the sentence (e.g., "the boy hit the ball," "the ball was hit by the boy," "the bat hit the ball").

Unlike images or concepts, propositions either have a truth value (in the case of a statement about something, asserting either a stative relation or an action) or can be meaningfully acted upon, in the case of a question or imperative. An image or concept cannot be true or false or be acted upon; it is merely a representation. On the other hand, a proposition asserts something, which may in reality be true or false, or requests a response, which may or may not be complied with.

Propositions have evolved as a very useful construct in studying linguistic information processing. Memory studies of prose are typically scored for the number of propositions recalled, rather than number of words or sentences. The number of propositions in a piece of prose is a better indicator than the number of words or sentences or the difficulty of reading level. Theoretical models of propositional learning continue to be developed and doubtlessly will have increasing impact on the study of information processing in the future.

Although the propositional representation of a sentence is the structural model of its meaning, sometimes the truth of an utterance is decided on surprising grounds (see Box 7.7).

PRAGMATICS

The last major aspect of language to be discussed is **pragmatics,** the relation of language to its context of use (Green, 1989). In actual language use, the context may radically alter the meaning, perhaps totally changing the "speech act" function of the utterance; for example, being ironic or sarcastic (33), turning a question into a command (34), or indicating a figurative intent by the speaker (35).

33. My, what a beautiful day!
    (Context: a blizzard)
34. John, are you able to reach the cookies?
    (Context: a hungry speaker out of reach of the cookies and John within reach of them)

■ **Box 7.7** ■

The Keats Heuristic: Where Beauty Really Becomes Truth

Psycholinguists Matthew McGlone and Jessica Tofighbakhsh (1999) have demonstrated some scientific truth to the poet Keats' old saying "beauty is truth, truth beauty." Their participants rated the comprehensibility and accuracy of 30 unfamiliar aphorisms that either rhymed ("Woes unite foes," "Beggars breed while rich men feed") or did not rhyme ("Woes unite enemies," "Beggars breed while rich men dine"). Although both forms were rated equally comprehensible, the rhyming aphorisms were rated as more "accurate descriptions of human behavior." Perhaps it is not surprising that people *liked* the rhyming forms better, but why should they think them to be more *true*? The authors suggest that the aesthetic quality may sometimes be used as a heuristic for assessing truth. What applications might this have? An intriguing, although admittedly speculative, example is defense lawyer Johnnie Cochran's plea to the jury in O.J. Simpson's 1995 double-murder trial "If the gloves don't fit, you must acquit!" Simpson was acquitted, in spite of much evidence and public sentiment to the contrary.

35. The troops marched on into battle for two hours.

(Context: a harried baby-sitter explaining children's rambunctious behavior to their parents upon their return)

Conversation

A conversation may be looked at in different ways, including an informal reasoning exercise (Rips, 1998) or as a type of game, consisting of a sequence of exchanges involving rule-governed processes (Weiner & Goodenough, 1977). Speakers make different *moves* with their remarks. These moves may either directly deal with the subject being discussed, or may add no new content but instead signal whether the speaker wants to change or to keep the current topic. For example, in a conversation between two people, a sequence of two so-called *passing moves,* like "okay," "uhhmm," and "all right," spoken with falling intonation (i.e., not as a question), usually signals a change in the topic being discussed, as desired by both speakers.

Forms of Address

Beyond the content of the conversation, even the way we address each other can indicate our relative social status or amount of shared experience with the person. Many languages have two forms of the second-person pronouns (French *tu-vous,* Spanish *tú-usted,* German *du-Sie*), one to be used with close friends and family members and one to be used with other adults. Modern English captures such differences only through the choice of the use of first name or a title and last name. However, English once did have a familiar second-person pronoun, *thou,* which is no longer used. Thus, certain distinctions are lost in modern English. For example, in Shakespeare's *Two Gentlemen of Verona* two friends, Proteus and Valentine, address each other with the familiar *thou* until one takes the other's girlfriend. The indignant friend then begins addressing his former buddy with *you,* a clear mark of distance to Elizabethan playgoers, but a signal likely to be missed by today's audiences.

Whether we use the formal or familiar form of address with another person may depend on how we perceive our relationship on one or both of two relevant dimensions. The first is **power.** A person in a position of greater power addresses a person of lesser power with the familiar form, but receives the formal in return. The basis of this power may take many forms: teacher-student, parent-child, employer-employee, and so forth.

The second dimension is **solidarity,** the degree of perceived commonality and shared experience. If this dimension is dominant, members of a group with something in common address each other with the familiar form, but address others outside the group with the formal form. These may be members of a family, a class, an office, or whatever. In the modern world, there is a gradual tendency for solidarity to assume relatively more importance in determining forms of address and power to assume somewhat less importance, but both are still important. If they come into conflict, the participants must resolve what forms to use; for example, should all workers in an office address each other with the familiar form or should the bosses expect to be addressed with the formal form?

Sometimes even the choice of what language to speak in a given situation has social or political implications (see Box 7.8).

■ Box 7.8 ■

Social Implications of Bilingualism

In spite of the strongly monolingual character of some major nations such as the United States, Japan, Brazil, and Great Britain, bilingualism (or multilingualism) is actually the rule rather than the exception in most areas of the world. The degree and character of bilingualism varies substantially, however. It is seldom the case that an individual is exactly equivalent in fluency in all aspects in two languages. For example, many people around the world can read English, which they have studied as an academic language, but they may have much less facility in speaking or in oral comprehension. Others have a conversational facility in a language, but they cannot read or write.

Although some nations like Switzerland have been happily multilingual for centuries, language can be a divisive force in a country. A good example is Canada, which is officially bilingual, but which has a majority of largely monolingual English-speakers. Predominantly French-speaking Quebec province passed anti-English laws, and very nearly voted to secede from Canada in 1995. Similarly, Belgium has had a long history of competition between the Dutch-speaking Flemings and the French-speaking Walloons of the north and south of the country, respectively. Unlike the situation in Canada, however, the Flemings and the Walloons have usually been closer to a numerical and power balance.

Sometimes a second language may be a source of regional consciousness and political tension, especially in cases where speakers perceive that a language is in danger of dying altogether. For example, in Wales there has been a great revival of Welsh over the last three decades. The old Celtic tongue is the first language of a sizable minority (10 to 20 percent) of Welsh people, especially in northern Wales, and the whole country has seen the introduction of bilingual signs and increased broadcast programming in Welsh. Although its sister tongue Irish is seldom spoken as a first language today, it is studied by all Irish schoolchildren in the Republic of Ireland.

Very common in many communities is a situation called diglossia, where there is a high-status formal language and a lower-status everyday language, with most of the people bilingual. This is very typical of immigrant communities of the first or second generation in immigrant societies like the United States, Canada, Brazil, Chile, and Australia; typically, in such situations, the original language is lost as the younger generations adopt the host country's language as its vernacular.

Sometimes the diglossia continues for many generations, especially in colonial settings. In colonial Africa, for example, residents learned English, French, or Portuguese as the high-status language, but continued to speak their indigenous languages at home. Diglossia has existed relatively unchanged for four centuries in parts of South America, where the everyday language is Quechua or Aymará in much of Peru and Bolivia and Guaraní in most of Paraguay, but where many, if not most, people know Spanish as well (de Groot & Kroll, 1997; Grosjean, 1982; Harris, 1992).

Maxims of Conversation

There are implicit rules that we all follow in conversation whether we realize it or not (Grice, 1975). One is to give enough information, but not too much. If a four-year-old asks where he or she came from, a response of "Go away" would be too little information, but a 10,000-word treatise on genetics would be too much. Certain conventional expressions carry strong expectations of just how much information to respond with. If someone asks "How are you?" that person really does not want a detailed medical report, and in fact such a response would typically not be appreciated, if even tolerated. Another implicit rule of conversation involves telling the truth, and assuming others are too, unless we have some compelling reason to suspect otherwise, or unless we recognize from the context that some sort of nonliteral conventional use of language is intended.

Irony and Sarcasm

Pragmatic considerations also help to determine if a statement is meant to be taken in some unusual, nonconventional fashion. For example, a statement exactly opposite of what is appropriate for the context may be meant as irony. Thus, if someone says (36) on a cold day after it has snowed all night, he or she is interpreted as being ironic, not psychotic. Interestingly enough, however, if someone labeled mentally ill made the same statement in the same situation, it might be labeled psychotic rather than ironic!

36. What lovely weather we're having!

Sometimes sarcasm may be used to communicate intentions and opinions of the speaker that have nothing at all to do with its surface, deep, or propositional structure. For example, if a student comes in and says her term paper fell in the mud and washed down a sewer on the way to class, the teacher could respond (37).

37. Yes, and I just got trampled by 15 purple elephants in the hall.

This statement has nothing whatever to do with elephants or hallways, but rather communicates to the student that the teacher does not believe the explanation of what happened to the term paper.

Gibbs (1986a) tested participants' comprehension and memory for statements like "You're a fine friend!" following a context suggesting either a literal or a sarcastic interpretation. People did not have to first comprehend the literal meaning and then compute the sarcastic one, when the latter was appropriate. In terms of memory, they remembered the sarcastic version of the same expression better than the literal equivalent. Gibbs (1984, 1986a) argued that there may not even be any such thing as literal, context-independent meaning; in real language use, every interpretation must take the context into consideration.

Jorgensen, Miller, and Sperber (1984); Clark and Gerrig (1984); and Kumon-Nakamura, Glucksberg, and Brown (1995) studied the psycholinguistics of irony, proposing three competing theories of how speakers and writers signify their intention to be ironic and how others perceive them to have done so. Even if there is no explicit cue such as intonation to indicate that someone is being sarcastic, people perceive that *others* detect the sarcasm if they have access to privileged information (e.g., overheard comments) indicating a sarcastic intent (Keysar, 1994). This is yet another example of how our natural egocentrism leads us to believe that others see the world more like we do than is in fact the case.

Indirect Speech Acts

When is a question not a question? When the context tells you it is a command. For example, suppose I am teaching a class where the room is getting very stuffy and I turn to one of the students near the window and say (38). In terms of surface structure, deep structure, and propositional content, that utterance is a question calling for a yes or no answer. However, a simple yes or no in this context would be interpreted as an inappropriate, perhaps even a highly discourteous, response. The context here has told us that what initially appears to be a question is, in fact, an imperative, just as surely as if I had said (39).

38. Can you reach the window?
39. Please open the window.

In some other context, such as my questioning an ailing student about how well he is gaining back his strength in his recently broken arm, (38) could indeed be intended to be a yes-no question. Sometimes the context of such expressions can even turn a negative into an affirmative and vice versa. For example, consider the same context as discussed previously and someone uttering (40) or (41).

40. Why not open the window?
41. Why open the window?

The negative (40) is really an affirmative imperative (Do open the window), and the affirmative (41) a negative imperative (Do not open the window)! According to Gibbs (1986b), requests in normal English conversation use these indirect, more polite forms more than 90 percent of the time, in contrast to apparently more direct languages like German or Polish (House & Casper, 1981; Wierzbicka, 1985). Speakers of languages that more commonly use the direct imperative form may appear to English speakers to be "bossy" or "rude" when speaking English in the style of their native language.

42. Haven't I been good to you?
43. Can any group compare to the Beatles?

Along the same line, an apparent question can actually be a statement. In many contexts (42), which is an apparent negative question, is, in fact, an affirmative statement (I have been good to you) while (43), which is an apparent affirmative question, is actually a negative declarative (No group can compare to the Beatles).

Gender and Conversation

Sociolinguist Deborah Tannen (1990) argues that men and women have different conversational styles that lead to miscommunication. While Tannen clearly acknowledges they are only generalizations, men are typically more interested in communicating information and maintaining independence and status, while women are more often concerned with establishing and nurturing relationships. When men gather and talk, the purpose is to do some activity, whereas women frequently gather for the expressed purpose of talking ("Come on over and visit"). Neither style is inherently better than the other, but rather both could gain by better understanding the other.

Although both men and women are interested in both maintaining their independence and developing intimacy in relationship to others, the biggest threat to men is a threat to their independence, and to women it is a threat to a relationship. For example, men are very reluctant to stop to ask for directions, which they see as a threat to their independence. Women are more likely than men to check with their spouse first before making a social commitment. To do so would threaten the independence of many men, whereas women see not doing it as expressing a lack of intimacy and concern about the relationship.

Men see themselves as having responsibility as problem solvers and see a woman's expression of distress as a request for a solution to some problem: Women, however, may be looking to men for an expression of emotional support, not advice. She may feel *lectured to* when he tries to solve the problem instead of connecting emotionally, while he may feel hurt that his sincere attempt to help her by suggesting solutions to her problem was not appreciated.

Men are more interested in maintaining their status and improving it relative to others, while women are more interested in establishing and maintaining affiliation with others. Thus, for example, when a husband says, "I didn't sleep very well last night" and his wife replies, "Oh, I didn't either," he may think she is trying to "one-up" him ("I lost more sleep than you did"), while she thinks she is trying to connect with him emotionally ("I understand how you feel; the same thing happened to me"). Each partner may misread the intent of the other's comments. A woman sees her suggestion ("Why don't we go out for pizza tonight?") as a discussion opener; her husband hears such a comment as telling him what to do, which threatens his status and independence. Women say "I'm sorry" to express empathy with a man, whereas men see it as an unnecessary and inappropriately subservient apology.

Contrary to the common belief that women talk more, men actually do, but the place matters. Men talk a lot in public but less so at home, whereas the reverse is true for women. Men see the public as a domain where they need to prove themselves and home as a place where proving oneself is not necessary, whereas women see home as a place to connect in terms of relationship and the public domain as a worse place to do that. Thus men talk more in public and less at home, while women do the reverse. These different styles also often lead to misunderstandings in the workplace (see Box 7.9).

Such differences start early. Videotape studies of children as young as second grade show very different conversational styles of girls and boys. Boys are more active and flit to many activities and topics of conversation. They seldom just sit and talk. Girls, on the other hand, are less active and often sit and talk. Their talk is very focused on relationships, with each other and third parties, with fewer topics in greater depth.

Now that we have examined the phonological, semantic, syntactic, and pragmatic components of language, we will apply these concepts by examining two of the major functions of language—reading and writing.

■ Box 7.9 ■

Talking at Work: Are Men and Women Speaking the Same Language?

Tannen (1994) sees many ways that men and women use language differently and misunderstand each other in the workplace. Women are more likely to speak with a more indirect style than men; while women perceive such a style as appropriately polite, some men may see it as indecisive or uncertain. Because men have been socialized to be more assertive verbally and otherwise, their ideas are more likely to be heard in an office meeting than a more soft-spoken woman's. On the other hand, a woman who is strongly assertive may be perceived by her male coworkers as "pushy" or even "bitchy." Men are often more comfortable than women with the "ritualistic debate" format common in graduate schools and many business settings. To many women, such sharp mutual criticism sounds biting and insensitive. Even sexual harassment may sometimes be a matter of gender miscommunication, with women interpreting sexual content to a remark not consciously intended that way by the male speaker. Part of the reason for the "glass ceiling," whereby women advance in the corporate world to a certain level but not beyond, may be that corporate communication styles are primarily the male styles, and women do not speak the language as well (and sometimes may choose not to).

READING AND WRITING

Writing Systems

Although writing is a newer invention than speech, it is hardly a recent phenomenon, with writing systems going back at least as far as 5000 B.C. in Mesopotamia, Egypt, and the Indus and Yangtze valleys. Earlier precursors probably included the use of pictures and tallies inscribed on stone (Olson, 1994).

The three different types of writing systems: **logographic, syllabic,** and **alphabetic,** differ in terms of whether one written symbol corresponds to a morpheme, a syllable, or a phoneme. While English and most other European languages are alphabetic, it is worth taking a brief look at logographic and syllabic writing systems, because our brains are also quite capable of reading in those systems.

In a **logographic** system, one symbol stands for a **morpheme,** the smallest *meaningful* unit of language. Chinese is the most widely used logographic system today. Compared to a syllabic or alphabetic system, logographic writing has a very large number of symbols (about 50,000 in Chinese, although only 1,000 or so account for about 90 percent of Chinese writing). The stage of learning to read where one learns the written symbols is much more complex in Chinese than in English, although Chinese is easier in the sense of not having any spelling-sound correlations to learn. Another interesting property of logographic systems is illustrated by the fact that all of China, the world's most populous country, uses the same logographic symbols, which are comprehensible anywhere in China. However, there are many spoken languages and dialects (as many as 1,800) that are often mutually incomprehensible, in spite of the fact that they all use the same written system. See Hoosain (1991) for a review of psycholinguistic studies of Chinese.

Although the written form of English and other European languages is alphabetic, logographic symbols are not totally outside the realm of our experience. For example, symbols like + , − , %, @, &, *, and $, are logographic symbols and translate directly to meaning, although in their spoken version, +, for example, might be read as "plus" by one person, "and" by another, and "added to" by a third.

A **syllabic** writing system, of which Japanese *kana* is a good example, uses one symbol to stand for a syllable. Japanese also uses some logographs called *kanji* borrowed from Chinese and also some transliterations into the Latin alphabet, for proper names or technical terms. The Japanese *kana* has about 100 consonant-vowel syllables, which are combined into words. Some notable ancient languages also used syllabic writing systems, most notably Akkadian of ancient Sumeria and the recently decoded Mayan script.

Alphabetic systems, of which the Latin, Cyrillic, Greek, Arabic, Hebrew, and the Indian Devanagari script are examples, have roughly one symbol per sound, although there are many systematic and idiosyncratic exceptions to this rule, such as the many ways of spelling the sound /ə/ in English or the many final consonants which are not pronounced in French. An alphabetic symbol has no meaning on its own and is meaningful only for the way it can combine with other symbols to form words. There have been 200 to 300 alphabets in the world, about half of them in India. The widely used Latin (Roman) alphabet was originally an adaptation of Greek, which evolved out of ancient Phoenician writing. There is even one language, Serbo-Croatian, which is written in two alphabets, the Latin alphabet in Croatia and the Cyrillic in Serbia (see Box 7.10).

■ Box 7.10 ■

Writing and Fighting in the Former Yugoslavia

When the former Yugoslavia disintegrated in the early 1990s after the end of the Cold War, a series of tragic regional wars ensued in Croatia, Bosnia, and Kosovo, all tapping into hatreds going back many centuries. Unlike the way they were sometimes presented, however, these difficulties were not due to language. The only two former Yugoslav states that had their own languages seceded peacefully and formed their own new nations (Slovenia in the northwest and Macedonia in the southeast). The rest of the former Yugoslavia (Bosnia-Herzegovina, Croatia, Serbia, and Montenegro) all speak the same language, traditionally called Serbo-Croatian. However, Serbo-Croatian has long been written in the Latin alphabet (like English) in Croatia and in the Cyrillic alphabet (like Russian) in Serbia and Montenegro. Bosnian Croats write in the Latin script, while Bosnian Serbs write the same language in Cyrillic.

This existence of one language and two different writing systems provides a unique opportunity for psycholinguistic research (see Lukatela and Turvey, 1998, for a review). For example, studies of "bialphabetic" readers, who can read Serbo-Croatian in either Latin or Cyrillic, suggest even more strongly than studies in English that readers often use an underlying phonological representation to identify words on the printed page.

As an ironic footnote, the term "Serbo-Croatian" may itself have become a casualty of the Yugoslav wars. Speakers now often choose to call their language "Serbian" or "Croatian" and sometimes refuse to answer someone speaking in the other dialect of their own language.

A sort of hybrid system is the Korean *hangul,* which is an alphabetic syllabary. It was invented around 1443 by King Sejong to replace the Chinese logographs, which were ill-suited to the polysyllabic and inflected Korean language. The symbols represent particular sounds (19 consonants, 21 vowels), but they are put together into around 2,000 syllable blocks (see Figure 7.1). This system makes reading very easy to learn, and according to Taylor and Taylor (1984), one finds virtually no illiteracy or remedial classes in Korea.

Although writing has been around for thousands of years, widespread literacy has not, and for most of human history reading and writing have been the province of the very few. With the development of printing in the Renaissance, forms of writing tended to become more standardized, with the most convenient forms gaining ascendancy and acceptance and other forms falling into disuse. Since that time, spelling has become more standardized and the rate of change in language has decreased.

The Psychology of Reading

Eye Movements in Reading

Studies of eye movements have shown that when people read, their eyes move in short jumps and hops, called **saccades.** Most people have a nearly constant rate of saccadic movement, about 3 to 4 saccades per second. What differentiates the good from the poor reader or the scanner from the studier is how much information is contained in each saccade. Though most eye movement is forward, there is occasional backward

FIGURE 7.1   Examples of different scripts.

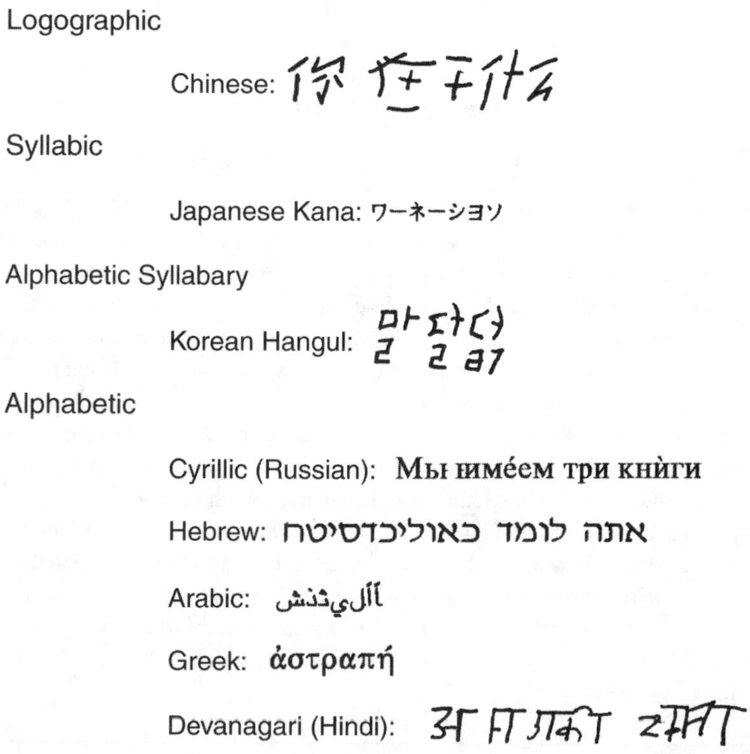

Logographic

Chinese: 你 任 干什名

Syllabic

Japanese Kana: ワーネーシヨソ

Alphabetic Syllabary

Korean Hangul: 마 쏘ㅏㄷ ㄹ ㄹ ㅌ

Alphabetic

Cyrillic (Russian): **Мы имéем три кнѝги**

Hebrew: אתה לומד כאוליכדסיטח

Arabic: اأَلىيذنش

Greek: ἀστραπή

Devanagari (Hindi): अ ग जाकी ग्गा

movement; for example, when the reader looks back to check the wording of a prior difficult phrase. The more difficult the text, the more such backward saccades occur and the slower the overall reading rate.

Essential Prereading Skills

Before a child can begin to read, he or she must have certain cognitive abilities that adults take for granted. For example, children have to be able to perceive speech and begin to understand the idea that speech is composed of smaller units and that the written symbols correspond to spoken sounds (or syllables or morphemes).

Parents can help prepare preschool children to read by reading to them. Not only does this model and motivate the use of the printed word (as opposed to television, for example), but it also helps them increase their vocabulary (Robbins & Ehri, 1994) and can expose children to stories and customs from different cultures and subcultures. When children actually do begin to learn to read, there is some controversy today about how to teach members of various linguistic minorities (see Box 7.11). Written and spoken language can actually be a significant part of one's social identity (Rubin, 1995).

Perception in Reading

Like so much other information processing, reading is a **constructive** process, not a simple mechanical bottom-up transmission of written symbols to the mind. As we read, we process information from beyond the immediate focus of our eyes. There is even a measure of how far the eye is ahead of the mouth in oral reading; this is called the **eye-voice span.** Better readers have longer eye-voice spans, and all readers have longer eye-voice spans for easier, as compared to more difficult, prose.

■ Box 7.11 ■

Bilingual and Bidialectal Education

A major controversy in education is the question of whether it is desirable to teach minority children to read in their own dialect or language or in the dominant language and dialect of the society. This is a complex issue with some strong proponents, especially among minorities, on both sides of the issue. In the United States, the debate usually centers on Black English vernacular or the Spanish language. On the one hand, members of these communities argue that teaching in so-called "standard English" puts the minority child at a disadvantage, because he or she is not as familiar with that type of speech, and, more seriously, that the very process denies the worth of their own dialect or language, thus relegating it and its speakers to an inferior status. On the opposite side, equally vocal spokespersons of the same minority groups argue that to teach the children in anything other than standard English language is to deny them forever the tools to get ahead in that society, which, for better or worse, will continue to use standard English. The debate continues. There are many common beliefs in regard to bilingual education and multiculturalism that are not consistent with research findings; these are nicely reviewed by Padilla and coworkers (1991) and in more detail by the readings in Crawford (1992). Bilingual education, in fact, leads to improved self-esteem and academic accomplishment of the minority child.

We know from the speed we can read that we could not possibly be processing each individual letter. We know that some letters, and some features of letters, are more important than others. Consonants are more important than vowels; that is, it is easier to construct missing vowels than missing consonants. Similarly, letters extending above or below the line tend to carry more information than those doing neither. The top halves of letters seem to be more important than the bottom halves. Eye fixations generally fall to the left of the center of words, suggesting that we are more likely to perceive the first parts of words and construct the last part than the reverse, at least in English.

The heart of the debate about the psychological nature of reading concerns the relationship between listening and reading. The basic issue is whether we go directly from the written symbol of the word to the meaning (**direct lexical access** hypothesis) or whether there is an intermediate step involving the sound (**phonological recoding** hypothesis). There is evidence for both processes; which predominates depends on the individual reader and the material being read.

Although direct lexical access is probably the primary process that occurs in reading logographic languages like Chinese (Leck, Weeks, & Chen, 1995), as well as logographic symbols like $ or =, it is not a very efficient method for reading alphabetic languages; each word would have to be a separate logogram and there would be no perceptual way to use the spelling-sound correspondence that exists in such languages. Individuals use the direct lexical access process to varying degrees. For example, adults who first learned to read using the *whole-word,* as opposed to the *phonics,* method are more likely to use direct access when reading. Thus, they do fine on identifying familiar words, but they have a more difficult time than the phonics-trained readers in identifying new words, because they have fewer skills for sounding them out. Direct access might be somewhat more useful with languages like English, with its many irregularities of spelling, or French, with its many unpronounced consonants, than it would be with a completely regular language like Spanish, whose spelling is almost perfectly predictable from its pronunciation.

The phonological recoding hypothesis argues that written symbols are converted to some sort of underlying sound representation. This is very rapid and not typically a conscious process, though readers may be aware of it to some small degree. A few readers will even noticeably move their lips during silent reading; this, however, is exceptional and clearly not necessary for reading. Although phonological recoding is probably not absolutely essential, there is nonetheless considerable evidence that it frequently occurs in reading alphabetical writing.

When people proofread, it is more difficult to catch silent letters that are incorrect or omitted than letters that represent some sound. Similarly, if an incorrect letter would make a sound identical to what the correct letter would make, it is difficult to catch in proofreading. For example, if someone had intended to write *work,* it is easiest to catch the error *wxrk* (unpronounceable in English), hardest to catch *werk* (pronounced identically to *work*), and of intermediate difficulty to catch *wark* (pronounceable, but with a different pronunciation from *work*). If direct lexical access occurred with no involvement of the phonological representation, such differences should not occur. Incidentally, the studies obtaining these differences have controlled for physical similarity of the letters and ruled that out as the critical factor.

The reading process has been studied extensively in psychology by presenting visual stimuli at very fast durations, even a small fraction of a second. Several such studies have shown the importance of phonological recoding in reading. For example, on exposures of 30 to 250 milliseconds, pronounceable nonwords (KIV) were perceived on shorter duration than nonpronounceable nonwords (QKU). While this is perhaps not too surprising, this difference occurred even when the unpronounceable nonword was highly meaningful and the pronounceable nonword was not; for example, BIM was perceived faster than IBM (Gibson, Bishop, Schiff, & Smith, 1964). This finding argues strongly for the importance of phonological recoding as primary over direct lexical access, at least at this early perceptual stage.

Another type of evidence for phonological recoding comes from the **lexical decision** task. In classifying strings of letters as words or nonwords, the reaction time can be measured. An unpronounceable nonword like *"sagm"* can be detected as a nonword faster than the pronounceable *"melp,"* which can in turn be detected faster than *"brane,"* which is also pronounceable but, unlike *"melp,"* has the sound identical to an English word (Rubenstein, Lewis, & Rubenstein, 1971). In classifying pairs of words as words or nonwords, rhyming sets like "set-wet," "handle-candle," and "bribe-tribe" are classified as words faster than sets like "few-sew," "lemon-demon," or "mint-pint," (Meyer, Schvaneveldt, & Ruddy, 1974). Because the direct lexical access hypothesis would predict no such difference, such findings suggest that phonological recoding occurs.

■ Box 7.12 ■

Why Lecturers Who Read Are Boring

Why is it always so boring to listen to someone read something aloud, even if it is very well read, where it is much more interesting to hear someone speak spontaneously, even if that speech is more halting and imperfect? Why does it bother us if actors in a play sound like they are reading their lines, rather than speaking them spontaneously? How can we tell the difference, anyway?

There are several ways that oral reading and spontaneous speech systematically differ. Oral reading is generally slower than speech, with speed increasing with the degree of informality. Oral reading contains very few false starts or filled pauses (place-holding interjections as *uh, well,* and *um*), while spontaneous speech contains many of both, especially in more informal speech. On the other hand, breathing pauses (places where we stop to breathe) occur almost entirely at major syntactic constituent boundaries in oral reading, but in many different places in spontaneous speech. If someone's breathing pauses are entirely at major syntactic boundaries, that is a strong clue that the person is reading directly from a text, where the constituents are already formed and available to allow for breathing in between.

Oral reading includes many words from one's passive vocabulary, that is, words that we comprehend but do not use in speech. Each of us has a large passive vocabulary that we do not use in speaking, even in formal situations.

Oral reading uses relatively flat intonation, while spontaneous speaking shows more variation in pitch and stress; the greater variety is one reason it is more interesting to listen to than oral reading. Enunciation is usually better in oral reading; however, often it is so good that it sounds unnatural.

If you need something to do during the next boring oral presentation you must listen to, try analyzing the language for the characteristics just described.

There is also evidence for the use of higher-order units in reading. For example, letters can be perceived faster in the context of a word than they can by themselves (Reicher, 1969; Wheeler, 1970). In a brief display of one of the six arrays in (44), followed by a marker where the N or R had been, participants correctly reported the letter after shorter exposure durations if the letter occurred in the context of a word (*bank* or *bark*) or pronounceable nonword (*zank* or *zark*) than if it had occurred by itself (*n* or *r*). While this may seem counterintuitive, since the word array contains four times as much stimulus information as the single-letter array, apparently we do not process each letter as a separate unit. There is something more "cognitively economical" about the pronounceable string in contrast to the individual letter.

44. N

R

BANK

BARK

ZANK

ZARK

In conclusion, reading may be viewed as a continual set of processes of constructing and testing hypotheses at several different levels: letter identification, sentence construction, and overall gist (Pressley & Afflerbach, 1995). As we have seen in every facet of information processing, top-down and bottom-up processes interact as we actively construct interpretations. Exactly what processes we use also depends on the purpose and situation in any given instance. Reading aloud is very different from spontaneous speech (see Box 7.12).

Control of Reading Rate

One important way that we control our reading habits is by controlling the speed and strategies used in our reading. Surprisingly, many college students and other people do not do this very effectively and thus they try to read novels, textbooks, newspapers, and scientific articles all in exactly the same way. Predictably, this often leads to frustration. Sometimes scanning or skimming is sufficient. Scanning (about 10,000 words per minute) is adequate when you need to search for a specific piece of information in a larger text, and that is all you care about; for example, scanning an article to see if there is any mention of Pavlov. There is no need to retain or even process any semantic information except the word "Pavlov." Skimming (about 800 to 1,500 words per minute) is used to extract the basic gist of a text without catching details. This would not be an adequate method of reading your psychology text initially, but it might be a useful technique for the very final review before an exam. Many so-called "speed-reading" courses really teach scanning and skimming. Insofar as you could learn to use these skills in ways you have not before, they might be useful. However, to believe you could learn to do all your reading at 10,000 (or even 1,000) words per minute and retain everything is unrealistic.

Control of reading rate and purpose is very helpful in professional reading. For instance, many journal articles in my field come across my desk, far more than I (RJH) have time to read even superficially. However, I can scan or skim them (or parts of them), depending on my purpose, and file them away (literally and figuratively) for future reference. If I am interested in seeing if an article deals with a particular topic, I could scan it for the appearance of that term. If I am interested in the procedural details of the study, because I am designing a similar one, I might read part of the method section very carefully and slowly, but scan or skim the rest of the article. Such strategies are necessary skills for a teacher or researcher to gain in order to keep on top of one's field professionally.

Sign Language

One type of reading that is very different from perceiving and interpreting words off a printed page involves interpreting handshapes and position by a person "speaking" **sign language.** Although many different types of sign language exist, we will focus on American Sign Language (ASL, or Ameslan), where one sign is approximately equivalent to one word or morpheme and thus has meaning in itself. Today, ASL is the first language of thousands of hearing-impaired people and an acquired second language of numerous others.

Sign language is not a degenerate or derivative form of spoken language. Sign language is not merely a system of gestures and is no more universal than any spoken language. Though there are some signs that physically resemble the thing they signify (e.g., sign for "drink" is making a fist with outstretched thumb moving toward mouth), many have no resemblance at all. Historically, ASL has progressed toward signs being less and less analogic in nature. Abstract concepts may be expressed in ASL just as in English, and there is as complex a set of syntactic rules as any language would have. Flexibility, ambiguity, sarcasm, and even wordplay is possible. For example, the sign for "milk" is made by holding both hands at forehead level and squeezing them. The sign for "pasteurized milk" is made using the same sign while moving across one's visual field; that is, "past your eyes"—a bilingual pun.

In virtually all ways, ASL has the complexity of spoken languages. For example, making the sign "happy" faster than other signs indicates "very happy." A question may be indicated by leaning forward toward the hearer, holding the final sign longer, or making a quizzical expression on one's face. Making a sign larger than normal shows emphasis, much like abnormally heavy stress in speaking. Past tense may be added to a verb by making that verb sign while holding one's hand over the shoulders; future tense may be indicated similarly by holding the hand farther than normal in front of the body.

Even though most of us never learn sign language, we are all capable of doing so given the right circumstances, just as we are capable of learning Chinese or English. In fact, deaf or hearing children born to signing parents will start *manual babbling* in sign language at a few months of age (Petitto & Marentette, 1991); this involves using handshapes that appear to be pieces of signs, much as a hearing child would babble phonemes which are "pieces of words." There are fewer ASL signs than there are English words, only a few thousand, but the list is ever growing. New or unfamiliar words or proper names may be communicated by fingerspelling, a type of sign language where each letter in a word of the spoken language is spelled quickly with the fingers. People can comprehend about the same amount of information (in propositions) per unit time from ASL as from English.

There are also some interesting findings in regard to where signs are processed in the brain. Just as most people perceive spoken language better in the left cerebral hemisphere than in the right, fluent signers are also left-hemisphere dominant for understanding signs; that is, their left hemispheres perceive the signs better than the right. However, both signers and nonsigners are right-hemisphere dominant for perceiving handshapes that are similar to ASL words but not actual words in the language (Virostek & Cutting, 1979), much as visual spatial perception for most people is right-hemisphere dominant. Left-hemisphere lesions in language areas interfere with ASL in the same way they interfere with spoken language (Kimura, 1981).

For a collection of papers on psychological research on sign language, see Siple and Fischer (1991); for readings on the linguistics of sign language, see Fischer and Siple (1990).

The Process of Writing

Let us now turn to the production of written language, namely, writing. Although it is a critical problem in cognitive psychology, writing has been studied surprisingly little. There is, happily, some evidence that this oversight is being corrected (see Bereiter & Scardamalia, 1987; Kellogg, 1994; Levy & Ransdell, 1996; Martlew, 1983; Nystrand, 1986).

Writing as a psychological process may be considered to have three stages: prewriting, drafting, and revising.

Prewriting

The **prewriting** stage (also called rehearsing, composing, or planning) deals with the generation, organization, and evaluation of ideas before any text is actually put on paper. This is sometimes conceptualized as the "internal dialogue" in the mind of the writer. Prewriting may involve conscious problem-solving procedures with oneself or others (brainstorming, outlining, note taking). Exercises to improve one's observational and perceptual skills may be useful in prewriting. Memory for very common objects that are seen frequently, but often are not directly attended to (for example, the design and details on a coin), is surprisingly poor (Nickerson & Adams, 1979).

During the prewriting stage, it is necessary always to keep in mind the audience for whom one is writing. Just as we talk very differently to different people on different occasions, so we should write differently in a research paper and a personal letter. Unfortunately, the prewriting stage is often sadly neglected in the teaching of writing. Many times students are expected to begin immediately to produce prose out of nothing on the blank paper in front of them, with those who cannot easily do so being made to feel inadequate. Producing prose is very difficult if there are no ideas to be expressed through it.

Drafting

The second stage of the writing process is **drafting,** or composition. This involves the actual generation of text, usually in prefinal draft form. The ideas generated and organized in the prewriting stage are here clothed in a surface structure of words and sentences. There are great individual differences in specific strategies for producing this prose. Sometimes it may even be produced initially in parallel with prewriting activities. For example, as I write this book, I am initially generating ideas while I write the first draft of these sentences into my computer. The crucial point is not so much whether or not one does prewriting and drafting serially or in parallel, but rather that both are done in some satisfactory way.

Revising

The third stage of writing is the **revising,** or editing, stage. This is where intermediate drafts are read and revised to be suitable for the final version of the writing. Several aspects of writing must be monitored during this stage. First of all, does it make sense? Are the ideas expressed good ones, containing truth and no contradictions? Is the writing well organized? In revising, one checks for overall coherence, including whether the organization selected in the drafting stage is in fact effective. Also, one examines the draft for so-called "connective tissue," that is, appropriate transitions between sections, statements of relationships, overview and summary statements, and headings. This aspect of composition is one of the most sorely neglected in college students' writing, and it is something that could be easily remedied, or at least vastly improved, with a more careful editing job.

Finally, the prose is edited and revised for elements of style, grammar, spelling, and usage. Verbose prose is condensed, inappropriate vocabulary is changed, and spelling and punctuation are corrected. Unfortunately, many students progress through their entire schooling thinking that writing is largely this last and most superficial aspect of the editing stage. Thus, they are often paralyzed from producing ideas because they are not sure how to spell words or use commas. Such matters, while not unimportant, are best handled at a much later stage than generation of ideas. Thinking you cannot write because you can't spell well is something like assuming you cannot build a house because you don't know how to lay carpet. There is a lot that can be done before the carpet is laid, just as there is much that can be done in writing before the final spelling is checked. Just as a carpet layer can be subcontracted, so can an editor (often in the form of a friend or colleague) check your writing for mechanical and technical correctness. See Box 7.13 for some examples where spelling errors have led to confusion and embarrassment.

Now that we have examined language in some detail, it is time to bring together themes of the last three chapters in the study of comprehension and discourse, the subject of Chapter 8.

■ Box 7.13 ■

Consequential Spelling Mistakes

Signs in laundromat: "No dying in these machines."

"Please leave your dog's outside."

Sports report: "There were some scoreless rumors about the star forward."

Ad: "9-inch osculating fan with push-button controls."

News story: "All soldiers are equipped with nerve agent anecdote kits."

Headlines: "Council Members to Open Flies to Public."

"Statewide Heroine Crackdown to Begin."

"78th career Grand Prick title for McEnroe."

"Track Teams Win in Duels vs. Idaho."

Do you think the writers may have meant to say *dyeing, dogs, scurrilous, oscillating, antidote, files, heroin, Grand Prix,* and *duals?*

SUGGESTED READINGS

Steven Pinker's (1994) *The Language Instinct* is the best-written overview of the psychological aspects of language, albeit with a strong nativist perspective and sometimes polemical tone. The best recent traditional texts on psycholinguistics are Carroll (1999), Harley (1996), and Whitney (1999). All give solid comprehensive views of the field without strong theoretical bias. For more detail and a model of psychological aspects of syntax, see Pinker's (1999) *Words and Rules.*

The best comprehensive texts on the psychology of reading are Smith (1994), Rayner and Pollatsek (1994), and Taylor and Taylor (1984). Gibson and Levin's (1975) text is also still worthwhile. As for the psychology of writing, Kellogg (1994) reviews the multidisciplinary research on writing, and Olson (1994) offers a fascinating look at the history of writing and its interaction with speech. For an interesting paper on expertise in reading and writing, see Scardamalia and Bereiter (1991).

For an extraordinarily interesting and comprehensive review of research on bilingualism, see François Grosjean's *Life with Two Languages* (1982). See de Groot and Kroll's *Tutorials in Bilingualism* (1997) for an outstanding collection of readings on cognitive processing in bilinguals.

8 Comprehension and Discourse

What does it mean to **comprehend** something? Very often people view the mind as some sort of organic camcorder, ready to make perfect, or nearly perfect, copies of everything it sees and hears. Something is thought to be comprehended if that perfect copy is made and is considered to have been not comprehended, or perhaps forgotten, if no such copy exists. As we saw in Chapter 6, however, our minds do not make such perfect choices.

The traditional view sees meaning as an inherent property of the stimulus. Just as a word has letters, or an object has color, so does each word or object contain meaning. Thus, meaning has been most often considered a property of the stimulus. However, this chapter takes a somewhat different and more dynamic approach to comprehension, considering meaning not as a property of the stimulus, but rather as an **emergent property** of the interaction of the stimulus and the mind of the comprehender. Both bottom-up and top-down processes are operating. Meaning arises as someone constructs an interpretation of a stimulus, and the meaning that one individual constructs will be somewhat different from what every other person constructs in response to that same stimulus. Such a perspective stresses the dynamic **interaction** of the active mind of the comprehender (top-down) and the particular external stimuli (bottom-up).

Much of the research on comprehension has involved the study of **discourse,** which is language in large enough units to involve a context that constrains interpretation. In most cases this means units longer than one sentence. Graesser, Millis, & Zwaan (1997) identify five levels of representation involved in discourse comprehension. First, the **surface code** is the actual sequence of words. Next, the **propositional textbase** is the construction of the basic meaning in propositional form. The retrieval of the appropriate knowledge structures with which to interpret that textbase and connect it to known information already in memory involves the third level, the **referential situation model.** The situation model (see Zwaan & Radvansky, 1998; Zwaan, 1999) comprises these knowledge structures necessary to interpret the discourse. Fourth, the **pragmatic communication level** involves the interpretation of the use, or possibly the violation of, pragmatic constraints. For example, an author might describe events in a backward time sequence instead of the usual forward fashion. Fifth and last, the **text genre** level involves consideration of the type of text that the discourse is. For example, we read fiction differently than we read an expository narrative.

Using this broad-based conceptualization of comprehension, this chapter examines the comprehension of primarily connected discourse and also nonlinguistic spatial or social stimuli. Comprehension of all these stimuli draws on principles of information processing, memory, and language from the last three chapters. The levels of primary concern will be textbase comprehension and situation model construction. Later in the chapter we shall examine some global models of comprehension and end with a brief look at **metacognition,** our cognition about our cognition.

TEXTBASE COMPREHENSION

As we saw in Chapter 7, language comprehension involves the parallel processing of linguistic information on the phonological, semantic, syntactic, and pragmatic levels. As well as being guided by the data-driven processes of the words themselves, comprehension is also simultaneously guided by the conceptually driven processes of **forming hypotheses** based on our expectations, prior knowledge, and contextual clues predicting what the speaker (or writer) will be saying.

Just as we cannot discuss memory totally apart from comprehension, it is impossible to discuss comprehension very long without considering memory. What we remember from prose is largely determined by how we understood it to begin with. Many studies reveal that information in separate but thematically related sentences is integrated into a single memory representation during the comprehension process. Later it is often difficult to remember the exact input sentences in subsequent memory tasks (see Bransford & Franks, 1971). For example, you might hear (1), but remember that you heard (2). The propositional representation in memory would be identical whether one had heard (1) or (2).

1a. The house was in the valley.
1b. The house was little.
1c. The valley was green.
1d. The house burned down.
2. The little house in the green valley burned down.

Most research has indicated that, after the meaning is comprehended, the surface code (exact wording and surface structure) is largely forgotten. There are, however, some cases where verbatim memory can be substantial (Hyman & Rubin, 1990; Keenan, Macwhinney, & Mayhew, 1977; Kintsch & Bates, 1977), especially in situations outside the laboratory. For example, we remember very well a humorous joke in a classroom lecture or a particularly emotional comment someone makes in a conversation.

Sometimes what we read does not fit in well with our natural language-comprehension processes; thus, we perceive that text to be difficult or poorly written. Box 8.1 discusses the case of legal language and what really makes it so difficult psychologically. Issues of language comprehensibility have some far-reaching legal and policy-making effects, for example, when people have been excused from legal responsibility when it was ruled that a contract they had signed was written in language far above their reading level.

SITUATION MODEL CONSTRUCTION

Retrieval of relevant information from long-term memory to aid ongoing comprehension of discourse involves the construction of a **situation model.** Several factors help determine how this model is constructed.

■ Box 8-1 ■
The Miscomprehension of Legal Language

Government agencies, insurance companies, and lawyers have frequently been under public criticism for writing documents that the intended readers, the general public, cannot reasonably hope to comprehend. The question is one of cognition and is empirically testable. How do people comprehend or fail to comprehend the intended message in legal documents? How could such documents be rewritten to improve comprehension?

Before examining what is wrong with legal language, it is helpful to look at its purpose. The overriding priority of legal language is conveying information, which is a higher value than aesthetic quality or brevity. The language must be explicit, both technically and legally precise, leaving minimal room for the reader to draw inferences other than those clearly intended by the writer. In this sense it is markedly different from artistic writing such as literature, poetry, or even humor, where the reader's imagination is heavily drawn upon. Although the defense of legal language is often made in a defensive manner itself, there is a valid point to the argument. If the information-conveying purpose is compromised, any additional improvement is worthless.

Georgetown University linguist Roger Shuy studied the language of insurance policies to find out exactly what it is that makes such language difficult to comprehend (Shuy, 1981; Shuy & Larkin, 1978). Shuy made several recommendations for making legal language more comprehensible. The first is the most general and the most important: Make better use of the natural strategies and expectations that we all bring to the language-comprehension process. For example, we are used to having given information signaled with the definite article "the"; if a contract replaces "the" with "such," this makes the given-new strategy (see Chapter 7) harder to apply. Also, much of the insurance contract language was extremely repetitive, so much so that it was unnatural. For example, legal language uses fewer pronouns relative to nouns than does ordinary language. While presumably this is done in order to reduce any possible ambiguity of figuring out who the pronouns refer to, it violates natural conversational rules and thus leads the reader to wonder why these are being violated.

Other types of constructions overused in legal language are passive verbs and nominalized constructions used instead of verbs. For example, contracts often use words like "as of the date of signing by the owner" instead of "when the owner signs it" or "at the time of receipt at the home office" instead of "when the home office receives it." The more natural way to say such ideas is often the active voice with an active verb. If such constructions can be employed with no accompanying loss in clarity, then it is desirable to do so.

Theme

One of the most important top-down factors in comprehension is the overall **theme** of the material. A comprehender's expectation of what a passage is about can serve as a framework for constructing the appropriate situation model for understanding the material. The overall theme of a passage can markedly affect almost every aspect of comprehension. It is very difficult to understand or remember much from prose such as (3) or (4), which may at first appear to have no theme (Bransford & Johnson, 1972, 1973; Dooling & Mullet, 1973).

3. The haystack was important because the cloth ripped.

4. "With hocked gems financing him, our hero bravely defied all scornful laughter that tried to prevent his scheme. 'Your eyes deceive,' he had said, 'an egg, not a table, typefies this unexplored planet.' Now three sturdy sisters sought proof, forging along through calm vastness, yet more often over turbulent peaks and valleys. Days become weeks as many doubters spread fearful rumors about the edge. At last from nowhere welcome winged creatures appeared signifying momentous success." (Dooling & Lachman, 1971, p. 217)

Participants told that (3) was about a parachute jump and (4) was about Christopher Columbus traveling to America understood the passages much better and remembered more than did those not given the appropriate theme. Supporting information is remembered better if it is relevant to the overall theme, and new but thematically consistent material is often falsely recognized as having been previously presented (Sulin & Dooling, 1974). This effect was also demonstrated pictorially with cartoons (Bower, Karlin, & Dueck, 1975; Bransford & McCarrell, 1974).

Both textbase comprehension and situation model construction are dependent on knowledge of the general semantic domain which is the topic of the prose. For example, participants with a high level of knowledge of baseball remembered more than low-knowledge participants after reading a summary of a baseball inning. High-knowledge participants were better able to integrate the new information with a goal structure in their stored knowledge of the game of baseball (Chiesi, Spilich, & Voss, 1979; Spilich, Vesonder, Chiesi, & Voss, 1979). Teachers would do well to remember that some students have trouble comprehending and remembering assigned reading because they have very little knowledge about that topic already in memory and thus have little previous information with which to connect the new material and construct a situation model.

Sometimes even readers with relatively little knowledge may construct a reasonably accurate textbase and falsely believe that they have a thorough understanding of the material. They may, however, lack an adequate situation model (Kintsch, 1994; Zwaan & Radvansky, 1998). That is, the connections of the new textbase to information already in the long-term memory of the high-knowledge reader may be many but in the low-knowledge reader these connections may be very few, even though both have understood the new passage at the textbase level. The comprehension of the low-knowledge reader may be much more shallow and less long-lasting, although the person may not always recognize this fact. Children are particularly likely to overestimate their understanding and the adequacy of their situation models.

Point of View

Knowledge can also be organized around a **point of view,** which then helps accept information thematically as it is comprehended. For example, Pichert and Anderson (1977) and Anderson and Pichert (1978) gave participants a story to read about two boys playing in an empty house. One group was told to read the story from the point of view of a burglar considering robbing the place; these people tended to remember details about valuable objects, isolation from surrounding houses, and other such details of interest to a potential burglar. The other group read the story from the point of view of a real estate agent; these people remembered details such as size and number of rooms, condition of the house, and landscaping. Different details were thus attended to and remembered as a function of the point of view. Such differing points of view may be the reason that sometimes two friends, or a parent and a child, might remember the same incident very differently.

Schema Theory

One important conceptual framework for building situation models comes out of **schema theory** (Alba & Hasher, 1983; Bloom, 1988; Brewer & Nakamura, 1984; Rumelhart, 1980; Thorndyke, 1984; Vandierendonck & Van Damme, 1988). The original notion of a **schema** dates back to the cognitive psychologist Sir Frederick Bartlett (1932), the physiologist Sir Henry Head (1920), and more indirectly back to the philosopher Immanuel Kant (1781), who argued that concepts only had meaning insofar as they could relate to knowledge the individual already possessed. Schema theory has also been heavily influenced by computer-science work in artificial intelligence (Abelson, 1981; Schank & Abelson, 1977) and as such became an important facet of the cognitive-science approach to studying the mind (Stillings et al., 1995). It generally assumes a model of comprehension of the sort outlined above in this chapter.

A **schema** (plural: schemas or schemata) may be defined somewhat informally as a structure of knowledge about some topic or, more technically, "a data structure for representing generic concepts in memory" (Rumelhart, 1980, p. 34). As such, a schema guides both information acceptance and information retrieval; it affects how we process new information and how we retrieve old information from long-term memory. Schemata may be as concrete as types of spatial diagram representations (Novick, Hurley, & Francis, 1999) or as abstract as ways of going on a date in a specific culture (Harris, Schoen, & Hensley, 1992).

Schemata in Encoding

Although there is some variability in the way that the term **schema** is used, Alba and Hasher (1983) suggest that most would agree with four basic principles of how schemata become involved in the encoding process: selection, abstraction, interpretation, and integration.

The principle of **selection** refers to the fact that, of all the information in a given event or message, only some of it will become incorporated into the memory representation that is constructed. Two factors are relevant in determining the selection of information for encoding. One is simply whether or not an appropriate schema already exists in memory. If no relevant schema is available, both comprehension and memory will be very poor, as in examples (3) and (4) above, where no theme is present.

A second reason that the appropriate schema might not be available would be that it may not be activated from long-term memory, even though it may exist there. The phenomenon of encoding specificity (see Chapter 6) may be reinterpreted as ensuring that the same schemata are available at retrieval that occurred at encoding. When the context has clarified the theme, this allows identification of some information as more highly related to that overall theme and thus more likely to be used in construction of the situation model. Such information will tend to be processed more deeply and be remembered better. Information that appears to be irrelevant or easily reconstructible will likely be forgotten. The accuracy of later recall will largely be a function of both how well the initial information was selected and how accurately it was later reconstructed. See Box 8.2 for two examples of how the choice of a schema greatly affects the meaning that one constructs.

Illustrations of a Schema's Effect on the Construction of Meaning

I. Conversation between A and B:

A: I'd agree with that. But experts sometimes forget.

B: I knew two beginners once. They were in a very large place. Open space all around. Their leader signaled them to raise their bows. They were ready to begin . . .

A: Did they follow through with proper timing?

B. Yes, but they kept missing the mark. I'm glad you didn't hear the terrible noises they were making!

A: Holding the bow the correct way takes years to learn.

B: An additional factor is tension.

A: A loose bow is a sure guarantee of failure.

B: Except when it's being stored—I almost ruined one once by forgetting to loosen it up after I was done using it.

A: And it should be drawn back evenly, with uniform motion.

B: That's not too hard if your bow is well-balanced and not warped. Otherwise there's not much that can be done.

Dubitsky (1980)

II. To start with, here is a set of guidelines:

1. Wait for a sunny day. Depending on where you live, you may want to carry out the procedures all year, although many people start in the spring.

2. Check the oil. Failure to monitor the amount of oil can create serious problems.

3. Do not take more than recommended limits. If you take too much, it's possible everything will become discolored. Color changes can be embarrassing, particularly if you worked hard to make everything look right.

4. One major concern will be bare patches. Sometimes, you'll fail to notice all of them at first. Then, as you proceed, you'll become painfully aware of uncovered sections. They will require special care. And you'll need a good supply of water, although if it starts to rain, you will want to stop immediately.

5. By autumn—again, depending on where you live—you may be tired of the ritual, and happy the season is ended. But generally, after a cold winter, you'll probably be pleased to start again.

Wittig and Williams (1984, p. 219)

Depending on which schema is activated and used to process the information, the conversation between A and B may be seen to be about either archery or playing a stringed instrument. Similarly, the "guidelines" may be either for mowing the grass, painting, or suntanning. Depending on which schema is activated, the meaning of each individual sentence is entirely different.

The second principle of encoding is **abstraction,** by which details tend to be lost in a reduction of information into main points, with the schema indicating relative importance of different pieces of information. For example, a friend may give you a lengthy account of last Saturday night's date. Later you may remember only that the couple went to see a movie and then went out for pizza.

The third principle, **interpretation,** results from the elaboration during or just after encoding. One major characteristic of schemata is that they have slots or variables where specific information is filled in when the schema is **instantiated,** that is, when it is used to accept or retrieve information about a particular instance. For example, we may use our schema about a California lifestyle to infer how Joe, from San Diego, must spend his time. When we make such inferences, we often are necessarily interpreting beyond the information given. The issue of inference-drawing will be discussed in more detail later in this chapter.

The fourth principle of encoding through schemata is **integration,** by which information is combined into relatively holistic representations. Inferences are drawn to relate previously unrelated information. Although integration is a principle that operates in everyone, there is some evidence that older people integrate information to an even greater degree than younger adults (Woodruff, 1983). This could be reflected in the fact that more senior professors frequently write theoretical and integrative professional writing (such as textbooks or review articles), whereas their younger colleagues frequently are more active in collecting data in specific experiments.

The activation or retrieval of relevant schemata may be triggered by almost anything from prior text to a nonverbal stimulus to a casual mention of a topic in a conversation. It may even be triggered by a metaphor. Allbritton, McKoon, and Gerrig (1995) presented subjects with metaphors like "crime is a disease," "an argument is a war," or "a business is a living organism." The knowledge schemata triggered by these metaphors facilitated recognition of schema-consistent sentences continuing the same metaphor (e.g., "crime epidemic was raging out of control" and "public officials desperately looked for a cure" for the "crime is a disease" case). Such a finding suggests that a major psychological function of figurative language may be to activate particular schemata to aid in construction of the appropriate situation model.

Schemata may sometimes be more personal or social in nature. For example, information may be organized around a motivational schema, a perceived overriding purpose or goal of a character (Owens, Bower, & Black, 1979). It may also be information about oneself, perhaps similar to the traditional personality construct of self (Fiske & Taylor, 1991; Markus & Nurius, 1986; Symons & Johnson, 1997). Finally, a schema may be information about particular actions or classes of actions. It is on this procedural schema called a **script** that we next focus our attention.

Scripts

Schemata about activities or processes are called **scripts.** They have all the properties of schemata already discussed, but are specifically concerned with actions (Abelson, 1981; Bower, Black, & Turner, 1979; Fayol & Monteil, 1988; Mandler & Murphy, 1983; Pohl, Colonius, & Thuring, 1985; Schank & Abelson, 1977). We have many scripts in our long-term memory for a variety of familiar activities, which may be looked at as complex action-concepts. A good example is Bower, Black, and Turner's (1979) restaurant script, which contains information about a typical visit to a restaurant (see Table 8.1). For example, there are certain *roles* to be filled (customer, server, cashier), certain *props* (silverware, food, dishes, check, napkins), and certain *activities* (sitting down, ordering, eating, paying the bill). Not every specific instantiation of this script would provide specific information to fill in all these variables. For example, friends telling you about their meal in a new restaurant might not mention all the specific food they ate or whether the napkins were cloth or paper. Still, we would infer that there were dishes, that someone acted as server, that the customer paid the bill, and so forth, even though we may not have been told so specifically.

The way a script operates can perhaps best be illustrated by examining what happens when the incoming information does not fit the apparently appropriate script. Assuming that you have a script for eating in a restaurant that is similar to the one in Table 8.1, how might you process the following story (Bransford, 1978, p. 184)?

TABLE 8.1   Theoretical Restaurant Script[a]

Roles:	Customer	Cashier	
	Server	Host	
Props:	Table	Check	Plates
	Menu	Money	Silverware
	Food	Tip	Napkins
Entry conditions:	Customer has money		
	Customer hungry		
	Restaurant is open		
Results:	Restaurant has more money		
	Customer has less money		
	Customer is not hungry		
Scene 1:	Entering		
	Customer enters restaurant		
	Customer (or Host) decides on table		
	Customer goes to table		
	Customer sits down		
Scene 2:	Ordering		
	Customer receives menu		
	Customer looks at menu		
	Customer orders food		
Scene 3:	Eating		
	Server brings food to customer		
	Customer eats food		
Scene 4:	Exiting		
	Server gives check to customer		
	Customer pays cashier		
	Customer leaves tip		
	Customer leaves restaurant		

[a] This is a general script. Each scene could be made more specific. This is a script for a general-service, family-type North American restaurant. Script would vary somewhat for a fast-food restaurant, nightclub, bar, or for restaurants in other cultures (see Box 8.3).

Source: Adapted from G. H. Bower, J. B. Black, and T. J. Turner, Scripts in memory for text, *Cognitive Psychology,* 1979, 11, 177–220. Reprinted by permission of Academic Press and the author.

Jim went to the restaurant and asked to be seated in the gallery. He was told that there would be a one-hour wait. Forty minutes later, the applause for his song indicated that he could proceed with the preparation. Twenty guests had ordered his favorite, a cheese souffle. Jim enjoyed the customers in the main dining area. After two hours, he ordered the specialty of the house—roast pheasant under glass. It was incredible to enjoy such exquisite cuisine and yet still have fifteen dollars. He would surely come back soon.

Although all the words make sense in this story, for most readers there is a problem. The text does not fit the restaurant script that we most naturally retrieve and try to use in processing the story. Specifically, it violates information about roles; the customer appears to be entertaining and cooking as well as eating, roles that are generally separate in this script. Suppose, however, that a new type of restaurant opens, thus introducing a new restaurant subscript into your memory, specifically the following:

Assume that Jim went to a very special type of restaurant. The owner allows people who can cook at least one special meal to compete for the honor of preparing their specialty for other customers who desire it. Those who wish to compete sit in the gallery rather than the main dining room (although a central stage is accessible to both). The competition centers on the competitor's entertaining the crowd, by singing, for example, or dancing or playing an instrument. The approval of the crowd is a prerequisite for allowing the person to announce his or her cooking specialty. The rest of the crowd then has the option of ordering it, and the person receives a certain amount of money for each meal prepared. After doing the cooking and serving the meal to the customers, the person can then order from the regular restaurant menu and pay for it out of the money received for cooking. (Bransford, 1978, pp. 186–187)

Now go back and reread the original story with this new script! Does it make more sense?

Schemata and scripts have proven to be useful constructs beyond traditional cognitive psychology. For example, social schemata can be very important in processing information about people in social situations (Fiske & Taylor, 1991; Rojahn & Pettigrew, 1992; Schneider, 1991), gender-role stereotyping (Bem, 1981; Markus, Crane, Bernstein, & Saladi, 1982; Payne, Connor, & Colletti, 1987), or responses to mass media (Harris, 1999). Prior attitudes and knowledge may also affect how we process, interpret, and remember events. For example, Wiseman and Morris (1995) showed believers and nonbelievers in paranormal psychic phenomena a videotape of a magician performing magic/psychic demonstrations (card-selecting and fork-bending). The nonbelievers noticed and remembered the trick used more than the believers and rated the incident as less paranormal than the believers did.

The construct of schema also may help shed light on certain kinds of misunderstandings due to cultural differences (Harris, Hensley, Lee, & Schoen, 1988; Harris, Schoen, & Hensley, 1992). Part of the knowledge that everyone shares by virtue of being a part of a given culture may be conceptualized as schemata or scripts required for construction of appropriate situation models. This is also what people joining that culture must learn as a part of being an immigrant or sojourner. See Boxes 8.3 and 8.4 for further discussion of the issue of culture.

LEARNING AND COGNITION

Cultural Knowledge as Scripts

People frequently speak of having to "learn the culture" when they move to another country, or perhaps even a different part of their own country. This knowledge may be conceptualized as scripts about activities in that culture. Many times the scripts will be similar to ones we already have from our own culture, but with a few differences in roles, activities, or conditions. Before proceeding further, read the following paragraph:

> Nelson and Sonia sat down at a table on the sidewalk. They were both starving, since it was already almost eleven o'clock. After looking at the menu full of delicious choices, they decided on the lasagna. It seemed to be an unusually large crowd for such a late hour. After the waiter had brought the plates, Nelson saw their friends Marcia and Rita a few tables away. He immediately went over and gave the two women a friendly kiss. They had not seen each other for several weeks. As they saw the waiter on his way with their food, Nelson and Sonia returned to their table, just in time to help themselves to some lasagna from the platter. Tasting it, Nelson added some more olive oil and then pronounced it delicious. Sonia thought it had a little too much ham, but she also enjoyed it. Some ragged children came to their table selling roses, but they told them no and turned away. Finally, the waiter chased them away altogether. What a delicious meal, and for a very reasonable cost too. Upon paying the check, Nelson had to use a large bill, and the waiter brought the change to the table. Nelson and Sonia left the restaurant satisfied and happy.

If you live in North America, you probably noticed a few details as being strange in this story. However, if you lived in Brazil, it would fit your script of what a restaurant is like. When I (RJH) lived and taught in Brazil and regularly ate at restaurants, I had to learn variations on the restaurant script, such as the fact that you must ask for the check before it is brought, food is always brought on platters to be served by the customers onto individual plates, and that you always pay the waiter and never the cashier. Certain activities, like poor children wandering from table to table selling roses or lottery tickets, occur frequently in Brazil. Such knowledge of "learning the culture" that an immigrant or long-term visitor must acquire as part of becoming "at home" in the new culture may be characterized as scripts or schemata (Harris, Schoen, & Lee, 1986; Harris, Schoen, & Hensley, 1992).

Narrative Schema

Graesser et al.'s (1997) highest representational level of **text genre** may be conceptualized as a type of schema. One especially important and generalizable schema or script in Western culture is the **narrative** (story) **schema** (Kintsch, 1977). The basic unit of the narrative schema is the **episode,** which consists of three parts, the exposition, complication, and resolution. The **exposition** introduces the characters and setting. The **complication** occurs when those characters encounter some problem that presents a barrier that must be overcome. Finally, the **resolution** is the process of overcoming the complication and wrapping up the story.

One major difference between children's and adults' stories is that children's stories more explicitly identify the components of the narrative schema and follow them more closely, whereas adult stories, while still following the same schema, may require the reader to use more inferential processes to make use of the schema. For

The Kyeah Schema*

New schemata may be learned through exposure to an example (instantiation) or by learning the abstract description of the schema. Some cultures (Korea, India) have a script for a co-operative buying activity called (in Korea) a "kyeah." American subjects of Ahn, Brewer, and Mooney (1992) were exposed either to an Example or an Abstract description of what was presumably a new script for them. The Example version was as follows:

> Tom, Sue, Jane, and Joe were all friends and each wanted to make a large purchase as soon as possible. Tom wanted a VCR, Sue wanted a microwave, Joe wanted a car stereo, and Jane wanted a compact disk player. However, after paying their expenses, they each only had $60 left at the end of every third month. Tom, Sue, Jane, and Joe all got together to solve the problem. They made four slips of paper with the numbers 1, 2, 3, and 4 written on them. They put them in a hat and each drew out one slip. Jane got the slip with the 4 written on it, and said, "Oh darn, I have to wait to get my CD player." Joe got the slip with the 1 written on it and said, "Great, I can get my car stereo right away!" Sue got the number 2, and Tom got number 3. In February, they each contributed the $60 they had left. Joe took the whole $240 and bought a Pioneer car stereo. In May, they each contributed their money again. This time, Sue used the $240 to buy a Sharp 600-watt, 1.5 cubic foot microwave. In August, all four again contributed $60. Tom took the money and bought a Sanyo VCR with wired remote. In November, Jane got the money and bought a Technics CD player.

The Abstract version was the following:

> Suppose there are a number of people (let the number be n) each of whom wants to make a large purchase but does not have enough cash on hand. They can cooperate to solve this problem by each donating an equal small amount of money to a common fund on a regular basis. (Let the amount donated by each member be m.) They meet at regular intervals to collect everyone's money. Each time money is collected, one member of the group is given all the money collected (n × m) and then with that money he or she can purchase what he or she wants. In order to be fair, the order in which people are given the money is determined randomly. The first person in the random ordering is therefore able to purchase their desired item immediately instead of having to wait until they save the needed amount of money. Although the last person does not get to buy their item early, this individual is no worse off than they would have been if they waited until they saved the money by themselves.

In several studies measuring learning of the schema from a single instance (Example group), college students showed that they had in fact learned the script on the basis of being exposed to just one story.

---

*Ahn, Brewer, & Mooney (1992).

example, fairy tales start out, "Once upon a time there was . . .", a very blatant signal that expository material is to follow. In contrast, an adult story might actually begin talking about the problem (complication) and only gradually complete the exposition later. Whereas an adult can make the appropriate inferences to instantiate the schema, a young child will have trouble doing so and thus will not fully comprehend (and probably will quickly lose interest in) the story. On the other hand, a children's story may be uninteresting and unchallenging to an adult, because relatively little cognitive effort is required for its comprehension; the surface form of the story fits the narrative schema so perfectly that it becomes too predictable. Besides literature, the narrative schema has many applications in other domains of our experience, for example, watching television (see Box 8.5).

Episodes may have different sorts of structure besides a simple exposition-complication-resolution format. For example, the complication of a story may contain an entire episode embedded within the larger episode, much as a subordinate clause might be embedded as the subject of a sentence (e.g., "What I want to do is to leave"). Another example might be the resolution containing two additional episodes embedded as the last part of the larger episode. In this way the narrative schema offers a sort of syntax for discourse, offering a structural analysis for connected prose, not unlike syntactic analyses of sentences discussed in the last chapter.

Some have even argued for the narrative as the underlying framework for all of comprehension and memory. Schank and Abelson (1995) present compelling arguments that most, if not all, knowledge is based on stories constructed around personal experiences. New experiences are interpreted in term of old stories. Specific content of the stories is affected by whether and how they are told to others, with the collective reconstituted memories forming the basis of the individual's **remembered self.**

■ Box 8.5 ■

The Narrative Schema on Television

The narrative schema occurs in modern Western society in many manifestations, including television and other mass entertainment media. Obviously, many television dramas are built around the narrative schema; first there is an introduction of the characters and situation (some of this may be assumed in cases of a series where viewers may already be very familiar with the characters); this is followed by some complication or problem, finally culminating with a resolution of that problem. This is the basic pattern of television dramas and situation comedies, as well as children's stories and fables. Sometimes a narrative schema may be intentionally incomplete in order to draw us back to the program. An example would be when a soap opera concludes at the end of the complication, the viewer must tune in the next day to discover the resolution. Our tendency to use the narrative schema is so strong that we are drawn back the next day to complete instantiating the schema.

Beyond television fiction, the narrative schema also applies to a sizable number of broadcast commercials, as well as to print advertising. Frequently the format of ads is one of "problem solving," that is, there is an exposition (Mary is about to do her wash), followed by a complication (her children's clothes are too stained for her detergent to clean), and a resolution (spray on some Scream Spot Remover to get out those tough stains). Such ads have basically the same format as a story where there is a villain who is overcome by a hero, except in this case the villain is usually dirt, stains, inferior taste, or excessive work, and the hero is almost always the product being sold. An advertiser can more easily communicate the message about the product by drawing on the viewers' readily available story structure, the narrative schema.

Repeated retelling of certain stories thus becomes the basis of memory, even memory for facts, beliefs, and what is traditionally considered as semantic memory. See Wyer (1995) for some papers offering elaboration, critique, and application of this model.

INFERENCE-DRAWING IN COMPREHENSION

Basic Processes

One major function of a situation model is to guide the drawing of inferences from discourse or a social situation. It is a natural process to draw inferences beyond the material actually presented (Clark, 1977; Graesser & Bower, 1990; Graesser & Zwaan, 1995; Harris, 1981; Rickheit & Strohner, 1985). Exactly which inferences will be drawn by any given individual in a given situation depends in part on what schemata are initially activated during comprehension. If the reader activates a schema about robberies in the context of hearing a description of a house and yard, very different inferences will be drawn from that description than if a schema about selling homes is activated. This inferred material is used to construct the situation model and becomes fully integrated with the new information stated directly. The constructed memory representation does not typically distinguish the new and inferred information (Graesser & Clark, 1985; Graesser, Singer, & Trabasso, 1994).

Functions of Inference-Drawing

The inferences drawn during comprehension fulfill two general functions (Warren, Nicholas, & Trabasso, 1979). On the one hand, they build connections within the new material and between this new information and knowledge already in memory. This allows for the integration of new material in memory representations of previously learned information and also helps to provide some organization and structure to the information. Secondly, inferences fill in empty slots in the overall structure. To illustrate, if a strongly implied instrument of some action is not explicitly mentioned ("Ed hit the nail"), it may be inferred and added to the memory representation ("Ed used a hammer"), just as if it had appeared explicitly (Corbett & Dosher, 1978; Johnson, Bransford, & Solomon, 1973; McKoon & Ratcliff, 1981). Although a natural and integral part of any comprehension process, inferences may be drawn even more frequently in response to inadequately developed prose, in an attempt to fill the many open slots needed to make an otherwise elliptical passage comprehensible (Glenn, 1978). In fact, there are many different conditions that may predict whether or not certain inferences will be drawn (Klin, Guzman, & Levine, 1999).

Default Inferences

If there is no value present for a given variable in the particular instance at hand, then a **default inference** is used to fill in the most typical value that is contained in the stored schema. For example, if we hear "the hungry python caught the mouse," we use our knowledge of pythons and hunger to make the default inference that the snake subsequently consumed the mouse. Such information was not stated in the text; rather, it was filled in by using a default inference and inferring, with no evidence to the contrary, that the catching was followed by eating. If we had heard "the hungry little girl caught the mouse," our small-child schema would probably not contain the default inference that, barring information to the contrary, little children who catch mice subsequently eat them. Although default inferences are a part of the information-accepting function of schemata, the memory representation constructed with them is then stored in memory and remembered as if it had been contained in the text itself.

Sometimes such an inference may be unwarranted. For example, in the python example above, if a person were subsequently questioned about the fate of the mouse, he or she would probably remember and respond that the mouse had been eaten, when it may have in fact escaped the snake's clutches. In this sense, memory is a by-product of the interpretation during the comprehension process; it is the residue left after the schemata have done their job of interpreting the new information or reconstructing old information during an attempt to remember.

Even a total lack of knowledge can be the basis for an inference. For example, in answering the question "Is Vanuatu a major oil-exporting country?" one may find no information about oil in one's stored information about Vanuatu (assuming any information at all about Vanuatu!). Therefore one might make the inference that the answer to the question is thus "no," because one has no knowledge of Vanuatu exporting oil and since one might expect to have that knowledge if it *were* a mjor oil exporter. In this case, such an inference would lead to the correct answer.

How Many Inferences Are Drawn?

A difficult theoretical question in the study of inferences is how to determine which of all the possible inferences will be generated on-line while reading or listening. The **Minimalist Hypothesis** (McKoon & Ratcliff, 1992, 1995) suggests that the only inferences which are encoded automatically are those absolutely necessary for establishing local coherence in the textbase. For example, we construct **anaphoric reference** like computing the referent of a pronoun or drawing connections with information in the previous sentence (e.g., understanding that, in "I did my homework. The algebra was hard," that algebra was among the homework). On the other hand, the **Constructionist Theory** (Graesser et al., 1994) argues that we generate on-line both text-connecting and extratextual inferences. The latter type is derived from relevant stored knowledge structures, which are then related to the text being processed in the construction of a situation model. Graesser et al. suggest thirteen classes of inferences generated on-line and off-line during reading.

Another way to conceptualize inference-drawing is in terms of its **readiness,** the momentary accessibility of certain information (Gerrig & McKoon, 1998). As we read, each new piece of linguistic information evokes related information from long-term memory. Certain information is more or less accessible—high or low in readiness—at any given moment in the on-line processing of the language. As the applicable moment for the use of that information passes, it fades in readiness. To take a very simple example from Gerrig and McKoon, suppose someone hears the message "It's me. It's here." on their voicemail. That will be understood, with appropriate inferences made, if and only if the listener has enough information *at that moment* to identify the referent of "me" and know what the second "it" refers to. By taking the approach that related knowledge varies moment-by-moment in readiness, this gets around the problem of having to decide what inferences are necessarily made (or not made) upon hearing or reading a certain string of words.

Inferences in Social Cognition

Cognitive inference processes operate more broadly than just in discourse comprehension settings. We also process social information by observing interpersonal behaviors and then drawing relevant inferences about those behaviors (Augustinos & Walker, 1995; Fiske & Taylor, 1991; Wyer & Radvansky, 1999).

Causal Inferences

One of the most common types of social inferences involves inferring a causal relationship of events. Owens et al. (1979) studied how the inference of a motive for behavior could guide causal attribution inferences drawn from a person's actions. Participants read a story about a woman doing a series of routine actions such as fixing a meal, attending a class, and visiting a doctor. Some participants received initial information describing a context that provided a motive for later behavior (e.g., discovering she was pregnant). On a free-recall task thirty minutes later, these people recalled more episodes and in better order than those not receiving this motive context. They also made more intrusions representing distortions to fit the inferred motive schema (remembering "usual medical procedures" as "pregnancy tests"). The knowledge of a motive helped integrate episodes into a coherent whole in comprehension.

This tendency to infer causes of observed events is the reason that we so frequently interpret correlated events as causally related. While it may be obvious that the number of deaths in Bangladesh is not causally related to the consumption of ice cream in Chicago (they are correlated, presumably due to seasonal temperature patterns in the Northern Hemisphere), it may be more difficult to realize that someone's death after taking an experimental drug may not necessarily be due to the drug. It appears that causality is an important category for structuring knowledge, and if information easily reflects causal categories, even if spurious ones, then information processing is facilitated (Noordman & Vonk, 1998).

Stereotyping

Social psychological studies of stereotyping have been reconceptualized in terms of schema theory (Hamilton & Sherman, 1994; Sherman, 1996). A stereotype that we hold of a certain group will affect how we process information about someone who is a member of that group. A very distinctive characteristic relative to other group members is more likely to be the basis of a social categorization than is a more common one; for example, the only Japanese baseball player in the United States is seen as primarily Japanese, or the only female CEO of a major corporation is seen primarily in terms of her gender (Nelson & Miller, 1995). Social schemata may have substantial consequences. See Box 8.6 for a description of the use of social cognition research on gender-role stereotyping in a sexual discrimination case that reached the U.S. Supreme Court.

Another area of great concern in regard to gender schemata has been their role in attributions about crimes such as rape or domestic violence. For example, certain myths have traditionally been associated with rape and its victims ("She must have been asking for it"; "attractive and provocatively dressed women are more likely to be raped"; "rape is a crime of unfulfilled sexual desires"). These myths may be seen as schemata. Thus, if we hear that someone has been raped, we tend to process and remember selectively, and even distort, information to be consistent with the rape

■ Box 8.6 ■

The Role of Social Cognition Research in Sex Discrimination Cases

In 1982 Ann Hopkins was an outstanding employee at the large accounting firm of Price Waterhouse. Although she was praised by clients and supporters, had more billable hours than any of the 87 other candidates (all men) proposed for partnership that year, she was denied that coveted position of partner. The reasons given were her interpersonal skills problems. Evaluators called her "macho" and said she "overcompensated for being a woman." They recommended a "course at charm school"; one colleague recommended that she walk, talk, and dress "more femininely." She took the firm to federal district court, alleging a civil rights violation of sex discrimination. The case eventually made it to the U.S. Supreme Court.

In this case social cognition researcher Susan Fiske testified as to the power of sex stereotyping and the conditions under which it is likely to be the greatest. Also, the American Psychological Association (APA) filed a friend of the court brief. This document argued for the validity of the stereotyping phenomenon, especially gender stereotyping, and tried to show how the findings from the psychological research indicated that a situation such as the organizational climate at Price Waterhouse could be expected to produce a high degree of stereotyping that would be brought to bear on decisions like Ms. Hopkins' partnership application. Fiske, Bersoff, Borgida, Deaux, and Heilman (1991) discuss this evidence in detail, and identify strengths and weaknesses of social cognition research, especially as applicable in the courtroom.

The Supreme Court decided that Ms. Hopkins had been evaluated as a *woman candidate* for partnership, not merely as a *candidate*. They concluded that an employer who acts on the belief that a woman "cannot be aggressive, or that she must not be, has acted on the basis of gender . . . An employer who objects to aggressiveness in women but whose positions require this trait places women in an intolerable Catch 22: out of a job if they behave aggressively and out of a job if they don't." (*Price Waterhouse v. Hopkins,* 1989, in Fiske et al., p. 1055).

myths (schemata) that we hold. Understanding the cognitive processes that contribute to the formation and maintenance of such inaccurate and inappropriate information may be an important first step toward changing people's attitudes about rape and its victims.

A parallel set of concerns exists for the way that we view domestic violence. If we know that a woman verbally provoked her husband before he battered her, this knowledge is used to interpret the whole incident, including making attributions that the assault was partly her responsibility (Kristiansen & Giulietti, 1990; Pierce & Harris, 1993). On the other hand, if we hear of a wife battering her husband, various schemata about gender and relationships are retrieved to discount the injury done to the male victim relative to the female victim in the more prototypical domestic battering case (Harris & Cook, 1994). A function of the testimony in a rape or domestic battering trial may be seen as providing critical, but highly selective, information to the jury so as to encourage it to make certain inferences about the event in question. By their selection of particular information and the withholding of other information, the defense and prosecuting attorneys attempt to guide the jurors' inference processes.

Gender schemata creep into our thinking in other more subtle ways less often acknowledged. For example, studies of press coverage of sex crimes show that women victims are typically described in terms of their appearance and sexuality, either around a theme of innocence (virgin) or seductress (vamp) (Benedict, 1992). Thus the public is encouraged to construct a situation model of either (1) a pure and innocent victim attacked by a vicious monster or (2) a seductive and loose woman bearing partial responsibility for her assault. Even cases of domestic violence are often described in terms of love (crimes of *passion*). Statements like "His love for her was so strong that jealousy took over and he killed her" encourage the hearer to retrieve schemata of love and relationship to understand a vicious violent crime that certainly reflects no love. In contrast, press descriptions of wartime rapes almost never describe victims in terms of their appearance or behavior but rather as the crimes of torture that they really are. Why are not individual acts of violence against women also so described?

Now let us move away from the drawing of inferences in social situations to the operation of such processes in the consumer's processing of advertising.

Cognition and Misleading Advertising

One interesting area where natural inference-drawing processes of language comprehension can lead us astray is the realm of advertising, especially in cases where ads may be misleading or deceptive. Each of us sees an average of around 500 ads every day, half of them television commercials (Wilson & Wilson, 1998). Advertising messages thus constitute a major type of stimulus in human experience, and the language of advertising raises some interesting information-processing issues (Geis, 1982; Harris, Sturm, Klassen, & Bechtold, 1986; Richards, 1990).

In exploring some issues in the processing of ads, Preston and Richards (1986) made a helpful distinction between miscomprehension and deceptiveness. **Miscomprehension** occurs when the meaning conveyed to the hearer is different from the literal content of the message. **Deceptiveness,** on the other hand, occurs if the conveyed meaning is inconsistent with the facts about the product, regardless of what the ad stated. From a cognitive perspective, the question is much more complex than merely determining the truth or falsity of the ad itself.

If both the literal and conveyed message are true, then there is neither miscomprehension nor deceptiveness. If the literal message is false and is clearly conveyed as if it were true, there is deceptiveness but no miscomprehension. The hearer constructes a meaning which is not consistent with reality, but not because he or she misunderstood the ad. For example, if an ad states an incorrect price for a product and we believe it, we have been deceived but have not miscomprehended the ad.

It is also possible to miscomprehend without being deceived. An ad may state a claim that is literally false, but we comprehend it in some nonliteral way that is consistent with reality. For example, the claim that "our cookies are made by elves" is unlikely to be comprehended literally; thus a "miscomprehension" will lead to *not* being deceived. This type of claim is fairly common (e.g., "a white tornado in every can," "at this price these cars will fly out the door"). Another type of false but probably nondeceptive ad would be some of the so-called mockups—photographic displays for print on television ads. Because of practicalities of studio photography, certain conventions are often used in some ads (see Box 8.7).

The type of advertising claim that is potentially the most damaging is the statement that is literally true but miscomprehended, thus deceiving consumers by inducing

───────── Advertising Mock-Ups: False—Yes, Deceptive—Maybe ─────────

That cool and sweet ice cream on television might really be mashed potatoes (because ice cream melts too fast under hot studio lights), or that foaming head on the cold beer in the magazine might in fact be shampoo (because soapsuds last longer for photographers than do beer heads). Sometimes such acceptable conventions may border on the deceptive. For example, there was a case many years ago where a soup company was censured for putting marbles in the bottom of the soup bowl during photography (Preston, 1975). Although the company argued that this was necessary to buoy up the solid ingredients and keep them all from sinking unseen to the bottom of the bowl while the photographers readied their cameras and lights, the courts ruled that this constituted a misleading implication that the soup contained more solid ingredients than it in fact did. In another famous case, a shaving cream manufacturer used grains of sand on clear plastic for a mock-up purporting to be a razor shaving sandpaper with its product. Although the razor would in fact shave **fine** sandpaper, fine sandpaper looks like flat paper when photographed. However, if coarse sandpaper was used, the razor wouldn't shave it; hence, the sand grains on clear plastic solution. Do you consider such a mock-up deceptive?

them to construct a meaning of the ad that is inconsistent with reality. There are several types of language constructions that, although true themselves, may imply something else that is not true (Burke, DeSarbo, Oliver, & Robertson, 1988; Harris, Dubitsky, & Bruno, 1983; Harris, Pounds, Maiorelle, & Mermis, 1993; Richards, 1990).

The first type of such statements are claims that contain a **hedge** word or phrase that seriously weakens the force of a claim; see examples (6) through (10). In all of these cases there is a word or phrase that qualifies and weakens the basic claim that is made. As such, the statement would be difficult, if not impossible, to prove false. However, if the hedge is not totally understood or remembered, the hearer might construct a much more optimistic interpretation of what the product can do.

6. Lavium Pills may help relieve tension (then again, they may not).
7. Spring Fluoride fights cavities (but it may fight and lose).
8. Bing detergent leaves dishes virtually spotless (whatever "virtually" means).
9. Mist shampoo helps control dandruff symptoms with regular use. (What is regular use? Does controlling the symptoms mean controlling the condition? Is helping to control sufficient to control?)
10. Nobody can promise you a good return on your investment, but try us and someday you too may be a millionaire (or you may not, and this is no promise anyway).

A second type of true but potentially deceptive claim is the **elliptical comparative.** Whenever an adjective or adverb is modified by "more" or an "-er" suffix, it involves a comparison with something else. This basis for comparison may or may not be stated directly, and if it is not, its absence may or may not be obvious to the inferring reader or listener. Sometimes in ads when the basis of the comparison is not stated, the strength of the claim could vary considerably depending on what that claim was. For example, consider (11). If there is anything at all, even cyanide capsules, that is worse to take than Snarfo, then (11) is not false. However, if the consumer infers that Snarfo is being compared to its competitors in the marketplace, miscomprehension may occur and the consumer will be deceived.

11. Snarfo makes you healthier.

Some years ago there was a case where an auto manufacturer claimed that its car was "700 percent quieter." When the FTC asked the manufacturer to produce the research evidence to back up this claim, it produced a study showing that the car was 700 percent quieter on the inside of the car than on the outside! Was that the basis of comparison that you inferred when you first read the claim? If you hear that a car "goes farther on a tank of gas," do you infer that it has better mileage than its competitors (which ones?) or that it has a larger gas tank? With advertising claims, more than one interpretation is possible.

A third category of true but potentially deceptive claims is **implied causation,** for example, through the use of two juxtaposed imperatives: (12) and (13). In these cases two imperatives are stated successively. Though no causal relationship of the two is necessary or stated, it is very easy to infer such a relationship, just as we saw with social cognition earlier in the chapter. Advertising copy frequently makes use of juxtaposed imperatives to imply a causal relationship, taking advantage of this natural information-processing tendency. Causal implications of a variety of sorts may be communicated through verbal advertising claims, pictorial material, or some combination of the two.

12. Get a beautiful tan this summer. Use Bronzoline.
13. Help your child get better grades. Buy an Addo computer.

Another type of literally true but potentially deceptive claim involves the citing of statistical or other scientific research information **(pseudoscience).** Any evidence of science tends to give an ad a greater aura of authority and prestige, but such statistics may often be a very slippery way to imply something quite different than what a claim directly states. One way this may be done is by reporting results of a survey only in terms of the absolute number or the percent, but not both: (14) and (15). Similarly, the number of respondents reporting may be mentioned with no consideration of the number questioned (16). Sometimes the competition in a comparative ad may be inadequately or inappropriately specified (17).

14. 5,000 doctors recommended Cashprin Aspirin. (5,000 out of how many?)
15. 75 percent of dentists recommended Fizzle Toothpaste (75 percent of how many? Four?)
16. 2,000 satisfied customers responding to our survey favored . . . (How many were questioned and didn't respond?)
17. Prince Scrubitoff Oven Cleaner has 40 percent more cleaning power than another popular brand. (What is cleaning power? What was popular about the other brand?)

Results may be reported in piecemeal fashion, with specific comparisons drawn comparing one's product to different competitors, but each on a different dimension. The overall set of comparisons may imply something far beyond what is stated directly.

For example, one might infer from (18) that the particular car was larger on all interior dimensions than any of its competitors, although that is not at all what is stated.

18. The Wallaby Medalist has more rear seat headroom than a Nissan Sentra, more leg room than a Ford Escort, a larger trunk than a Toyota Corolla, and more hip room than a Honda Civic.

Sometimes an ad can make an **implied slur** about the competition without stating it directly, as in examples (19) through (22). Even if all of the statements are verifiably true, the inferences one is invited to make are considerably more questionable.

19. Tipsi-Cola Lite has no cancer-causing artificial sweetener. (But maybe the competition does?)
20. S&M Schlock will accompany you to an audit if the IRS questions a tax return we prepare. (But any tax preparer by law must do so.)
21. Wouldn't it be terrible to be stuck somewhere with some of those traveler's checks that don't give refunds easily? (But all do give refunds.)
22. Slurpo Mushroom Soup—there's no asbestos in our mushrooms! (But beware the other brands.)

So far we have discussed several types of advertising claims that may imply more than they state directly and thus possibly deceive through inducing miscomprehension. Do people in fact infer the (perhaps false) inferences which go beyond what is directly stated? Yes, they do. When people hear or read a claim like (23), they are much more likely to remember it as (24) than they are to remember (24) as (23). People reading implied claims frequently understand and remember a stronger version of that claim, whereas stronger claims are seldom remembered as weaker ones (Harris, Dubitsky, & Bruno, 1983; Harris, Trusty, Bechtold, & Wasinger, 1989).

23. Lytenol fights colds.
24. Lytenol cures colds.

Other extensions of this work tried to train people not to draw such unwarranted inferences from radio ads (Bruno & Harris, 1980). This is difficult to do and, although some progress was achieved through small group interactive training, it is very hard to stop this general information-processing activity from occurring. The most effective training required participants themselves to generate alternative interpretations besides the obvious implied claim.

We now turn to a brief examination of two global models of comprehension, John Anderson's ACT and Walter Kintsch's Construction-Integration model. Both are extremely complicated, and we only present the basic highlights here.

ANDERSON'S ACT MODEL

One of the most influential global models of comprehension has been the series of **ACT** (Adaptive Control of Thought) models of John R. Anderson. Beginning with the earliest ACT model (Anderson, 1976), and later definitively revised and elaborated in ACT* ("Act-Star") by Anderson (1983), it has most recently culminated in ACT-R

(Anderson, 1993, 1996). ACT is a very comprehensive model, a computer simulation as well as a psychological model. Anderson argues that "all there is to intelligence is the simple accrual and tuning of many small units of knowledge that in total produce complex cognition" (Anderson, 1996, p. 356). ACT deals broadly with both "knowledge acquisition" (e.g., learning, recognition) and "knowledge deployment" (e.g., categorization, problem solving).

ACT has three major components. The first is **working memory,** encompassing more or less the traditional view of this construct (see Chapter 5). The second component is **declarative memory,** including both episodic memory, represented as **token** nodes (specific instances), and semantic memory, represented as **type** nodes (general concepts). This network of nodes is connected by relations and accessed by spreading activation. Knowledge codes may be of three types. Propositional relationships encode idea units with component *arguments,* like AGENT, ACTION, OBJECT, or INSTRUMENT. Temporal strings encode the order of events. Finally, spatial images encode pictorial information.

The third, and most original, component of ACT is **production memory,** the long-term store for procedural knowledge. Here the unit of representation is the **production,** a set of condition-action (IF-THEN) pairs. These productions may be either motor skills, such as riding a bicycle or shooting a basketball, or purely internal events like conjugating a verb or using a mathematical algorithm to solve a problem.

The actual processing is done through a process of matching IF conditions in working memory with those in production memory and, if those conditions are met, executing the THEN action. Productions are continually being modified by application to new situations. Trying to match a production sometimes leads to errors, which then result in changing the production to fit the new reality. Often productions are used in a series, together becoming a single process, such as riding a bike or tying one's shoe. Automaticity comes as the initial declarative knowledge is gradually replaced with productions that perform behavior directly (proceduralization process). The series of productions is then triggered as a unit without the necessity of conscious attention.

Anderson argues that ACT has many applications. One is in learning, which he argues has been neglected by many cognitive theories. ACT accounts for procedural as well as declarative knowledge and describes the transfer from deliberate to automatic processing that occurs with increasing practice. ACT has the advantage of being a very global model, yet it is extremely complex and hard to definitively test or falsify. A model so powerful and so generalizable across situations runs the risk of being untestable. Whether ACT has this problem to a critical degree awaits further research.

KINTSCH'S CONSTRUCTION-INTEGRATION MODEL

Like ACT, the **Construction-Integration (CI)** model evolved out of earlier work (Kintsch, 1974, 1992, 1994; van Dijk & Kintsch, 1983). By far its most detailed and systematic presentation, however, is found in Kintsch's (1998) book *Comprehension.* More strongly rooted in language comprehension than is ACT, CI nonetheless also aspires to be a generalized model of comprehension of all sorts of information.

The core knowledge representation in CI is the proposition (see Chapter 7), although imagery representations are also permitted. Propositions derived directly from the text constitute the **textbase.** However, complete comprehension almost always requires elaboration beyond the textbase, drawing on one's long-term memory and interpretations of the textbase propositions. This complete structure including both the textbase and associated elaborations is the **situation model** (Zwaan, 1999; Zwaan & Radvansky, 1998). In fact, "language comprehension necessarily involves construction of representation of the state of affairs described in a text" (p. 162). Comprehension thus is achieved by building this mental model. In so doing, the textbase is very strongly constrained by the text, while the situation model is much less constrained, given that each person's knowledge and experience is different.

A major component of the CI model are the **construction rules.** There are rules for the construction of propositions, rules for interconnecting the propositions in a network (see Chapter 6), rules for the activation of knowledge, and rules for constructing inferences. Once a network of propositions is constructed, it is stabilized and integrated through a spreading activation process. As new propositions or imagery representations are formed, they are further integrated into the existing network being formed in working memory. See Kintsch (1998) for reporting of several experiments supporting CI theory in the areas of language comprehension, arithmetic word problems, and problem solving. As with ACT, the CI model still requires further testing to establish its generality and limiting conditions, as well as explore its falsifiability.

We now conclude this chapter with a look at **metacognition,** cognition about cognition.

METACOGNITION

The knowledge, awareness, and monitoring of one's own cognitions is called **metacognition.** Knowledge of more specific cognitive processes may be described as metamemory, metalinguistics, or metareasoning.

Metacognition may be divided into three broad conceptual categories. **Autobiographical information,** accumulated gradually about one's own cognitions, makes up one large class (Johnson, Foley, Suengas, & Ray, 1988; see also Autobiographical Memory in Chapter 6).

A second category is the ongoing **monitoring of one's own cognitions,** including feeling-of-knowing (FOK) judgments (Nelson, 1988; Vesonder & Voss, 1985), comprehension calibration and the illusion of knowing (Glenberg, Sanocki, Epstein, & Morris, 1987; Maki, Foley, Kajer, Thompson, & Wilert, 1990; Weaver, 1990), monitoring during problem solving (Metcalfe, 1986), and reality monitoring, the discrimination of external versus imagined information (Johnson, 1988; Johnson & Raye, 1981; Suengas & Johnson, 1988).

The third category is the ongoing **control of one's own cognitions,** such as allocation of self-paced study time (Mazzoni, Cornoldi, & Marchitelli, 1990; Nelson & Leonesio, 1988), the selection and monitoring of encoding strategies in memory (Justice & Weaver-McDougall, 1989; Pressley, Levin, & Ghatala, 1984), and the metacognitive control of the termination of retrieval (Anderson & Milson, 1989; Nelson & Narens, 1990; Reder, 1988).

One important consideration in regard to metacognition is the developmental aspect. How do children develop the ability to think about their thinking? Young children frequently overestimate what they know and how well they can think. They may also confuse what they know with what someone else knows (Flavell, Green, Flavell, & Grossman, 1997; Jenkins & Astington, 1996). While most psychologists and parents have assumed that this cognitive immaturity is a sort of deficit or inefficiency, some have argued that this inaccurate metacognition may actually be adaptive by motivating children to practice their thought processes and motor skills more widely, thus improving their performance (Bjorklund & Green, 1992).

CONCLUSION

At the beginning of this chapter, we introduced an interactionist model of comprehension, whereby meaning is not a property of the stimulus, but rather emerges from top-down and bottom-up processing through the interaction of the stimulus and the active mind and memory of the person. In comprehension, the sounds (listening) or letters (reading) are perceived and recognized and then constructed into words. These words are then decoded to meanings, using information in the mental lexicon and the syntactic structure of the words. In constructing the meaning of a whole sequence of words, one retrieves knowledge schemata from memory and draws inferences based on such knowledge to construct a situation model, taking into account pragmatic considerations surrounding the utterance or text. Information of different sorts (phonetic, lexical, syntactic, pragmatic) is processed in parallel during the comprehension process as the meaning is constructed. In this way comprehension involves top-down and bottom-up processing and is a multifaceted set of processes, not an all-or-none operation.

SUGGESTED READINGS

The material in this chapter is usually discussed at least briefly in chapters on memory or language in cognition texts. For good integrative discussions of schema theory, see the articles by Rumelhart (1980), Alba and Hasher (1983), Brewer and Nakamura (1984), and Thorndyke (1984). See Fiske and Taylor's (1991) *Social Cognition* for a thorough review of social cognition. A highly readable, entertaining, and fact-filled discussion of deceptive advertising is Ivan Preston's (1975) *The Great American Blow-Up: Puffery in Advertising and Selling;* for a more recent and experimental approach, see Jef Richard's (1990) *Deceptive Advertising.* Scott (1994) offers a thorough and provocative discussion of advertising as a type of text to be processed by the consumer. For an excellent comprehensive set of readings on metacognition, see Nelson (1992). For sets of readings on discourse processing, see Weaver, Mannes, and Fletcher (1995) and Britton and Graesser (1996); for readings on inference processing, see Graesser and Bower (1990).

9 Thinking: Problem Solving, Reasoning, and Decision Making

A panel of psychologists interviewed and administered personality tests to 30 engineers and 70 lawyers, all successful in their respective fields. On the basis of this information, thumbnail descriptions of the 30 engineers and 70 lawyers were written. Following are three descriptions, chosen at random from the 100 available descriptions. For each description, please indicate, on a scale from 0 to 100, what you think the probability is that the person described is an engineer (adapted from Kahneman & Tversky, 1973, p. 241):

1. Rich is a 30-year-old man. He is married with no children. A man of high ability and high motivation, he promises to be quite successful in his field. He is well liked by his colleagues. (p. 242)
   Probability Rich is one of the 30 engineers out of the 100 people _____?

2. Jack is a 45-year-old man. He is married and has four children. He is generally conservative, careful, and ambitious. He shows no interest in political and social issues and spends most of his free time on his many hobbies, which include home carpentry, sailing, and mathematical puzzles. (p. 241)
   Probability that Jack is one of the 30 engineers out of the 100 people _____?

3. No information provided on Fred.
   Probability that Fred is one of the 30 engineers out of the 100 people _____?

The participants studied by Kahneman and Tversky guessed that the probability that Rich is an engineer is about 50 percent, that Jack is an engineer is about 95 percent, and that Fred is an engineer is about 30 percent. Only one of these estimates—the last one—is correct.

In the above example, if a person is chosen at random from a group of 30 engineers and 70 lawyers, he or she is much more likely to be a lawyer than an engineer, and so we estimate the chances that Fred is an engineer, correctly, at 30/100, or 30 percent. But as soon as people are given a personality description, they forget about the **objective probabilities** (base rates). The description of Rich is worthless; it could describe any professional person—doctor, lawyer, engineer, politician, scientist, or professor. There is no reason to think Rich is more likely to be an engineer than a lawyer, so we set an estimate of 50 percent—equally likely to be a lawyer or an engineer—quite forgetting the population distribution of 30 engineers and 70 lawyers. We ought to treat Rich like Fred and estimate 30 percent, but few of us do.

With Jack we go even further astray. His profile fits the stereotype (schema) of the engineer we have in long-term memory, and we jump to the conclusion that he must be an engineer, again ignoring the objective probabilities. Even if the engineer schema is accurate—which it very likely is not—there are only 30 engineers in the group to begin with, so that any randomly sampled person will most likely be a lawyer. Whether told there were 30 of 100 engineers or 70 of 100 engineers, both groups gave the same estimate that Jack is an engineer (95%), thus showing that they ignored the base rates and followed their intuitive personality theories.

In this chapter we will find that, as this example illustrates, human thinking is much more imperfect than we would like to believe. We ignore important relevant information, rely far too much on stereotypes and personal experience, jump to conclusions, fail to challenge dubious facts, and even have trouble reasoning according to the rules of logic. This chapter will examine the psychological study of problem solving, reasoning (inductive, deductive, and scientific), and decision making.

PROBLEM SOLVING

In discussing problem solving, we may define a **problem** broadly as the "gap that separates the present state and the goal state" (Hayes, 1978). Obviously, this includes a wide variety of situations. Although problem solving has most often been studied by psychologists using little puzzles of some sort, the principles of problem solving have broad application beyond puzzles and games to the many problems we face in our daily lives. Our discussion of problem solving will take a broad approach considering both types of problems.

The topic of problem solving has been studied in diverse traditions in psychology. Gestalt psychologists examined it many years ago, with emphasis on holistic aspects like restructuring the problem and combining elements in new ways. The behaviorist tradition studied problem solving from the perspective of analyzing it into simple processes of learning responses to stimuli and acquiring solutions incrementally (see Chapter 3). Finally, the computer-influenced information-processing tradition has dominated recent research, which has been active especially since Newell and Simon's (1972) landmark book, *Human Problem Solving*. It is generally this information-processing approach that is taken in this section, since that best represents current thinking on the topic. We also, however, bring in insights from other traditions, especially Gestalt psychology.

Understanding the Problem

The overall problem situation may be subdivided into (1) understanding the problem, and (2) solving the problem. Contrary to what might be your first impression, understanding the problem is far from trivial. Many of the barriers to solving a problem stem not from inappropriate strategies in trying to solve it but rather from inappropriate conceptualizations of what the problem is all about.

Considering a problem as a sequence of continually changing states from the start to the finish, there are several aspects to understanding the problem. The initial situation (start state) must be understood. What are the "givens" at the start of the problem? These givens would include a full description of the context of the problem and all of the parameters under which one must operate in solving the problem. This would include, among other information, a description of the operators (moves) available for changing the state of the problem. For example, a description of all the allowable moves of each piece in chess would completely define the operators for that game. In contrast to puzzles and games, many real-world problems do not have the operators so well defined. It may take a depressed person several sessions of counseling just to identify operators that might be available for changing one's life.

Another important aspect of understanding the problem is defining the goal state. While this is sometimes very clear, such as in games or many puzzles, often it is not; this lack of specificity of the goal state becomes part of the difficulty of the problem. For example, students who have difficulty concentrating in school and who feel lethargic and apathetic may not have a clear goal state for their problem. It is hard to make much progress toward a goal if you do not know what that goal is. Merely knowing that you want to change from the start state is not sufficient. Problem solving must be goal-directed, even though that goal may not always be achieved.

The ongoing construction of mental representations of a problem as we are understanding it is a comprehension process. It initially involves working memory and also draws heavily on long-term memory, especially processes of retrieving schemata and drawing inferences, as discussed in Chapter 8. The extent and character of our knowledge about a specific problem area naturally affects how we understand the problem. For example, if you have considerable mechanical knowledge, you are probably better able to describe the givens and recognize available operators at your disposal to solve the problem of your car dying at the side of the road. A person with little mechanical knowledge could not describe the problem nearly so completely.

Solving the Problem

Actually solving the problem may be viewed as a process of searching through the **"problem space"** for a "solution path," a path connecting the start state and the goal state. There may be one or several solution paths; usually the discovery of one good solution path is sufficient. Very often there is a huge number of possible solution paths for a given problem. For example, a 40-move chess game has around 10^{20} solution paths! Ridding yourself of depression has some unknown number of solution paths.

Algorithms and Heuristics

Procedures used in solving problems may be either algorithms or heuristics. **Algorithms** are strategies guaranteed to produce a solution, whereas **heuristics** are knowledge-based strategies which involve hunches, good guesses, and past experience.

Algorithms are most useful for well-defined, highly structured problems. For example, a division algorithm is used to solve long-division problems. Very often no algorithm exists (e.g., you are shy and want to be more popular socially) or the algorithm is so cumbersome that it would be of no real help to use it. For instance, anagrams (scrambled words) could be solved by the algorithm of rearranging the letters in all the possible permutations. However, the number of such permutations is huge; the eight-letter anagram THREAGUD has 40,320 possible rearrangements of all its letters! To start writing these out would be pretty futile. Instead, we draw on our knowledge of English spelling rules to eliminate a large majority of those 40,320 possibilities (e.g., words that start out RG or GD need not be considered). Thus, we use heuristics, in this case drawing on our knowledge of the English language. In such a case, heuristics are much more efficient strategies than the available algorithm, although the latter might work better in a computer program.

Sometimes the distinction is made between **well-defined** and **ill-defined** problems. Well-defined problems typically have an explicit goal state and clearly defined operators, as found in most games. On the other hand, ill-defined problems are much less structured, and part of the challenge for the problem solver is to provide structure for the problem. Well-defined problems are often, though not always, amenable to algorithmic solutions, whereas ill-defined problems almost never are. Most of the real problems we face in our jobs and personal lives are largely ill-defined.

One good general heuristic in problem solving is **subgoaling,** that is dividing a problem into subproblems to be worked on one at a time. Very often an entire problem can seem forbidding ("I don't know where to begin") and subgoaling can help. For example, I start writing a book by first making an overall outline, then an outline of a particular chapter, then writing a part of the chapter, and so on. Sometimes a counselor can help a client to subgoal a personal problem, for example, to divide the problem of excessive shyness into subproblems of excessive anxiety, a poor self-image, and a lack of social skills in conversation. It is easier to work on each of these one at a time than it is to work generally on being less shy.

If you have a problem of feeling uptight from having too many responsibilities, you could subgoal the problem into particular tasks and work on each separately (your psychology paper due Friday, the chemistry exam Monday, showing your little sister around campus next Saturday). You might also identify particular aspects of your personality to reevaluate (you accept responsibilities too quickly, perhaps from an excessive desire to please others). Such subgoaling can often help move the person off the unproductive dead center of feeling totally immobilized and defeated by the problem ("Where do I begin?").

Another general problem-solving heuristic is **means-ends analysis,** where one continually compares the goal state with the present state and tries to reduce the distance. A particular type of means-ends analysis is **hill climbing,** where one operates by the rule that "anything that gets me closer to the goal than I am now is good," based on the metaphor of climbing the mountain where any step *up* is good. Although hill climbing is often useful, especially in cases where there is no other well-motivated strategy available, it is not possible to solve all problems this way. Sometimes we must go *backward* at some point and actually be temporarily *farther* from the goal than where we started. For example, the road to drug addiction rehab sometimes must go through a withdrawal period where one is even more miserable than being on drugs. Even in climbing a mountain, sometimes we must detour down to get around some uncrossable landform.

Finally, we can use general heuristics of **working backward** from the goal to find a solution path or use **analogies** from previous problems to solve the current one. Depending on the particular problem, these heuristics may or may not be useful. Working backward tends to be most useful in cases with a limited number of solution paths. Using analogies is highly dependent on choosing appropriate past problems as models. If you choose something that is superficially similar but fundamentally different, the analogy could actually be a distracting diversion rather than a useful heuristic.

Restructuring

Sometimes it may be necessary to restructure the problem in order to solve it. It was this aspect of problem solving that was extensively studied by the Gestalt psychologists, who were interested in holistic approaches to thought. For example, consider the following conversation between a server (S) and a customer (C):

C: DUFNEX?
S: ESVFX.
C: NEM?
S: ESVFM2.
C: DUFT?
S: EST2.
C: OK10, LFMNXNT.

The problem is: What was the customer ordering? As long as you understand and structure this problem incorrectly, it is impossible to solve. For example, you may experience **mental set** of being able to think of the letters only as letters spelling words (or perhaps as initials or cryptograms). You have to think of the letters in a new way, that is, overcome mental set, in order to discover the solution. A more specific type of mental set is **functional fixedness,** the barrier of seeing something as being used only in one way and not seeing other possibilities.

This failure to see objects in a novel way is a common barrier in problem solution. Restructuring may be necessary to remove the mental set or functional fixedness. Such restructuring frequently comes in a moment of "insight." There has been a long debate in the psychology of problem solving over whether problem solving occurs incrementally as a result of trial and error, as the behaviorists argued, or suddenly in a moment of **insight,** the "aha" experience, as the Gestalt psychologists called it. This turned out in many ways to be a spurious issue, since support for each process was obtained, depending on the task used. Insight has qualities of dramatic suddenness, at least in terms of conscious experience. It also tends to produce a novel solution that is a complete one, at least to a major subpart of the problem. A very recent line of neuroscience research has suggested that insight tends to occur after right hemisphere activation (Bowden & Beeman, 1998).

Sometimes insight occurs after a period of **incubation,** when one takes a break from working on a problem after a period of intense work on it. Why insight sometimes, but not always, comes after a period of incubation is a matter of some debate. It may be that the brain is rested and able to think more productively, or it may be that a mental set established in the earlier period of work on the problem has weakened after the rest and thus the problem solver is able to see the problem in a new way. Box 9.1 gives some additional problems where you may experience mental set or functional fixedness and need some insight to restructure the problem. The answers to those problems and the answer to what the customer ordered in the preceding example can be found in Box 9.11, at the end of the chapter.

Creativity

One characteristic of problem solving that most see as desirable is **creativity,** a construct that has proven exceptionally difficult to define operationally. While creativity is generally considered to be a *process,* it is usually only the *product* of creativity that is available to study. Creativity has been studied in a wide variety of disciplines,

Other Examples of Problems Requiring Restructuring

A. In days of old, two knights were competing for the hand of the king's daughter. The king, being an ingenious old man, decided to settle the competition in a unique type of horse race. The two knights would be required to race against each other on horseback, but with the unusual stipulation that whoever horse crossed the finish line **last** would be the winner and would thus marry the princess. How could the knights make sure that this race wouldn't be the slowest race in history?

B. In Italy during World War II, U.S. soldiers found standing on the ground small wooden billboards about two feet high. They looked like the figure below. What was the purpose of these boards?

C. What is the only English four-letter word ending in -eny?

D. Given the circle in the figure below, with radius 2, find the length of line c.

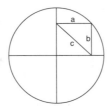

particularly in education and psychometrics, where it is often studied in conjunction with intelligence and testing. There is general agreement that a creative solution to a problem must be both novel (original) and useful or valuable in some way. Defining creativity purely in terms of novelty might leave the delusional schizophrenic as the most creative among us.

There are several radically different ways of defining or conceptualizing creativity. One way is the **divergent thinking** view of J. P. Guilford (1956, 1986). Here one starts with some piece of information and works outward in several directions. For example, the Alternate Uses Test gives a common item and its most common use ("a newspaper—for reading"). One is asked to give up to six alternate uses, which are scored for their infrequency in the normative sample, the less frequent responses being considered the most creative. Along a similar line, projective tests like the Rorschach Inkblot Test or the Thematic Apperception Test (TAT) may have their responses scored for originality (i.e., infrequency).

A completely different approach to creativity comes out of S-R associationism and views creativity as a process of **convergent thinking** (Mednick, 1962). Here one begins with highly disparate, weakly associated elements and finds some connection between them. The more remote the original items that one can conceptually connect, the more creative one is. This understanding of creativity is measured by the Remote Associates Test (RAT) (Mednick & Mednick, 1967). This test presents triads of unrelated words for which one must find a common associate. For example, for "elephant," "tree," and "luggage," the correct answer is "trunk." For "worm," "scotch," and "red," the answer is "tape." Although this task may seem somewhat odd, it is not unlike many crossword puzzle clues. Notice, however, the idea that creativity is defined here as finding the *right* answer, a useful skill but very unlike the divergent thinking approach.

Yet another approach to creativity involves case studies of artistic and scientific creativity (Gardner, 1993; Gruber & Davis, 1988). While these narratives are intriguing and sometimes useful, they are by nature highly idiosyncratic and make heavy use of peer judgments, which may reflect factors other than creativity. Particular in the realm of art, and to a lesser extent in science, there are always different opinions of what is a creative piece of work. In fact, Weisberg (1986) argues that much of what people commonly believe about creativity, especially those in the divergent thinking and case study traditions, simply is not so (see Box 9.2).

One of the most recent theories of creativity attempts to combine some earlier perspectives. Sternberg and Lubart's (1995, 1996) **investment theory of creativity** sees creativity as taking a "buy-low, sell-high approach to ideas." In "buying low," the creative person sees great potential in ideas that have been passed over or undervalued by others. He or she takes these ideas and develops them into a meaningful, significant contribution. Once the idea has been developed and its worth recognized by others, the creative person "sells high" by moving on to other undervalued ideas.

Thus it is clear that psychologists do not agree what makes a person or some product of thought *creative*. Each of these approaches identifies some useful cognitive process. Just which of these, or which combination, is the heart of creativity is not yet clear. Aside from these models, other factors also play a large role in creativity, including motivation (Amabile, 1996), insight (Finke, 1995; Smith, 1995), and the context of the creative act (Csikszentmihalyi, 1996).

Next we will examine a type of problem solving of a more specific and structured sort, reasoning.

REASONING

An important component of thinking is **reasoning,** the process of drawing logical conclusions from evidence or from given premises. There are two kinds of reasoning recognized by philosophers and mathematicians: inductive reasoning and deductive reasoning. **Inductive reasoning** involves drawing a general conclusion from a set of data; **deductive reasoning** involves drawing a conclusion from a given set of initial statements, or premises. We will look at the psychology of these logics in turn, and then consider scientific reasoning, which involves both deduction and induction.

Is Creativity a Myth?

Common belief holds that certain people are capable of extraordinary thought processes, which produce insightful solutions that come suddenly out of nowhere. Cognitive psychologist Robert Weisberg, examining these beliefs very critically, identifies four "myths" about creativity.

The first is the myth of the unconscious. The fact that people often cannot report their thought processes leading to a solution does not warrant assuming that they involve unconscious processing. The frequent anecdotal reports of solving a problem after a period of incubation, an inactive period after working unsuccessfully on a problem, do not hold up under careful scrutiny. For example, Mozart's notebooks contain many uncompleted pieces and show that he had a prodigious knowledge of music. Experimental tests have consistently failed to demonstrate the facility of a period of unconscious working on a problem during incubation.

Weisberg's second myth is the myth of insight (the "aha" experience). This construct grew out of the Gestalt psychologists' emphasis on perception but has not been confirmed by research, which tends to support a more incremental process. Weisberg argues that restructuring is most often demonstrated in the artificial "trick" laboratory situations and is much less typical of real problems. He argues that the great role of knowledge is a much larger determinant in creative problem solving.

Third, Weisberg identifies the myth of divergent thinking. He particularly attacks the assumptions of the technique of brainstorming, whereby a group solving a problem has two discrete stages of (a) generating ideas and (b) critiquing the ideas. This technique assumes that the group generates more and better ideas than individuals. Weisberg disputes this, arguing that the larger the group, the more interference with good ideas that occurs. Secondly, brainstorming assumes that criticism inhibits the free expression of ideas. Weisberg presents evidence from several experimental studies, showing that withholding judgment during the idea-generation phase, the hallmark of brainstorming, did not improve the quality of ideas generated.

Finally, Weisberg identifies the myth of genius, the belief that certain individuals possess extraordinary mental qualities. This position assumes that these so-called geniuses possess some characteristics not present (or not present as much) in others, yet it has been difficult if not impossible to identify these characteristics. Being creative is not a permanent characteristic enduring throughout life. Even most creative people have low times, and they are not consistently recognized by others as creative. If genius is a measurable psychological characteristic (or a set of them), there is no consensus on what it is.

As an alternative view of creativity, Weisberg suggests that a creative solution evolves out of earlier attempts. To support this, he argues that actual scientific creativity proceeds gradually, with no one moment of great advance or insight. He uses case studies of Watson and Crick's discovery of the structure of DNA and Darwin's development of the theory of evolution as examples. Even Picasso's Guernica, one of the great artworks of the twentieth century, developed through various trials, as preserved through sketches and in-progress photos. Johann Sebastian Bach drew greatly from the music of his time but made it better. Creative solutions to problems depend on the solvers' knowledge and how they use the knowledge from others that preceded them (Weisberg, 1986).

Inductive Reasoning

Consider the number series completion problem: "The three numbers, 2, 4, 6, conform to a simple rule. Your task is to discover the rule by generating successive triads of numbers. After generating each triad, you will be told whether the triad fits the rule or not. Announce the rule when you are highly confident it is correct, and I will then provide feedback" (Wason & Johnson-Laird, 1972). Typically, participants will generate triads and hypotheses like "8, 10, 12—adding 2 each time" but then will be told their hypothesis is incorrect. Puzzled, they may try similar triads or perhaps more complex ones like "2, 6, 10—The middle number is the arithmetic mean of the other two," or "0, 3, 6—Three added each time," only to hear that these hypotheses are also incorrect.

The real rule (any three numbers in order of magnitude) is extremely simple and broad, so that many more specific rules generate triads consistent with it. The only way to solve the problem, unless one stumbles on the right answer immediately, as many children—unaccustomed to the subtleties of number series problems—do, is to test one's hypothesis by attempting to **falsify** it by generating triads inconsistent with one's hypothesis. However, this is exactly what most people fail to do. Instead, they set out to **verify** their hypothesis by generating triads consistent with their rule. But since many rules are consistent with the true rule, one can spend quite some time receiving "confirmations" of an incorrect hypothesis. Mistakes can be discovered much more quickly by seeking falsification rather than verification (Klayman & Ha, 1989). This tendency to try to verify instead of falsify (**confirmation bias**) is a recurring theme behind many errors of reasoning and decision making.

The effect of a single, vivid, confirming piece of evidence can be compelling. Some politicians have exploited our willingness to believe a compelling anecdote and our resistance to falsifying statistics, tendencies demonstrated in an experiment reported by Nisbett and Ross (1980). Three groups of participants completed questionnaires evaluating their attitudes toward welfare recipients. A control group was then given correct statistics about people on welfare, including, for example, that the median stay on welfare is two years and that only 10 percent of welfare recipients remain on the rolls for as long as four years. These participants—who believed initially that the average stay was ten years—were unaffected by the evidence, expressing the same negative attitudes on a second questionnaire.

Two experimental groups read a description of a welfare mother that the experimenters had adapted from the *New Yorker* magazine. As described by Nisbett and Ross (1980, p. 57):

> An obese, friendly, emotional, and irresponsible woman had been on welfare for many years. Middle-aged now, she had lived with a succession of husbands, typically also unemployed, and had borne children by each of them. Her home was a nightmare of dirty and dilapidated plastic furniture bought on time at outrageous prices, filthy kitchen appliances, and cockroaches walking about in the daylight. Her children showed little promise of rising above their origins. They attended school off and on and had begun to run afoul of the law in their early teens, with the other children now thoroughly enmeshed in a life of heroin, numbers-running, and welfare.

The experimental groups were then given information making the woman's case seem either (falsely) typical, or (correctly) atypical. In the first condition, the woman's very long stay on welfare was characterized as typical: The average length of time on welfare for recipients between the ages of 40 and 55 was reported to be 15 years, with 90 percent on welfare for at least 8 years. In the second condition, the woman's time on welfare was made to seem abnormally long: The average time on welfare was presented as 2 years, with 90 percent of these people off welfare in 4 years (Nisbett & Ross, 1980, p. 86).

The effect of the single, vivid case that confirmed entrenched stereotypes (social schemata—see Chapter 8) was dramatic. The experimental groups reported increased negative attitudes toward welfare recipients on the second test, regardless of whether they had been led to believe the case was typical or not. So not only do we have stereotypes about engineers and "welfare queens," but these stereotypes also resist change, and are strengthened by isolated, *confirming* instances, no matter if these instances are atypical or even totally apocryphal.

Nor does presenting fair, balanced discussion reflecting both sides of controversial issues necessarily help people on each side to understand each other better. Nisbett and Ross (1980; see also Lord, Ross, & Lepper, 1979) describe a study suggesting that fair presentations of both sides of an issue, what every news reporter aims at, may actually strengthen preexisting opinions rather than create an atmosphere of tolerance. Students who were either strongly for or strongly against capital punishment read two articles describing studies either supporting or refuting the deterrent effect of execution. Half read the confirming study first; half read the falsifying one first. Everyone filled out an attitude questionnaire on capital punishment after reading the first article, and again after the second.

Results showed that participants displayed strong confirmation bias, judging the study that supported them as sound and valid, and dismissing the disconfirming study as sloppy and poorly conducted. Reading a confirming study strengthened their original opinion, while reading a disconfirming study had little impact. The consequence of these tendencies was polarization of opinion after reading the balanced package of both articles. Since disconfirming evidence had no effect and confirming evidence a strengthening effect, participants had stronger opinions about capital punishment at the end of the study than at the beginning.

The disturbing conclusion is that presentation of both sides of an issue does not reduce differences between holders of opposing opinions, but actually widens them. People are not swayed by the balance of the evidence but tend to pick and choose only what conforms to their views and reject what does not, all the while growing ever surer that they are correct and that those who differ with them must be fools. Some have argued that such polarization is a growing and widespread tendency of modern society (see Box 9.3).

Induction is merely learning from experience. What the above experiments seem to show is that we learn from experience in a highly selective fashion. Once we form a belief we are loath to give it up, and grasp eagerly for any confirming evidence, no matter how isolated or atypical.

Deductive Reasoning

As the philosopher David Hume showed two centuries ago, no inductive generalization is ever certain, because tomorrow's experience may prove it wrong. For certainty and proof we must go to deductive reasoning, where we can deduce conclusions from given propositions in accordance with formal rules, and show that the conclusions *must* follow from the premises.

The Argument Culture

Sociolinguist Deborah Tannen (1998) has written a provocative book *The Argument Culture,* promoting the thesis that debate and discourse at all levels in contemporary culture, at least in the United States, has become more polarized in recent years. Everything is framed as a battle of opposing sides. Journalists attack those in power with a dogged relentlessness not seen previously. The "attack mode" is used to investigate sports figures, nominees for public office, and even persons interviewed on talk shows. Politics becomes nastier, and cynical voters tune out in increasing numbers. People routinely turn to litigation in the adversarial court system to settle differences. The end result is often a general loss of respect and credibility for all concerned. For example, although U.S. President Bill Clinton was acquitted in his 1999 impeachment trial, he was widely believed to have lied to the nation about the Monica Lewinsky affair. Nor was there much more respect for Lewinsky, Special Prosecutor Kenneth Starr, Linda Tripp, or other figures in the affair. Other alleged victims of presidential sexual harassment, such as Paula Jones, were also attacked and ridiculed. Everyone was tainted.

For example, if I assert the premise (4) and then receive the information in (5), I may validly deduce the conclusion (6).

4. If a person is 21, then he or she may legally drink wine.
5. Fred is 21.
6. Fred may legally drink wine.

It is important to bear in mind about deductive reasoning that following the rules of logic guarantees only that the conclusion is **valid,** that is, follows logically from the given premises; there is no guarantee that the conclusion is true. The premises may be false. So the argument (7), (8), (9) is just as valid as (4), (5), (6), even though it is absurd.

7. If Mickey Mouse is president, then horses are purple.
8. Mickey Mouse is president.
9. Therefore, horses are purple.

Although deductive logic cannot assure us that our conclusions are *true,* it is still an essential component in reasoning. For when we reason, we assemble what we know about a problem; in logical terms, we establish a set of premises from which we make inferences. It is important that we reason logically; otherwise, we may fall into error with even the truest of premises.

Of the various kinds of deductive logic and types of logical rules, we will consider just one here, reasoning with *if . . . then* statements (conditional reasoning), which has been investigated by researchers over the past several decades. Sample problems from their experiments are given in Boxes 9.4 and 9.5; the correct answers are found in Box 9.6. Please read these boxes and do the problems before going on to read about the research results.

■ Box 9.4 ■

Peter Wason's Four-Card Problem

The cards in the figure below have information on both sides. On one side of a card is a letter, and on the other side is a number.

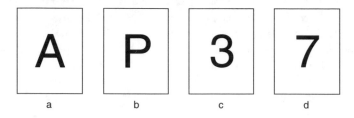

Here is a rule: If a card has an "A" on one side, then it has a "3" on the other side.

Select those cards that you definitely need to turn over to determine whether or not the cards are violating the rule.*

---

* Instructions from Cox & Griggs, 1982.

This basic **selection task** in its original, abstract form (Box 9.4), is especially difficult. Only about 10 percent of participants make the correct choices when the problem is presented as in Box 9.4. The most common error is to choose cards a and c (see Evans, 1982; Johnson-Laird & Byrne, 1991, 1999; Oaksford & Chater, 1994, and Rips, 1994, for reviews). Similarly, when given an abstract rule and asked to draw

■ Box 9.5 ■

Richard Griggs' Drinking Age Problem

On this task imagine you are a police officer on duty. It is your job to ensure that people conform to certain rules. The cards in the figure below have information about four people sitting at a table. On one side of a card is a person's age and on the other side of the card is what a person is drinking. Here is a rule:

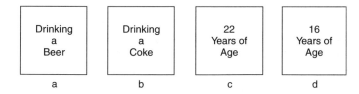

If a person is drinking beer, then the person must be over 21. Select those cards that you definitely need to turn over to determine whether or not the people are violating the rule.*

---

* Instructions from Cox & Griggs, 1982.

Answers to the Problems in Boxes 9.4 and 9.5

The correct answer in each case is to turn over only cards *a* and *d;* if you are like most U.S. undergraduates, you probably got Box 9.4 incorrect and Box 9.5 correct. Remember that you were told to falsify—not verify—the rule. Turning over card *a* can do this, since in 9.4 if (say) a 2 is on the other side, the rule is violated, and in 9.5 if the other side says, "Sixteen years of age," the rule is violated. Turning over card *b* cannot falsify the rule, because it does not satisfy the "if . . . " part of the rule, called the antecedent. So no matter what is on the other side, the rule stands unviolated. Card *c* is similarly unhelpful: In 9.5 it does not matter what the 22-year-old is drinking; he can't be violating the drinking law. Similarly, in 9.4 it doesn't matter what is on the other side of the 3; the rule cannot be violated. Finally, card *d* can violate the rule: If the 16-year-old is drinking beer, the rule is violated; if there is an A on the other side of the card in Box 9.4, the rule is falsified.

While the two problems differ in content, they both have the same logical structure, and therefore the same logically correct answer. The formal justification for the correct choices comes from the truth table (as logicians call it) for conditional reasoning, which specifies the conditions under which a statement, of whatever content, is to be judged true or false. The following truth table summarizes the four possible deductions:

Logical Rule	Premise	Conclusion	Deduction Name	Logical Status
If p, then q	p	therefore q	modus ponens	valid
If p, then q	not-q	therefore not-p	modus tollens	valid
If p, then q	q	therefore p	affirming the consequent	not valid
If p, then q	not-p	therefore not-q	denying the antecedent	not valid

In the four-card task, the logical rule is something like "if there is an A on the front (p), then there is a 3 on the back (q)" or "If the person is drinking beer (p), then he or she must be over 21 (q)."

In the two tasks in Boxes 9.4 and 9.5, only choosing cards *a* and *d* can possibly falsify the rule. The choice of *a* (premise p) involves the modus ponens deduction, which is a valid inference, because assuming the premise is true, as one must do in deductive reasoning, if *p* is true, *q* must be true also. The choice of card *d* (premise not-*q*) is the modus tollens deduction. This deduction is also valid, but this time we reason by falsification. Again, assuming the rule is true, given that *q* is false, it must be the case that *p* is false.

There are, however, also two fallacious deductions with conditional reasoning, denying the antecedent and affirming the consequent. Denying the antecedent (e.g., checking the age of the person drinking the coke) actually says nothing about testing the rule, nor does affirming the consequent (e.g., checking what the 22-year-old is drinking). Both deductions (turning over both "cards") are fallacious because what is on the other side is irrelevant to testing the truth of the rule. However, in the research described in the text, people frequently made one or both fallacious inferences, especially in the abstract forms of the task.

inferences from it in combination with propositions forming the argument patterns in Box 9.6, they show poor command of conditional reasoning. Such erroneous reasoning has proved most difficult to modify, even through taking a semester-long logic course (Cheng, Holyoak, Nisbett, & Oliver, 1986)!

When the problem is presented in meaningful verbal form, as in Box 9.5, the results have been exceedingly varied. Early results (summarized in Wason & Johnson-Laird, 1972) showed that verbal formulations produced superior performance, even in these who could not do the abstract version, suggesting that people understood the conditional logic but just could not bring it to bear on abstract material. However, these findings could not always be replicated and further research by Griggs and his colleagues (Cox & Griggs, 1982; Griggs & Cox, 1982, 1993) showed why. The verbal formulation yielded improved performance only when the rule and its manner of testing were already familiar to the participants. So, for example, the drinking age problem (Box 9.5) facilitated performance among American undergraduates familiar with alcoholic beverage rules, even though the same students did poorly with the abstract problem and with concrete versions involving British postal rules or travel between British cities, problems on which British students had done well.

Such results have been explained in several ways, each of which suggests that people do not reason as logically as they suppose, when they reason at all. One factor is the confirmation bias, the tendency of people to verify a rule, rather than attempt to falsify it, leading them to choose cards a and c, hoping to find verifying cases (Wason & Johnson-Laird, 1972). Another possible explanation for the superiority of concrete versions of the selection task is that they facilitate people's mental construction of concrete mental models that embody the task structure. Rather than reasoning, participants simply read the answer off the mental model (Byrne & Johnson-Laird, 1990; Johnson-Laird, 1999).

On the other hand, Griggs and Cox (1983, 1993) argued that the two versions of the selection task are not in fact the same type of problem. Griggs proposed that superior performance on the concrete tasks is due not to better application of logical abilities, but to sheer familiarity. Specifically, on the familiar, concrete problems people do not actually reason the correct answers, but rather already know them from experience. Undergraduates in the United States know all about drinking age rules, and can recall the conditions that violate such rules, but do badly on unfamiliar problems concerning British postage and rail travel. Thus, what may appear to be superior reasoning on such concrete problems may not really be superior deduction.

Recently, other researchers have suggested in different ways that better performance on real-life scenarios than abstract versions of the selection task is caused not by familiarity or concreteness, but rather by engaging innate (Cosmides, 1989), probabilistic (Oaksford & Chater, 1994), pragmatic social (Cheng & Holyoak, 1985, 1989), necessity versus sufficiency (Ahn & Graham, 1999), or moral (Gigerenzer & Hug, 1992; Manktelow & Over, 1990) reasoning schemata. For example, Manktelow and Over (1990, p. 155) asked participants to imagine themselves as store managers who were to "inspect the receipts at the end of the day to be certain that they were properly filled out. The rule is that, if any purchase exceeded \$30, the receipt must have the signature of the department manager on the back." In this case, 70 percent of the participants made the two correct choices. The version of the selection task that people perform the best is one that is unfamiliar but engages moral thought. In Chapter 14, we will see that most theorizing about the evolution of intelligence today proposes that human intelligence evolved to facilitate reasoning about social situations. The legacy of that evolutionary heritage is that, even now, in the age of science, humans reason best about social and moral situations.

Scientific Reasoning

In practice, inductive and deductive reasoning are rarely used in isolation. In the induction problems we studied, participants must draw a generalization from experience, that is, they must use induction, but then they must test the hypothesis by deducing from it predictions about future experience. Similarly, in the four-card selection task, people have to deduce what would falsify the given premise, and evaluate it against potential evidence. Such interweaving of induction and deduction, prediction and proof, is at the center of science. Moreover, because science prides itself on being rational, logical, and orderly, we should examine scientific reasoning in light of findings that people are less rational, logical, and orderly than we usually suppose.

Scientists as Reasoners

To start, let us ask if scientists, trained in the rigorous methodology of their discipline, are better at reasoning than the lay people that psychologists study. Kern, Mirels, and Hinshaw (1983) administered the Wason selection task to university scientists in three fields. While physicists did slightly better (21%–25% correct) than biologists (8%–13%) or psychologists (13%–17%), no group did really well, and performance overall was only marginally better than college students, even among those scientists with some training in logic (12%–16% correct). Mahoney and DeMonbreun (1981) presented Wason's 2, 4, 6 problem to two groups of university scientists (physicists and psychologists) and to a group of Protestant ministers. The results found few differences across the groups.

Perhaps most troubling is the persistence of incorrect beliefs in areas in which scientists are specifically trained. Consider the "gambler's fallacy." Suppose we take a coin known to be fair having a 50 percent chance of turning up either heads (H) or tails (T), and flip the following sequence: T, T, T, T, T, T, T, T, T; what is the probability the next flip will be a head? Most people commit the **gambler's fallacy** and think heads is more likely to turn up than 0.5, the correct answer; they think the coin is "due" to turn up heads. This is, of course, a fallacy, since, given that it is a fair coin, the probability of heads is 0.5 on each flip. Each toss is independent of every other toss. Tversky and Kahneman (1981) discovered that the gambler's fallacy persisted even among psychologists, who are trained in statistics and should have known better. When questioned on a number of statistical problems, psychologists showed themselves prone to such errors.

The Layperson as Scientist

Experiments by Doherty, Mynatt, Tweney, and Schiavo (1981), and Mynatt, Doherty, and Tweney (1981) asked college students to pretend to be scientists (archaeologists or physicists) and then placed them in simulated research environments that required them to formulate and test scientific hypotheses. In the physics experiment, some were given indoctrination concerning falsification as the optimum scientific strategy. Regardless of instructions, however, participants shared a strong tendency to confirm rather than disconfirm their hypotheses, persisted in repeatedly testing disconfirmed hypotheses, and especially in the archaeology experiment, were poor at choosing the best data for confirming or disconfirming their hypotheses.

In social situations—where we conduct "experiments" to find out about strangers—confirmation bias is so strong that it creates self-fulfilling hypotheses. Snyder, Tanke, and Berscheid (1977; reported by Nisbett & Ross, 1980) had men talk over an intercom with an unseen woman whom they had been led to believe was either attractive or unattractive. Another group of men listened to tapes made of the woman's side of the conversation only and—without seeing her or knowing what the first man had been told about her appearance—rated her attractiveness. Evidently, the questions and probes used by the conversing man had elicited verbal evidence of attractiveness or unattractiveness, because the second group of men followed the first group's hypotheses. If the woman had been labeled "attractive," her verbal behavior made her seem attractive, even to the blind raters in the second part of the experiment. The reverse held for "unattractive" women. So the hypothesis led to questions that created confirming behavior in the answers, creating a self-fulfilling circle of hypothesis and evidence.

Conclusion

By now you may want to ask, as did a reader of Nisbett and Ross (1980): "If we're so dumb, how come we made it to the moon?" One answer—not Nisbett and Ross'—is that rationality should not be equated with logic (Toulmin, 1972), and that disconfirmation is not really the best way to do science. Science does work; its success is established. Yet the major result of work in history and philosophy of science over the past few decades has been that scientists are not logical automata; the work we have surveyed in this chapter already supports such a conclusion. Moreover, it seems wise to argue (see Kuhn, 1970) that science succeeds not despite its deviations from falsificationist logic but because of them (Leahey & Leahey, 1983). In the simulated physics experiment conducted by Mynatt et al. (1981), participants who performed best quickly formulated a partially correct hypothesis and then stuck to it, using disconfirmation to gradually modify the wrong parts. The results described by Mahoney and DeMonbreun suggest that real scientists do likewise.

DECISION MAKING

When we talk about decision making, we consider how people *should* make decisions (normative approach) or how they actually *do* make decisions (descriptive approach). While the psychologist's approach to the problem is most often descriptive, nuances of the normative creep in frequently, particularly in discussions of particular mathematical models of decision making, which are largely beyond the scope of this book. In recent years the emphasis has been increasingly on a more descriptive approach to decision making, which will be the emphasis in our treatment of decision making that follows.

Rationality

When we discuss decision making, the assumption is usually made that decisions are rational. We like to think that thought is rational, but there is some disagreement on what being rational actually means. For a review of different approaches to defining and studying rationality, see Jungermann (1983). Many of these approaches assume some common set of principles of rational thought.

First of all, a rational decision is one that is made from a set of alternatives that have been identified. Part of making a good decision is first identifying all the reasonable alternative choices. If a highly desirable or likely choice is not included among the possibilities considered, then the final choice may not be the best one. Second, a rational decision follows the principle of transitivity. For example, if, on a given afternoon, you would choose to play tennis rather than golf and golf rather than jogging, then you should also choose tennis over jogging, given that binary choice.

Third, a rational decision is intended to maximize utility for the person. **Utility,** a central construct in decision making, is the value to a person of a particular outcome. Utility is a psychological, subjective concept and is related, but not identical, to the concept of value. An outcome of the same value may have two different utilities to two different people. For example, bending down to pick up a dollar bill off the sidewalk has the same value to anyone ($1); however, it would have a much greater utility to a poor college student than to a millionaire. The higher utility in the one case might lead to the student's deciding to pick it up, while the millionaire might walk on by.

Finally, a rational decision is one that is made based on the relevant, but not the irrelevant, information available. Whenever we make a decision, we consider some information that is relevant, or diagnostic, while we ignore (or at least intend to ignore) other information that is irrelevant (or **nondiagnostic**). As we shall see later, ignoring nondiagnostic information is not as easy as you might think. Box 9.7 uses the concept of utility to analyze and use diagnostic information to come to a decision about a personal course of action. You may find this approach useful in your own life.

When we make any kind of decision, the diagnostic information is combined in various ways. Some researchers in decision making focus their studies on what information is combined and how it is combined. Norman Anderson (1981, 1982, 1991) used the term "cognitive algebra" to refer to the mathematical laws that describe how we integrate various pieces of information together to come up with a decision. For example, if Amy were trying to decide whether to go out with Kevin, she might have an impression of his personality and his appearance. For purposes of research, we could have Amy quantify these impressions. She could combine these two pieces of information according to an additive (or perhaps an averaging) model if she considered both personality and appearance more or less equally (though this could be changed by introducing weighting factors in the model; for example, weight personality 75 percent and appearance 25 percent).

On the other hand, she could combine the pieces of information multiplicatively. In this case, if Kevin scored high on both personality and appearance, Nancy's total impression of him would be much better than if he were merely moderately high on both. On the other hand, if he were very low on either measure, that would pull her overall impression of him way down, even if he were very high on the second measure (great looks but a zero personality). A multiplicative model fits well with the intuitive notion that the worth of someone with personality = 0 is still 0, even if he or she is extremely attractive. In such a case the model is **noncompensatory,** meaning that a high value on one attribute cannot compensate for a very low value on another.

Estimating Likelihoods of Occurrence

Some events have **objective probabilities** of occurrence. For example, the probability of throwing a six on any given toss of a fair die is ⅙. The probability of drawing the six of clubs from a deck of 52 cards is ¹⁄₅₂. The probability as we estimate it is

Multiattribute Utility (MAU) Analysis

This is a technique for analyzing a decision with several possible outcomes and several attributes on which to consider each outcome. It also uses the concept of subjective utility.

To understand the MAU approach, let's take a sample problem. Suppose you are trying to decide what car to purchase. The following discussion will explain the technique through the use of this example. In reality, of course, the development of the example would be different for each individual.

1. The first step is to define the different alternatives (outcomes). Be sure to consider all the alternatives that would be real possibilities. For this example, suppose the cars listed across the top of the table below were the appropriate alternatives, determined through comparative shopping.

2. Next, identify the relevant attributes for making your decision. As with the alternatives, be sure not to leave out an important attribute. These are the criteria on which you expect to make your decision.

3. Third, assign utility values to each alternative X attribute combination on a 9-point evaluation scale, where 1 = bad and 9 = good. These are the values that attribute or that alternative has to you. For example, on the attribute of age, a 2001 Bronco rates a higher utility than an older car, though it rates more poorly on initial cost, because it is more expensive. (Remember that 9 is good and 1 is bad; this is not a cost scale!)

4. Fourth, assign weight values to each attribute based on that attribute's importance to you. The weights must sum to 100. In the example below, we chose to weight initial cost and gas mileage much higher than style. The weights, of course, reflect your personal attitudes and values.

5. Next, multiply each utility by the weight value for that attribute. These products appear in the table below after the slash (/).

6. Add the totals of these products for each alternative.

7. Compare the totals for each alternative. The alternative with the highest total should be your best choice. In the example below, that is the Ford Bronco.

8. Now try the MAU approach for a decision you face in your own life.

ALTERNATIVES with Utilities/Weighted Utilities for Each Case

Attributes	2001 Ford Bronco	1998 Jeep Cherokee	1994 Pontiac Trans Am	1983 Chevy Impala	Weight
Age	$8/160$	$5/100$	$3/60$	$3/60$	20
Initial cost	$2/70$	$4/140$	$7/245$	$8/280$	35
Mileage	$9/360$	$5/200$	$4/160$	$2/80$	40
Style	$4/20$	$5/25$	$7/35$	$1/5$	5
Sum	610	465	500	425	100

called **subjective probability,** which may or may not be equal, or even close to, the objective probability. Casinos and lotteries make a lot of money on patrons using inflated subjective probabilities of winning. Feelings of being "on a roll" or "my luck's got to change" are merely subjective, not objective, probabilities. Many times there are no objective probabilities, and we must rely on subjective estimates. Many real-world decisions are like this. For example, Gilchurch, Vallone, and Tversky (1985) have shown that, contrary to fans' and players' belief, the "hot hand" in basketball is a myth.

The Availability Heuristic

It has become clear in the psychology of decision making that people do not make choices as mathematical laws would predict (Kahneman, Slovic, & Tversky, 1982), just as they do not reason according to laws of formal logic. Rather, they frequently use heuristics, or practical strategies, for decision making. Tversky and Kahneman have identified several of these.

One heuristic very widely used is **availability** (Kahneman & Tversky, 1982; Tversky & Kahneman, 1973). In such cases we estimate the likelihood or frequency of occurrence of some event based on the ease with which instances or associations can be brought to mind. Certainly, we always make decisions by retrieving appropriate schemata from long-term memory, but if we interpret our own experience and examples as being more typical than they really are, then we are biased by the availability heuristic.

For example, when people were asked to say if the letter K is more likely to appear in the first or third position in a five-letter word in English, about two-thirds of the participants responded "first," although, in fact, K is much more common in the third position. It is easier to generate examples of words starting with K than those with K in the middle, however. Consider how much easier a crossword clue is when we know only the first letter (K _ _ _ _) than when we know only a letter in the middle (_ _ K _ _).

Looking at availability more generally, we tend to underestimate the probability of even a very likely event if it has never occurred before, because there is not a readily available instance to use in constructing a scenario. One current issue concerns the rapid depletion of the water table in the once-abundant groundwater of the Ogallala Aquifer that underlies much of the western United States Great Plains. Scientists warn that unless agriculture reduces its rate of groundwater pumping to irrigate thirsty but profitable crops like corn, this rich agricultural region could revert to a desert in the next half century. Though this is a highly probable event if policies do not change, many find the scenario hard to imagine, just as people in the United States found a projected gasoline scarcity difficult to imagine before the first Arab oil embargo of 1973. Once the event occurs, however, people may err and overestimate the probability of its recurrence, as when people leave an area after a very unusual flood that occurred once but would (mathematically) probably not recur in their lifetime. Another example of a likely but never-before-occurring event that people do not take very seriously is global warming, which may raise the level of oceans worldwide and flood coastal areas in the twenty-first century.

Media coverage of an event introduces an available scenario that increases our subjective probability estimations of the likelihood of its future occurrence. When Slovic, Fischhoff, and Lichtenstein (1982) studied participants' perceptions of the likelihood of different causes of death, certain causes were consistently overestimated and others consistently underestimated, and the difference was not particularly related to overall actual frequency (objective probability). For example, people overestimated the likelihood of dying from tornadoes, floods, venomous bites or stings, and car accidents. Even one death from such causes is likely to make the front page or the TV evening news. On the other hand, participants consistently underestimated the probability of dying from chronic unglamorous diseases like asthma, emphysema, diabetes, strokes, and tuberculosis. Some kinds of cancer were overestimated and other kinds underestimated, with differences related to media coverage and intensity of recent public discussion.

Sometimes the overestimation of subjective probabilities may be socially useful. For example, when young drivers are shown gory films of auto accidents, they may revise upward their probabilities of having such an accident themselves and consequently may drive more carefully. In such a case, the most accurate mathematical estimate would not be the most useful social choice, just as the most logical scientific reasoning discussed earlier in the chapter was not always the best.

Another way that the availability heuristic manifests itself is in **illusory correlation.** People may infer that a causative relationship exists simply because a readily available correlated event with some face validity as a causal agent exists. For example, suppose a man receives a new treatment for cancer and subsequently dies. The survivors try to sue the doctor and hospital for causing the death of their loved one. Who is to say, however, that the treatment had any effect at all? Perhaps the treatment was the cause of the death, but perhaps also the availability heuristic mentally assigned a convenient cause for a tragedy that people wanted very much to explain, to keep within the bounds of their rational model of the world. Often courts are called on to make very difficult decisions, in part involving questions of how we process information, particularly our inferring of causal relationships.

The Anchoring-Adjustment Heuristic

Another heuristic is the **anchoring-adjustment heuristic** (Chapman & Johnson, 1994; Slovic & Lichtenstein, 1971; Tversky & Kahneman, 1974). In these cases some initial estimate (first impression) is made and later revised upward or downward according to new information. However, the bias enters when that initial estimate (**anchor**) is not **adjusted** sufficiently; thus we are overly biased by the original estimation. Personality studies show that we often are unduly biased by our first impression of a person. For example, students may feel that poor performance on the first exam in a class may forever brand them as stupid in the teacher's eyes, even if later test performance is much better. If the teacher is, in fact, thinking this way, the anchoring-adjustment heuristic may be operating. The teacher's schema of that student would have been formed initially from highly negative information, and that becomes the prototype anchor.

Another type of example of anchoring-adjustment bias comes from cost and duration estimates for construction projects. Cost overruns and delays are quite frequent in construction. When project costs are figured, they are initially figured at current cost levels and assuming that construction will proceed as planned. That overall figure is then revised upward by some amount to account for projected inflation, labor problems, delivery delays, weather, and other factors. Often, however, this *adjustment is not sufficient;* that is, there is *too much reliance on the initial estimate.*

The anchor value may reflect past experience at using contextual information, or it may be purely arbitrary (Wallsten, Fillenbaum, & Cox, 1986). For example,

LEARNING AND COGNITION

McGlone and Reed (1998) found that apparently "completely arbitrary" percentages pulled out of a bag (6% for a low condition, 94% for high) as anchors affected people's interpretations of probability expressions like "slight chance" or "likely" in a medical decision-making task. This has implications for the wording of survey questions, where choices of distractors might serve as anchors and inadvertently affect responses.

Hindsight

Another heuristic is **hindsight,** or "creeping determinism," studied experimentally by Fischhoff (1975, 1977; Fischhoff & Beyth, 1975). Fischhoff demonstrated that people are overly biased by the knowledge of how an event came out, that is, hindsight. When participants who already knew how an event came out were asked to estimate the prior probability that that event would have occurred, answered from the point of view of someone answering *before* the event had occurred, people did not ignore their own knowledge of the outcome, even when specifically told to do so. The event was seen as more predictable than had in fact been the case.

After an unfortunate event occurs, people often look back and say, "We should have seen that coming." People retrospectively said the Japanese attack on Pearl Harbor in 1941 should have been foreseen. A prisoner on parole commits another crime; people will say the parole officer should have foreseen that. Often people in responsible positions receive the blame or even lose their jobs after such events occur. Sometimes they may have been at fault and the event should have been anticipated. On the other hand, it is also likely that the hindsight bias is operating in some of these cases, and the unfortunate event really may not have been predictable before it happened. Maybe the decision made *at the time* really was the best one with the available information. Research has tried to identify specific conditions under which such effects occur (Hasher, Attig, & Alba, 1981).

Slovic and Fischhoff (1977) have demonstrated that hindsight also operates in interpreting psychological research. For example, we overestimate the likelihood of replicating preliminary results. One disturbing theme has been the way mathematicians and scientists are almost as vulnerable as anyone else to distorted thinking through use of judgment heuristics (cf. results of scientific reasoning studies discussed previously).

Critique of Heuristics Approach

The heuristics and biases research has frequently been criticized for taking a purely descriptive, atheoretical approach to studying decisions and for implicitly defining decision making by what it is not. Some have examined decision processes using a more theoretical, model-testing approach. For example, Downing, Sternberg, and Ross (1985) used multiple regression techniques to test several models of making inferences about causality in multicausal situations. Medin and Bazerman (1999) offer a model based on multiple levels of cognitive processing satisfying multiple goals in decision making.

One disturbing trend about the heuristics and biases literature is that the effects are often highly specific to the particular task on which they were originally obtained. A similar task—or even almost the same one with the wording slightly changed—obtains completely different results. One can describe patterns of behavior in such tasks with certain labels like "availability," or "anchoring and adjustment," but identifying the causal mechanism behind the strategy or specifying the limiting conditions under which it operates (and does not operate) is more difficult. This, however, is where much current decision-making research is headed (Gigerenzer, 1991, 1992, 1993).

Public Policy Decision Making

We have examined how the research psychologist studies decision making. Does this research have anything to contribute toward the making of actual public policy decisions of the sort that government officials or corporate officers must make?

Psychological Issues in Cost/Risk-Benefit Analysis

Many policy decisions involve some evaluation of relative merits of risks or costs versus benefits of some course of action. There are several psychological considerations in such risk (cost)-benefit analysis.

First, how safe is safe enough? While $p = .05$ may be an adequate criterion for many psychology experiments, being 95 percent certain (or even 99% certain) that there will not be a meltdown at a nuclear power plant is unlikely to be very comforting. That plant can never be made 100 percent safe, with absolutely no probability of accident, and setting the criterion for how safe it must be in order to be acceptable is a psychological question.

Second, how do we balance a "known life" versus a "statistical life"? If terrorists take ten people hostage and threaten to kill them if certain demands are not granted, how do we balance ten known lives against some unknown number of lives that may be lost in future incidents if the terrorists are appeased in this case? This question is complicated even more by the fact that in some cases the toll in statistical lives may remain unknown for many years and perhaps never be definitely established, as in the case of cancer deaths from radiation exposure many years earlier.

Third, how do we balance economic and noneconomic costs and benefits? This question arises particularly in discussions of preserving jobs versus the environment, or supplying needs for wilderness versus energy. Fourth, how do we deal with unforeseen outcomes? Few predicted the depletion of the ozone layer or the collapse of the Soviet Union. It is hard to plan for scenarios that are not even envisioned as possible alternatives.

Finally, how do we communicate such scientific concerns to the public? It is difficult to teach people to think probabilistically rather than deterministically; this may be the reason many psychology students (and others) have trouble with statistics. The general public wants to reduce the risk of risky choices to zero, but this is impossible. All of the choices involve how to balance the risk or cost of some policy with the benefit gained.

Facts versus Values

Hammond, Harvey, and Hastie (1992) argue that the confusion of scientific issues of facts with public policy issues of values has seriously hindered the productive application of scientific results of decision making under uncertainty to public policymaking. Science has a contribution to make to policymaking, but it is the policymakers who must make the final policy decision. For example, the two parameters of strength/accuracy and criterion from signal detection theory (see Chapter 5) may be viewed as the scenario/fact and value/policy component, respectively. For example, the science of weather forecasting may predict the probability of a hurricane, but it is the job of policymakers to evaluate that information to set the criterion to decide whether to issue an evacuation order for coastal areas.

Science may figure the accuracy of polygraph readers in judging whether a person is lying. It is up to the policymakers, however, to decide what criterion is acceptable. Hammond et al. suggest that decision-making research would do well to explain to polygraph users the difference between accuracy and criterion measures. Perhaps then they would see that setting the criterion to a level consistent with the "beyond reasonable doubt" standard of the legal system would yield a very high miss rate, while a lower criterion would produce an alarmingly high false alarm rate. Still, the scientist does not make the policy decision.

Decision Making in Foreign Policy

Can cognitive psychologists have some impact on foreign policy decision making? Tetlow (1986) suggests that they can. Researchers who have studied social-judgment and decision-making processes may help identify strategies used in foreign-policy decision making and identify points at which error and bias enter.

Assuming a more-or-less rational model of decision making, certain psychological variables leading to deviations from this rational model may be identified. For example, some personality variables irrelevant to the policy issues could affect decisions, as when a relatively authoritarian person may endorse harder-line measures than a less authoritarian person would do under the same circumstances. Small-group dynamics, such as implicit pressures to conform and encourage group solidarity, may limit the options and views considered and inhibit self-criticism, especially of popular views. National leaders, for example, often should explicitly encourage their staffs to share divergent and unpopular views in meetings, in order to avoid having conformity and group cohesiveness inhibit the expression of a variety of policy options (groupthink).

More germane for our discussion here are the cognitive variables affecting decision making. Top-down processes may be overused relative to bottom-up processes (see Chapter 5); for example, a local disturbance somewhere may be quickly identified as "racially motivated," without closely examining the specific facts of the situation. Superficial and simplistic analogies may be drawn from history without adequate recognition of differences of the current and historical situations; for example, looking at civil unrest somewhere and quickly reacting "another Cuba!" "another Kosovo!" or "another Vietnam!" Sometimes the political and situational constraints on one's adversaries are not fully recognized and taken into account, partially because of the difficulty of obtaining knowledge of such information. Additionally, people tend to be overly confident in the correctness of their own judgments. Also, errors and bias tend to be worse in times of high stress than under less stressful conditions. Identifying such possible sources of bias and error may be the first step toward reducing them. However, the need for such analysis may not be easy to sell to the policymakers in question (Hammond & Grassia, 1985). For an innovative and sobering analysis of the behind-the-scenes decision making that brought the world back from the brink of nuclear war, see Box 9.8.

Economic Decision Making

How people make economic decisions—defined broadly as "any decision framed in terms of costs and benefits, monetary or not,"—has long been a concern of philosophers

─── **Decision Making in the White House During the Cuban Missile Crisis** ───

In October 1962 the world came closer than ever to nuclear war between the United States and the Soviet Union. Soviet leader Nikita Khrushchev had placed nuclear missiles in Fidel Castro's Cuba, just 90 miles from the United States. In response, U.S. President John F. Kennedy ordered a blockade around Cuba. The USSR was given a deadline to pull missiles out, or they would be taken out by force, a move that both sides realized would very likely begin a nuclear war. After several very tense days, the Soviets backed down at the last minute and removed the missiles.

Political psychologist James Blight (1990) identifies two popular, and totally opposite, theories about how decision making proceeds in such a crisis. One such theory is that everyone is cold and calculating, oblivious to the enormous risks, merely playing a cosmic chess game with the lives of the world. An alternative view holds that everyone involved is completely irrational and out of control. Blight used a very ingenious methodology to argue that neither of these extremes characterized decision making in President Kennedy's inner circle during the Cuban Missile Crisis. Blight compared tapes of White House conversations declassified in the late 1980s with the memories of the still living participants in those meetings, including their reactions as they listened to the tapes.

Blight's conclusion was that, far from being either absent or causing participants to be totally irrational and out of control, the strong emotion of fear was acutely felt by both sides and actually was the force that drove them to desperately search for a solution. Both sides realized they would have to take dramatic steps to prevent a catastrophic, perhaps apocalyptic, war.

and psychologists. The most important approach to economic decision making is utility theory, first proposed by Jeremy Bentham in 1789. Bentham proposed that, when people make a decision involving costs and benefits, they evaluate the goodness of various outcomes and weight them by each outcome's probability of occurrence.

Let us consider a simple example, that is, whether to take an umbrella on a possibly rainy day. According to utility theory, the decision may be framed as a 2 by 2 table based on the two possible choices and two possible weather scenarios. Either you take or do not take your umbrella and either it rains or does not rain. According to utility theory, one begins by evaluating the four possible outcomes in terms of how happy one would be with each one. In the present case, the utilities are subjective, depending on the feelings and taste of each individual decider. The version of utility theory employing subjective evaluations of happiness is called subjective expected utility (SEU) theory. According to SEU, then, everyone goes through the same decision-making process but may not always reach the same conclusion if their subjective utilities are different. SEU also assumes that subjective utilities can be scientifically quantified. Although in real life we do not assign numbers to our evaluations of happiness, SEU theory says that in principle we could do so, improving our decision making. In any event, SEU claims that even without exact quantification, human decision making follows its processes in a general way.

Returning to our example, the decision maker evaluates the possible outcomes of the decision. If she takes the umbrella and it rains, she'll stay dry, which will make her moderately happy. If she takes the umbrella and it doesn't rain, she'll be made mildly unhappy by the inconvenience of lugging it around all day. If she doesn't take the umbrella and it rains, she'll be very unhappily wet. Finally, if she doesn't take the umbrella and it doesn't rain, she'll be dry and moderately happy.

The next step is to calculate the expected utilities of each option. To do this, we need an estimate of the probability of each outcome. Here, we can find the probability of rain or no rain from a weather forecast. Then, we multiply each cell's utility by the probability of each event's occurrence, and sum across the outcomes of each decision. The choice we make should be the one that maximizes our net utility or, more informally, leads to the greatest amount of happiness.

In economic decision making, utility theory—especially when the utilities can be quantified as dollars or precise units of happiness—is a normative theory. That is, it prescribes how one ought to reason about cost-benefit outcomes, just as logic prescribes how one ought to reason about deductive and inductive problems. Moreover, economists since Bentham have assumed that utility theory also describes, at least in a rough way, how people do in fact reason. As we learned in our study of conditional reasoning, however, psychologists have challenged the assumption that humans reason using logical rules, and they also challenge the psychological reality of utility theory. As with formal logic, psychologists concede that utility theory is normative—it does indeed tell us how we ought to decide—but argue that it fails to describe ordinary economic decision making.

The first significant challenge to the economist's assumption that utility theory describes ordinary people and situations was offered by Herbert Simon's (e.g., 1955, 1982) theory of **bounded rationality.** A person who follows the principles of utility theory and formal logic will be optimally rational. However, people are rarely able to make optimal decisions because of constraints (bounds) of time, money, or other resources. Consider, for example, a corporation president who needs to hire an executive assistant (Dawes, 1988). Optimally, the president should hire the best possible person for the job, but doing so would take enormous amounts of time and money. So one realistic procedure is to carefully define the job requirements and search until someone who meets them is found. Another way might be to form a reasonably sized pool of applicants, and choose the best person from the pool. Neither procedure is optimal, because the ideal executive assistant would probably not be found, but each should produce a suitable candidate. According to Simon, then, because human beings are boundedly, not optimally, rational, they do not **optimize** their outcomes, as utility theory says they should, but rather they **satisfice.** Our corporate president has not found the optimal assistant but has found a satisfactory one. People and companies do not strive for optimal outcomes but settle for satisfactory ones.

Experimental evidence has accumulated that, as in the case of logical reasoning, human beings do not make economic decisions according to the principles of utility theory (Arkes & Hammond, 1986; Dawes, 1988). For example, consider the choice between a sure win of $30 and an 80 percent chance to win $45. Applying utility theory, we should choose the second bet, because $45 × 0.80 = $36, greater than $30. However, most people choose the first bet (Kahneman & Tversky, 1981). Humans **satisfice,** settling for the satisfactory sure thing, rather than optimizing and making the risky choice. This sort of finding has been replicated many times, and illustrates a nonnormative bias called **risk aversion.** When choices involve gains, people prefer risk-free gains to risky, but more optimal, ones. On the other hand, when choices involve losses, people often become **risk-seeking,** preferring risky but less dangerous choices to certain bad outcomes (Jou, Shanteau, & Harris, 1996; Kahneman & Tversky, 1981; Slovic, 1995). There is also evidence that we reason differently when dealing with problems of human life than with property (Jou et al., 1996). Such issues become especially difficult and important when dealing with health appeals and decisions (Rothman & Salovey, 1997) and life and death judgments (see Box 9.9).

Economic reasoning has been extensively studied by Nisbett and his colleagues, who have shown that normative economic reasoning can be taught (Larrick, Morgan, & Nisbett, 1990). Nisbett proposed three normative rules of cost-benefit decision making that hold across a wide range of choices:

- The greatest net benefit principle. Choose the action with the greatest positive difference between the total benefit of the outcome and the cost of its performance. This is the same as choosing the outcome with greatest expected utility.

- The opportunity cost principle. Choosing one action means foregoing others. Thus in calculating the costs of an action one should include the benefits lost by not taking the others. For example, a person who saves money by mowing his or her own lawn may really be losing money by taking time away from some more lucrative activity.

- The sunk cost principle. Consider only future benefits and costs, not past unchangeable ones. What is done is done, and past—sunk—costs are lost forever no matter what happens.

To illustrate, we will discuss research on the sunk cost principle. Dawes (1988) offers a nice example of how people fall into sunk cost traps. Imagine a couple who have placed a large, nonrefundable deposit on a resort vacation. The day before they

■ Box 9.9 ■

Death Penalty Decisions by Juries

One of the cornerstones of the Anglo-American legal system is the right to a trial by a jury of one's peers. But how do juries make decisions? Psychologist-lawyer Sherry Diamond (1995) studied what she calls the "most difficult legal decisions made by amateurs," decisions to invoke the death penalty in the United States, the only western democratic nation to retain capital punishment. Although historically selected for their expertise, modern juries often seem more selected for their ignorance, with knowledgeable people such as criminology scholars and crime victims excluded from participation. Attitudes are also a selection factor; prosecutors routinely exclude people from capital juries if they have attitudes against the death penalty, although those strongly favoring the death penalty are less often excluded. Diamond's research studying real jurors found that verdicts are a function both of the evidence presented and the jurors' prior attitudes about the death penalty. There is also a lack of trust in other alternatives; for example, in one study 53 percent of juror subjects believed that someone sentenced to "life in prison with no possibility of parole" would be released someday. Juries can also be more lenient than the evidence calls for; in a "nullification of evidence" case, a jury acquits a defendant for reasons of values or emotions rather than evidence as such. For example, it is very difficult to obtain a conviction for a so-called "mercy killing," where someone helps a loved one in great pain to die.

are to drive to the resort, they become ill with the flu. The couple believe that they would be happier and better off spending the weekend at home, but go anyway because "we've already paid the deposit, and it will go to waste if we don't go." As Dawes points out, the couple is paying money to be where they do not want to be. The deposit is a sunk cost that cannot be recovered no matter what happens. It therefore should be irrelevant to deciding where to spend the weekend, and the couple is making themselves sicker and more miserable for no gain.

There are many real life examples of falling into the sunk cost trap. One of the most expensive concerns the Anglo-French supersonic transport, the Concorde. The British and French governments spent millions developing the Concorde in the 1970s, but about half-way through, it became apparent that the Concorde would never turn a profit. Nevertheless, they went ahead and completed the Concordes, throwing good money after bad. They fell into the sunk cost trap, spending still more money only because they had already spent so much. The Concorde and its occasional flights are still money losers and were all grounded due to safety concerns in 2000.

Experiments confirm that people are prone to falling into sunk cost traps (Larrick et al., 1990). Imagine you're a basketball fan and have bought a ticket to see your team play the Chicago Bulls. On the night in question, it's snowing and the man you want to see—Michael Jordan—is injured and won't play. Would you go? In experimental versions of this question, most people said they would because they had paid for the ticket. A way to reframe the problem to see past the sunk cost trap is to imagine not having bought a ticket and being called the night of the game and being offered a free ticket to the game. Put this way, we look at the problem only in terms of future costs, risks, and benefits, and will properly decide to go or not. Similarly, suppose you've bought a $20 ticket to see your favorite play, but lost it on the way to the theater, with no way to replace it. Should you buy another ticket? Many people fall into the sunk cost trap and say no, since it seems that seeing the play will then cost $40. But the original $20 is gone no matter what happens: it's a sunk cost. Again, reframing the problem helps see past the trap (Larrick et al., 1990). Imagine having lost a $20 bill on the way to the theater. Put this way, most people will go see the play, although in both scenarios the cost is $40.

EXPERTISE

Although all of us regularly reason, solve problems, and make decisions in our daily lives, some people are particular effective at doing so. What makes **experts** so good at the problem solving, reasoning, or decision making that they do? The basic question is, how does someone who is very good at a task perform differently from a novice (someone who knows the rules and can do the task but is not highly skilled) or naive person (someone who knows nothing about the area)? Psychologists generally presume expertise to be acquired, not innate, although in some domains this assumption may be questionable. A major dilemma is how to define expertise in a non-domain-specific way.

Characteristics of Experts

Shanteau (1992) identified several psychological characteristics of experts. Although not all these characteristics may describe every expert in every domain, they have a large degree of generality.

First are several general cognitive characteristics. Experts are unusually perceptive, that is, able to extract information that others cannot. An expert detective may see an important clue that a novice would miss. Second, an expert is able to readily distinguish diagnostic from nondiagnostic information and quickly focus on the former. Third, an expert can simplify, chunk, and organize information efficiently and develop subgoals in problem solving.

In addition to these cognitive characteristics, experts effectively communicate their standing as experts to those who might call on that expertise. They are self-confident with belief in their abilities. They handle adversity and stress well, in part by planning ahead. They are flexible and make exceptions when necessary; they know when to follow rules rigidly and when not to. They are adaptable, adjusting their strategies to fit a constantly changing situation. Finally, they are creative, in the ways discussed earlier in this chapter.

Perhaps most important of all, experts possess an extensive knowledge base in their domain of expertise. Having such knowledge does not ensure that they will be an expert, but not having it is likely to ensure that they cannot be an expert. They also make greater use of automatic and parallel processing, saving valuable attentional resources for more subtle and complex thinking. There are, however, occasions when being an expert can be a disadvantage. For example, experts underestimate how long novices will take to complete a task (Hinds, 1999).

Most experimental research on expertise has examined specific knowledge domains. Let us now look briefly at a few of these.

Sample Studies of Expertise by Area

One of the most heavily studied domains in terms of expertise is chess (see Charness, 1991, for a review). Chess masters, compared to novices, use larger chunks in working memory, building on their knowledge of the game. Thus they are able to easily encode the present configurations of pieces in the game and leave more attentional resources for allocation to more subtle aspects of play. Experts' memory is better than novices' but only for real chess positions; when random placements of chess pieces on the board were shown to both groups, the chess masters were no better than novices in their memory (Chase & Simon, 1973). Masters also have a much greater long-term memory for chess positions, with up to 50,000 patterns and possible productions stored in memory (Simon & Gilmartin, 1973)! This prodigious memory leads to fewer errors in play, because the correct solutions are also stored. A superior ability to recognize patterns in chess games might be more critical to chess masters than the ability to plan many moves ahead (Gobet & Simon, 1996).

In studies of physics professors (experts) and physics students (novices), novices were found to work backward, while experts worked forward in solving problems (Larkin, 1981). Also, experts classified the problems more abstractly, noting more abstract conceptual similarities among problems (Chi, Feltovich, & Glaser, 1981). Similar results were found in studies of novice and expert computer programmers (Jeffries, Turner, Polson, & Atwood, 1981). Novices think in language-specific terms; experts think more abstractly. Experts develop solutions breadth first, while novices do them depth first. As in chess, experts have better memory for features of computer programs (McKeithen, Reitman, Reuter, & Hirtle, 1981).

Studies of expertise in medicine have particularly centered around the issue of medical diagnosis. One approach has examined verbal protocols from a doctor (expert)

LEARNING AND COGNITION

or novice upon hearing the patient's description of symptoms (Elstein, Shulman, & Sprafka, 1978). Four components of the decision process have been identified. Information is obtained, plausible hypotheses are generated, the data are interpreted in light of these hypotheses, and finally the hypotheses are evaluated to see if any of them are confirmed or disconfirmed by the data. Results have shown both experts and novices to go through these stages but the two groups show vastly different knowledge bases. There is also a bias toward seeking information to confirm the initial hypothesis generated, along with a tendency to continue to seek information even after enough is available to select one of the competing hypotheses. A second approach examines both free recall of symptoms and the diagnosis itself, concluding that true forward reasoning of going from the symptoms toward specific hypotheses is found only in top experts (Groen & Patel, 1990; Patel & Groen, 1991).

Medical decision making also occurs in decision makers other than the physicians or other medical professionals. The medical consumer makes decisions about when and where to seek medical treatment (e.g., see Janis, 1984; Matthews, Kuller, Siegel, Thompson, & Varat, 1983). Sometimes such decisions have potential life-and-death consequences, as in choosing the appropriate form of cancer therapy. In other

■ Box 9.10 ■

To Donate or Not to Donate Someone's Organs: How Do We Decide?

Why is it that almost everyone recognizes that there is a great need for donor organs, yet relatively few people have signed a donor card, frequently made very convenient by being on the back of a driver's license? Some of the reasons lie in psychological factors of fear, misunderstandings, and deep-seated emotions and attitudes (see Shanteau & Harris, 1990, for a series of readings on these issues). In fact, however, transplant physicians will not use organs even from a signed donor without the consent of the next-of-kin after the death. On what bases do families make decisions to consent to the use of their loved one's organs?

Harris, Jasper, Lee, and Miller (1991) used an experimental approach to answer this question. Participants read a series of scenarios about families in crisis and were asked to make a recommendation of "yes," "no," or "not sure" in regard to whether the survivors should consent to donate organs. The information was systematically varied across versions of the scenario, identical except for one critical piece of information. The influence of many types of information was examined, but by far the most important variable was the perception of the wishes of the deceased. If that person had signed a donor card or had otherwise clearly indicated wishes to have his or her organs donated should the situation arise, almost everyone agreed to donate, even if the next-of-kin opposed donation and even if the participants themselves opposed organ donation. Similarly, if the deceased had been clearly on record as being opposed to organ donation, people respected those wishes to not donate, even if the next-of-kin and the participants themselves favored donation. If the attitude of the potential donor was not clearly known, people tried to infer it from other information such as his/her attitude toward physicians or religious beliefs. The findings suggest that signing an organ donor card is in fact very important, though not for the reason most people think it is. It will not permit the organs to be taken (although it does so legally), but it does make the person's wishes completely clear, thus aiding the surviving family in their consent decision.

instances the decision that must be made is a difficult choice on behalf of some third party unable to make that decision, such as the decision to terminate life-support for a brain-dead relative or deciding whether to donate the organs of a next-of-kin who has tragically died in an accident (see Box 9.10 on page 281).

Decision making by expert auditors has been studied by Bédard and Chi (1994) and Shanteau (1989, 1993). The importance of the training of experts is crucial. Experts are better than novices at distinguishing diagnostic from nondiagnostic information and especially at translating that knowledge into practice. Mid-level auditing novices are comparable to experts in their knowledge base but they apply it less effectively.

Finally, attempts have been made to model expertise on the computer (Benfer, Brent, & Furbee, 1991; Stefik, 1995). **Expert systems** is the branch of artificial intelligence in computer science that tries to build computer models of expertise. These computer programs are written to behave as human experts. However, this has often been far more difficult to do than was initially expected. There is especially a bottleneck at the point in such programs where they must describe the acquisition of knowledge, that is, learning. This essentially psychological problem has proven the most intractable for expert systems.

CONCLUSION

The study of problem solving, reasoning, and decision making encompasses a wide range of problems and issues. There is no comprehensive theory or even theoretical framework that can claim to describe or explain all of these processes, nor is there likely to be such a theory in the near future. Still, cognitive psychology has managed to shed many important insights on these complex and often mysterious thought processes.

LEARNING AND COGNITION

SUGGESTED READINGS

Problem solving is covered in most cognitive texts cited at the end of Chapter 4, and reasoning and decision making are covered in many of them. Baron (1988) offers a text heavy on decision making (including applications) and much lighter on problem solving, reasoning, creativity, and other topics. Newstead and Evans (1995) offer a book of readings of research on reasoning. Dawes (1988) offers a good introduction to decision making, while Arkes and Hammond (1986) and Kahneman, Slovic, and Tversky (1982) give good selections of primary source readings in decision making. For a good review of research on decision making in traditional and alternative frameworks, see Mellers, Schwartz, and Cooke (1998). For a good selection of papers studying creativity from a variety of approaches, see Sternberg (1988). For books of readings on the psychological study of expertise, see Hoffman (1994), Ericsson and Smith (1991), Wright and Bolger (1992), and Chi, Glaser, and Farr (1988). Bransford and Stein (1984), Levine (1994), and Sternberg (1986) attempt to apply problem-solving research to daily life. Beyth-Marom and Lichtenstein (1984) and Piatelli-Palmarini (1994) do the same for various judgmental biases in decision making. For readable introductions to scientific reasoning, see Levy (1997) and Stanovich (1998).

PART V

DEVELOPMENT

10 Cognitive Development

DEFINING DEVELOPMENT

One of the most remarkable facts about living creatures is their orderly development. We plant one kind of seed and we get a tomato plant; another seed produces marigolds. There are two features of this kind of growth that are deeply important and challenge scientific explanation. First, the growth from seed to mature plant is not simply mechanical change. When we build a house out of lumber, the wood of which the lumber is made is cut and rearranged into the shape of a house, but its nature is not fundamentally altered. In the growth of a seed to a plant, the matter of the seed not only increases in mass but also is altered qualitatively into different types of cells; a tomato is not a tomato seed. Second, the growth of the plant is somehow directed from within. A carpenter imposes the form of a house on lumber, but the form of a tomato plant emerges spontaneously. All we need do is nourish the plant, and nature does the rest. Moreover, each seed seems to contain a unique plan of development. Tomato seeds yield only tomato plants and marigold seeds yield only marigold plants.

Inner-directed development seems mysterious because we cannot see its causes, as they lie within the organism. The first scientist to offer an explanation of development was the Greek philosopher Aristotle. He envisioned the development of any living being as the unfolding of a preexisting plan of development (called an *entelechy*) that brought an organism from seed to mature plant, from egg to adult bird, from embryo to mature animal, from fetus to mature human being. Like many Greeks and Romans, Aristotle believed that nature was inherently purposeful, moving in things big and small toward a final end of perfection.

The teleological view of the universe was overthrown by the Scientific Revolution (Leahey, 2000). Instead of being seen as a divine organism moving toward perfection, the physical universe came to be seen as a magnificent clockwork governed by Newton's eternal laws of motion. Beginning with Descartes, the clockwork conception of nature was extended from the inorganic to the organic world; animal bodies were seen as being like the mechanical figures one sees on some clock towers, who come out on the hour and strike a bell. This mechanical approach to living organisms raised a host of problems (Leahey, 2000), but was widely accepted by the nineteenth century.

One of the greatest challenges it faced was explaining the spontaneous development of living things. Aristotle had not needed to posit a mechanism of development, because he thought that teleological development was a fundamental property of nature. Because it sees nature as a machine (or collection of machines) modern science requires that development be explained, not taken for granted. Providing mechanical explanations of living processes—including development—was a major preoccupation of twentieth-century biology.

While the problem arose in biology, explaining development also came to occupy social scientists, including psychologists. Human history is a story of change. Is it also a story of development? Does human history have a direction? A child changes psychologically as well as biologically from infancy to adulthood. Is this change development? Does cognitive development have a direction? In nineteenth-century Europe—the birthplace of much of psychology—these two questions came together almost as one. Although teleological thinking was dying in biology, some theorists, especially Germans, defended it in philosophy and social science. They proposed that just as a human being passes from the simple and primitive thoughts and feelings of infancy to the sophisticated thinking and nuanced emotion of adulthood, so human societies progress from simple and primitive tribalism to the sophistication of the Western nation-state. Usually, it was hoped that one stage yet remained: achievement of a harmonious brotherhood of all people under a peaceful world government. Karl Marx's theory of history is the best-known example of such historicism today; Marx envisioned history as an inevitable progression through a series of stages from barbarism to feudalism to capitalism and finally to world socialism, at which point history ends. For Marx, the autonomous force directing historical development was economic change, specifically changes in who owns the means of production characteristic of each stage. Moreover, each system of ownership (save socialism) possesses internal contradictions that ensure its eventual overthrow and replacement by a superior one. History, according to Marx, is the inevitable progress of humankind to economic and social maturity as the logic of economic change unfolds.

Historicism did much to reinforce and preserve the teleological concept of human development against mechanistic criticism, and it is therefore not surprising that shortly after psychology began there appeared in Europe historicist-developmentalist theories of human development. For example, there are interesting parallels between Marx's theory of history and Piaget's and Kohlberg's theories of cognitive and moral development. They propose that cognition and morality develop through fixed sequences of stages such that each stage (save the last) contains inconsistencies that bring about its overthrow and replacement by a more adequate one. Human development is therefore the inevitable progress of a child to cognitive and moral maturity as the logic of development unfolds.

The theorist who most emphatically distinguished between mere change and true development, and who applied the concept of development to everything from perception to history was Heinz Werner (1890–1964). Werner was educated in Germany, steeped in the German historical-developmental tradition, before fleeing the Nazis and settling in the United States. Werner studied the processes of development from an organismic-teleological perspective as manifested in children and adults, primitives and moderns, and in psychotics and normals (Baldwin, 1980; Langer, 1970; Werner, 1978).

Werner carefully distinguished development from change or growth. Not all change is development, for change may be regressive. Nor is all growth development; a savings account "grows" as interest is added, but this does not constitute development because no qualitative improvement takes place. Werner (1978) borrowed the term orthogenesis from embryology to define development:

It is an orthogenetic principle which states that whenever development occurs it proceeds from a state of relative globality and lack of differentiation to a state of increasing differentiation, articulation, and hierarchic integration. (Werner, 1957, p. 126)

The principle naturally fits embryogenesis. What begins as a single nonspecialized cell gradually develops into an organism, a collection of specialized cells (differentiation) structurally organized (articulation) into an efficient system under central control (hierarchic integration). Werner thought that the same functional principles of development characterized not only the development of the embryo, but the evolutionary history of a species (phylogenesis), the long-term development of a person (orthogenesis), the short-term development of thinking, emotion, and perception (microgenesis), the development of societies (ethnogenesis), and the development of psychopathology (pathogenesis). Although the material basis (what develops) in each case is different, Werner believed the orthogenetic principles of development—the teleological drive to differentiation, articulation, and integration—could be found in each case (Langer, 1970).

Controversies

Unsurprisingly, teleological and historicist approaches have been controversial. In biology, mechanism trumped teleology when the structure and function of DNA were revealed. The building plan for each organism is encoded in the DNA, and it directs development by amazingly complex and subtle—but unmysterious—biochemical processes. In history, it's possible to deny that history has a direction. Henry Ford once said that history is just one damn thing after another, and historian Edward Gibbon said history was a tale of human folly.

Likewise, in psychology empiricists deny that cognitive change has a direction. Radical behaviorists say that children are simply shaped by reinforcement; whatever direction cognitive development has is imposed by parents and society the way a carpenter builds a house. Information-processing theories likewise tend to see development as the gradual accumulation of expertise, while connectionists see it as the gradual training of the brain's neural network. Additionally, cognitive development interacts with biological development. If cognitive development is directed, the genes might direct it as they direct bodily development, there being no special form of inner psychological development. Thus the adult mind would be a product of genetic tendencies interacting with environmental experience.

In this chapter we begin with theorists who defended the teleological-historicist approach to cognitive development. Jean Piaget and Lawrence Kohlberg both proposed that cognitive and moral development are directed from within as psychological processes unfolded in a series of orderly stages. Their theories fully embraced the two distinctive features of development we discussed earlier. First, development involves qualitative, not just quantitative, change. They proposed that the mind does not grow by accumulation like a bank account or expert system, but proceeds through a series of stages such that the thinking of each stage is unique and qualitatively different from the stage it succeeds. Second, Piaget and Kohlberg believed that mental development is directed from within by autonomous psychological processes, not by the genes or by shaping forces in the environment. They recognized that genes and learning have roles to play in cognitive development, but that they are not the whole—or even most—of the story.

DEVELOPMENTALIST STAGE THEORIES OF COGNITIVE DEVELOPMENT

Genetic Epistemology

Piaget as Philosopher

Jean Piaget was one of the towering psychological theorists of the twentieth century, yet his ideas are often misunderstood and misrepresented. One reason for this is that Piaget represents the European developmentalist tradition alluded to already. Specifically, he belongs in what Blumenthal (1980), following Brett (1912) calls the Leibnizian (European) tradition in philosophy. Gottfried Leibniz (1646–1716) described the mind as an active entity, developing itself through inner-directed principles toward ever-greater perfection. The Leibnizian tradition stands in contrast to the English empiricist tradition that depicts the mind as passive, building up knowledge by receiving and copying sense impressions as if it were clay to be molded (compare Skinner's term "shaping"). Because Americans are raised in the empiricist tradition, it is hardly surprising that Piaget's theory may strike us as odd and hard to understand. Piaget was also greatly influenced by the German historicist philosopher Georg Wilhelm Friederich Hegel (1770–1831). Hegel claimed that human history was directed by the inner dialectic development of a "world-spirit" whose ideas manifested themselves in historical events. Hegel's student Marx turned Hegel upside down by seeing material, economic forces as in the driver's seat of history. Piaget brought Hegel's orientation to history to cognitive development, seeing it as a dialectical interaction between child and environment.

The other main reason for misunderstanding Piaget is less often acknowledged: In an important sense Piaget—despite collecting data and theorizing about cognition—was not a psychologist at all. He called what he did genetic epistemology, the study of the origins (genesis) of knowledge (epistemology), specifically in child development. But the term epistemology needs closer attention, because it was Piaget's concerns as an epistemologist that led to his developmentalism.

Epistemology is the branch of philosophy concerned with knowledge—what it is and how we acquire it. Naively, we think that knowledge is true belief; I can say I know that George Washington was the first president because it is true. But this cannot be all that knowledge is. On an American history test you might be asked, "Who was the third president?" and be unable to remember. So you recall the name of the only president after Washington and before Lincoln you can remember, namely, Jefferson, and write that down. The answer happens to be correct, but we would not say that you knew Jefferson was the third president even though you expressed the true belief that he was. Philosophers concede that knowledge is more than simply true belief, but what that "more" is remains elusive.

Some have even given up the quest altogether and asserted that there is no knowledge, only workable beliefs that may nevertheless eventually be proven wrong. This was the view of the Scottish philosopher David Hume and the American philosopher and psychologist William James, so it is part of Americans' intellectual heritage.

Piaget, however, is among those philosophers who did not give up the quest, and he proposed his genetic epistemology as an answer to this central problem of epistemology. One old candidate (going back to Plato) for what is needed to make true belief knowledge is provable certainty. To count as knowledge, something must have the character of a mathematical or logical theorem—it can be proven true by deductive logic.

Manifestly, any generalization from experience cannot have this characteristic of provable certainty, as David Hume showed in the eighteenth century. No matter how confident I may be that all swans are white from having examined 2,000 of them, I must realize that I could be wrong, that the 2,001st swan may be some other color. Therefore, while experience may yield up true beliefs, it cannot yield up knowledge.

Another move in the search for knowledge was tried by many thinkers from Plato down to the present. It is to claim that human knowledge is innate. So, for example, the eighteenth-century Scottish philosopher Thomas Reid (1710–1796) held that humans possess God-given beliefs and cognitive processes, which, since God made us in His image, cannot be mistaken. These, therefore, constitute knowledge.

However, in light of modern evolutionary theory such a comfortable nativism is no longer convincing. Whatever human propensities and abilities may be innate, they were selected by the nondirective happenstances of natural and sexual selection. They are not necessarily true; had our ancient ecology been different, our human nature would be different. In a sense, innate ideas are not very different from ideas drawn from experience—useful, but the product of whatever experience our ancestors had and therefore not certain, not knowledge.

Now none of this need bother a psychologist; he or she can study what's innate and what's learned without caring whether our beliefs are ultimately true or not. In this the psychologist would resemble Hume or James. But Piaget, even as a teenager, wanted certainty, and his genetic epistemology is in his view a third way to knowledge through development rather than through learning or heredity.

Piaget's approach to epistemology was strongly influenced by another German philosopher, Immanual Kant (1724–1804). One can look at the directedness of development in an epistemological way. Barring accidents or a hideous environment, every tomato plant turns out pretty much the same. Knowledge has a similar character. Everyone everywhere shares a common stock of knowledge, so common it's often overlooked. All humans believe that space is three-dimensional, that time moves along a single irreversible dimension, that events have causes, that objects continue to exist when we do not see them, and so on. Empiricists believed that people share these beliefs because we share the same world, and experience writes the same truths on the blank slate of the mind. Religious nativists, on the other hand, claimed that beliefs held universally were given by God. Kant proposed a third answer that was neither exactly nativist nor empiricist. He said—and claimed to have proved—that the mind must have a certain cognitive structure such that all experiences exist in three-dimensional space, move along an irreversible time line, and so on. Kant differed from the empiricists when he said that the mind possesses a structure prior to experience: It is not clay shaped by experience. He differed from contemporary nativists when he said that the prior structure of the mind was a logical necessity for any kind of experience: It was not given by God. He also differed from both nativists and empiricists by abandoning the notion of innate ideas. Empiricists and nativists tended to argue about whether specific ideas such as the idea of God were innate or learned. Kant, however, focussed on the cognitive structure of the mind instead of its ideas. The inherent structures of the mind organize experience into coherent ideas, he said. They are not themselves ideas, but the constructor of ideas. For Kant, ideas are given neither by experience alone (the empiricist view) nor by God (or genes) alone (the nativist view) but by the interplay of both.

Piaget turned Kant's epistemology into a theory of cognitive development. Kant thought that the cognitive structures of the mind are logically necessary and present at birth. Piaget proposed that they are not present from birth but developmentally unfold in much the way a logical argument unfolds, step by step in a logically necessary sequence of stages and substages. The child's cognitive structures might be regarded at any moment as a set of logical premises. Experience provides information that children can use to make deductions from their premises, resulting in a new set of premises or logical structures, from which further deductions are made in the light of experience, and so on until an adequate set of structures is achieved that can deal effectively and creatively with the environment. Piaget retained Kant's emphasis on logical structure as the core of the mind, but stretched its development out over years rather than seeing it as given *a priori*.

According to Piaget, cognitive development has the character of a logical argument, moving step by step to a provably certain conclusion. In short, cognitive development is the construction of knowledge, and Piaget's approach to cognitive development is called constructivism. We see, then, that epistemological concerns led Piaget to postulate autonomous developmental forces beside maturation (nativism) and experience (empiricism), and it is these concerns, together with his inheritance of the Leibnizian tradition, that can make him so hard to understand.

Stages of Development

Thinking of development in terms of stages, is quite common, occurring in all the developmentalists surveyed in this chapter. The intuitive appeal of stages is evident in our commonsense usage: We divide life into infancy, childhood, adolescence, adulthood, and old age. However, we mean by these things no more than convenient descriptions—the terrible twos—and do not take them to be real entities in any fundamental sense. But Piaget does; his stages are proposed as psychological realities, not convenient sketches of age-typical behavior. We will sketch Paiget's proposed stages of development in Table 10.1, and then discuss the developmental forces that move the child from stage to stage.* You may investigate stages of development by doing the simple experiment described in Box 10.1.

Processes of Development

Piaget's area of earliest interest and university training was biology, so he brought a strong biological, adaptationist influence to developmental psychology. In fact, his goal was to make epistemology a science along biological lines. He viewed intelligence—cognitive structures and processes—as an organ of biological adaptation like the hand or the eye. The only unique thing about intelligence as an adaptation is that it is mental and behavioral rather than morphological. Intelligence, especially

---

* The following discussion of Piaget's theory is based primarily on the following sources: Piaget (1963, 1965, 1967a, 1967b, 1969, 1970a, 1970b, 1971a, 1971b, 1971c, 1972, 1973, 1976); Piaget and Inhelder (1969a, 1969b, 1969c, 1971, 1973); Inhelder and Piaget (1958). Secondary sources consulted include Elkind and Flavell (1969), Baldwin (1980), Furth (1969). An interesting attempt to picture Piaget as a learning theorist is Gallagher and Reid (1981). A good single source for reading Piaget is Gruber and Voneche (1977), which contains extracts from Piaget's leading work over his entire lifetime, together with thoughtful and insightful commentary.

TABLE 10.1 Piaget's Stages of Intellectual Development

I.   SENSORIMOTOR INTELLIGENCE (0 TO 24 MOS.)

Adaptation is "practical," oriented to the here and now, based on behavioral schemes only—few if any mental representations present. Interiorization, coordination, and enriching of sensorimotor schemes provide basis for operational thought. Six substages:

1. *Modification of innate reflexes* (0 to 1 mos.)   Initially fixed S-R reflexes become adaptive schemes as they assimilate objects and accommodate reality.

2. *Acquisition of new habits* (1 to 4 mos.)   First new schemes, primary circular reactions, learned. Child discovers some behavior centering on its own body that has interesting effects (e.g., sucking a thumb) and it learns to reinstate it.

3. *Secondary circular reactions* (4 to 10 mos.)   Reinstatement of interesting effect taking place in outside world (e.g., Jacqueline and the mobile). First signs of object concept; for example, child will now continue to track the trajectory of a previously visible, now occluded, object.

4. *Coordination of secondary schemes* (4 to 12 mos.)   First indication of true intentional intelligence and first step toward general knowledge. Infant can now detach an old scheme from its familiar context (e.g., hitting things to see them move or hear them make noise) and use it as a means to a more remote end (e.g., striking an obstacle to the grasping of an interesting object). Object concept much more developed: Child will now search for a vanished object, showing it now knows that objects continue to exist even when they cannot be sensed.

5. *Tertiary circular reactions* (12 to 18 mos.)   Secondary circular reactions with systematic variation to explore the effect of behavior on the world instead of just repeating an old effect, as before. New schemes invented on the spot to solve problems instead of use of older scheme in new context.

6. *Beginnings of thought* (18 to 24 mos.)   Transition to next major stage as semiotic function—the ability to represent mentally—begins to appear, insightful problem solution—the result of the precorrection of errors—now possible as solutions are first tried mentally before being translated into behavior. Full development of the object concept as child can now infer location of a hidden object from witnessing a series of both visible and invisible displacements.

II.   PREOPERATIONAL INTELLIGENCE (2 TO 7 YRS.)

With the acquisition of the semiotic function [marked by appearance of delayed imitation, symbolic play (pretending), drawing, mental images, and above all by language acquisition] real thinking, the manipulation of a mental world begins. During this period, schemes are interiorized into operations as concrete operational intelligence is constructed. Two substages.

A. *Preconceptual* (2 to 4 yrs.)   Interiorization of schemes just beginning, so that a child can do many things in reality but not with representations. For example, a four-year-old may be able to navigate a path between its house and nursery school, but be unable to tell anyone else how to do it, even with the aid of a realistic map on which are set the principle landmarks.

(continued)

Cognitive Development   **Chapter 10**   **293**

TABLE 10.1   *(Continued)*

B.   *Intuitive, or Functional* (5 to 7 yrs.)   Operations beginning to appear but are not yet integrated and coordinated into an overall logical structure. Child intuitively understands certain functional relations but fails tests of deeper understanding. For example, shown a nail driven into a board with a string running around it at right angles such as this:

The child understands that if one pulls on the end of string at A, the distance B-C will shorten and vice-versa, that is, that lengths A-C and B-C are functionally (inversely) related. But this understanding is not fully coordinated, for the child will deny that the total length of the string A-C is unchanged by moving the string around the nail. Child does not yet conserve length.

III.   CONCRETE OPERATIONAL INTELLIGENCE (7 TO 12 YRS.)

Appearance of logically integrated thought. The logic at this stage is the logic of classes, similar to formal syllogistic logic. That is, the child can reason about logically defined classes defined over objects (hence, concrete operational), and can represent (and internally manipulate) concrete, familiar objects competently and adaptively, so errors are precorrected. Two substages.

A.   (8 to 9 yrs.)   Operations coordinated into a logical system. Onset best marked by the first appearance of the conservations, the knowledge that physical quantities do not change despite changes in appearance. An example is conservation of amount, or continuous quantity. A child is shown two identical glasses filled with identical amounts of water, A1 and A2, and an empty vessel B, much narrower but taller than A. The water in A2 is poured into B, and the child is asked if there is still the same amount in A1 and B. At IIA, the child denies this, claiming B has more because it's taller. At IIB the child may answer correctly but be unable to justify its response, even though it does conserve the water's identity, recognizing that the water in B is the same water that was in A2; it was merely poured. At IIIA, the child can justify his or her response.

B.   (10 to 12 yrs.)   Continuation of the consolidation of concrete operations into an equilibrated system; more conservations mastered. Limitations to concrete logic can be seen. Most importantly, the child cannot think hypothetically about all the things that might be done in a given situation so that they might be explored systematically. For example, given a set of clear liquid chemicals and told that some combination of them will produce a yellow color, the child proceeds haphazardly, combining pairs of chemicals at random (never trying three), so that even if the solution is achieved, it likely cannot be explained or repeated. Possibility is still subordinate to reality.

IV.   FORMAL OPERATIONAL INTELLIGENCE (12 YRS. ON)

Operations become yet more abstract and formal, dealing not with objects at all but with formally stated relations or hypotheses. The logic of this stage is propositional logic, in which what is understood and manipulated are not classes of objects (concepts) but whole statements or propositions. The power of this stage is that in language—propositions—one

continued

TABLE 10.1 *(Continued)*

can state anything, whether true or false, real or imaginary, so that reality becomes just an instantiation of one among many possible worlds. Einstein's elevator (Box 10.2) is an excellent example of formal thinking at its best. Adolescents' involvement with novel political systems, utopias, and their identity crises are partly the outcome of formal operational thinking, as the teenager is both exhilarated and confused by what he or she and society may be, and angry and resentful of what he or she and society are. Reality becomes subordinate to possibility, and the imagined possible gleams like utopia from the future. But remember, u-topia means "no-where."

Substages are not clearly marked, but around 12 years the child shows the ability to think hypothetically. In the chemical combination task the subject of formal operations will work systematically through all possible combinations, keeping records of what was done as all possibilities are exhausted. He or she will be able to explain his or her strategy and repeat the solution if asked. There is now a great deal of evidence, some of it reviewed in the chapter (9) on Thinking, that for most (perhaps all) people, formal operational thinking remains more an occasionally reached ideal than an everyday actuality, manifesting itself only in familiar domains, but not everyday in every decision. This may be just as well, since weighing all possible pros and cons of every decision is probably not adaptive. It is said that the great philosopher Immanuel Kant—a formal operational reasoner, surely—took so long to weigh the pros and cons of marriage that by the time he decided to propose, his intended was already wed!

One final note on Piaget's stages. The ages given are approximations only, and are not to be taken as norms in any sense. There will be wide individual variation from child to child in the speed with which the stages are traversed. What matters to Piaget is the invariant sequence of the stages, not their age of acquisition.

■ Box 10.1 ■

Tilting a Bottle: Procedure

One interesting pencil-and-paper Piagetian task that is easily done is his water-level problem. Draw a picture of a table from a side view, with a glass on it, as shown in the figure below:

Now draw a bottle or pitcher pouring water into the glass, and be sure to show some water remaining in the bottle or pitcher. Collect as many as possible such drawings from friends and classmates before reading Box 10.2, which discusses the usual results.

Tilting a Bottle: Results

When Piaget asked children to do a task similar to that described in Box 10.1, he reported results as shown in the figure below:

Stage	Age	Drawing
I	4 yrs.	
IIA	5	
IIB	6	
IIB–IIIA	6+	or
IIIB	7	correct

From Piaget and Inhelder (1948/1967)

Interestingly, however, when groups of adults are given this problem [having been a subject once, one of us (THL) has done this as a class demonstration for years] few of them get it right. Although no one gives the preschooler's response (Stage I), their responses cover Piaget's entire range of drawings, the most common being the IIB drawing and the IIB-IIIA drawings.

Piaget interpreted his results as reflecting decentration, the increasing ability of children to consider an ever larger frame of reference for their activities. The young child of five focuses (centers) narrowly on the bottle itself, defines the frame of reference for water level as the sides of the bottle, and maintains the familiar right-angle relationship of water surface and bottle side of a bottle standing up, even when the child is drawing a tilted bottle. This centration only gradually breaks up through intermediate stages, as the child realizes that something happens to the water's surface, but cannot yet grasp the correct frame of reference. That frame of reference is the surface of the Earth: Water responds to gravity and so maintains a surface parallel to the ground whatever the orientation of the bottle.

If your results are typical, you caught many subjects' cognitive processes napping. Clearly a moment's reflection would reveal the absurdity of one's response to an adult who drew a Stage II drawing, but it appears that when they are not careful, people lapse back into earlier forms of thought. Such findings suggest again that real-world reasoning is a mixed bag of hunches, fancies, and misconceptions tainting a larger set of correct information processed in a rather haphazard fashion.

Read Jean Piaget and Bärbel Inhelder, *The Child's Conception of Space* (New York: Norton, 1967; originally published 1948).

human intelligence, is the most powerful organ of adaptation there is, and we reflected on its evolutionary origins in Chapter 2. Piaget is concerned with the evolution of intelligence in the individual child as he or she attains mature cognition, perfect adaptation to the environment, and certain knowledge.

Piaget drew a sharp and significant distinction between physical (or empirical) and logico-mathematical knowledge, which correspond to learning and development respectively (see Table 10.2). Empirical knowledge has to do with facts—knowledge of the outside world—and how we represent them internally, which Piaget calls figurativity. Logico-mathematical knowledge has to do with our actions on the world or its internal representations, which Piaget calls operativity in an unconscious echo of Skinner's coinage "operant." Both Piaget and Skinner thereby emphasized an organism's activity and study how it operates on the world it lives in.

The source of empirical knowledge is experienced objects. As we perceive and interact with the objects in our environment we learn about them through perception and the cognitive process of empirical abstraction, which gives rise to concepts. For example, a child meets many small furry animals and must learn to group them into distinct conceptual categories such as dog, cat, and gerbil. Each class will have features in common with the other—dogs, cats, and gerbils are all furry; all of them eat, drink, and move; many are brown. Other features distinguish each class from the others. Dogs chase cats and cats chase gerbils; dogs bark, cats meow, and gerbils (occasionally) squeak. What the child does is to abstract from each particular animal the features that define its class, and so builds up a concept of DOG, of CAT, of GERBIL. This process Piaget calls empirical (sometimes physical) abstraction, because it is an abstraction from the perceived physical world. The child is also able to represent the world internally, both as memory of his particular experiences (e.g., an image of a pet gerbil) and as concepts representing general classes (what gerbils are). Developing representations is an internalization of one's experience, and the representations themselves are called schemas. This represents learning for Piaget.

Now while this kind of knowledge is important, useful, and adaptive, it is less important than logico-mathematical knowledge to Piaget. To begin with, it falls short of the universality Piaget seeks in true knowledge. Indian children learn about dacoits, dhotis, and Krishna, while American children learn about muggers, suits, and Jehova: Empirical knowledge—facts—are culture-specific and particular. More importantly, facts are meaningless and unlearnable without actions and cognitive processes, and these change over time while objects do not. To an infant, a gerbil is an interesting moving object; to a 6-year-old it is a beloved pet coming from a mysterious place called Mongolia; to a biology student a gerbil is a member of the class of rodents along with mice and rats, with certain unique properties resulting from its evolution in a specific ecological niche. So Piaget rejects the copy theory; concepts and schemas are not simply given by experience impressing itself on a child, but depend on the child's preexisting and changing cognitive structures. Piaget's work has concentrated on these cognitive structures that he believes are human universals that pass through an invariant sequence of development.

Cognitive structures comprise human logico-mathematical knowledge and are rooted in action rather than the perception of objects. Piaget tells a story about a mathematician friend of his who, as a child, had a great insight one day playing with pebbles. The boy found that if he lined up ten pebbles in a row, he had ten; if he changed the line to a circle, still ten; to a square, still ten. He discovered what Piaget

TABLE 10.2 Processes and Units of Learning and Development in Piaget's Theory. Terms Internalization and Interiorization Are Furth's (1969) Clarifications of Piaget's French Usage

Type of Change	Type of Knowledge	Source	Processes of Transformation				
			Type of Abstraction	Behavioral Basis	Mentalization Process	Mental Units	Process of Change
Learning	Empirical Field of Figurativity	Objects	Empirical	Perception	Internalization	Schemas (representations, concepts)	Learning
Development	Logico-mathematical Field of Operativity	Actions	Reflective	Schemes (abstracted actions)	Interiorization	Operations (mental actions)	Assimilation Accommodation Equilibration

298

calls conservation of number, that no matter how a group of objects is arranged, their number remains the same. This piece of knowledge is logico-mathematical knowledge, and it is far more general and certain than empirical knowledge, for it is capable of proof and applies to pebbles, rocks, bricks, children, dacoits, U.S. senators, and stars.

Naturally, the boy was gaining empirical knowledge about the pebbles, too. He had schemas (images) of the pebbles he was using, and doubtless had a schema (concept) of the PEBBLE, abstracting away the features common to all pebbles. The generalization about conservation of number did not derive from the pebbles, since the same insight could have come from playing with leaves, Lego pieces, toy soldiers, or pieces of candy. Piaget maintains that logico-mathematical knowledge is an abstraction, called reflective abstraction, from a child's actions. The young mathematician could have arranged pebbles, leaves, Lego pieces the same way, and what would be the same in each case, and therefore abstractable as a generalization, is the acts of arranging and counting, getting the same number in each configuration. Again, observe that the actions like conservation of number, are quite general, applying to any countable objects, and operative on the world. Logico-mathematical knowledge is operative knowledge and constitutes an organ of adaptation, because it is able to deal effectively with virtually every concrete situation and is not limited to any given context or culture.

Reflective abstraction creates two units of operative intelligence corresponding to sensorimotor, or behavioral, and mental intelligence, respectively; these units are the scheme and the operation. Schemes are sensorimotor ways of knowing the world by direct perception or action. Attentive looking or grasping qualify as schemes. Schemes are rather like Skinnerian operants, in that they are defined by their consequences or purposes, not by their topography. Thus, schemes, like operants, are not specific muscle movements but are purposive actions. Piaget (1963) describes an incident involving his infant daughter, Jacqueline, that illustrates how schemes are to be understood. Piaget arranged a mobile over her crib and tied one end of a string to the mobile and taped the other end to her right arm. Like all infants, Jacqueline would wiggle; she discovered that her wiggling would jerk the mobile about, which she found fascinating. After a great deal of trial and error she learned to move the mobile just by pulling on the string with her right arm. Piaget then taped the string to the left arm. If Jacqueline had acquired only a specific muscular response, she would have had to relearn it with her left arm. However, she immediately began to use her left arm to work the mobile, showing that she had learned something more general and goal-defined, namely, a scheme.

Schemes provide the original behavioral foundations of later mental actions. Schemes operate on immediately given physical objects; objects are internalized into mental schemas, and as such they are subject to mental action by interiorized schemes, called operations. For example, infants "classify" objects by what can be done to them—that is, what schemes apply to them. Some objects can be sucked on, others hit, some picked up, and so on. This constitutes a primitive, sensorimotor sort of classification of objects into overlapping classes. Piaget believes that his sensori motor "classification" becomes interiorized and more general, providing the cognitive structures underlying classification of objects under conceptual heads in later childhood and adulthood. As he does with all thought, Piaget thus views classification as action—mental action—whereby objects are actively sorted into groups; classes are not given by nature and imposed on a passive organism.

The adaptive virtue of operations as opposed to schemes—and therefore the source of the evolutionary advantage—is that they make possible mental trial-and-error learning, enhancing adaptive coping. At the sensorimotor level one can only act and then discover—perhaps to one's great, even fatal cost—that the act was unwise. Operations encourage prudence, because one can try out a line of action (operations) on one's mental world (schemas), estimating its likelihood of success or failure. Piaget calls this the precorrection of errors made possible by operational thought.

Individual schemes and operations develop because of two processes, assimilation and accommodation. Assimilation and accommodation come into play when a child (or adult) encounters a new object or situation requiring adaptive mastery. Piagetian organisms, being active learners, seek out new learning opportunities, boldly going where they have not been before. Assimilation refers to the organism bringing a new object, concept, or situation within the competence of its schemes or operations. An infant coming across a keyring for the first time (infants find them fascinating) fumbles with it for a while until it can securely grasp it, rattle it, and pass it from hand to hand (all schemes). This process may take days, and to the Piagetian-informed parent is fascinating to watch. When all these things can be done smoothly and competently, the object is assimilated to the schemes and will soon become boring.

At a more mature level, you fumbled with the concept "parental investment" until you mastered it (we hope), thereby assimilating it to your operations. Neither you nor the baby was unchanged during all of this. The infant's schemes were tested and refined by the encounter with the keyring, improving its adaptive fit to the environment and better equipping it for future challenges. Encountering "parental investment" tested and refined your intellectual operations, improving your adaptive fit to your academic environment, and better equipping you for future challenges whether in psychology or in marriage. A change to schemes and operations taking place during an adaptive learning encounter Piaget calls accommodation, which always takes place alongside assimilation. In fact, Piaget maintains that while we can conceptually separate them, assimilation and accommodation are inextricably intertwined in the actual development of infant, child, and adult.

There is one final development process, shown in Table 10.3, equilibration. Equilibration is the master developmental process, lying behind assimilation and accommodation and being responsible for transitions between Piaget's well-known stages of cognitive development. As for theorists of evolution, so with development for Piaget: He needs to find a motor to move it forward. In evolution, the orthodox motor (Chapter 12) of the neo-Darwinians is the struggle for existence and natural selection. In development, the common alternatives are maturation, espoused by nativists (Piaget calls them preformationists) or the environment, which simply shapes the organism through learning, according to empiricists and behaviorists.

We have seen that for Skinner the process of learning is the same as the process of evolution, selection by the environment among random variations emitted by organisms. Piaget agrees that evolution and development (not learning) are based on the same process, but seeks, as usual, a via media between learning and maturation, proposing a basic process quite different from Skinner's: equilibration (Piaget, 1971a, 1978). Equilibration refers to what Piaget also calls the auto-regulation of behavior and behavior change. He maintains with Lamarck that organisms do not just respond passively to a selecting environment, but actively strive to improve their adaptation. They seek not just an adequate level of adaptation, but the best adaptation possible (Flanagan, 1983).

TABLE 10.3 Decalage in the Development of Physical Quantity Conservation Problems

Approximate Age Acquired		Task Description
1	6	*Conservation of discontinuous quantity* Child fills two identical vessels with the same number of discrete objects, such as marbles; experimenter pours contents of one glass into a differently shaped one and asks if contents are still same in amount.
2	6½	*Conservation of substance* Child shown two identical balls of clay that he or she acknowledges to be the same in amount (or they are adjusted); experimenter transforms one ball into a sausage and asks if there is still just as much clay in each piece.
3	7	*Conservation of continuous quantity* Same as (1) except begin with vessels identically filled with a liquid.
4	9 to 10	*Conservation of weight* Same as (2) except questions concern weight of clay pieces.
5	10 to 11 (some data indicate concept not present in all college freshmen)	*Conservation of volume* Begin with identical glasses of liquid and balls of clay. First ball placed in a glass; liquid level rises. Second ball deformed; subject asked (1) if deformed piece placed in glass how high will liquid rise? and (2) do the two pieces take up same amount of space?

Auto-regulation (a term Piaget in his last works preferred to equilibration; Furth, 1969/1981) captures what Piaget means—organisms regulate their own behavior, their own adaptive fit; it is not blindly imposed on them by either environment (as empiricists argue) or genes (as maturationists say).

Cognitive development is driven by equilibration: assimilation and accommodation, reflective abstraction, and interiorization are all processes that alter the child's understanding, schemes, and operations in search of superior logico-mathematical knowledge, which uses the facts and concepts gleaned from experience. Therefore, equilibration and its various processes of logico-mathematical development are far more important than learning in accounting for intellectual development; from first to last it is equilibration that shapes perception, concept formation, and behavior. Auto-regulation is also responsible for the general restructuring of logico-mathematical knowledge that occurs three times in a child's life. Piaget believes that logico-mathematical knowledge can be described as a set of logical structures of schemes and/or operations, and that these structures are assembled in distinct ways at different points in cognitive development, moving from immediate, context-bound knowledge to abstract, context-free creative knowledge. Each structured ensemble of logico-mathematical structures defines a distinct stage in cognitive development.

Lawrence Kohlberg's Cognitive Stage Theory of Moral Development

One of Sigmund Freud's legacies to psychology was his treatment of morality as part of emotional and personality development. His focus on the feelings associated with morality, especially shame and guilt, has continued to be the focus of even anti-Freudian developmental psychologists. But as almost any philosopher of ethics would remind us, morality has a strong intellectual element, at the very least in weighing moral ends and calculating the best means to them. Influenced more by Piaget than Freud, Lawrence Kohlberg has redressed the imbalance by offering a cognitive developmental view of moral development.

One of Piaget's methods for investigating children's levels of moral understanding was to present them with a little moral anecdote and then ask the child questions about it. So the child might be told that while helping her parents prepare for a party, Sarah inadvertently broke a dozen records, while in a contrasting case Becky broke one record while playing in a closet she knew was forbidden to her. Subjects are asked which child had done the naughtier deed, which should be punished more, and why? Up until about age nine, children, in Piaget's terms, are moral realists, weighing right and wrong solely in relation to the objective damage done. So in the story above, Sarah is more in the wrong and more to be punished because she broke more records than Becky. After about age nine, children become moral relativists, judging actions more in relation to the virtue of the intent behind them. The moral relativist reverses the judgment of the moral realist, recognizing that Sarah was trying to be helpful, breaking the records out of clumsiness only, and condemning Becky's willful flouting of a clear rule, however slight the actual damage.

Beginning in 1958, Kohlberg (1958, 1971, 1969/1976; Kohlberg & Kramer, 1969; Rosen, 1980) has developed the Piagetian cognitive-developmental approach to morality into a comprehensive theory of moral development, including the assessment of stage of moral reasoning, a theory of stage-change, and plans for improving individuals' moral judgments.

Kohlberg's assessment instrument is a more structured form of Piaget's clinical method. A child (or adult) is presented with a series of dilemmas turning on a moral issue (e.g., is it right for a poor man to steal a rapaciously priced drug in order to save his dying wife?) and has to choose and defined a particular course of action, or condemn its opposite. These dilemmas are meant to measure a person's moral reasoning only, and not his likely moral behavior. Indeed, the same style of moral reasoning may yield different prescriptions for moral action.

Stages of Development

What emerged from Kohlberg's research was a multistage theory of the development of moral reasoning rather more complex than Piaget's. Kohlberg proposed somewhat different stage sequences in different publications over the years (Kohlberg, 1971; Kohlberg & Kramer, 1969; Rosen, 1980) and we list every stage ever proposed. There are three levels of morality, divided into two or three substages each (Table 10.4). Empirically, the preconventional levels are found in childhood, the conventional levels in most adults, and postconventional levels in a few superior men and women.

Positing a Stage 4½ (sometimes called 4B) was an awkward step forced on Kohlberg by the depth of his commitment to the cognitive-developmental research program. One of the central assumptions of Piaget's stage theory was that cognitive development proceeds universally through a fixed series of stages showing no regression from an attained higher stage to a lower one. However, in following Kohlberg's initial adolescent sample (Kohlberg, 1958) into their thirties, Kohlberg and Kramer (1969/1976) found evidence that many subjects who had initially tested as solid Stage 4 or even Stage 5 now seemed to reason at Stage 2! Unwilling to abandon

TABLE 10.4 Definition of Moral Stages

I. PRECONVENTIONAL LEVEL

At this level the child is responsive to cultural rules and labels of good and bad, right or wrong, but interprets these labels in terms of either the physical or the hedonistic consequences of action (punishment, reward, exchange of favors), or in terms of the physical power of those who enunciate the rules and labels. The level is divided into the following two stages:

STAGE 1: The punishment and obedience orientation. The physical consequences of action determine its goodness or badness regardless of the human meaning or value of these consequences. Avoidance of punishment and unquestioning deference to power are valued in their own right, not in terms of respect for underlying moral order supported by punishment and authority (the latter being Stage 4).

STAGE 2: The instrumental relativist orientation. Right action consists of that which instrumentally satisfies one's own needs and occasionally the needs of others. Human relations are viewed in terms like those of the market place. Elements of fairness, of reciprocity, and of equal sharing are present, but they are always interpreted in a physical, pragmatic way. Reciprocity is a matter of "you scratch my back and I'll scratch yours," not of loyalty, gratitude, or justice.

II. CONVENTIONAL LEVEL

At this level, maintaining the expectations of the individual's family, group, or nation is perceived as valuable in its own right, regardless of immediate and obvious consequences. The attitude is not only one of conformity to personal expectations and social order, but of loyalty to it, of actively maintaining, supporting, and justifying the order, and of identifying with the persons or group involved in it. At this level, there are the following three stages:

STAGE 3: The interpersonal concordance of "good boy–nice girl" orientation. Good behavior is that which pleases or helps others and is approved by them. There is much conformity to stereotypical images of what is majority or "natural" behavior. Behavior is frequently judged by intention— "he means well" becomes important for the first time. One earns approval by being "nice."

STAGE 4: The "law and order" orientation. There is orientation toward authority, fixed rules, and the maintenance of the social order. Right behavior consists of doing one's duty, showing respect for authority, and maintaining the given social order for its own sake.

STAGE 4½: Ethical egoistic orientation. Apparent Stage 2 reasoning by previously conventional Stage 4 person. Argues that all moral judgments are relative, that there are no moral absolutes, and that moral judgments are primarily emotional, not rational. Moral terms such as "duty" are dismissed as meaningless. Represents breaking up of conventional morality in preparation for Stage 5.

III. POSTCONVENTIONAL, AUTONOMOUS, OR PRINCIPLED LEVEL

At this level, there is a clear effort to define moral values and principles that have validity and application apart from the authority of the groups or persons holding these principles, and apart from the individual's own identification with these groups. This level again has three stages:

STAGE 5: The social-contract legalistic orientation, generally with utilitarian overtones. Right action tends to be defined in terms of general individual rights and standards, which have been critically examined and agreed upon by the whole society. There is a clear awareness of the relativism of personal values and opinions and a corresponding emphasis upon procedural rules for reaching consensus. Aside from what is constitutionally and democratically

(continued)

TABLE 10.4 *(Continued)*

agreed upon, the right is a matter of personal "values" and "opinion." The result is an emphasis upon the "legal point of view," but with an emphasis upon the possibility of changing law in terms of rational considerations of social utility (rather than freezing it in terms of Stage 4 "law and order"). Outside the legal realm, free agreement and contract is the binding element of obligation. This is the "official" morality of the American government and Constitution.

STAGE 6: The universal ethical principle orientation. Right is defined by the decision of conscience in accord with self-chosen ethical principles appealing to logical comprehensiveness, universality, and consistency. These principles are abstract and ethical (the Gold Rule, the categorical imperative); they are not concrete moral rules like the Ten Commandments. At heart, these are universal principles of justice, of the reciprocity and equality of human rights, and of respect for the dignity of human beings as individual persons. The Declaration of Independence is at Stage 6.

Source: Kohlberg (1971) except for the description of Stage 4½, which is based primarily on Kohlberg & Kramer (1969) and Rosen (1980).

the fixed-stage concept, Kohlberg denied that any of his subjects regressed, undergoing instead what he calls *retrogression* (Kohlberg & Kramer, 1969/1976).

Kohlberg argues that the subjects he tested had never really achieved Stage 4 or Stage 5 to begin with, and that their seeming to do so was a failing of the initial test instrument. Kohlberg's revised scoring system corrects those alleged errors. Stage 4½ represents a transitional stage between conventional and postconventional thinking, resulting from the breaking up of rigid, social-oriented conventional morality preparatory to the individual-rights centered philosophy of Stage 5. But in the meantime, there is an apparent return to egoism and a questioning of all absolutes. Kohlberg defends his view by pointing out that unlike real Stage 2 subjects, the Stage 4½ subjects still understand Stages 3 and 4, and can reason at those levels if asked to do so.

Kohlberg's rethinking of his scoring procedures also had the effect of eliminating Stage 6. It remains an ideal to be aimed at, and perhaps has been achieved by great minds such as Thomas Jefferson, author of the Declaration of Independence (and a slave-owner), but it no longer is the achievement of any of Kohlberg's subjects (Levine, Kohlberg, & Hewer, 1985).

Processes of Development

Kohlberg tended to see his theory of moral development as an extension of Piaget's theory into the moral realm, so he used Piaget's proposed processes of cognitive development to explain moral development. However, unlike Piaget, who rejected the American idea of trying to speed up cognitive development, Kohlberg's ultimate goal was to facilitate moral development. Kohlberg believed that it was possible to deliberately induce the process of equilibration and thus cause moral development to occur. Studies by Kohlberg and others (see Turiel, 1973) claimed that if presented with an array of answers to a moral dilemma, subjects typically chose as the best answer one that represented thinking from the next stage of moral development beyond their own. If, as cognitive developmental theory maintains, development is a process of successive equilibrations in resolution of cognitive conflict, this finding suggests that the best way to foster moral development is quite simple: promote discussions of moral issues. Any sufficiently heterogeneous group (a high school class, for example) will have members at almost all levels (save the first and the last), so that a person at Stage X will give arguments of that stage that will help another at Stage X + 1 move up, and will be exposed to argument at Stage X + 1, advancing his or her own development.

Testing Stage Theories of Development

Criteria for Evaluating Stage Theories

Piaget offered various criteria for defining true stages, and they have been usefully assembled by Pinard and Laurendeau (1969), Brainerd (1978a, 1978b), and Flanagan (1983):

1. Each stage must be **qualitatively different** and **more complex** from the previous stage. Piaget maintains that the growth of knowledge is more than the slow accumulation of facts and skills, but that the way children think at a given stage is qualitatively different from other stages. So at IIB there is a logic of functions, at IIIB a logic of classes, and at IV a logic of propositions.

2. Each stage is **more adequate,** that is, more adaptive, than the previous one.

3. The stages must follow each other in an **ordered sequence** such that
   a. the sequence is culturally universal
   b. it occurs in the **same order** for everyone
   c. all normal children **reach the last stage**
   d. there is **never regression** from a higher to a lower stage.

4. Each stage **subsumes** and **integrates** the abilities of the previous stage. The stages thus form a hierarchy such that the mental structures of the formal operational stage include and reintegrate concrete operational structures, which included and reintegrated functional and sensorimotor structures. Abilities from earlier stages are not lost or erased, therefore, but take a new place in the higher form of intelligence.

5. Each stage's schemes and operations form a **structured whole.** The schemes and operations do not exist simply as a collection of loosely connected parts but are integrated into a larger, overall structure, that is, the logic of classes or the logic of propositions.

Taken together, Piaget's claims assert that the development of intelligence is not a continuous process of growth, but is marked by leaps from one mode of knowing to a distinct, more adequate one, and that these leaps are made by all individuals in all cultures without backward steps. While development is thus not continuous, it is cumulative, since the structures of earlier stages are not abolished by later ones, but are restructured into a new and more adaptive way of knowing.

Evaluating Piaget's Theory of Cognitive Development

Piaget's genetic epistemology has naturally attracted a great deal of criticism, ranging from accusations of poor design and sloppy methodology (Gruen, 1966) to findings that his formulation of symbolic logic is inadequate (Parsons, 1960). Here, we will focus on attacks on Piaget's stage concept of development. Followers of Piaget have termed it a "key" part of the overall theory (Pinard & Laurendeau, 1969), and stage-thinking is characteristic of developmentalists generally. The central developmental force of equilibration is closely tied to the stages, for stage transitions come about because of equilibration, not learning. The postulation of real, explanatory stages is therefore perhaps the major issue that separates developmentalists from nondevelopmentalists.

Beginning with the simpler and more testable criteria, those concerning the ordered sequence of stages, we find that the empirical evidence is mixed. Criteria 3a and 3b from the list of criteria defining a true stage theory say the stage sequence must be culturally universal, and most cross-cultural Piagetian research indicates that children do pass through the stages up through concrete operations in the same sequence, with the speed of acquisition varying from culture to culture, usually as a function of degree of Westernization (Dasen, 1972). However, reaching the stage of formal operations is not a cross-culturally universal achievement, and the findings we discussed in Chapter 9 ("Thinking") suggest that formal operations are not routinely used even by scientists. Therefore, criterion 3c is not met, formal operations remaining an ideal to be aimed at, rather than a realistically achievable goal. Criterion 3d states there must be no regression from a higher stage to a lower. Temporary regression has been observed by Inhelder, Sinclair, and Bovet (1974) in experiments challenging the thought of early concrete operational children, by replicators of Piaget's memory studies (Liben, 1977), and suggested by a cross-sectional study of acquisition of conservation of liquid problems (Leahey, 1977c). While permanent regression would be a serious blow to Piaget's theory, temporary regressions may be only a sign of confused thought during the restructuring of cognitive structures taking place at stage transitions. On the other hand, an information-processing perspective could see temporary regressions as similar overgeneralization phenomena in language acquisition when learning a new rule leads to apparent loss of mastery of irregular forms. So regression could be the result of an incremental learning process and not a mark of stage boundaries. On the whole, data regarding criterion 3 is equivocal, offering neither clear support nor disproof of Piaget's stage hypothesis.

Criterion 2 claims that each stage is more adequate than the previous one. This criterion is more philosophical than empirical, and seems uncontroversial (Flanagan, 1983). Piaget's stages are so constituted that if they are real, clearly formal operations are more adequate—more adaptive—than concrete operations, which in turn, is an advance over sensorimotor intelligence.

The remaining criteria—that the stages are qualitatively different (1), that they form a hierarchy (4), and that each stage's structures form a structured whole (5)—are much more difficult to test and have been the subject of much controversy (Brainerd, 1978b, and subsequent commentary). Most observers agree that taken together, these criteria suggest that stages should appear relatively abruptly, as equilibration restructures thinking according to a new logic now applied to all experience. Three lines of research have been brought to bear on this empirical prediction: training studies, studies modifying the content of the standard Piagetian tasks, and studies of horizontal decalages, differences in the ages at which the same children master closely related cognitive tasks.

When Piaget attracted the attention of American psychologists during the cognitive revolution of the 1960s, they asked him a question that had not arisen during decades of research in Europe. The "American question," as Piaget called it, was: "How can we make the stages go faster?" Besides illustrating the American character, this question raises important issues about the unity of the stages (criterion 5) and the reality of equilibration. For if mastery of some Piagetian task (e.g., conservation of liquid) can be taught, it would undermine the concept of stages as structured wholes—only a single task is mastered—and support a learning as opposed to an equilibration account of development. Success in training would also suggest that various cognitive skills are learned piecemeal rather than appearing as part of an overall stage change.

For both practical and theoretical reasons, therefore, studies attempting to train children on Piagetian tasks became very popular (Brainerd & Allen, 1971) and were even carried out at Geneva by Inhelder and her colleagues (Inhelder and others, 1974). Overall, the studies show that a wide variety of techniques can be used to turn preoperational into operational reasoners for some skill area in a short period of time. However, interpreting these findings is difficult, since the results may be assimilated to Piagetian theory, and because there may be differences between trained and untrained children despite superficial similarities (Cromer, 1981).

Consider the classic training experiment by Smedslund (1961/1968), who trained children on conservation of weight. In the standard Piagetian form, a child is shown two identical balls of clay that the child acknowledges to be of the same weight. Then one ball is transformed, typically by rolling it into a sausage, and the question is repeated. The preoperational subject will now deny equality of weight, usually claiming that the sausage shape is lighter because longer, even when the child can pick up the pieces. The concrete operational child conserves weight, pointing out that the experimenter only altered the appearance of the clay, not its weight.

Smedslund pretested children on the standard task and then put the nonconservers through a training phase in which he used a balance to demonstrate several times that weight is unaffected by shape, the two pieces of clay remaining equal in weight before and after transformation. The nonconservers came to say that weight remains unchanged in the standard task. Smedslund now repeated the standard task with all subjects, except he secretly removed some clay during the transformation and used the balance to show a difference in weight. Smedslund found that trained conservers quickly reverted to nonconservation, concluding that sometimes weight does change when shape is changed. Natural conservers, on the other hand, stood their ground, insisting that weight must remain the same and that the experimenter must have somehow cheated.

Smedslund's results suggest that even if a training program appears to be successful, it may have had only a surface effect, engaging a child's verbal agreement but leaving untouched the deeper cognitive processes that change with development. Inhelder and co-workers (1974) argue, and provide data to show, that training can be successful only when, first the child is nearing stage transition anyway, and second, when it induces cognitive conflict by challenging the child's preoperational understanding. By creating disequilibrium, equilibration is brought into play, and the child is accelerated into operational structures. Therefore, the successful training studies can be explained as the creation of superficial verbal change or acceleration of a deeper change already underway.

Another empirical difficulty for the unified stage hypothesis is that different methods of assessment from those of Piaget's often find Piagetian concepts at much earlier ages than the standard tasks. For example, Gelman (1972) used conjuring techniques to violate conservation rules. Gelman found that very young children who failed ordinary number conservation tasks could detect when one penny was secretly removed from a small collection of coins (three or four), causing them to unfairly lose a game played with the experimenter, which indicates a sense of number conservation with small, but not large, arrays. There is now a large amount of data demonstrating similar effects for many Piagetian concepts (Gelman, 1978, 1983). Critics take such findings to indicate that concrete operational cognitive abilities are present very early in a child's life and grow slowly and incrementally, Piaget's apparently discrete stages being artifacts of his particular measurement tasks (Gelman, 1978; Donaldson, 1978). While these studies showed that some abilities appear much earlier than Piaget thought, other investigators found that adults do not understand some things they should (see Box 10.3).

This problem is linked to the broader and most serious one of what Genevans call *horizontal decalages,* or differences in the age of acquisition of behaviors supposedly depending on the same operational structures. A well-established decalage involves the conservations, all of which depend on concrete operational structures, according to Piaget. Table 10.3 shows the sequence of acquisition—stretching over at least five years—for several physical quantity conservations. Observe that all the tasks have the same structure: two quantities are established as equal, the shape of one is changed, and the subject asked if the quantity is still the same. Conservation of substance and weight are especially similar, yet appear about three years apart. Even slight changes in the material used can change the child's response from non-conservation to conservation (Uzgiris, 1964/1968).

The existence of decalages such as these suggests that cognitive development is not a very stagelike affair, proceeding, instead, in an incremental, but still orderly, way. Many critics of Piaget's stage concept have simply concluded that his stages should be taken as descriptive only, and that equilibration is an unnecessary and seemingly mysterious force (Brainerd, 1974a, 1974b, 1978a, 1978b; Flavell, 1971, 1977; Flavell & Wohlwill, 1969; Macnamara, 1976; Toulmin, 1971). Some neo-Piagetians have backed away from the stage hypothesis, asserting that while invariant sequence in the acquisition is an important part of Piaget's theory, the existence of large comprehensive stages is not (Gruber & Voneche, 1977), or have moved toward an information-processing view of cognitive development (Cellerier, 1971; Inhelder, 1972).

Evaluating Kohlberg's Theory of Moral Development

Kohlberg's theory is well known, influential, and controversial (Modgil & Modgil, 1986). Texts in introductory or developmental psychology discuss it at least briefly. Questions on teacher competence exams concerning ways to foster morality are based on the theory. Nevertheless, Kohlberg's work has serious deficiencies and some vocal detractors (for reviews see Flanagan, 1983; Kurtines & Greif, 1974; reply in Levine, Kohlberg, & Hewer, 1985).

To begin with, as a cognitive-developmental theory closely modeled on Piaget's, it faces all the difficulties of the latter, such as the problem of decalage. A subject's responses to Kohlberg's instrument may scatter over three or more stages, making it hard to determine the subject's "dominant" stage (Kurtines & Greif, 1974). A student of Kohlberg's, James Rest (Rest, 1986) has responded to such criticisms by creating a more structured assessment instrument, the Defining Issues Test. Rest is also less committed to stages than is Kohlberg.

Two special problems within the cognitive-developmental framework arise for Kohlberg's theory as compared with Piaget's. First, Kohlberg runs up against the intuitive and reasonable idea that development of reasoning about morals is different from development of reasoning about physical concepts (Flanagan, 1982a, 1982b).

LEARNING AND COGNITION

Intuitive Physics

As children, most of us tied something heavy to a string, twirled it around our heads, and then let it go. How much do we actually understand about such a familiar bit of physics? Even if we learn to hit a target with our primitive sling, do we grasp the principles underlying our behavior? The figure below shows a man twirling a ball on a string and releasing it when the ball is at the point of the filled-in circle. Which path shown will the ball subsequently take, Path 1 (left) or Path 2 (right)?

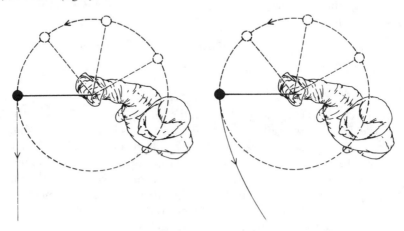

Michael McCloskey (1983) asked college students this and other questions testing their intuitive knowledge of physics, specifically concerning the laws of objects in motion. Fifty-one percent correctly chose Path 1, 30 percent incorrectly chose Path 2, and 19 percent made other errors. Path 1 is correct because according to Newton's laws of motion an object once set in motion will continue in a straight line unless acted on by an outside force. As long as it is held, the string acts as such a force and the ball moves in a circle. When the string is released its constraining force vanishes and the ball moves in a straight line. Path 2 would be expected from medieval impetus theory, which held that the circular motion would persist after the string was released, resulting in a curved trajectory. In other experiments, McCloskey found that many, sometimes most, of his well-educated subjects' intuitive physics was closer to medieval natural philosophy than to modern physics. Even having passed physics courses did little to alter students' folk beliefs.

Such findings pose a special problem for Piagetian theory, especially its account of formal operations. For here are familiar situations (every child has spun objects on a string, thrown and caught balls, and dropped objects while moving, providing rich opportunities for accommodation, assimilation, and reflective abstraction), yet conscious understanding of such activities is weak. They may be done—sensorimotorically—very well, even brilliantly as by sports stars, yet they are reflectively known very poorly.

In Piagetian terms, McCloskey's results provide further evidence that formal operations are not a universal achievement, Piaget has always held that at earlier stages consciousness

(continued)

knows only the products of cognitive operations, not the operations themselves. Here we see how hard it is for people to understand what they may do very well, and conscious understanding is a formal operational achievement.

More broadly, we again are reminded of the surprising gulf between behavior and insight. Much of what we do is learned effortlessly and without tuition. Yet being able to explain what we do, to understand it consciously, requires great effort, the insights of genius and deliberate education. And it is disappointing to the professor and scientist to find that years of education leave many young people back in the Middle Ages, behind Newton and far behind Einstein.*

* Read Michael McCloskey, "Intuitive Physics," *Scientific American,* April 1983, 248 (4), 122–130.

Every child everywhere grows up in the same physical universe—the laws of motion, matter, and mathematics are indifferent to a culture's beliefs. But not every child grows up in the same moral world. Each culture and subculture has its own values, religious beliefs, notions of justice, and procedures for righting wrongs; there is no underlying physical reality common to everyone in this domain. So our astonishment at Kohlberg's claim of universality and the data he offers to support it may be so great to make us doubt his test and his theory rather than doubt our belief that human cultures are morally heterogeneous (Reid, 1984).

The other problem faced by Kohlberg more than by Piaget is his claim that the final stage in his hierarchy is the most adequate. Whether or not Piaget has correctly described the most adequate form of scientific reasoning with his model of formal operations, at least it is easy to decide what kind of reasoning is more adequate when dealing with physical concepts: Which level of reasoning gives the better scientific answers, concrete or formal operations? Clearly, formal operations are more scientifically adequate. Kohlberg, however, has to claim that Stage 6 (or the newly combined Stages 5–6) is the most morally adequate stage.

From the time of David Hume, philosophers have agreed that one cannot derive moral principles (*ought*) from facts about nature (*is*). For example, smallpox is natural—it exists—but we do not conclude that we ought not eradicate it. Erroneously reasoning from *is* to *ought* is called the naturalistic fallacy, and Kohlberg, in his own words, tries "to commit the naturalistic fallacy and get away with it" (Kohlberg, 1971, p. 151). The incoherence of moving from "is" to "ought" is easily found in Kohlberg's theory. For years he argued that Stage 6 was clearly the highest form of morality but now says that almost no one reaches that stage, so now there is no "is" on which to base the "ought." And what about Stage 7? Furthermore, how can we assess any claim that the last stage is morally best? Kohlberg likes to point to a convergence between his Stage 6 and philosopher John Rawls' book *A Theory of Justice.* This, however, is just an appeal to authority that settles nothing. Another well-regarded Harvard philosopher is Robert Nozick, whose ethical theory *Anarchy, State, and Utopia* is libertarian, and looks like Stage 2. Perhaps, as Kohlberg (Levine, Kohlberg, & Hewer, 1985) once seemed to concede, his theory contains hidden ethical assumptions, and that it is therefore not a scientific theory in the usual sense. If this is true, he has recognized the futility of trying to commit the naturalistic fallacy, but at the same time withdrawn his theory from the realm of empirical evaluation.

Difficulties of claiming moral superiority for a given stage are pointed out by two arguments having a rather evolutionary air about them (unintended by their proponents, but see MacDonald, 1988, for an evolutionary psychology perspective on Kohlberg's work). Consider the following moral problem. A mother is on the shore watching her child and a stranger's child rowing a boat out on the lake. Suddenly, the boat capsizes and the helpless children are flipped into the water. The mother can save only one child. She swims out and saves the stranger's child, justifying her action with the clear Stage 6 assertion that all human lives are of equal value, so she flipped a coin saying, "Heads my child, tails the other child." Tails came up and she saved the other child (Flanagan, 1983). How do we feel about the mother and her actions? Flanagan and the people he has queried on this problem felt strongly that the mother did the wrong thing and that they would feel very strange around such a person.

What our example reveals is an important limitation on Kohlberg's theory; there is more to morality than the impersonal equal distribution of justice. In particular, it suggests that Kohlberg's highest stages represent the best way to administer justice in a particular social world, specifically our own modern, industrialized, impersonal West (Flanagan, 1983). In Chapter 2 we saw how modern society is quite unlike the societies that shaped human evolution and in which most people still live. In those societies, kinship still plays the most important role in regulating human affairs (see Chapter 14), and certain contemporary problems can be traced to the breakdown of kin ties. Our example reveals that kinship still plays a role in our concepts of right and wrong. Stages 5 and 6 describe right and wrong in a society of strangers—but not all human beings are unrelated strangers.

The second evolutionary-sounding difficulty concerns the claim made by Kohlberg's former student Carol Gilligan that women score lower than men on Kohlberg's scale. Now it seems extraordinarily unlikely that women are really less moral than men are. Gilligan (1977, 1979, 1982), has argued that Kohlberg's scale—based on the initial testing and continued following of 84 males—is sex-biased. She argues that men's concepts of morality focus on stern, abstract principles of justice rationally arrived at, whereas women are more attuned to personal relationships, to feelings, and to the unique context of particular moral problems. Gilligan states:

> Whereas the rights conception of morality that informs Kohlberg's principled level (Stages 5 and 6) is geared to arriving at an objectively fair or just resolution to the moral dilemmas to which "all rational men can agree," the responsibility conception focuses instead on the limitation of any particular resolution and describes the conflicts that remain . . . a woman in her thirties . . . says that her guiding principle in making moral decisions has to do with "responsibility and caring about yourself and others, not just a principle that once you take hold of, you settle (the moral problem)." The principle put into practice is still going to leave you with conflict. (1977, p. 482)

We can detect in this contrast of male and female moral styles the same sorts of sex differences surveyed in Chapter 14. From the earliest days, girls are more alert to emotional expression and nuances of feeling than are boys, and in women and men this carries through to a wide range of differences, including, we now find, differing conceptions of morality and justice. We should not conclude that women are less (or more) moral than men but that, to borrow Gilligan's phrase, they speak "in a different voice" about moral issues. If it is correct that much of human violence is instigated or at least abetted by moral imperialism—crusades against those labeled "evil"—as Alexander suggested (Chapter 14), then a voice of compassion and feeling is one that is well heeded. Impersonal abstract justice easily becomes persecution; morality erected on intimate personal ties does not.

Of the various deficiencies that mark Kohlberg's cognitive-developmental theory of moral development, the one that troubles most psychologists is its indifference to behavior. What practical good is high moral reasoning if it does little to reduce crime and war? Concern with moral behavior and its causes has characterized the major alternative to Kohlberg's stage theory, social learning theory.

In sharp contrast to Kohlberg's developmentalism, social-learning theory views personality and morality as learned, part of the overall socialization of children. Social-learning theory began some decades ago as an attempt to marry what were then seen as the artful insights of psychoanalysis with the scientific rigor of behaviorism (Dollard, Doob, Miller, Mower, & Sears, 1939; Dollard & Miller, 1950; Miller & Dollard, 1941; Whiting & Child, 1953). Over the years social-learning theory has changed, moving away from its Freudian roots and becoming, along with the rest of psychology, more cognitive (Bandura, 1982; Mitchell & Mitchell, 1976). Nevertheless, despite these changes and despite often strong disagreement among its proponents on theoretical details (Graham, 1972), the social-learning perspective maintains its emphasis on moral behavior and learning. In this section we will focus on the living and lively controversy (Wren, 1982), and following papers between social-learning and cognitive developmental theories of morality.

From a dynamic psychoanalytic perspective, conscience is built on feelings of shame, guilt, and moral rightness that are internalizations of parental punishment and reward. This accords well with any behavioral perspective, which holds that, because moral behavior is behavior, it must follow the usual laws of punishment and reinforcement. Morality, therefore, consists in learning to inhibit actions that are punished, and to perform those that are rewarded. So, for example, Aronfreed (1976) reports that children punished for choosing the more attractive of a series of toys quickly learn not to choose them. Furthermore in keeping with the standard laws of learning, this inhibition, or resistance to temptation, generalizes best to a test situation when the child is alone, if the punishment is delivered immediately after the "wrong" choice, rather than delayed. An inner moral agent—a conscience—is formed as the child internalizes moral rules and learns to regulate his or her own behavior rather than having to receive actual rewards and punishment (Aronfreed, 1976; Mischel & Mischel, 1976). That both cognition and affect are part of internal moral regulation is indicated by Aronfreed's further finding that punishment delivered with a plausible rationale was more effective in inducing later resistance to temptation than punishment alone.

Freud and the other psychoanalysts placed great stress on identification as a source of morality. Children identify with their parents first because they depend on them to meet their needs (anaclitic identification) and then because they fear them as punishing agents (identification with the aggressor); the latter is especially strong in boys' Oedipal period. Identification leads to imitation of the parents and the adoption (introjection) of the parents' values. While learning theorists play down the role of identification in socialization and speak of imitation as a direct behavioral copying of a model (Bandura, 1967), they agree with Freud that parents and others provide models of moral behavior from which their children learn right and wrong (Bandura, 1967; Bandura & Walters, 1963; Miller & Dollard, 1941; Rushton, 1982a, 1982b).

One particularly interesting source of models intensively studied by social-learning theorists is one Freud did not have to worry about: the mass media, especially television (Eron, 1982; Liebert & Poulos, 1976; Roberts & Bachen, 1981). Television and movies provide a wide range of possible models to imitate for good or ill. Social-learning theorists have investigated whether films as well as parents can influence behavior, and whether what children actually see on television does influence their behavior.

Beginning with the work of Bandura and his colleagues around 1960 (see Bandura, Ross, & Ross, 1961), the answer to the first question is quite clear. Laboratory experiments soon showed that viewing films or video can have dramatic impact on children's behavior. If children see an adult or another child being aggressive, especially if the actor is rewarded or not punished, children will later act aggressively in remarkably similar ways (Bandura, 1967).

While the results are not as dramatically unequivocal, it also appears that children's behavior is, in fact, affected by their exposure to real television, which is many hours each day. Most field research has focused on television violence, asking if it leads to increased levels of aggression or toleration for aggression in children (Eron, 1982) or even adults (Roberts & Bachen, 1981). The consensus of researchers is that it does (APA Monitor, 1983). Of particular concern is the self-reinforcing nature of aggressiveness and television watching: Children proven to be aggressive watch more violent television (Eron, 1982).

In contrast to Kohlberg's search for universal moral forms, social-learning theorists view morality as relative. Different cultures have different values and practices, so that people in different cultures espouse different moralities (Garbarino & Bronfenbrenner, 1976; Whiting & Child, 1953). Because parents have different child-rearing practices, different effects on moral learning should occur. For example, parents who use love-withdrawal rather than physical punishment as a discipline technique produce more moral children (Hoffman, 1976, 1979; Hoffman & Saltzstein, 1967), and this is particularly true of those who are authoritative—firm, but giving explanations of their actions—as opposed to authoritarian or permissive parents (Baumrind, 1971).

Finally, because social-learning theory focuses on the environmental determinants of behavior, social-learning theorists expect moral behavior to be situation-specific rather than consistent across situations. An especially distressing example of the situational specificity of morality is an experiment by Haney, Banks, and Zimbardo (1973). They built a simulated prison in the basement of the psychology department at Stanford University, and chose a group of male students to be either "prisoners" or "guards" for several weeks in this pretend prison. The subjects were screened for emotional stability and assigned randomly as "prisoners" or "guards." The researchers were shocked to discover that very quickly the "guards" became guards—brutal, domineering, and inhumane—and the "prisoners" became prisoners—fearful yet hostile, prepared to riot and rebel, or to go into depressive withdrawal. So vicious did the situation become that the experiment was ended very early. This study and others (see Milgram, 1974) seem to show that morality—indeed, perhaps personality—is not a permanent, enduring part of an individual, but a momentary product of his or her surroundings.

COGNITIVE DEVELOPMENT IN THE ARCHITECTURES OF COGNITION

The Symbol-System Architecture

Cognitive Development

Since the early 1970s [see McShane (1991) and Siegler (1998) for reviews], information-processing concepts have been applied to cognitive development as cognitive science extended its influence over human experimental psychology (Gopnik, 1996). While as yet there is no generally accepted theory of development from this perspective, two lines of research have been pursued by cognitive scientists: writing information-processing accounts of Piagetian problems and studying the development of standard information-processing topics such as memory (Brainerd & Pressley, 1987; Kail, 1984; Schneider, 1989), concept learning (Keil, 1989), and problem solving (Bjorklund, 1990; Siegler, 1999).

As an example of the former approach (rethinking Piaget) we may take the work of Klahr and Wallace (1973, 1976; Klahr, 1984; Klahr, Langley, & Neches, 1987; Wallace, Klahr, & Bluff, 1987) on the development of conservation. They view conservation as the induction of general rules—statements of conservations—reflecting what is learned about the invariance of physical properties despite apparent transformation.

Klahr and Wallace endow the young information processor with three quantification operators whose operations provide the data base for learning conservation rules. The first operator to appear in subitizing, an innate quantifier which applies only to very small arrays of discrete objects, never more than four. Subjects presented with such small displays just see without counting that there are 1, 2, 3, or 4 objects, even with very brief display times. The next quantification operator is counting, dependent on social learning, applicable in principle to any array of discrete objects, but that under time constaints is abandoned in favor of the third operator, estimation: No one tries to count the beans in a jar of jelly beans. Estimation also applies to continuous quantities, such as liquid amount, which cannot be quantified by subitizing or counting.

In each of its domains, conservation rule learning develops in the following manner. The child quantifies an array (e.g., two rows of six jelly beans each, by counting), sees one altered, as in the usual Piagetian task, and quantifies again, getting the same result. Eventually, repeated experience leads to rule induction: Number (or whatever attribute is at issue) remains invariant despite changes in appearance. The motivation for forming conservation rules is economy of processing. Simply knowing that a property is conserved eliminates the need for constant qualifications and comparisons.

The rule-learning approach easily explains some of the data—particularly the decalages—so troublesome for Piaget. Since development is seen as gradual (the slow accumulation of conservation rules) there is no reason to be troubled by an absence of sharp stage boundaries. Moreover, the observed decalages fit well with the theory. Subitizing is the most primitive quantification operator, possessed before counting is taught, and he found that very young children conserve small arrays but not larger ones. At the other extreme, a quantity like volume is very hard to estimate and is the last conservation learned, while more tangible, estimatable quantities such as weight form a middle ground between number and volume.

The detailed development of various cognitive domains has been extensively studied from the information-processing perspective (Gopnik, 1996; Siegler, 1998). The general picture that emerges has two main features: Piaget underestimated children's cognitive abilities and decalage is the rule rather than the exception. If one uses the right tasks, virtually any cognitive ability can be found in nascent form in infancy and it develops steadily and gradually over time.

Development of Memory

Let us take long-term memory as an example. In adults, long-term memory is typically studied using language (see Chapters 6 and 8). In many experiments, the materials to be learned are verbal, such as lists of words or passages of prose. When the experiences to be remembered are not verbal—as in the study of flashbulb memories—psychologists nevertheless ask subjects to recall the event and describe it in words. Such procedures obviously cannot tap the early development of memory, and developmental psychologists have devised nonverbal methods to study memory in infancy. Rovee-Collier (e.g., 1999), for example, developed overlapping tasks to measure memory in infants from 2 to 18 months old. The first, suitable for the youngest children, aged 2 to 6 months, was adapted from Piaget's informal experiments with Jacqueline described earlier. Babies lying in cribs have taped to their legs a string that can move a mobile suspended above them. Infants 6 months and older are trained to press a bar to make a small train run around a track in front of them. It is then possible to later re-present the same stimulus—mobile or train—and see if the baby recognizes it—that is, responds to it the same way. For both tasks, Rovee-Collier found a gradual increase in the length of time over which infants remember their earlier training.

Other lines of investigation have shown that all the various forms of short (Gathercole, 1999) and long (Rovee-Collier, 1999) memory are present in infants and young children, and that all the variables that influence adult memory influence children's memory. These findings make infantile amnesia—the fact that we remember little or nothing from the first few years of life—very difficult to explain (Eacott, 1999).

Since the time of Freud, psychologists have been puzzled by infantile amnesia, the fact that no one has good memories for the earliest years of his life. Freud thought that infantile amnesia was caused by wholesale repression meant to conceal sexual feelings for one's parents during early childhood. Freud claimed to have discovered in his own autobiographical memory a deeply hidden memory of feeling lust for his mother during a train trip at the age of $1\frac{1}{2}$, and immediately concluded it was a universal event in everyone's childhood, repressed because incestuous thoughts are deeply distressing. Cognitive psychologists are skeptical of repression and tend to regard Freud as a fantasist rather than a scientist. They look elsewhere for the cause of infantile amnesia.

Yet, as is so often the case with interesting but real-life psychological phenomena, infantile amnesia is hard to study scientifically. The first question is to determine when the period of amnesia ends. Freud thought that the primal repression of infantile memories took place at about six years, but modern studies asking people to report their first memory place the offset of infantile amnesia at about $3\frac{1}{2}$ to 4 years (Loftus, 1993).

However, it is hard to determine what weight to place on these reports, or to determine why some events are remembered and others are not. My wife's first memory, of being in a kitchen with her mother, cannot be true because their kitchen was arranged differently at the age she remembers. On the other hand, my parents confirmed the reality of my first memory from toddlerhood, of being lifted over a fence into a playground while a woman in an adjoining apartment—who had caused the playground to be fenced off—screamed at us. I remember that unique event, but I have not the slightest memory—even recognition memory—of the little blonde girl who my parents say was my closest companion that same year. A further puzzle of infantile amnesia is that while toddlers can remember events that happened some months before, these memories are lost in adulthood (Nelson, 1993).

Recently, Usher and Neisser (1993) have attempted to use a different technique, *targeted recall,* to probe early memories, assess their accuracy, and determine why some events are recalled and others are not. They located subjects who had experienced at least one of four target experiences that could be dated and verified, the birth of a sibling, a hospital stay of at least one night, the death of a family member, or a family move to a new home. The subjects were then asked a set of standardized questions about each event. Contrary to earlier studies, Usher and Neisser found that some memories—specifically those of a sibling's birth or a hospital stay—may be remembered from age 2, but not before. Memory onset for the other targets, death of a family member and moving, were in line with earlier studies. Thus one determinant of the offset of childhood amnesia is the nature of the remembered event.

Usher and Neisser propose that infantile amnesia has two sources. First, as we shall see, the hippocampus plays a key role in memory formation, but it is not fully developed until about two years of age, explaining amnesia for events before that date. Later amnesia occurs because early memories do not fit the schemas that adults use to encode and retrieve memories. It has been shown (Nelson, 1993) that young children tend to talk about the most mundane aspects of a day's experiences, not the surprising ones that adults fix on. Usher and Neisser suggest that parents carefully prepare children for hospital stays and sibling's births, naturally doing so from an adult point of view and therefore providing children with adult schemas to use to organize their experience. Because these memories are encoded in more adult form than other memories, they are more available when we are adults than memories encoded by childish schemas.

As is true of all psychological research, Usher and Neisser's study is useful, but not definitive (Loftus, 1993). For example, our earliest memories may be recalled not because of the effects of schemas, but because they are rehearsed later in life. I know that I discussed my memory of being lifted into the playground several times with my parents, but apparently never discussed my blonde friend. Therefore, it might be the later rehearsals of the event—like the later rehearsals of flashbulb memory—that keep some memories alive while others languish and die. One interesting suggestion is that the cause of infantile amnesia is more social than psychological (Nelson, 1992, 1993). We learned above that infants and young children do not lack any of the forms and processes of adult memory. However, while they store events, they do not structure them into coherent autobiographical narratives until middle childhood (Eacott, 1999). Telling chronological stories is a social skill that animals do not need, but which is important for human social interaction. Therefore it is possible that adults, whose lives are ordered along an autobiographical timeline—the story of the self in social context—have lost access to earlier memories which were not autobiographically encoded.

The issue of childhood memory is currently of great public interest because of well-publicized cases in which people in therapy claim to have remembered childhood abuse, typically sexual abuse, sometimes resulting in legal proceedings against the alleged perpetrators (see Chapter 6). The accuracy of these supposed repressed memories has become a highly controversial issue both in the public arena and in psychology. By and large, experimental psychologists, drawing on the kind of research on memory discussed in this chapter, tend to think that repressed memories are fantasies suggested by therapists and believed to be memories by patients. Clinical practitioners, on the other hand, tend to believe the stories, and to believe there is a long hidden epidemic of child abuse. Interestingly, Freud himself was told tales of childhood sexual abuse by his patients, and initially believed them, only to conclude later that they were disguised sexual fantasies, not real events. (Leahey, 2000).

Moral Development

Thomas R. Schultz (e.g., Darley & Schultz, 1990) has developed a production system theory for the study of moral judgment. As we have learned, Piaget's theory of cognitive development has been shown to underestimate children's cognitive abilities because of the difficult nature of the tasks he employed. Schultz advances a similar argument against Kohlberg. Kohlberg's findings suggested that moral development is very slow, and indeed is never completed in most individuals. However, to bring out his subject's reasoning, Kohlberg presented his subjects with difficult, even intractable, moral dilemmas to which there is no clear right answer. In his own work, Schultz studies reasoning about law-based cases that are concrete and straightforward, finding, as have others, that even young children show a good grasp of moral principles (Darley & Schultz, 1990).

Schultz's own model is called the Moral Reasoner (MR). The heart of the model is 39 if . . . then production rules such as this (modified from Darley & Schultz, 1990, p. 538):

If the protagonist [in a legal case] produced the harm,
and the protagonist's action was not accidental,
and the protagonist's action was voluntary,
and the harm was a foreseeable consequence of the protagonist's action,
and there was no intervening cause of the harm,
then the protagonist is morally responsible for the harm.

The model is then presented with cases like those presented to human subjects, coded for relevant variables such as the foreseeability of the harm in the case, and then reasons about issues such as responsibility, blame, and punishment. MR has been found to reach conclusions similar to those of human reasoners, for example, concluding that, if the harm was not foreseeable, the person who caused it should not be found responsible.

Development of Folk Psychology (Theory of Mind)

In Chapters 1 and 2 we discussed the idea that folk psychology—the theory of mind that we use everyday to explain our own and others behavior—might be an innate mental module whose evolution was crucial to the success of modern *Homo sapiens*. Research into the development of theory of mind in children has obvious bearing on these claims, and has been the single most active research area in cognitive development in recent years (Flavell, 1999).

The most widely used task for studying development of theory of mind is the false belief task. A child is told a story, sometimes aided by pictures, puppets, or videotape, which requires that he or she be able to attribute a false belief to a child in a story. For example, the subject sees a child put some chocolates in a green kitchen cabinet before going out to play. Then the child's mother moves the chocolates to another, blue, cabinet. The child returns home. The subject is then asked where the child will look for the chocolates. Passing this test requires a fairly sophisticated theory of mind. Even infants can distinguish intentional actions from mechanical ones (Johnson, 2000) and young children understand that people act so as to get what they want (Perner & Lang, 1999). However, passing the false belief task requires that the subject appreciate that the child in the story will act against his or her desires, looking for the chocolates in the wrong place. Typically, until about age 4 subjects say the child in the story will look in the blue cabinet, where they really are, rather than in the green cabinet where they were left. Some of the innocence we associate with young children may stem from their not yet having a theory of mind. Because they can't attribute false beliefs to other people, toddlers do not lie or deceive (Penner & Lang, 1999).

Interestingly, children and adults with autism (see Chapter 2; Frith, 1997) and the related disorder of Asperger's syndrome (Ellis & Gunter, 1999) show severe deficits on theory of mind tests, and, like children, are incapable of deceit and are easily taken advantage of (Sacks, 1995). Theory of mind deficits are also seen in some children with abnormalities other than autism. Peterson & Siegel (1999) administered theory of mind tests to normal, autistic, and deaf children who had different experiences with sign language and vocal language. One group of deaf children came from hearing families, and used sign language only in school. The second group was native signers—that is, at least one parent signed and so the children learned and experienced sign language at home from infancy onward. The third group of deaf children had hearing loss that could be corrected with hearing aids, and so had learned verbal language. As expected, autistic children did significantly worse than controls on the theory of mind tests. Among the deaf children, only the first group—children from hearing, non-signing families—showed a theory of mind deficit, doing about as well as autistics. Peterson and Siegel (1999) observe that autistic children almost never speak about mental states despite talking fluently about other topics. Similarly, deaf children who cannot converse with their parents at home will be similarly deprived of discussions of mental states, and may therefore fall behind in acquisition of theory of mind.

Development of theory of mind seems to be linked to development of self-control. For example, children who fail to pass the false belief test do poorly on tests that measure self-control such as a card-sorting task. Subjects are given a deck of cards with figures on then that might be sorted in a number of ways. The cards might show different geometrical forms also varying in size and color. The subject is told initially to sort the cards according to one rule (e.g., put the blue figures in one pile and the red ones in the other pile). After a while the rule is changed (e.g., put all the squares in one pile and all the triangles into the other). When the rule is shifted, children who fail the false belief task tend to *perseverate,* sorting by the old rule even when they can state the old rule. Autistics and people suffering from frontal lobe damage (see Chapter 12) show the same deficit.

The leading theoretical dispute concerning theory of mind and its development concerns whether it is a distinct and innate mental module or not. Autistics' unique theory of mind deficit supports the modularity thesis (Baron-Cohen, 1995). As we saw in Chapter 2, it seems likely that early *Homo sapiens* were strongly selected for skill at folk psychology, further supporting the idea that theory of mind is an innate and unique endowment of modern humans. Other psychologists resist the modularity thesis. Connectionists characteristically reject it, proposing that apparently innate, modular abilities emerge out of brain-environment interaction (Karmiloff-Smith, 1998). Happe (1999) argues that autism is a broad cognitive style rather than a specific deficit in theory of mind. She observes that autistics often have special abilities, such as skill at drawing or assembling jigsaw puzzles (see also Chapter 1, Mindblindness Box). They are also less fooled by some visual illusions, particularly those in which the illusion is created by surrounding context, such as the Titchener circles in Figure 10.1. Happe proposes that autistics possess weak "central coherence," meaning they tend to focus on the details of experience rather than the surrounding context. Similarly, Ellis and Gunter (1999) think that Asperger's syndrome, and perhaps autism, is caused by defective white matter in the cerebral hemispheres.

Support for the modularity of theory of mind comes from a quantitative genetic study of the development of theory of mind in a set of 238 monozygotic (MZ, or "identical") and dizygotic (DZ, or "fraternal") twins (Hughes & Cutting. 1999). Such studies make it possible to estimate how much a measurable biological or psychological trait is influenced by genetic factors, how much by shared environmental factors (aspects of twin's experience are the same for both, such as growing up in the same household), and how much by nonshared environmental factors (aspects of experience that are unique to each twin such as going to different schools)(Martin, Boomsma, & Machin, 1997). The researchers assembled ten tasks that measure theory of mind and administered the resulting scale to the twins, for whom IQ scores were also available.

FIGURE 10.1   Titchener Circles. The circles in the middle are the same size.

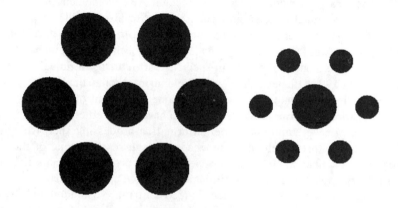

Correlations between MZ twins' scores ($r = .66$) on the theory of mind test were much higher than correlations between DZ twins ($r = .32$). They concluded that the primary influence on theory of mind performance was genetic, followed by the influence of the nonshared environment, with the shared environment having no measurable influence. Moreover, performance on the theory of mind scale was mostly independent of verbal IQ score. These conclusions suggest that development of theory of mind is independent of the development of general intelligence; being good at folk psychology is not simply a matter of being smart. It is important to note that the twins studied did not suffer from any psychopathology such as autism. This means that in the normal population there are natural differences in expertise at folk psychology. Indeed, Baron-Cohen (1998) thinks that all males are somewhat autistic.

Explaining Cognitive Change

The greatest challenge facing the cognitive scientist studying development is explaining how the processor changes (Sternberg, 1984). It is easy to write a simulation of the age 4 nonconserver and of the age 10 conserver; it is very much harder to get model 1 to change by itself into model 2, as the developing child does.

A sketch of an answer—it is no more than a sketch—has been essayed by Kail and Bisanz (1982). As we learned in earlier chapters, the major bottleneck in human information processing is the limited amount of attentional resources we have to allocate to different tasks. In the view of Kail and Bisanz, cognitive development is driven by dealing with this bottleneck, through maturational growth in total amount of resources (as the brain matures), or through increased availability of resources within an unchanging capacity as mental processes that were once conscious become unconscious and automatic—automatized—reducing their demand for attention.

Increased availability of attentional resources both facilitates and is made possible by knowledge modification processes. These are the agents of cognitive development, and they consist of two main operations; first, adding or deleting memory nodes and connections (representations) in LTM, or control processes; and second, strengthening or weakening connections in LTM. Change is abetted by the performance monitors that detect inconsistencies to be eliminated, such as believing whales are fishes while knowing they are warm blooded and nurse live-born young, or regularities that can be more simply handled (as when a conservation rule is induced based on observed regularities in quantification operations), in the Klahr and Wallace model of conservation. Information-processing theories of cognitive development invoking similar mechanisms are offered by the authors collected by Sternberg (1984).

Cognitive schema theory has been applied to cognitive development by Vosniadou and Brewer (1987). Following Carey (1985), they distinguish between global restructuring of thought and domain-specific restructuring of thought (see also Wellman & Gelman, 1992). Piaget's theory of development through qualitatively different stages involves global restructuring, when the mode of thought of a new stage supplants the mode of thought of the previous stage. We have reviewed evidence that casts doubt on the stage concept, and like other information-processing theorists, Vosniadou and Brewer argue that development proceeds through restructuring of thought limited to specific content areas. In their view, development proceeds piecemeal, as children master different tasks and domains through experience and teaching.

As examples of domain-specific restructuring, Vosniadou and Brewer cite studies of the novice-expert shift carried out with adults. Cognitive scientists have studied in a variety of fields from chess to physics the differences between novices and experts. Two kinds of change seem to take place as one acquires expertise. Weak restructuring is the accumulation of knowledge in an area; radical restructuring involves the creation of new schemas to organize knowledge. Thus, experts are different from novices not only in how much they know about their field, but also in how they think about and perceive it. As information-processing theorists, Vosniadou and Brewer do not distinguish between child mind and adult mind, suggesting that cognitive development proceeds through the same kinds of domain-specific restructurings, both weak and radical, that characterize the novice-expert shift. In short, children are novices at everything, and become experts at adult life through episodes of domain-specific restructuring. Vosniadou and Brewer advocate teaching through analogy— application of familiar schemes to new domains, and Socratic dialogue—helping the child find and resolve inconsistencies in his or her understanding of a topic—as the best ways of fostering radical restructuring.

To what extent are information-processing theories of cognitive development truly developmentalist? Klahr (1984) argues that information-processing theories that posit self-modifying mechanisms of cognitive change, such as his, Kail and Bisanz's (1982), and Vosniadou and Brewer's, capture "the essence of development" and are not simply theories of learning. He points out that such models involve internally based mechanisms that produce spontaneous change not caused by reinforcement, and that the changes produced are qualitative and structural, not just quantitative and local. Thus Klahr's own theory of conservation acquisition posits an internal mechanism that monitors past and present quantitative transformations looking for consistencies that can be used to formulate conservation rules going beyond the currently given information.

Against Klahr's position, however, stand two important differences between information-processing theories and traditional developmentalist theories such as Piaget's. As we have seen, information-processing theories propose that cognitive change is domain-specific, not global, denying the existence of the stages that are the hallmark of developmentalist theorizing. More important, developmentalist theories are heirs to historicism, holding that development is guided toward a final goal by an autonomous process pressing thought to progress to the best possible cognitive adaptation. Information-processing theories are not teleological, seeking at best only adequate, not ideal, adaptation. Lacking a teleological drive for perfection, information-processing models are driven more by experience and teaching than are developmentalist models. Klahr is no doubt correct in asserting that self-modifying information-processing theories are more developmental than behaviorist-conditioning theories, but they are still much less developmental than Piaget's.

One fundamental issue remains unresolved by the information-processing perspective. Piaget's stage theory claimed that cognitive development preceded by global restructuring through qualitatively different stages, is denied by the information-processing theory (Darley & Schultz, 1990). However, what remains disputed is how much qualitative developmental change occurs if we reject the stage conception of cognitive growth. On one end of the controversy, a number of developmental psychologists have embraced a neonativist (Fischer & Bidell, 1991) conception of development (Karmiloff-Smith, 1991) in which the core of cognitive abilities is given innately, and these are simply enriched and improved, but not fundamentally changed, by experience (Spelke, 1991).

On the other hand, Carey (1991), argues that, while cognitive change is domain-specific, genuine conceptual change takes place within domains, so that in partial accord with Piaget, children think differently at different ages. For example, Carey argues that young children fail to distinguish density and weight, holding an undifferentiated concept of weight/density. Until they are 12, few children can order a set of objects separately by weight and by density, even with scales present. Older children and adults can separate the two, suggesting that the weight/density concept of children is qualitatively different from adult concepts of density or weight.

Resolving this issue will prove difficult, since it is impossible to directly penetrate children's minds. As Carey (1991) points out, when a young child tells us that a grain of rice has no weight, we can interpret his or her belief in two ways. On the Spelke view, the child has a false belief about the weight of rice, but basically understands weight the way adults do, and will correct his or her belief about rice eventually. On Carey's interpretation, the child possesses a different conception of weight from adults, and his or her belief about the rice is true given his or her understanding of weight. Deciding between these interpretations has long bedeviled the history and philosophy of science, as Carey points out, and now confronts developmental psychologists.

THE BIOLOGY OF DEVELOPMENT

The Connectionist Perspective

Connectionist models of development have been proposed in a number of domains, but they are too technical to review here (see Plunkett & Elman, 1997 for working examples). More importantly, connectionists have proposed ways to rethink controversies over innateness and directed development. It is in the areas of cognitive and language development that the connectionist architecture still sharply challenges rival theoretical frameworks (Elman et al., 1997; Johnson, 1997).

Given the nature of connectionist models, it is no surprise to find that connectionists view development as taking place gradually instead of in stages. As we learned in Chapter 2, neural networks are slowly shaped by training into organized structures. Therefore, connectionists reject Piaget's idea that development is an inner-directed process of unfolding logical structures. Instead, they see development as subject to constraints whose collective effect is to seemingly "direct" cognitive development to its final, adult, form. Connectionists identify four types of constraints on cognitive development (Elman et al., 1997):

1. *Representational constraints.* Connectionists wish to ban the term "innate" from the study of development (Johnson, 1997), but "representational constraints" refer to the traditional concept of innate ideas (Elman et al., 1997). Like empiricists and Piaget, connectionists reject the existence of innate ideas, and are especially critical of Chomsky's Cartesian linguistics (see Chapter 11). The only form of innate "representations" they accept are innate weightings of the human neural network, the brain. In Chapter 2 we saw that in AI work neural networks' connection weights are randomized before training. As the existence of prepared and contraprepared learning (see Chapter 3) demonstrates, the synaptic connections of animal brains are not set at random values. In connectionist terms, many of the connections between neurons come with preset values, so that some associations are easy to learn while others are hard to learn.

2. *Architectural constraints.* Throughout this book we have discussed theories that view the brain/mind as a connection of domain-specific "modules" dedicated to solving particular problems or processing certain kinds of information. Connectionists vehemently reject the idea of innate mental modules; indeed it is their central theoretical claim (Elman et al., 1997). Like Piaget, they believe that the brain is a general-purpose device, though its purpose is not logical thinking as it was for Piaget, but connection-making. They believe that modularity emerges from the self-organization of initially diffuse neural networks: "modularization [i]s the end product of development rather than its starting point" (Elman et al., 1997, p. 115). The architectural constraints recognized by connectionists have to do with the structure of the brain as an organ, from the structure and types of different nerve cells, to the columnar architecture of much of the cortex, to the larger structures such as the limbic system and the lobes of the cortex.

3. *Chronotopic constraints.* Biological development often occurs on genetically controlled time schedules. The most obvious example is puberty, which does not occur at random in human lives, but at about 12–13 years, when a cascade of processes occur together. Similar processes operate in the development of the brain and nervous system, and are only now beginning to be understood. For example, it used to be thought that the brain changed very little after infancy, but this is not so. Recent research shows that the brain undergoes dramatic transformations in different areas at different ages from infancy to adolescence (Suplee, 2000, March 9). For example, neuron growth in the frontal lobes, responsible for rational thought and planning (see Chapter 12), explodes at the beginning of adolescence, and is pruned back in the 20s. Thus, "The teenage years," says neuroscientist Jay Giedd, "are a kind of critical time to optimize the brain" (Suplee, 2000, March 9, p. A14).

4. *The primal environment.* Connectionists tend to be empiricists, seeing the mind as mostly shaped by experience rather than innate factors. Like empiricists, connectionists point out that while some features of the environment differ from place to place on Earth, many do not. All humans experience the same gravity, the same basic natural materials (earth, air, fire, water, etc), the same sun and moon, the same bodily feelings, and so on; these common features constitute the *primal environment* (Johnson, 1997). Thus, as empiricists held that experience writes the same truths on the human mind, connectionists hold that all human minds are subject to nearly identical training sets, and so come to resemble one another.

In general, although they disagree with Piaget on the existence of stages of development and on the existence of psychological forces such as equilibration, connectionists see themselves as constructivists (Johnson, 1997), specifically, neuro-constructivists (Karmiloff-Smith, 1998). Like Piaget, their thinking is influenced by the biologist Waddington's idea of *probabilistic epigenesis* (Johnson, 1997, see Figure 10.2). As the ball rolls down the hill, there are several paths it might take, but some are more likely than others. Moreover, taking a certain earlier path forecloses taking certain later ones. These paths represent the various constraints on development. Development does not follow a linear path to a foretold, necessary end, but some developmental outcomes are more likely than others, and the environment can nudge—but not strictly control—what the final outcome will be. The end result of development is thus a complicated and drawn out interaction between what is given innately, inputs from the environment, and the accumulating effects of learning. Epigenesis represents a middle path between radical empiricism, in which

FIGURE 10.2 The epigenetic landscape.

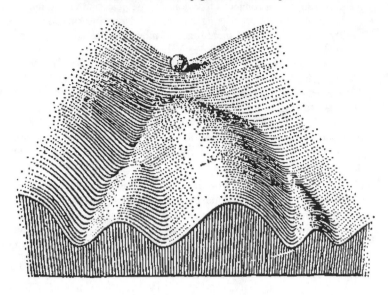

the environment determines everything, and strong nativism, in which the genes determine everything.

BIOLOGY OF DEVELOPMENT

Neural Development

Along with the rest of the body, the nervous system continues to develop after birth (Siegler, 1998). To illustrate the neuropsychology of development, we will review findings from two experimental paradigms: depriving young animals of visual experience during early stages of visual development, and rearing animals in varying conditions of environmental richness. In both cases, investigators try to assess the effects of experience on the structures of the nervous system (see Black & Greenough, 1991, for a review).

Mammals reared in the dark show abnormal visually guided behavior. For example, one test of depth perception is the visual cliff, which invites animals placed on the top of a laboratory cliff to step off into space, the animal being protected from harm by a layer of glass. Normally reared kittens refuse to step over the cliff, but kittens reared since birth in the dark go right ahead. In a study of more specific deprivation, kittens were reared in a contrived environment that keeps them from seeing vertical lines. The kittens developed into cats who walked into table legs and who didn't play with strings dangled in front of them, but could jump onto chair seats and tables, suggesting that they simply did not see vertical lines. Kittens reared in environments without horizontal lines show reverse defects.

Not surprisingly, visual deprivation causes quantitative and structural changes in the brain. Neurons in the visual cortex of visually deprived cats have fewer dendritic branches and fewer synapses per neuron than in normal cats. The orientation of dendrites in Layer III pyramidal cells of the visual cortex was differentially affected in the kittens raised in oppositely striped environments. Dendrites were oriented in one direction only, perpendicular to the lines to which the kittens were exposed, so that the kittens in each group had oppositely oriented dendrites.

A number of studies have examined the effects of rearing rats alone in normal laboratory cages (deprived condition), in groups in normal laboratory cages (deprived-social condition), and in groups living in large cages with toys that are changed every day (enriched condition). Profound behavioral differences result from differential rearing: Enriched-condition animals are superior at learning mazes under almost all conditions, with deprived-social rats showing only modest superiority to deprived rats. Behavioral differences are mirrored in changes to the rats' brains. Compared to either group of deprived rats, the brains of enriched-condition rats are heavier, possess more dendrites and have larger dendritic fields, have larger cell bodies, possess more glial cells, and have more synapses per neuron. Differences between deprived and deprived-social rats' brains have been found to be small to nonexistent. These effects are not dependent on age, but can occur when animals are differentially raised beginning in adolescence. Finally, active use of the enriched environment is necessary to cause changes to the brain; rats raised as a group in a small cage inside an enriched environment had brains identical to those of deprived rats.

It is clear that the mammalian nervous system does not simply mature independently of experience, but is affected by the kind of environment in which the growing young animal lives. Black and Greenough (1991) propose that there are two kinds of neural plasticity underlying nervous systems' response to the environment, namely, experience-expectant plasticity and experience-dependent plasticity. Because many features of the world are stable from generation to generation, organisms have evolved to expect certain kinds of experiences to be reliably available, providing input to activate preadapted parts of the brain. For example, in any normal environment visual lines of all orientation are found, and different pyramidal cells of the cat's visual cortex have evolved to be activated by and attuned to these different kinds of visual input. This is experience-expectant plasticity: Parts of the nervous system expect and are sensitive to standard, expectable, environmental events. On the other hand, an animal's brain must be able to master novel problems and be appropriately changed by unique and unfamiliar aspects of the particular environment in which an individual organism happens to be born. Such neural plasticity is what we usually call learning, but is what Black and Greenough dub experience-dependent plasticity.

Black and Greenough propose that different mechanisms of neural change underlie the two types of plasticity. With regard to experience-expectant plasticity, studies of the maturation of mammalian nervous systems (including the human) have shown that the number of dendrites and synapses in many parts of the brain peak sometime in childhood and then fall off in number as the organism enters adulthood. Connections in the nervous system seem thus to be at first overproduced and then weeded out as development proceeds. The nervous system appears to prepare for expected experience by proliferating neural interconnections from which experience, acting like natural selection in evolution, eliminates unneeded connections and preserves useful ones. The mechanisms of experience-dependent plasticity involve growing new synapses between neurons, thus encoding permanent memories.

CONCLUSION: CONSTRAINTS ON DEVELOPMENT

Piaget began to study development when, as a young man, he administered intelligence tests to children. He observed that children of about the same age who missed the same item nevertheless give similar or identical wrong answers. This is surprising, because although there is only one right answer to a question, there are many wrong answers, yet children only gave one. The same remarkable point emerges from Piaget's studies of development, which elaborated and explored his youthful finding. Consider conservation of amount, for example: Before Piaget no one had even noticed that young children believe that the amount of water changes when you pour it; of course, children have never been instructed about conservation, yet all children in all cultures move through the identical sequence of conservation acquisition. It appears that cognitive development proceeds the same way everywhere on the globe, independent of teaching and culture. Although no two children are exactly alike, general process of development appears to be uniform. Contrary to behaviorists, it seems clear that children are not simply shaped by reinforcement contingencies, which led Piaget to propose his teleological equilibration model of development through stages.

But teleology is suspect among scientists, and we have seen that Piaget's claim of qualitatively different stages of thought is shaky and is being abandoned in favor of information-processing theories of cognitive development. Yet information-processing psychologists must face Piaget's great insight that development is remarkably uniform and individual differences narrow. Biological thinking has supplied an answer to similar phenomena in other areas. Language acquisition appears to move along similar lines in all children, and it is plausible to suppose that this is so because of innate constraints on the kinds of languages humans can learn and be exposed to. Similarly, learning psychologists have come to recognize that what and how an animal learns is constrained by the genetic legacy of its environmental history. Perhaps the concept of biological constraints can be fruitfully applied to development, seeing it as a process or set of processes operating within biologically given constraints, such that development is guided—without stages and without a Lamarckian goal—within a range of possible individual differences. Frank Keil (1981, 1984) has proposed just such an approach to cognitive development.

Keil offers a quotation from the American philosopher Charles Sanders Peirce (1839–1914), who first proposed the constraints approach, nicely summarizing its basic argument:

> Suppose a being from some remote part of the universe, where the conditions of existence are inconceivably different from ours, to be presented with a United States Census Report which is for us a mine of valuable inductions, so vast as almost to give that epithet a new signification. He begins, perhaps, by comparing the ratio of indebtedness to deaths by consumption in counties whose names begin with different letters of the alphabet. It is safe to say that he would find the ratio everywhere the same, and thus his inquiry would lead to nothing. The stranger to this planet might go on for some time asking inductive questions that the Census would faithfully answer without learning anything except that certain conditions were independent of others. . . . Nature is a far vaster and less clearly arranged repertoire of facts than a Census report; and if men had not come to it with special aptitudes for guessing right, it may well be doubted whether in the ten or twenty thousand years that they may have existed their greatest mind would have

attained the amount of knowledge which is actually possessed by the lowest idiot. But, in point of fact, not man merely, but all animals derive by inheritance (presumably by natural selection) . . . classes of ideas which adapt them to their environment.

Side by side, then, with the well-established proposition that all knowledge is based on experience, and that science is only advanced by the experimental verifications of theories, we have to place this other equally important truth, that all human knowledge, up to the highest flights of science, is but the development of our inborn animal instincts. (Keil, 1981, p. 199)

There is nothing very mysterious about Keil's argument that cognitive ontogeny is subject to innate constraints, for it, along with the language-learning constraints theory of Chomsky and Wexler and Cullicover, is simply an extension of well-established views in sociobiology and animal learning applied to human beings. In Chapter 4 we saw that animal learning is constrained—some things are easy for a given species to learn, others difficult. It is important to see that the idea of modern nativism departs from the stereotypical view of innate behaviors as rigidly preprogrammed. Conditioned nausea is both learned, as experience is needed to learn what causes illness, and innate, as rats, by virtue of their evolution, learn to avoid poisonous foods by taste cues, while birds, by virtue of their evolution, learn to avoid them by visual cues.

Richard Coss' (1985) investigations of the evolution and learning of ground squirrel antisnake behaviors provide a good example of how evolution constrains development, and how experience affects the course of evolution. Ground squirrels living in many parts of North America are subject to predation by gopher snakes and rattlesnakes, the latter being more dangerous because they are poisonous as well as carnivorous. Ground squirrels in snake-infested habitats respond with alarm calls, tail waving, and a variety of harassing attacks, including throwing dirt and sticks at the predator. However, in some areas either rattlesnakes, gopher snakes, or both are no longer threats to squirrels, and Coss has studied how evolving in different habitats for different amounts of time has affected ground-squirrel behavior.

In one experiment, Coss compared the antisnake behaviors of two groups of squirrels, one caught in a habitat infested with both rattlesnakes and gopher snakes and the other group caught from an area free of rattlers but not of gopher snakes. Squirrels from the latter area were much bolder in approaching the three kinds of snakes to which they were exposed, rattlers, gopher snakes, and garter snakes, reflecting the greater threat of rattlers. That these differences were primarily hereditary was shown by exposing a garter snake to laboratory-reared pups born from each. Pups from the population predated by both rattlers and gopher snakes were much more cautious in approaching the test snake than were pups from the rattler-free population.

An additional study shed more light on the evolution—specifically, the loss— of antisnake behavior. Three groups were studied: The first group was caught in Folsom State Park, where rattlesnakes are common but gopher snakes are quite rare. A second was trapped at Lake Tahoe, free of both kinds of snake. The third group came from the Sacramento delta, where there are no rattlers, but some gopher snakes. Using molecular clock techniques (see Chapter 12), it was determined that the first two groups had been isolated for about 35,000 years, the third for about 85,000 years. After living for nine months in laboratory enclosures simulating wild conditions, each group was exposed over several trials to either rattlesnakes or gopher snakes. Persistence of genetic knowledge over thousands of years was revealed by the Lake Tahoe squirrels, who reacted to both kinds of snakes in typical ways, including jumping back after approaching a rattler in order to avoid its venomous strike. Thus, ground squirrels' innate knowledge of rattlesnakes included not just response to it as a threat, but knowledge of what rattlers do. Experience can modify genetic patterns, however, as shown by the Folsom squirrels, whose experience with rattlesnakes in the wild had made them wary, approaching snakes cautiously and soon avoiding them altogether. The behavior of the Delta population revealed antisnake behavior in the process of being lost. Some of the animals behaved toward snake threats in the same excited way as the Folsom group, whereas others engaged in antisnake tactics only sluggishly, and seemed to habituate to the snake's presence, ceasing to regard it as a threat. It appears that genetic knowledge of snakes persists at least 35,000 years, but begins to be lost after 85,000 years.

Follow-up research was conducted with other groups of ground squirrels. Arctic ground squirrels have lived without snake predation for 3 million years. When tested, they responded to rattlesnakes as interesting novel objects despite numerous strikes and rattled warnings, suggesting that innate knowledge of snakes as threats can persist for perhaps 100,000 years, but not 3 million. In a related experiment, two groups of pups from two ground-squirrel groups were tested. One group came from a population exposed only to gopher snakes, the second to both types of snakes; the populations had diverged about 3,000 years ago. Pups from the second group distinguished between the two species of snake, regarding rattlers as the greater menace. The first group was vigilant about both kinds of snakes, but did not treat the rattlesnakes differently from the gopher snakes. Because these were lab-reared, snake-inexperienced pups, it appears that knowledge about snakes can begin to be affected differentially by evolution in fewer than 3,000 years, a remarkably brief span of time on the evolutionary time scale.

Coss concludes that "learning is part of a continuum of adjustment over phylogenetic [evolutionary], ontogenetic [developmental], and proximate [immediate response] time scales." An organism's adjustment to—knowledge of—its environment is based first of all on its genetic heritage, which is shaped by evolution over thousands of years to its subspecies' habitat. Thus, even as pups without experience of snakes, different subspecies of ground squirrels react differently to snakes. The individual's genetic base guides development, combining innate knowledge with individual experience to produce an adult whose behavior is well tuned to its own surroundings. Hence, adults in snake-infested areas, equipped with antisnake behavior by their genes, have learned to be wary of snakes, attacking them less vigorously than inexperienced pups. Finally, the developed organism must constantly monitor its immediate, short-term environment for challenges and opportunities. Thus, mature ground squirrels when they encounter a snake muster their genetic resources and learned caution to treat it as the serious threat it is.

If outmoded ideas about evolution and genetics can be discarded, developmentalists and cognitive-learning theorists may be reconciled. Like the defensive behaviors of ground squirrels, human knowledge, personality, and even morality are both innate and learned; they develop through universal patterns set by genetic constraints within which learning acts to produce each individual's path of development.

SUGGESTED READINGS

The best general survey of theories of development is Alfred Baldwin's *Theories of Child Development,* 2nd ed., 1980. Baldwin is weak on the information-processing view that now dominates cognitive development, but a fine survey is provided by McShane (1991), who carefully considers the issue of levels of theory in cognitive development, and Siegler (1990), who takes a broader perspective. On the intersection of evolution and development, see Butterworth, Rutkowska, and Scaife (1985). Two recent collections survey the interface between cognitive development and biology: Carey and Gelman (1991) focus on conceptual and theoretical issues, while Gibson and Petersen (1991) focus on empirical findings from neurophysiology and genetics.

11   Language Development

Whatever else may be unique about the human species, there is no doubt that our most important single possession is language. Language makes human culture possible, creating the coevolution of biology and society that is uniquely human. We can express and explore ideas and feelings in ways unknown to the animal world. With language we can communicate, entertain, and rhapsodize. Without language we would surely not be human.

But important as language is, is it special? Is human language a particular and unique species-specific human trait—as is the opposable thumb—or is language a consequence of other, more general learning and cognitive abilities, and therefore unique to humans (if it is unique) only because our conceptual powers are so highly developed? This question, which is very old but still controversial, will occupy us in this chapter.

BEHAVIORISM AND LANGUAGE

The shared attitude of the behaviorists (see Mowrer, 1954; Osgood, 1963/1967; Skinner, 1957) was that "we neither wish nor require any special theory for language" (Osgood, 1963/1967, p. 110). Language was viewed as just another (albeit complex) behavior to be explained by behavior theoretic principles, and its acquisition was explained as processes of classical and/or operant conditioning. For example, Mowrer (1954) described semantics in terms of classical conditioning. Word meanings are acquired as CSs paired with the objects or actions they designate (USs) with the result that some component of one's reactions to objects and actions comes to be elicited by words; this component is the word's "meaning." B. F. Skinner, on the other hand, described language learning as a process of operant conditioning, as we saw in Chapter 4.

What we have already learned about language in earlier chapters suggests that behaviorist accounts of language are implausible at best (Chomsky, 1959). Interestingly, though, whatever their other differences with behaviorists, cognitive psychologists by and large agree that language is not special, but is just an expression of complex information-processing abilities. In this they differ from the followers of Noam Chomsky, the major modern proponent of the idea that language is a unique, species-specific human adaptive organ.

COULD LANGUAGE BE INNATE?

Noam Chomsky calls himself a **Cartesian linguist** (Chomsky, 1965b) for believing in language's uniqueness to human beings and its creative power. René Descartes

(1596–1650) followed the older rationalist philosophical tradition of Plato in maintaining that some of our ideas are **innate.** For example, Descartes held that one's idea of God is innate for we know about God without ever having met God. Similarly, many mathematical truths are known without being based on experience. If $A = B$ and $B = C$, we know immediately that $A = C$, and this is an abstract truth not derived from experience. It is an unlearned, innate truth. Of course Descartes, like Plato before him, did not think that little babies can do math. Rationalists allow a role for experience as an activator of innate ideas, a concept quite in keeping with modern genetic thinking.

Unlike Plato, Descartes—and Chomsky—assigned a special role to language. Descartes argued that only human beings think, have ideas to express, and so only human beings have language, which is the expression of thought. Language is therefore specific to the human species, because animals do not think. A later Cartesian, Julien Offroy de la Mettrie (1709–1751), however, proposed that at least some animals could think and therefore could learn language. Specifically, he suggested teaching language to an ape, making him a "perfect little gentlemen." La Mettrie's research proposal was finally carried out some two centuries later, as we shall see.

While Chomsky's proposal that language is innate is in the Cartesian tradition (but see Aarslef, 1982), he views language as even more special than Descartes did. Descartes viewed language as the expression of cognitive processes unique to humans, thereby making language unique to humans. But as la Mettrie's argument shows, if animals can think, however simply, they can possess language, however simple. Chomsky goes further, proposing that language has the general properties of an organ of the body (Chomsky, 1976, in following discussion). For Chomsky, then, language is something very special indeed—the function of an innate language faculty—and not the result of anything else, of learning or cognition, or thinking.

Chomsky's major contribution to linguistics is his powerful analysis of syntax, transformational grammar. There are several insights from the study of syntax that he brings to bear on formulating the problem of language acquisition.

To begin with, as we learned in Chapter 7, language possesses an invisible structure—**syntax**—that is not given by spoken words themselves, but must be applied by the listener. The hidden syntactic structure of language is important to defining the language acquisition problem in two ways. First, since as adults we use syntax to understand sentences, we must have acquired these rules somehow as children. In our society we tend to think we were taught them directly; we all remember grammar drills at school and being corrected for certain grammatical errors ("Me and Jimmy went . . ."). However, in preliterate cultures, grammar is not taught. Natives do not know the rules of their own language; it takes an anthropologist months or years to work out the rules. Moreover, even in our own culture children begin to speak in sentences before they go to school and before anyone fusses over their grammar.

The second way that syntax defines the language acquisition problem is more important for Chomsky's thesis. It is the fact that the syntactic structure of the sentences a child hears is not in the words themselves. Grammar is an invisible organizer of words into sentences, and somehow children must figure out their language's syntax without direct exposure to it. This suggests that children already know something about grammar, furnishing a basis for constructing the rules of their individual grammar.

So far, we have only discussed the surface structure of sentences. But underneath the surface structure of each sentence lies its more remote deep structure, and these deep-structure rules must also be learned. Since deep-structure rules are far removed from the words of sentences, learning them is an especially difficult task, thus reinforcing the notion that the child brings to the task of language acquisition more than just an ability to make associations, possessing some innate faculty for constructing linguistic rules.

In tackling this formidable task, the child faces two additional problems also faced by an anthropologist trying to unravel a novel language. First, it is generally the case that given any finite set of sentences that a child has heard—or an anthropologist has recorded—up to a given moment, more than one grammar can be written to describe their structures. The anthropologist's problem (and the child's) is to decide which grammar is correct. It would help if certain universal features of all human languages existed to help rule out certain grammars as simply impossible. Such universals do, in fact exist—the agent/object distinction, for example—and Chomsky argues that they reflect innately invariant properties of the language faculty, and place constraints on the kinds of grammars the child will construct. Since all speakers of a given language appear to have learned the same rules, even though many rules may be consistent with the data, Chomsky believes that a universal language faculty is at work. At this juncture it should be pointed out that Chomsky does not think that the Chinese child comes prepared to learn Chinese, the French child to learn French, and so on; obviously, this is false. Rather, Chomsky claims that human children come prepared to learn a human language, and the language faculty already knows, in a sense, what human languages are like, setting out of bounds other plausible, but nonhuman syntactic systems.

The second problem shared by both anthropologist and child is that actual speech, what one can listen to and record, is influenced by factors irrelevant to the grammar of the language. An analogy may be made to hearing a symphony. If a musician records each note as it is played in performance (and does not have the Score) what he or she writes down will not be the symphony itself. The performers may be tired, may be unfamiliar with the conductor, may be playing from memory, or may have varying degrees of talent. All these factors, which are irrelevant to the symphony, will lead to mistakes, so that the performance is not a true representation of the symphony, but a distortion of it. And mistakes are inevitable.

In language the situation is similar. Anyone who has read unedited speech, or listened carefully to it, knows that speech is influenced by many extra linguistic factors: memory, change in the point one wanted to make, false starts, hesitations, and so on. Although speakers know the rules of their language, their actual performance—like musicians—is a distorted embodiment of them. So the anthropologist and child must somehow ignore or correct the errors. Indeed, they must first figure out what is error and what is correct syntax before they can uncover both the surface and deep structures of the language they are confronting. Again, this learning would be greatly facilitated by some preexisting knowledge of human language to be applied to one's specific situation. And the child—who learns most of his or her syntax between ages two and five—does not have the anthropologist's professional training, so that the child's preexisting knowledge must be innate.

Chomsky calls the difference between people's knowledge of their grammar and their actual use of it the **competence/performance distinction,** and we may now formulate the problem of language acquisition as Chomsky sees it.

The problem is to account for the acquisition by a child of linguistic competence in his or her native tongue. Acquisition of language is based on limited exposure to primary linguistic input flawed by deficiencies in adult performance, from which a child between the ages of two and five must nevertheless correctly abstract surface and deep-structure rules without direct teaching. The magnitude of the problem suggests that children are born with a language faculty, or, in more modern terms, a language acquisition device (LAD), richly furnished with knowledge of human language in general. This LAD constrains and makes manageable the child's task. Children do not begin to acquire language before 15 months of age or so, and acquisition of a second language in adolescence or adulthood is a markedly different and more difficult process. These facts indicate that there is a critical period in which the LAD is active and during which language acquisition must take place. All of this adds up to the proposal that language is a species-specific human faculty rooted in our biological ancestry (Crain, 1991; Lightfoot, 1989).

Criticisms of Chomsky's Thesis

Complaints and criticisms concerning Chomsky's proposal have been numerous and varied, ranging from philosophers who find it unintelligible to psychologists who find it intelligible and interesting, but who cannot reconcile it with the data. The usual alternative offered to Chomsky's rationalism is an empiricist cognitive hypothesis (see Bever, 1970; Eliot, 1981). What these scientists offer is the view (specifics, of course, vary) that a child possesses certain general cognitive abilities related to perception, learning, reasoning, and so on, that the child can also apply to learning language. What is learned on this account is thus neither competence (linguistic grammar) nor even mental grammar, but rather the application of information-processing abilities to the domain of language. Psychologically speaking, then, there is no such thing as grammar at all, only the processing of linguistic information (MacWhinney & MacDonald, 1991) with the goal of achieving communication (Bates & MacWhinney, 1987; Gleason, Hay, & Cain, 1989).

ANIMAL COMMUNICATION

One important question that Chomsky tends to ignore in his rationalist emphasis on human uniqueness is what continuities, if any, exist between human language and animal communication systems.

Patterns of Animal Communication

Defining communication is surprisingly difficult. As I write this I am communicating—I hope!—with the reader. What if I sneeze? Someone who hears me may find out that I have a cold. But have I communicated with that person? Or suppose I sneeze deliberately in my wife's presence to let her know I have a cold and so elicit her sympathy; this would seem to be communication, for it is intentional, even if I have not used language. Finally, however, a psychoanalyst might claim an "accidental" sneeze near my wife is really an unconscious but real communication, a reaching out for sympathy that my conscious mind, not wanting to feel dependent, rejects. Much of our nonverbal communication is just like this: unconscious and often beyond our willful control—except, of course, for the actor or poker player.

We should recognize a continuum of communication from verbal language used purposefully to unconscious, nonverbal communication. In the case of animals, defining communication is especially problematic because we can assess intention only with difficulty, and are reluctant to attribute intentions to lightning bugs, for example, who not only communicate, but even lie (see Box 11.1).

Green and Marler (1979) have proposed a useful definition of animal communication. To count as communication, a signal or set of signals must meet three criteria. First, the signals must be nonconstant, that is, emitted only on some occasions. This rules out signals such as coloration or shape, which convey information such as species identity, but are not communication in any useful sense. Second, the signal must be specialized to serve a communicative function. Third, there must be internal processing, the encoding and decoding of signals. Green and Marler's criteria seem to formalize our intuitive notion of communication while allowing room for doubtful cases such as the unconscious sneeze.

Functions of Communication

However we define it, communication serves many important functions in animal life, for species ranging from the slime mold—who reproduce in hard times by emitting a pheromone that gathers a crowd of fellows who temporarily form themselves into a large fruiting body (Gould, 1982)—to human beings. Table 11.1 (on page 336) lists some of the functions of communication adduced by Wilson (1980) with some examples. One can see that communication is involved in every aspect of animals' lives from birth to death, serving many functions essential to survival. Animal communication must, therefore, have a strong innate component.

Evolution of Communication

Because communication is so important to individual and group survival, signaling and receiving systems and behaviors are under strong selective pressure (Green & Marler, 1979). On the sending side, an individual must be able to send appropriate and perceivable messages so that natural selection acts on the morphology, behavior, and even cognitive abilities of organisms. For example, signals designed to attract a mate must be locatable, so that the prospective mate can find the signaler. On the other hand, an alarm call should be hard to locate so as not to attract a predator's attention. Thus, selection tends to develop the ability to produce distinctive kinds of calls, and the ability to use each appropriately.

On the receiving side, selection favors sensory abilities and acuities involved in communication. Thus, any animal's most acute range of sensory discrimination generally coincides with the range of signals. In both cases the physical environment—and changes in environment produce evolution—is important, for signals must strive and be received despite noise, obstacles, aquatic thermoclines, and other hazards. So each species' characteristic mode and manner of signaling—chemical, visual, auditory, tactile, or electric—will evolve in accordance with its environment and way of life (Wilson, 1980).

The most important process involved in the evolution of communication is what ethologists call ritualization (Hinde, 1974; Wilson, 1980). Ritualization transforms preexisting behaviors unrelated to communication into stereotyped, patterned behaviors that can serve as distinct signals. The process is also called semanticization (Wilson, 1980) because the essential change taking place during ritualization is that the behavior acquires meaning, and is no longer just a behavior occurring because of some external or internal cause. A ritualized behavior becomes a signal that affects another's behavior rather than one's own.

■ Box 11.1 ■
Do Animals Lie?

One thing we learn from sociobiology is to analyze the costs and benefits of different classes of behavior. And nothing costs less than sending a message: Talk is cheap. Since there are obvious benefits to be gained from lying, we might expect to find many cases of deceitful communication in nature, and our expectations are amply confirmed (Barash, 1982). For example, monarch butterflies feed on milkweed plants, which contain a toxin not digested but stored within the butterfly. Birds who eat monarchs get violently ill and, in an example of conditioned food aversion (Chapter 4), avoid eating monarchs thereafter. The distinctive coloring of the monarch signals danger, an honest communication adaptive to both predator and butterfly. But then there is the viceroy butterfly that does not eat milkweed and contains no toxin, but has evolved to look like the monarch. It sends a false message of danger, and since this message is heeded by wary predators, natural selection has favored the viceroy's deceitful coloration. Such mimicry is fairly common among insects, and it was partly his consideration of mimicry in Amazonian insects that put A. R. Wallace onto the theory of evolution.

A particularly interesting form of deceit occurs among fireflies (Gould, 1982). Fireflies' flashing lights serve two adaptive functions. Like monarch butterflies, fireflies contain toxic cardiac glycerides (although they make their own) and the flashing warns predators that they are poisonous. More importantly, firefly males and females locate each other for mating by exchanging coded signals, and each of the many firefly species has its own characteristic code. Females remain stationary as the males fly around flashing. Females—sensing a species' correct flashing pattern in the air—return the males' signals, and the distinctive timing of the return flash lets the male know of an appropriate conspecific female. He lands near her, and perhaps using smell and shape as a final test that she is the correct species, copulates with her.

Females of the species photuris versicolor have learned to lie to their own benefit. After mating with a conspecific male, preparing to bear and hatch offspring, the photuris female begins to attract males of other species by mimicing the code of their females. The unwitting male firefly is lured to photuris by her deceptive signal and approaches, learning too late that he is going to be a meal, not a mate. Photuris females in this way gain an excellent source of protein for very little work: Talk is cheap.

By the way, you can perform the same trick yourself with a penlight (Gould, 1982). Try various delay times between the offset of a flying (and therefore male) firefly and when you turn on your penlight in return. Some trial and error will give you the right latency, and then you can lure in the male. Of course, you won't smell right and so he won't try to mate with you, or the flashlight.

Fortunately, deceit is not rampant in nature because false signals often exact costs—the liar is found out and his or her fitness reduced. Moreover, natural selection has evolved various reliability signs into many messages (Barash, 1982). For example, the loudness and the low pitch of aggressive roaring among many males—including species as different as Fowler's toad and red deer—correlate well with fighting ability, since a strong male is large and well-muscled. Such correlations help establish truth-in-advertising in the wild kingdom.

TABLE 11.1 Some Functions of Communication among Animals

Function	Description and Examples
Contact	Signals that maintain contact between members of a group. *Example:* Under condition of poor visibility (e.g., dense vegetation) South American tapirs emit a short squeal to stay in touch with their herd.
Individual and class recognition	Signals that identify a particular individual and/or his or her (or its) class. *Example:* Pheremones emitted by queens in ant, termite, and bee nests cause workers to act in special ways toward her.
Status signaling	Signals that communicate the rank of an individual in a status hierarchy. *Example:* Dominant rhesus monkeys walk with head and tail erect, low-ranking males with tail and head drooping.
Begging and offering of food	Signals that indicate readiness to share food or that elicit sharing. *Example:* Open mouth gape of baby bird in nest triggers parents placing food in mouth.
Grooming	While it may also serve hygienic functions, allogrooming—the grooming of others—can be a social signal. *Example:* Grooming among primates forestalls aggression and reinforces status hierarchies.
Alarm	Signals indicating danger and mobilizing some response. *Example:* Alarm calls in birds and ground squirrels.
Threat, submission, and appeasement	Signals occurring in connection with aggression. *Example:* The fluffing-up of a cat's fur in the presence of an enemy.
Sexual behavior	Signals associated with sexual activity, such as courtship rituals. *Examples:* See Chapter 14.

Two Examples: Honeybees and Birds.

Nature offers two highly developed forms of communication that approach human language in many respects. One is the language of the honeybees, one of the most famous discoveries of ethology, and the other is birdsong, long beloved but only recently the object of scientific scrutiny.

That bees can communicate to each other the location of pollen had long been suspected. Aristotle thought that a bee who finds a trove of pollen returns to the hive and recruits her fellows into following her to the pollen site. Early comparative psychology quickly disproved Aristotle's theory. Discoverer bees were marked when they discovered pollen, allowed to return to the hive but captured upon reemergence. Nevertheless, the other workers made straight for the newly found pollen (Gould,

1982). It remained for German ethologist Karl von Frisch to unravel this mystery, showing that bees communicate the location of pollen through a language of dance.

When the bee returns to the hive, she announces her find by dancing in a figure-eight pattern with a waggle in the middle during which the bee shakes rapidly back and forth and gives off a buzzing sound by vibrating her wings. Other workers gather around her, touching her, and soon begin to take off for the new food source, locating it with remarkable accuracy. It is the waggle part of the dance that communicates the location of food. The length of the waggle portion and the rapidity of waggling are graded signals indicating distance to the food site, while the angle of the dance with respect to the sun (if outside) or the gravitational vertical (if within the hive) indicates the direction with respect to the sun along which the food will be found. There are different dialects of honeybee language, so that different species code distance differently into their waggling (Gould, 1982).

Considering the simplicity of the bee's nervous system, all of this is a remarkable—and clearly quite adaptive—achievement. How much it resembles human language is open to debate, however. There is symbolism in that the waggling run represents time (specifically, the effort needed to make the flight; Gould, 1982) and direction to the food, while the quality and the quantity of food are indicated by whether or not dancing occurs at all. The symbolism is abstract in that the object "talked about" is not present, and partly, arbitrary (like human words) in that distance is marked by dialect-specific waggle-lengths and speeds. Finally, there is some creativity in that a dancer can "say" new things, reporting unique locations.

On the other hand, honeybee language is quite restricted compared to human language (Wilson, 1980). Most importantly, bees can only communicate about one thing: food location. Bees cannot break out of this rigid context and use language in a truly creative way. Their language is too preprogrammed and innate to admit any flexibility and creativity. Nonetheless, we should respect the language of the bees as a wonderful example of the subtleties of natural selection (Corballis, 1991).

Another remarkable achievement of evolution is birdsong, which serves many functions in most bird species: courtship, mate location, establishment of territory, alarms. While lovers of nature and bird enthusiasts have long appreciated birdsong as an art, it is only since World War II that birdsong has been studied scientifically. Research on how birds learn to sing may provide a model for discussing human language acquisition, for we may do experiments on birds that we may not morally perform on children. W. H. Thorpe and then Peter Marler (see, Marler, 1970, 1991; Marler & Peters, 1981) conducted brilliant sets of research showing that birdsong (at least in the species studied by them) is both innate and learned.

Many experiments have been performed by Thorpe, Marler, and others, but the basic results are summarized in Figure 11.1, from Gould (1982). After hatching, baby birds are reared in isolation, and during the critical period for song-learning, the youngsters are either played tapes of birdsong, or hear nothing. In Case A, the babies heard both their own species' (the white-crowned sparrow) song and that of a related species, the song-sparrow, whose songs are within their vocal capabilities. Then, for many weeks the birds heard nothing (research has shown that exposure after 50 days or so has no effect) and were silent. Then, after 100 days, the birds break out into their subsong, a sort of practice period preceding appearance of the full song. Case A is analogous to the situation in the wild in that more than one sound is heard, and development is normal.

FIGURE 11.1   White-crowned sparrows learn their species' song during a critical period from 10 to 50 days of age. At about 150 days they begin to vocalize and practice making syllable sounds. By 200 days they have developed a stable song which closely matches the song heard during the critical period. The song learning is selective, so that if offered a choice, birds will learn only their own species' song (A); and if offered the wrong song (B) or no song at all (C), the bird will learn nothing and sing only a simple tune. If deafened before he begins to practice (D) the bird will never sing anything melodic while if deafened after the song "crystallizes," subsequent singing is perfect. These visual displays of the songs were made with a sound spectograph, a device which represents frequency on the vertical axis, time on the horizontal axis, and indicates intensity by the darkness of the trace. (Reproduced from *Ethology, The Mechanisms and Evolution of Behavior,* by James L. Gould, by permission of W. W. Norton & Co. Copyright © 1982 by James L. Gould.)

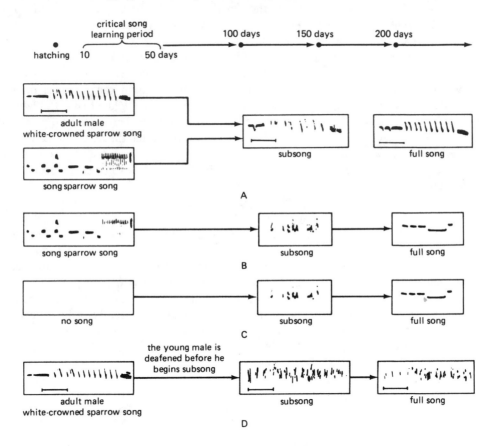

In Case B only the song sparrow song is played during the critical period, and we see that the subsong is abnormal, and the full song, while structured, does not resemble the normal song. This case rules out simple imitation as the basis of song learning, since the white-crowned sparrows do not learn the song sparrow song.

Case C represents total acoustic isolation, the results of which are identical with hearing the wrong song. Therefore, song singing is not the result of simple maturation, in which an innate program simply expresses itself at maturity, as in bees.

Finally, Case D reveals the importance of practice and feedback during the subsong phase. Here, the young bird is exposed to the correct song, but is deafened prior to beginning subsong. In this case both subsong and full song are disorganized peeps.

These findings beautifully illustrate the complex and subtle interplay between the innate and the experienced at the base of all learning. Any simply maturational model of birdsong development is untenable. Equally untenable is any behaviorist reinforcement theory, since there is no reinforcement during initial exposure or subsong phases. Nor are the constraints on song learning merely peripheral, being set only by what the bird can hear or the notes it can utter, since songs of physically similar birds of different species are unlearnable.

There must be in species such as the sparrow central constraints on learning. As in humans, bird language is a specialized function of the left hemisphere of the brain, and it is there that natural selection has acted to constrain birdsong learning. It appears that the songbird is born with a template active only during a critical period early in the baby bird's life (Konishi, 1985; Marler, 1970). The template contains a sort of model of the appropriate song of the species. The model is not specified in precise detail, because songbirds develop dialects peculiar to different geographic regions, and young birds can learn any dialect of their songs. The template acts as a filter, directing the brain's attention to the biologically important sounds in the helpless infant's environment: its species' song. Sounds of passing 747s, of owls, robins, and other kinds of sparrows are models which, if followed, would lead to an adult male unable to attract a mate. (Females do not sing unless injected with testosterone; their knowledge of the song is adaptive in causing recognition of a true conspecific.) The template thus becomes a model of the correct song against which the adolescent bird can later check his vocalizing during the subsong phase. Feedback checked against the model leads to adjustments and the emergence of full song (Marler, 1991).

Conclusion

While there is no question animals communicate, it is doubtful that they have anything like human language. Human language exploits the arbitrariness of the sign, the fact that words do not resemble what they represent. Bees, however, directly encode direction into the angle they dance on the wall and amount of effort needed to fly to the pollen site into the speed of the dance. Bees can therefore "speak" about nothing but time and effort, while human language considers all things visible in Heaven or earth, and all things fair and good. Vervet monkeys possess a system of calls that signal presence of predators. However, vervet monkeys lack syntax. They cannot combine their calls in structured strings to say new things; they cannot say "Remember that stupid eagle we saw yesterday—you know, the one that couldn't even catch old Harry?—well, it's perched in the oak where you mated with Francine." Moreover, the calls of vervet monkeys are controlled by the primitive limbic system of the brain, while most human language is controlled by the cortex. There remains a great gulf between human and animal communication.

ACQUISITION OF LANGUAGE

Behavioral Theories

Behavioral reinforcement and modeling theories of language acquisition are untenable. Studies of parent-child interaction have shown that, aside from a few pet language peeves we all remember, such as "ain't," parents pay more attention to—that is, reinforce or punish—the content of what their children say than to its grammatical form. Moskowitz (1978) reports a charming example of this. A mother hearing her son, Stevie, say, "Tommy fall my truck down?" quickly turned to Tommy and asked, "Did you fall Stevie's truck down?" The mother was clearly more concerned about the truth of Stevie's claim, and the moral issues it raised, than with its syntactic correctness. Since this is generally true, it follows, as Brown (1973) points out, that if the contingencies of reinforcement shaped language, we should find ungrammatical but truth-telling adults. Obviously, though, what develops is people who lie with good grammar.

Imitation, too, has been found to be a less important process in language acquisition than most people and psychologists have believed. Bloom, Hood, and Lightbown (1974; Bloom, 1991; Tager-Flusberg & Calkins, 1990) showed that there is considerable difference between children in whether or not they imitated utterances they had heard. Some children imitate very little, yet learn language as quickly as their peers who imitate a great deal. More generally, imitation is ruled out by the fact that as children construct their grammatical rules—which, of course, should not exist according to behaviorist theory—they use rules at first that differ from adult rules, and create utterances that they cannot have heard.

The phenomenon of overregularization offers a nice example establishing that language is rule-learning, because it requires invoking cognitive structures underlying behavior, and cannot be due to imitation. Language is based on rules, but the rules have exceptions, and children must learn what they are. For example, most verbs in English convert to the past tense by adding the morpheme *-ed*. However, there are many common exceptions to this rule, such as fall-fell or go-went. As they learn language, children typically first learn both the regular and irregular verbs correctly, and can say, "I went home." Then, however, they formulate the general rule but overapply it: "I goed home." Now they cannot be imitating goed, nor has it been shaped by reinforcement. Instead, the child has induced a general rule and overgeneralized it, losing the correct, reinforced form and suddenly emitting a new, deviant form in its place. Later, perhaps after a phase of saying "I wented home," the child learns the exceptions and returns to the correct form, "I went home" (Moskowitz, 1978; Rice, 1989).

Nativist Theories

The leading exponent of the view that language is a species-specific biological capacity of *Homo sapiens,* and that much of language acquisition is simply maturation, was Eric Lenneberg (1964, 1965, 1967, 1969/1972; see also Corballis, 1991; Lieberman, 1989; Maratsos, 1989). We may list some of the more important reasons Lenneberg adduced in support of his thesis:

- Humans possess many anatomical specializations related to language use from the shape and placement of the larynx to specialization of language functions in the left hemisphere of the brain. (See Marshall, 1980, for a more recent review.)

- Damage to certain parts of the brain (in the left hemisphere only) lead to damaged or lost linguistic abilities. Moreover, time of damage during childhood is related to clinical outcome. Damage to the left hemisphere during the first few years of life can be overcome; after puberty it cannot be. Recent research shows Lenneberg to have conceded too much to the environment. Woods (1980) provides evidence of very early left hemisphere specialization for language. Dennis (1980) has found that infants who have their right hemispheres removed at birth develop normal language, while those who lose their left hemispheres have only imperfect (though usable) language all their lives.

- Language cannot be suppressed. Studies of completely untutored deaf children found that they spontaneously invent a gestural language whose structure and acquisition parallel normal child language (Goldin-Meadow, 1999; Goldin-Meadow & Mylander, 1991; Mylander & Goldin-Meadow, 1990). Teaching signing to chimps is hard work, but children learn language by themselves (Miller, 1981). On the other hand, language learning cannot be speeded up by more than a few days, as training studies have shown (Moskowitz, 1978).

- The time of onset and early steps of language learning are universal around the world.

- The early sequence of language acquisition is closely correlated with motor development, which is known to be due entirely to maturation. Just as swaddled children begin to walk at the same time as unswaddled children. Lenneberg reports a baby at the babbling stage who was tracheostomized for six months, and who picked up babbling not where she left off but where she should have been when the tracheostomy was reversed.

- Language cannot be taught to any other species. Although this claim is controversial, it is not clearly false.

- Linguistic universals do exist.

- Certain forms of aphasia (disordered language) are inheritable (Gopnik, 1991).

- Timing of speech onset and onset of speech deficits (if any) are more similar between identical than between fraternal twins.

- So-called wolf-children denied access to speech until adolescence cannot learn language despite intensive tutoring (Jeffrey, 1980), while similar children discovered at an earlier age can learn language. The later one begins to learn a first or second language, the poorer one's performance will be (Newport, 1991).

- Language is present in all cultures.

To Lenneberg's list we can add some further considerations:

- There is a clear difference between learning a second language in adulthood and first language learning, whether spoken or sign (Eichen & Mayberry, 1991). We learn our primary language without thinking: most of us struggle through language classes with great difficulty, despite adult cognitive skills and careful instruction. Vocabulary learning provides a dramatic contrast. The adult language learner struggles to master a few new words a week. Without trying, the average six-year-old learns 22 new words a day (Bloom & Markson, 1998)! As Miller (1981) puts it: "Their minds are like little vacuum pumps designed by nature to suck up words" (p. 119).

- Both children and adults suffering from aphasia can learn Premack's token "language," indicating that the problem-solving, but not linguistic, parts of their brains are intact (Cromer, 1981).

- Neonates (12 hours old) show "interactional synchrony" with spoken language (Bower, 1977; Condon & Sander, 1974; Rice, 1989). When they hear human language—any human language—but not when they hear other sounds, they move their bodies in a regular rhythmic fashion following the sound pattern of what they hear. Speech is clearly a special sound to even the youngest human.

- Human speech perception is categorical (Chapter 5), and there is evidence that these categories are innate. Eimas, Siqueland, Jusczyk, and Vigorito (1971) and Miller and Eimas (1983) showed that prelinguistic infants show the same kind of categorical perception, and they proposed that infants have innate human speech detectors. Subsequent research has shown that some other (but not all) distinctive features are recognized by infants including features not used in their natural language (see Blumenstein, 1980, for a review).

On the other hand, nonhuman species perceive categorically, too (Eilers, 1980): Chinchillas, like adult and infant humans, categorically perceive (ba) and (pa). So the species-specificity of this ability is unclear. Evolution may have incorporated preexisting perceptual abilities into the human language system.

Taken together, these considerations suggest that human language acquisition is a biologically based, genetically constrained and directed form of learning that takes place during a fixed critical period ending at adolescence (Corballis, 1991; Hurford, 1991; Maratsos, 1989). The analogy to birdsong is striking. In both cases language does not simply mature, but requires input and practice that must occur in a certain period of time. In both cases there is a range of languages (or dialects) that may be learned, but certain kinds of languages may not be learned. In both, there is cerebral (left hemisphere) specialization of language function.

Cognitive Theories

The cognitivist counter-proposal is based essentially on negative reasoning: It is not necessary to postulate specifically linguistic innate processes and structures (Atkinson, 1982; MacWhinney, 1987; Pinker, 1987; Rumelhart & McClellan 1987). With regard to neurology, it is claimed that hemispheric specialization is really for two broad types of cognitive abilities, linear (left hemisphere) and holistic (right hemisphere) so that language winds up in the left hemisphere by virtue of being a linear processing task (Bever, 1980). With regard to the work on categorical speech perception in infants, the cognitivists maintain that since not all distinctive features are innate, and some distinctive features that are innate are found in nonhuman perceptual systems, there is no linguistic specialization at work (Aslin & Pisoni, 1980). This is an objection of limited force, since as Gould (1982) points out, evolution is a great opportunist, and in building language it took advantage of older, preexisting abilities. In general, communication systems show a careful tuning between already present sensory abilities and characteristics of the message (Wilson, 1980).

Although the cognitivist hypothesis is the favorite among current psychologists (Elkind, 1981; Moskowitz, 1978; Rice, 1989), a careful review of their claims (Cromer, 1981) shows it to be flawed (Pinker, 1994, 1999). The general problem with the cognitivist approach is oversimplification. It assumes that once a cognitive strategy or concept is acquired it is immediately translated into language. But Cromer argues that the translation is not a trivial automatic affair, and is likely to involve specifically linguistic processes, perhaps innate ones. In any event, despite its popularity with psychologists, there is no cognitive theory of language learning as detailed as the nativist hypothesis (Campbell, 1986).

On the empirical side, evidence indicates that cognitive and linguistic development can be almost completely decoupled, suggesting separate developmental paths. Cromer cites a study with two subjects in whom such decoupling took place in opposite ways. One subject was a 20-year-old female deprived of language until age 12, and who despite intensive instruction had still not acquired language beyond a 2-year-old level; nevertheless, her general cognitive ability was much higher, at Piaget's level of concrete operations (7 to 12 years old). Another subject—a child—did poorly on cognitive tests, but spoke using highly complex syntactic constructions. The content of his speech—clearly depending on thinking—was often nonsense, but his grammatical skills were high. In this connection we may again mention the ape language projects, because chimpanzees have (relatively) sophisticated intelligence, but acquire only rudimentary language at best.

One of the major findings making the cognitivist hypothesis attractive has been the discovery of baby talk, called child-directed speech (Snow, 1986), or "motherese." Chomsky alleged that children heard only fragmentary, ill-formed utterances, from which only an innate language faculty could extract linguistic competence. However, studies (see Snow, 1972/1978) of parental speech to children showed that it differed from speech to adults, and was in general well formed and framed in short sentences. From this, advocates of cognitivism concluded that children were getting a sort of tutorial in language, and that Chomsky's nativism was unnecessary.

However, Cromer uses a careful study of motherese (Newport, Gleitman, & Gleitman, 1977) to undermine the cognitivist claim. One problem with the idea that motherese is used to teach children language is that baby talk, motherese, could have other functions than teaching: to express affection (it is used between lovers), to facilitate communication (it is used with foreigners), or to assert power (nurses use it with patients). Against the tutorial view Newport and others (1977) found that while motherese sentences are short, they are syntactically complex, by some measures more complex than speech between adults. Moreover, the "lessons" seem ill designed to teach syntax. For example, the canonical form of English sentences is a declarative sentence in subject-verb-object word order: 87 percent of adult-adult sentences are of this type; but only 30 percent of sentences directed to children are, there being many more commands and questions. In investigating the influence of motherese or subsequent child speech, Newport and others (1977) found that motherese affected the acquisition only of English-language specific structures, and had no impact on the rate of acquisition of more universal aspects of language.

Furthermore, "motherese" is not something to which all children are exposed. "Motherese" is used almost exclusively by attentive middle-class mothers (Rice, 1989); yet all normal children of whatever class or nation learn language. Moreover, the verbal models to which children are exposed, and the feedback they receive about their own utterances, may be in principle ill-suited to nurture language were there no innate language acquisition device (Lightfoot, 1989).

More recent studies of child-directed speech have focused on its semantic properties. Early views of motherese assumed that mothers were giving their babies lessons in syntax, overlooking the fact that mothers were really trying simply to communicate with their children, to convey and understand information, not to teach grammar (Snow, 1986). Therefore, utterances to children are simple because the ideas being dealt with are simple, not because the parents' sentences are designed to teach language. The shift in researchers' focus from syntax to semantics revealed that how parents speak to their children may speed up language acquisition. In particular, when parents talk at length about what their child is doing—even when an infant is too young to respond linguistically—the rate of language learning is accelerated.

CAN CHIMPS READ?

To propose an analogy between songbirds and humans is to do one form of evolutionary psychology, in approaching humans via a perhaps distant species that, nevertheless, is similar ecologically and functionally. Like human babies, altricial (helpless at birth) bird nestlings are helpless but must anyway learn a sophisticated signaling system essential to later reproductive success. The other kind of analogy one can draw is between humans and their most closely related relatives—primates—especially chimpanzees and gorillas. This is the controversial strategy of the various research teams engaged in teaching language to apes.

Ape Language Projects

Early attempts to teach apes language failed. Best known was the charming endeavor by a married pair of psychologists to teach a chimpanzee language by raising it with their own child. This attempt was bound to fail if only because chimps' vocal apparatus is ill-suited to language. La Mettrie's challenge to Descartes was not carried out until the 1960s in response to Chomsky's revived Cartesian linguistics.

There is no doubt that monkeys and apes communicate in the wild, both vocally and nonvocally, often sending fairly elaborate messages. For example, the alarm calls of the vervet monkey, a small monkey relatively distant from *Homo sapiens,* are remarkably sophisticated. The calls can designate different predators, and can distinguish moving from nonmoving predators. Vervet monkeys are therefore able to convey a lot about the location and type of predator, thus ensuring behavior adaptively nuanced as a result.

Several research teams have investigated the acquisition of language by great apes, primarily chimpanzees. Since it is clear chimpanzees and gorillas cannot acquire vocal language, researchers have had to devise nonvocal languages to teach to their subjects. David Premack invented a visual "language" in which chimp and human communicate by placing plastic tokens (roughly equivalent to words) on a board following specified grammatical rules. At the Yerkes Primate Research Center, Georgia, E. S. Savage-Rumbaugh and Duane Rumbaugh use an artificial language called Yerkish, in which a chimp "talks" with a computer by pressing symbolic keys—lexigrams— (roughly equal to words) following rules of syntax. The system allows the computer both to "talk" to the chimp, and to provide human-chimp and chimp-chimp interaction.

The best-known projects, however, follow up an old suggestion made by the great primate psychologist Robert Yerkes in the 1920s, using the American sign language of the deaf (ASL) as the medium of communication. The pioneer project was carried out by Beatrice and Allan Gardner at the University of Nevada at Reno with a chimp named Washoe. Work with Washoe and others was carried on by Roger Fouts in Kansas, while, in New York, Herbert Terrace and his associates taught ASL to Neam Chimsky (!) or Nim; Francine Patterson in California taught it to a gorilla, Koko. It should be pointed out that in addition to skill and patience, these projects require real courage, Chimps grow up to weigh nearly as much as a large man, and they are three times as strong, and can—even inadvertently—do real harm to people and property. Many of the projects can only last a few years, until the chimp reaches puberty and becomes a potential danger.

Whatever method was used, the findings of the ape-language projects establish beyond doubt that apes can express themselves symbolically. They can make requests, convey their feelings, and discuss the past. Other experiments have shown that apes can invent new sign or lexigram strings, can name objects, and can communicate about things such as a tool needed to get a piece of food. However, the exact significance of these findings remains unclear and controversial. Have any of the apes learned language, not just a new communication system? Can these projects tell us anything about the evolution of human language? How similar is an ape's acquisition of signing (or lexigram use) to the acquisition of language by children?

Controversy

Is It Language?

From their inception, the ape-language projects provoked controversy, primarily over the issue of whether or not what apes acquired was language (it was clearly communication) and, consequently, whether their learning processes were the same as a child's learning language. Roger Brown (1970), a pioneer in the study of human language acquisition (see R. Brown, 1973), argued that the Gardner's Washoe did not seem to possess syntax. That is, she constructed utterances out of random aggregations of signs rather than showing any following of word (sign) order rules, namely, syntax. This implied the important conclusion that Washoe did not have semantic intentions while signing, but instead just emitted behaviors until reinforcement was forthcoming. Later, Brown (1973) modified his view, conceding that Washoe did have semantic intentions, without word order, because of his finding that children learning languages that are less strict about word order than English speak intentionally without exhibiting regular syntax.

Using data from Nim, Terrace and colleagues (1980) directly investigated the question of rule-governed combination of signs, and found that while Nim assembled multisign utterances, there was no evidence there of regular sign-order. They concluded that Nim was just a random sign-generator, emitting signs until they had some desired effect. Similarly, the Yerkes group has tempered earlier claims that its chimps showed syntactic structure in their utterances (Ristau & Robbins, 1982). Because their computer language requires linear symbol-by-symbol production, it should be ideal for eliciting syntax in apes; in fact, it might produce syntax as an artifact of the experiment. So if there is poor evidence of grammar acquisition in Yerkish, it seems syntax is difficult, perhaps impossible, for chimps to acquire.

The issue of grammar is quite important, for it is syntax that gives human language its infinite expressive and productive powers. Without syntax, only the most rudimentary thoughts or desires can be expressed, and communication must remain tied to an immediate concrete context. With syntax, nuances of expression become possible, and intellect is freed from the immediate and concrete and can soar to the distant and imaginary.

Is It Problem Solving?

It was not about chimps learning sign language that it was first said "that an animal can think in human ways and can express human ideas in human language" (Hediger, 1981, p. 1). The animal in question was Clever Hans, a horse, who early in the twentieth century fooled many people, including a panel of eminent scientists, and his owner himself, into believing he could do mathematics, think, and understand spoken and written language. It took the clever research of a young psychologist, Oskar Pfungst, to show that apparently in teaching Hans arithmetic and language, his owner had really taught him to attend to subtle, unconscious, nonverbal cues given off by his questioner. Clever Hans should remind us that a very plausible imitation of language is not language itself (Heil, 1982).

Accusations that the linguistic apes were in effect simian Clever Hanses have been raised by Terrace (Terrace, 1979a, 1979b, 1979c, 1982; Terrace, Petitto, Sanders,

& Bever, 1979), who argues that the apes did not really learn language, but only to gesture (or arrange plastic tokens, or push computer lexigrams) to satisfy their masters and get things they want. Sebeok and Umiker-Sebeok (1979, 1980; Sebeok, 1980) also make this claim. This new aspect to the ape language controversy has engendered a bitter debate between skeptics and most of the project directors (Benderly, 1980). Indeed, at a conference devoted to the Clever Hans phenomenon with respect to the ape language projects (Sebeok & Rosenthal, 1981) the phrase "witch hunt" was used by Duane Rumbaugh (1981; see also Linden, 1981).

Unfortunately, evaluating claims of deceptive communication is difficult because of the methodological deficiencies of the various studies (Ristau & Robbins, 1982). In general, the database from all the projects—save Nim's—is very poor. The Gardner's data (1969/1972) consist of diaries, and one study showed serious errors in recording the apes' signing. The Yerkes project only recorded what the apes punched on their keyboard, but not the possibly cuing activities of the trainers. Sarah, the Premack chimp, was drilled in such a way that she could have functioned by rote-learning of symbol sequences rather than language-rule learning. Most of the famous and persuasive creative utterances of the chimps are merely anecdotal, and open to other interpretations than those given by the investigators, who, of course, wanted the apes to have language. The best-known of these events was Washoe's signing "water bird" upon seeing a swan on a river. Advocates of chimp language (e.g., Lieberman, 1984; Linden, 1981) see this as creative naming—calling the swan a "water-bird." Skeptics see it as two separate signs under distinct stimulus control, "water" (water was present) and "bird."

The only project with adequate records was Terrace's Nim project, where extensive videotapes were made. Terrace for a long time believed Nim had learned language until he started studying the videotapes after the project ended. Among other things, he detected the Clever Hans phenomena, specifically cuing in the form of signs that Nim could imitate. Apparently, Nim's trainers were unaware of their cuing, for they expressed surprise on seeing the tapes.

The currently most active ape language project involves the rarest of the great apes, pygmy chimpanzees (*Pan paniscus*) (Savage-Rumbaugh, 1990, 1997; Savage-Rumbaugh et al., 1986). Pygmy chimps are brighter and socially more like us than are ordinary chimps (*Pan troglodytes*). Among pygmy chimpanzees, in contrast to ordinary chimpanzees, male-female bonds are strong and fathers help rear offspring. Moreover, pygmy chimps in the wild possess a much larger repertoire of vocal and gestural symbols than do *Pan troglodytes*. They are, perhaps, much better candidates for language learning than gorillas and *Pan troglodytes* (de Waal & Lanting, 1998).

The most important subject of Savage-Rumbaugh's study is Kanzi (Savage-Rumbaugh, Lewin, & Savage-Rumbaugh, 1996), male offspring of a female pygmy chimpanzee who was taught Yerkish. He acquired Yerkish spontaneously, simply by being exposed to its use between his mother and her trainers. Continuing to work with—but not instruct or reward—the youngster, Savage-Rumbaugh and her associates found that Kanzi was an active learner, rapidly mastering Yerkish and able to apply it in novel contexts, such as guiding a blind researcher around an enclosed forest. Unlike the chimps who had learned Yerkish, Kanzi began to understand the English vocal names for the lexigrams, although of course he could not learn to speak. Most significantly, unlike the Yerkish chimpanzees and unlike Nim, who just signed to get something for themselves, the pygmy chimpanzee came to use Yerkish unselfishly. He often used Yerkish to request that the experimenters do something for the other chimp, or for another person. The investigators conclude that pygmy chimpanzees master Yerkish in a completely different manner from ordinary chimpanzees, and draw parallels between human language acquisition and their subjects' Yerkish acquisition. They also harshly criticize the Cartesian tradition of maintaining that language is a uniquely human ability (Savage-Rumbaugh, Shanker, Taylor, & Savage-Rumbaugh, 1999).

Kanzi's considerable communicative achievements may have blurred the line between animal and human language acquisition. However, important differences remain (Goldin-Meadow, 1996). For example, Kanzi, like Nim, uses language almost exclusively to accomplish things rather than to chat. As anyone who has been around them knows, young children keep up a constant stream of social conversation. Moreover, although Kanzi learned language without direct teaching, he was extensively exposed to language. Human children deprived for one reason or another of human language will actively invent language-like ways of communicating. Deaf children, for example, use gestures to communicate and these gestures have a linguistic structure to them (Goldin-Meadow & Mylander, 1990). Human children seem to possess a communicative-linguistic drive and creative ability absent in chimpanzees.

As we have seen, language, communication, and the use of symbols are overlapping but non-identical abilities. Some recent studies have attempted to explore similarities and differences between children and apes in all these areas, and they have begun to implicate theory of mind—or lack of it—as a critical difference between apes and humans. As just mentioned, children, in common with all humans, communicate by gestures as well as words. Our simplest symbolic gesture is pointing, yet it is perhaps the evolutionary origin of symbolic thought (see Chapter 2), because it designates some object or action that it does not resemble. Lower animals do not understand pointing. I have often thrown a treat for one of our cats that the cat doesn't see; in mounting frustration I point at the treat on the floor while the cat stares at the end of my finger. Two and 3-year-old children easily understand pointing as a clue to finding hidden treats, but chimpanzees generally do not (Povinelli, Reaux, Bierschwale, Allain, & Simon, 1997; Tomasello, Call, & Gluckman, 1997). Naïve chimpanzees never follow pointing, although sometimes apes who have been trained about pointing do. Tomasello et al. (1997) also indicated to subjects hidden treats by putting markers (a wooden cube) or plastic replicas of the treats on boxes containing them. Children could use these cues, albeit with more difficulty than pointing, but apes never did. Children, but not apes, also can follow gazes as cues to objects' locations (Povinelli, Bierschwale, & Cech, 1999).

Taken together, these findings suggest the following picture: Critical to the human way of life is theory of mind (see Chapters 2 and 10), including the ability to "mind read": to know what other people think, what they want, what they want to communicate, and even to attribute to them false beliefs. Without a grasp of another's intention, pointing and glancing are mere movements like coughing or breathing, having no symbolic values whatever. Tomasello (1999) calls apes such as Kanzi, who have had significant amounts of exposure to human ways of life, enculturated apes. It appears that natural apes are devoid of theory of mind, and so cannot understand pointing and glancing. Enculturated apes may have picked up some aspects of human theory of mind, but are not as skilled at mind reading as normal 3-year-old children. Thus, even if we put aside issues of syntax and focus only on communicative skills and use of symbols, there is still a large gap between ape and human. Apes do not develop language, communication, or symbol use on their own; they can acquire rudiments of all these with training and experience; but even when they do, they use them only for practical ends, to get what they want. They do not converse for its own sake or even point to draw attention to the wonders of the world.

Conclusion

Chomsky's remarks (1979, 1980a) on the linguistic apes raise the crucial issue: What is language and what is human language? For it is not clear that even if the various apes do in fact acquire language that they have acquired human language.

Confounding the two runs all the way through our interpretation of what the apes are doing. Consider interpreting two- and three-word sentences—assuming even that they are sentences—such as "water bird." Children, too, pass through a two-word stage, and we assume that their utterances are simple language. Defenders of the linguistic capacity of apes have said that skeptics apply a double standard, requiring more of the ape than of the child to call these utterances "language." Chomsky's analysis suggests the double standard is not misplaced: We call the children's two-word sentences language in view of what they later will achieve, not by virtue of their present linguistic sophistication, which indeed is no greater than the apes'. Terrace's data support Chomsky's argument, since he found the mean length of Nim's utterances got stuck at three or four words, while children's—even of comparable stages of linguistic experience—continued to grow.

Chomsky points out that no matter how sophisticated chimp or gorilla language may be, there is (at present) no strong reason to see it as incipient human language. It is more likely to be a separate cognitive activity not closely related to normal human language. Chomsky (1979) cites studies in which patients with damage to the language centers of their brains are able to acquire symbol-systems akin to the apes, and whose use of these systems seems much like the use of signing and symbols by the apes. If Chomsky's parallel is valid, it means that the ape-language projects may tell us much about ape mentality, but can offer us little insight into human language. The analogy from apes to humans is tempting, but should be regarded skeptically. Even if apes can be taught rudiments of language and theory of mind, it does not follow that their language and theory of the mind are the *same* as ours (Povinelli, 1999, Povinelli, Povinelli, & Giambrone, 1998). The problem is similar to those we encountered in discussing artificial intelligence. It may be possible to program a computer to do things that humans do—such as play chess—but it does so in truly artificial ways. Enculturated apes may be organic forms of artificial intelligence, programmed by their encounter by people to act in human-like ways, but human-like is not the same as human identical.

Language Acquisition in the Architectures of Cognition

It is primarily in the domain of cognitive development that the battle between symbol-system and connectionist brands of cognitive science continues. The arena in which the battle is fiercest is the study of language acquisition. Here the battle lines are most clearly drawn and the stakes are highest. If any aspect of human thought appears to be based on rules rather than associations, it is language, so that learning syntax ought to be the paradigm case of learning rules rather than connections. The stakes are the highest because, as with the ape language projects, the argument is over human uniqueness. The battle between the symbolic and connectionist treatments of language and language acquisition elevated the battle between behaviorism and cognitive psychology to new heights. Is language a specialized mental module unique to the human brain/mind depending for its proper development on an innate LAD?

The details of this debate quickly become technical both with regard to neo-Chomskian linguistic theory and connectionist modeling. The strategy of the combatants, however, is clear. Connectionists create artificial neural networks that mimic how children learn language—such as the acquisition of irregular verbs, including overregularization—and then claim that because general-purpose neural networks can acquire linguistic forms without invoking symbolic rules, that is how human language acquisition works as well (McCelland & Plaut, 1999; Rumelhart & McClelland, 1986; Seidenberg & Elman, 1999). Defenders of traditional rule-based linguistics reply that connectionist models rely upon unrealistic assumptions about the nature of language and language learning input (Marcus, 1999a, 1999b, 1999c; Pinker, 1999). For example, as we learned in Chapter 2, connectionist models learn by careful training, in which they receive explicit feedback about the correctness of their output given the stimulus. Children, however, are not so carefully trained (Pinker, 1999). Earlier, we noted that parents correct the contents of their children's language more than they correct their grammar, yet children acquire syntax more readily than morality. In addition, connectionist networks are concerned only with the phonology of language, not meaning or syntax, both of which are important cues children use to acquire language, including its phonology (Pinker, 1999).

Unsurprisingly, the argument spills over into experimental and clinical neuroscience. Advocates of the modular view of language argue that there exist heritable disorders that afflict syntax alone (Gopnik, 1997; van der Lely, 1999), and that the patterns of aphasia—language disorders—seen in spoken language are duplicated in aphasias of sign language (Hickok, Bellugi, & Klima, 1998). Both sets of findings suggest that language is a dedicated modular brain system constructed by specific genes and which is primarily concerned with syntax and meaning, not sound, since the same areas of the brain seem to control spoken and signed language. Critics of the traditional modular view of language deny that the deficits are specific to grammar (Tomblin & Pandich, 1999).

To an outsider at least, connectionist arguments seem beside the point. Let's return to the reverse-engineering computer model of psychology discussed in Chapter 2. We find an alien computer and try to figure out how it works and what it is for. Figuring out its mechanical and electronic workings is a legitimate task, but it would be absurd to claim that that is all we should do because at bottom the computer is just silicon and metal obeying physical laws, and therefore one ought not ask what programs the alien computer is running. In this debate, connectionists (e.g., Tomblin & Pandich) seem to be saying that because at bottom the brain is just a collection of proteins following biological laws, it is illegitimate to ask what rules the brain is computing. It may be that linguistic rules are embodied in connectionist networks (Marcus, 1999a; Pinker, 1999), but connectionists stoutly resist the idea (Seidenberg & Elman, 1999).

CONCLUSION: THE BIOLOGICAL BASIS OF LANGUAGE

Let us reflect once again on the difference between child and chimp. The child learns language naturally, with little or no tutoring and with little visible effort. The chimp is carefully taught by a team of intelligent, dedicated researchers who want very much to succeed and who work as hard as possible to give their subjects language. Yet the chimp—despite such heroic efforts—acquires no more than the simplest language, and perhaps not even that.

Whatever else may be innate, it is quite clear that human children have a powerful drive to learn language (Gould, 1982; Maratsos, 1987; Mylander & Goldin-Meadow, 1990). Even if all the mechanisms of language acquisition should turn out to be those of general intelligence—which, as we have seen, is by no means clear—evolution has provided at least this much: To learn human language is one of a child's deepest needs.

Whatever the details of the evolution of symbolic language, there is no doubt that it wrought a great sea-change in *Homo sapiens'* way of life. It freed our thought from the shackles of mental imagery. We could begin to think about the physically distant and the unexperienced future. We could think about abstract concepts such as truth and justice, souls and god, that cannot be expressed or thought as images. Moreover, we could share our thoughts with others, enriching all our minds in a new kind of intellectual cooperation. With the appearance of writing, ideas could be shared across generations and cultures. Symbolic thought made possible the formation of human cooperative groups much larger than 150 (Dunbar, 1993). Language, in short, created the symbolic world of culture in which we among all animals uniquely dwell. Language changed *Homo sapiens* into human beings.

SUGGESTED READINGS

The full range of mammalian communication systems from hedgehogs to humans is presented in Roger Peters' *Mammalian Communication* (1980). A good place for the student interested in Chomsky's work to start is with his *Language and Mind* (1968; enlarged ed., 1972). The references list many popular books on the ape-language studies. For language acquisition, see Steven Pinker, Language acquisition, in L. R. Gleitman, M. Liberman, and D. N. Osherson (Eds.), *An Invitation to Cognitive Science,* 2nd ed. Volume 1: Language. Cambridge, MA: MIT Press, 1995; *The Language Instinct* (New York: HarperCollins, 1999), and *Words and Rules* (New York: Basic, 1999).

PART VI

COGNITIVE NEUROSCIENCE

12 Neurophysiology of Learning and Cognition

The 1990s was the Decade of the Brain. During that decade tremendous progress was made in understanding the human brain, giving rise to the interdisciplinary field of cognitive neuroscience (Gazzinaga, Ivry, & Mangun, 1998). It is impossible in a short chapter to do proper justice to this exciting new field. What we will do is go over some of the cognitive processes we have discussed in earlier chapters, approaching them from the neurophysiological perspective. The next chapter will take a more extended look at one of the most important new areas in cognitive science and cognitive neuroscience, emotion.

EARLY INFORMATION PROCESSING

Attention

Over the past decade, Michael Posner and his colleagues (e.g., Posner & Petersen, 1990; Posner, 1992) have carried out extensive studies of attention using the PET technique, and we will briefly review their findings as an example of this exciting new area.

In PET scans, subjects are injected with a small amount of a harmless radioactive substance with a very short half-life, which is carried to the brain. When an area of the brain goes to work, blood flow to the area increases. If a subject is given a task to perform, such as thinking about the meaning of a word, the amount of radiation from all areas of the brain can be measured, and the area with the greatest activity will be the part carrying out the assigned task.

Using PET scans, Posner has delineated two attentional systems in the brains of monkeys and humans. One system is located in the rear (posterior) lobes of the brain. When a subject attends to one part of the visual field, blood flow to the opposite parietal lobe increases. Patients with damage to one parietal lobe suffer from "neglect"—inattention to—the opposite visual field, and even with improvement show difficulty shifting attention from an object in the unimpaired visual field to the other. Subcortical areas are also involved with the parietal attentional system. An area called the superior colliculus takes part in attentional shifts, while a part of the thalamus called the pulvinar maintains attention to a stimulus once the shift has occurred. In general, then, the posterior attentional system is responsible for shifting and focussing attention on different parts of the visual field.

The other attentional network is centered in the front (anterior) part of the brain, and is responsible for detecting events in the attended area. Most of Posner's work has focused on word recognition. An area at the lower front of the left side of the brain (left ventral occipital lobe) is activated by looking at words or nonwords, but not strings of consonants. While this area is thus involved in word recognition, it does not know the meanings of words, since nonsense but pronounceable nonwords (e.g., *tweal*) activate it. Meaning seems to reside in the left prefrontal cortex, which becomes active when subjects think about word meanings. Nearby and related areas are involved in other, nonattentional tasks with or without language. It may be that the attentional deficits suffered by schizophrenics are caused by malfunction of the anterior attentional system.

Attention is psychologically and neurophysiologically real. But as we learned in Chapter 5, there is evidence that material outside the focus of attention may be processed, and that this processing may be remarkably sophisticated. Studies of the clinical syndrome called *neglect* are especially revealing in this area. When patients suffers from neglect, they do not consciously perceive the left or right half of their visual field; neglect can even extend to perception of the body, so that patients with left neglect, for example, do not recognize their left arms and legs as their own. Nevertheless, there is evidence that stimuli in the neglected visual hemisphere may be perceived outside of consciousness. Patients can, when prodded, say if two stimuli in the neglected hemisphere are the same or different. If a word is presented to the dark hemisphere, it may nevertheless prime (see Chapter 5 and below) perception of a later word presented to the conscious hemisphere. Thus, if *doctor* is presented in the dark field, later perception of *nurse* in the good field will be enhanced (Gazzinaga, Ivry, & Mangun, 1998). This finding demonstrates that the stimulus *doctor* was processed for meaning despite not being perceived in consciousness.

The paradoxes of attention remain. Clearly, we actively perceive and process some things—attended things—more than others. Yet at the same time, we must be alert to things outside attention, because they might be important. If a bird watcher in the woods locked her attention so tightly on a rare bird that she did not hear a rattlesnake, she might die. Survival demands alertness to what's unattended, but the limitations of conscious experience—working memory—equally demand a mechanism for ignoring the currently irrelevant. We will return to this problem in Chapter 13.

Pattern Recognition

As we learned in Chapter 5, pattern recognition is one of the most important cognitive processes, because it is through pattern recognition that we perceive and thus know the distinct objects that make up the world. We also learned that how pattern recognition works is not fully understood. Perceiving an object is not an easy task. Consider, for example, recognizing your grandmother. You can recognize her from different angles, in different clothes, at different ages, in black and white as well as color photographs. The perceptual features which make up each presentation of your grandmother differ greatly, yet somehow you can effortlessly pull them together into the single pattern, or concept, called "grandmother."

One of the computational approaches to pattern recognition discussed in Chapter 5 is feature analysis. According to feature analysis theories, an object is defined by a set of distinctive perceptual features. Thus, your grandmother might be defined by her distinctive eyes, shape of nose, hairline, gait, and so on. When you see all these features, you perceive your grandmother. We found that there are difficulties with feature analysis theories, one of the most important being how the individual features are brought together in consciousness as perception of a whole integrated object (see also Box 12.1). The same problem exists at the neurophysiological level.

There is ample evidence that there are cells and ganglia in the brain which respond selectively to certain perceptual features such as edges or movement or size. There are also cells that respond selectively to organized percepts such as a hand regardless of its orientation, but not to hand-like stimuli such as a 4-pronged fork (Gazzinaga, Ivry, & Mangun, 1998). This has led to the suggestion that object perception might be arranged hierarchically. At the lowest level there are cells that perceive simple features such as vertical and horizontal edges. These would feed to cells that recognize conjunctions of features such as corners. These would provide input to cells that put the corners together into a rectangular surface, and so on until a master object cell is reached that represents an entire object, such as a table. Such object cells are called "gnostic" cells, from the Greek word for knowing, gnosis (see also Box 12.2).

Gnostic cells are also known informally among neuroscientists as "grandmother cells," a name that puts its finger on the key problem with the idea (Gazzaniga, Ivry, & Mangun, 1998). If grandmother cells existed in the way just described, you would have to have a distinct gnostic cell for every single object you can recognize. A cell for each grandmother; for each grandfather; for each parent; for each sibling; for each book you own; for each tune you know; for each friend you have; for each distinct automobile you recognize (not just Escort vs. Saturn, but each car you recognize as an individual, such as your rich uncle's Porsche); for every word you know, and so on. While such specific gnostic cells remain a theoretical possibility, few neuroscientists believe they exist, because we would have to have so many of them and be capable of adding to them through learning.

The main alternative theory is called *ensemble coding* (Gazzinaga, Ivry, & Mangun, 1998). It gives up on the idea of object perception being a hierarchical process culminating in the activation of a single "grandmother cell." Instead, it says that objects are defined by the simultaneous activation of a set of defining properties. Thus, your grandmother is defined by the co-occurrence in perception of a set of features, the activation of a cell assembly. Exactly how the integration is done remains a topic of investigation.

Clinical neuroscience shows that failures of object perception may be extremely fine-grained. Patients with Balint's syndrome can only perceive one object at a time. Thus, if they are shown an array of dots that are half red and half green, they report seeing only one color or the other, because they only see one dot at a time and each dot is only one color. Yet if a line is drawn connecting two differently colored dots, they now report seeing the two colors. The mere drawing of the line has made the separate objects into a single object, a dumbbell, which has two perceivable features!

The Frontal Lobes: Working Memory and Executive Control

The most developed parts of the human brain compared to the brains of even our closest primate relatives are the frontal lobes. Due to their importance, the functions of the frontal lobes have been extensively investigated, but because they are large and structurally complex, an understanding of their functions in detail is just beginning to

■ Box 12.1 ■

Singing in the Brain

One of the key problems in the neuroscience of perception, consciousness, and memory is *the binding problem*. The world of conscious experience is a unified place: sights, sounds, smells, tastes, and feelings are integrated into coherent conscious experience. Episodic memories are similarly structured. Yet the different aspects of experience are processed in different parts of the brain. The binding problem refers to the unsolved mystery of how different brain processes are bound together into consciousness. If the brain has a modular structure, as many cognitive scientists believe, the problem is compounded, because each module processes only information of concern to it, the output of the modules are integrated into a general cognitive understanding of the world and our actions in it. One motivation for connectionism is to minimize the binding problem. To the extent that the brain is a large neural network, there is no need for coordinating the outputs of separate mental modules.

Songs provide an interesting vehicle for investigating the binding problem and the issue of modularity. Songs have a linguistic component—lyrics—and a purely auditory-sensory component—melody. Our experience of songs integrates the two into an exciting whole. But what goes on in the brain? Are words and melody processed separately, as a modular approach would suggest, or together, as connectionists would have it?

French scientists studied the perception of songs from operas by professional musicians from the Marseilles opera house using the evoked potential technique (Besson, Faita, Peretz, Bonnel, & Requin, 1998). The subject wears what looks like a shower cap that has a standard set of electrodes that pick up brain wave activity from different locations on the scalp. It is known that different types of stimuli provoke different kinds of electrophysiological patterns of activity. In the present study, the relevant evoked brain waves (potentials) were the N400 wave, which reflects semantic processing, and the P300 wave, which reflects sensory processing. Subjects listened to 200 short passages from well-known French operas, sung by a professional singer *a cappella*. The key stimulus was the last word in the passage, which was either semantically incongruous (e.g., BLOOD when the word should have been WIND) or sung off key or both or neither (control condition).

The investigators found that semantic incongruity alone provoked a strong N400 wave over most of the brain, no different from N400 waves provoked by semantic incongruity in speech. Off-key singing alone produced P300 waves mostly in the parietal regions, no different from P300 waves provoked by missed notes in pure music. Off-key semantically inappropriate words provoked both N400 and P300 waves, but there was no interaction, the effects of the two variables were additive. Off-key singing did not change the semantic N400 wave and semantic inappropriateness did not affect the P300 wave. These results support modularity. Processing of semantic information is not affected by being embedded in song, and processing of musical information is unaffected by being accompanied by words.

Modularity with regard to the perception and understanding of melodies is supported by another study by the same group of scientists (Peretz et al., 1994). A 35-year-old Canadian nurse suffered from aneurysms which had to be treated by surgery, resulting in limited damage to her auditory cortex. After surgery, her ability to understand non-musical sounds such as speech, tones, or animal noises was unimpaired. However, she complained that her perception of music was changed. She could not recognize tunes taken from her personal record collection, she could not name popular tunes, including the Canadian national anthem. She could recognize the songs if given the lyrics and could name the composers of named pieces of classical music.

It appears that our perception of songs rests on two separate modules of the brain. *How* words and melody are integrated remains an open question.

LEARNING AND COGNITION

■ Box 12.2 ■

Agnosia

Agnosia was a term coined by Sigmund Freud during his early days as a neurologist. It means not-knowing. Agnosias represent failures of object recognition. For example, the patient in Box 12.1 who lost the ability to hear melodies suffered from *amusia,* not-knowing music.

Agnosias come in many different forms, and provide some of the most dramatic evidence for the modularity of the brain/mind. For example, one patient could not name individual objects that overlapped in a black and white drawing, but could color each one in with crayons. An artist afflicted with agnosia could not name objects but could still draw them. Another patient was given a card that could be inserted in a horizontal slot. When asked to hold the card in the correct position for insertion, she held it vertically, but could actually insert the card in the slot when told to do so. Agnosia is not simply memory failure. A patient whose memory is failing would not recognize a given object such as a set of keys however it's presented, while an agnosic patient might fail to recognize the keys by sight but could recognize them if put in the hand.

Perhaps the most dramatic form of agnosia is prosopagnosia, the inability to see faces as faces, such as the famous man who mistook his wife for a hat (Sacks, 1985). Although such patients have no trouble recognizing objects, including facial features, such as eyes, nose, lips, and so on, they do not see faces as faces. One patient could not recognize his wife or photographs of famous people. One day at a club he saw someone laughing and asked who it was, to be told it was himself, seen in a mirror. The existence of prosopagnosia suggests that the brain possesses a module dedicated to seeing faces as wholes apart from their parts. Against this it has been argued that prosopagnosia reflects a breakdown in the ability to distinguish subtly different objects of any type. After all, all faces are basically similar, and only small physical differences make Tom Arnold's and Bill Clinton's faces distinguishable. However, this line of reasoning was undermined by a sheep farmer who suffered from prosopagnosia. He could not recognize faces of well-known people, but he could easily distinguish photos of his own sheep and learn to distinguish new sheep. Neurologically, it has been found that certain cells in the brain, most importantly in the amygdala, fire only in response to faces and not to other complex stimuli. In addition, certain cells fire only in response to certain emotional expressions in faces (Adolphs, 1999). We will look at facial expression of emotion in Chapter 13.

Exactly how the brain detects "faceness" is unclear, but the survival value of a module for face processing is quite clear. As we learned in Chapter 2, early human beings survived by virtue of expertise at social interaction. Key to sophisticated social skills is being able to identify fellow human beings as individuals—to recognize one's mate, one's enemies, one's friends, and so on. Moreover, faces are important to the exercise of theory of mind, because faces provide us cues to other people's states of mind: their feelings, attitudes, and intentions toward us. Face-reading is a vital part of mind-reading.

See Gazzaniga, Ivry, and Mangun (1998) and Sacks (1985).

---

emerge. Here, we will just touch on two psychological aspects of the frontal lobes: their role in memory and complex behavioral control.

The prefrontal cortex is the site of working memory. Monkeys with lesions to the prefrontal cortex fail a delayed memory test. They see food placed in one of two wells in a board placed in front of their cage. Then a barrier is lowered so the monkey cannot see the board, and identical cards are placed over the two wells. To retrieve the food, the monkey must maintain its location in working memory and lift the appropriate cover. Which well will be baited with food is chosen randomly on each trial, so the monkey cannot learn to simply choose left or right. Normal monkeys pass this test, but prefrontally lesioned monkeys choose covers at random. Their deficit is not a deficit in learning. In a variant of the test, a distinctive card is placed on the baited well. So a card with a cross on it might always cover the baited well and a card with a circle always covers the empty well. Mastering this trial requires learning and thus long-term memory, and prefrontally lesioned animals can learn to always choose the well with the cross. Variants on this learning task have been used to study long-term memory.

Patients with damage to the prefrontal cortex behave like the lesioned monkeys on a similar task, the Wisconsin card-sorting task. In this test, a pack of cards is given showing a variety of geometric figures varying as to shape, color, and number. Thus, one card may have one red triangle, another two blue circles, third four red stars and so on. The subject is asked to sort the cards into piles according to some rule. Thus, the subject might be told to sort by color, or by number, or by shape, or by combinations of these. There are obviously many rules one might follow, and the rule is periodically changed in the course of testing. Normal subjects can adjust to the changes in rules, holding each one in working memory as appropriate. Subjects with prefrontal lesions, however, tend to perseverate, returning to an earlier rule because they cannot hold the current one temporarily in working memory to guide their behavior.

The prefrontal cortex is also involved in source-monitoring of memories. In Chapter 6 we studied eyewitness testimony and learned that one problem with eyewitness recollection stems from source-monitoring failures. For example, a subject might see a film of an auto accident in which no stop sign is present, but is later asked a question suggesting the presence of the stop sign. If the subject fails to separate the two sources of information in memory, he or she may testify to seeing a stop sign in the original film. Glisky, Polster, and Routhuieaux (1995) used standard neuropsychological tests to measure the frontal lobe functioning of normal subjects. Some subjects showed relatively poor frontal lobe function, though still well above the performance of patients with actual frontal lobe damage. The subjects listened to a series of sentences read either by a male or a female voice. Recognition memory for the sentences was tested by presenting the subjects with pairs of sentences and asking them to choose the one they had heard. Source memory was tested by having the subjects listen to previously heard sentences read by each voice and then choosing the voice that had originally read the sentence. Subjects with low frontal lobe scores did not score above chance on the source memory test, although their scores on sentence-recognition were normal.

Patients with frontal lobe damage show difficulties in making appropriate—especially socially appropriate—decisions. For example, their behavior is dominated to a highly exaggerated degree by the physical cues present in a situation. A French neuropsychologist, Lhermitte, has demonstrated this tendency in somewhat grotesque experiments (see Gazzinaga, Ivry, & Mangun, 1998). He might greet a patient coming to his office by placing on a table a hammer, a nail, and a framed picture. The patient spontaneously uses the hammer to drive the nail into the wall and hang the picture. Another patient found a hypodermic on the table. When Lhermitte turned and dropped his pants, the patient gave him a shot in the buttocks! Monkeys with frontal lesions lose social skills and find themselves ostracized by their troop. We will return to the role of the frontal lobes in decision making in Chapter 13.

LONG-TERM MEMORY AND LEARNING

The idea that memories are stored in the brain is very old. Medieval Islamic and, later, Christian physicians believed that the brain was divided into separate compartments, or ventricles, each of which was responsible for a different psychological function. Experiences were thought to be processed from the senses through a series of four to seven ventricles, finally coming to reside in the ventricle for memory. Even Descartes, who thought that soul and body were distinct substances (the former spiritual and the latter material), believed that memories are stored in the brain, not the soul. In the seventeenth and eighteenth centuries it was discovered that the ventricles of the medieval doctors—who had been forbidden by their religions to dissect the body—did not exist, and the search for the biological basis of learning and memory had to start over again.

Modern neuroscience began with the research and theories of Franz Joseph Gall (1758–1828). Gall performed the first modern anatomical and comparative studies of human and animal brains, believing that different psychological functions were located in distinct organs of the brain. For example, he located Lust in the cerebellum, Murder just above the ears, and Location and Language behind the eyes. While Gall agreed with the medieval physicians that each psychological function had its distinct organ in the brain, he did not believe that memory was a separate mental power, and he located memories throughout the brain. Gall thought that memories were stored in the organ whose function had been involved with a particular experience. So, for example, memories of sexual experience would be stored with the organ for Lust, while memories for places would be stored in Location.

Unfortunately for the development of neuroscience, Gall's basically correct view of the brain turned into the pseudoscience of phrenology. Gall was followed by enthusiasts rather than scientists, and his system became a sort of parlor game of diagnosing people's personalities from the bumps on their skulls, and so phrenology, as it came to be called, fell into disrepute in scientific circles. Gall had been an extreme localizationalist, believing that psychological functions could be localized to precisely definable parts of the brain. Partly in reaction to Gall, a rival view arose that maintained that the brain acts as a whole, with psychological functions being distributed throughout the entire brain. The tension between localizationalist and distributionist views of mental function has generated controversy and creativity in neuroscience down to the present day.

The distributionist view gained credence from the research of Pierre Jean Marie Flourens (1794–1867), Gall's harshest critic and the leading physiologist of the day. Flourens performed ablation experiments, in which he removed (ablated) or destroyed (lesioned) different parts and amounts of animals' brains. He claimed that destruction of parts of the brain resulted in the loss not of specific functions, as phrenology predicted, but of a general capacity for adaptive behavior, suggesting that the brain acts as a whole; thus, as more brain is removed, the stupider the animal becomes. Phrenologists protested, rightly, that Flourens' method was like investigating the functions of an unknown machine by taking an ax to part of it and then observing what the machine does not do. Notwithstanding the crudity of his methods, Flourens' prestige ensured that the distributionist view of brain function would remain dominant for some decades.

The localizationist view began to revive with the clinical findings of Pierre Paul Broca (1824–1880). In his hospital, Broca observed that patients with a certain kind of aphasia—difficulty with speech or language—proved, upon autopsy, to have lesions in the left front neocortex of their brains. Broca hypothesized that this area—today called Broca's area—was responsible for language, just as the phrenologists had said. In 1870, two German investigators showed that application of mild electrical currents to the brains of living animals resulted in specific muscular responses. As a result of these findings, a sort of "new phrenology" was born. It turned out that Gall had been correct that the brain possessed specialized areas for specific functions, but had been wrong about the sort of functions the brain served. Instead of broad psychological traits such as Lust and Theft, the specialized areas of the brain were responsible for specific sensory or motor functions, such as registering a sound or moving a limb.

However, these discoveries of the late nineteenth century left the physiological basis of learning as mysterious as ever. Was there a brain center for Memory? Were specific memories stored in specific parts of the brain? These questions remained unanswered. As the localizational view gained dominance around the turn of the century, the biologist Richard Semon coined the term "engram" to refer to the trace in the brain storing a particular memory (Squire, 1987). The search for the engram has dominated the physiological study of learning ever since (Donegan & Thompson, 1991).

In the first half of the twentieth century, the most diligent searcher for the engram was the psychologist Karl Lashley, a student of John B. Watson's. Lashley had collaborated with Watson on a series of classical conditioning studies—the first ever performed in the United States—and believed that the future of behaviorist psychology lay in the reduction of psychological laws to physiology (Lashley, 1923); hence his ultimately futile search for the engram. Lashley reasoned that if engrams existed at specific sites in the brain—the localizationist hypothesis about learning—removal of the site of the engram would abolish specific memories. Therefore, Lashley adopted Flourens' ablation method, hoping to remove, and thus find, the engram.

Over years of difficult investigation, Lashley had rats learn mazes, ablating varying amounts and location of brain matter either before or after learning. Lashley's results and conclusions echoed Flourens': The ability to learn was not impaired by lesions to any specific site in the brain, but was gradually lost as greater amounts of brain were removed; similarly, memory for the maze seemed not to reside in any particular part of the brain, but seemed to be gradually erased as more and more brain was removed. In looking back on his search, Lashley ruefully but wryly concluded that, according to his findings, "learning is just not possible. It is difficult to conceive of a mechanism which can satisfy the conditions set for it. Nevertheless, in spite of such evidence against it, learning does sometimes occur" (Lashley, 1950, pp. 477–478). Lashley embraced, as Flourens had, the distributionist, or mass-action, view of the brain, proposing that learning is an activity of the whole brain and that individual memories are stored in the whole brain, not at distinct sites, or engrams. Despite difficulties and controversies over the interpretation of his results (Squire, 1987)—he was, after all, still attacking a delicate mechanism with what amounted to a jackhammer—Lashley's results, when published in 1929, virtually brought to a halt the investigation of the neural substrates of learning and memory (Donegan & Thompson, 1991).

A virtue of the localizationist, engram theory had been that it held out the hope of finding discrete mechanisms of learning and memory, and it pointed the way to investigations searching for them. But Lashley's findings had destroyed the localizationist view. His replacement, mass action, seemed to make finding the neural basis of memory a hopeless task, for there seemed to be no place to look for it. However, in 1949, Donald Hebb, a student of Lashley's, revived the field and gave it its modern form with his concept of the cell assembly. The cell-assembly concept respected Lashley's findings while reintroducing the localizational hypothesis in modified form. The failing of the old engram view had been its narrowness, essentially claiming that individual memories resided in individual neurons, a hypothesis rendered untenable by Lashley's studies. Hebb proposed instead that the mechanisms of learning, and the sites of memory storage, lay not in isolated neurons but in organized groups, or assemblies, of neurons. Moreover, these assemblies need not involve cells adjacent to one another, but might involve connections between cells in different parts of the brain. According to Hebb, memories were both distributed, as engrams are not found in single cells, and localized, as learning does not involve the whole brain (Donegan & Thompson, 1991; Squire, 1987). Thus, ablation of some piece of brain tissue could not remove a single engram but it might damage part of the circuitries responsible for learning and memory storage, weakening, but not abolishing, learning, as Lashley had found. By proposing that there were mechanisms of learning to be found, Hebb gave new inspiration to the neuropsychology of learning.

The concept of the cell assembly helps show how difficult it is to interpret ablation findings (Olton, 1991). Any given piece of behavior involves what Richard Thompson (Donegan & Thompson, 1991) calls a sensory-motor circuit, beginning with peripheral stimulation and ending with overt motor response. Somewhere in between is the structure or structures—the cell assemblies—responsible for learning, Thompson's memory trace circuit. The memory structures must be plastic, capable of modification by experience, and of retaining this modification for a period of time. But finding the central, plastic part of the sensory-motor circuit is difficult, for experiments looking for the memory trace circuit may change behavior by altering structures not involved in learning. For example, ablation may accidentally destroy tissue necessary for making a classically conditioned motor response, but it would be a mistake to think that because the response has disappeared that one has found the memory trace. Ablation experiments are thus no longer the mainstay of researchers on the neural basis of memory.

There are several logically possible sources of neural plasticity (Squire, 1987). One is growing new neurons. The development of the brain and the nervous system is taken up in Chapter 10; this chapter will treat learning and memory in adult organisms. Until recently, it was thought that the adult brain is incapable of growing new cells, but recent research suggests that this is not so. However, these findings have not yet affected investigation into the neural bases of learning and memory. One disproved possibility is that memory was stored in the complex organic molecules found in neural tissue. This hypothesis was popular for a while in the 1960s and led to hopes for learning by taking pills, but the initially exciting findings did not pan out. Most research today focuses on changes to the synapses that connect existing neurons. Experience may induce growth of new synapses or alter the neurochemistry and/or the structure of existing synapses. Thus, the modern "search for the engram" involves, first, locating the plastic structures of the brain that change with learning, and then identifying the cellular mechanisms in these structures that cause learning. Great advances in answering both questions have been made.

Neurophysiological studies of learning and memory proceed at a fine level of detail, and primarily investigate evolutionarily old, noncortical parts of the brain. Higher cognitive functions, however, are carried out by the cortex, and are harder to investigate. Recent advances in the ability to scan brain activity in real time, as opposed to taking a momentary snapshot of brain structures with conventional X-rays or CAT scans, have made feasible the first investigations of the cortex as it goes about its work. The most important of these new techniques are MRI (magnetic resonance imaging), functional MRI, and PET (positron emission tomography) scans.

Amnesia

Perhaps the most dramatic evidence that learning and memory depend on the brain is organic amnesia, when damage to the brain erases old memories and makes it difficult or impossible to form new ones. The study of amnesia, while necessarily less precise than experimental studies of the biology of memory, has nevertheless contributed important information concerning the sites of memory formation in storage (for a review, see Verfaellie & Cermak, 1991). In this section we will focus on the irreversible amnesic syndrome; temporary amnesia is treated in Box 12.3. Amnesic syndrome is defined by four symptoms (Butters & Miliotis, 1985; Groves & Rebec, 1988). The first is anterograde amnesia, the difficulty or inability to form new memories. Second is retrograde amnesia, the loss of some memories prior to the event causing the brain damage

■ Box 12.3 ■

Temporary Amnesia and Consolidation

The amnesic syndrome involves permanent impairment to the ability to form new memories. Memory loss, including retrograde and anterograde amnesia, can also occur following brain trauma that does not create amnesic syndrome.

The most important aspect of temporary amnesia from the standpoint of the study of learning and memory is the gradual recovery from retrograde amnesia for events lying many years before the brain insult. For example, five months after trauma one patient suffered total retrograde amnesia for all events occurring less than two years before the accident, but gradually memory returned, so that the patient permanently lost memories for events occurring only two weeks or less before brain insult. Memories are recovered from the oldest memories to the most recent. Findings such as these have led to the concept of *consolidation*, the hypothesis that memory formation is a remarkably gradual process taking weeks or even months. When the process is disrupted, consolidation is slowed, as in the present case for all memories within two years of brain damage, or even blocked entirely, as for the events occurring two weeks or less before injury. The concept of consolidation challenges our commonsense ideas about memory, which suggest that one immediately stores memories the way a VCR does. A better analogy might be to a Polaroid picture that takes not seconds but months to develop. Memories may be laid down when we have experiences, but it takes a long time for the information to be fixed permanently, and it is possible for the fixation process to be altered by damage to the brain mechanisms responsible for it.

LEARNING AND COGNITION

responsible for the amnesia. The retrograde amnesia is graded, so that the more remote a memory is from the traumatic event the more likely it is to be remembered. The third symptom is confabulation: When asked to recall an event lost to memory, amnesiacs may make up a story instead. Finally, amnesics' difficulties are restricted to memory, for they possess normal intelligence.

The most famous and most extensively researched case of amnesic syndrome is the patient H.M. (Cotman & McGaugh, 1980; Squire, 1987). H.M. had suffered from epilepsy from age 16, and in 1953, at age 27, the epilepsy having become uncontrollable by medication, surgery was performed in an effort to relieve the patient's seizures. The operation was successful in controlling the epilepsy, but accidentally and unfortunately it caused total anterograde amnesia. H.M.'s intelligence (IQ 117), personality, and working memory are intact—he has a normal digit span of 6 to 7 items—but he can form no new memories: Even after 25 presentations of a long word list he cannot recall more than the 6 items storable in working memory, and he shows no primacy effect. As H.M. says, "Every day is alone in itself . . . everything looks clear to me, but what happened just before? . . . It's like waking from a dream. I just don't remember" (quoted by Cotman & McGaugh, 1980, p. 334). H.M. cannot even recognize a current photograph of himself, and he needs constant custodial care. We sometimes wish we could forget, but life without memory is horrible.

Cases of amnesia have proven valuable in distinguishing between various forms and processes of memory. The distinction between working and long-term memory (LTM) is supported by the amnesic syndrome. H.M. is typical among amnesics in having a normal digit span, and thus intact working memory, while being unable to lay down memories in LTM. Amnesia also shows that we must distinguish between the site of memory storage and the sites of the processes and mechanisms that create memories. H.M. can recall remote events, so we know that his permanent memory-storage sites were not damaged by surgery, but he cannot form new memories, so we know that the structures responsible for memory creation were damaged. Moreover, the graded nature of retrograde amnesia suggests that memory consolidation is a drawn out but time-limited process in which some structures of the brain participate in laying down memories in some other part of the brain with which contact is eventually broken off (Squire, 1987).

One remarkable finding with H.M., and confirmed in other cases of amnesia, supports important distinctions between types of long-term memory. H.M. shows essentially normal rates of learning for a variety of motor skills, such as mirror drawing, even though each time he performs the task he says he has never done it before! Amnesics also show normal acquisition of simple Pavlovian responses without memory of the apparatus, although complex Pavlovian phenomena such as latent inhibition and reversal learning are impaired. Such learning without memory even extends to some problem-solving tasks such as the *Tower of Hanoi* puzzle (see Chapter 2), in which washers of different sizes making a pyramid shape over the first of three posts must be moved, one at a time and without placing a larger on a smaller, to make the pyramid on the third post, and indicates that there are at least two forms of long-term memory, one of which is spared in the amnesic syndrome. Squire (1987) adopts the distinction between declarative and procedural memory, made by philosophy and artificial intelligence (see Chapters 2 and 6). Amnesics lack declarative memory, conscious recall of past events, but retain procedural memory, the ability to learn new behaviors. Thus, mirror drawing remains ever new to H.M. even as he gets better and better at it.

Recent research also reveals that amnesics show near normal to normal priming effects (Schachter, 1985, 1986a, 1986b, 1987). Usually, memory for a list of words is tested by asking subjects to recall the list or to say whether presented words were on the list or not (recognition). However, if subjects learn a list of words and are later presented even two or three weeks later with a list of word fragments to complete, and are told nothing about any connection between the word fragments and the earlier list, they are more likely than controls to complete the word fragments if the fragments make words that were on the earlier list, and if the fragments have more than one solution, they are more likely than controls to complete the fragment with a word from the earlier list. A related phenomenon occurs when subjects are shown a word and then later are tachistoscopically shown words at extremely brief presentation times, and it is found that the word or words shown to the subject are recognized at much shorter presentation intervals than control words. It appears that mere exposure to a word somehow "primes" that word in memory so that it is much more available than other words for some time.

When amnesics are shown a list of words and then tested on it by the usual means, they do very poorly, showing anterograde amnesia. But if they are simply given word fragments to complete, they show priming for words on the list. This occurs only when they are not told of any connection between the two lists: When they are told that the fragments are hints that will help them remember the earlier list, they again do poorly. The distinction between recognition and priming is dramatically emphasized by research with sufferers from Alzheimer's disease, whose amnesic syndrome grows progressively worse. Alzheimer's subjects show a steady loss in the ability to recognize words from earlier presented lists, but show essentially normal priming (Schachter, 1985).

The existence of intact priming makes possible some learning by amnesics, but within very rigid limits. For example, after extensive drilling, a group of amnesics learned 30 items of computer terminology and retained it over the months of the experiment. They could also learn to write a very simple program. However, their knowledge could only be brought out when test questions were almost exactly the same as the wording of items and definitions at the time of learning. For example, one subject learned to respond "save" to the definition "to store a program," but after having written his simple program and being told to save it, he was unable to do so until prompted with the letter s.

As a result of these and other findings, Daniel Schachter (1985, 1987, 1995) has distinguished between explicit and implicit long-term memory. Explicit memory requires conscious awareness of a previous event, and is lost in amnesia; implicit memory does not require conscious awareness and is spared by amnesia. The existence and classification of multiple memory systems will be discussed in the next sections.

We have now reviewed the behavioral psychology of amnesia. What structures of the brain are responsible for amnesic syndrome? H.M.'s surgery involved the removal of structures from the medio-temporal areas of the brain: two-thirds of the hippocampus, the parahippocampal gyrus, the uncus, and the amygdala (Cotman & McGaugh, 1980). The medio-temporal structures are closely interconnected, appearing to form a functional system within the brain, called the limbic system. One case of human amnesia implicates the hippocampus as the most important structure responsible for learning, because unlike H.M., patient R.B. suffered damage only to area CA1 of the hippocampus, yet developed a severe case of the amnesic syndrome

(Squire, 1987). Human amnesia can also result from damage to the diencephalic midline of the brain, including the thalamus, hypothalamus, and mammilary bodies (Markowitsch, 1995), as happens in Korsakoff's syndrome, which follows upon some cases of severe alcoholism.

While cases of amnesia may suggest which structures of the brain are involved in learning, they cannot answer more precise questions about how various structures operate and interact while forming, storing, and retrieving memories. Amnesic's brains may be damaged in ways not always apparent at autopsy, and many amnesics such as H.M., who had suffered epilepsy, and those acquiring amnesia from disease, such as Korsakoff's patients, may have incurred other physiological damage, making identification of memory structures tentative (see Box 12.4). Investigators into the biological bases of learning and memory have therefore tried to develop experimental animal

■ Box 12.4 ■

Permanent Memory?

Once a memory is completely consolidated, can it be lost? This important question has been much contested in cognitive psychology. While it is obvious that we cannot remember everything we have been exposed to—otherwise we would never get less than 100 percent on college tests—there are two reasons this might be so. On the one hand, memories might be lost even after complete consolidation, perhaps because memory traces in the brain simply decay over the years. On the other hand, memories might be permanent, and our loss of them is really a loss of ability to retrieve them from storage.

Support for the second point of view seemed to come from serendipitous findings by the neurosurgeon Wilder Penfield in the 1950s. Penfield performed operations on the brains of epilepsy patients in hope of relieving their symptoms. Part of brain surgery—which is always done on awake patients—involves stimulating the brain to discover the precise location of important abilities, so that they will not be damaged by surgery. Penfield reported that in the course of his explorations of the brain, his patients would sometimes seem to relive remote events as if they were being experienced anew. For example, one patient reported hearing music being played, although of course no music was to be heard in the operating room. Penfield and others have argued that these experiences are an accurate reliving of past experience permanently etched in the brain.

However, closer examination of Penfield's findings casts doubt on his interpretation. To begin with, only a tiny minority of Penfield's patients ever reported memorylike experiences. Those who did often reported that they were more like dreams than like real experiences, having either the unreal or fantastic character of dreams or involving experiences the patient could not have had. Moreover, we should bear in mind that Penfield's patients all suffered from epilepsy, a disorder of the brain, and many of the "recollections" were connected with the patient's epileptic symptoms. For example, one patient's seizures were regularly preceded by a (false) image of a robber approaching him; during surgery he reported the vivid experience of being attacked by robbers in the operating room! It thus seems likely that Penfield's patients were reporting not memories, but artificial experiences created by electrical stimulation of the brain (Squire, 1987). Whether or not memories are permanent remains an open question.

models of human amnesia to pinpoint more precisely the structures involved in learning and memory (Ridley & Baker, 1991; Rolls, 1990).

Squire (1992) reviewed attempts to replicate the human amnesic syndrome by lesioning in rats and monkeys the various parts of the brain found to be implicated in human amnesic syndrome. Squire concluded that the key structures involved in the formation of long-term memory are the hippocampus and associated cortical tissue (especially the perirhinal cortex and the parahippocampal gyrus).

The Biology of Long-Term Memory

Multiple Memory Systems

Psychologists have drawn many distinctions between forms of long-term memory (Kesner, 1991), such as episodic-semantic or explicit-implicit. A perennial question has been whether these different psychological memory systems would prove to be neurologically distinct as well. Squire (1992, 1994, 1995; Squire & Knowlton, 1995) has proposed a classification of memory systems based on extensive findings on the neurophysiology of learning and memory.

The Critical Role of the Hippocampus

The most studied neurological memory structure is the hippocampus and its related cortical structures, which many psychologists believe is uniquely involved in forming declarative memories. Squire (1992) proposes that the essential psychological function of the hippocampus is to rapidly—often on a single trial—establish links between ordinarily unrelated patterns of events by establishing flexible representations of multiple stimuli, which then become available to multiple response systems. The hippocampus is thus involved in general purpose learning, while the learning systems spared in amnesia are special purpose, reflexive, rigid, and slow.

Recent research on the hippocampus has begun to focus on the different roles played in learning and memory by different hippocampal structures, especially the parahippocampal gyrus and the hippocampus proper (Eichenbaum, Otto, & Cohen, 1994; Eichenbaum & Bunsey, 1995; Gluck & Myers, 1995). Figure 12.1 shows a simplified structural flow diagram of how the structures of the hippocampus relate to the brain. Observe that the hippocampus proper is self-contained and connects with the rest of the brain only through the parahippocampal structures.

Early psychologists distinguished two ways in which ideas might be bound together by learning and stored in memory. One way was called **fusion.** In fusion, the ideas blend together so perfectly that they can no longer be separated. An example is our perception of a harmonious chord played on a piano. Played alone, we can distinguish two or three notes, but if they are played together as a chord, we experience them so blended that we no longer can hear each note separately. The other form of the binding of ideas was **association** as we have discussed earlier. In an association each idea retains its identity and representation in memory, but a link is formed between them. For example, in an old-fashioned paired associate learning task I might learn to say BOK when I see DIV presented on the memory drum, but the nonsense syllables do not blend together in an inextricable tangle the way the notes in a chord do. While their theories are somewhat different, Eichenbaum and his colleagues (Eichenbaum & Bunsey, 1995; Eichenbaum, Otto, & Cohen, 1994; and Gluck &

FIGURE 12.1 Simplified block diagram showing information flows between the hippocampus, its related structures in the parahippocampal gyrus, and the rest of the brain. From "Representation and Association in Memory: A Neurocomputational View of Hippocampal Function" by M. A. Gluck and C. E. Myers. *Current Directions in Psychological Science, 4,* 1995. Reprinted with the permission of Cambridge University Press.

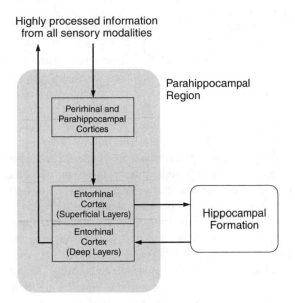

Myers, 1995) propose that the hippocampus proper forms associations while the parahippocampal gyrus forms fusions.

For example, Eichenbaum and Bunsey (1995) report a series of experiments with rats using a variation on the old paired-associate learning paradigm used with humans in the Golden Age of Theory. The rats were either normal or had their parahippocampus lesioned (thus also cutting off the hippocampus from the brain), or had their hippocampi proper lesioned. The task involved learning to bar-press for reinforcement only when certain pairs of odors were presented in a sniff tube in either order. Thus pairs such as A-B, or C-D, or B-A, or D-C were followed by reward, while other pairings were not. Nonreinforced (foil) pairs were of two types, mispairings or nonrelational sequences. Mispairings were pairs of odors that occurred in the list of paired associates but which were not paired with each other, such as A-D. Nonrelational sequences were pairings of a familiar odor with a new one that had never been presented, for example B-X, or pairings of completely new odors.

Normal rats learned to distinguish between paired associates and mispairings and nonrelational sequences. That is, they learned to bar-press only when presented with the former but not the latter two. Rats with parahippocampal lesions (which also rendered the hippocampus inoperative) never learned to distinguish paired associates from mispairings but they did learn to distinguish paired associates from nonrelational sequences. It appears that rats without a functional hippocampus can tell novelty when they see it (and thus reject nonrelational sequences, which always involve at least one new odor), but cannot distinguish between pairs of familiar odors. They are thus like the amnesic who laughed at a joke the first time he heard it, but thought it stupid and unfunny the second time, even though he thought he'd never heard it before. The finding is also consistent with Squire's view that nonassociative learning does not depend on the hippocampus.

Rats with lesions to the hippocampus alone behaved differently from normal or parahippocampal lesioned rats. Like both, they learned to ignore nonrelational sequences. However, they were even better at distinguishing paired associates from mispairs than were normal animals.

Eichenbaum concluded from these findings that the hippocampus is critically involved in associative learning, but that the two hippocampal structures form different sorts of association. The hippocampus forms associations while the parahippocampal gyrus forms fusions. Rats with lesions to the parahippocampal gyrus, that is, with no effective hippocampus at all, cannot learn any associations at all, but can recognize novelty. Rats with lesions to the hippocampus can form fusions, and thus can readily distinguish pairs from mispairs, because the fusions of, for example, A-B and A-C are recognizably different. Interestingly, human amnesics can, with effort, learn rigidly defined question and answer pairs, as we saw earlier. For example, they can learn to answer questions about baseball, but only if the question asked is repeated exactly the same on each occasion. Eichenbaum suggests that they form fusions, not associations, between the ideas in the question and answer. Change even one part of the fused idea, and it cannot be retrieved from memory.

Although the hippocampus is involved in forming memories, it is not the site of engrams. Amnesics can remember their past despite losing their hippocampal function. Thus the role of the hippocampus in laying down memories is time-limited (Squire, 1992). The hippocampus thus seems to play the central role in memory consolidation as revealed in temporary amnesia. Indeed, in temporary amnesia, memory formation is disrupted as long as hippocampal function is impaired (Squire, 1992). McClelland, McNaughton, and O'Reilly (1995) have proposed that the hippocampus causes consolidation of memory by repeatedly presenting connectionist theory-like "training pairs" to the cortex. Roughly speaking, as the cortex forms the cell assemblies that will eventually store a given memory, it tests them against a record stored temporarily in the hippocampus, and corrects itself by connectionist weight-modification methods until it correctly represents the memory. Eventually, the hippocampal memory vanishes, leaving only the cortical representation. Thus amnesia is temporally graded, as we have seen. Old memories are intact because the hippocampus had finished training the cortex; memories just before and after trauma are lost because the hippocampus was completely out of operation; and memories for events in between are partially lost because the hippocampus was active for a while and then damaged, only partially training the cell assemblies of the cortex.

Connectionist Model of Hippocampal Function. As we saw in the last chapter, one of the promises of connectionism is to bring closer together psychological theories about the intuitive processor with neurological understanding of brain functioning. Schmajuk and his colleagues (e.g., Schmajuk & DiCarlo, 1992) have proposed a connectionist theory of learning and memory that can be mapped onto neural pathways of learning.

Figure 12.2 shows Schmajuk's "brain-mapped" neural network. Ignoring the hippocampus for the moment, Schmajuk's network is an only slightly more complex

FIGURE 12.2 The S-D (Schmajuk-DiCarlo) connectionist neural model of Pavlovian conditioning: Diagram of the network showing error signals sent to the hidden units and output units. (CS = conditioned stimulus; CN = configural stimulus; US = unconditioned stimulus; VS = CS-US association; VN = CN-US associations; VH = CS-CN association; B = aggregate prediction; CR = conditioned response; EH = error signal for hidden units; EO = error signal for output units. Arrows represent fixed synapses. Solid circles represent variable synapses. Anatomical areas indicated in parentheses refer to the mapping of different nodes in the network onto various brain regions. CX = context.)

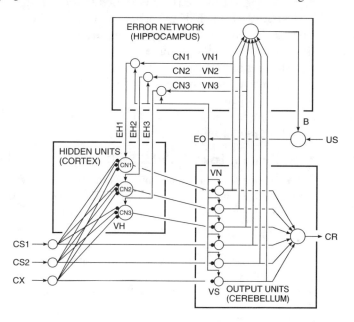

version of the three-layer Pavlovian conditioning network discussed in Chapter 10. The network is of the feedforward type and has four layers: (1) an input layer for conditioned stimuli and contextual stimuli, (2) a layer of hidden units for representing configural stimuli, (3) a hidden layer of output units converging on (4) a final single unit layer responsible for the CR. The first layer of hidden units is presumed to be in the cortex, where stimuli are represented, and both response layers are located in the cerebellum, which is where conditioned responses take place. As we have seen, animals and humans without functioning hippocampi are capable of conditioning and skill learning, but not of complex forms of declarative memory. Without its hippocampal units, Schmajuk's model likewise simulates conditioning but not memory.

Squire and Schmajuk both believe that the hippocampus is crucial for memory, but Schmajuk assigns a somewhat different role to the hippocampus than does Squire. One of the shortcomings of neural networks, we learned in the last chapter, is the biologically implausible nature of back-propagation. Schmajuk's account of hippocampal functioning represents a way to carry out back-propagation's job—sending error messages to the neural network so that it can adjust its connection strengths and learn—in a physiologically realistic way. The hippocampus in this model acts as an additional neural network laid over the first, whose role is to carry error signals from the cerebellum's motor units to the hidden units in the cortex, adjusting their weights until the network produces the desired output.

Recall that in the Holyoak, Koh, and Nisbett (1989) model of Pavlovian conditioning presented in Chapter 3, the system predicted the occurrence or nonoccurrence of the US, and production rules gained or lost strength depending on their ability to make correct predictions. Similarly, Schmajuk assigns to the hippocampus the role of generating a prediction (B in Figure 12.2) about US occurrence, computing the error (EO in the figure) between prediction and reality, and using the discrepancy, if any, to tune the network toward better predictions by sending error signals (EH in the figure) to the hidden cortical units. Schmajuk and Dicarlo review extensive neurophysiological and behavioral literature to support their hypothesized network and its mapping onto the brain, and report extensive simulations showing that the model correctly predicts conditioning and amnesic phenomena.

The Schmajuk model is a good example of trends in the neurophysiology of learning and memory. It incorporates cognitive ideas from the symbol-manipulation tradition, aims for biological plausibility, and proposes a model at a level of analysis between pure symbol-systems and pure physiology.

Learning at the Cellular Level: Model Systems

We now move down by one level of the nervous system, from the structures of the brain to the individual neurons of which they are composed, looking for the neural circuits that lay down and store memories. Research on the cellular mechanisms of learning has advanced rapidly in the past few years. For reasons that will become apparent, investigations of learning at the cellular level use very simple animal models—especially invertebrates—and concern simple forms of conditioning. Psychologists hope that, because neurons and synapses are the same in all animals, including humans, the exciting findings from research on invertebrates will prove true of humans too.

Neural Circuits for Conditioning

We cannot morally or ethically study human neural circuitry at work; nor is it practical to do so, given the human nervous system's size and complexity. However, marine invertebrates and insects have simple nervous systems made up of large neurons, making it possible to study how each neuron works and how neural connections are modified during learning. Several research programs employ such subjects (see Byrne & Crow, 1991, or Krasne & Glanzman, 1995, for reviews).

Perhaps the most prominent of these research programs is Eric Kandel's investigations of Pavlovian conditioning in the gastropod *Aplysia* (e.g., Bailey & Kandel, 1995; Hawkins & Kandel, 1986; Schacher et al., 1990). *Aplysia* is a simple sluglike creature that crawls along the sea floor ingesting water through a siphon projecting from its front. Until Kandel began his work, it was generally believed that *Aplysia* was incapable of even simple learning, and in fact it took Kandel and his associates months of study before they found a behavior they could condition, the gill and siphon withdrawal reflex. If *Aplysia*'s siphon is stimulated by a touch, it withdraws siphon and gill into its body to protect them. This reflex proved to be modifiable. If the siphon is repeatedly stimulated with a mild, nonthreatening stimulus, the withdrawal reflex weakens and disappears to that stimulus, demonstrating habituation. The reflex demonstrates sensitization when repeated strong noxious stimulation of *Aplysia*'s tail enhances the withdrawal reflex to even the mildest of touches to the siphon. Pavlovian conditioning occurs when a strong shock (US) is applied to the tail one-half second after a weak touch (CS) is applied to the siphon, and after some pairings the withdrawal reflex to the touch is greatly increased. This result is specific to the CS and is not just the result of sensitization to all stimuli, because discrimination learning occurs in *Aplysia*. A touch to another part of the body is unpaired with the shock while the touch to the siphon is paired with the shock, resulting in withdrawal to the siphon CS alone. A learned CR of withdrawal also extinguishes.

Learning circuits get considerably more complex in mammals (Pascoe, Supple, & Kapp, 1991). Richard Thompson and his colleagues (Thompson, 1991; Thompson & Donegan, 1986) have for some years investigated Pavlovian conditioning in the rabbit, focusing in particular on the nictating membrane response as a UR. This is a defensive response in which a rabbit's inner eyelid (the nictating membrane) closes in response to a threatening stimulus such as a puff of air. Neurologically, conditioning the nictating membrane proves to be quite primitive, as animals whose cerebral cortexes have been completely removed nevertheless learn! Thompson believes that the site of nictating membrane conditioning is the cerebellum, an ancient structure of the brain covering the brain stem.

Although the cerebellum's best-known function is coordination of movement, Thompson and his colleagues believe that it is the site of association formation in Pavlovian conditioning, at least for the responses they have studied. The key association cells are probably the Purkinje cells, because they bring together the inputs from the CS and the US, and also connect to the eye blink and leg-flexion motor program cell assemblies. Thus this model, along with the invertebrate-based models, support the hypothesis advanced at the beginning of the section on the neural basis of learning that the brain contains from the outset all the circuits involved in learning. Learning does not take place because new neurons are created but because new connections between existing neurons are created or existing ones are modified.

The models of learning circuits that have been proposed to date are interesting and exciting as first steps toward unraveling the mysteries of how the brain learns, but they are first steps. The invertebrate circuits are extraordinarily simple; when we move to mammals with Thompson's model of Pavlovian conditioning in the rabbit, the circuits become much more complex, but still do not involve the cerebral hemispheres. It seems likely that many years, perhaps decades, of research will be required before the first circuits for complex human learning can be proposed. Of perhaps greater immediate importance are recent findings about the processes that take place within neurons as synapses are created and modified. Because all neurons work according to similar chemical and biophysical principles, findings about learning at the cellular level in simple animals may very well apply to all forms of learning, however complex. Human learning circuitry may be incredibly complex, but the processes of association formation may be the same everywhere.

Cellular Processes in Conditioning

Everything we have learned so far leads to the conclusion that learning must occur by modifying the connections between neurons—the synapses. Neurons communicate chemically, when the activation of a neuron releases neurotransmitters at its synaptic terminal, which travel across the synaptic cleft to the dendrite of another neuron. There, the neurotransmitter binds onto sites in the dendrite specific to that neurotransmitter, and if enough of the neurotransmitter binds to the dendrite of the receiving neuron, it fires an action potential, releasing neurotransmitters at its terminal, and so on from neuron to neuron throughout some neural circuit. Changes to synapses that occur with learning must involve relatively stable alterations of the functioning either of the presynaptic neuron (the one that sends the transmitter), or to the postsynaptic (receiving) neuron, or perhaps both (Crutcher, 1991). Investigating the cellular basis of learning and memory is an intensely active area of research in biology and physiological psychology. We will present here an example of research in the field, from Eric Kandel's work with conditioning in *Aplysia*.

Kandel and his associates (Bailey & Kandel, 1995; Hawkins & Kandel, 1986) have proposed cellular biophysical mechanisms for habituation, sensitization, and Pavlovian conditioning in *Aplysia*. Because the models for sensitization and Pavlovian conditioning are quite complex, we will discuss only the model for habituation, to illustrate the general approach of the invertebrate model-systems approach to the problem.

Kandel's theory of habituation in *Aplysia* proposes that habituation (and also sensitization and conditioning) takes place by means of changes to the presynaptic neuron alone, by inhibiting its production of neurotransmitters at the synaptic site, thus slowing the build-up of transmitter at the binding sites of the postsynaptic dendrites, and in turn slowing the rate of firing of the postsynaptic motor neuron. Inhibition is accomplished by reducing the rate at which calcium ions (Ca^{++}) enter the presynaptic, sensory neuron. Neurons work hard to keep calcium at very low concentration in their intracellular fluid, but when an axon potential travels down a cell's axon, channels in the cell membrane briefly open, permitting calcium to rush into the cell. The calcium in turn triggers the production of the neurotransmitter to be released at the synapse. Repeated stimulation of the sensory presynaptic neuron reduces the permeability of the calcium channels during later action potentials, reducing the influx of calcium, and consequently the production of neurotransmitters, reducing the firing rate of the postsynaptic, response neuron. Sensitization involves more complex processes that facilitate calcium inflows during presynaptic firings, increasing production of neurotransmitter and firing of the postsynaptic neuron. Pavlovian conditioning builds on the cellular mechanisms of sensitization, as US stimulation facilitates the increased permeability of the calcium channels in the sensory neuron. Sensitization and conditioning processes are much more complex than habituation, involving more chemical changes mediating the action of the calcium channels.

These models of learning involve only short-term memory, because the neural changes are unstable and temporary. Kandel has recently elucidated complex mechanisms by which neurotransmitters affect cause individual neurons' genes to induce growth of new synapses (Bailey & Kandel, 1995). However, while gene-sustained structural changes to neurons may explain long-term memory in *Aplysia,* it is unlikely to be a model for long-term memory in more complex creatures, who, as we have seen, deploy brain structures not possessed by marine invertebrates (Krasne & Glanzman, 1995). Moreover, a limitation of all lines of model systems research is that while they illuminate how individual cells change in response to various forms of stimulation, the actual sites and mechanisms of learning vary considerably from animal to animal (Krasne & Glanzman, 1995). While the results have their own importance, the possibility of generalizing to human learning and memory remains obscure.

Long-Term Potentiation

We have already found that the hippocampus, although not the site of memory storage, plays an important role in creating memories. Some years ago it was found that when neurons from the mammalian hippocampus are repeatedly stimulated, they become more sensitive to subsequent stimulation, and that this sensitivity is relatively long-lasting, coming to be called long-term potentiation (see Massicote, 1991, for a review). Because LTP is durable but ultimately time-limited, it was hoped that long-term potentiation may be part of the mechanism by which the hippocampus participates in learning and memory formation. However, while LTP remains a fascinating phenomenon and a focus of research (e.g., Davis, Butcher, & Morris, 1992; del Cerro, Larson, Oliver, & Lynch, 1990; Huang, Colino, Selig, & Malenka, 1992; Lynch, 1985, 1986; McGaugh, Weinberger, & Lynch, 1995), many neuroscientists have become skeptical about its importance to learning and memory (McGaugh, Weinberger, and Lynch, 1995).

THE HIGHER MENTAL PROCESSES

Intelligence

While cognitive psychologists have focused on specific forms of learning, memory, and expertise, psychometric psychologists have proposed that humans possess a form of general intelligence, or *g,* separate from knowledge of particular skills, facts, or bodies of knowledge. The idea of general intelligence sprang from the observation that there are strong correlations between performance on tests of various mental abilities (Brody, 1992). However, psychometricians always hoped that *g* had a physical basis in the brain. For example, the English psychologist Charles Spearman thought that *g* was a sort of nervous energy that powered the brain. Many approaches to finding the physiological basis of intelligence have been taken (see Brody, 1992 for a review), but we will consider here the work of Richard Haier (1994), who has done extensive work on intelligence using PET scans.

The modest positive correlation of brain size with intelligence (Brody, 1992) suggests that brains vary in their structural **capacity** for information-processing, but Haier has shown that brains also differ in their information processing **efficiency.** For example, Haier et al. (1988) found a negative correlation between overall brain activity as measured by a PET scan and scores on an IQ test. While taking an IQ test, the brains of retarded subjects showed much higher rates of glucose use than the brains of subjects who attained higher IQs. Less intelligent brains appear to be less efficient at processing information than more intelligent brains, and thus must work harder to keep up.

The idea that IQ depends upon information-processing efficiency was supported by an experiment on the effects of learning on glucose consumption by the brain. Haier et al. (1992) had subjects unfamiliar with it play the computer game *Tetris*™, and measured their glucose consumption rate with a PET scan. The scans showed very active, hardworking brains. The subjects then practiced *Tetris* everyday for several weeks, becoming very good at it. When they were scanned again after playing *Tetris,* their brains were remarkably quiet looking, even though they were carrying out rapid calculations and making lightning moves with their hands. With experience, the brain becomes more efficient at processing information, and as a result does not have to work as hard as when the task was being learned.

Reasoning

Neuroscientists have begun to study specific reasoning tasks such as the Wason four-card task (see Chapter 9) using both imaging and clinical methods (see Wharton &

Grafman, 1998, for a review). This research is in its early stages, and we will discuss two studies that address one of the main issues discussed in Chapter 9. We saw there that the difficulty of a reasoning task varies with its content. In its abstract form, the Wason four-card task is enormously difficult. When given content it becomes easier, though the exact nature of the content affects performance a great deal. One important variable was familiarity. Subjects did better with familiar content than unfamiliar content, leading to the possibility that they did not reason at all, but simply retrieved the correct answer from memory.

Although it did not use the Wason task, a study conducted on Russian patients undergoing electroshock therapy (ECT) bears on the question of how content affects reasoning. In modern ECT only one-half of the brain is subjected to shock. For 10 to 15 minutes after shock, functions in the targeted hemisphere are suppressed and functions in the other hemisphere are enhanced. During this period, patients were asked to solve syllogisms involving familiar (e.g., There are traffic lights in all major streets. Dybenko Street is a major street. Does it have traffic lights?) or unfamiliar (Every state has a flag. Zambia is a state. Does Zambia have a flag?) content. The experimenters were interested in how the subjects justified their answers. "Theoretical" answers appealed to the logical structure of the problem with minimal reference to content; "empirical" answers appealed to the subject's personal knowledge. Theoretical answers therefore suggest reasoning while empirical answers suggest consulting memory. Before ECT, 86 percent of patients gave theoretical answers, reflecting reasoning. After right-hemisphere ECT, the same percentage gave theoretical answers, but they were given with more confidence and fluidity. Following left-hemisphere ECT 70 percent of subjects gave empirical answers, a considerable shift. In a related study, patients were given syllogisms with familiar content but false premises (e.g., Dybenko Street is a minor street). To be successful on such a problem, one must accept the false premises despite one's knowledge and reason entirely with logic. Following right-hemisphere ECT, patients accepted the false premises without objection and did well. Following left-hemisphere ECT, on the other hand, patients rejected the premises out of hand as inconsistent with what they knew to be true.

These findings suggest that the left hemisphere is responsible for abstract reasoning detached from familiar content, while the right hemisphere functions on the basis of knowledge rather than logic. They are consistent with the general picture of the differences between the right and left hemispheres, which implicate the left hemisphere in language and other generally linear processes, while the right hemisphere tends to be more oriented to spatial and purely sensory information.

Another study (Adophs, 1999) presented abstract and familiar, social-contract versions of the Wason task to normal controls and to patients with lesions to the ventromedial frontal lobes (i.e., central along the divide separating the hemispheres). See Chapter 9 for examples of the different type of tasks. As usual, normal subjects did much better on the familiar version (90% correct) of the four-card task than on the abstract versions (40% correct). However, the ventromedial patients did much better on the abstract version (70% correct) than controls, and much worse (60%) than normals on the familiar versions. Earlier, we saw that the frontal lobes are important for controlling the social appropriateness of behavior, and in the next chapter we will see that the ventromedial frontal area is strongly implicated in the emotional modulation of reasoning. These results are consistent with these ideas. When the ventromedial area is damaged, context-independent thinking is facilitated, but reasoning rooted in social contexts is impaired.

Language

Research on the neurophysiological basis of language is perhaps the oldest field in cognitive neuroscience. Indeed, one of the first great breakthroughs in the understanding of the brain began with the studies of language disorders by Broca and Wernicke. Their work supported the seemingly discredited idea of Gall that the brain is a collection of specialized organs each devoted to a particular psychological task. Specifically, it appeared that Broca's area was responsible for grammar and Wernicke's for making semantic sense. Until recently, that simple picture of the neural basis of language held. However, current research has begun to show that the Broca-Wernicke picture is simplistic. Increasingly, the brain is being seen as a collection of small modules, each of which performs a single well-defined task. Not too differently from Gall, Broca and Wernicke looked upon language as a single faculty (or at most two faculties) well localized in the brain. However, it turns out that areas of the brain outside Broca's and Wernicke's large areas play a role in language use, and that particular areas of the brain fulfill rather narrow linguistic functions.

Some of the most suggestive evidence supporting the modular view of language functioning comes from the same source as Broca's and Wernicke's pioneering work, the study of the aphasias, disorders of language functioning caused by damage to the brain. These new studies report remarkably specific deficits to specific abilities. Here are some of the more dramatic, reported by Rapp & Caramazza (1995) and Damasio and Damasio (1993):

- Access to a specific name or word (**word-form**) can be lost even though the meaning of the word remains. Patient, AN, showed a picture of a raccoon could describe the creatures habits ("It is a nasty animal. It will come and rummage in the back-yard. . . .") but be unable to name it. This is the tip-of-the-tongue state made permanent. The deficit can extend to reading. Shown the word STEAK, patient EST said "I'm going to eat something . . . it's beef. . . . " but could not say "steak."

- The reverse is also possible, retention of word-forms but loss of meaning. Patient JJ could read correctly 75 percent of words that he could not correctly define.

- Reading and writing can be separately damaged from oral speech. Patient RGB could not say words he read, but clearly understood their meanings. Presented RECORDS, he read "radio," but described the word, "You play 'em on a phonograph . . . can also mean notes you take and keep." This means that word meanings in the mental lexicon are separately access by reading and hearing. Knowing the meaning of a written word does not require being able to pronounce it.

- It is possible to lose access to some classes of the mental lexicon but not others. Several patients have been found who have retained the ability to define inanimate words such as *tent, briefcase,* or *compass,* but not animate words such as *wasp, duck,* and *snail.* Extremely narrow semantic defects have also been found, such as loss of concepts connected with fruits and vegetables only.

- Proper nouns can be selectively lost. Patient AN, shown a picture of Marilyn Monroe could give a thumbnail biography but could not name her.

- Conceptual loss can cut along syntactic lines. Patients with noun problems such as those described so far, typically show no difficulty understanding verbs, while some other patients have trouble with verbs but not nouns. Selective noun or verb loss can even be specific to writing or saying. Patient SJD could say nouns and verbs equally well, but showed impairment when writing verbs. Patient HW could write nouns and verbs equally well but had trouble saying verbs.

- Syntactic skills can be selectively affected, too. Some aphasics have unique trouble with reversible passive sentences. A reversible passive sentence is one in which either noun can be the actor or the recipient of the action, as in *The boy kissed the girl.* Thus these patients had no trouble with nonreversible passives such as *The apple was eaten by the boy* or active sentences such as *The boy kissed the girl,* but were confused by reversible passives such as *The girl was kissed by the boy.*

Taken as a whole, these findings lead to the conclusion that in the brain different parts of language are handled by distinct parts of the brain, so that loss to one brain area results in loss to a narrowly definable linguistic ability.

As a case study, let us take the understanding of color and the names for color, extensively studied by Damasio and Damasio (e.g., 1993).

Achromatopsia is a disorder in which people lose the ability to perceive color, not from damage to cones in the retina, but to damage to the visual cortex. Interestingly, these patients lose the ability even to imagine color; their private images as well as their perceptions are shades of gray.

As with other semantic areas, word-forms for color can be lost even if knowledge of the color remains. This results from damage to the word-form area.

Finally, some patients have **color anomia.** They still perceive and understand colors, because they can match color swatches exactly, and can place a green chip next to a black and white picture of grass and a yellow chip next to a picture of a banana. However, shown a color chip and asked to name the color they give hopelessly wrong responses such as "blue" for red. They understand color and have color word-forms, but they can no longer link the two. Color anomia comes from damage to the left lingual gyrus near the visual color area.

As we have learned, there is no single place in the brain that stores the whole of a concept or memory. Our stored knowledge of the world—and our ability to use it in spoken and written language—requires the cooperative effort and proper operation of multiple sites spread over the entire brain.

Studies of the deaf have shown that the cerebral sites for language are located in the same regions as in hearing people, not in areas responsible for manual dexterity (Damasio & Damasio, 1993). This supports Chomsky's idea that language is innate (see Chapter 11): whatever the mode in which language is expressed, its neural workings remain the same. Nevertheless there are some systematic differences in the location of language in the brain. Recently a neuroimaging team led by Shaywitz and Shaywitz (Shaywitz et al., 1995) has revealed differences in how men and women process language at the first level of phonology. Right-handed subjects were shown pairs of words and asked if they were the same or different in terms of sound—did they rhyme?—or semantic category—were they synonyms? On the phonological task, PET scans showed that male brains' activity was closely focused in the right hemisphere, while the brains of women were showed activity over larger areas and in both hemispheres. Please note that because on the semantic task men and women showed no difference, this study does *not* demonstrate that men and women "think differently" as has been suggested by some popular stories in the media.

While research on the biological bases of higher mental functions is new and takes place at a cruder level of analysis than studies of learning and memory, preliminary findings are promising. Different cognitive functions are carried out in different parts of the brain, and we can hope to fill in the details as research continues.

SUGGESTED READINGS

Understanding the brain is one of the scientific adventure stories of our times, and there are several good popular books on the subject. For those who would like to teach themselves neuroanatomy, see *The Human Brain Coloring Book,* by M. C. Diamond, B. Scheibel, and L. M. Elson (New York: Barnes & Noble, 1985). Do not be put off by the fact that it is a coloring book: It is a serious, adult text designed for and used by universities and medical schools. A standard text has appeared by Gazzinaga, Ivry, and Mangun (1998). The amazing and sometimes tragic quirks of the damaged brain are humanely and humanistically described by clinical neuropsychiatrist Oliver Sacks in his various books such as *The Man Who Mistook His Wife for a Hat and Other Clinical Tales* (New York: Summit Books, 1985) or *An Anthropologist on Mars: Seven Paradoxical Tales* (New York: Knopf, 1995). Susan Allport tells the story of *Explorers of the Black Box: The Search for the Cellular Basis of Memory* (New York: Norton, 1986). Her book not only provides a good introduction to the model systems theorists, but is an instructive and revealing study of the human side of science, as we learn about the intense rivalry and competition to be first, which helps drive natural science forward. Kandel shared the 2000 Nobel Prize in Physiology and Medicine for his work on learning in *Aplysia*. Less gossipy but more detailed is Steven Rose, *The Making of Memory: From Molecules to Mind* (New York: Anchor Books, 1992). Peirce J. Howard, *The Owner's Manual for the Brain* (Austin, TX: Leornian Press) provides a readable overview of cognitive neuroscience with an emphasis on practical uses.

13 Emotion

Beatrice appeared dressed in the most patrician of colors, a subdued and decorous crimson, bound round and adorned in a style suitable to her years. At that moment, I say truly that the vital spirit, the one that dwells in the most secret chamber of the heart, began to tremble so violently that even the least pulses of my body were strangely affected; and trembling, it spoke these words: "Here is a god stronger than I, who shall come to rule over me." At that point the animal spirit, the one abiding in the high chamber to which all the senses bring their perceptions, was stricken with amazement, and speaking directly to the spirits of sight, said these words: "Now your bliss has appeared." At that moment the natural spirit, the one which lives in that part where our food is worked on, began to weep, and weeping, said these words: "Alas, wretch that I am, from now on I shall be interfered with often." Let me say that from that time on Love governed my soul, which became so readily devoted to him and over which he reigned with such assurance and lordship given him through the power of my imagination that it became necessary for me to tend to his every pleasure. . . . And though her image, which remained constantly with me, was Love's assurance of holding me, it was of such a pure quality that never did it permit me to be ruled by Love without the trusted counsel of reason (regarding those things wherein such advice would profitably be heeded). [Dante Alighieri (1265–1321), *La Vita Nuova*, c. 1293]

Can love be explained? Dante offers a poet's explanation, cast in the scientific vocabulary of his times. Dante deploys the faculty psychology and animal spirit neurophysiology that was current in the Middle Ages and Renaissance. In this passage from *La Vita Nuova*—one of the greatest love poems in literature—Dante makes two points central to today's psychological study of emotion. First, emotion and motivation are intimately connected. Having gained control of his faculty of imagination, Love commands Dante to seek out his beloved Beatrice. Second, the degree to which emotion and reason (cognition) get along is debated. Dante says that his love for Beatrice was so pure that he could be ruled by it without offending reason, but this suggests that some other, less pure love might blind him to "the trusted counsel of reason." From ancient times to the present, emotion has challenged philosophers, poets, and now, psychological scientists.

EMOTION IN WESTERN CULTURE

The place of emotion in human life has divided the great thinkers of Western and Eastern thought. In the Greek, Hellenistic, and Roman eras, emotion was sometimes condemned and sometimes praised. Plato, for example, teaches in the *Phaedrus* that emotions are like powerful horses, beasts of our bodies that must be tamed and guided by the reason of the immortal soul. Yet in the *Symposium,* he teaches that erotic love is the essential first motive that leads us to know and love truth. We love first a beautiful person, then the idea of Beauty, and finally the idea of Truth. The poet John Keats (1795–1821) echoed Plato when he wrote:

> Beauty is truth, truth beauty,—that is all
> Ye know on earth and all ye need to know.
>
> *Ode on a Grecian Urn,* Stanza 4

In the Hellenistic and Roman eras, philosophers tended to believe that emotion was the main source of human unhappiness and taught their followers recipes for achieving *ataraxia,* an austere kind of happiness defined as freedom from disturbance. The most influential of these ancient therapies of desire (Nussbaum, 1994) was Stoicism, which exerted great influence on the leaders of Rome and, through them, Christianity. Stoics taught that the path to *ataraxia* was extirpation of all emotional reactions. As the Stoic philosopher Epictetus (C.E. 50–138) wrote:

> Men are disturbed not by the things which happen, but by the opinions [i.e., emotions] about the things. For example, death is nothing terrible, for if it were, it would have seemed so to Socrates; for the opinion about death, that it is terrible, is the terrible thing. When, then, we are impeded or disturbed or grieved, let us never blame others, but ourselves, that is, our opinions. It is the act of an ill-instructed man to blame others for his own bad condition; it is the act of one who has begun to be instructed, to lay the blame on himself; and of one whose instruction is completed, neither to blame another nor himself.

Similar advice may be found in Eastern religions such as Buddhism and Daoism, which teach that reason should master the passions; that strong feeling is to be avoided as disturbing.

Ancient ambiguity about emotion passed through the Christian era to the philosophers of the eighteenth century who began to create psychology. Like Plato, Descartes sharply divided the soul from the body, defining the soul as a thing that thinks rather than a thing that feels. The German philosopher Kant taught that moral action should be based on pure rational calculation of universal good.

On the other hand, some philosophers found wisdom in our passions, the name for emotions prior to the nineteenth century. Against Descartes, Pascal wrote, "The heart has its reasons that reason does not understand." Scottish philosophers, who exerted enormous influence in America until the 1870s (Leahey, 2000), believed that reason by itself was an inadequate guide to life. David Hume said, "Reason is, and ought only to be, the slave of the passions." Our emotions determine our goals, and thinking's job is only to calculate the best means to achieve them. Contrary to Kant, Hume and other Scottish philosophers also saw emotion as the basis of morality. They believed that each of us possesses an innate *moral sense.* When we see someone doing something virtuous, we automatically (i.e., without pondering the matter) feel approval; when we see an immoral act, we feel disapproval. The eighteenth century ended with the emotional outburst of Romanticism, which elevated the heart over the head, passion over reason. The German writer Herder inverted Descartes when he proclaimed, "I feel! I am!"

EMOTION IN PSYCHOLOGY

If emotion has challenged poets, philosophers, and writers, it has daunted psychologists. In their classic 1954 *Experimental Psychology,* Woodworth and Schlosberg (1954, p. 107) wrote, "The topic of Emotion has perhaps generated more unprofitable controversy among psychologists than any other with which they have concerned themselves." One of today's leading psychologists of emotion, George Mandler (1987, p. 219), writes, "Emotion is a topic that, more than any other, has bedeviled students of mental life."

Emotion is an especially difficult subject for modern psychology because it does not fit easily into the behavioral approach to psychology. Psychologists have found that they can ignore consciousness and fruitfully study topics such as learning, memory, and personality in terms of behavior alone. However, when it comes to emotion, consciousness cannot be avoided, because emotions are subjective feelings, not objective, publicly observable behaviors. However, psychology cannot simply pass the emotions by because, as their embroidery by artists attests, emotions are important to us.

The James-Lange Theory of Emotion

Modern psychological thinking about emotion began with William James and the **James-Lange theory of emotion,** proposed independently by William James in 1884 and the Dutch physiologist Carl Lange (1834–1900) in 1885. The James-Lange theory of emotion has influenced every psychologist who has tackled the topic of emotion and is still widely discussed today.

As a psychologist of consciousness, James wanted to explain how and why emotions arise in conscious experience. James contrasted his theory of emotions with that of folk psychology, admitting that, at least at first glance, his was less plausible (James, *Principles of Psychology,* 1892/1992, p. 352):

> Our natural way of thinking about . . . emotions is that the mental perception of some fact excites the mental affection called the emotion, and that this latter state of mind gives rise to the bodily expression. My theory, on the contrary, is that the bodily changes follow directly the perception of the exciting fact, and that our feeling of the same changes as they occur is the emotion. Common-sense says, we lose our fortune, are sorry and weep; we meet a bear, are frightened and run; we are insulted by a rival, are angry and strike. The hypothesis here to be defended says that this order of sequence is incorrect, that the one mental state is not immediately induced by the other, that the bodily manifestations must first be interposed between, and that the more rational statement is that we feel sorry because we cry, angry because we strike, afraid because we tremble, and not that we cry, strike, or tremble because we are sorry, angry, or fearful, as the case may be. Without the bodily states following on the perception, the latter would be purely cognitive in form, pale, colorless, destitute of emotional warmth. We might then see the bear and judge it best to run, receive the insult and deem it right to strike, but we should not actually feel afraid or angry. Stated in this crude way, the hypothesis is pretty sure to meet with immediate disbelief. And yet neither many nor far-fetched considerations are required to mitigate its paradoxical character, and possibly to produce conviction of its truth.

Issues in the Psychology of Emotion

In formulating his theory of emotion, James wrestled with issues that remain unresolved today. The first issue is the most basic, "What *is* an emotion?" Many, perhaps most, of our perceptions are "purely cognitive in form." The perceptions of my fax machine, my mouse pad, a box of floppy disks on my desk are "pale, colorless, destitute of emotional warmth." It is certainly true should I meet a bear in the woods my perception of it will be warm (to say the least), but in what does this warmth—the *emotion* of fear—consist? What is added to consciousness in the case of the bear that is not added in the case of the fax machine?

James' answer was dictated by the view of the brain and nervous system reigning when he wrote. In the late nineteenth century, the brain was seen as being rather like a telephone switchboard, providing connections between stimulus and response, but incapable of originating experience, feeling, or action on its own. James gave this rather mechanical view of the brain a dynamic twist, holding that any perceived stimulus acts on the nervous system to automatically bring about some adaptive bodily response, whether learned or innate. Thus if a large animal rears up and roars at me, I possess an innate and automatic tendency to run away. When I am driving and a traffic light turns red, I have a learned and automatic tendency to step on my car's brakes (see Figure 13.1).

To understand some of the important arguments about emotion and cognition, we should remember that what's evolutionarily adaptive in this sequence of events is my running away. Whatever I may subjectively feel upon seeing the bear is completely irrelevant as long as I escape from its clutches. I could, as James says, see the bear and coolly reason that running away is the wise thing to do, feeling nothing at all. Robots have been built that seek out some objects and avoid others, but they feel neither desire nor fear.

Yet because we humans do feel emotions, it is the psychologist's job to figure out what emotions are and what they are for. When I feel an emotion, what is added to consciousness that is absent when cognition is cold? James proposed that the emotional something extra is the registration in consciousness of the state and activity of our body caused by emotional stimuli such as the bear in the woods. Because he thought of the brain as merely a device for connecting stimulus and response, James located emotions not in the brain itself but outside the brain, in the viscera (our stomach churns with fear) and the muscles that work to take us away from the bear. With regard to simple emotions like fear or lust (as opposed to subtler emotions like envy or love), James

FIGURE 13.1 William James' theory of emotion. An emotional stimulus is registered by the sensory systems of the brain, which is turn activate bodily responses. These bodily reponses give emotional color to the experience of the stimulus in consciousness. Adapted from LeDoux (1996, p. 80).

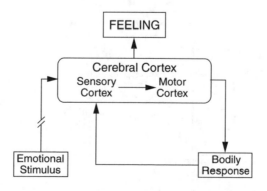

believed that the most important bodily feelings that comprise emotions arise in the viscera. In summary, according to the James-Lange theory of emotion, fear does not *cause* our intestines to churn and our legs to run, nor do churning intestines and running legs *cause* us to feel fear; instead fear simply *is* our churning innards and running legs. Emotions are states of the body.

Are There Specific and Basic Emotions?

In ordinary language, we distinguish many emotions: fear, love, awe, envy, anger, grief, pride, and so on. However, it is not always easy to give a precise description of each emotion or to tell them apart. Defining love has occupied poets for generations, and telling apart love, liking, lust, infatuation, and having a crush on someone is not always easy. James' theory of emotions provides one possible way of defining specific emotions, namely that each emotion is constituted by a specific constellation of bodily feelings.

Related to the question of how uniquely to define each emotion is the question of whether some emotions might be more basic than others. Basic emotions would be hardwired into the brain, would be universally experienced in all human cultures, and would provide components for the creation of less basic, culture-specific emotions. James did not address this issue, but today it is one of the most contentious issues in the psychology of emotion.

Historically, the generation that followed James developed a theory of emotion that viewed emotions as diffuse bodily states given different labels by different societies.

William Cannon and his student Philip Bard attacked James' bodily feedback theory by performing a series of experiments on rats. They focused on the emotion of rage and showed that while the cortex was not necessary for rage to occur the hypothalamus was. Emotion, they argued, was generated in the brain, specifically the hypothalamus, without any need for feedback from visceral or motor responses (Figure 13.2). As a result, psychologists came to think of emotion as essentially a state of

FIGURE 13.2 The Cannon-Bard theory of emotion. Emotion is arousal of subcortical brain structures, especially the hypothalamus, whose activation leads to both emotional behavior and the feeling of an emotion in the cortex. Adapted from Le Doux (1996, p. 83).

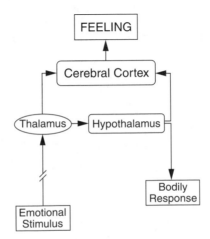

LEARNING AND COGNITION

activation or arousal in the nervous system, mediated by ancient subcortical structures, most importantly, the hypothalamus (Woodworth & Schlosberg, 1954).

Because of the work of Cannon and Bard, psychologists came to believe that each emotion was defined not, as James said, by a specific constellation of bodily feelings, but by how a person interpreted his or her feeling of arousal. Interpretation of arousal was guided by the social context in which the arousal occurred. Thus according to this theory, there are no specific emotions at the biological level, and there are no basic emotions, since simple arousal is not usually counted as an emotion.

A famous attribution theory experiment performed by social psychologists Schachter and Singer (1962) seemed to support the arousal plus interpretation theory. Subjects were injected either with a placebo or with epinephrine (which causes autonomic arousal). Subjects receiving the epinephrine were either told or not told about its arousing effects, and were then placed in a room with a confederate of the experimenters who acted either happy or angry. They predicted that subjects injected with epinephrine who were informed about epinephrine's arousing effects would report feeling no emotion because they could attribute their feelings to the injection and therefore would not use situational cues to interpret their aroused states. On the other hand, subjects not informed about the effects of the injection would feel aroused and seek its cause in their environment. Thus, subjects confronted with an angry confederate would feel anger, and subjects confronted with a happy confederate would feel happy. Although Schachter and Singer reported results consistent with their hypotheses, their results have not been consistently replicated (Frijda, 1986). Moreover, as we will learn later, there is increasing evidence that specific emotions are mediated by different parts of the brain.

Few psychologists now believe that emotion is nothing more than arousal. However, lively controversies persist about what emotions are, how they are differentiated, and what, if any, emotions are basic. They also continue to debate the usefulness of emotions.

What Are Emotions For?

This is the key evolutionary question about emotion. Given that getting away from the bear is the important thing from the standpoint of survival, why do we in addition feel conscious fear of the bear? Are emotions parts of evolution's design of human nature, or just decorative accidents of no evolutionary value?

In James' time, some psychologists and physiologists believed that emotions have no Darwinian function. We learned in Chapter 1 about the automaton theory of consciousness advanced by various thinkers in the nineteenth century. They held that animals—including human beings—are just machines, and that consciousness—and therefore emotion—is a by-product of brain processes and behavior, playing no role in causing our thought or actions. A similar view of emotion is held by radical behaviorists today. James, however, rejected the automaton theory as "an impertinence," arguing that consciousness, including emotion, has adaptive value.

According to James, consciousness gives its bearer interests, turning survival into "an imperative decree." Of all aspects of consciousness, emotions are the foremost creators of self-interest, and thus of the will to survive. Emotions create motives. If we love someone, we will be moved to help him or her; if we hate someone, we will be moved to harm him or her. Without emotions we would be indifferent to our survival, and so would probably fail in the struggle for existence.

While James strenuously objected to the automaton theory, his theory of emotion came perilously close to endorsing it. It is easy to read James as saying that the emotion of fear arises only after one has run away from the bear, and therefore fear played no role in causing the running to take place. James objected to this interpretation of his theory, but nevertheless it became the view generally attributed to him (Myers, 1987).

Theories of Emotion in Psychology Today

While psychologists have proposed many theories of emotion, they tend to fall into two broad classes, **cognitive-social theories of emotion** and **biosocial theories of emotion** (Izard, 1988). Cognitive-social theories are more sophisticated and refined versions of the activation-arousal theories we just discussed. Cognitive-social theories continue to look at emotions as biologically diffuse, proposing that experienced emotions are cognitively constructed out of our interpretations of situations in which we find ourselves. In contrast, biosocial theories propose that there are biologically specific basic emotions whose nature is largely genetically determined. Theories of emotion are also beginning to emerge from evolutionary psychology; they try to spell out in detail why human nature is equipped with its particular repertoire of emotions.

EMOTION AND COGNITION: COGNITIVE-SOCIAL THEORIES OF EMOTION

The fundamental issue separating the cognitive-social and biosocial approaches to emotion is whether or not cognitive information processing is necessary to produce a given emotion. Roughly speaking, psychologists in the biosocial camp believe that basic emotions are hardwired into our brain by evolution and are automatically felt with little or no intervention of thought processes. In certain respects, advocates of the biosocial view continue the Jamesian tradition of rooting emotions in the body, although unlike James, they look less to the body than to the brain, as we will see later. Psychologists in the cognitive-social camp, on the other hand, continue Cannon's tradition, believing that while emotions have a biological basis—arousal separates hot emotion from cold cognition (Lazarus, 1991)—what emotion we feel in an aroused state depends on how we interpret events that happen to us.

The central and distinctive concept of cognitive-social theories of emotion is **appraisal.** Cognitive-social theorists agree with James that emotions are connected with our interests. Our interests create motives, and motives create goals. Emotions arise when, and only when, events have some bearing on our welfare, either facilitating or impairing us in pursuit of our goals. Thus, right now my perception of my fax machine is coolly cognitive, "destitute of emotional warmth," because it is irrelevant to my currently active goals. If I am trying to send a fax, however, and the machine doesn't work properly, I will become upset, and, depending on how I interpret the situation, will feel frustration and, perhaps, anger.

Cognitive-social theories of emotion say that emotions arise from the following series of steps (Howard, 1994):

1. An event occurs.
2. You perceive the event.

3. You appraise the event. Is the event relevant to any of my current goals? If it is, how is it relevant?

4. Filtering the appraisal. Our current bodily state or mood influences the intensity of the appraisal.

5. Reaction to the appraisal. Our emotion moves us to react in some way to the event, coping with the challenge or opportunity the event provides.

One important issue in the study of emotion for which we do not have space in this chapter is distinguishing emotions from other mental states that have to do with feeling (affect). One such distinction is that between an *emotion* and a *mood*. Most psychologists agree that moods endure over longer periods of time than emotions, though how to draw precise boundaries is more contentious. Some psychologists propose further that emotions are intentional—in the sense of directed at someone or some thing (see Chapter 1)—whereas moods are not. Thus, for example, being happy or sad are moods, because they have no clear object (though they may have specific causes), but being in love or angry are emotions, being directed at some person or object (Ekman & Davidson, 1994).

To illustrate cognitive-social theory, let's go back in the woods with James:

1. *Event:* A bear rises up in front of you.

2. *You see the bear.* In a case such as this one, perception of the event is straightforward. In more subtle cases, however, events may occur but be misperceived or not perceived at all. Engrossed in looking at a bird we might not hear a twig snap as a bear approaches from behind, or we may think it's just the friend we're out birding with.

3. *You appraise the significance of the bear's sudden appearance to your current goals.* One goal is survival: We appraise the bear's appearance as threatening that goal, and so we feel fear. On the other hand, if we are biologists looking for a bear to study it, we will appraise its appearance as positive with respect to our goal as scientists, and may feel joy at success tinged with fear of death. As one journalist said about enduring danger in the interests of a good story, "Bad for me, good for the piece."

4. *Mood or bodily state filters the appraisal.* If we've had a wonderful day in the woods and feel on top of the world, we may be slower to feel fear or feel less fear than if we have been worrying all day about all the dangers that lurk in the woods: insects, snakes, poison ivy, and, of course, bears.

5. *We cope with the bear.* If we are bird hunting, we run away. On the other hand, if we are biologists looking for a bear, we might raise our tranquilizer gun to stun it, or if we are nature journalists, raise our camera to photograph it. In all three cases, we will feel fear because a bear threatens our survival, but in the latter two cases we will cope with the bear differently because its sudden appearance engages goals other than biological survival.

Cognition Defines Emotions

According to the cognitive-social view, whatever emotion we feel as a result of a given event is primarily determined by how we appraise that event. Because we do not have to respond to them, events that are not goal-related are not appraised, and hence we feel no emotion when they occur. Events that are goal-related either help us reach some goal, in which case they provoke a positive emotion, or they hinder us in reaching some goal, in which case they provoke a negative emotion.

We experience many more emotions than simply feeling good or bad about what happens to us. In the cognitive-social views, specific emotions result from the complexities of the appraisal process. For example, according to Ortony, Clore, and Collins (1988), emotions are defined primarily by what we focus on in an event. According to them, emotions are **valenced** reactions to consequences of events, the actions of agents (whether people, animals, or things), or to aspects of objects. The term valence simply refers to evaluating an event as *good for me* (or someone else)(positive valence) or *bad for me* (or someone else)(negative valence).

Events either please us or displease us, but the precise nature of our pleasure or displeasure depends on what aspect of the event we focus on and on various preexisting **attitudes.** Thus if we focus on an event's good or bad consequences for someone else, our pleasure will be felt as being happy for the other if we like him or her, or as gloating if we dislike them; displeasure will similarly be felt as resentment or pity. If we focus on an event's consequences for us, emotions depend first on whether the event is anticipated or unanticipated. When we anticipate an event that helps us achieve a goal, we feel hope; when we anticipate an event that will harm us, we feel fear. When events simply occur without anticipation, our well-being is felt as either joy or distress.

Actions of agents relevant to our goals excite our approval or disapproval. If we focus on our own actions, we will make emotional self-attributions of pride or shame, depending on whether what we have done is good or bad. Similarly, we make emotional attributions of admiration or reproach when we focus on the actions of others. Finally, emotional attributions and well-being emotions may combine to create more complex emotions. For example, pride and joy lead to feeling gratified about ourselves, while joy and admiration lead us to feel gratitude to another.

Aspects of objects either attract or repel us, leading us to feel emotions such as liking, love, disliking and hatred, based primarily on the intensity of the attraction or repulsion exerted.

Perhaps the most difficult empirical problem in studying the emotions is deciding if there are certain emotions that are basic to human nature, found around the world in all cultures and in all human beings. Not only does this issue divide cognitive-social theorists from biosocial theorists, it also divides cognitive-social theorists among themselves.

There is evidence that the folk psychology of English-speaking people defines a few basic emotions, which are embroidered into a rich emotional vocabulary consisting of several hundred terms. Using a technique called cluster analysis, Shaver, Schwartz, Kirson, and O'Conner extracted a list of five basic emotions—*love, joy, surprise, anger, sadness,* and *fear*—from subjects' ratings of over 200 emotionally related words.

It is more difficult to determine if this list of emotions (or some other list) is basic—that is, is part of human nature. No one disputes that different languages capture different emotional nuances. For example, there is no word in English exactly equivalent to the German *Schadenfreude*. It is typically translated as "gloating," but the two words are not quite equivalent. Gloating is typically a state of unalloyed happiness—feeling real joy at an enemy's suffering. However, the German word *schade* is an interjection expressing pity, meaning roughly, "too bad." *Freude* means joy. Therefore, *Schadenfreude* means feeling joy at another's misfortune tempered by a degree of sorrow, a sort of subdued and sympathetic gloating. In fact, German possesses no verb equivalent for "to gloat." The hard questions are deciding if Germans feel joy at others' misfortune differently than we do, if Germans, Americans (and all people) feel the same emotions even if we do not always have exactly equivalent ways of naming and describing them, and if culturally different emotions are but variations on a basic human emotional palette.

Cognitive-social theorists do not agree on the answers to these questions. Some believe that there are a few basic emotions. However, unlike biosocial theorists, they believe that the basic emotions are not created by a universal human nature. Instead, they propose that there are a limited number of ways in which events can help or hinder us in pursuing our goals, and hence a limited number of patterns of human appraisals of goal-relevant events. Lazarus (1991) enumerated a list of 15 basic emotions based on each emotion's "core relational theme," that is, the central harm or benefit that any event may bring us. For example, love's "core relational theme" is "desiring or participating in affection, usually but not necessarily reciprocated"; and hope is "fearing the worst but yearning for the better" (Lazarus, 1991, p. 122).

On the other hand, some psychologists believe there are no basic emotions, whether defined by biology or defined by universal human experience. For example, Schweder (1994) proposed that human emotions are cultural constructions, so that the emotional lives of the various human cultures may be radically different, sharing nothing in common beyond the activities of feeding, fighting, fleeing, and sexual reproduction that humans share by virtue of being mammals. For Schweder, emotions are **schemas** (see Chapter 8) people use to interpret their experience. Cultures can provide quite different schemas for interpreting experience, so, Schweder concludes, people in different cultures may feel profoundly different emotions.

For example, Schweder argues that the raw material of experience described by Dante may be interpreted differently by members of different cultures. In his culture, Dante's feelings were usually experienced as love and many Westerners would agree. In another culture, perhaps lacking the concept of romantic love, they might be interpreted as disease. In a third, they might be interpreted as bewitchment, as symptoms of attack by a witch or sorcerer. Indeed, an old jazz song refers to the "black magic called love." No one reading of experience is "right," says Schweder. All are plausible and culturally determined ways of experiencing.

Between psychologists such as Lazarus and Schweder are theorists who believe that while there are some universal building blocks of emotion, there are no universal full-blown emotions (Ortony, Clore, & Collins, 1988). They believe that the concept of "basic emotion" is too vague to be scientifically useful. They canvas 14 emotion theorists, showing that each proposed a different list of basic emotions. They point out that in addition to disagreeing on what the basic emotions are, theorists disagree on what makes a basic emotion basic. For biosocial theorists, the criteria are biological; for cognitive theorists like Lazarus, the criteria are psychological. It is hard to tell, however, if Ortony, Clore, and Collins are seeking the truth in the middle of extreme views, or simply ducking a difficult issue by arguing about words. Muddle on so central a question as the existence of basic emotions is typical of the psychology of emotion.

Emotions Shape Cognitions

Do our emotions affect how we think and remember? While it may seem obvious that they do, scientific investigation of the question is quite difficult. Emotional experiences are fleeting and unpredictable, making them hard to study experimentally, and it is difficult (and unethical if the emotion is a strong one) to make people feel an emotion by some experimental manipulation.

Two techniques have been used to study the effect of emotion on cognition (see Smith & Kemp-Wheeler, 1996). In one, attempts are made to induce (mild) emotions in normal subjects, and measure the effects on information processing. For example, subjects might be asked to remember a happy or sad event, read a happy or sad story, or see a happy, or distressing video clip. Most such studies have found that when happy states are induced, a cheerful cognitive bias results: Compared to control subjects experiencing no emotion induction, experimental subjects are more likely to recall happy events, to rate themselves highly on scales of self-confidence and social skills, and to judge others more favorably on everything from attractiveness to honesty. Subjects in whom negative emotions have been induced show little, if any, cognitive biasing in an unhappy direction.

The other method for investigating the effects of emotion on cognition involves studying people suffering from an emotional disorder such as chronic anxiety or depression (Mathews, Mackintosh, & Fulcher, 1997). One study examined how chronic anxiety biases the understanding of semantically ambiguous (see Chapter 7) words in a priming (see Chapters 5 and 12) task. Subjects were presented with a priming word whose meaning is ambiguous, such as *arms,* which can mean either what your hands are attached to or military weapons. For all the priming words, one meaning was either neutral or positive in emotional connotation, while the other was negative. Then, after a brief pause, subjects were presented with a word or nonword (e.g. tweal) and had to say if it was a word or not. In word trials, the target word was related to one or the other meaning of the priming word (e.g., *leg* vs. *shield*).

Compared to normal, non-anxious subjects, anxious subjects showed much greater priming to target words linked to the negative meaning of the priming word. That is, the time it took them to identify as a word the word linked to the prime's negative meaning was shorter than the time it took them to identify as a word the word linked to the prime's less threatening meaning. It appears that chronically anxious subjects are more likely than normal people to see their world as threatening and hostile.

EMOTION AND BIOLOGY: BIOSOCIAL THEORIES OF EMOTION

According to cognitive-social theorists, "cognition is both a necessary and sufficient condition of emotion" (Lazarus, 1991). That is, without cognitive appraisal of an event we will experience no emotion (cognition is *necessary* for an emotion to be felt), and cognitive appraisal by itself can generate emotions (cognition is *sufficient* to cause an emotion).

In contrast, because biosocial theorists believe that emotions are generated by the most evolutionary ancient parts of our brains, they believe that emotions can be produced without cognitive information processing, and that cognition by itself produces no emotion.

Some support for the biosocial view comes from clinical evidence (Damasio, 1996; Le Doux, 1996):

■ Early in the twentieth century, the physician and psychologist Edouard Claparede examined a female patient suffering from amnesic syndrome (see Chapter 12). Each time he saw her, he had to reintroduce himself. On one visit he secreted a pin in his right hand, and pricked her with it when they shook hands. On his next visit, she still did not recognize Claparede, but she refused to shake his hand.

- Patient P. S., a split-brain patient (see Chapter 12) was unusual in that he retained some receptive vocabulary in his right hemisphere. That is, his right hemisphere could recognize many words, but it could not speak. When emotionally loaded words were presented to the right hemisphere, he could appropriately label them as "good" or "bad." Thus *mom* was called "good" and *devil* was called "bad." Nevertheless, P. S.—or, more precisely, P. S.'s left hemisphere—had no idea what words he had seen.

- Normal human beings exhibit Pavlovian fear conditioning (see Chapter 3). Presented with several pairings of a tone that signals an obnoxious and fear producing noise, they soon feel fear when the tone is presented. However, a patient with frontal lobe damage did not acquire conditioned fear. He learned that the tone is followed by the noise, but fear never became attached to the tone.

In each of these patients, the normal connection between cognition and emotion has been severed. Because of her amnesia, Claparede's patient could form no memory of him—but she did become afraid of him. P. S. could evaluate as good or bad, stimuli of which he never became consciously aware. In these patients, we see emotion in the absence of cognition, suggesting that cognition is not necessary for emotion. In the last patient, we see the reverse, cognition without emotion, suggesting that cognition is not sufficient for emotion. He knew the connection between CS and US, but never acquired fear of the CS.

Experimental findings also suggest that emotion can occur without cognition. The most dramatic evidence comes from studies in which people's feelings about a stimulus are affected by simple exposure to it, sometimes even when the stimulus is not registered in consciousness.

Simple exposure to a novel stimulus can make us like it. For example, subjects asked to rate how much they liked Chinese ideograms preferred the ones they had seen in an earlier phase of the experiment. The effect of pre-exposure is *greater* when the initial presentation of the ideogram is **masked** (see Chapter 5) so that it never enters consciousness.

Masked emotionally loaded stimuli cause **priming** (see Chapters 5 and 12) of affect. Subjects were asked to rate how much they liked Chinese ideograms. Before seeing each ideogram, subjects were exposed to a masked stimulus of a smiling or a frowning face. Ideograms preceded by the smiling faces were liked better than those preceded by frowning faces.

Mere exposure to affect-arousing stimuli can influence behavior in surprising ways. For example, subjects in one experiment unscrambled sentences that referred to elderly people, while other subjects unscrambled different sentences. When leaving the experiment, subjects in the former group walked more slowly down the hall than subjects in the latter group, even though the sentences had said nothing about elderly people being slow. Mere exposure to sentences about the elderly automatically activated the whole stereotype. In another experiment, two groups unscrambled sentences dealing either with "assertiveness" or "politeness." All subjects were then sent to deliver a message to the experimenter, who by prearrangement was engaged in a conversation when the subject arrived. Subjects who had unscrambled the assertiveness sentences interrupted the conversation more quickly than the politeness subjects did.

These findings suggest that emotions may be produced without the involvement of cognitive appraisal processes. In the first case, stimuli acquired positive affective value by mere exposure, without needing to be cognitively appraised at all. When stimuli are masked, cognitive appraisal cannot occur, because masked stimuli never reach the visual cortex, yet they may affect us anyway. In the last case, even though subjects were not asked to direct their attention to the content of the sentences they unscrambled, stereotypes of the elderly were activated and subjects were made more or less assertive.

We will soon learn that although these findings may be counterintuitive, they are consistent with the modular structure of the brain. Thinking and feeling run on distinct neural pathways.

Evidence for Basic Emotions

Some social-cognitive theorists, such as Schweder, believe there are no basic emotions. Some, such as Lazarus, believe there are basic emotions, although they owe nothing to the body or the brain, being defined by situational appraisal rather than by evolutionary biology.

Because they believe that emotions are biological rather than cognitive phenomena (Le Doux, 1996), biosocial theorists believe that there are basic emotions shared by humans and other animals. Biosocial theorists do not dispute that human beings experience more complex and subtle emotions than animals, or that cultures do not shape emotions at all, but they do think there is a core set of universal human emotions. One argument for the existence of basic universal emotions comes from neurobiology. If emotions are caused by specific (and ancient) brain structures, then we should expect to find them throughout the animal world and in all intact human beings. We will explore this argument in the next section. Another argument that basic emotions exist involves one of the oldest scientific topics in the study of emotion, the expression of emotion in behavior, especially the human face.

The first scientific study of the emotions from the biological point of view was Charles Darwin's own *Expression of Emotion in Man and Animals* (1872). Darwin argued that human beings and animals have innately fixed ways of expressing their emotions in posture, gestures, and facial expression. If there are biologically universal ways of expressing emotions in all human beings, then it seems plausible that there are universal basic emotions felt by all human beings. For example, Darwin pointed out that the facial expression of fear in cats and humans is similar. In each the mouth is open, the brow is wrinkled, and in general the face is pulled taut. That fear should be expressed similarly in cats and humans is not surprising. The fear center of the brain is the amygdala, one of the oldest brain structures. Darwin showed a human face to 24 people, asking them what emotion it expressed. Without prompting, twenty answered "extreme fright" or "terror," three said pain, and one said extreme discomfort. Darwin carried out similar informal studies with photographs of many different emotional expressions, including happiness, disgust, disdain, and misery, with similar results. Darwin concluded, "all the chief expressions exhibited by man are the same throughout the world" (p. 359).

Darwin's conclusion fell into disrepute during the behaviorist era, when psychologists ceased to believe in human or animal nature, but modern students of emotion, have powerfully revived it. Paul Ekman (1982) and his colleagues have done extensive studies showing that the same emotions are expressed the same way in different cultures. Ekman studied a remote tribe in New Guinea, the South Fore. The Fore live in remote and isolated villages uninfluenced by Western media. Nonetheless, they readily recognized emotions shown in photographs of Westerners, and American subjects readily recognized the facial expression of emotions in the Fore natives.

One of Ekman's most revealing experiments compared emotional expression in American and Japanese subjects. Japanese culture prizes self-control and emotional reticence, which is why Americans tend to find them "inscrutable" (Ekman, 1982). The same experiment was run at the University of California at Berkeley and at Waseda University in Tokyo. Subjects watched travelogues (the control condition) and a film known to induce distress while their facial responses were secretly taped. Stress-inducing films are typically vivid with detailed records of painful surgical procedures. Subjects watched the films either alone or with an experimenter in a white lab coat. Later, other subjects who did not know the original subjects, the nature of the film being viewed, or the condition in which it was viewed coded the recorded facial expressions for emotional content.

Ekman found that when the stress-inducing films were watched alone, Japanese and American facial expressions were virtually identical. Presence of the experimenter made little difference to the facial expression of distress among the American subjects, but among Japanese subjects, emotional expression was more polite and there was much more smiling. When the tapes of the Japanese facial expression were played in extreme slow motion, however, coders detected initial spontaneous expressions of stress quickly overlaid by a more subdued expression. For example, a nose wrinkle (a common sigh of distress) would be turned into a smile.

Ekman and other biosocial theorists propose that there are innate motor programs for expressing basic emotions, but that cultures can modify the programs by teaching **display-rules** that regulate how emotions are displayed. Thus, Japanese and Americans are equally distressed by the same experiences and have the same innate motor programs for expressing distress, but Japanese culture frowns on public display of emotion, and Japanese people learn to replace signs of private distress with a public smile (see Box 13.1).

What are our basic emotions? Biosocial theorists have proposed different lists, but Plutchik (1980) has offered one influential classification. He arranges eight basic emotions in a circle; depending on their positions in the circle, basic emotions may combine in pairs (dyads) to produce higher order, nonbasic emotions. These nonbasic emotions may very well be uniquely human (see Figure 13.3 on page 394). In Plutchik's scheme, emotions that are next to one another readily combine to make complex emotions, while more distant pairs combine less readily, creating a more conflicted higher order emotion. Fear and surprise, for example, readily combine to create alarm. Fear and joy are separated by acceptance, and combine less well to create guilt, that uneasy blending of doing what we want (joy) but worrying about its consequences (fear).

Proximate Causes: The Neurobiology of Emotion

Because biosocial theorists regard emotions as modularized functions of the brain, they have not proposed a general theory of "emotion," but instead study single emotions, trying to detail the biological processes that give rise to each one. Due primarily to the investigations of Joseph Le Doux (1996), the emotion of fear is now well understood at the neurological level.

■ Box 13.1 ■

Emotional Control

We learned in Chapter 9 that we have limited control over our mental processes, especially automatic ones. Cognitive-social and biosocial theorists agree that emotions are largely automatic processes and therefore should be hard to control. Certainly our own experiences with emotions demonstrate that emotions are difficult, if not impossible, to control. We would prefer not to feel anxious at the dentist's office and to control feelings of stress and fear during important tests. Ability to control emotions is therefore useful, especially in helping people suffering from emotional disorders. The ancient Stoic philosophers thought happiness was to be found in emotional self-control, and taught their students how to achieve it. Was their project impossible: Can we control our emotions? Should we control our emotions?

As the experiment performed by Ekman with American and Japanese subjects showed, there is no question that human beings can control how they express emotions. Whether or not people can control subjective emotional feelings and their physiological counterparts is less clear. One experiment (Gross, 1995) illustrates the complexities of research findings on emotional control. Subjects watched a distressing film—the amputation of a limb (the same film Ekman's subjects watched). They were instructed either to suppress their emotions (the experimental group) or to simply watch the film (the control group).

The researchers found that Americans could, if instructed, suppress facial expressions of disgust, though the suppression was imperfect. However, the experimental subjects did not succeed in controlling their feelings; they did not differ from control subjects when asked how disgusted the film made them feel. Physiological measures of emotion in the experimental group presented a mixed picture. On some measures of physiological disturbance, such as heart rate, the experimental group seemed to have succeeded in emotional control: heart rates in the experimental group were slower than those in the control group. On other physiological measures such as skin moisture (a standard measure of anxiety), the experimental group displayed ironic effects: their skin moisture was greater than that in the control group. In summary, this experiment suggests that while people can control how much they express emotions, they have little if any natural control on how much they feel emotion, and that the physiological effects of attempted emotional control are sometimes good and sometimes bad.

Psychological research also suggests that emotional self-control is an important ingredient to achieving happiness, just as the Stoics thought. People who ruminate over their feelings following the death of a spouse from cancer experience longer and deeper periods of depression than those who do not (Hoeksma, 1995). Rumination makes depression worse by causing people to remember more depressing memories and by interfering with coping by blocking effective problem-solving thought. Subjects in these experiments who were given distracting tasks to do—to prevent useless rumination—became less depressed.

As the Stoics would have expected, health is adversely affected by frequent states of emotional arousal (Levenson, 1995). One arena in which unpleasant (as well as pleasant) arousal is common is marriage. Every marriage needs a good emotional regulator to preserve the mental and emotional health of each spouse.

Studies have reliably shown that married men are healthier and happier than unmarried men, whatever the quality of the marriage, while women's health and happiness depend on being in a good marriage. Levenson (1995) set out to find out why, focusing on the role emotional control plays in marriage.

Levenson found that experiencing and expressing anger did not damage marriages; feelings of fear and sadness (depression) do. Worst for marriages are feelings and verbal expressions of judgmental negative emotions such as disgust and contempt. Of all the emotions, presence of these best predicts divorce, because they lead to making unforgivable statements. The health of the marriage depends on preventing anger from escalating into disgust and contempt.

Some successful couples achieve this by simply avoiding conflict. In other successful couples, escalating tensions are broken by one of the spouses turning away from saying negative things to saying something positive, such as, "In spite of our problems, I still love you," or, "You're really wonderful." Levenson found that it was usually the wife who was the emotional regulator of the marriage, breaking escalating tensions with emotionally positive statements.

Levenson now had the answer to his question. His study (and many others) showed that husbands reduce emotional tension by simply mentally and emotionally withdrawing from conflicts. This strategy means they can protect their health from the dangers of continual arousal whether the marriage is good or bad. As active emotional regulators, on the other hand, women actively engage in and cope with conflict. Thus, how much conflict they experience—with its concomitant arousal—depends on how happy the marriage is. If conflicts are rare, then the wife's arousal is rare, and her health will be good (all other things being equal). If conflicts are frequent, then arousal will be frequent, and her health will suffer. If the wife is a good conflict manager, the marriage will endure, because anger will not become disgust and contempt, but she will pay a price for her success.

Levenson offers this advice to young people. If you are male, marry early, and, if necessary, often. If you are female, and you marry, choose your husband carefully.

It appears that even with little training or social support, people have some control over their emotions. It also appears that emotional self-control is a key to happiness. The Stoics may not have been right to teach the suppression of all emotion—we've learned in this chapter that emotion is an important part of human intelligence—but they were right that emotion can be, and should be, controlled.

How Does Fear Work? Fear Conditioning

Le Doux set out to study the neurophysiological details of the Pavlovian conditioning (see Chapter 3) of fear. Recall that Pavlovian conditioning involves an animal or person learning that a previously neutral stimulus reliably predicts the occurrence of a biologically important stimulus. During fear conditioning, a conditional stimulus, such as a tone or a visual pattern, is made to reliably precede a biologically threatening—and hence fear-producing—stimulus, such as electric shock. As a result, the conditional stimulus comes itself to elicit fear. Le Doux wanted to know what brain structures and circuits took part in such conditioning of fear, with specific reference to auditory CSs.

FIGURE 13.3 Plutchik's (1980) theory of basic emotions and their combinations into nonbasic dyads.

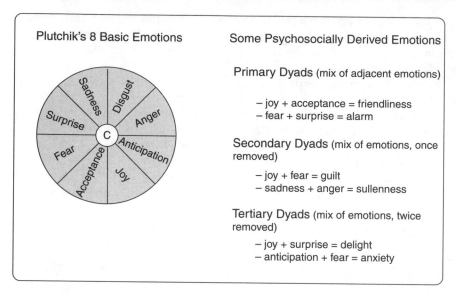

Plutchik's 8 Basic Emotions

Some Psychosocially Derived Emotions

Primary Dyads (mix of adjacent emotions)

    – joy + acceptance = friendliness
    – fear + surprise = alarm

Secondary Dyads (mix of emotions, once removed)

    – joy + fear = guilt
    – sadness + anger = sullenness

Tertiary Dyads (mix of emotions, twice removed)

    – joy + surprise = delight
    – anticipation + fear = anxiety

He began by studying the auditory pathways that connect the ears to the sensory cortex. Auditory stimuli are registered in the ear and then pass through a series of waystations, the most important of which is the thalamus, until they are registered in the sensory cortex, and perceived. In a series of experiments, Le Doux found that severing the connection between the auditory thalamus and the auditory cortex did not disrupt Pavlovian fear conditioning, but that lesions to the auditory thalamus or earlier in the auditory circuit abolished fear conditioning. It appears that the actual perception of a stimulus is not necessary for us to associate it with shock, and therefore for it to cause fear.

Further investigations established that the crucial brain structure that causes and controls fear and fear behavior is the **amygdala.** Via projections to other parts of the brain, the amygdala controls the various behavioral responses to fear, including freezing in place, increase in blood pressure, release of hormones related to stress, and the startle reflex.

Le Doux also found that the auditory thalamus projects separately to the amygdala and to the auditory cortex, by what he calls the "high road" to the cortex and the "low road" to the amygdala (see Figure 13.4). It now became clear why fear conditioning could take place when the thalamus's projections to the cortex were severed. The behaviors elicited by fear (i.e., the various unconditional responses to a fear producing US such as shock) were controlled by the amygdala, and could therefore be activated by projections directly from the thalamus, which also registered the auditory CS. Thus CS and US could be associated without involvement of the sensory cortex, and the CS could come to provoke fearful behaviors without being experienced.

We can now explain the three cases we discussed earlier in which cognition and emotion were disconnected by damage to the brain. In Claparede's patient and P. S., the subcortical connections between the thalamus and amygdala were intact, but connections between the amygdala and the cortex had been cut. Thus Claparede's patient

FIGURE 13.4 Critical pathways involved in experiencing and responding to fear.

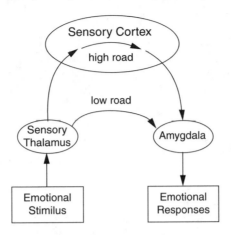

never learned to recognize him (a cortical memory function) but did learn to fear him (a subcortical amygdala function). P. S. could not identify the words he saw because his left (language) cortex was no longer connected to his right hemisphere. However, within the right brain, amygdala-cortex connections remained, so that P. S. could tell when the words he had seen were good or bad. Finally, the patient who knew that tones predicted unpleasant noises had lost his amygdala. He was fully (cortically) aware of CS and US, but could no longer feel, or learn, fear.

Recall that in our discussion of the neural bases of learning and memory (Chapter 12), we found that the simplest forms of learning do not involve the cortex, but that more complex forms of learning and memory do. That same pattern holds true for fear conditioning. In addition to simple Pavlovian conditioning of fear, animals can learn to discriminate stimuli that predict danger from those that do not. For example, an animal can learn that one tone predicts shock while another tone does not, and it exhibits fear to the first but not to the second. If we teach a rat to make such a discrimination and then sever the connection between the thalamus and the cortex, the discrimination is lost, and the animal responds fearfully to both stimuli.

Physiologically, the reason is clear. Thalamic projections to the cortex are very fine-grained, representing stimuli in precise detail. Projections to the thalamus are much cruder. Roughly speaking, thalamic projections to the cortex tell it, "This is a middle C," or "This is a D-flat above high C," while projections to the thalamus simply say, "A noise is happening." If the fine-grained thalamic-cortex connection is cut, the rat can no longer tell one tone from another, and feels fear of both, because all it hears is "noise happening."

How Does Fear Work? Emotional Memories

Not only does fear affect procedural (implicit) learning, as Le Doux's work shows, it also can affect the formation of declarative (explicit) memories, as shown by investigations carried out by McGaugh and his associates (reported by Haier, 1997).

McGaugh's basic experimental paradigm involves showing subjects either emotionally neutral or emotionally distressing films, and later testing the subjects' memories for them. He found that long-term memories (over several days or a week) for the distressing films were much better than for the neutral films. Suspecting that fear and the amygdala were responsible for the improved memory of scary films, McGaugh conducted two further experiments. One of the stress hormones produced by an activated amygdala is adrenaline, which McGaugh hypothesized might affect memory formation. He therefore conducted an experiment in which before seeing the film, subjects were injected with a beta-blocker, a drug that does not prevent release of adrenaline but which interferes with adrenaline's effects on the cortex. Subjects who received the beta-blocker remembered the frightening film no better than the boring film, supporting the hypothesis. Finally, the role of the amygdala in enhancing emotional memory was directly established by use of PET scanning. Subjects saw either a neutral or a distressing film and then were PET scanned. When memories were tested days later, among subjects who saw the distressing film there was a correlation of +.93 between how much they recalled of the film and how active was their amygdala while viewing it.

McGaugh's research may throw neurophysiological light on the flashbulb memories we discussed in Chapter 6. Flashbulb memories typically involve distressing events, such as assassinations and wars. It is possible, therefore, that flashbulb memories are more vivid in our minds because when they were first laid down our amygdalas were active, causing adrenaline to enhance learning. In addition, the amygdala projects directly to the hippocampus, which we have learned is the part of the brain that is crucial for forming memories. On the other hand, flashbulb memories are not always more accurate than other memories. We have also learned the unexpressed emotional memories can cause poor health (Box 13.2).

ULTIMATE CAUSES: WHAT ARE EMOTIONS FOR?

Why are emotions part of human nature? Perhaps emotions are just accidental by-products of the fact that we are made of living tissue rather than computers' plastic and metal. The automaton theory rejected by James held the view that emotions serve no evolutionary function at all.

Perhaps we would be better off without emotions. When world chess champion Gary Kasparov was defeated by computer program *Deep Blue* in 1997, he blamed his defeat on human emotional vulnerability. He was deeply disturbed by the subtlety of *Deep Blue*'s play in the second game, and had been unable to recover his usual courage. In the final and decisive game, Kasparov was so emotionally upset that he misplayed a simple opening sequence he had played hundreds of times before, and resigned early in anger. He said that *Deep Blue* won because it did not care if it lost; it did not care if it won; it just played. Commenting on the match and worried about cold-blooded machine intelligence, the *The Weekly Standard* said on the cover, "Be afraid. Be very afraid."

On the other hand, leading AI researcher Marvin Minsky wrote in *Society of Mind,* "The question is not whether intelligent machines can have any emotions, but whether machines can be intelligent without any emotions." Chess provides a poor test of intelligence—whether natural or artificial—because it requires taking no physical action in the world (*Deep Blue*'s helpers moved its pieces) and because the universe of chess, though large, is logically simple, being constrained by the board and the formal rules that players must obey. Computer-controlled robots are still

LEARNING AND COGNITION

■ Box 13.2 ■

Emotional Letting-Go and Health

The Greek philosopher Aristotle said that tragic plays appeal to us because they bring *catharsis,* a purging of negative emotions. James Pennebaker (1989, 1995), a social psychologist, has experimentally demonstrated that catharsis—cognitively infused release of suppressed emotion—provides considerable benefits to mental and even physical health.

His procedure is disarmingly simple. Pennebaker asks subjects to write about the most emotionally upsetting events in their lives, events that they have kept private. The nature of the events varied widely. One young man recounted being beaten repeatedly by his stepfather; despairing, he tried to commit suicide with his stepfather's gun, and was ridiculed by his stepfather for failing. A young woman told of being told at age ten to clean her room because her grandmother was going to visit; she did not, and the grandmother slipped on one of the girl's toys, broke her hip, and died during surgery.

Pennebaker has looked at the short- and long-term health effects of inhibiting and disinhibiting traumatic experiences. People who have had such experiences and kept them to themselves are more likely than people who either had no such experiences or revealed them to others to contract cancer, hypertension, ulcers, and even the flu. Subjects in Pennebaker's experiments who inhibited traumatic memories showed physiological signs of stress and had compromised immune systems when compared to others. Students in one study who confided traumatic experiences visited the student health center less frequently than others over a six-month period. Similar results were found in a study of Holocaust survivors who described experiences more horrific than anything students disclosed.

In the context of cognitive psychology two points about Pennebaker's findings are worthy of note. First, the traumas recounted by his subjects were *not* repressed in a psychoanalytic sense. Indeed, Pennebaker emphasizes that the deleterious consequences of nondisclosure stem from ongoing *conscious* refusal to think about the upsetting events. Second, simple venting of unpleasant emotions heightened them instead of reducing them, and conferred no benefits to Pennebaker's subjects. In order to benefit from disclosure, subjects had to disclose thoughts as well as feelings and achieve a sense of perspective on the trauma that they experienced. Such subjects reported achieving cognitive insight, saying, "It helped me look at myself from the outside," or "It was a chance to sort out my thoughts."

Again, here is an important contrast between Pennebaker's findings and popularized versions of psychoanalysis. Early in his career, Sigmund Freud and his mentor Joseph Breuer (1895) proposed that neuroses could be cured by the dramatic release—abreaction—of so-called "strangulated affect" associated with a supposedly repressed memory.* Many people now believe that simple ventilation of unpleasant emotions will achieve mental health. Pennebaker has shown that thinking about the unpleasant past is needed, and most modern forms of therapy value insight over simple emotional expression.

---

* Breuer and Freud's most famous patient Anna O., who was supposedly cured only when she ventilated the emotion associated with a "repressed" memory. Historical research has revealed that Anna O. did not ventilate her emotions, but simply recalled previous distressing experiences. There was no abreaction (Ellenberger, 1970; Leahey, 2000; Macmillan, 1997).

remarkably stupid, unable to move efficiently through space, and unable to cope with problems that are not well defined.

Specifically, robots have not yet solved the real-time problem and the frame problem. Confronted by a bear, you must respond quickly. This is the real-time problem: In the real world, success and survival depend on solving problems quickly, not eventually.

In addition, if we meet a menacing bear, it is important to apprehend that the bear is the problem with which we must cope, not the bird flying by at the same time, or the rabbit fleeing the bear. This is the frame problem: In the real world, many things invite our attention, but we must zero in quickly on the right thing. That the bear is the right thing to fear is obvious to us, but it would not be obvious to a robot.

Emotions help us solve both the real-time and frame problems. In addition, emotion plays an important role in effective social behavior. As we learned in the chapter on intelligence, the evolutionary roots of human intelligence are social in origin, and emotion plays a key role in solving problems of interacting with other people. Biosocial and cognitive social theorists agree with Minsky that emotions are a functional part of human nature.

Individual Emotional Intelligence

Solving the Real-Time Problem

Reference to Figure 13.4 shows how the fear pathways of the brain solve the real-time problem with respect to situations of danger, such as seeing a bear—or a snake—while on a stroll in the woods. Since Ledoux studied Pavlovian conditioning of sound, let us imagine a hiker in the woods who hears a rattlesnake's warning. The sound of the snake is processed by the thalamus, which sends two streams of information to other parts of the brain. A quick and dirty signal saying little more than "Danger!" is sent to the amygdala, causing the stroller to feel fear without yet recognizing the source of his fear. More detailed information is sent by the slower pathway to the cortex, which assembles a conscious representation of the snake.

Fear generated by the amygdala elicits an innate response of freezing. Freezing prevents us from moving into greater danger, buying time for the cortex to consciously recognize the threat and implement a coping strategy. Pavlovian fear conditioning may occur, too. Since the rattler's sound precedes threat, the sound will become a CS predicting danger. In future, the sound alone will be enough to cause fear and inspire freezing and flight. Furthermore, the experience of fear will change instrumental behavior, too. The hiker will probably avoid the same area of the woods in the future, or will at least be more cautious. Similarly, a mugging victim will avoid the neighborhood where he was mugged, and may be reluctant to venture out at night.

Our detailed knowledge of the adaptive nature of fear conditioning suggests an adaptive role for all the basic emotions (Ledoux, 1996; Simon, 1967). Consciousness is a serial processing system and when we focus our attention on one stimulus, our conscious perceptions of other stimuli are degraded. Yet, as the dangers of a walk in the woods suggest, significant events that we ignore at our peril may occur outside the focus of consciousness. Therefore, the brain possesses unconscious circuits operating in parallel to conscious thinking. These unconscious processes detect important events outside focal attention, albeit in crude and simple ways, and emotion is the signal they send to consciousness to capture its attention and engage its more sophisticated cognitive resources.

In sum, humans and other animals use emotion to help solve the real-time problem. Simple brain processes running in parallel to and outside consciousness constantly monitor the environment, looking for evidence of biologically important events (the sight of a bear, the cry of a child, the voice of one's beloved). When such events are detected, emotion arises to disengage consciousness from a less important task to deal with a more important one.

Solving the Frame Problem

I was discussing with the . . . patient when his next visit to the laboratory should take place. I suggested two alternative dates, both in the coming month and just a few days apart from each other. The patient pulled out his appointment book and began consulting the calendar. The behavior that ensued, which was witnessed by several investigators, was remarkable. For the better part of a half-hour, the patient enumerated reasons for and against each of the two dates: previous engagements, proximity to other engagements, possible meteorological conditions, virtually anything that one could reasonably think about concerning a simple date. Just as calmly as he had driven over the ice [see below], and recounted that episode, he was now walking us through a tiresome cost-benefit analysis, an endless outlining and fruitless comparison of options and possible consequences. It took enormous discipline to listen to all of this without pounding on the table and telling him to stop, but we finally did tell him, quietly, that he should come on the second of the alternative dates. His response was equally calm and prompt. He simply said: "That's fine." Back the appointment book went into his pocket, and then he was off. This behavior is a good example of the limits of pure reason. It is also a good example of the calamitous consequence of not having automated mechanisms of decision making. (Damasio, 1996)

The patient in question had experienced damage to the emotional parts of the brain we have been discussing in this chapter. As a consequence he, like computers, is beset by the frame problem. Presented with a simple task, he becomes "sicklied o're by the pale cast of thought." His reasoning was intact, and he was able to calculate all the possible things that might interfere with a given day's appointment. But reason could not choose between the two dates. Bereft of emotion, the patient could not cut decisively through the fog of possibilities, choose one date, and go on with life, until the psychologists—upset with him—decided for him.

Just as emotion helps us solve the real-time problem, it helps us solve the frame problem. As David Hume noted two centuries ago, "reason is and ought only to be the slave of the passions." Reason can formulate alternative plans of action, but reason alone provides no basis for choosing among them. By giving us motives, emotions move us to act rather than simply think.

At the same time, this patient shows that, as Kasparov found, sometimes being emotional can be a drawback. The day before the appointment episode, Damasio, like the patient, had had to drive to the laboratory on dangerously icy roads. Unlike Damasio, who had felt frightened and panicky, his patient had been unperturbed, calmly describing how to drive on the ice and calmly describing the misfortunes of those who had driven less rationally than he.

Social Emotional Intelligence

Solving the Commitment Problem

Source: Calvin and Hobbs, United Media. Reprinted by permission.

As we learned in Chapter 8, people tend to focus on the immediate consequences of their decisions and neglect gains and losses that may accrue to a decision over the long term. Frequently we would be better off by committing ourselves to a long-term strategy whose immediate benefits may be meager, but whose long-term benefits are great. Economist Robert Frank (1988) calls this the *commitment problem.*

In the cartoon, Calvin is being a good evolutionary psychologist. He suggests that love is a proximate psychological mechanism ("biochemical reaction") designed to help us reproduce ("make sure our genes get passed on"). His mother's answer confirms Calvin's speculation, and shows that mother love is a way of solving the commitment problem. Her immediate temptation is to get rid of what has disturbed her sleep, but her love for her son has committed her to a long-term adaptive strategy of raising a successful child. Through the emotion of love, she has acted more intelligently than if she were a simple calculator of immediate costs and benefits.

In a series of experiments, Damasio (1994) has shown that patients with medial frontal lobe damage, such as the patient described earlier, have a hard time formulating and acting on strategies that benefit them in the long as opposed to the short term. Damasio compared normal and medial frontal lobe patients on a complex gambling game in which one set of wagers earned occasional big payoffs but more frequent disastrous losses, while the other set of wagers brought consistent small but steady wins and occasional small losses. Normal subjects initially were attracted by the big payoffs of the first strategy, but ultimately stuck to the safer long-term strategy. The patients, however, never learned the lesson and lost large sums on the game. Their reasoning was intact, but lacking emotion, they never learned from their painful mistakes.

Emotional Communication

The commitment problem involves social interactions, and therefore an important aspect of solving the commitment problem is communicating our emotional commitments to other people. If people do not believe we are committed to a certain course of action, our interests may suffer (Frank, 1988).

Consider the cartoon (Figure 13.5). Normally we assume that we can pass beggars by with impunity. However, this beggar, through his sign and the expression on his face suggests that he is so irrational that he will use the whip on anyone who fails to "buy" a pencil from him. Thus, he will collect more money than will another beggar who gives no such sign of irrational tendencies to violence. The very signs of his irrationality serve his rational self-interest.

There are many examples from life demonstrating that seeming irrationality may ultimately serve our best interests. In poker, a purely rational player who carefully calculates the odds that his or her hand is best will never place large bets on a weak hand. Bluffing, however, involves placing a large bet on a weak hand. The success of bluffing depends on other, purely rational, players reasoning that large bets mean strong hands, so that they fold. Box 13.3 disucsses a poker-like game investigated by experimental economists.

The cold-war strategy of Mutually Assured Destruction was well described by its acronym, MAD. The United States and the Soviet Union each maintained large stockpiles of nuclear weapons sufficient to obliterate the other many times over, and each pledged to retaliate for any first nuclear strike by the other. However, retaliation would be manifestly irrational. If attacked, one's own country would stand in ruins, and to then atomize the other would be an act of irrational spite, killing millions and perhaps destroying the whole planet. Therefore, each side had to believe the other was irrational enough to carry out their threat, and therefore each had to occasionally send signals indicating such irrationality. One such signal was spending great sums of money buying so many more weapons than actually needed for successful retaliation. MAD was indeed mad, but that was the secret of its success—neither side dared launch a first strike against the other, fearing the other would be so mad as to blow up the planet.

Communicating emotional commitment is also important in less frightening affairs such as personal relationships. From an economic perspective, searching for a spouse is like searching for an apartment (Frank, 1988). One wants the ideal mate (or apartment) but one cannot take the time to carry out an optimizing exhaustive search, but must satisfice, marrying an acceptable but less than ideal spouse (see Chapter 9). Successful marriage, which is in the long-term interests of husband and wife, requires long-term commitment to the raising of children and the accumulation of jointly held property that may be difficult to divide. On what can such a commitment be based? Short-term rationality suggests avoiding marriage: a better partner might come along, the other might become disabled and so on. Moreover, one must worry about the other partner's commitment to the marriage, because he or she has the same

Homo Economicus and the Ultimatum Game

Of all the social sciences, economics is the most wedded to the idea that people always act to maximize their utility (see Chapter 9). The economists' ideal person is sometimes called—with a degree of sarcasm—*Homo economicus.* Traditionally, economists have based their theories on aggregate statistical data collected by governments and corporations about the economic activities of thousands and millions of people. *Homo economicus* is therefore an abstraction, existing only in the mathematical models of economic forecasters.

However, there is an emerging interdisciplinary field called experimental economics in which psychologists' laboratory methods are used to test economic theories (Perlstein, 1997). By looking at individuals, often in cooperation with psychologists, experimental economists can determine to what degree real people act like economists' *Homo economicus.* Typically, they do this by setting up games that subjects play for money, examining how much the subjects' behavior conforms to economic predictions.

One game has gathered a great deal of attention from economists and social psychologists because it casts great doubt on economists' assumption that people are rational utility maximizers (Frank, 1988; Perlstein, 1997; Ridley, 1996).

The Ultimatum Game is a variation on the Prisoner's Dilemma (Chapter 9). In the standard version two players play the game once. One player is called the Proposer, the other is the Acceptor. The Proposor is given some amount of money, typically $10 (though one version of the game played in a poor country had stakes equivalent to two weeks wages without changing the outcomes I'll describe). The Proposer must then offer some amount of money to the Acceptor. If the Acceptor takes the offer, both players get to keep what they have; if the Acceptor refuses the offer, neither player gets to keep any money. In what follows, I will assume that the Proposer is given 10 one-dollar bills. What would you do in each role?

Traditional economists were so sure of the outcome of the Ultimatum Game that they scoffed at experimental economists for even running the experiment. According to economic theory, each player, being a *Homo economicus,* will act so as to maximize the amount of money with which he or she will leave the experiment. The Proposer will thus offer as little as possible, $1, expecting to keep $9. The Acceptor will now have the choice of leaving with $1 or with nothing, and should choose to accept the $1. However, in experiments of the type just described, people deviate from economic expectations. Typically, most Proposers propose a 50–50 split or close to it, while Acceptors reject offers of less than about $3. Very few Proposers offer only $1. These results shook the economic community (Perlstein, 1997), and continue to inspire research and controversy.

One interpretation of the results is that people in this situation are motivated less by cold-blooded calculations of economic gain than by emotional concerns about social fairness (Frank, 1988; Ridley, 1996). The economic prediction completely ignores the social aspects of the game. Imagine that you went to an experiment and the experimenter simply offered you a dollar, which you could refuse to take. I am sure the vast majority of people would take the dollar. Economists believe that in the Ultimatum Game players should do the same, taking the dollar rather than leaving with nothing. However, this ignores the emotional question of social fairness. The Acceptor knows that the Proposer could offer more and refuses to take the dollar because it's an unfair split of the money given by the researcher. Proposers, too, are motivated by fairness, and split the money about evenly.

Further evidence in favor of the fairness theory comes from an experiment in which a second round followed the first. Subjects who had not played in the first round were now paired with subjects who they knew had either proposed a fair split in the first round, or had proposed an unfair split. The new subjects then had to choose between splitting $12 evenly with an unfair Proposer or $10 evenly with a fair Proposer. Of the subjects, 74 percent made the latter choice. Again, this behavior is not that of the purely self-interested *Homo economicus*. From a selfish perspective, one should take the $6 split rather than the $5 split, but instead, subjects were willing to forgo $1 to punish someone known to be unfair. The emotional moral sense of altruism overrides the greed of self-interest (Frank, 1988).

We should note, however, that people are not always fair; sometimes greed trumps altruism. For example, if the $10 is given to the Proposer in an envelope so that only he or she knows how much is at stake, he or she tends to offer only $1, and the Acceptor tends to accept it. This suggests that possibly in the standard game, Proposers offer even splits because they want to *appear* to be fair in the eyes of others (the Acceptor and the experimenter, a professor who may one day have power over them) rather than because they simply wanted to be fair. Interestingly, unlike the classic Prisoner's Dilemma, in which repeated play tends to make people act more altruistically, in the Ultimatum Game repeated play moves subjects into acting more and more like *Homo economicus,* though it is unclear why (Perlstein, 1997).

Finally, it is interesting to observe differences between the social sciences. Economists have often been actively hostile to psychologists who throw cold water on their belief in *Homo economicus* (Slovic, 1995). Sometimes they have conducted studies designed to "discredit psychologists' works as applied to economics" (Grether & Plott, 1979, p. 623). More psychologically minded economists admit their field suffers from dogmatism (Hausman, 1991).

Economics and psychology are supposed to be sciences of human behavior, and therefore should make similar predictions about human behavior. I described the Ultimatum Game to three colleagues in social psychology who had not heard of it and asked them to predict what would happen. None predicted what economists had so confidently expected. Two predicted the actual results, though on intuition rather than psychological theory. The third, to whom I described a version of the game played by the same subjects for 10 rounds, predicted that in the end the Proposer would have to offer $9, because the Acceptor has all the power, able to coerce the Proposer into giving up most of the money. This has never been reported.

Some differences between economists and psychologists may be a matter of personality. Carter (1991) compared the behavior of economics majors with other subjects in the Ultimatum Game, finding that economics majors were more likely to propose unfair splits. He concluded that selfish people were drawn to economics rather than that taking economics makes people selfish. Perhaps "scientific" theories reflect personal biases; certainly a unified science of human nature is a long way off.

short-term reasons for avoiding marriage, or might desert if a more attractive partner becomes available.

Like many poets and song writers, Dante described love as a kind of madness. But as with MAD, there is long-term intelligence in love. As with Calvin's mother, love overcomes one's immediate rational calculations and commits one to a course of action that is in one's long-term best interests. And signs of being in love communicate to one's beloved that one is so committed. Laws against divorce are meant to shore up commitment to marriage during weak moments, but love keeps partners together.

As Shakespeare (Sonnet 116) wrote:

> Love is not love
> Which alters when it alteration finds,
> Or bends with the remover to remove;
> O, no! it is an ever-fixed mark,
> That looks on tempests and is never shaken.

SUGGESTED READINGS

A good general survey of psychological findings regarding emotional intelligence is Daniel Goleman, *Emotional Intelligence: Why It Can Matter More Than IQ* (New York: Bantam Books, 1995). Le Doux (1996) is the best general treatment of emotion from the biosocial perspective, while Lazarus (1991) is a good statement of one cognitive-social theory. To see both perspectives set at odds in a useful series of debates, see Paul Ekman and Richard J. Davidson, *The Nature of Emotion: Fundamental Questions* (New York: Oxford University Press, 1994). Neuroscientist Antonio Damasio has written two accessible books about the neuroscience of emotion. The first, *Descartes' Error* (1996), argued for the important adaptive value of emotion against its rationalist critics; the second, *The Feeling of What Happens: Body and Emotion in the Making of Consciousness* (New York: Harcourt Brace, 1999), focuses on the "somatic marker hypothesis," his neo-Jamesian theory of how emotions are felt.

14 Evolutionary Psychology

In Chapter 2 we covered the basics of evolutionary theory, the evolutionary path of human beings, and the selective forces that led to the evolution of human intelligence and language. In this chapter we take up the evolutionary basis for a number of human social traits, looking not only at humans but at the same traits in other animals.

ALTRUISM

Helping another at some risk to one's self—**altruism**—appears to fly in the face of natural selection. How can there be a gene that puts its bearer, and thus itself, at risk of death? If the organism dies, so do its genes, and so it appears quite impossible for natural selection to have favored altruistic, suicidal genes. The answer lies in gene-thinking: The altruist is the tool of a selfish gene.

Forms of Altruism

Altruism and Kin-Selection

A number of insect species, including the familiar honeybee and the summer house pest, the paper wasp, have evolved what biologists call eusociality, a highly organized social structure including a distinct caste of sterile female workers. Such a caste represents the height of altruism, for these workers give up having offspring of their own and toil "for the good of the hive." Altruism of this order was recognized by Darwin himself as a serious challenge to natural selection, and a solution of the problem (Hamilton, 1964/1980; Samuelson, 1983; Trivers & Hare, 1976/1980) represented a triumph for gene-thinking.

What was first most suggestive about eusociality was that of the two dozen or so species that display it, all but one (certain termites) are of the order Hymenoptera, which possesses a very unusual genetic system called haplodiploidy. In the haplodiploid species the paper wasp (shown in Figure 14.1), a female mates once with a male and stores his sperm inside her body, and then goes on to found a colony. When she fertilizes an egg and deposits it in the nest, it becomes a female; when she deposits an egg without fertilizing it, it becomes a male.

The vast majority of living things are like the female wasp: They are diploid, possessing two sets of chromosomes, one set from each parent. For simplicity's sake, only two chromosomes, A and B, are considered in Figure 14.1. In the female the pairs of A chromosomes are called A_1 and A_2, the pairs of B chromosomes are B_1 and B_2; thus, the queen carries four chromosomes altogether. Male wasps, however, are haploid: Since they develop from an unfertilized egg, they possess only one set of

FIGURE 14.1 The genetics of haplodiploid insects. (Adapted from Alcock, 1979.)

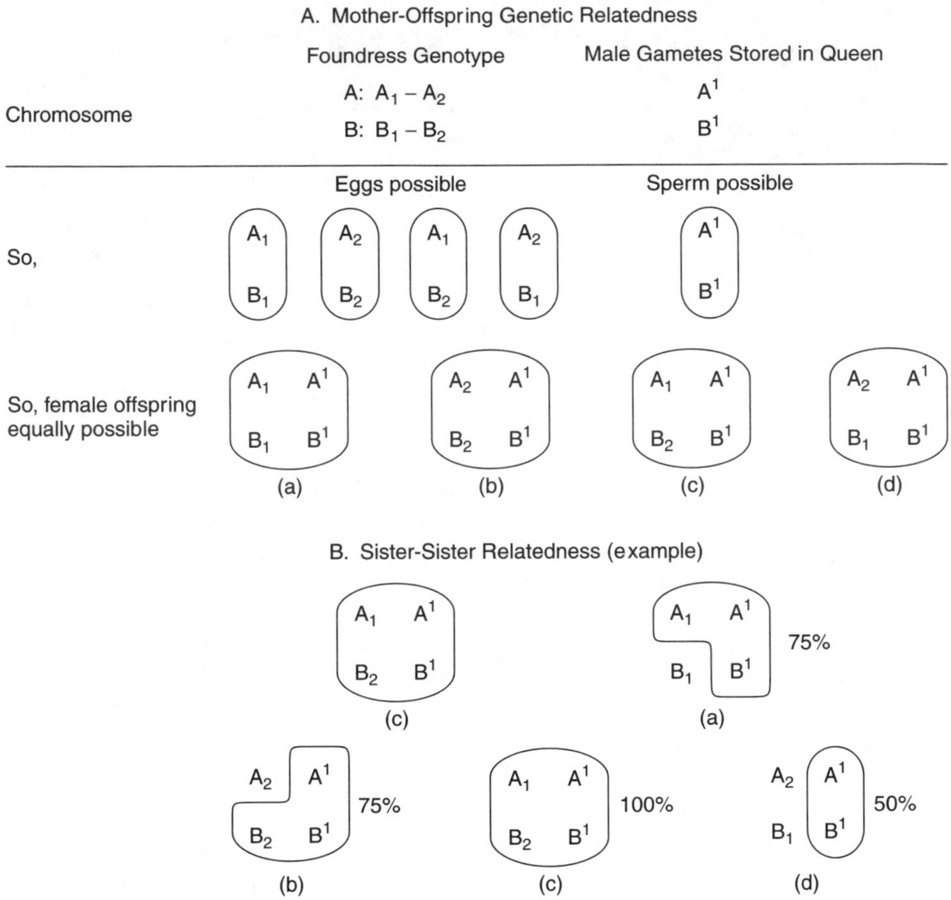

A. Mother-Offspring Genetic Relatedness

B. Sister-Sister Relatedness (example)

chromosomes, not two sets. In Figure 14.1, the male carries only two chromosomes, A' and B'.

When the queen forms an egg from her genotype, taking half the chromosomes, four possible eggs can result, as shown. However, the sperm she carries are all identical—the male must contribute all of his genotype to each sperm, not just half of it as diploid creatures do. This simple fact does odd things to the genetic relatedness of the sisters produced by the queen. Figure 14.1 shows the four possible genotypes that can be formed from each mating of sperm and egg, and then picks one possible female and measures her degree of relatedness to her sisters. In diploid genetic systems, siblings are related by half their genes; however, in the haplodiploid system all sisters begin with the same genes gotten from the haploid father and add some degree of relatedness through their mother. As Figure 14.1 shows, each female is on average 75 percent related to her sisters.

These calculations make possible a kin-selection explanation of female sterility in eusocial insects. If a sister has her own offspring, she will be related to them by 50 percent of her genes (just as they are related to the queen). But she is related to her sisters by sharing 75 percent of their genes. Therefore, her genes will do better in the struggle for existence—increasing their numbers in the wasp gene pool—by helping the queen produce other sisters who share 75 percent of their genes, than by having their own offspring, who would share only 50 percent of their genes. In this way **kin-selection** produces selfish altruism. In sacrificing their own individual fitness by "altruistically" remaining sterile and helping their mother run the colony and raise her offspring, worker wasps (and bees) are really acting in the (selfish) interest of their own genes. Selection acts through kin, specifically sisters in this case, rather than through an individual's own offspring.

The kin-selection explanation of altruism can be, and has been, extended to other species including mammals. It may explain why ground squirrels give predator alarm calls when they are near close relatives but not otherwise, why wild turkeys form brother-brother pairs while looking for mates, and why young male Florida scrub jays often help their parents rear more offspring. In general, kin-selection of altruistic behavior may be invoked whenever we wish to explain a behavior that reduces one's own fitness but enhances that of relatives. Whenever the risk to your own genes is outweighed by the benefit to your genes carried by relatives, then kin-selection may take place.

Parental Manipulation Altruism

Parents may train—or try to train—their offspring to be altruistic toward each other (being "fair") or to the parents, beyond the altruism based on kin-selection. For example, termites are eusocial but diploid. It appears that by pheromones the queen termite suppresses female workers' reproduction and guides their solicitude for her and the termite colony. By forcing her workers to be sterile, she reserves all rights of genetic reproduction to herself.

Reciprocal Altruism

Even in the animal world not all altruism is directed at or controlled by close relatives. Can evolutionary psychology explain the evolution of behavior that immediately benefits neither the individual nor his or her relatives but some total stranger? Perhaps it can (see Trivers, 1971/1980). If one offers aid to another, one likely expects future aid in return. This is **reciprocal altruism:** You scratch my back and I will scratch yours. Reciprocal altruism can evolve whenever individuals, at small cost to themselves, can aid another and expect a great genetic return. In baboon troops a male may enlist the aid of another male to defeat a higher status male and steal his mate. Later, the helper is similarly aided by his co-conspirator. Again, evolutionary psychology says that phenotypic altruism is genetically selfish: I will help you only if I can expect to benefit later on.

The evolution of reciprocal altruism may be an engine of cognitive evolution. Imagine a species that cannot recognize its fellows as distinct individuals. An altruist in such a species would blindly aid whoever asked for aid. Quickly a conniving counter-strategy would evolve to prey upon the saintly sucker: Get aid from the altruist but never return it. Only a smart altruist could avoid extinction by the new egotists. He or she would give aid when called upon, but never to one who had earlier cheated by refusing aid. Mathematical models indicate that the smart, reciprocal altruist would soon become the dominant type (Dawkins, 1976). But the strategy of reciprocal altruism necessitates concomitant cognitive evolution. The reciprocal altruist would need to be able to discern individual differences in appearance; be able to remember each individual and associate that individual with acts of helping or cheating; be able to base a behavioral decision on memory and calculation of a risk/benefit ratio. Thus, evolution of one social trait—altruism—may fuel the evolution of cognitive abilities, and as these grow they may in turn feed back on social development. Perhaps intellect originated in just this way; if so, in humans it has ironically expanded to the point of finding reciprocal altruism cynical, and constructed truly nonselfish systems of ethics.

Reciprocal altruism may be seen as a more specific form of a broader class of mutual helping, **mutualism** (Maynard Smith, 1982a; Wrangham, 1982). Mutualism occurs whenever several individuals cooperate for the immediate benefit of all under circumstances in which no individual can exploit a given situation. So, for example, orb weaver spiders, unable alone to throw a web across a stream to catch the many insects flying above, may cooperate with others in the initial spanning of the stream. Then, each spider builds its own nest. Here, unrelated individuals cooperate in order that each spider may enjoy a rich payoff, which is why the behavior has evolved. Since the mutual cooperation occurs at the same time, controls on cheating are unnecessary, so mutualism is simpler than reciprocal altruism. But it remains truly altruistic; although each spider gains an individual reward (each catches its own prey and does not share) it succeeds by aiding and without exploiting its fellows, as occurs with individually selected "altruism."

Beyond the scope of our introduction to evolutionary psychology lies the sophisticated analysis of altruism using game theory (see Box 14.1).

Altruism and Individual Selection

Finally, it is possible for apparent altruism to be entirely selfish, and to be subject to individual selection. Consider alarm calls in birds. A flock is on the ground eating and a cat stalks up. The first bird to see the cat gives a cry of alarm, and the flock flutters off. The alarm-giver appears to risk calling the cat's attention to itself while "altruistically" warning the flock. But appearances deceive. The caller knows that the flock will take off when it cries (and so the flock benefits), but the caller benefits even more because it knows where the predator is and can position itself

■ Box 14.1 ■

Evolutionary Psychology and Game Theory

Game theory is a branch of utility theory (see Chapter 9) that has occasionally been applied to psychology; for example, in social psychology's studies of the prisoner's dilemma. Game theory describes the outcomes of interactions between individuals who adopt different strategies in their encounters, and it evaluates the outcomes of each encounter by weighing the relative costs and benefits of adopting each strategy. As is clear already, evolutionary psychology makes extensive use of cost/benefit analysis, and game theory is becoming its most powerful mathematical tool for understanding the strategies genes adopt and the games they play to survive. While the formal refinements of game theory lie well beyond the scope of our book, we will present here a simple and brief analysis of altruism in game theory terms.

Consider a population of organisms, say birds (Dawkins, 1976), who pick lice from each other's heads. We begin with the whole population being suckers, who groom any head presented to them—they are completely altruistic. Now imagining we can quantify inclusive fitness, let us assume that the benefit of being groomed is 5 fitness units, and the cost (time lost from foraging or mating while grooming another) is 2 units. Each grooming interaction is beneficial: $5 - 2 = 3$; the payoff exceeds the cost. However, this happy state of affairs is not an evolutionarily stable strategy, or ESS, because a mutant gene may easily arise, creating a new strategy, cheating. The cheat presents his or her head for grooming and is groomed by suckers, but never grooms in return. The resulting costs and benefits may be summarized in this payoff matrix, showing the result of each possible interaction of strategy:

	Sucker	*Cheat*	*Net Payoff*
Sucker	$5 - 2 = 3$	$0 - 2 = -2$	1
Cheat	$5 - 0 = 5$	$0 - 0 = 0$	5

Cheating is a superior strategy, for the cheat gets groomed without ever paying the cost, and the sucker is constantly wasting time grooming cheats. This new pattern is not stable either, because the cheating strategy works too well. Early cheats will flourish among the many suckers, but as cheats multiply (and suckers diminish) the actual payoff of cheating declines, as each cheat finds it harder to get groomed. So the ratio of cheats-to-suckers population may oscillate; pure sucker strategy isn't stable, as a few cheats flourish; pure cheating isn't stable, because then no one gets groomed.

While there may be a stable population ratio of suckers to cheats, this is unlikely, since the optimum strategy, the ESS, is reciprocal altruism; let us call it the bourgeois strategy. The bourgeois grooms the heads of those who present themselves—except those known to have cheated in the past! We can construct the following payoff matrix, omitting for simplicity's sake the occasional interaction between a new cheat and a bourgeois:

	Sucker	*Cheat*	*Bourgeois*	*Net Payoff*
Sucker	$5 - 2 = 3$	$0 - 2 = -2$	$5 - 2 = 3$	4
Cheat	$5 - 0 = 5$	$0 - 0 = 0$	$0 - 0 = 0$	5
Bourgeois	$5 - 2 = 3$	$0 - 0 = 0$	$5 - 2 = 3$	6

The bourgeois strategy is superior to either cheating or being a sucker, and depending on the actual cost/benefit values, an evolutionarily stable situation should be reached, since no new, superior strategy should arise to displace the bourgeoisie.

Game theory is now being applied to every area of evolutionary psychology—aggressive interactions, altruism, mating strategies, parent-child interactions, population size, and so on—and promises to bring mathematical rigor to the field. An introduction to game theory and ESSs may be found in the second edition (not the first) of Barash's *Evolutionary Psychology and Behavior* (1982), while the more serious student may see *Evolution and the Theory of Games* by John Maynard Smith (1982b), the pioneer in applying game theory to evolutionary psychology (Maynard Smith, 1982a). For a history, see William Poundstone, *Prisoners Dilemma* (New York: Doubleday, 1992).

advantageously in the confusing swarm of birds, and so increase its own chances of escape (Alcock, 1979). Altruism in this case is totally selfish: The herd is manipulated by a single member for its own advantage. The existence of such strategies suggests caution about too readily seeing various behaviors as altruistic.

Human Altruism

While readers of this book live in large, impersonal, modern societies, humans evolved—and most people today still live—under very different conditions in which relationship with an extended community of kin was a major factor in determining social success or failure. Such conditions naturally favor kin-selected altruism. The fitness of any individual gene carrier is greatly enhanced by cooperating with relatives in such matters, say, as negotiating marriage. Conversely, the relative's fitness is also increased because the individual carries some of each relative's genes, which will be increased by the marriage. It pays your genes to help others who carry those genes. The closer blood ties are, the greater altruism is kin-selected, and is simply what we normally call nepotism: One's inclusive fitness is enhanced by helping one's relatives. The larger the social organization, the more distant kin ties become, and altruism is less and less kin-selected, but must be based on mutualism and reciprocity—reciprocal altruism.

Studies of traditional cultures support the evolutionary psychological contention that cooperative social interaction is a relatively direct function of degree of genetic relatedness, while conflict splits societies at the weakest links in the chain of relatives. (See Chagnon, 1981; Chagnon & Irons, 1979; Flinn, 1982; Irons, 1982; and van der Berghe & Barash, 1977/1980 for extensive discussions.) To take a simple example, Hames (1979) studied the amount of social interaction between pairs of individuals as a function of their degree of genetic relatedness; this was done among the Ye'kwana of Venezuela's upper Orinoco basin. Hames found a remarkably precise relationship between kinship and amount of interaction, frequency of interaction increasing linearly with degree of relatedness. One's reaction to Hames' finding is likely to be: Well of course, people naturally want to help their relatives, so they live together and must interact more frequently. But remember that evolutionary psychology seeks ultimate causes, to know why sugar tastes sweet and why we "naturally" are fond of our relatives. Hames argues that living together—and, by implication, the desire to live together—is the proximate mechanism by which human kin-selection operates. Only if people live in related groups can they help the genes they share with relatives.

For it is not obvious to reason that we ought to favor our relatives. Selfish egoistic reason would dictate that I ought to treat everyone impersonally as a means to my own gratification: as temporary allies or enemies. Unselfish moral reason would dictate that I ought to treat everyone impersonally as autonomous human beings: each person to be cherished as such and treated equally. But traditional societies—where humans evolved—do not work in these ways. In them people want to help and be helped by their kin, to establish new kin relations as a means to social peace and harmony, and they want to hurt alien kin groups. In these natural preferences we see the hand of natural (kin) selection. People are, by nature, neither egoists nor saints.

This brings us to reciprocal altruism and the problem of mass societies. As the circles of interaction widen from village to tribe and beyond to the nation state and the urban civilization modern Western people live in, ties of kin weaken, and kin-selected altruism becomes irrelevant. Relations with strangers cannot be based on shared genetic interest; they must rest on reciprocal altruism, or reciprocity: I will cooperate with others insofar as I can expect they will cooperate with me.

But reciprocal altruism encourages cheating, or "negative reciprocity." I take a risk when I help another, and he or she may cheat me by not returning my help. Especially in mass societies when people are likely to interact only once (making it hard to learn who the cheaters are), fraud and deception become serious problems. Just consider commercial transactions. You hand over money at the same time the merchant gives you your purchase: Neither one has to trust the other, for you reciprocate at the same moment. Hence, the merchant's distrust of checks—he or she has learned by experience that, like the empty balloon with which the male hanging fly woos his mate, some people's checks signify nothing of value. Thus, the consumer's distrust of mail-order business, since one entrusts one's money to strangers with no guarantee it will buy anything. In urban societies, altruism may even become maladaptive (MacDonald, 1984).

It is thus not surprising that the most stable form of reciprocal altruism occurs when people interact over time. Axelrod (1984) has shown that there is a simple, but powerful, strategy for enforcing reciprocal altruism, the tit-for-tat strategy. In your first interaction with a person, be cooperative. However, if in any future interaction the other person cheats you, retaliate. This simple strategy has been shown to be more effective than ones that are considerably more complicated, and it therefore has the virtue of being evolutionarily stable; it defeats any other possible strategy.

But reciprocity is the only social cement that holds urban society together. Cultural evolution in Western civilization has produced complex mechanisms for enforcing reciprocity: government, police, the law. In the absence of kin ties we bind ourselves with the impersonal ties of rules and regulations. Biological evolution has given us a conscience and guilt (Trivers, 1971/1980). Guilt motivates a cheater to make amends, and restores his or her position in society. A cheater with no guilt, on the other hand, would be ostracized by society; unrepentant cheaters' genes will die with them. The guilty cheater returns and may prosper; his or her guilt-feeling genes survive him or her.

Besides the theoretical arguments that altruism can be an innate human trait, there is now direct evidence that it is (Pines, 1979). Some infants as young as one year of age, before any appreciable degree of social learning can take place, attempt to console or even help people who are crying or in pain. Differences in altruism at one year persisted in a follow-up study five years later: One-year-old altruists became six-year-old altruists. There was also evidence of parental correlates of baby altruism. Parents who forcefully and emotionally explained how their child had hurt someone had more altruistic children, as did parents who were themselves altruists. It is unclear however, if these parental behaviors caused the children to be altruistic, or if they simply reinforced a predisposition toward altruism shared by parent and child alike. The early appearance of altruistic behavior, individual differences in altruism, and its temporal stability, all point to some genetic basis for this important human trait, based perhaps on a genetic propensity to become affectionate with those who raise us and with whom we are raised (MacDonald, 1984), and to like those whom we resemble (Glassman, Packel, & Brown, 1981).

AGGRESSION

Animal Aggression

Why aggression occurs has a simple evolutionary psychological answer—sometimes it benefits an individual's inclusive fitness. Aggression can enhance fitness in many ways. It is usually males who are aggressive, and their fitness may be improved by fighting for a territory to control and to live off, for one or more females to mate, or for high status in a dominance hierarchy and the access to females that this ensures. Excluding parental discipline and predator-prey aggression most aggression is a form of competition for resources, typically either for scarce natural resources or for a limited supply of females.

Thus success at aggressive competition enhances fitness. The successful aggressor with a good territory and many mates will pass his genes on into the next generation in greater numbers than the vanquished will. If this be so, why is aggression restrained at all? Surely the best strategy would be for a male to kill all his rivals, ensuring that their genes have no hope of survival.

The answer to this apparent puzzle is that aggression always entails risks. As with altruism, evolutionary psychology holds that an organism acts as if it calculates the ratio between the benefits of aggression against its costs. To enter an all-out fight to the death is to risk losing everything; even should one win, one might be so damaged that later fitness is reduced. A drive for lethal aggression would be so detrimental to its holders that a gene for it cannot evolve. Moreover, even losers in aggressive interchanges benefit from controlled aggression. If one dies, one's genes die too. But if one loses nonfatally, one can hope to be more successful later.

Aggression exists in nature, therefore, in a kind of compromised state. Aggressiveness enhances fitness, so it has evolved; at the same time too much aggressiveness reduces fitness, so constraints on aggression have evolved. The result is the evolution of a set of behavioral mechanisms that give individuals of many species the capacity to fight, but which limit the aggression to the establishment of competitive superiority—for a territory or for females—without resulting in the death of the loser. In the animal world, nature is red in tooth and claw, but within certain evolutionary constrained boundaries.

Human Aggression

Ever since Cain slew Abel, aggression has been the dark side of human nature. The men of Homer's *Iliad* seem to enjoy killing and worship the glory to be won in war. The seventeenth-century political philosopher Thomas Hobbes observed that without society—and a strong ruler—human life would be solitary, nasty, brutish, and short. This view of human aggression as an impulse barely checked by repressive civilization was shared after World War I by Sigmund Freud, who had previously rejected it. And, of course, the background to all philosophical and scientific speculation—and no one has gone much beyond speculation—on human aggression is our species' history of murder, torture, war, and genocide.

In the modern era, but before evolutionary psychology, proponents of theories of human aggression had divided into two quarrelsome camps. On one side was the ethological neo-Freudian view whose scientific spokesman was Konrad Lorenz (1966) and whose able publicist was author and screenwriter Robert Ardrey (1966). Like Freud, Lorenz claimed that aggression was a distinct innate drive, a need to be aggressive that constantly seeks expression. Unlike Freud, in the ethological perspective the aggressive drive was only a "so-called evil" (the subtitle of Lorenz's book in German), since aggression was recognized to have the adaptive properties discussed earlier. For Lorenz, the problem of human aggression was that the drive was no longer under the control of the mechanisms that in animals constrain it short of murder, a problem multiplied many times by humankind's inventive technology of death. The solution to the problem of aggression was to rechannel aggressiveness into moral equivalents of war—activities that, like space exploration, provide the thrills, glory, heroism, and solidarity of war within a socially constructive context. For Lorenz and his followers, then, aggressiveness was an ineradicable part of human nature, a drive that could not be escaped but could be redirected.

The other side viewed aggression as alien to the human condition (Montague, 1968), a view represented in psychology by the social learning tradition (e.g., Bandura & Walters, 1963). Like Lorenz's view, this camp developed in part from psychoanalysis, following Freud's earlier idea that aggression was not an autonomous drive but derived from frustration of other drives such as sex or hunger and from infantile oral-aggressive sexuality. So the Montague camp argued against Lorenz that aggression was a product of culture and not of biology. Through imitation of observed aggression, especially when it was seen to pay off, and reinforcement of aggressive acts, a child was molded by its environment into an aggressive adult. According to these environmentalists, aggression was nothing more than a set of learned skills that could be unlearned by an adult and, of course, not taught to children. A pacific utopia is to be achieved not by redirecting aggression but by refusing to model it and refusing to let it pay; aggression could go the way of the bustle.

The evolutionary psychological view is, in effect, a compromise between Lorenz's adaptive aggressive drive and social learning's set of learned skills. Rejecting any notion that aggression is an instinctive drive, evolutionary psychology holds that aggression results instead from competition. Whenever resources are in limited supply—be they food, space, or mates—aggression becomes an adaptive response. Thus, for the evolutionary theorist, aggression is an innate set of skills, or an innate disposition to learn aggressive skills, which evolved because it has been adaptive in the past. Evolutionary psychology shares with Lorenz the insight that aggression is not a purely gratuitous evil, but shares with the social learners the insight that aggression is a capacity, not a drive, whose learning and manifestation depend on environmental circumstances.

Some anthropological evidence indicates that human aggression occurs for the same reasons as aggression between animals. To begin with, aggression may stem from efforts to establish dominance. People, especially males, struggle to establish power over others in our numerous hierarchical organizations. Status displays, such as joining the country club or buying a Rolls-Royce, are peaceful ways of showing one's superior dominance position. As in animals, human aggression sometimes—but all too rarely—is channeled into ritualized mock combat, as in medieval jousts, when one knight established his superiority over his rivals.

Human aggression and warfare are also caused by resource competition. The Munducurú of Brazil fight frequent wars with their neighbors, wars that appeared quite senseless until fitted to an evolutionary psychological model (Durham, 1976). As were human beings for most of their evolutionary history, the Munducurú are hunter-gatherers who rely on hunting as their primary source of high quality protein.

The mere existence of other tribes—in Munducurú the word for enemy means all who are not Munducurú—threatens their supply of game. So their propensity for war is adaptive for each and every individual of their tribe by helping assure a plentiful supply of protein. The individual fitness of the best warriors is directly increased through increase in social status and lavish gifts. The most outstanding warrior in a particular battle is by no evolutionary psychological accident called "mother of the peccary": one who increases valued game by killing those who might diminish it. Where women are a scarce resource, as in periods of rapid geographical and population expansion (e.g., among the Yanamamö of Brazil and Venezuela) men fight for opportunities to take wives. In short, where some resource is in short supply, aggression occurs, even among groups that are otherwise quite pacific (Eibl-Eibesfeldt, 1975); Western children's fights over toys are regulated by the same factors as among the Munducurú (Weigel, 1984).

Factors that tend to inhibit aggression are also explicable in evolutionary psychological terms. Medieval rulers arranged marriages to make alliances with each other, reducing the likelihood of war between them, a practice pursued by many primitive groups as well. One is less likely to kill kin than to kill strangers, for kin carry one's genes, and their murder would harm one's own inclusive fitness. Reciprocal altruism, too, can check forces pushing toward aggression. Where people and groups of people can cooperate to increase their fitness over what each alone could achieve through aggression, aggression will no longer pay and would be shunned.

Apart from these general tendencies that humans share with other animals, tendencies that lead us at once toward and away from fighting, evolutionary psychologists have considered the unique problem of human aggression. First, however, it should be pointed out that there may not be a special problem of human aggressiveness, despite Lorenz. Human technology makes humans uniquely efficient killers, but it does not follow that we are the most aggressive—even if we are the most dangerous—species on earth. Wilson (1975a) has catalogued among animals' brutalities extending to cannibalism. As Wilson (p. 107) observes, "If hamadryas baboons had nuclear weapons they would destroy the world in a week. And alongside ants, which conduct assassinations, skirmishes, and pitched battles as routine business, men are all but tranquilized pacifists."

Nevertheless, human aggression does possess certain unique features. The naked (human) ape is an ill-equipped killer. Our teeth and our claws, or fingernails, are poor offensive weapons set alongside the natural equipment of the lion or wolf. Unfortunately, as Lorenz originally suggested, this means during our early evolution in the pretechnological past it was so unlikely that man could kill another that we lack the reflexive aggression-inhibiting responses possessed by lions and wolves. So give a human a weapon, and death can follow all too readily. It is not surprising, then, that while ritual aggression is common in the rest of the animal kingdom, knightly mock combat occurs but seldom. Human intelligence and our capacity for morality (or at least for moralizing) create the unique human capacity for moralistic aggression (Trivers, 1971/1980). Human history is replete with crusades, massacres, and orgies of execution in the name of a higher moral power, be it God, Allah, the State, or Reason. The suggestion here is not that moral reasons are just rationalizations for innate bloodthirsty behavior. Quite the contrary. Evolutionary psychology says that we are driven not to kill but to be moral, to cooperate with our in-group. Morality is a human imperative that makes us want to kill the immoral, the out-group. Morality causes aggression; it does not rationalize it.

The main evolutionary roots of human aggression can be traced to our long period spent as technologically primitive hunter-gatherers. Since most of our evolution occurred in this stage, evolutionary psychologists look there for the ecological pressures that created human nature. As humans moved from the trees to the plains, they began to hunt game and to be exposed to predators who hunted them. Given the poor fighting equipment of the individual human, survival became possible only by cohesive group living and the ability of human beings to cooperate. Now while cooperation is one of our most admirable traits, it also made warfare possible and intensified the human capacity for certain forms of aggression. Groups now competed for resources and resource-rich territory, creating warrior groups and warfare. Sex-based division of labor also occurred, with consequences to be explored later.

Cooperativeness and the tendency to form dominance hierarchies created in people tendencies toward social compliance and obedience toward superiors. The shocking dangers of compliance and obedience have been amply demonstrated by Stanley Milgram's (1974) classic experiments. Milgram has shown that while no one thinks he or she would deliberately injure another person just because a researcher tells that person to, a great many people will, in fact, do so. When told to administer intense electric shocks to a "learner" for failing to learn a paired-associate list, most subjects did so, despite screams of pain from the learner (really a confederate of Milgram's) in the next room. Even when the "learner" was in the same room with the "teacher," and the real subject, (the "teacher") could see the agony he was (apparently) inflicting, 40 percent of the subjects nevertheless delivered the maximum shock (450 volts) as ordered; 30 percent did so when they had to hold the "learner" to the shock-delivering electrode.

SEXUAL BEHAVIOR

The Master Key: Parental Investment

Sex is the essence of individual fitness. Therefore, we must expect the struggle for existence to have strongly shaped the way animals attract mates and reproduce.

The first significant fact about evolution and sexual behavior is that the struggle for existence—or more precisely in this context, the struggle to mate—has fallen much harder on males than females. Studies and experiments on many species from insects to apes have shown that every female has opportunities to mate and produce offspring, but that only some males get such opportunities. In the vast majority of animal species, females represent a limited resource for which males compete. Therefore, male sexual behavior, being under evolutionary pressure, has been more strongly shaped than female behavior.

Once sex itself appeared on earth (see Box 14.2) millions of years ago—for reasons that are still unclear—the basic fact underlying male-female differences emerged. This is the fact that the **parental investment** (Trivers, 1972/1978) of each parent in its offspring is quite radically different. The male gametes (sperm) are small, biologically cheap to produce, highly mobile, and can be made continuously in huge numbers; the sperm in one male human ejaculate are enough to fertilize every woman in North America. The female gamete, or egg, on the other hand, is larger and biologically more

Why Is There Sex?

We tend to take the existence of sexual reproduction for granted because it is so common. However, from an evolutionary standpoint the existence of sex as a means of reproduction is a serious puzzle. The simplest and most direct way of reproducing one's genes is fission: creating a copy of yourself the way many simple organisms do. Moreover, sexual reproduction incurs many costs. One has to find a mate, which takes time and effort, and one has to risk mingling one's genes with another individual's, about whose fitness one is uncertain. As we will see, animals have to go to great lengths to find mates, choose the best mates, and try to guarantee that the offspring are one's own. Withal, sexual reproduction is a costly and risky business. Why then does it not only exist, but exist in so many species?

The question has been addressed by many theories over the years. The central feature of sexual reproduction that almost all theories focus on is the fact that sexual reproduction introduces variation into nature. Unlike fissioning or cloning, sexual reproduction reshuffles genes into new combinations, so that offspring are quite different from either parent. The currently favored account of the evolutionary value of such reshuffling is the "Red Queen" theory, named after the character in *Alice in Wonderland*. According to the Red Queen theory, the gene reshuffling brought about by sex keeps us one step ahead of our most dangerous enemies: viruses, bacteria, and parasites.

Imagine owning a home threatened by clever burglars. You put locks on doors, but the burglars figure out how the locks work and get in. Our immune systems are the locks that our bodies use to repel invading microorganisms and parasites. They are the burglars who figure out how to pick the locks. Now, if we reproduced by fission, our offspring would be exact copies of ourselves, possessing the same locks of the immune system as we had. Soon, viruses, bacteria, and parasites would evolve into perfect adaptation with our immune system, and we would be defenseless against disease. However, if we shuffle our genes when reproducing, new immune systems—new locks against the burglars—will be created, and we will gain protection against the organisms who had adapted themselves to our last generation. Of course, they will in turn catch up to us, and we have to keep running away to stay just ahead of them. Hence the "Red Queen" name for the theory.

The Red Queen turns up in many areas of evolution. Any time organisms interact competitively, the Red Queen may be found. Each competitor evolves to adapt to the strategies of the other, who in turn evolves new strategies of defense.

See Matt Ridley, *The Red Queen: Sex and the Evolution of Human Nature* (New York: Macmillan, 1993).

expensive to make, since it contains both genetic material and nourishment for the developing organism. The egg is also incapable of movement, and is produced in smaller quantities only at certain periods of the female biological cycle.

Additionally, in mammals the female must bear and nurse her young, a task spared the male. We see, then, that the biological investment of male and female parents in their offspring is vastly different. A male can sire many offspring in many females quickly and cheaply, while a female must invest, especially if a mammal, a great deal of energy and time in each of her young. We can add to this basic difference a further, related fact, that a female knows with certainty that its offspring are her own and must carry her genes, while a male can never know with certainty that "his" offspring truly carry his genes.

Putting all these considerations together we should expect to find—and do find—that evolution has produced very different strategies by which males and females go about the business of reproducing. The most dramatic illustration of this difference, at least in animals, is called the Coolidge effect, from the following story:

> One day the President and Mrs. Coolidge were visiting a government farm. Soon after their arrival they were taken off on separate tours. When Mrs. Coolidge passed the chicken pens she paused to ask the man in charge if the rooster copulates more than once each day. "Dozens of times" was the reply. "Please tell that to the President," Mrs. Coolidge requested. When the President passed the pens and was told about the rooster, he asked, "Same hen every time?" "Oh, no, Mr. President, a different one each time." The President nodded slowly, then said, "Tell that to Mrs. Coolidge." (Berment, 1976, pp. 76–77)

In a great many mammals, a male will mount a given female only a few times and then lose interest. But if a new female is introduced he mounts her just as enthusiastically as the first. This pattern can be repeated over and over. Males are also remarkably hard to fool into re-mating with an already inseminated female: They have sex indiscriminately but are nonetheless discriminating about the condition of their partners (Symons, 1979). The Coolidge effect is almost absent in females.

This makes a great deal of evolutionary sense given the basic difference between egg and sperm. Once fertilized, a female has nothing to gain by further copulation with any male at all; her genes are now developing (along with the father's) into a new member of the species. For her, further sexual activity is pointless at best and risky at worst. On the male side, further copulation with a female he has just fertilized is pointless for the same reason, and he should lose interest in her; further copulation just wastes time, effort, and sperm, thereby reducing fitness. But it would pay to have sex with new, unfertilized females. Sperm are cheap and continuously produced, so further opportunities for sex with new females should be seized to increase individual fitness by impregnating them. So it is genetically profitable for males, but not for females, to desire and perform sex with many partners. The reproductive strategies of male and female thus share their mentalities and desires in different directions.

All these differences create two different kinds of selection pressure on the further evolution of sexuality. First, females become for males a desirable resource to control. If a male can collect many females—which he is likely to desire—and impregnate them himself to the exclusion of other males—which he is capable of doing—then his individual fitness will be enhanced and the fitness of others harmed. He will gain in the struggle for existence. Males will therefore compete for possession of females, creating intrasexual selection: Males who successfully compete will be selected and their fitness enhanced.

For a female the situation is rather different. A male can have profligate sex with many females whose own fitness may be high or low. But this is of small moment, for some of his sperm will impregnate some fit females, and so his genes will survive. But a female is putting up a large investment when she copulates, a large investment of biological matter (her eggs) and time and effort in bearing, nursing, and raising her offspring. Should she mate with an unfit male her fitness will be correspondingly harmed.

So in the struggle for existence it pays for females to be choosy, to mate only with the fittest available male in order to protect her large (and his small) investment. And females can be choosy because they are a scarce resource. The criteria for their choices create a selection pressure, called by Darwin sexual selection, but now called epigamic selection. Genes carried by male survival machines that meet female criteria will prosper, while those carried by losers will go extinct. Male appearance and behavior will thus be pushed in the direction of pleasing the female.

In this way is born the stratagem and counter-stratagem of the war between the sexes. Females set criteria for male fitness, and males try to meet them or deceive females into thinking they have met them. Females see through the ruses and set new tests; new, craftier deceptions evolve, and so on through an endless and fascinating cycle.

Sexual Selection

Intrasexual Selection

Competition among males (and in a very few species, females) has resulted in a number of adaptations that serve each competitor, summarized in Table 14.1.

The first set of adaptations help a male compete for access to females. First (A), males, much more than females, are easily aroused and sexually promiscuous; males need not be choosy and need to be ready to seize every opportunity, while females must be more cautious. Second (B), in many group-living species the males fight one another, generally without bloodshed, to establish a dominance hierarchy, which runs from the dominant "alpha" male who can defeat everyone else, to a lowest ranking male who defers to everyone else. Dominance expresses itself in reproductive success in the ways listed in Table 14.1.

Third [C], subordinate males have strategies open to them that give their genes a chance at survival. As we mentioned earlier in discussing aggression, submitting now in a dominance fight leaves open the possibility of later success as practice perfects competitive abilities and dominant males weaken or die. Or males may try to court (2) or secretly copulate (3) with females when a dominant male is absent or occupied. Finally, there is the possibility of rape, which, contrary to general opinion, is by no means confined to humans (Shields & Shields, 1983).

The second set of male adaptations produced by intrasexual selection has evolved to help a male be sure it is his sperm that fertilize a female's egg, since in many species it is not the first male whose sperm succeeds, but rather the last male's. Even when this is not the case, it is in a male's interest to increase his certainty of paternity. To accomplish these ends, males can guard their mates (A) either just long enough to ensure insemination (1) or more permanently through monogamous union or harem keeping (2). Other behaviors may be used to keep females from mating again (B). In some species, including the familiar rat, a male inserts a plug in the female after copulation that at once retains his own sperm and excludes others (1). In some species a male may use chemical or behavioral signals that automatically reduce a female's receptivity after mating (2). It appears that male lions do this by gently biting the neck of their mate during copulation, signaling her that she is inseminated.

Finally, there are adaptations that directly lower other males' reproductive success. Males can interfere with other males' courtship or copulations (A,1), perhaps by attacking them in flagrante. In a few species, for example, the salamander Plethodon jordani, males pretend to be females and induce other males to waste time,

TABLE 14.1   Results of Intrasexual Selection on the Evolution of Male Behavior

ADAPTATIONS THAT PLAY A ROLE IN THE COMPETITION TO SECURE COPULATIONS

A. A low threshold for mating attempts
B. Dominance behavior (the monopolization of females)—the exclusion of other males from:
    1. The vicinity of a female that is or will become receptive
    2. A harem of females
    3. Positions of high status in multimale groups
    4. Areas with useful resources attractive to females
    5. Display sites attractive to females
C. Subordinate behavior (coping with dominant males)
    1. Submissive behavior and the (temporary) postponement of attempts to reproduce
    2. Courtship of females only when dominant males are absent or occupied
    3. Sneak copulations
    4. Rape

ADAPTATIONS THAT HELP A MALE ENSURE THAT HIS SPERM WILL BE USED BY FEMALES HE HAS INSEMINATED

A. Guarding behavior
    1. Temporary guarding of a recently inseminated female
    2. Prolonged protection of a female or harem against other males
B. Behavior that reduces the likelihood that an unguarded female will copulate again
    1. The insertion of mating plugs in females after copulation
    2. The use of biochemical or behavioral signals to activate mechanisms within the female that reduce her receptivity

ADAPTATIONS THAT LOWER THE REPRODUCTIVE SUCCESS OF COMPETITORS

A. Sexual interference
    1. Interruption of another male's courtship
    2. Female mimicry by males that induces other males to waste time, energy, or sperm
B. Attempts to injure competitors
    1. Assault on other males, including homosexual rape
    2. Assault on mates or offspring of other males

Adopted from Alcock (1979).

effort, and sperm (A,2) to the detriment of their fitness. And, of course, males can turn red in tooth and claw and try to injure each other or each other's mates (B,2), or to kill the offspring of other males, as langurs and lions do. Homosexual rape may be included here (B,1), which takes a particularly bizarre form in an insect species wherein a male may rape another male, depositing his sperm in his victim's genitals, seeing to it that if the victim later mates with a female it will be the rapist's semen and genes that survive, not the poor victim's!

We can summarize the effects of intrasexual selection by saying that most of the evolutionary pressures favor males who are aggressive with each other and their mates, are easily aroused and sexually promiscuous, and who jealously watch over their mates. The sole countervailing pressure is the advantage of monogamy in heightening certainty of paternity. Whether and in what ways these pressures have affected male human sexuality will be explored later in this chapter.

Epigamic Selection

Because of the differences between egg and sperm, female behavior has been very differently affected by evolution. A female must exercise great care in selection of a mate; she must be cautious, willing to test out possible suitors before committing her eggs to his sperm. Table 14.2, based on Trivers (1972/1978) and Alcock (1979), summarizes criteria suggested by evolutionary theorists, especially Trivers, that females can use in choosing a mate.

The first set of criteria (I) are used by all females but especially those of the many species in which the male does nothing to help raise his offspring. The most basic question is whether a given male can, in fact, fertilize the female's eggs (A), as indicated by the four listed criteria. Doing this is not always as obvious as it seems. Many insects resemble each other, especially if they are related species or members of a species that practices mimicry. Usually, the male's courtship behavior, which is often highly elaborate and ritualized, indicates yes answers to all these questions, so the female can then choose among qualified males. Thus, the fact of female choice becomes a pressure on male behavior: Male courtship rituals have evolved precisely because of the need to convince females that a male is ready, willing, and able to perform his role.

Next, in order not to waste her precious eggs on an unfit mate, the female must assess her suitor's individual fitness (B). She can ask if he possesses (and thereby his genes ought to possess) high survival ability (B,1). The most obvious measure of fitness is age: A young male is untested while an older male has, by definition, survived. So a female should prefer an older to a younger suitor. Gene quality may also be measured through dominance (B,2). Dominance hierarchies, in those species that have

TABLE 14.2   Criteria Used by Females for Choosing Mates

I.   Criteria used by females of all species, but especially those where males offer little parental care.

   A.   Can he fertilize my eggs?
   1.   Is he of the correct species?
   2.   Is he of the correct sex?
   3.   Is he mature?
   4.   Is he sexually competent?

   B.   What is the quality of his genes?
   1.   Does he show high survival ability?
   2.   Can he dominate other males?
      (a)   as shown by high dominance ranking
      (b)   by fighting well when I incite him

II.   Criteria used by females of species whose males offer parental care.

   A.   What will be the quality of his care?
   1.   Is he able to control needed resources?
   2.   Is he willing to share these resources?
   3.   Is he willing to protect me and my offspring?

Adapted from Trivers (1972) and Alcock (1979).

them, provide a direct measure of fitness. Lacking a hierarchy, females might get males to fight each other and pick the winner.

Additional criteria come into play if a female can choose a mate who will invest in his offspring (II). Now she must weigh the quality of his parental care. Can he control resources (A,1) needed by her and her offspring? In territorial species females will prefer males having environmentally rich territories. Will he share resources (A,2)? In many species males give females valuable presents, especially food, to induce them to mate. Finally, can he protect me and my offspring (A,3)? Often these criteria boil down to assessing general genetic fitness, discussed previously.

Two important observations need to be made about this last class of criteria. First, to the degree that males invest in caring for their offspring they risk lowering their fitness by giving up possible copulations with other females. Therefore, to the extent they invest in offspring they must act like females and be choosy about their mates. If, for example, a species is really monogamous, the male has just as much invested—everything—in his offspring as his mate. Both he and she must be equally careful in choosing a partner for life, or even for a breeding season. In a very few species such as doves and giant water bugs this process has gone so far that males invest more in offspring than females do, and the usual roles are reversed, males being cautious and sexually reserved while the females are aggressive and promiscuous. Such apparent exceptions to the general run of things in fact support Trivers's evolutionary psychological analysis: Sexual behavior depends on the degree of biological investment in offspring. To the degree an individual's investment is large and lasting, the usual "female" strategy will be adopted; to the degree that investment is small and fleeting, the usual "male" strategy will be adopted.

The second observation about this last class of female criteria is that it gives rise to the stratagem and counter-stratagem of the war of the sexes, for males may pretend to be more fit than they are. They may share resources only long enough to copulate and then abandon the female; especially if the female can rear her young alone, this becomes an important male option for it frees him to increase his fitness with other females. Fortunately for females, if they all require long courtship and monogamous mating, abandonment will not pay, for lengthy courtship reduces male fitness, and monogamy reduces the population of available females. Under these circumstances, deception may arise, as males pretend to be more willing to invest than they are, and females attempt to see through the deceptions, which only calls forth more male cunning—and so on.

Deception is well illustrated by the hanging fly, whose species exhibit a gradation from male sincerity to flattery to fraud. In one species, the male brings a present of food, a blowfly he has caught. She feeds on it during copulation, which enhances her fitness and keeps him from being eaten in the way male praying mantises are. In another (more advanced?) species the male makes the present more attractive by wrapping it in a balloon of silvery webbing. The female unwraps the present, which gives the male a little longer, and feeds. In another species she opens the wrapping and finds a fly already sucked dry—too late, for the male is gone. Finally, in the highest (?) species, the female unwraps her balloon to find . . . nothing!

Mating Systems

All these varied factors that play a part in evolving sexuality have resulted in a variety of stable mating systems; the ecology of male investment that gives rise to

TABLE 14.3   The Ecology of Mating Systems. Different Mating Systems Reflect Ecological Factors That Determine How Much a Male Can Help His Mate Produce and Rear Offspring and How Much Males of a Species Vary in Their Ability to Assist Their Mates

	Male Ability to Provide Useful Services to Mate	Female Choice	Mating System
Males can monopolize useful resources or provide parental care	Most males offer same medium-to-high assistance	Females prefer unmated males	Monogamy robins, foxes
	Some males offer much more than others	Females prefer superior helpers	Parental investment polygyny redwing black-bird, impala
Ecology of species	Male's parental ability exceeds that of female	Females invest in egg production only, mating with several males	Polyandry stickleback fish, tinamou
Males cannot provide useful assistance to females	Males compete to demonstrate genetic quality to females or to monopolize group of females	Females choose the competitively superior male	Pure dominance polygyny manakins, elephants

Adapted from Trivers (1972) and Alcock (1979).

these systems are summarized in Table 14.3, which shows the synthesizing power of evolutionary psychology. It allows us to give a useful classification of a complex and varied set of behaviors (mating arrangements) and account for the classification on a few quantifiable principles, primarily the degree of male investment in offspring. Even the unusual case of polyandry fits neatly in place, not as an exception, but as the logical outcome of more male than female investment. Examples are given of each mating system. Where do people fit in?

Human Sexuality*

We have found that the parental investment of males in most species is much less than that of females. Consequently, natural selection has produced males who are aggressive with each other and toward prospective mates, who are easily aroused and sexually promiscuous, and who watch jealously over their mates. Additionally, males are high-variance gambles in the struggle for existence: Many males do not mate at all

---

* In addition to the standard evolutionary psychological works cited in the animal section, the present account of sexuality draws especially on Symons (1979), Daly and Wilson (1978), and van den Berghe (1979). For views contrary to Symons, see Hrdy (1981). Hrdy (1979) reviewed Symons's book, and Symons (1983) reviewed Hrdy's.

and are evolutionary failures, while some males are spectacularly successful, siring large numbers of offspring. Females, on the other hand, have been selected to be un-aggressive, sexually reserved, and choosy about their mates. Females are safe but low-paying evolutionary investments: Every female can find a mate, but the number of offspring she may have is small compared to males. We will now consider whether this common pattern fits human beings.

Sex Differences

Aggressiveness. One of the few generally acknowledged sex differences is that males are inherently more aggressive than females (Maccoby & Jacklin, 1974). The general division of labor in cultures around the world reflects this fact: Men hunt, make weapons, and go to war, while women gather and prepare food. In our own society, violent crime is committed almost exclusively by impoverished young males, those old enough to seek mates but who find themselves denied the usual signs of fit-ness awarded by our society, namely, education, wealth, status, and prospects for ad-vancement. Among the middle class, competition for women is nonviolent and indirect; among the poor and disenfranchised, nature turns red in tooth and claw, and male youths seek female attention through toughness, machismo, and dominance within a male gang (Alexander, 1979a).

Viewed from the standpoint of evolutionary psychology, the human pattern makes sense. The young male must fight to become a man, whether through actual physical competition with others, through indirect status-competition, or through the ritualized torture of initiation rites unknown to females (Barash, 1979). Only through competition can males earn females, thus ensuring their fitness, while fe-males need but choose the successful competitor. Unfortunately, as among animals, human males may turn to rape as an adaptive strategy, especially when the cost is low (Shields & Shields, 1983; Thornhill & Thornhill, 1983).

The proximate mechanism of male aggressiveness is the male hormone testos-terone, produced by the testes. Testosterone creates the male pattern, an energy-consuming, active, and aggression-prone way of life; female animals injected with testosterone become more active and aggressive. But testosterone also contributes to characteristic male vulnerability. By driving the male toward activity and ag-gression—the basic male fitness strategy—it makes him more likely to be killed (Daly & Wilson, 1978). Males also tend to suffer higher rates of embryonic, fetal, and infantile mortality, and to senesce more rapidly than females (Alexander, Hoogland, Howard, Noonan, & Sherman, 1979).

Contrary to popular beliefs, cultural sex-typing falls more heavily on males than on females, for sexual stereotypes are more rigidly imposed on males. Even contemporary American couples consciously trying to raise their children apart from sexist stereotypes find it easier to do so for girls. The girl playing with a fire truck is applauded, but the boy playing with dolls is often not (Katchadourian, 1979).

Cultural expectation reflects and magnifies the underlying biological reality that males are risk-taking, aggressive people who must struggle for success, for bio-logical fitness. Girls will become women and find mates as a matter of course, so cul-ture need not teach any particular role. These differences are evident even when we determinedly try to change. Contemporary sexual liberation has usually meant women becoming free to act like men—seeking places in business, industry, and the professions, where aggressiveness and risk-taking pay—rather than the other way around. The househusband is much more a curiosity than the female stockbroker.

Arousability. Observation of the contemporary American scene also suggests that human males are, like most males, easily aroused sexually, while human females, like most females, are not. Pornography—manufactured sexual stimulation—is a huge business run by men for men. Sales of everything from Playboy to hardcore pornographic magazines run to about $2 billion a year, and are made for men, whether heterosexual or homosexual, while attempts to sell pornography to women of any orientation have proved unsuccessful. There is evidence that the modest success of the one magazine that aims pictures of naked men at women partly results from sales to homosexual men, while lesbians find magazines such as *Playboy* rather silly and puzzle that men enjoy them (Symons, 1979).

Some recent research has suggested that women can be aroused by sexually explicit materials at least as much as men, at least in experimental settings in which subjects view or read erotica and have their arousal measured through self-report or physical monitoring. These results have been taken to cast doubt on traditional stereotypes of the "turned-on" man and "frigid" woman. However, a closer look reveals features that support evolutionary psychological hypotheses.

To begin with, close analysis of one such experiment (Heiman, 1975, reanalyzed by Symons, 1979), showed that men responded more strongly than women to tapes depicting sexual activity. Moreover, men, but not women, responded (at least initially) about as strongly to control tapes—a discussion between a male and female student about choice of college major—as to any explicit tape. Males are clearly more easily and strongly aroused by any situation in which sex might play a part. Women often complain that on dates any word or gesture meant as general friendliness is taken as expressing sexual interest, a real-life finding well grounded in evolutionary psychology.

Analysis of these studies also shows that the proximate psychological mechanisms of sexual arousal are entirely different in males and females (Money & Erhardt, 1972; Symons, 1979). A man responds directly to the image of the woman photographed or described, and fantasizes about having sex with her. A woman, if aroused at all, is aroused by identifying with a photograph of a naked woman, and imagines herself to be similarly desirable. In erotica with male-female interaction, she is likely again to identify with the woman to learn ways in which she can be arousing and sexually skilled herself. So sexual arousal from erotic literature is possible for both men and women, but the thoughts that connect erotic depiction to actual arousal are not the same in men and women.

Men and women also respond differently to first appearances (Hill, Nocks, & Gardner, 1987). Males distinguish between a female's sexual attractiveness and her potential as a marriage partner. When shown pictures of women varying in both sexiness of dress and socioeconomic status display, men rated low status but sexily dressed women as desirable sex partners but as undesirable mates. High-status women were regarded favorably as potential wives regardless of sexiness of appearance. Women evaluating male models, in contrast, preferred high-status, unsexily dressed men both as potential sex partners and as husbands. In fact, women seemed to a degree turned off by male displays emphasizing the body.

Finally, we must remember that only men seek arousal through pornography. This is not a cultural artifact created by sleazy adult bookstores that socially inhibited women fear to enter. Kenrick, Stringfield, Wagenhals, Dahl, & Ransdell (1980) called male and female college students and asked if they would volunteer to participate in experiments involving seeing geometric figures, soft-core "loving" erotica, or hard-core "lustful" erotica. Women were less likely than men in every case to volunteer for the erotic experiment, and, when they did choose erotica, they preferred the soft-core description. As the marketplace indicates, men seek arousal while women do not.

All of this suggests that we must make an important distinction between appetitive sexuality, or an actual sex drive, and sexual responsiveness. Once they are in a sexual situation, women are at least as sexually responsive as men, and perhaps even more so, given the female ability to have multiple orgasms (Hrdy, 1979). Nevertheless, women seem not to have the driven sexual appetite of men; they do not seek out arousal through pornography. There are cultures in which the female orgasm is unknown, indicating that women do not have a drive to seek sexual outlet as men do (Symons, 1979). Again, the proximate mechanism seems to be testosterone. Women who for medical reasons have high levels of this hormone show characteristically male patterns of sexuality, becoming much more sexually aggressive. When treated, such women express relief at being able to return to "normal"—that is, nondriven, sexuality (Money & Erhardt, 1972; Symons, 1979).

Promiscuity. We come naturally, then, to promiscuity, a characteristic male trait in nonhuman animals. There is good evidence that men—whose minimum parental investment is so much less than women's—seek sexual variety. They fantasize about sex with many different women through pornography. While adultery rates for men and women may be equalizing, men still have more partners than women do, and they are more likely to have one-night stands; the roving male seeks sex, the female is looking for a better partner. The Coolidge effect appears to apply to humans. The frequency of intercourse falls off after a couple is married, and wives are often puzzled by male adultery when they are always available to their husbands. Sexual autobiographies suggest that males are readily re-aroused by a new woman shortly after intercourse with another, who may instantaneously be transformed from alluring to repulsive (Symons, 1979). "Swinging" is largely a male-instigated practice, and most frequently involves adding a new woman to a married couple, sometimes a merger of couples, and almost never the addition of a new man (van den Berghe, 1979).

Patterns of homosexual conduct reinforce our picture of this pattern. Indeed, Symons (1979) has suggested that homosexuals represent the "acid test" of theories of sexuality, for in a homosexual encounter male and female strategies will be directly revealed, there being no need to compromise with or manipulate the other sex's strategy. Male homosexuals are quite promiscuous, and even though they desire permanent, stable relationships, they find them difficult to maintain, and often institutionalize sex with another partner outside the relationship. Male homosexuals seek out quick, anonymous, orgasmic encounters, even finding many in one night with multiple partners. The lesbian pattern is quite different. Relationships between couples are more stable and more frequent, there is little compulsive seeking of new partners, and lesbian sex is more extended and does not center on the orgasm (Symons, 1979).

Jealousy. Although jealousy is clearly an emotion experienced by both men and women, the evidence is that it is a more powerful emotion in men (Daly, Wilson, & Weghorst, 1982). The enraged husband slaying his wife and her lover (and getting off) is well known; the reverse is not. This pattern—the classic double-standard—is found in almost all cultures (Daly, Wilson, & Weghorst, 1982; Symons, 1979). That males should be especially jealous makes good biological sense. Men can never be certain of paternity, and adultery by their wives (who they know in their hearts can find willing partners) reduces their fitness. So evolution has produced men who feel sexual jealousy and become outraged by their wives' affairs, even while they themselves aim to seduce their neighbor's wife. Male sexual jealousy is perhaps the leading cause of familial assault and murder (Daly, Wilson, & Weghorst, 1982). Women, on the other hand, are certain of maternity, and their fitness is not harmed by any purely sexual liaisons their husbands might have. The natural female fear is being abandoned for another woman, losing valuable male investment in child-rearing. Therefore, jealousy has a different, more biologically remote basis in women, and is less purely sexual.

Male uncertainty of paternity and sexual jealousy also leads to attempts by men to control female reproduction, just as male animals do. There are practices designed to isolate women from men who are neither husbands nor fathers; they help increase male certainty of paternity and thus have a biological basis not always apparent to the culture, which often views them as "protection" of women. Some such practices are:

- *Chinese footbinding.* From an early age chinese girls' feet were tightly bound, preventing proper growth of the foot, resulting in tiny, misshapen feet. Chinese men thought of this as a technique for enhancing women's sexual attractiveness, but it kept women literally hobbled and mostly at home (Dickemann, 1982).

- *Claustration and veiling (Purdah).* This practice involves the isolation of women from men other than kin or husband, and the covering of their bodies when they do go abroad. The Koran explains this as a means by which women "may be recognized and not annoyed" (Dickemann, 1982), but it serves men's reproductive control of women.

- *Surgical procedures such as sewing up of the vagina (until the husband wants access) or castration of the clitoris.* The former is usually recognized as a means of reproductive control, while the latter may be explained, as in the nineteenth century, as a way to prevent masturbation (Barker-Benfield, 1976).

What all of these practices really accomplish is control of women's reproduction in the interest of male genes.

Mate Choice

So far we have catalogued differences between men and women on arousability, sex drive, promiscuity, jealousy, and probable degree of reproductive success, focusing on the consequences of minimum male parental investment. Now we look at the consequences of human female parental investment. In our species it is especially large. A woman produces a single protein-rich egg once a month for about 35 years and can have at most 20 or so children regardless of how many partners she has. (This is in stark contrast to the male whose cheap sperm may father hundreds of children in many women.) She must then bear the child for nine increasingly difficult months, followed by several more months of nursing. The child who is born is singularly helpless, needing prolonged care, supervision, and education. Child-rearing would be easier with continuing male interest after marriage.

It is therefore of paramount importance in our species—as in other slowly reproducing species—for females to be choosy about their mates. While modern contraception distinguishes choice of sexual partner from choice of father for one's children, people did not evolve with contraceptives.

The criteria for women's choices adduced by evolutionary psychologists are human versions of most of the criteria used by females of other animal species in which males may offer care of offspring. First, it is a cultural universal that close relatives are not suitable mates—Freud's famous incest taboo. There is a good biological basis for it, since it prevents incestuous inbreeding that would likely result in combining recessive lethal genes, reducing fitness of offspring (van den Berghe, 1983). A woman must gauge the willingness of a man to provide parental investment, which may be indicated by his behavior toward her and his general reputation—a uniquely human possession. As with many other animals, it is quite common in all cultures for a man to woo a woman with gifts, especially meat from the hunt in traditional cultures. Such behavior shows, at least on the surface, a willingness to share resources. Human females—like hanging fly females—may find male gifts deceiving. Finally, not only must a man be willing to share resources, but he must also possess resources to share, and a woman must estimate these by judging the quality of his gifts, his wealth, his status, and his intelligence, or as our Victorian ancestors might have called it—his "prospects." Cross-cultural research has confirmed that the sorts of traits listed by Alcock are in fact those used by women and/or their relatives in the choice of a husband. Physical appearance counts for relatively little (Hill, Nocks, & Gardner, 1987).

Given the importance of female choice to their individual fitness, we can readily see that it is most adaptive for women to be less arousable than men and to largely lack appetitive sexuality. A woman driven by constant stimulation and an autonomous sex urge would be relatively unable to test and evaluate men's fitness. Women find it relatively easy to control their sexual desires with strangers, and this is of great adaptive value. Males, on the other hand, benefit—in ultimate terms—from their constant sexual stimulability and sex drive, for it makes it possible for them to search for and seize opportunities to mate, and so enhance their fitness. This does not justify their doing so, but it does mean that the tendency is an inherent part of male human nature and must be controlled, not wished away.

What about male choice? From what we have learned about male sexuality, we would expect their criteria to be simple physical attractiveness, which research and cross-cultural studies strongly support. Precisely because men are primed for quick physical arousal, they will judge a woman by her looks, by how arousing she is. Because his minimal parental investment is so low—simple insemination—a man is not likely to evaluate a woman on any deeper criteria. The basic male strategy is the high-risk one: impregnate many women (which he desires to do) and his genes are bound to survive.

The evolutionary psychological result of these differences between men and women is the war between the sexes. A woman evaluates the fitness of a man and tries to get him to invest in her to show whether he will invest in offspring after birth. A man wishes to impress females, trying to act fitter than he is, and to invest just enough in a woman to seduce her but without committing himself and without giving up opportunities to enhance his fitness with other women. Popular songs are full of the battles between the sperm and the egg—the man who professes his love as a tactic of seduction versus the woman who hopes to turn the tactic into a reality.

Changing cultural environment may change the rules of the game. In a strongly monogamous environment, men will act more like women. A long courtship followed by a permanent marriage multiplies the male's actual parental investment many times over his minimal one. So men will be choosy not about whom they bed but whom they wed. They will look for maternal and perhaps economic qualities that will ensure their offspring's fitness. In our culture, to cite another example, men have traditionally sought female approbation through swaggering machismo—advertising their fitness by (at least apparent) toughness. But as times change machismo may become a losing strategy, and the man who wants to attract the new woman would do well to cultivate sensitivity and emotional vulnerability.

Recent studies of personal advertisement in newspapers support evolutionary psychological theories about the criteria men and women use to choose mates (Dunbar, 1995; Thiessen, Young, & Borroughs, 1993). Especially when they are young, women overwhelmingly advertise for men who have financial and other resources and high social status, while men scarcely mention them until they are over age 60. Men, on the other hand, seek physical attractiveness in potential dates, even when they get old. To meet men's demands, women advertise their physical attractiveness. Men tend to overrate the importance of their own physical attractiveness to women, and undervalue emotional commitment. These rather informal findings have been supported by extensive experimental and survey research in cultures around the world (Buss, 1994). There have been some historical changes: As health has improved, emphasis on good looks has increased since the Depression, although men still emphasize looks more than women (Buss, 1994).

Women's Unique Sexuality

There are two features of *Homo sapiens'* sexuality—specifically, women's sexuality—that, while not entirely unique among animals, have been carried to a high pitch among our species. Women are unusual in experiencing orgasms, and in concealing ovulation, that is, not entering a period known generally as "heat" (technically estrus) when they advertise fertility and sexual availability. There is a lively controversy within evolutionary psychology about the significance and possible adaptive value, if any, of these female traits.

The most popular hypothesis, possessing roots in ethology, is the theory that both female orgasm and loss of estrus are adaptations creating a male-female pair-bond, which in turn creates the basic nuclear family (see Barash, 1979; van den Berghe, 1979; Wilson, 1978). According to this reasoning, loss of estrus makes a woman continuously sexually available to a male partner, who then has less need to look elsewhere for sexual satisfaction, creating a bond between him and her. The bond is reciprocated by the woman's deriving pleasure from sex with her partner. Thus is created—so the pair-bond story goes—the intimate loving attachment between husband and wife that is the rock of the nuclear family, enhancing the fitness of both mother and father.

Consoling as this idea may be, there are good reasons to think it fable rather than fact (Hrdy, 1979, 1981; Symons, 1979). As Wilson pointed out in his book *Evolutionary Psychology*—notwithstanding his later belief in the pair-bond theory—sex is a divisive, not a solidifying, force in animal or human society. In the animal world, monogamous species are hyposexual—engaging in little sexual activity—a characterization that hardly fits *Homo sapiens*. Primates copulate throughout the sexual cycle and have not developed monogamy (Daniels, 1983). In the vast majority of societies, marriages are arranged on calculations of gain to the partners and (especially the man's) kin group, not on grounds of mutual satisfaction. Finally, in most cultures couples stay together despite quarrels over sexuality (mutual recriminations concerning adultery and abandonment) and when marriages become happy they do so late in life, when sexual fires are dampened. In the general run of human experience, then, it appears that marriage—the pair-bond—is not built on sexuality but endures when it does in spite of sexuality. Human sexuality seems instead to be an adaptation to a cultural environment in which marriage is ubiquitous, the man seeking outside opportunities to increase his fitness and the woman seeking to increase her husband's parental investment.

Unfortunately, although the pair-bond theory may be challenged, evolutionary psychologists do not agree on the origins of the family, the adaptiveness of women's concealment of ovulation, or their ability to have orgasms. Symons (1979) argues that female orgasm is a physiological accident rather than an adaptation, pointing to the fact that unlike the male orgasm it is not necessary to procreation, hence plays no role in fitness and cannot have been selected. In some societies female orgasm is unknown; in most it is highly variable between and within women; and in those societies in which it is expected as normal, it only comes about from men being carefully trained in the arts of love.

On the other hand, Alexander (1979b) thinks that orgasm, through its outward manifestations, is an adaptive signal from the woman to her lover that she finds him sexually satisfying and is unlikely to cuckold him, reassuring his feeling of paternity. Hrdy (1979, 1981) suggests that the capacity to have orgasm makes a woman have many lovers, all of whom may invest in her offspring.

With regard to concealment of ovulation, evolutionary psychological theories are even more at odds. The problem is simple but intractable: When women ceased to go into estrus did they thereby stop advertising their sexual availability, or did they begin to continuously advertise their availability? Alexander (1979b; Alexander & Noonan, 1979) adopts the former line of reasoning. He argues that by concealing ovulation women enticed men into an extended consortship, for since neither he nor his mate knew when she was fertile, he would have to remain with her to keep inseminating her and guarding against insemination by other males. At the same time, by no longer going into estrus, the woman reassured her mate's sense of paternity by making her less likely to seek or attract adulterous partners during "heat." One might call Alexander's theory the Machiavellian pair-bond based on uncertainty and manipulation.

Symons (1979) and Hrdy (1979), on the other hand, think that women continuously advertise their sexuality, reducing their mate's certainty of paternity, since she is always available for sex with another male. Symons offers two scenarios by which loss of estrus might be adaptive and have evolved. In the first, continuously advertising women would be more successful than estrus women in obtaining meat from males to exchange for sex. In the second, continuous availability is adaptive by allowing a woman to be fertilized by presumably fitter males other than her husband. Hrdy (1979) suggests additionally that loss of estrus made it easier for a woman to manipulate men's uncertainty about paternity, entangling them in a web of parental investment, serving her own genetic fitness.

Finally, Daniels (1983) suggests that loss of estrus promotes general social solidarity. Open estrus would constantly incite men to competition not cooperation, and would divert female attention from social tasks such as child-rearing and food gathering.

Conclusion

Evolutionary psychology offers a picture of human sexuality that conforms to the more firmly established evolutionary psychology of nonhuman creatures, that makes sense of our own observation of our everyday lives, and is reasonably supported by cross-cultural data and research results from social psychology. Many may find it an unpleasant picture, preferring to think of differences in sexuality as cultural products, especially of our own "sexist" society. The account is also disturbing in its suggestion that in such an intimate arena men and woman are so different that they almost cannot communicate, cannot intuitively understand one another. Nevertheless, if we share our sexuality with the animals, evolutionary psychology likely describes our condition. It will take the resources of humankind's master trait—intelligence—to bridge the gap between man and woman through art, poetry, writing, science, and a determined effort to understand and respect those with whom we share our lives.

Evolution of Western Sexual Behavior and Mores

One of the important considerations in evolutionary psychology is the difference between the era of evolutionary adaptation (EEA) and later periods of human history. Our basic human nature, especially in its emotional aspects, evolved millions of years ago, but now must cope with a radically different environment. This is especially true with regard to human sexuality. Because reproduction is so important to evolution, sexual feelings and behavior have been heavily shaped by natural selection, and we have just tried to show the deep continuity between mammalian and human sexuality. As Midgely said, we are not just like the animals, we are animals. However, we are animals who construct and live in cultures, and these cultures establish values, traditions, and rules that create a unique environment beyond the physical one. All societies seek to control sexual behavior, as we have seen. Recently, and from very different backgrounds, anthropologist Helen Fisher (1992) and Federal Court Judge Richard Posner (1992) have tried to describe how changing social arrangements in the history of the West have changed Western social behavior in an interesting circular pattern.

The Period of Evolutionary Adaptation: Australopithecus Afarensis to *Homo Habilis*—Evolution of the Basic Human Pattern

Fisher (1992) explains how human sexuality was shaped during the early stages of human evolution when we survived by being gatherer-hunters. Most food was vegetables, fruits, and grains gathered by females, while males gained occasional rich prizes of protein by hunting. Fisher proposes that during this period humans evolved their basic reproductive strategy, a temporary pair-bond between a male and female that lasted until their child did not need both parents. Such a pattern is common in nature, especially among birds, who pair off for a single breeding season. Because human infants are helpless for so long, the human pair-bond must last for four to six years. Today, the pair-bond is called "falling in love." Fisher has found that the maximum risk of divorce for a married couple is at about the time the old pair-bond would have dissolved, and successful married couples know that the first glow of romance fades with time. Interestingly, many people never fall in love, or experience what Tennov (1979) calls limerence. For them, a happy marriage is always friendship plus sex.

Fisher believes the ancient pair-bond was real. That is, short-term monogamy, not polygyny, is the human norm. Nevertheless, the pair-bond is punctuated by episodes of adultery. However, the genetic logic of adultery is different in males and females. As among animals, males seek sexual variety as a simple way of spreading genes and are motivated to have sex with any available female. The motives for female adultery are more mixed and more complex. By committing adultery, females may:

- Gain supplementary subsistence from males who "pay" for sex with food.
- Gain insurance against the death of her pair-bonded mate by making an emotional connection with a male who might replace him.
- Gain better genes for her offspring by having sex with a biologically superior male, especially if the original mate can be induced to raise the child.
- Gain investment in her offspring by several males, all of whom contribute something to her and her children. Moreover, links to other males (including the pair-bonded partner) created links to their relatives, and such extended kin networks can help care for children.

Recent studies suggest that men and women have evolved biological mechanisms for facilitating and coping with adultery. Women having affairs tend to schedule copulations with their lovers to the period in their menstrual cycle when they are most likely to conceive. Men, on the other hand, produce many times more sperm when they are away from their wives than when they are spending all their time with them. Thus, when they return home, copulation is more likely to result in an insemination with their own child (Buss, 1994).

Further, Fisher proposes that along with the pair-bond evolved the unique features of female orgasm and loss of estrus. Factors involved include the following:

- Having orgasms motivates the female to have sex to help create and maintain the pair-bond and to seek out adaptive adulterous liaisons. The pair-bond is also facilitated by the unique human practice of having face-to-face sex. Unlike animals, humans copulate with each others as individuals and sexual pleasure builds an emotional bond between partners.
- Orgasm signals enjoyment to the female's pair-bonded partner, making him less likely to suspect adultery and desert.
- Fertilization is facilitated by lying down.
- Having an orgasm indicates that the male is sexually competent. Orgasm is thus a sort of "Mr. Right" detector.
- Loss of estrus gives females more control over their own behavior, making it easier to rationally choose mates.

The Modern Period: The Coming of Agriculture to About 1970—Enforcing Long-Term Monogamy

Period of Noncompanionate Marriage (Classical World to the Rise of Christianity). The most important change in sexual mores came when society sought to enforce a permanent pair-bond through **indissoluble marriage.** Fisher believes the key development was changing from gathering-hunting to agricultural economies. In the EEA it was easy for couples to break up, because each could take his or her possessions and move out, there being no difficulty with the division of accumulated wealth. However, with agriculture, a couple's wealth resides in their land and becomes hard to divide, tying the couple together with economic bonds. Moreover, males become the main suppliers of subsistence, because farming requires male physical strength to control draught animals and work heavy plows. Posner adds that since men are now the primary source of economic wealth, their relative level of investment in each offspring increases. Men thus seek to control female sexuality through the means we have seen. Women must become careful to "sell" their reproductive capacity to a man with substantial resources. While such conditions tend to the creation of polygyny, its development is inhibited by governments because it threatens to place too much power in hands of small numbers of powerful families.

Posner offers an example—Classical Greece. Men married very late to much younger women for the sole purpose of furnishing an "heir and a spare" as a nineteenth-century American heiress married to a Duke of Marlborough put it. Because it is difficult for men to form bonds of friendship with women so much younger than themselves and because Greek culture called for men and women to live separate lives, homosexuality became common. Because homosexual relationships were taken for granted, there was little or no recognition of a separate class of life-long homosexuals.

Period of Companionate Marriage (Middle Ages to c. 1970).
Seeking to improve the status of women, the Christian Church encouraged companionate marriage: lifelong union between man and woman not simply as sexual partners, but in intimate friendship and partnership. Women's status rises because they now must consent to wed and cannot be abandoned as divorce is made very difficult. Early marriage was encouraged to promote chastity by channeling sex into marriage. In the seventeenth century, Puritan morals became even stricter, encouraging men to devote more time to productive labor, setting off the rise of capitalism. A recognizable homosexual class, for whom companionate marriage is difficult, appears for the first time.

Future Sex: Emerging Patterns

Fisher and Posner agree that the traditional idea of life-long marriage is under strain, if not breaking down entirely. Moreover, each believes that the key to this development is the increasing economic independence of women, which, ironically, makes the emerging scene resemble that of the EEA. As women enter the workplace, they become productive, as they were as gatherers, and the opportunity cost of (unpaid) housework rises. With the potential to be self-supporting, women will be more likely to leave a bad marriage, especially if their are no or few children. Likewise, expecting that their marriage may not last, men invest less heavily emotionally in their marriages and offspring. Moreover, since their children's mother is working, she may be able to support the children herself, making abandonment for a younger woman with whom to have more children more attractive. Were divorce difficult and women unwilling to marry divorced men, it would be more attractive to stay married and help ensure the success of one's first family. Thus man and women have motives for divorce, and the divorce rate rises. Likewise, adultery becomes common, as it was in the EEA and prostitution declines as men are more likely to be able to obtain sex without paying for it.

Posner sees these changes as being abetted by government programs supporting single or cohabiting women. If a woman can obtain "parental" investment from government, husbands become dispensable. This is the pattern in Sweden, which provides generous child-support programs for unmarried women, tied to a woman's having a job. There is intensive contraception training in home and at schools, and hence much premarital sex at young ages, but there is little teenage pregnancy. Most couples cohabit rather than marry, and the divorce and couple dissolution rate is high, and there are many single adult mothers. Inner city America resembles the Swedish situation, although government programs are less lavish, and there are fewer disincentives to teen pregnancy.

As men invest less in family, at-home fathers become fewer, as it pays to father children elsewhere to be supported by working women or by government programs. Posner says the question we need to ask about our future is not the effect of having fathers at home or not, but having the government act as children's "fathers." In Sweden especially, the state is replacing the father, regulating the treatment of children (e.g., forbidding spanking) and instituting a system of rules allowing children legal recourse against parents. The psychological consequences of fewer fathers at home is unclear, but in order to pay for extensive social services, Swedish tax rates are extortionate by American standards.

Families

Parental Care

Once mating has occurred and young are born, what happens? In many species the young are left entirely on their own, to fend for themselves or die. This lack of parental care usually occurs in species living in unstable, unpredictable environments, which produces r-selection. Species subject to r-selection generally adopt a strategy of producing a huge number of offspring all at once (and sometimes only once), and completely neglecting them. Although most will die, enough offspring—the toughest and luckiest—will survive to reproduce.

Degrees of parental care evolve under K-selection, which occurs in stable, predictable environments. K-selection leads to larger size and longer life, giving parents the capability of extended child care. It leads to smaller brood sizes as animals reproduce many times in a longer life, giving parents a greater investment in each child than under r-selection. K-selection, therefore, is likely to lead to increased parental care. It may be helped along by a dangerous environment requiring parental protection, and also by the evolution of offspring who are helpless long after birth and who thereby need parental care if they (the holders of the parents' genes) are to survive at all.

Once parental care has evolved, however, it is usually the female who bears the burden of child-rearing. Only in the most strictly monogamous species (a small minority) is child care about equally shared. Otherwise, the male does much less, because his investment is much less. Females always have a high investment in their offspring, as we have seen, and for them parental care always pays. Males, however, typically have a lower degree of investment and so typically care less to begin with; furthermore, they are less certain a given child is theirs, taking some of the edge off the desire to care for what may be an imposter. Moreover, in nonmonogamous species, the male's (or females' under polyandry) fitness is better served by begetting more offspring with more females, as in a harem, than by caring extensively for one mate's small brood. Thus, many animal families resemble the lion's pride. The females possess the territory (passed by inheritance through a group of sisters), care for the young, and do all the hunting (although the male of the pride gets to eat first). The male's role lies in protecting the pride from occasional harm, begetting offspring, and ensuring that cubs get a share of hunted prey.

Evolutionary psychological analysis can be extended to parent-offspring interactions, as Trivers (1974) has done with his parental investment concept. Attachment—the bond between parent and child—is a much studied phenomenon of human and animal behavior. It must have biological roots because it is so fitness-enhancing. Emotional attachment is the proximate motivator of parental care, and has evolved to protect the parents' investment in their offspring and, of course, the offspring's investment in itself.

Given this, we might expect parent-offspring behavior to be harmonious, which every parent knows is not true. Trivers's analysis suggests why. Certainly a parent has an investment in his or her offspring, for it carries his or her genes—but only 50 percent. A child, on the other hand, has a 100 percent investment in itself. This differential investment means there will be times when the parents' genetic interest and the child's are not identical.

Trivers's analysis suggests a further point, increasingly (and independently) recognized by developmental psychologists, that contrary to the usual view, the parent-child relationship is not a one-way affair in which the parent molds a passively dependent child. Parents and child differ in their investments in each other and themselves rendering conflict inevitable. Although it appears that the parents have all the power, children are not without resources. Consider the attachment bond. Every human parent knows the ineffable joy of an infant's smile, which can wash away anger and resentment; of course that smile is sweet—for the same reason sugar is sweet. A child can manipulate a parent with that smile and through attachment. Many a parent has been gulled into doing something against his or her better judgment by the cute demeanor and innocent smile of his or her three-year-old! Just as deception and a war of stratagem and counter-stratagem occurs between the sexes, so does it occur between parent and child.

Human Families

Surveys of the world's cultures find that polygyny in some form is the most common marital arrangement (when polygyny is "usual," most men have or want to have two or three wives; when it is "occasional," a few high-status men secure a large number of wives, leaving few women for other men to marry). Monogamy is uncommon, and was quite rare until the coming of religions that impose it as a moral requirement. Polyandry is practically unknown; as among other species it occurs only in rare ecological situations and is viewed by its participants as making the best of a bad deal (van den Berghe, 1979). Humans also display the sexual dimorphism of a mildly polygynous species: Generally speaking, the greater the difference in bodily size between males and females of a given species, the greater is their degree of polygyny, and among humans, men are on average slightly larger than women (Alexander, Hoogland, Howard, Noonan, & Sherman, 1979). If we use data on sexual dimorphism we can calculate that on average men should want about two or three wives, as is the case with "usual" polygynous societies, and in the nominally "monogamous" ones that allow a man to keep concubines. These data, taken together with human hypersexuality, indicate that as far as nature is concerned, human beings are polygynous, not monogamous.

One should remember that this represents the ideal state of affairs for men only, since they, but not women, can increase their fitness by holding many mates, at once gaining women to impregnate and keeping other men from finding wives. Women, on the other hand, are hurt by polygyny, since female fitness declines in polygynous marriages among all species (Daly & Wilson, 1978). Emotionally, too, women prefer monogamy, since in general women see sex as part of a deep, intimate, and loving relationship with another person, not as an end in itself or as superficial recreation (Symons, 1979). Therefore, if we apply human intelligence to the question of marriage systems we may freely disagree with natural selection's production of natural human polygyny, and say that monogamous union based on love, respect, and personal intimacy is the ideal for which we should aim.

Within the family, parent-offspring conflict—even child abuse (Box 14.3)—can be expected to occur. The rudiments of parent-offspring conflict were covered earlier. Those simpler forms of conflict should apply to humans as to other species. But human intelligence increases the sophistication of the conflict. For example, conflict should arise between parents and children over altruism between siblings. A pair of siblings share 50 percent of their genes, which motivates kin-selected altruism

■ Box 14.3 ■

Child Abuse and Evolution

Most evolutionary psychological theories about families attempt to understand why families work—why parents and children love each other, how children are socialized, how parent-offspring conflict is mediated. But as we know all too well today, families don't always work; child abuse and neglect are tragically commonplace even among animals. Can evolutionary psychology shed any light on abnormal family patterns? Daly and Wilson (1982) think it can, that patterns of abuse and neglect can be explained in terms of biologically likely variables.

For example, degree of paternal investment in offspring after birth, throughout the animal kingdom, is a function of confidence of paternity. The more a species' behavior or ecology makes it possible for a male to be sure a female's offspring are his, the more likely is he to help raise them. From the standpoint of fitness, this is quite sensible, since raising offspring not your own would injure your own fitness and increase that of someone else. Daly and Wilson present data showing that abuse and neglect are more common between step-parents and children than in intact families, and is more likely perpetrated by men than women. Other factors that vary with child abuse and neglect also are compatible with evolutionary psychological reasoning: Neglect and abuse are more likely when resources are scarce or when the child is abnormal, cases in which a parent may estimate that the reproductive capacity of the child as an adult will be low, making awaiting new times or a new child a reproductively more attractive option. Finally, factors that disrupt mother-child bonding—the proximate cause of maternal love—are likely to lead to later neglect or abuse. Such factors include prematurity or congenital disease, indicators of poor reproductive potential.

Observe that in each case, parents' behavior is adaptive or at least not maladaptive for them. The father who suspects a child is not his own is likely to abandon it and its mother for reproductive success elsewhere. A child whose life is at risk due to malnutrition, disease, prematurity, or defect is a poor reproductive investment. Morally, child abuse and neglect are abhorrent, and we all must strive to eliminate these ills. But to do so, we should first understand them, see that there are explicable causes to bring about abuse and neglect, in order to act effectively. Shrinking back in horror and condemnation is unlikely to lead to effective action. For example, an important proximate cause of mother-infant bonding appears to be very early contact—in the first hours after birth—between mother and child. Hospitals should encourage such contact, especially in the case of children born prematurely, who are often kept for days away from mother in an incubator. Similarly, presence at birth of the father may stimulate father-child bonding. We may think such measures trivially obvious—such conclusions are just "natural." The perspective of evolutionary biology lets us see why they are natural.

between them. But a given child has a 100 percent genetic investment in one's self and will be altruistic only when the benefit to one's brother or sister is at least twice the cost to one's self. But parents are equally (50 percent investment) interested in all their children and will encourage sibling altruism whenever costs and benefits between them are equal. Conflict is inevitable: Parents will emphasize precise sharing and "fairness," treating each sibling equally, while each individual child will want something more than his or her exact fair share (Trivers, 1974/1980). Socialization plays an important proximate role for the parent. Parents and cultures value honesty, fairness, openness, generosity, self-denial, and sharing, and when parents teach these values they are passing their culture on to their children and their children are becoming members of the culture. At the same time, however, the parents are furthering their genetic investment in all their children, because mutual aid and support ensure that all the children will be able to reproduce.

CONCLUSION

Genetics or Learning?

It is on the issue of genetic determinism that evolutionary psychology conflicts with the psychology of learning. Psychologists assumed for many years that animals, including people, are behaviorally a sort of putty to be shaped—Skinner's term—by the environment acting through reinforcement and punishment. However, evolutionary psychology seems to suggest—especially if we read genetic determinism into it—that learning does not accomplish very much, that males grow into men and females into women. But no evolutionary psychologist denies the role of the environment, culture, and learning in determining human behavior. They insist, as all modern geneticists do, that development is not an either-learning-or-genes proposition, but is instead a complex interaction between genetic givens and cultural shaping.

For example, Alexander (1979a) maintains that social learning is a proximate mechanism serving adaptive ends. We may illustrate this with the incest taboo. In both animals and humans, close inbreeding is genetically dangerous, and that therefore we ought to have evolved to innately avoid sex and marriage with close relatives. In human beings, social learning may be the proximate mechanism that prevents brother-sister incest.

In traditional Israeli kibbutzes, groups of similar-aged but unrelated children are reared together collectively. Now although it is certainly in the interest of the kibbutz to get these children to marry one another as adults, and there is pressure for them to do so, marriages between such children simply do not occur, nor does sex between adolescent age-mates seem to occur.

Clearly this is a form of learning. It appears that boys and girls who grow up together on an intimate, everyday, familial basis learn to not feel sexual desire for each other later on. Such learning under normal family circumstances would keep brother-sister incest from happening, and so it is a useful proximate mechanism serving the ultimate end of outbreeding. In the kibbutz, the learning misfires, but in so doing reveals itself to us.

So incest avoidance is both genetic and learned. Our species is so constructed by evolution to avoid close inbreeding (ultimate cause) by having its members learn (proximate cause) to inhibit sexual desire toward intimate age-mates (van den Berghe, 1983). The species was shaped by evolution, but the particular individual learns to avoid sex with certain other particular individuals. This situation reminds us of the constraints on animal learning discussed in Chapter 3. Biology makes certain kinds of learning easier than others, and now we see evidence of the same thing in people. The "whisperings within" may constrain learning, but they do not substitute robotic preprogramming for the flexible and adaptive patterns of learning.

In people flexibility and learning are most highly developed, as all evolutionary psychologists recognize. The vast majority of human adaptation is cultural; there are no genes for building airplanes, telephones, or computers, or for writing books and attending classes. What we have evolved is an enormous capacity to be flexibly clever. We adapt by what we make, rather than by changing our bodies, and by turning our cleverness on the world itself, making it serve our ends rather than we serve its ends.

Uniquely Human: Co-Evolution

Recently, the notion of **cultural-biological co-evolution** has been proposed by various authors (Axelrod, 1987; Ball, 1984; Cavalli-Sforza, Feldman, Chen, & Dornbusch, 1982; Durham, 1978, 1982; Flinn & Alexander, 1982; Lumsden & Wilson, 1981; Rindos, 1985, 1986a, 1986b; Ruse, 1979; for criticism of the approach, see Hallpike, 1985; and Kitcher, 1985).

Co-evolutionary theory recognizes that natural selection has produced in human beings a creature whose nature is much less constrained by the genes than is that of other animals. Human beings' abilities to learn, to speak, and to build culture have evolved because they have worked in the struggle for existence. Therefore, while natural selection has evolved an open and flexible human nature (within broad limits), it has thereby created a new selection pressure, cultural selection, which acts on cultural practices, ideas, and institutions. Any given human trait is the joint product of natural selection, which gives us our genetic dispositions, and cultural selection, which gives us our individual ideas and dispositions (Boyd & Richerson, 1985).

Ruse (1979) offers an informative example of this in the case of sexuality. The fact that a male is sexually aroused by the female form is an obvious (and obviously adaptive) biological disposition. Yet a contemporary Western male will be (if he is typical) especially aroused by large breasts (which may be habitually uncovered in another culture) but unmoved by the bare female ankle (which may have driven his Victorian great-grand-father to feverish lust). Biology and culture meet to determine the concrete mind of the individual in society.

Co-evolution, however, is more than a simple juxtaposing of biological and social sciences, for it emphasizes the pervasiveness of selection. Natural selection favors genes that promote survival; cultural selection favors ideas, practices, and institutions that promote survival. In either case, the scientist must ask questions new to the social sciences: Whom does culture benefit and how? Cultures that violate selection too wantonly cannot survive. The Shakers refused, on moral grounds, to reproduce, so their moral ideas went extinct. In both the biological and cultural realms, co-evolutionary theory focuses our attention on selection, on how human traits, whatever their source, help or hinder our ability to survive and grow.

Finally, co-evolutionary theory points out that cultural and natural evolution must interact in important ways so that we can never again consider each in isolation. Cultural evolution must ultimately serve reproduction and survival, or the culture will become extinct. Cultural change cannot wander too far from the underlying biological imperatives of human nature. At the same time, once culture is created it imposes new selection pressures on biological evolution. Culture is the most important part of the environment in which humans develop, mate, and raise children. Therefore, cultural pressures for or against aggression, for or against altruism, for or against traditional sex roles, will act on the underlying genotypes and change their relative frequencies. So not only can *Homo sapiens* construct their own social nature, but their own nature as an animal.

Evolutionary Psychology and the Deep Recesses of the Mind

Evolutionary psychology is, at least potentially, not only a theory about behavior. For evolutionary psychology may be able to explain the ultimate causes of a species' mentality. This is not readily apparent in talking about animals to whom we ordinarily feel uncomfortable attributing mental states such as wants and desires. However, when we talk about human beings in evolutionary psychological terms, our discussion soon embraces mental life. The Coolidge Effect only leads us to attribute a disposition to enjoy female variety to male animals, but when we turn to male humans we may want to say men desire female variety. Such attributions of mentality strike us as uncomfortably presumptuous. We do not like to be told that our most intimate likes and dislikes, desires and schemes, have a merely genetic ultimate causation. Controversy boils to white heat when evolutionary psychologists' claims of what constitutes "natural" mentality run counter to cultural orthodoxies. You should remember, however—and bear it in mind during any discussion about the biological basis of behavior—not to confuse the natural with the good. Polio is natural; vaccination is unnatural.

SUGGESTED READINGS

The ambitious reader may want to tackle E. O. Wilson's *Sociobiology* (Harvard University Press, 1975), the founding modern document for applying Darwinian theory to social behavior; it is surprisingly readable, especially in its abridged paperback edition, from which the more fearsome mathematics was pruned. Two other lively secondary primers are available— Richard Dawkins' *The Selfish Gene* (Oxford University Press, 1976), which is the most aggressive evolutionary psychology work, and David Barash's *Evolutionary Psychology and Behavior* (Elsevier, 1977, 2nd ed., 1982), which is written with clarity and grace. Finally, students of animal behavior should read John Alcock's *Animal Behavior: An Evolutionary Approach* (Sinauer Associates, 1979), a truly excellent book on which this chapter relied for much of the data on animal behavior. Alcock does a superb job summarizing data and theory for all areas of animal behavior, not just evolutionary psychology. An excellent introduction to human evolutionary psychology is Barash's *The Whisperings Within* (Penguin, 1979). Robert Wright surveys evolutionary psychology in *The Moral Animal: Why We Are the Way We Are: The New Science of Evolutionary Psychology* (New York: Pantheon, 1994). For a fascinating survey of the role of sex in our evolution, see Matt Ridley, *The Red Queen: Sex and the Evolution of Human Nature* (New York: Macmillan, 1993).

References

Aarsleff, H. (1976). An outline of language origin theories since the Renaissance. In S. R. Harnad, H. Steklis, &J. Lancaster (Eds.), *Annals of the New York Academy of Sciences* (Vol. 280). New York: New York Academy of Sciences.

Aarsleff, H. (1982). The history of linguistics and professor Chomsky. In H. Aarsleff, *From Locke to Saussure*. Minneapolis: University of Minnesota Press.

Abelson, R. P. (1981). Psychological status of the script concept. *American Psychologist, 36,* 715–729.

Ader, R. (1985). Conditioned immunopharmacological effects in animals: Implications for a conditioning model of pharmacotherapy. In L. White, B. Tursky, & G. E. Schwartz (Eds.), *Placebo: Theory, research, and mechanisms*. Westport, CT: Guilford.

Ader, R., & Cohen, N. (1982). Behaviorally conditioned immunosuppression and murine systemic lupus erythematosus. *Science, 215,* 1534–1536.

Ader, R., & Cohen, N. (1985). CNS-immune system interactions: Conditioning phenomena. *Behavioral and Brain Sciences, 8,* 379–426.

Adolphs, R. (1999). Social cognition in the human brain. *Trends in Cognitive Sciences, 3,* 469–479.

Adolphs, R., Russell, J. A. & Tranel, D. (1999). A role for the human amygdala in recognizing emotional arousal from unpleasant stimuli. *Psychological Science, 10,* 167–171.

Adolphs, R., Tranel, D., Damasio, H., & Damaio, A. (1994). Impaired recognition of emotion in facial expressions following bilateral damage to the amygdala. *Nature, 372,* 669–672.

Ahn, W. -K., Brewer, W. F., & Mooney, R. J. (1992). Schema acquisition from a single example. *Journal of Experimental Psychology: Learning, Memory, and Cognition, 18,* 391–412.

Ahn, W. -K., & Graham, L. M. (1999). The impact of necessity and sufficiency in the Wason four-card selection task. *Psychological Science, 10,* 237–242.

Alba, J. W., & Hasher, L. (1983). Is memory schematic? *Psychological Bulletin, 93,* 203–231.

Alcock, J. (1979). *Animal behavior* (2nd ed.). Sunderland, MA: Sinauer Associates.

Alesandrini, K. L. (1983). Strategies that influence memory for advertising communications. In R. J. Harris (Ed.), *Information processing research in advertising*. Hillsdale, NJ: Erlbaum.

Alexander, R. D. (1979a). *Darwinisin and human affairs*. Seattle: University of Washington Press.

Alexander, R. D. (1979b). Sexuality and sociality in humans and other primates. In H. A. Katchadourian (Ed.), *Human sexuality: A comparative and developmental process*. Berkeley: University of California Press.

Alexander, R. D. (1987). *The biology of moral systems*. Hawthorne, NY: Aldine.

Alexander, R. D., Hoogland, J. L., Howard, R. D., Noonan, K. M., & Sherman, P. W. (1979). Sexual dimorphisms and breeding systems in pinnipeds, ungulates, primates, and humans. In N. A. Chagnon & W. Irons (Eds.), *Evolutionary biology and human social behavior.* North Scituate, MA: Duxbury Press.

Alexander, R. D., & Noonan, K. M. (1979). Concealment of ovulation, parental care, and human social evolution. In N. A. Chagnon & W. Irons (Eds.), *Evolutionary biology and human social behavior.* North Scituate, MA: Duxbury Press.

Alexander, R. D., & Tinkle, D. (Eds.). (1982). *Natural selection and social behavior.* New York: Chiron Press.

Alkon, D. L. (1985). Conditioning-induced changes of Hermissenda channels: Relevance to mammalian brain function. In N. M. Weinberger, J. L. McGaugh, & G. Lynch (Eds.), *Memory systems of the brain: Animal and human cognitive processes.* New York: Guilford.

Alkon, D. L. (1987). *Memory traces in the brain.* Cambridge, England: Cambridge University Press.

Alkon, D. L., & Farley, J. (Eds.). (1984). *Primary neural substrates of learning and behavior change.* New York: Cambridge University Press.

Allbritton, D. W., McKoon, G., & Gerrig, R. J. (1995). Metaphor-based schemas and text representations: Making connections through conceptual metaphors. *Journal of Experimental Psychology: Learning, Memory, and Cognition, 21,* 1–14.

Allen, C., & Saidel, E. (1998). The evolution of reference. In D. D. Cummins & C. Allen (Eds.), *The evolution of mind* (pp. 183–203). New York: Oxford University Press.

Allison, J. (1989). The nature of reinforcement. In S. B. Klein & R. R. Mowrer (Eds.), *Contemporary learning theories: Instrumental conditioning theory and the impact of biological constraints on learning* (pp. 13–39). Hillsdale, NJ: Erlbaum.

Alloy, L. B., & Abramson, L. Y. (1982). Learned helplessness, depression, and the illusion of control. *Journal of Personality and Social Psychology, 42,* 1114–1126.

Allport, S. (1986). *Explorers of the black box: The search for the cellular basis of memory.* New York: Norton.

Altmann, G. (Ed.). (1990). *Parsing and interpretation.* Hillsdale, NJ: Erlbaum.

Amabile, T. M. (1996). *Creativity in context.* Boulder, CO: Westview Press.

Aman, R. (1982). Interlingual taboos in advertising: How not to name your product. In H. DiPietro (Ed.), *Linguistics and the professions.* Norwood, NJ: Ablex.

American Psychiatric Association. (1980). Diagnostic and statistical manual of mental disorders (3rd ed.). Washington, DC: American Psychiatric Association.

Amsel, A. (1958). The role of frustrative nonreward in noncontinuous reward situations. *Psychological Bulletin, 55,* 102–119.

Amsel, A. (1962). Frustrative nonreward in partial reinforcement and discrimination learning. *Psychological Review, 69,* 306–328.

Amsel, A. (1967). Partial reinforcement effects on vigor and persistence. In K. W. Spence & J. T. Spence (Eds.), *The psychology of learning and motivation* (Vol. I). New York: Academic Press.

Amsel, E., Langer, R., & Loutzenheizer, L. (1991). Do lawyers reason differently from psychologists? A comparative design for studying expertise. In R. J. Sternberg & P. A. Frensch (Eds.), *Complex problem solving: Principles and mechanisms.* Hillsdale, NJ: Erlbaum.

Anderson, D. R., & Burns, J. (1991). Paying attention to television. In J. Bryant & D. Zillmann (Eds.), *Responding to the screen: Reception and reaction processes* (pp. 3–25). Hillsdale, NJ: Erlbaum.

Anderson, D. R., & Field, D. E. (1991). Online and offline assessment of the television audience. In J. Bryant & D. Zillmann (Eds.), *Responding to the screen: Reception and reaction processes* (pp. 199–216). Hillsdale, NJ: Erlbaum.

Anderson, J. R. (1976). *Language, memory, and thought.* Hillsdale, NJ: Erlbaum.

Anderson, J. R. (1983). *The architecture of cognition.* Cambridge, MA: Harvard University Press.

Anderson, J. R. (1984). Spreading activation. In J. R. Anderson & S. M. Rosslyn (Eds.), *Tutorials in learning and memory* (pp. 61–90). San Francisco: Freeman.

Anderson, J. R. (1985). *Cognitive psychology and its implications* (2nd ed.). New York: Freeman.

Anderson, J. R. (1993). *Rules of the mind.* Hillsdale, NJ: Erlbaum.

Anderson, J. R. (1996). ACT: A simple theory of complex cognition. *American Psychologist, 51,* 355–363.

Anderson, J. R., & Bower, G. H. (1973). *Human associative memory.* Washington, DC: Winston.

Anderson, J. R., & Milson, R. (1989). Human memory: An adaptive perspective. *Psychological Review, 96,* 708–719.

Anderson, N. H. (1981). *Foundations of information integration theory.* New York: Academic Press.

Anderson, N. H. (1982). *Methods of infor4mation integration theory.* New York: Academic Press.

Anderson, N. H. (Ed.). (1991). *Contributions to information integration theory.* Hillsdale, NJ: Erlbaum.

Anderson, R. C., & Ortony, R. (1975). On putting apples into bottles—problem of polysemy. *Cognitive Psychology, 7,* 167–180.

Anderson, R. C., & Pichert, J. W. (1978). Recall of previously unrecallable information following a shift in perspective. *Journal of Verbal Learning and Verbal Behavior, 17,* 1–12.

Antinucci, F. (Ed.). (1989). *Cognitive structure and development in nonhuman primates.* Hillsdale, NJ: Erlbaum.

APA. (1983, May). Monitor. Caution: TV on. Letter from 43 psychologists and communications researchers. *APA Monitor, 14*(5), 4.

Ardrey, R. (1966). *The territorial imperative.* New York: Atheneum.

Arensburg, B., & Tillier, A. M. (1991). Speech and the Neanderthals. *Endeavour, 15,* 26–28.

Arkes, H. R., & Hammond, K. R. (Eds.). (1986). *Judgment and decision making: An interdisciplinary reader.* Cambridge, England: Cambridge University Press.

Armstrong, T. (1995). *The mystery of the A.D.D. child.* New York: Dutton.

Armstrong, D. F., Stokoe, W. C., & Wilcox, S. E. (1994). Signs of the origin of syntax. *Current Anthropology, 35,* 349–358.

Aronfreed, J. (1976). Moral development from the standpoint of a general psychological theory. In T. Lickona (Ed.), *Moral development and behavior.* New York: Holt, Rinehart & Winston.

Ashcraft, M. A. (1993). *Human memory and cognition* (2nd ed.). New York: HarperCollins.

Aslin, R. N., & Pisoni, D. B. (1980). Some developmental processes in speech perception. In G. H. Yeni-Komshian, J. F. Kavanaugh, & C. A. Ferguson (Eds.), *Child phonology. Vol. 2: Perception.* New York: Academic Press.

Atkinson, M. (1982). *Explanations in the study of child language development.* Cambridge, England: Cambridge University Press.

Atkinson, M. (1986). Learnability. In P. Fletcher & M. Garman (Eds.), *Language acquisition* (2nd ed.). Cambridge, England: Cambridge University Press.

Atkinson, R. C. (1975). Mnemotechnics in second-language learning. *American Psychologist, 30,* 821–828.

Atkinson, R. C., & Raugh, M. R. (1975). An application of the mnemonic keyword method to the acquisition of Russian vocabulary. *Journal of Experimental Psychology: Human Learning and Memory, 104,* 126–133.

Atkinson, R. C., & Shiffrin, R. M. (1968). Human memory: A proposed system and its control processes. In K. Spence & J. Spence (Eds.), *The psychology of learning and motivation* (Vol. 2). New York: Academic Press.

Augustinos, M., & Walker, I. (1995). *Social cognition: An integrated perspective.* Thousand Oaks, CA: Sage.

Axelrod, R. (1984). *The evolution of cooperation.* New York: Basic Books.

Axelrod, R. (1987, March/April). Laws of life: How standards evolve. *The Sciences,* 44–51.

Ayers, M. S., & Reder, L. M. (1998). A theoretical review of the misinformation effect: Predictions from an activation-based memory model. *Psychonomic Bulletin and Review, 5,* 1–21.

Azrin, N. H., Holz, W., Ulrich, R., & Goldiamond, I. (1961). The control of the content of conversation through reinforcement. *Journal of the Experimental Analysis of Behavior, 4,* 25–30.

Baba, M. L., Darga, L., & Goodman, M. (1982). Recent advances in molecular evolution of the primates. In A. Chiarelli & R. Corruccini (Eds.), *Advanced views in primate biology.* Berlin: Springer-Verlag.

Baddeley, A. (1990). *Human memory: Theory and practice.* Boston: Allyn & Bacon.

Baddeley, A. (1992). Working memory. *Science, 255,* 556–559.

Baddeley, A. D. (1978). The trouble with levels: A reexamination of Crail and Lockhart's framework for memory research. *Psychological Review, 85,* 139–152.

Baddeley, A. D., Gathercole, S., & Papagno, C. (1998). The phonological loop as a language learning device. *Psychological Review, 105,* 158–173.

Bahrick, H. P. (1984). Semantic memory content in permastore: Fifty years of memory for Spanish learned in school. *Journal of Experimental Psychology: General, 113,* 1–29.

Bahrick, H. P., Bahrick, P. O., & Wittlinger, R. P. (1975). Fifty years of memory for names and faces: A cross-sectional approach. *Journal of Experimental Psychology: General, 114,* 54–75.

Bahrick, H. P., & Phelps, E. (1987). Retention of the Spanish vocabulary over 8 years. *Journal of Experimental Psychology: Learning, Memory, and Cognition, 13,* 344–349.

Bailey, C. H., & Kandel, E. R. (1995). Molecular and structural mechanisms underlying long-term memory. In M. S. Gazzinaga (Ed.), *The cognitive neurosciences* (pp. 19–36). Cambridge, MA: MIT Press.

Baker, A. G., & Mercier, P. (1989). Attention, retrospective processing, and cognitive representations. In S. B. Klein & R. R. Mowrer (Eds.), *Contemporary learning theories: Pavlovian conditioning and the status of traditional learning theory* (pp. 85–116). Hillsdale, NJ: Erlbaum.

Baker, L., & Wagner, J. L. (1987). Evaluating information for truthfulness. The effects of logical subordination. *Memory and Cognition, 15,* 247–255.

Balch, W. R., Bowman, K., & Mohler, L. A. (1992). Music-dependent memory in immediate and delayed recall. *Memory and Cognition, 20,* 21–28.

Baldwin, A. (1980). *Theories of child development* (2nd ed.). New York: Wiley.

Ball, J. A. (1984). Memes as replicators. *Ethology and Sociobiology, 5,* 145–161.

Balota, D. A., Flores d'Arcais, G. B., & Rayner, K. (Eds.). (1990). *Comprehension processes in reading.* Hillsdale, NJ: Erlbaum.

Bandura, A. (1967). The role of modeling processes in personality development. In W. Hartup (Ed.), *The young child: Reviews of research.* Washington, DC: National Association for Education of Young Children.

Bandura, A. (1974). Behavior theory and the models of man. *American Psychologist, 29,* 859–869.

Bandura, A. (1978). The self-system in reciprocal determinism. *American Psychologist, 33,* 344–358.

Bandura, A. (1982). Self-efficacy mechanism in human agency. *American Psychologist, 37,* 122–147.

Bandura, A., Ross, D., & Ross, S. (1961). Transmission of aggression through imitation of aggressive models. *Journal of Abnormal and Social Psychology, 63,* 575–582.

Bandura, A., & Walters, R. (1963). *Social learning and personality development.* New York: Holt, Rinehart & Winston.

Banich, M. T. (1997). *Neuropsychology: The neural base of mental function.* New York: Houghton Mifflin.

Bar-Adon, A., & Leopold, W. F. (Eds.). (1971). *Child language: A book of readings.* Englewood Cliffs, NJ: Prentice Hall.

Barash, D. P. (1977). *Sociobiology and behavior* (1st ed.). New York: Elsevier.

Barash, D. P. (1979). *The whisperings within.* New York: Penguin.

Barash, D. P. (1982). *Sociobiology and behavior* (2nd ed.). New York: Elsevier.

Barclay, C. R. (1986). Schematization of autobiographical memory. In D. C. Rubin (Ed.), *Autobiographical memory* (pp. 82–99). Cambridge, England: Cambridge University Press.

Barclay, C. R. (1988). Truth and accuracy in autobiographical memory. In M. M. Gruneberg, P. E. Morris, & R. N. Sykes (Eds.), *Practical aspects of memory: Current research and issues. Vol. I. Memory in everyday life* (pp. 289–294). Chichester, England: Wiley.

Barclay, J. R., Bransford, J. D., Franks, J. J., McCarrell, N. S., & Nitsch, K. (1974). Comprehension and semantic flexibility. *Journal of Verbal Learning and Verbal Behavior, 13,* 471–481.

Barclay, R. A. (1997). *ADHD and the nature of self-control.* New York: Guilford Press.

Barker-Benfield, G. J. (1976). *The horrors of the half-known life.* New York: Harper Colophon.

Barkley, R. A. (1990). *Attention deficit hyperactivity disorder: A handbook for diagnosis and treatment.* New York: Guilford.

Barkley, R. A. (1995). *Taking charge of ADHD: The complete, authoritative guide for parents.* New York: Guilford.

Barkow, J. H., Cosmides, L., & Tooby, J. (Eds.). (1992). *The adapted mind: Evolutionary psychology and the direction of culture.* New York: Oxford University Press.

Barlow, G. W., & Silverberg, J. (Eds.). (1980). *Sociobiology: Beyond nature/nurture?* Boulder, CO: Westview Press, (AAAS Selected Symposium 35).

Barlow, H., Blakemore, C., & Weston-Smith, M. (Eds.). (1990). *Images and understanding.* Cambridge, England: Cambridge University Press.

Baron, A., Kaufman, A., & Stauber, K. (1969). Effects of instructions and reinforcement-feedback on human operant behavior maintained by fixed-internal reinforcement. *Journal of the Experimental Analysis of Behavior, 12,* 701–712.

Baron, J. (1988). *Thinking and deciding.* Cambridge, England: Cambridge University Press.

Baron-Cohen, S. (1995). *Mindblindness: An essay on autism and theory of mind.* Cambridge, MA: MIT Press.

Baron-Cohen, S. (1998). Is autism an extreme form of male brain? In R. Carter, *Mapping the mind.* Berkeley: University of California Press, pp. 77–79.

Barr, A., Feigenbaum, E. A., & Cohen, P. R. (1982–1989). *The handbook of artificial intelligence* (Vols. 1–4). Reading, MA: Addison-Wesley.

Barsalou, L. S. (1983). Ad hoc categories. *Memory and Cognition, 11,* 211–227.

Barsalou, L. W. (1992). *Cognitive psychology: An overview for cognitive scientists.* Hillsdale, NJ: Erlbaum.

Barsalou, L. W. (1999a). Language comprehension: Archival memory or preparation for situated action? *Discourse Processes, 28,* 61–80.

Barsalou, L. W. (1999b). Perceptual symbol systems. *Behavioral and Brain Sciences, 22,* 577–660.

Bartlett, F. C. (1932). *Remembering: A study in experimental and social psychology.* London: Cambridge University Press.

Bass, E., & Davis, L. (1988). *The courage to heal: A guide to women survivors of child sexual abuse.* New York: Harper & Row.

Bates, E., & MacWhinney, B. (1987). Competition, variation, and language learning. In B. MacWhinney (Ed.), *Mechanisms of language acquisition.* Hillsdale, NJ: Erlbaum.

Bateson, P. (1985). Problems and possibilities of fusing developmental and evolutionary thought. In G. Butterworth, J. Rutkowska, & M. Scaife (Eds.), *Evolution and developmental psychology.* New York: St. Martin's Press.

Battan, J. F. (1983). The "new narcissism" in 20th-century America: The shadow and substance of social change. *Journal of Social History, 17,* 199–220.

Baumrind, D. (1971). Harmonious parents and their preschool children. *Developmental Psychology, 4,* 63–72.

Beals, K. L., Smith, C. L., & Dodd, S. M. (1984). Brain size, cranial morphology, climate, and time machines. *Current Anthropology, 25,* 301–320.

Beaton, A. A., Gruneberg, M. M., & Ellis, N. (1995). Retention and foreign vocabulary learned using the keyword method: A ten-year follow-up. *Second Language Research, 11*(2), 112–120.

Bechtel, W., & Abrahamsen, A. (1991). *Connectionism and the mind: An introduction to parallel processing in networks.* Cambridge, MA: Basil Blackwell.

Beck, B. (1983, April 10). *Tools and intelligence.* Paper presented at the Second National Zoological Park Symposium, Animal Intelligence, Washington, DC.

Bédard, J., & Chi, M. T. H. (1994). Expertise in auditing. *Auditing: A Journal of Practice and Theory, 13*(Supplement), 21–45.

Begg, I., & Paivio, A. (1969). Concreteness and imagery in sentence meaning. *Journal of Verbal Learning and Verbal Behavior, 8,* 821–827.

Beilin, H. (1980). Piaget's theory: Refinement, rejection, or revision? In R. H. Kluwe & H. Spada (Eds.), *Developmental models of thinking.* New York: Academic Press.

Beit-Hallahmi, B., & Rabin, A. (1977). The kibbutz as a social experiment and as child-bearing laboratory. *American Psychologist, 32,* 532–541.

Bekerian, D. A., & Dennett, J. L. (1993). The cognitive interview technique: Reviving the issues. *Applied Cognitive Psychology, 7,* 275–297.

Bem, D. (1967). Self-perception: An alternative interpretation of cognitive dissonance. *Psychological Review, 24,* 183–200.

Benderly, B. L. (1980). The great ape debate. *Science, 80, 1*(5), 60–65.

Benedict, H. (1992). *Virgin or vamp: How the press covers sex crimes.* New York: Oxford University Press.

Benfer, R. A., Brent, E. E., Jr., & Furbee, L. (1991). *Expert systems.* Newbury Park, CA: Sage.

Bennett, H. L., Davis, H. S., & Giannini, J. A. (1985). Nonverbal response to intraoperative conversation. *British Journal of Anaesthesia, 57,* 174–179.

Bentham, J. (1843). An introduction to the principles of moral legislation. The works of Jeremy Bentham, 11 vols., Vol. I. Partially reprinted in P. Gay (Ed.), *The enlightenment: A comprehensive anthology.* New York: Simon & Schuster. (Original work published 1789)

Bereiter, C., & Scardamalia, M. (1987). *The psychology of written composition.* Hillsdale, NJ: Erlbaum.

Berko Gleason, J., Hay, D., & Cain, L. (1989). Social and affective determinants of language acquisition. In M. L. Rice & R. L. Schiefelbusch (Eds.), *The teachability of language.* Baltimore: Paul H. Brooks.

Berlin, B., & Kay, P. (1969). *Basic color terms: Their universality and evolution.* Berkeley: University of California Press.

Bermant, G. (1976). Sexual behavior: Hard times with the Coolidge Effect. In M. Siegel & H. Zigler (Eds.), *Psychological research: The inside story.* New York: Harper & Row.

Berne, E. (1964). *Games people play.* New York: Grove Press.

Bernstein, B. (1964). Aspects of language and learning in the genesis of the social process. In D. Hymes (Ed.), *Language in culture and society* (pp. 251–263). New York: Harper & Row.

Bernstein, I. L. (1985). Learned food aversions in the progression of cancer. *Annals of the New York Academy of Sciences, 443,* 365–380.

Besner, D., & Humphreys, G. (Eds.). (1990). *Basic processes in reading: Visual word recognition.* Hillsdale, NJ: Erlbaum.

Besson, M., Falta, F., Peretz, I., Bonnel, A. -M., & Requin, J. (1998). Singing in the brain: Independence of lyrics and tunes. *Psychological Science, 9,* 494–497.

Best, J. B. (1999). *Cognitive psychology* (5th ed.). St. Paul: West.

Bethel-Fox, C. E., & Shepard, R. N. (1988). Mental rotation: Effects of stimulus complexity and familiarity. *Journal of Experimental Psychology: Human Perception and Performance, 14,* 12–23.

Bethell, T. (1980). Burning Darwin to save Marx. *Harper's, 257*(1543), 31–38, 91–92.

Bever, T. G. (1970). The cognitive basis for linguistic structures. In J. R. Hayes (Ed.), *Cognition and the development of language.* New York: Wiley.

Bever, T. G. (1980). Broca and Lashley were right: Cerebral dominance is an accident of growth. In D. Caplan (Ed.), *Biological studies of mental processes.* Cambridge, MA: MIT Press.

Beyth-Marom, R., & Lichtenstein, S. (1984). *An elementary approach to thinking under uncertainty.* Hillsdale, NJ: Erlbaum.

Bickerton, D. (1990). *Language and species.* Chicago: University of Chicago Press.

Bickerton, D. (1995). *Language and human behavior.* Seattle: University of Washington Press.

Biederman, I., Cooper, E. E., & Fox, P. W. (1992). Unexceptional spatial memory in an exceptional memorist. *Journal of Experimental Psychology: Learning, Memory, and Cognition, 18,* 654–657.

Bijou, S. (1976). *Child development: The basic stage of early childhood.* Englewood Cliffs, NJ: Prentice Hall.

Bijou, S., & Baer, D. M. (1968). *Child development: Readings in behavior analysis.* New York: Appleton-Century-Crofts.

Bingham, R. (1980). Trivers in Jamaica. *Science, 80, 1*(3), 56–67.

Bjorklund, D. F. (Ed.). (1990). *Children's strategies: Contemporary views of cognitive development.* Hillsdale, NJ: Erlbaum.

Bjorklund, D. F., & Green, B. L. (1992). The adaptive nature of cognitive immaturity. *American Psychologist, 47,* 46–54.

Black, A., Cott, A., & Pavloski, R. (1977). The operating learning theory approach to biofeedback training. In G. Schwartz & J. Beatty (Eds.), *Biofeedback: Theory and research.* New York: Academic Press.

Black, J. E., & Greenough, W. T. (1986). Developmental approaches to the memory process. In J. L. Martinez & R. P. Kesner (Eds.), *Learning and memory: A psychological view.* Orlando, FL: Academic Press.

Black, J. E., & Greenough, W. T. (1991). Developmental approaches to the memory process. In J. L. Martinez & R. P. Kesner, *Learning and memory: A biological view* (2nd ed.). San Diego: Academic Press.

Black, S. (1994). Different kinds of smart. *The Executive Educator,* 24–27.

Blanchard, E., & Epstein, L. (1978). *A biofeedback primer.* Reading, MA: Addison-Wesley.

Blight, J. G. (1990). *The shattered crystal ball: Fear and learning in the Cuban missile crisis.* Savage, MD: Rowman & Littlefield.

Bloch, M. (1991). Language, anthropology, and cognitive science. *Man, 26,* 183–198.

Blodgett, H. S. (1929). The effect of the introduction of reward upon the maze performance of rats. *University of California Publications in Psychology, 4,* 113–134.

Bloom, C. P. (1988). The roles of schemata in memory for text. *Discourse Processes, 11,* 305–318.

Bloom, L. (Ed.). (1978). *Readings in language development.* New York: Wiley.

Bloom, L. (1991). *Language and development from two to three.* Cambridge, England: Cambridge University Press.

Bloom, L., Hood, L., & Lightbown, P. (1974). Imitation in language development: If, when, and why. *Cognitive Psychology, 6,* 380–420.

Bloom, L., & Lahey, M. (1978). *Language development and language disorders.* New York: Wiley.

Bloom, P. (1998). Some issues in the evolution of language and thought. In D. D. Cummins & C. Allen (Eds.), *The evolution of mind* (pp. 204–223). New York: Oxford University Press.

Bloom, P., & Markson, L. (1998). Capacities underlying word learning. *Trends in Cognitive Sciences, 2,* 67–73.

Blume, E. S. (1990). *Secret survivors: Uncovering incest and its aftereffects in women.* New York: Ballantine.

Blumenberg, B. (1983). The evolution of the advanced hominid brain. *Current Anthropology, 24,* 589–623.

Blumenstein, S. E. (1980). Speech perception: An overview. In G. H. Yeni-Komshian, J. F. Kavanaugh, & C. A. Ferguson (Eds.), *Child phonology. Vol. 2: Perception.* New York: Academic Press.

Blumenthal, A. (1980). Wilhelm Wundt and early American psychology: A clash of cultures. In R. W. Rieber (Ed.), *Wilhelm Wundt and the making of a scientific psychology.* New York: Plenum.

Boden, M. A. (Ed.). (1990). *The philosophy of artificial intelligence.* Oxford: Oxford University Press.

Bohannon, J. N. (1988). Flashbulb memories for the space shuttle disaster: A tale of two theories. *Cognition, 29,* 179–196.

Bolles, R. C. (1971). Species-specific defense reactions. In R. F. Brush (Ed.), *Aversive learning and conditioning.* New York: Academic Press.

Bolles, R. C. (1975). Learning, motivation, and cognition. In W. K. Estes (Ed.), *Handbook of learning and cognitive processes* (Vol. I). Hillsdale, NJ: Erlbaum.

Bouton, M. (1991). Context and retrieval in extinction and in other examples of interference and simple associative learning. In L. Dachowski & C. F. Flaherty (Eds.), *Current topics in animal learning: Brain, emotion, and cognition* (pp. 25–53). Hillsdale, NJ: Erlbaum.

Bowden, E. M., & Beeman, M. J. (1998). Getting the right idea: Semantic activation in the right hemisphere may help solve insight problems. *Psychological Science, 9,* 435–440.

Bower, G. H. (1981). Mood and memory. *American Psychologist, 36,* 129–148.

Bower, G. H., Black, J. B., & Turner, T. J. (1979). Scripts in memory for text. *Cognitive Psychology, 11,* 177–220.

Bower, G. H., Karlin, M. B., & Dueck, A. (1975). Comprehension and memory for pictures. *Memory and Cognition, 3,* 216–220.

Bower, G. H., Monteiro, K. P., & Gilligan, S. G. (1978). Emotional mood as a context for learning and recall. *Journal of Verbal Learning and Verbal Behavior, 17,* 573–587.

Bower, T. G. R. (1974). *Development in infancy.* San Francisco: Freeman.

Bower, T. G. R. (1977). *A primer of infant development.* San Francisco: Freeman.

Bower, T. G. R. (1979). *Human development.* San Francisco: Freeman.

Bowers, K. S., & Farvolden, P. (1996). Revisiting a century-old Freudian slip: From suggestion disavowed to the truth repressed. *Psychological Bulletin, 119,* 355–380.

Boyd, R., & Richerson, P. J. (1985). *Culture and the evolutionary process.* Chicago; University of Chicago Press.

Bradshaw, J. (1991). Animal asymmetry and human heredity: Dextrality, tool use, and language in evolution—10 years after Walker (1980). *British Journal of Psychology, 82,* 39–59.

Brainerd, C. J. (1974a). Neo-Piagetian training experiments revisited: Is there any support for the cognitive-developmental stage hypotheses? *Cognition, 2,* 349–376.

Brainerd, C. J. (1974b, June). Structures of the whole: Is there any glue to hold the concrete operational "stage" together? Paper presented at the annual meeting of the Canadian Psychological Association, Windsor, Ontario, Canada.

Brainerd, C. J. (1978a). *Piaget's theory of intelligence.* Englewood Cliffs, NJ: Prentice Hall.

Brainerd, C. J. (1978b). The stage question in cognitive developmental theory. *Behavioral and Brain Sciences, 1,* 173–213.

Brainerd, C. J., & Allen, T. W. (1971). Experimental inductions of the conservation of "first order" quantitative invariants. *Psychological Bulletin, 75,* 125–144.

Brainerd, C. J., & Pressley, M. (Eds.). (1987). *Basic processes in memory development.* New York: Springer.

Brandon, R. N., & Burian, R. (Eds.). (1984). *Genes, organisms and populations: Controversies over the units of selection.* Cambridge: MIT Press.

Bransford, J. D. (1978). *Human cognition.* Belmont, CA: Wadsworth.

Bransford, J. D., & Franks, J. J. (1971). The abstraction of linguistic ideas. *Cognitive Psychology, 2,* 331–350.

Bransford, J. D., & Johnson, M. K. (1972). Contextual prerequisites for understanding: Some investigations of comprehension and recall. *Journal of Verbal Learning and Verbal Behavior, 11,* 717–726.

Bransford, J. D., & Johnson, M. K. (1973). Considerations of some problems of comprehension. In W. Chase (Ed.), *Visual information processing.* New York: Academic Press.

Bransford, J. D., & McCarrell, N. S. (1974). A cognitive approach to comprehension: Some thoughts about understanding what it means to comprehend. In W. B. Weimer & D. S. Palermo (Eds.), *Cognition and the symbolic processes.* Hillsdale, NJ: Erlbaum.

Bransford, J. D., & Stein, B. S. (1984). *The ideal problem solver.* New York: Freeman.

Breland, K., & Breland, M. (1972). The misbehavior of organisms. In M. E. P. Seligman & J. L. Hager (Eds.), *Biological boundaries of learning.* New York: Appleton-Century-Crofts. (Original work published 1961)

Brett, G. S. (1912). *A history of psychology* (Vol. 2). London: Allen.

Brewer, W. F. (1974). There is no convincing evidence for operant or classical conditioning in adult humans. In W. Weimer & D. Palermo (Eds.), *Cognition and the symbolic processes.* Hillsdale, NJ: Erlbaum.

Brewer, W. F. (1986). What is autobiographical memory? In D. C. Rubin (Ed.), *Autobiographical memory* (pp. 25–49). Cambridge, England: Cambridge University Press.

Brewer, W. F. (1987). Schemas versus mental models in human memory. In P. Morris (Ed.), *Modelling cognition: Proceedings of the International Workshop on Modelling Cognition.* New York: Wiley.

Brewer, W. F. (1988). A qualitative analysis of the recalls of randomly sampled autobiographical events. In M. M. Gruneberg, P. E. Morris, & R. N. Sykes (Eds.), *Practical aspects of memory: Current research and issues. Vol. I. Memory in everyday life* (pp. 263–268). Chichester, England: Wiley.

Brewer, W. F. (1995). What is recollective memory? In D. C. Rubin (Ed.), *Remembering our past: Studies in autobiographical memory.* Cambridge, England: Cambridge University Press.

Brewer, W. F., & Harris, R. J. (1974). Memory for deictic elements in sentences. *Journal of Verbal Learning and Verbal Behavior, 13,* 321–327.

Brewer, W. F., & Nakamura, G. V. (1984). The nature and functions of schemas. In R. S. Wyer & T. K. Srull (Eds.), *Handbook of social cognition.* Hillsdale, NJ: Erlbaum.

Brewin, C. R. (1998). Intrusive autobiographical memories in depression and post-traumatic stress disorder. *Applied Cognitive Psychology, 12,* 359–370.

Brigham, J. C., Maas, A., Snyder, L. D., & Spaulding, K. (1982). Accuracy of eyewitness identification in a field study. *Journal of Personality and Social Psychology, 42,* 673–681.

Britton, B. K., & Graesser, A. C. (Eds.). (1996). *Models of understanding text.* Mahwah, NJ: Erlbaum.

Broadbent, D. (1958). *Perception and communication.* New York: Pergamon Press.

Broadbent, D. (1982). Task combination and selective intake of information. *Acta Psychologica, 50,* 253–290.

Brodbeck, D. R., Burack, O. R., & Shettleworth, S. J. (1992). One-trial associative memory in black-capped chickadees. *Journal of Experimental Psychology: Animal Behavior Processes, 18,* 12–21.

Brown, A. S. (1991). A review of the tip-of-the-tongue phenomenon. *Psychological Bulletin, 109,* 204–233.

Brown, J. A. (1958). Some tests of the decay theory of immediate memory. *Quarterly Journal of Experimental Psychology, 10,* 12–21.

Brown, J. L., & Brown, E. R. (1981). Kin selection and individual selection in babblers. In R. D. Alexander & D. Tinkle (Eds.), *Natural selection and social behavior.* New York: Chiron Press.

Brown, M. (1992). Does a cognitive map guide choices in the radial-arm maze? *Journal of Experimental Psychology: Animal Behavior Processes, 18,* 56–66.

Brown, N. R., & Schopflocher, D. (1998). Event clusters: An organization of personal events in autobiographical memory. *Psychological Science, 9,* 470–475.

Brown, P. C., & Jenkins, H. M. (1968). Autoshaping of the pigeon's key peck. *Journal of the Experimental Analysis of Behavior, 11,* 1–8.

Brown, R. (1970). The first sentences of child and chimpanzee. In *Psycholinguistics: Selected papers.* New York: Free Press. Reprinted in T. A. Sebeok & J. Umiker-Sebeok (1980).

Brown, R. (1973). *A first language.* Cambridge, MA: Harvard University Press.

Brown, R., & Kulick, J. (1977). Flashbulb memories. *Cognition, 5,* 73–99.

Brown, R., & McNeill, D. (1966). The "tip of the tongue" phenomenon. *Journal of Verbal Learning and Verbal Behavior, 5,* 325–337.

Bruck, M., Cavanagh, P., & Ceci, S. J. (1991). Fortysomething: Recognizing faces at one's 25th reunion. *Memory and Cognition, 19,* 221–228.

Bruno, K. J., & Harris, R. J. (1980). The effect of repetition on the discrimination of asserted and implied claims in advertising. *Applied Psycholinguistics, 1,* 307–321.

Bryant, P. (1974). *Perception and understanding in young children.* New York: Basic Books.

Buckner, R. (1996). Beyond HERA: Contributions of specific prefrontal areas to long-term memory. *Psychonomic Bulletin and Review, 3,* 149–158.

Burenhult, G. (Ed.). (1993). *The first humans: Human origins and history to 10,000 B.C.* New York: HarperSanFrancisco.

Burke, R. R., Desarbo, W. S., Oliver, R. L., & Robertson, T. S. (1988). Deception by implication: An experimental investigation. *Journal of Consumer Research, 14,* 483–494.

Burling, R. (1993). Primate call, human language, and nonverbal communication. *Current Anthropology, 34,* 25–37.

Burt, C. B. B. (1992). Reconstruction of the duration of autobiographical events. *Memory and Cognition, 20,* 124–132.

Burt, C. D. B., Watt, S. C., Mitchell, D. A., & Conway, M. A. (1998). Retrieving the sequence of autobiographical event components. *Applied Cognitive Psychology, 12,* 305–320.

Buss, D. M. (1994). *The evolution of desire: Strategies of human mating.* New York: Basic.

Butters, N., & Miliotis, P. (1985). In K. Heilman & E. Valenstein (Eds.), *Clinical neuropsychology.* New York: Oxford University Press.

Butterworth, G., Rutkowska, J., & Scaife, M. (Eds.). (1985). *Evolution and developmental psychology.* New York: St. Martin's Press.

Byrne, J. H., & Crow, T. (1991). Examples of mechanistic analyses of learning and memory in invertebrates. In J. L. Martinez & R. P. Kesner (Eds.), *Learning and memory: A biological view* (2nd ed.). San Diego: Academic Press.

Byrne, R. M. J. (1991). The psychology of thinking. *The Psychologist, 4,* 297–300.

Byrne, R. M. J., & Johnson-Laird, P. M. (1990). Models and deductive reasoning. In K. H. Gilhooly, M. T. G. Keane, R. H. Logie, & G. Erdos (Eds.), *Lines of thinking: Reflections on the psychology of thought. Vol. I. Representation, reasoning, analogy, and decision making.* New York: Wiley.

Byrne, R. W., & Whiten, A. (Eds.). (1988). *Machiavellian intelligence*. Oxford: Oxford University Press.

Cabeza, R., & Nyberg, L. (1997). Imaging cognition: An empirical review of PET studies with normal subjects. *Journal of Cognitive Neuroscience, 9,* 1–26.

Cacciari, C. (1998). Why do we think metaphorically? Reflections on the functions of metaphor in discourse and reasoning. In A. N. Katz, C. Cacciari, R. W. Gibbs, Jr., & M. Turner (Eds.), *Figurative language and thought* (pp. 119–157). New York: Oxford University Press.

Cahill, L., Haier, R. J., & McGaugh, J. (1996). Amygdala activity at encoding correlated with long-term free recall of emotional information. *Proceedings of the National Academy of Sciences, 93,* 8016–8321.

Cairns, R. B., & Valsiner, J. (1984). Child psychology. *Annual Review of Psychology, 35,* 553–577.

Calkins, M. W. (1894). Association. *Psychological Review, 1,* 476–483.

Calogero, M., & Nelson, T. O. (1992). Utilization of base-rate information during feeling-of-knowing judgments. *American Journal of Psychology, 105,* 565–573.

Calvin, W. H. (1982). Did throwing stones shape hominid brain evolution? *Ethology and Sociobiology, 3,* 115–124.

Calvin, W. H. (1990). *The ascent of mind: Ice age climates and the evolution of intelligence.* New York: Bantam Books.

Calvin, W. H. (1993). The unitary hypothesis: A common neural circuitry for novel manipulations, language, plan-ahead, and throwing. In K. R. Gibson & T. Ingold (Eds.), *Tools, language, and cognition in human evolution* (pp. 230–250). Cambridge, England: Cambridge University Press.

Calvin, W. H. (1994, October). The emergence of intelligence. *Scientific American, 261,* 101–107.

Campbell, R. N. (1986). Language acquisition and cognition. In P. Fletcher & M. Garman (Eds.), *Language acquisition* (2nd ed.). Cambridge, England: Cambridge University Press.

Cann, A., & Ross, D. A. (1989). Olfactory stimuli as context cues in human memory. *American Journal of Psychology, 2,* 91–102.

Capaldi, E. J. (1966). Partial reinforcement: An hypothesis of sequential effects. *Psychological Review, 73,* 459–477.

Capaldi, E. J. (1971). Memory and learning: A sequential viewpoint. In W. Honig & P. James (Eds.), *Animal memory*. New York: Academic Press.

Caplan, A. L. (1978). *The sociobiology debate*. New York: Harper Colophon.

Caplan, D. (Ed.). (1980). *Biological studies of mental processes*. Cambridge, MA: MIT Press.

Carey, S. (1985). *Conceptual change in childhood*. Cambridge, MA: MIT Press.

Carey, S. (1991). Knowledge acquisition: Enrichment or conceptual change? In S. Carey & R. Gelman (Eds.), *The epigenesis of mind: Essays on biology and cognition*. Hillsdale, NJ: Erlbaum.

Carey, S., & Gelman, R. (Eds.). (1991). *The epigenesis of mind: Essays on biology and cognition*. Hillsdale, NJ: Erlbaum.

Carpenter, P. A., & Just, M. A. (1989). The role of working memory in language comprehension. In D. Klahr & K. Kotovsky (Eds.), *Complex information processing: The impact of Herbert A. Simon* (pp. 31–68). Hillsdale, NJ: Erlbaum.

Carroll, D. W. (1999). *Psychology of language* (3rd ed.). Monterey, CA: Brooks/Cole.

Carter, J. R. (1991). Are economists different, and if so, why? *Journal of Economic Perspectives, 5,* 171–177.

Cartmill, D., Pilbeam, D., & Isaac, G. (1986). One hundred years of paleoanthropology. *American Scientist, 74,* 410–422.

Cavalli-Sforza, L., Feldman, M., Chen, K., & Dornbusch, S. (1982). Theory and observation in cultural transmission. *Science, 218,* 19–27.

Cavalli-Sforza, L. L. (1991). Genes, peoples, and languages. *Scientific American, 265*(5), 104–110.

Cavalli-Sforza, L. L., Menozzi, P., & Piazza, A. (1994). *The history and geography of human genes.* Princeton, NJ: Princeton University Press.

Cavanaugh, J. C., & Perlmutter, M. (1982). Metamemory: A critical examination. *Child Development, 53,* 1–28.

Ceci, S. J., & Loftus, E. F. (1994). "Memory work": A royal road to false memories? *Applied Cognitive Psychology, 8,* 351–364.

Cellerier, G. (1972). Information processing tendencies in recent experiments in cognitive learning: Theoretical implication. In S. Farnham-Diggory (Ed.), *Information processing in children.* New York: Academic Press.

Chagnon, N. A. (1980). Kin-selection theory, kinship, marriage and fitness among the Yanomamo Indians. In G. W. Barlow & J. Silverberg (Eds.), *Sociobiology: Beyond nature/nurture?* Boulder, CO: Westview Press, (AAAS Selected Symposium 35).

Chagnon, N. A. (1981). Terminological kinship, genealogical relatedness and village fissioning among the Yanomamo Indians. In R. D. Alexander & D. Tinkle (Eds.), *Natural selection and social behavior.* New York: Chiron Press.

Chagnon, N. A., & Irons, W. (Eds.). (1979). *Evolutionary biology and human social behavior.* North Scituate, MA: Duxbury Press.

Chalmers, D. J. (1995, December). The puzzle of conscious experience. *Scientific American, 273,* 80–86.

Chang, T. M. (1986). Semantic memory: Facts and models. *Psychological Bulletin, 99,* 199–220.

Chapin, J. K., Moxon, K. A., Markowitz, R. S., & Nicolelis, A. C. (1999). Real-time control of a robot arm using simultaneously recorded neurons in the motor cortex. *Nature Neuroscience, 2,* 664–670.

Chapman, G. B., & Johnson, E. J. (1994). The limits of anchoring. *Journal of Behavioral Decision Making, 7,* 223–242.

Chapman, L. J., & Chapman, J. P. (1967). Genesis of popular, but erroneous diagnostic observations. *Journal of Abnormal Psychology, 72,* 193–204.

Chapman, L. J., & Chapman, J. P. (1969). Illusory correlation as an obstacle to the use of valid diagnostic signs. *Journal of Abnormal Psychology, 74,* 271–280.

Chapman, P., & Underwood, G. (2000). Forgetting near-accidents: The roles of severity, culpability and experience in the poor recall of dangerous driving situations. *Applied Cognitive Psychology, 14,* 31–44.

Charness, N. (1991). Expertise in chess: The balance between knowledge and search. In K. A. Ericsson & J. Smith (Eds.), *Toward a general theory of expertise* (pp. 39–63). Cambridge, England: Cambridge University Press.

Charrow, R. P., & Charrow, V. R. (1979). Making legal language understandable: A psycholinguistic study of jury instructions. *Columbia Law Review, 79,* 1306–1374.

Charrow, V. R. (1982). Linguistic theory and the study of legal and bureaucratic language. In L. K. Obler & L. Menn (Eds.), *Exceptional language and linguistics.* New York: Academic Press.

Chase, W. G. (1973). *Visual information processing.* New York: Academic Press.

Chase, W. G., & Simon, H. A. (1973). The mind's eye in chess. In W. G. Chase (Ed.), *Visual information processing*. New York: Academic Press.

Cheney, D. L., & Seyfarth, R. M. (1990). *How monkeys see the world*. Chicago: Chicago University Press.

Cheney, D. L., & Seyfarth, R. M. (1992). Multiple book review of how monkeys see the world. *Behavioral and Brain Sciences, 15,* 135–182.

Cheng, P. W., & Holyoak, K. J. (1985). Pragmatic reasoning schemas. *Cognitive Psychology, 17,* 391–416.

Cheng, P. W., & Holyoak, K. J. (1989). On the natural selection of reasoning theories. *Cognition, 33,* 285–313.

Cheng, P. W., Holyoak, K. J., Nisbett, R. J., & Oliver, L. M. (1986). Pragmatic versus syntactic approaches to training deductive reasoning. *Cognitive Psychology, 18,* 293–328.

Cherry, E. C. (1953). Some experiments on the recognition of speech with one and two ears. *Journal of the Acoustical Society of America, 25,* 975–979.

Chevalier-Skolniroff, S., & Poirier, F. (Eds.). (1977). *Primate bio-social development*. New York: Garland.

Chi, M. T. H., Feltovich, P. J., & Glaser, R. (1981). Categorization and representation of physics problems by experts and novices. *Cognitive Science, 5,* 121–152.

Chi, M. T. H., Glaser, R., & Farr, M. J. (Eds.). (1988). *The nature of expertise*. Hillsdale, NJ: Erlbaum.

Chiesi, H. L., Spilich, G. J., & Voss, J. F. (1979). Acquisition of domain-related information in relation to high and low domain knowledge. *Journal of Verbal Learning and Verbal Behavior, 18,* 257–273.

Chomsky, N. (1957). *Syntactic structures*. The Hague: Mouton.

Chomsky, N. (1959). Review of Skinner's Verbal Behavior. *Language, 35,* 26–58.

Chomsky, N. (1965a). *Aspects of the theory of syntax*. Cambridge, MA: MIT Press.

Chomsky, N. (1965b). *Cartesian linguistics*. Cambridge, MA: MIT Press.

Chomsky, N. (1972). *Language and mind* (Enlarged ed.). New York: Harcourt Brace Jovanovich.

Chomsky, N. (1976). On the nature of language. In S. R. Harnad, H. Steklis, & J. Lancaster (Eds.), *Annals of the New York Academy of Sciences* (Vol. 280). New York: New York Academy of Sciences.

Chomsky, N. (1979). Human language and other semiotic systems. *Semiotica,* 31–44.

Chomsky, N. (1980). *Rules and representations*. New York: Columbia University Press.

Christianson, S. -A. (1989). Flashbulb memories: Special, but not so special. *Memory and Cognition, 17,* 435–443.

Christianson, S. -A. (Ed.). (1992). *The handbook of emotion and memory: Research and theory*. Hillsdale, NJ: Erlbaum.

Churchland, P. M., & Churchland, P. S. (1990, January). Could a machine think? *Scientific American, 262,* 32–37.

Churchland, P. S. (1987, May 6). *Epistemology in the age of neuroscience*. Paper presented at a conference on The Brain: Philosophy, Psychology, and Artificial Intelligence. University of Pittsburgh, Pittsburgh, PA.

Clark, A. (1990). *Microcognition*. Cambridge, MA: MIT Press.

Clark, E. V., & Hecht, B. F. (1983). Comprehension, production and language acquisition. *Annual Review of Psychology, 34,* 325–350.

Clark, H. H. (1977). Inferences in comprehension. In D. Laberge & S. J. Samuels (Eds.), *Basic processes in reading: Perception and comprehension.* Hillsdale, NJ: Erlbaum.

Clark, H. H., & Gerrig, R. J. (1984). On the pretense theory of irony. *Journal of Experimental Psychology: General, 113,* 121–126.

Clark, H. H., & Haviland, S. E. (1977). Comprehension and the given-new contract. In R. O. Freedle (Ed.), *Discourse production and comprehension.* Norwood, NJ: Ablex.

Clutton-Brock, T. H., & Harvey, P. H. (Eds.). (1978). *Readings in sociobiology.* San Francisco: Freeman.

Cohen, D. (1979). *J. B. Watson.* London: Routledge & Kegan Paul.

Cohen, G., Conway, M. A., & Maylor, E. A. (1994). Flashbulb memories in older adults. *Psychology and Aging, 9,* 454–463.

Collier, G., Johnson, D. F., & Morgan, C. (1992). The magnitude of reinforcement function in closed and open economies. *Journal of the Experimental Analysis of Behavior, 57,* 81–89.

Collins, A. M., Gathercole, S. E., Conway, M., & Morris, P. E. (1993). *Theories of memory.* Hillsdale, NJ: Erlbaum.

Collins, A. M., & Loftus, E. F. (1975). A spreading-activation theory of semantic processing. *Psychological Review, 82,* 407–428.

Collins, A. M., & Quillian, M. R. (1969). Retrieval time from semantic memory. *Journal of Verbal Learning and Verbal Behavior, 8,* 240–247.

Colwill, R. M., & Rescorla, R. A. (1986). Associative structures in instrumental learning. *Psychology of Learning and Motivation, 20,* 55–104.

Condon, W. S., & Sander, L. (1974). Neonate movement is synchronized with adult speech: Interactional participation and language acquisition. *Science, 183,* 99–101.

Conrad, R. (1964). Acoustic confusions in immediate memory. *British Journal of Psychology, 55,* 75–84.

Conway, M. (1995). *Flashbulb memories.* Hillsdale, NJ: Erlbaum.

Conway, M. A., Bruce, D., & Sehulster, J. R. (1998). New directions in autobiographical memory research. *Applied Cognitive Psychology, 12,* 297–303.

Conway, M. A., Cohen, G., & Stanhope, N. (1991). On the very long-term retention of knowledge acquired through formal education: Twelve years of cognitive psychology. *Journal of Experimental Psychology: General, 120,* 395–409.

Cook, D. G., Stopfer, M., & Carew, T. J. (1991). Identification of a reinforcement pathway necessary for operant conditioning of head waving in Aplysia Californica. *Behavioral and Neural Biology, 55,* 313–337.

Corballis, M. C. (1991). *The lopsided ape: Evolution of the generative mind.* New York: Oxford University Press.

Corbett, A. T., & Dosher, B. A. (1978). Instrument inferences in sentence encoding. *Journal of Verbal Learning and Verbal Behavior, 17,* 479–491.

Cosmides, L. (1987). The logic of social exchange: Has natural selection shaped how humans reason? *Cognition, 31,* 187–276.

Cosmides, L., & Tooby, J. (1997). The modular nature of human intelligence. In A. B. Scheibel & J. W. Schopf (Eds.), *The origin and evolution of intelligence* (pp. 71–102). Sudbury, MA: Jones & Bartlett.

Coss, R. G. (1985). Comparative restraints on learning: Phylogenetic and synaptic interpretations. In N. M. Weinberger, J. L. McGaugh, & G. Lynch (Eds.), *Memory systems of the brain: Animal and human cognitive processes.* New York: Guilford.

Cotman, C., & McGaugh, J. E. (1980). *Behavioral neuroscience: An introduction.* Orlando, FL: Academic Press.

Cotton, J. W. (1955). On making predictions from Hull's theory. *Psychological Review, 62,* 303–314.

Coughlin, W. J. (1953, March). The great mokusatsu mistake. *Harper's.*

Cox, J. R., & Griggs, R. A. (1982). The effects of experience on performance in Wason's selection task. *Memory and Cognition, 10,* 496–502.

Craik, F. I. M. (1979). Human memory. *Annual Review of Psychology, 30,* 63–102.

Craik, F. I. M., & Lockhart, R. S. (1972). Levels of processing: A framework for memory research. *Journal of Verbal Learning and Verbal Behavior, 11,* 671–684.

Craik, F. I. M., & McIntyre, J. S. (1986, November). *Age differences in memory for facts and their sources.* Paper presented at meeting of the Psychonomic Society, New Orleans, LA.

Craik, F. I. M., Moroz, T. M., Moscovitch, M., Stuss, D. T., Winocur, G., Tulving, E., & Kapur, S. (1999). In search of the self: A positron emission tomography study. *Psychological Science, 10,* 26–34.

Craik, F. I. M., & Tulving, E. (1975). Depth of processing and the retention of words in episodic memory. *Journal of Experimental Psychology: General, 104,* 268–294.

Crain, S. (1991). Language acquisition in the absence of experience. *Behavioral and Brain Sciences, 14,* 597–650.

Crawford, C. (1983). *Sociobiology: Of what value to psychology?* Paper presented at the annual meeting of the American Psychological Association, Anaheim, CA.

Crawford, J. (Eds.). (1992). *Language loyalties: A source book on the Official English controversy.* Chicago: University of Chicago Press.

Crick, F. (1994). *The astonishing hypothesis: The scientific search for the soul.* New York: Scribners's.

Cromer, R. F. (1974). The development of language and cognition: The cognition hypothesis. In B. Foss (Ed.), *New perspectives in child development.* Baltimore: Penguin.

Cromer, R. F. (1981). Reconceptualizing language acquisition and cognitive development. In R. L. Schiefelbusch & D. D. Bricker (Eds.), *Early language: Acquisition and intervention.* Baltimore: University Park Press.

Crutcher, K. A. (1991). Anatomical correlates of neural plasticity. In J. L. Martinez & R. P. Kesner (Eds.), *Learning and memory: A biological view* (2nd ed.). San Diego: Academic Press.

Csikszentmihalyi, M. (1996). *Creativity.* New York: HarperCollins.

Cummins, D. D. (1998). Social norms and other minds: The evolutionary roots of higher cognition. In D. D. Cummins & C. Allen (Eds.), *The evolution of mind* (pp. 30–50). New York: Oxford University Press.

Cummins, D. D., & Allen, C. (Eds.). (1998). *The evolution of mind.* New York: Oxford University Press.

Curtis, H. (1968). *Biology.* New York: Worth.

Dachowski, L., & Flaherty, C. F. (Eds.). (1991). *Current topics in animal learning: Brain, emotion, and cognition.* Hillsdale, NJ: Erlbaum.

Dale, P. S. (1976). *Language development* (2nd ed.). New York: Holt, Rinehart & Winston.

Daly, M., & Wilson, M. (1978). *Sex, evolution and behavior: Adaptations for reproduction.* North Scituate, MA: Duxbury Press.

Daly, M., & Wilson, M. (1982). Abuse and neglect of children in evolutionary perspective. In R. D. Alexander & D. Tinkle (Eds.), *Natural selection and social behavior.* New York: Chiron Press.

Daly, M., Wilson, M., & Weghorst, S. (1982). Male sexual jealousy. *Ethology and Sociobiology, 3,* 11–27.

Damasio, A. (1994). *Descartes' Error: Emotion, reason and the human brain.* New York: G. P. Putnam.

Damasio, A. R., & Damasio, H. (1993). Brain and language. In Anon. (Ed.), *Mind and Brain.* New York: Freeman.

Daniels, D. (1983). The evolution of concealed ovulation and self-deception. *Ethology and Sociobiology, 4,* 69–87.

Danks, J. H., & Griffin, J. (1997). Reading and translation: A psycholinguistic perspective. In J. H. Danks, G. M. Shreve, S. B. Fountain, & M. K. McBeath (Eds.), *Cognitive processes in translation and interpreting* (pp. 161–175). Thousand Oaks, CA: Sage.

Danks, J. H., Shreve, G. M., Fountain, S. B., & McBeath, M. K. (Eds.). (1997). *Cognitive processes in translation and interpreting.* Thousand Oaks, CA: Sage.

D'Aquili, E. G. (1978). The neurobiological bases of myth and concepts of deity. *Zygon, 13,* 257–275.

Darwin, C. (1965). *The expression of emotion in man and animals.* Chicago: University of Chicago Press. (Original work published 1872)

Darwin, C. J., Turvey, M. T., & Crowder, R. G. (1972). The auditory analogue of the Sperling partial report procedure: Evidence for brief auditory storage. *Cognitive Psychology, 3,* 225–267.

Dasen, P. R. (1972). Cross-cultural Piagetian research: A summary. *Journal of Cross-Cultural Psychology, 3,* 23–39. Reprinted in J. Berry & P. Dasen (Eds.), *Culture and cognition: Readings in cross-cultural psychology.* London: Methuen, 1974.

Davey, G. C. L. (Ed.). (1987a). *Cognitive processes and Pavlovian conditioning in humans.* New York: Wiley.

Davey, G. C. L. (1987b). An integration of human and animal models of conditioning: Associations, cognitions, and attributions. In G. C. L. Davey (Ed.), *Cognitive processes and Pavlovian conditioning in humans.* New York: Wiley.

Davidson, I. (1991). The archeology of language origins: A review. *Antiquity, 65,* 39–48.

Davidson, I., & Noble, W. (1993a). When did language begin. In G. Burenhalt (Ed.), *The first humans: Human origins and history to 10,000 B.C.* (p. 46). New York: HarperSanFrancisco.

Davidson, I., & Noble, W. (1993b). Tools and language in human evolution. In K. R. Gibson & T. Ingold (Eds.), *Tools, language, and cognition in human evolution* (pp. 363–388). Cambridge, England: Cambridge University Press.

Davis, S., Butcher, S. P., & Morris, R. G. (1992). NMDA receptor antagonist D-2amino-5-phosphonopentanoate (D-AP) impairs spatial learning and LTP in vivo at intracerebral concentrations comparable to those that block LTP in vitro. *Journal of Neuroscience, 12,* 21–34.

Davis, W. J. (1986). Invertebrate model systems. In J. L. Martinez & R. P. Kesner (Eds.), *Learning and memory: A psychological view.* Orlando, FL: Academic Press.

Dawes, R. M. (1988). *Rational choice in an uncertain world.* San Diego: Harcourt Brace Jovanovich.

Dawkins, R. (1976). *The selfish gene.* New York: Oxford University Press.

Dawkins, R. (1996). *Climbing Mount Improbable.* New York: Norton.

Dawson, M. E., & Schell, A. M. (1987). Human autonomic conditioning and skeletal classical conditioning: The role of conscious cognitive factors. In G. C. L. Davey (Ed.), *Cognitive processes and Pavlovian conditioning in humans* (pp. 27–55). New York: Wiley.

D'Azevedo, W. L. (1962). Uses of the past in Gola discourse. *Journal of African History, 3,* 11–34.

Deacon, T. W. (1992). The human brain. In S. Jones, R. Martin, & D. Pilbeam (Eds.), *The Cambridge encyclopedia of evolution* (pp. 115–123). Cambridge, England: Cambridge University Press.

Deacon, T. W. (1992). Biological aspects of language. In S. Jones, R. Martin, & D. Pilbeam (Eds.), *The Cambridge encyclopedia of evolution* (pp. 128–133). Cambridge, England: Cambridge University Press.

Deacon, T. W. (1997). Evolution and intelligence—Beyond the argument from design. In A. B. Scheibel & J. W. Schopf (Eds.), *The origin and evolution of intelligence* (pp. 103–136). Sudbury, MA: Jones & Bartlett.

Dean, D. (1993). Vocal grooming: Man the schmoozer. *Behavioral and Brain Sciences, 16,* 699–700.

Dean, J. (1998). Animats and what they can tell us. *Trends in Cognitive Sciences, 2,* 60–67.

De Castro, J., Arsuaga, H., Carbonell, E., Rosas, A., Martinez, I., & Mosquera, M. (1997). A homonid from the lower Pleistocene of Atapuerca, Spain: Possible ancestor to Neandertals and modern humans. *Science, 276,* 1392–1395.

D'Esposito, M., Zarahn, E., & Aguirre, G. K. (1999). Event-related functional MRI: Implications for cognitive psychology. *Psychological Bulletin, 125,* 155–164.

Deffenbacher, K. A. (1991). A maturing of research on the behaviour of eyewitnesses. *Applied Cognitive Psychology, 5,* 377–402.

de Groot, A. M. B. (1997). The cognitive study of translation and interpretation: Three approaches. In J. H. Danks, G. M. Shreve, S. B. Fountain, & M. K. McBeath (Eds.), *Cognitive processes in translation and interpreting* (pp. 25–56). Thousand Oaks, CA: Sage.

de Groot, A. M. B., & Kroll, J. F. (Eds.). (1997). *Tutorials in bilingualism: Psycholinguistic perspectives.* Mahwah, NJ: Erlbaum.

Del Cerro, S., Larson, J., Oliver, M. W., & Lynch, G. (1990). Development of hippocampal long-term potentiation is reduced by recently introduced calpain inhibitors. *Brain Research, 530,* 91–95.

Delgado, J. (1969). *Physical control of the mind.* New York: Harper & Row.

Delgado, J. (1976). New orientations in brain stimulation in man. In A. Wauquier & E. Rolls (Eds.), *Brain-stimulation reward.* Amsterdam: North Holland.

Delson, E. (Ed.). (1985). *Ancestors: The hard evidence.* New York: Alan R. Liss.

Dennett, D. (1978). *Brainstorms.* Cambridge, MA: Bradford/MIT Press.

Dennett, D. (1978). Skinner skinned. In D. Dennett (Ed.), *Brainstorms.* Cambridge, MA: Bradford/MIT.

Dennett, D. C. (1991). *Consciousness explained.* Boston: Little, Brown.

Dennett, D. C., & Kinsbourne, M. (1992). Time and the observer: The where and when of consciousness in the brain. *Behavioral and Brain Sciences, 15,* 183–248.

Dennis, M. (1980). Language acquisition in a single hemisphere: Semantic organization. In D. Caplan (Ed.), *Biological studies of mental processes.* Cambridge, MA: MIT Press.

Derwing, B. L. (1973). *Transformational grammar as a theory of language acquisition.* Cambridge, England: Cambridge University Press.

Desimone, R. (1992). The physiology of memory: Recording of things past. *Science, 258,* 245–246.

de Sousa, R. (1991). *The rationality of emotion.* Cambridge, MA: MIT Press.

Desrochers, A., Gelinas, C., & Wieland, L. D. (1989). An application of the mnemonic keyword method to the acquisition of German nouns and their grammatical gender. *Journal of Educational Psychology, 81,* 25–32.

Desrochers, A., Wieland, L. D., & Cote, M. (1991). Instructional effects in the use of the mnemonic keyword method for learning German nouns and their grammatical gender. *Applied Cognitive Psychology, 5,* 19–36.

Deutsch, J. A. (1956). The inadequacy of the Hullian derivations of reasoning and latent learning. *Psychological Review, 63,* 389–399.

De Villiers, J. G., & De Villiers, P. A. (1978). *Language acquisition.* Cambridge, MA: Harvard University Press.

de Waal, F., & Lanting, F. (1998). *Bonobo: The forgotten ape.* Los Angeles: University of California Press.

Dewsbury, D. A. (1981). Effects of novelty on copulatory behavior: The Coolidge Effect and related phenomena. *Psychological Bulletin, 89,* 464–482.

Diamond, S. S. (1995, July). *The clash between values and evidence in death penalty decisions.* Paper presented at Interamerican Congress of Psychology, San Juan, Puerto Rico.

Dickemann, M. (1982). Paternal confidence and dowry competition: A biocultural analysis of Purdah. In R. D. Alexander & D. Tinkle (Eds.), *Natural selection and social behavior.* New York: Chiron Press.

Dickenson, A. (1989). Expectancy theory in animal classical conditioning. In S. B. Klein & R. R. Mowrer (Eds.), *Contemporary learning theories: Pavlovian conditioning and the status of traditional learning theory* (pp. 279–308). Hillsdale, NJ: Erlbaum.

Dixon, T. R., & Horton, D. L. (Eds.). (1968). *Verbal behavior and general behavior theory.* Englewood Cliffs, NJ: Prentice Hall.

Dodds, E. R. (1951). *The Greeks and the irrational.* Los Angeles: University of California Press.

Dollard, J., Doob, L., Miller, N., Mowrer, O., & Sears, R. (1939). *Frustration and aggression.* New Haven, CT: Yale University Press.

Dollard, J., & Miller, N. (1950). *Personality and psychotherapy.* New York: McGraw-Hill.

Domjon, M. (1980). *Ingestional aversion learning: Unique and general processes. Advances in the study of behavior* (Vol. II). New York: Academic Press.

Domjon, M. (1987). Animal learning comes of age. *American Psychologist, 42,* 56–64.

Donald, M. (1991). *Origins of the modern mind: Three stages in the evolution of culture and cognition.* Cambridge, MA: Harvard University Press.

Donald, M. (1993). Precis of Origins of the modern mind: Three stages in the evolution of culture and cognition. *Behavioral and Brain Sciences, 16,* 737–791.

Donaldson, M. (1978). *Children's minds.* New York: Norton.

Donders, F. C. (1969). Over de snelheid van psychische processen. Ondenoikingen gedaan in het Psychologish Laboratorium der Utrechtsche Hoogeschool: 1868–1869. *Tweede Reeks, 11,* 92–120. In W. G. Koster (Ed. & trans.), Attention and performance 11. *Acta Psychologica, 30,* 412–431.

Donegan, N. H., & Thompson, R. F. (1991). The search for the engram. In J. L. Martinez & R. P. Kesner (Eds.), *Learning and memory: A biological view* (2nd ed.). San Diego: Academic Press.

Dooling, D. J., & Lachman, R. (1971). Effects of comprehension on retention of prose. *Journal of Experimental Psychology, 88,* 216–222.

Dooling, D. J., & Mullet, R. L. (1973). Locus of thematic effects in retention of prose. *Journal of Experimental Psychology, 97,* 404–406.

Doolittle, W., & Sapienza, C. (1980). Selfish genes, the phenotype paradigm and gene evolution. *Nature, 284,* 601–603.

Doris, J. (Ed.). (1991). *The suggestibility of children's recollections: Implications for eyewitness testimony.* Washington, DC: American Psychological Association.

Downing, D. J., Sternberg, R. J., & Ross, B. H. (1985). Multicausal inference: Evaluation of evidence in causally complex situations. *Journal of Experimental Psychology: General, 114,* 239–263.

Dreyfus, H., & Dreyfus, S. (1990). Making a mind vs. modelling the brain: Artificial intelligence at a branch-point. *Artificial Intelligence, 117.* Reprinted in Boden (1990). (Original work published 1988)

Dreyfus, H. L., & Dreyfus, S. E. (1990). *Mind over machine: The power of human intuition and expertise in the era of the computer.* New York: The Free Press.

Dubitsky, T. M. (1980). *The effects of contextual knowledge on drawing inferences from conversation.* Master's thesis, Kansas State University.

Duchan, J. F., Bruder, G. A., & Hewitt, L. E. (Eds.). (1995). *Deixis in narrative: A cognitive science perspective.* Hillsdale, NJ: Erlbaum.

Dunbar, R. (1995, February 11). Are you lonesome tonight? *New Scientist, 145,* 26–31.

Dunbar, R. I. M. (1993). Coevolution of neocortical size, group size, and language in humans. *Behavioral and Brain Sciences, 16,* 681–737.

Durham, W. H. (1976). Resource competition and human aggression. *Quarterly Review of Biology, 51,* 385–415.

Durham, W. H. (1978). Toward a coevolutionary theory of human biology and culture. In D. Caplan (Ed.), *Biological studies of mental processes.* Cambridge, MA: MIT Press.

Durham, W. H. (1982). Interactions of genetic and cultural evolution: Models and examples. *Human Ecology, 10,* 289–323.

Durlach, P. J. (1989). Learning and performance in Pavlovian conditioning: Are failures of contiguity failures of learning or performance? In S. B. Klein & R. R. Mowrer (Eds.), *Contemporary learning theories: Pavlovian conditioning and the status of traditional learning theory* (pp. 19–59). Hillsdale, NJ: Erlbaum.

Eacott, M. J. (1999). Memory for the events of early childhood. *Current Directions in Psychological Science, 8,* 45–49.

Ebbinghaus, H. (1964). *Memory.* New York: Dover. (Original work published 1885)

Eibl-Eibesfeldt, I. (1975). *Ethology* (2nd ed.). New York: Holt, Rinehart & Winston.

Eich, E. (1995). Searching for mood dependent memory. *Psychological Science, 6,* 67–75.

Eichen, E. B., & Mayberry, R. I. (1991). The long-lasting advantage of learning sign language in childhood: Another look at the critical period for language acquisition. *Journal of Memory and Language, 30,* 486–512.

Eichenbaum, H., & Bunsey, M. (1995). On the binding of associations in memory: Clues from studies on the role of the hippocampal region in paired-associate learning. *Current Directions in Psychological Science, 4,* 19–23.

Eichenbaum, H., Otto, T., & Cohen, N. J. (1994). Two functional components of the hippocampal memory system. *Behavioral and Brain Sciences, 17,* 449–518.

Eilers, R. E. (1980). Infant speech perception: History and mystery. In G. H. Yeni-Komshian, J. F. Kavanaugh, & C. A. Ferguson (Eds.), *Child phonology. Vol. 2: Perception.* New York: Academic Press.

Eimas, P. D., Siqueland, J. R., Jusczyk, P., & Vigorito, J. (1971). Speech perception in infants. *Science, 171,* 303–306.

Einstein, G. O., & McDaniel, M. A. (1996). Retrieval processes in prospective memory: Theoretical approaches and some new empirical findings. In M. Brandimonte, G. Einstein, & M. McDaniel (Eds.), *Prospective memory: Theory and applications* (pp. 115–142). Mahwah, NJ: Erlbaum.

Ekman, P. (1982). *Emotion in the human face.* New York: Cambridge University Press.

Ekman, P., & Davidson, R. (Eds.). (1994). *Nature of emotion: Basic questions.* New York: Oxford University Press.

Eliot, A. J. (1981). *Child language.* New York: Cambridge University Press.

Elkind, D. (1981). Recent research in cognitive and language development. In L. T. Benjamin (Ed.), *The G. Stanley Hall lecture series* (Vol. I). Washington, DC: American Psychological Association.

Elkind, D., & Flavell, J. H. (1969). *Studies in cognitive development.* New York: Oxford University Press.

Ellenberger, H. (1970). *The discovery of the unconscious.* New York: Basic Books.

Ellis, H. C. (1991). Focussed attention and depressive deficits in memory. *Journal of Experimental Psychology: General, 120,* 310–312.

Ellis, H. C., & Ashbrook, P. W. (1989). The "state" of mood and memory research: A selective review. *Journal of Social Behavior and Personality, 4,* 1–21.

Ellis, H. D., & Gunter, H. L. (1999). Asperger syndrome: A simple matter of white matter. *Trends in Cognitive Sciences, 3,* 192–200.

Elman, J. L., Bates, E. A., Johnson, M., Karmiloff-Smith, A., Parisis, D., & Plunkett, K. (1997). *Rethinking innateness: A connectionist perspective on development.* Cambridge, MA: MIT Press.

Elstein, A. S., Shulman, L. S., & Sprafka, S. A. (1978). *Medical problem solving: An analysis of clinical reasoning.* Cambridge, MA: Harvard University Press.

Elwork, A., & Sales, B. D. (1985). Jury Instructions. In S. M. Kassin & L. S. Wrightsman (Eds.), *The psychology of evidence and trial procedure* (pp. 280–297). Beverly Hills, CA: Sage.

Enns, J. T. (Ed.). (1990). *The development of attention.* Amsterdam: North-Holland.

Epstein, R. (1991). Skinner, creativity, and the problem of spontaneous behavior. *Psychological Science, 2,* 362–370.

Erickson, T. D., & Mattson, M. E. (1981). From words to meaning: A semantic illusion. *Journal of Verbal Learning and Verbal Behavior, 20,* 540–551.

Ericsson, K. A., & Kintsch, W. (1995). Long-term working memory. *Psychological Review, 102,* 211–245.

Ericsson, K. A., & Polson, P. G. (1988a). A cognitive analysis of exceptional memory for restaurant orders. In M. T. H. Chi, R. Glaser, & M. J. Farr (Eds.), *The nature of expertise.* Hillsdale, NJ: Erlbaum.

Ericsson, K. A., & Polson, P. G. (1988b). An experimental analysis of the mechanisms of a memory skill. *Journal of Experimental Psychology: Learning, Memory, and Cognition, 14,* 305–316.

Ericsson, K. A., & Smith, J. (Eds.). (1991). *Toward a general theory of expertise: Prospects and limits.* Cambridge, England: Cambridge University Press.

Erikson, E. (1939). Observations on Sioux education. *Journal of Psychology, 7,* 101–156.

Erikson, E. H. (1963). *Childhood and society* (2nd ed.). New York: Norton.

Eron, L. (1982). Parent-child interactions, television violence, and aggression of children. *American Psychologist, 37,* 197–211.

Essock-Vitale, S. M. (1984). The reproductive success of wealthy Americans. *Ethology and Sociobiology, 5,* 4–49.

Estes, W. K. (1950). Toward a statistical theory of learning. *Psychological Review, 57,* 94–107.

Estes, W. K. (1972). Reinforcement in human behavior. *American Scientist, 60,* 723–729.

Estes, W. K. (1991a). What is cognitive science? *Psychological Science, 2,* 282.

Estes, W. K. (1991b). Cognitive architectures from the standpoint of an experimental psychologist. *Annual Review of Psychology, 42,* 1–28.

Estes, W. K., Koch, S., MacCorquodale, K., Meehl, P., Mueller, C. G., Schoenfeld, W. N., & Verplanck, W. S. (1954). *Modern learning theory.* New York: Appleton-Century-Crofts.

Evans, J. St. B. T. (1982). *The psychology of deductive reasoning.* London: Routledge & Kegan Paul.

Falk, D. (1992). *Braindance: New discoveries about human brain evolution.* New York: Holt.

Falk, D. (1987). Hominid paleoneurology. *Annual Review of Anthropology, 16,* 13–30.

Farb, P. (1978). *Humankind.* Boston: Houghton Mifflin.

Farber, S. (1981). Telltale behavior of twins. *Psychology Today, 15*(1), 58–62, 79–80.

Farley, J., & Alkon, D. L. (1985). Cellular mechanisms of learning, memory, and information storage. *Annual Review of Psychology, 36,* 419–494.

Farnham-Diggory, S. (Ed.). (1972). *Information processing in children.* New York: Academic Press.

Faux, S. F., & Miller, H. L. (1984). Evolutionary speculations on the oligarchic development of Mormon polygyny. *Ethology and Sociobiology, 5,* 15–31.

Fayol, M., & Montell, J. -M. (1988). The notion of script: From general to developmental and social psychology. *European Bulletin of Cognitive Psychology, 8,* 335–361.

Ferster, C. B., & Skinner, B. F. (1957). *Schedules of reinforcement.* Englewood Cliffs, NJ: Prentice Hall.

Fillmore, C. J. (1968). The case for case. In E. Bach & R. Harms (Eds.), *Universals in linguistic theory.* New York: Holt, Rinehart & Winston.

Fillmore, C. J. (1971). Verbs of judging: An exercise in semantic description. In C. J. Fillmore & D. T. Langendoen (Eds.), *Studies in linguistic semantics.* New York: Holt, Rinehart & Winston.

Finke, R. A. (1989). *Principles of mental imagery.* Cambridge: MIT Press.

Finke, R. A. (1995). Creative insight and preinventive forms. in R. J. Sternberg & J. E. Davidson (Eds.), *The nature of insight.* (pp. 255–280). Cambridge MA: MIT Press.

Finkenauer, C., Luminet, O., Gisle, L., El-Ahmadi, A., van der Linden, M., & Philippot, P. (1998). Flashbulb memories and the underlying mechanisms of their formation: Toward an emotional-integrative model. *Memory and Cognition, 26,* 516–531.

Fischer, S. D., & Siple, P. (Eds.). (1990). *Theoretical issues in sign language research. Vol. I. Linguistics.* Chicago: University of Chicago Press.

Fischhoff, B. (1975). Hindsight and foresight: The effect of outcome knowledge on judgment under uncertainty. *Journal of Experimental Psychology: Human Perception and Performance, 1,* 288–299.

Fischhoff, B. (1977). Perceived informativeness of facts. *Journal of Experimental Psychology: Human Perception and Performance, 3,* 349–358.

Fischhoff, B., & Beyth, R. (1975). "I knew it would happen"—Remember probabilities of once-future things. *Organizational Behavior and Human Performance, 13,* 1–16.

Fishbein, H. D. (1976). *Evolution, development and children's learning*. Santa Monica, CA: Goodyear.

Fisher, G., & Cummings, R. (1990). *The survival guide for kids with LD*. Minneapolis, MN: Free Spirit Publishing, Inc.

Fisher, H. E. (1992). *Anatomy of love: The natural history of monogamy, adultery, and divorce*. New York: Norton.

Fisher, R. P., & Geiselman, R. E. (1988). Enhancing eyewitness memory with the cognitive interview. In M. M. Gruneberg, P. E. Morris, & R. N. Sykes (Eds.), *Practical aspects of memory: Current research and issues. Vol. I. Memory in everyday life* (pp. 34–39). Chichester, England: Wiley.

Fiske, S. T., Bersoff, D. N., Borgida, E., Deaux, K., & Hellman, M. E. (1991). Social science research on trial: Use of sex stereotyping research in Price Waterhouse v. Hopkins. *American Psychologist, 46,* 1049–1060.

Fiske, S. T., & Taylor, S. E. (1990). *Social cognition* (2nd ed.). Reading, MA: Addison-Wesley.

Fitzgerald, J. M. (1986). Autobiographical memory: A developmental perspective. In D. C. Rubin (Ed.), *Autobiographical memory* (pp. 122–133). Cambridge, England: Cambridge University Press.

Fitzgerald, J. M., & Lawrence, R. (1984). Autobiographical memory across the life span. *Journal of Gerontology, 39,* 692–699.

Fivush, R., & Schwarzmueller, A. (1998). Children remember childhood: Implications for childhood amnesia. *Applied Cognitive Psychology, 12,* 455–473.

Flanagan, O. (1981, June 12). *The Freud-Lamarck connections: The philosophical foundations of the penis-envy hypothesis*. Paper presented at Cheiron XIII, River Falls, WI.

Flanagan, O. (1982a). Virtue, sex and gender: Some philosophical reflections on the moral psychology debate. *Ethics, 92,* 499–512.

Flanagan, O. (1982b). A reply to Lawrence Kohlberg. *Ethics, 92,* 529–532.

Flanagan, O. (1982c). Moral structures? *Philosophy of the Social Sciences, 12,* 255–270.

Flanagan, O. (1983). *The sciences of the mind*. Cambridge, MA: MIT Press.

Flanagan, O. (1993). *Consciousness reconsidered*. Cambridge, MA: MIT Press/A Bradford Book.

Flavell, J. H. (1971). Stage related properties of cognitive development. *Cognitive Psychology, 2,* 421–453.

Flavell, J. H. (1977). *Cognitive development*. Englewood Cliffs, NJ: Prentice Hall.

Flavell, J. H. (1979). Metacognition and cognitive monitoring. A new area of cognitive developmental inquiry. *American Psychologist, 34,* 906–911.

Flavell, J. H. (1982). On cognitive development. *Child Development, 53,* 1–10.

Flavell, J. H. (1999). Cognitive development: Children's knowledge about the mind. *Annual Review of Psychology, 50,* 21–45.

Flavell, J. H., Green, F. L., Flavell, E. R., & Grossman, J. B. (1997). The development of children's knowledge about inner speech. *Child Development, 68,* 39–47.

Flavell, J. H., & Wellman, H. M. (1977). Metamemory. In R. Kail & J. Hogen (Eds.), *Perspectives on the development of memory and cognition*. Hillsdale, NJ: Erlbaum.

Flavell, J. H., & Wohlwill, J. (1969). Formal and functional aspects of cognitive development. In D. Elkind & J. H. Flavell, *Studies in cognitive development*. New York: Oxford University Press.

Fletcher, P., & Garman, M. (Eds.). (1986). *Language acquisition* (2nd ed.). Cambridge, England: Cambridge University Press.

Flinn, M. (1982). Uterine vs. agnatic kinship variability and associated cousin marriage preferences: An evolutionary biological analysis. In R. D. Alexander & D. Tinkle (Eds.), *Natural selection and social behavior.* New York: Chiron Press.

Flinn, M. V., & Alexander, R. D. (1982). Culture theory: The developing synthesis from biology. *Human Ecology, 10,* 383–400.

Fodor, J., & Pylyshyn, Z. W. (1988). Connectionism and cognitive architecture: A Critical analysis. *Cognition, 28,* 3–71.

Fodor, J. D., & Crain, S. (1987). Simplicity and generality of rules in language acquisition. In B. MacWhinney (Ed.), *Mechanisms of language acquisition.* Hillsdale, NJ: Erlbaum.

Foley, R. (1998). The context of human genetic evolution. *Genome Research, 8,* 339–347.

Foley, R. A. (1991). The silence of the past. *Nature, 353,* 114–115.

Fouts, R. S., & Rigby, R. L. (1980). Man-chimpanzee communication. In T. A. Sebeok & J. Umiker-Sebeok (Eds.), *Speaking of apes: A critical anthology of two-way communication with man.* New York: Plenum.

Fox, J. L. (1983). Debate on learning theory is shifting. *Science, 222,* 1219–1222.

Frank, R. H. (1988). *Passions within reason: The strategic role of the emotions.* New York: Norton.

Frederick, B. P., & Olmi, D. J. (1994). Children with attention-deficit/hyperactivity disorder: A review of the literature on social skills deficits. *Psychology in the Schools, 31,* 288–296.

Frederickson, R. (1992). *Repressed memories: A journey to recovery from sexual abuse.* New York: Simon & Schuster.

Freedman, D. G. (1974). *Human infancy: A biological perspective.* Hillsdale, NJ: Erlbaum.

French, R. M. (1999). Catastrophic forgetting in connectionist networks. *Trends in Cognitive Sciences, 3,* 128–135.

Freud, S., & Breuer, J. (1895/1966). *Studies in hysteria.* New York: Avon.

Frijda, N. (1986). *The emotions.* Cambridge, England: Cambridge University Press.

Frith, U. (1997). The neurocognitive basis of autism. *Trends in Cognitive Sciences, 1,* 73–77.

Furedy, J. J., & Riley, D. M. (1987). Human Pavlovian autonomic conditioning and the cognitive paradigm. In G. C. L. Davey (Ed.), *Cognitive processes and Pavlovian conditioning in humans* (pp. 1–25). New York: Wiley.

Furth, H. G. (1969). *Piaget and knowledge: Theoretical foundations.* Englewood Cliffs, NJ: Prentice Hall, (2nd ed.). Chicago: University of Chicago Press, 1981.

Gabriel, M., Sparenborc, S. P., & Stolar, N. (1986). The neurobiology of memory. In J. E. LeDoux & W. Hirst (Eds.), *Mind and brain: Dialogues in cognitive neuroscience.* Cambridge, England: Cambridge University Press.

Gabrieli, J. D. E. (1998). Cognitive neuroscience of human memory. *Annual Review of Psychology, 49,* 87–115.

Gabrieli, J. D. E., Fleischman, D. A., Keane, M. M., Reminger, S. L., & Morrell, F. (1995). Double dissociation between memory systems underlying explicit and implicit memory in the human brain. *Psychological Science, 6,* 76–82.

Gabunia, L., & Vekus, A. (1995). A Plio-Pleistocene hominid from Dmanisi, East Georgia, Caucasus. *Nature, 373,* 509–511.

Galef, B. (1983, April 10). *Tradition and social learning in animals.* Paper presented at the second National Zoological Park Symposium, Washington, DC.

Galizio, M. (1979). Contingency-shaped and rule-governed behavior: Instructional control of human loss avoidance. *Journal of the Experimental Analysis of Behavior, 31,* 53–70.

Gallacher, J. M., & Reid, D. K. (1981). *The learning theory of Piaget and Inhelder.* Monterey, CA: Brooks/Cole.

Gallagher, S. (2000). Philosophical concepts of the self: Implications for cognitive science. *Trends in Cognitive Sciences, 4,* 14–21.

Gallup, G. G. (1977). Self-recognition in primates: A comparison approach to the bidirectional properties of consciousness. *American Psychologist, 32,* 329–338.

Galotti, K. M. (1989). Approaches to studying formal and everyday reasoning. *Psychological Bulletin, 105,* 331–351.

Galotti, K. M. (1999). *Cognitive psychology in and out of the laboratory* (2nd ed). Belmont, CA: Brooks-Cole.

Garbarino, J., & Bronfenbrenner, U. (1976). The socialization of moral judgment and behavior in cross-cultural perspective. In T. Lickona (Ed.), *Moral development and behavior.* New York: Holt, Rinehart & Winston.

Garcia, J. (1981). Tilting at the windmills of academe. *American Psychologist, 36,* 149–158.

Garcia, J., Brett, L. P., & Rusniak, K. W. (1989). Limits of Darwinian conditioning. In S. B. Klein & R. R. Mowrer (Eds.), *Contemporary learning theories: Instrumental conditioning theory and the impact of biological constraints on learning* (pp. 181–203). Hillsdale, NJ: Erlbaum.

Garcia, J., Clarke, J., & Hanlins, W. (1973). Natural responses to schedule rewards. In P. Bateson & P. Klopfer (Eds.), *Perspectives in ethology.* New York: Plenum.

Garcia, J., McGowan, B., & Green, K. (1972). Biological constraints on conditioning. In M. E. P. Seligman & J. L. Hager (Eds.), *Biological boundaries of learning.* New York: Appleton-Century-Crofts.

Garcia, J., Quicle, D., & White, G. (1984). Conditioned disgust and fear from mollusk to monkey. In D. L. Alkon & J. Farley (Eds.), *Primary neural substrates of learning and behavior change.* New York: Cambridge University Press.

Gardner, H. (1993). *Creating minds: An anatomy of creativity seen through the lives of Freud, Einstein, Picasso, Stravinsky, Eliot, Graham, and Gandhi.* New York: HarperCollins.

Gardner, R. A., & Gardner, B. T. (1969). Teaching sign language to a chimpanzee. *Science, 165,* 664–672.

Gardner, R. A., & Gardner, B. T. (1980a). Comparative psychology and language acquisition. In T. A. Sebeok & J. Umiker-Sebeok (Eds.), *Speaking of apes: A critical anthology of two-way communication with man.* New York: Plenum.

Gardner, R. A., & Gardner, B. T. (1980b). Two comparative psychologists look at language acquisition. In K. E. Nelson (Ed.), *Children's language* (Vol. 2). New York: Gardner Press.

Gardner, R. A., & Gardner, B. T. (1988). Feedforward vs. feedbackward: An ethological alternative to the law of effect (with commentary). *Behavioral and Brain Sciences, 11,* 429–493.

Garry, M., Manning, C. G., Loftus, E. L., & Sherman, S. J. (1996). Imagination inflation: Imagining a childhood event inflates confidence that it occurred. *Psychonomic Bulletin and Review, 3,* 208–214.

Gathercole, S. E. (1999). Cognitive approaches to the study of short-term memory. *Trends in Cognitive Sciences, 3,* 410–419.

Gathercole, S. E., & Baddeley, A. D. (1993). *Working memory and language.* Hove, England: Erlbaum.

Gaukroger, S. (1995). *Descartes: An intellectual biography.* Oxford: Oxford University Press.

Gazzaniga, M. S. (Ed.). (1995). *The cognitive neurosciences.* Cambridge, MA: MIT Press.

Gazzinaga, M., Ivry, R. B., & Mangun, G. R. (1998). *Cognitive neuroscience: The biology of the mind.* New York: Norton.

Gee, H. (1995). Uprooting the human family tree. *Nature, 373,* 15.

Geis, M. L. (1982). *The language of television advertising.* New York: Academic Press.

Geiselman, R. E. (1988). Improving eyewitness memory through reinstatement of context. In G. M. Davies & D. M. Thomson (Eds.), *Memory in context: Context in memory* (pp. 245–266). Chichester, England: Wiley.

Geiselman, R. E., Fisher, R. P., MacKinnon, D. P., & Holland, H. L. (1985). Eyewitness memory enhancement in the police interview: Cognitive retrieval mnemonics versus hypnosis. *Journal of Applied Psychology, 70,* 401–412.

Geiselman, R. E., Fisher, R. P., MacKinnon, D. P., & Holland, H. L. (1986). Enhancement of eyewitness memory with the cognitive interview. *American Journal of Psychology, 99,* 385–401.

Gelman, R. (1972). The nature and development of early number concepts. In H. Reese (Ed.), *Advances in child development and behavior* (Vol. 7). New York: Academic Press.

Gelman, R. (1978). Cognitive development. *Annual Review of Psychology, 29,* 297–332.

Gelman, R. (1983). Recent trends in cognitive development. In G. Scherrer & A. M. Rogers (Eds.), *The G. Stanley Hall lecture series* (Vol. 3). Washington, DC: American Psychological Association.

Genter, D., & Grudin, J. (1985). The evolution of mental metaphors in psychology: A 90-year retrospective. *American Psychologist, 40,* 181–192.

Gerrig, R. J., & McKoon, G. (1998). The readiness is all: The functionality of memory-based text processing. *Discourse Processes, 26,* 67–86.

Gewirtz, J. L., & Stingle, K. (1968). Learning of generalized imitations as the basis for identification. *Psychological Review, 75,* 374–397.

Ghiselin, M. (1974). *The economy of nature and the evolution of sex.* Berkeley: University of California Press.

Gibbons, A. (1992). Neandertal language debate: Tongues wag anew. *Science, 256,* 33–34.

Gibbons, A. (1994). Anthropologists take the measure of humanity. *Science, 264,* 350–351.

Gibbs, R. W., Jr. (1984). Literal meaning and psychological theory. *Cognitive Science, 8,* 275–304.

Gibbs, R. W., Jr. (1986a). On the psycholinguistics of sarcasm. *Journal of Experimental Psychology: General, 115,* 3–15.

Gibbs, R. W., Jr. (1986b). What makes some indirect speech acts conventional? *Journal of Memory and Language, 25,* 181–196.

Gibbs, R. W., Jr. (1994). *The poetics of mind: Figurative thought, language, and understanding.* Cambridge, England: Cambridge University Press.

Gibbs, R. W., Jr. (1998). The fight over metaphor in thought and language. In A. N. Katz, C. Cacciari, R. W. Gibbs, Jr., & Turner, M. (Eds.), *Figurative language and thought* (pp. 88–118). New York: Oxford University Press.

Gibbs, R. W., Jr., & Bogdonovitch, J. (1999). Mental imagery in interpreting poetic metaphor. *Metaphor and Symbol, 14,* 37–44.

Gibson, E. J., Bishop, C., Schiff, W., & Smith, J. (1964). Comparison of meaningfulness and pronounceability as grouping principles in the perception and retention of verbal material. *Journal of Experimental Psychology, 67,* 173–182.

Gibson, E. J., & Levin, H. (1975). *The psychology of reading.* Cambridge, MA: MIT Press.

Gibson, K. (1985). Has the evolution of intelligence stagnated since Neanderthal man? In G. Butterworth, J. Rutkowska, & M. Scaife (Eds.), *Evolution and developmental psychology.* New York: St. Martin's Press.

Gibson, K. (1991). Tools, language, and intelligence: Evolutionary implications. *Man, 26,* 255–264.

Gibson, K. R., & Ingold, T. (Eds.). (1993). *Tools, language, and cognition in human evolution.* Cambridge, England: Cambridge University Press.

Gibson, K. R., & Petersen, A. C. (Eds.). (1991). *Brain maturation and cognitive development.* New York: Aldine de Gruyter.

Gigerenzer, G. (1991). How to make cognitive illusions disappear: Beyond "heuristics and biases." In W. Stroebe & M. Hewstone (Eds.), *European Review of Social Psychology, Vol 2* (pp. 83–115). London: Wiley.

Gigerenzer, G. (1992). Discovery in cognitive psychology: New tools inspire new theories. *Science in Context, 5,* 329–350.

Gigerenzer, G. (1993). The superego, the ego, and the id in statistical reasoning. In G. Keren and C. Lewis (Eds.), *A handbook for data analysis in the behavioral sciences: Methodological issues* (pp. 311–339). Hillsdale, NJ: Erlbaum.

Gigerenzer, G., & Hug, K. (1992). Domain-specific reasoning: Social contracts, cheating, and perspective change. *Cognition, 43,* 127–171.

Gilhooly, K. H., Keane, M. T. G., Logie, R. H., & Erdos, G. (Eds.). (1990). *Lines of thinking: Reflections on the psychology of thought. Vol. I. Representation, reasoning, analogy, and decision making.* New York: Wiley.

Gilhooly, K. J. (Ed.). (1989). *Human and machine problem solving.* New York: Plenum.

Gilligan, C. (1977). In a different voice. Women's conception of self and morality. *Harvard Educational Review, 47,* 481–517.

Gilligan, C. (1979). Woman's place in man's life cycle. *Harvard Educational Review, 59,* 431–446.

Gilligan, C. (1982). *In a different voice.* Cambridge, MA: Harvard University Press.

Gilligan, S. G., & Bower, G. H. (1984). Cognitive consequences of emotional arousal. In C. E. Izard, J. Kagan, & R. B. Zajonc (Eds.), *Emotions, cognition, and behavior.* Cambridge, England: Cambridge University Press.

Gilovich, T., Vallone, R., & Tversky, A. (1985). The hot hand in basketball: On the misperception of random sequences. *Cognitive Psychology, 17,* 295–314.

Ginsberg, A. (1954). Does Hullian theory provide the adequate foundations for a comprehensive theory of human behavior? *Journal of General Psychology, 51,* 301–330.

Glass, A. L. (1984). Effect of memory set on reaction time. In J. R. Anderson & S. M. Kosslyn (Eds.), *Tutorials in learning and memory* (pp. 119–136). San Francisco: Freeman.

Glassman, R., Packel, E., & Brown, D. (1986). Green beards and kindred spirits: A preliminary mathematical model of altruism toward nonkin who bear similarities to the giver. *Ethology and Sociobiology, 7,* 107–115.

Glenberg, A., Sanocki, T., Epstein, W., & Morris, C. (1987). Enhancing calibration of comprehension. *Journal of Experimental Psychology: General, 116,* 119–136.

Glenberg, A. M., & Robertson, D. A. (1999). Indexical understanding of instructions. *Discourse Processes, 28,* 1–26.

Glenberg, A. M., & Robertson, D. A. (in press). Symbol grounding and meaning: A comparison of high-dimensional and embodied theories of meaning. *Journal of Memory and Language.*

Glenn, C. G. (1978). The role of episodic structure and story length in children's recall of simple stories. *Journal of Verbal Learning and Verbal Behavior, 17,* 229–247.

Glitsky, E. L., Polster, M. R., & Routhuieaux, B. C. (1995). Double dissociation between item and source memory. *Neuropsychology, 9,* 229–235.

Gluck, M. A., & Myers, C. E. (1995). Representation and association in memory: A neuro-computational view of hippocampal function. *Current Directions in Psychological Science, 4,* 23–29.

Gluck, M. A., & Thompson, R. F. (1987). Modeling the neural substrates of learning: A computational approach. *Psychological Review, 94,* 176–191.

Glucksberg, S. (1991). Beyond literal meanings: The psychology of allusion. *Psychological Science, 2,* 146–152.

Glucksberg, S., & Keysar, B. (1990). Understanding metaphorical comparisons: Beyond similarity. *Psychological Review, 97,* 3–18.

Glucksberg, S., Manfredi, D. A., & McGlone, M. S. (1997). Metaphor comprehension: How metaphors create new categories. In T. B. Ward, S. M. Smith, & J. Vaid (Eds.), *Creative thought* (pp. 327–350). Washington, DC: American Psychological Association.

Gobet, F., & Simon, H. A. (1996). The roles of recognition processes and look-ahead search in time-constrained expert chess problem solving: Evidence from grand-master-level chess. *Psychological Science, 7,* 52–55.

Godden, D. R., & Baddeley, A. D. (1975). Context-dependent memory in two natural environments: On land and underwater. *British Journal of Psychology, 66,* 325–331.

Goff, L. M., & Roediger, H. L. (1998). Imagination inflation for action events: Repeated imaginings lead to illusory recollections. *Memory and Cognition, 26,* 20–33.

Goldin-Meadow, S. (1996). Review of Kanzi: Ape at the brink of the human mind. *International Journal of Primatology, 17,* 145–148.

Goldin-Meadow, S. (1999). The role of gesture in communication and thinking. *Trends in Cognitive Sciences, 3,* 419–429.

Goldin-Meadow, S., & Mylander, C. (1990). Beyond the input given: The child's role in the acquisition of language. *Language, 66,* 323–355.

Goldin-Meadow, S., & Mylander, C. (1991). Levels of structure in a communication system developed without a language model. In K. R. Gibson & A. C. Petersen (Eds.), *Tools, language, and cognition in human evolution.* Cambridge, England: Cambridge University Press.

Goldmann, L., Shah, M. V., & Hebden, M. W. (1987). Memory of cardiac anesthesia. Psychological sequelae in cardiac patients of intraoperative suggestion and operating room conversation. *Anesthesia, 42,* 596–603.

Gomez, K. M., & Cole, C. L. (1991). Attention deficit hyperactivity disorder: A review of treatment alternatives. *Elementary School Guidance and Counseling, 26,* 106–114.

Goodwin, D. W., Powell, B., Bremer, D., Hoine, H., & Stern, J. (1969). Alcohol and recall: State-dependent effects in man. *Science, 163,* 1358.

Gopnik, A. (1996). The post-Piagetian era. *Psychological Science, 7,* 221–225.

Gopnik, A., & Crago, M. B. (1991). Familial aggregation of a developmental disorder. *Cognition, 39,* 1–58.

Gopnik, M. (1997). Language deficits and genetic factors. *Trends in Cognitive Sciences, 1,* 5–9.

Goss, A. (1961). Early behaviorism and verbal mediating responses. *American Psychologist, 16,* 285–298.

Gould, J. E., & Gould, C. (1981). The instinct to learn. *Science, 81*(2), 44–50.

Gould, J. L. (1982). *Ethology.* New York: Norton.

Gould, J. L., & Marler, P. (1987, January). Learning by instinct. *Scientific American, 256,* 42–50.

Gould, P., & White, R. (1974). *Mental maps.* Harmondswonh, England: Penguin.

Gowlett, J. A. J. (1992). Early human mental abilities. In S. Jones, R. Martin, & D. Pilbeam (Eds.), *The Cambridge encyclopedia of evolution* (pp. 341–345). Cambridge, England: Cambridge University Press.

Graesser, A. C., & Bower, G. H. (Eds.). (1990). *Inferences and text comprehension.* San Diego: Academic Press.

Graesser, A. C., & Clark, L. F. (1985). The generation of knowledge-based inferences during narrative comprehension. In G. Rickheit & H. Strohner (Eds.), *Inferences in text processing* (pp. 53–94). Amsterdam: Elsevier (North-Holland).

Graesser, A. C., Millis, K. K., & Zwaan, R. A. (1997). Discourse comprehension. *Annual Review of Psychology, 48,* 163–189.

Graesser, A. C., Singer, M., & Trabasso, T. (1994). Constructing inferences during narrative text comprehension. *Psychological Review, 101,* 371–395.

Graesser, A. C., & Zwaan, R. A. (1995). Inference generation and the construction of situation models. In C. A. Weaver, S. Mannes, & C. R. Fletcher (Eds.), *Discourse comprehension: Essays in honor of Walter Kintsch* (pp. 117–139). Hillsdale, NJ: Erlbaum.

Graf, P., & Masson, M. E. J. (Eds.). (1993). *Implicit memory.* Hillsdale, NJ: Erlbaum.

Graf, P., & Schacter, D. L. (1985). Implicit and explicit memory for new associations in normal and amnesic subjects. *Journal of Experimental Psychology: Learning, Memory Cognition, 11,* 501–518.

Graham, D. (1972). *Moral learning and development: Theory and research.* New York: Wiley-Interscience.

Granger, R. H., & Schlimmer, J. C. (1986). The computation of contingency in classical conditioning. *Psychology of Learning and Motivation, 20,* 137–192.

Graves, P. (1994). Flakes and ladders: What the archaeological record cannot tell us about the origins of language. *World Archaeology, 26,* 158–171.

Green, G. M. (1989). *Pragmatics and natural language understanding.* Hillsdale, NJ: Erlbaum.

Green, S., & Marler, P. (1979). The analysis of animal communication. In P. Marler & J. G. Vandenberg (Eds.), *Handbook of Behavioral Neurobiology. Vol. 3. Social behavior and communication.* New York: Plenum.

Greene, E. (1988). Judge's instruction on eyewitness testimony: Evaluation and revision. *Journal of Applied Social Psychology, 18,* 252–276.

Greenfield, P. M. (1991). Language, tools, and the brain: The ontogeny and phylogeny of hierarchically sequential behavior. *Behavioral and Brain Sciences, 14,* 531–596.

Greenspoon, J. (1955). The reinforcing effect of two spoken sounds on the frequency of two responses. *American Journal of Psychology, 68,* 409–416.

Gregory, M. S., Silvers, A., & Sutch, D. (Eds.). (1978). *Sociobiology and human nature.* San Francisco: Jossey-Bass.

Grether, D. M., & Plott, C. (1979). Economic theory of choice and the preference reversal phenomemna. *American Economic Review, 69,* 623–638.

Grice, J. P. (1975). Logic and conversation. In P. Cole & J. L. Morgan (Eds.), *Syntax and semantics III: Speech acts.* New York: Academic Press.

Griggs, R. A. (1983). The role of problem content in the selection task and THOG problem. In J. St. B. T. Evans (Ed.), *Thinking and reasoning: Psychological approaches.* London: Routledge & Kegan Paul.

Griggs, R. A., & Cox, J. R. (1982). The elusive thematic materials effect in Wason's selection task. *British Journal of Psychology, 73,* 407–420.

Griggs, R. A., & Cox, J. R. (1983). The effect of problem content on strategies in Wason's selection task. *Quarterly Journal of Experimental Psychology, 35,* 519–534.

Griggs, R. A., & Cox, J. R. (1993). Permission schemas and the selection task. *Quarterly Journal of Experimental Psychology, 46A,* 637–651.

Groen, G. J., & Patel, V. L. (1990). Professional and novice expertise in medicine. In M. Smith (Ed.), *Toward a unified theory of problem solving: Views from content domains* (pp. 35–44). Hillsdale, NJ: Erlbaum.

Grosjean, F. (1982). *Life with two languages.* Cambridge, MA: Harvard University Press.

Gross, J. (1995, June). The acute effects of emotional regulation. Paper presented at the 7th annual meeting of the American Psychological Society, New York.

Grotevant, H., Scarr, S., & Weinberg, R. (1978). Are career interests inheritable? *Psychology Today, 11*(10), 88–90.

Groves, P. M., & Rebec, G. V. (1988). *Introduction to biological psychology* (3rd ed.). Dubuque, IA: Wm. C. Brown.

Gruber, H. E., & Davis, S. N. (1988). Inching our way up Mount Olympus: The evolving systems approach to creative thinking. In R. J. Sternberg (Ed.), *The nature of creativity* (pp. 243–270). Cambridge, England: Cambridge University Press.

Gruber, H. E., & Voneche, J. J. (Eds.). (1977). *The essential Piaget.* New York: Basic Books.

Gruen, G. E. (1966). Note on conservation: Methodological and definitional considerations. *Child Development, 37,* 977–983. Reprinted in Sigel & Hooper (1968).

Gruneberg, M. M. (1998). A commentary on the criticism of the keyword method of learning foreign languages. *Applied Cognitive Psychology, 12,* 529–532.

Grusser, O. J. (1983). Mother-child holding patterns in Western art: A developmental study. *Ethology and Sociobiology, 4,* 89–94.

Guilford, J. P. (1956). Structure of intellect. *Psychological Bulletin, 53,* 267–293.

Guilford, J. P. (1986). *Creative talents: Their nature, uses, and development.* Buffalo, NY: Bearly Limited.

Gurin, J. (1976). Is society hereditary? *Harvard Magazine, 79*(2), 21–25.

Guthrie, E. R. (1930). Conditioning as a principle of learning. *Psychological Review, 37,* 412–428.

Guthrie, E. R. (1933). Association as a function of the time-interval. *Psychological Review, 40,* 355–367.

Guthrie, E. R. (1934). Reward and punishment. *Psychological Review, 41,* 450–460.

Guthrie, E. R. (1939). The effect of outcome on learning. *Psychological Review, 46,* 480–484.

Guthrie, E. R. (1940). Association and the law of effect. *Psychological Review, 47,* 127–148.

Guthrie, E. R. (1952). *The psychology of learning* (2nd ed.). New York: Harper & Row.

Guthrie, E. R., & Horton, G. (1946). *Cats in a puzzle box.* New York: Rinehart Press.

Haber, R. N. (1983). The impending demise of the icon: A critique of the iconic storage in visual information processing. *Behavioral and Brain Sciences, 6,* 1–54.

Haber, R. N. (1985). An icon can have no worth in the real world: Comments on Loftus, Johnson, and Shimamura's "How much is an icon worth?" *Journal of Experimental Psychology: Human Perception and Performance, 11,* 374–378.

Hagen, J. W. (1972). Strategies for remembering. In S. Farnham-Diggory (Ed.), *Information processing in children.* New York: Academic Press.

Hahn, M., Jensen, C., & Duder, B. (Eds.). (1979). *The development and evolution of brain size: Behavioral implications.* New York: Academic Press.

Haier, R. J. (1994, July 1). *PET studies of intelligence and mental retardation: Mental effort and brain efficiency.* Paper presented at the 6th annual convention of the American Psychological Society, Washington, DC.

Haier, R. J. (1997, May 24). *Brain imaging experiments of thinking, memory, and consciousness.* Paper presented at the annual meeting of the American Psychological Society, Washington, DC.

Haier, R. J., Siegel, B. V., Neuchterlein, K. N., Hazlett, E., Wu, J. C., Paek, J., Browning, H. L., & Buchsbaum, M. S. (1988). Cortical glucose metabolic rate correlates of abstract reasoning and attention studied with positron emission tomography. *Intelligence, 12,* 199–217.

Haier, R. J., Siegel, B., Tang, C., Abel, L., & Buchsbaum, M. S. (1992). Intelligence and changes in regional cerebral glucose matabolic rate following learning. *Intelligence, 16,* 415–426.

Haley, A. (1976). *Roots.* New York: Doubleday.

Hall, G., & Honey, R. (1989). Perceptual and associative learning. In S. B. Klein & R. R. Mowrer (Eds.), *Contemporary learning theories: Pavlovian conditioning and the status of traditional learning theory* (pp. 117–147). Hillsdale, NJ: Erlbaum.

Hallpike, C. R. (1985). Social and biological evolution. I. Darwinism and social evolution. *Journal of Social and Biological Structures, 8,* 129–146.

Hames, R. B. (1979). Relatedness and interaction among the Ye'kwana: A preliminary analysis. In N. A. Chagnon & W. Irons (Eds.), *Evolutionary biology and human social behavior.* North Scituate, MA: Duxbury Press.

Hamilton, D. L. (1989). Understanding impression formation: What has memory research contributed? In P. R. Solomon, G. R. Goethals, C. M. Kelley, & B. R. Stephens (Eds.), *Memory: Interdisciplinary approaches* (pp. 221–242). New York: Springer-Verlag.

Hamilton, D. L., & Sherman, J. W. (1994). Stereotypes. In R. S. Wyer & T. K. Srull (Eds.), *Handbook of social cognition* (2nd ed., Vol. 2, pp. 1–68).

Hamilton, W. D. (1964). The genetic evolution of social behaviour. *Journal of Theroetical Biology, 7,* 1–53.

Hammersley, R., & Read, J. D. (1986). What is integration? Remembering a story and remembering false implications about the story. *British Journal of Psychology, 77,* 329–341.

Hammond, K. R., & Grassi, A. J. (1985). The cognitive side of conflict: From theory to resolution of policy disputes. In S. Oskamp (Ed.), *Applied social psychology annual* (Vol. 6, pp. 233–254). Beverly Hills, CA: Sage.

Hammond, K. R., Harvey, L. O., Jr., & Hastie, R. (1992). Making better use of scientific knowledge: Separating truth from justice. *Psychological Science, 3,* 80–87.

Haney, C., Banks, C., & Zimbardo, P. (1973). Interpersonal dynamics in a simulated prison. *International Journal of Criminology and Penology, 1,* 69–97.

Hanson, S. J., & Burr, D. J. (1990). What connectionist networks learn: Learning and representation in connectionist networks. *Behavioral and Brain Sciences, 13,* 471–518.

Happe, F. (1999). Autism: Cognitive deficit or cognitive style. *Trends in Cognitive Sciences, 3,* 216–222.

Harkness, S. (1990). A cultural model for the acquisition of language: Implications for the innateness debate. *Developmental Psychobiology, 23,* 727–740.

Harley, T. A. (1996). *Psychology of language: From data to theory.* Hove, England: Erlbaum.

Harnad, S. R., Steklis, H., & Lancaster, J. (1976). Origins and evolution of language and speech. *Annals of the New York Academy of Sciences* (Vol. 280). New York: New York Academy of Sciences.

Harris, B. (1979). What ever happened to Little Albert? *American Psychologist, 34,* 151–160.

Harris, R. J. (1977). The teacher as actor. *Teaching of Psychology, 4,* 185–187.

Harris, R. J. (1981). Inferences in information processing. In G. H. Bower (Ed.), *The psychology of learning and motivation* (Vol. 15). New York: Academic Press.

Harris, R. J. (1984). An autobiographical longitudinal study of event memory and affect during second-language acquisition. *Journal of Multilingual and Multi-cultural Development, 5,* 159–173.

Harris, R. J. (Ed.). (1992). *Cognitive processing in bilinguals.* Amsterdam: North-Holland.

Harris, R. J. (1999). *A cognitive psychology of mass communication.* (3rd ed.) Hillsdale, NJ: Erlbaum.

Harris, R. J., & Cook, C. A. (1994). Attributions about spouse abuse: It matters who the batterers and victims are. *Sex Roles, 30,* 553–565.

Harris, R. J., Dubitsky, T. M., & Bruno, K. J. (1983). Psycholinguistic studies of misleading advertising. In R. J. Harris (Ed.), *Information processing research in advertising.* Hillsdale, NJ: Erlbaum.

Harris, R. J., Jasper, J. D., Lee, B. C., & Miller, K. E. (1991). Consenting to donate organs: Whose wishes carry the most weight? *Journal of Applied Social Psychology, 21,* 3–14.

Harris, R. J., Lahey, M. A., & Marsalek, F. (1980). Metaphors and images: Rating, responding, and remembering. In R. P. Honeck & R. R. Hoffman (Eds.), *Cognition and figurative language.* Hillsdale, NJ: Erlbaum.

Harris, R. J., Lee, D. J., Hensley, D., & Schoen, L. M. (1988). The effect of cultural script knowledge on memory for stories over time. *Discourse Processes, 11,* 413–431.

Harris, R. J., Pounds, J. C., Maiorelle, M. J., & Mermis, M. (1993). The effect of linguistic form and buying history on the drawing of pragmatic inferences from advertising claims. *Journal of Consumer Psychology, 2,* 83–95.

Harris, R. J., Schoen, L. M., & Hensley, D. (1992). A cross-cultural study of story memory. *Journal of Cross-Cultural Psychology, 23,* 133–147.

Harris, R. J., Schoen, L. M., & Lee, D. J. (1986). Culture-based distortion in memory for stories. In J. L. Armagost (Ed.), *Papers from the 1985 Mid-America Linguistics Conference* (pp. 84–91). Manhattan, KS: Kansas State University Department of Speech.

Harris, R. J., Sturm, R. E., Klassen, M. L., & Bechtold, J. E. (1986). Language in advertising: A psycholinguistic approach. *Current Issues and Research in Advertising, 9,* 1–26.

Harris, R. J., Trusty, M. L., Bechtold, J. I., & Wasinger, L. (1989). Memory for implied versus directly stated claims in advertising. *Psychology and Marketing, 6,* 87–96.

Hasher, L., Attig, M. S., & Alba, J. W. (1981). I knew it all along: Or did I? *Journal of Verbal Learning and Verbal Behavior, 20,* 86–96.

Haugeland, J. (Ed.). (1981). *Mind design.* Cambridge, MA: Bradford/MIT Press.

Haugeland, J. (1985). *Artificial intelligence: The very idea.* Cambridge, MA: Bradford/MIT Press.

Hausman, D. (1991). On dogmatism in economics: The case of preference reversals. *Journal of Socio-Economics, 20,* 205–225.

Haviland, S. E., & Clark, H. H. (1974). What's new? Acquiring new information as a process of comprehension. *Journal of Verbal Learning and Verbal Behavior, 13,* 512–521.

Hawkins, R. D., & Kandel, E. R. (1986). Steps toward a cell-biological alphabet for elementary forms of learning. In G. Lynch, J. L. McGaugh, & N. M. Weinberger (Eds.), *Neurobiology of learning and memory.* New York: Guilford.

Hayes, J. R. (Ed.). (1970). *Cognition and the development of language.* New York: Wiley.

Hayes, J. R. (1978). *Cognitive psychology.* Homewood, IL: Dorsey Press.

Head, H. (1920). *Studies in neurology.* Oxford: Oxford University Press.

Heaps, C., & Nash, M. (1999). Individual differences in imagination inflation. *Psychonomic Bulletin and Review, 6,* 313–318.

Hearst, E. (1975). The classical-instrumental distinction: Reflexes, voluntary behavior, and categories of associative learning. In W. K. Estes (Ed.), *Handbook of learning and cognitive processes* (Vol. 2). Hillsdale, NJ: Erlbaum.

Hedicer, H. K. P. (1981). The Clever Hans Phenomenon from an animal psychologist's point of view. In T. A. Sebeok & R. Rosenthal (Eds.), The clever Hans phenomenon. *Annals of the New York Academy of Sciences* (Vol. 364). New York: New York Academy of Sciences.

Heil, J. (1982). Speechless brutes. *Philosophy and Phenomenological Research, 42,* 400–406.

Heilbrun, A. B. (1981). *Human sex-role behavior.* New York: Pergamon Press.

Heiman, J. R. (1975, April). The physiology of erotica: Women's sexual arousal. *Psychology Today, 8,* 90–94.

Herrmann, D. J., & Gruneberg, M. M. (1999). *How to cure your memory failures.* London: Blandford.

Hertel, P. T., & Rude, S. S. (1991). Depressive deficits in memory: Focusing attention improves subsequent recall. *Journal of Experimental Psychology: General, 120,* 301–309.

Hewes, G. W. (1975, August 30). *The evolutionary significance of pongid sign language acquisition.* Paper presented at the Annual Meeting of the American Psychological Association, Chicago.

Hewes, G. W. (1976). The current status of the gestural theory of language origin. In S. R. Harnad, H. Steklls, & J. Lancaster (Eds.), *Annals of the New York Academy of Sciences* (Vol. 280). New York: New York Academy of Sciences.

Heyman, G. E., & Oldfather, C. M. (1992). Inelastic preference for ethanol in rats: An analysis of ethanol's reinforcing effects. *Psychological Science, 3,* 122–130.

Hickok, G., Bellugi, U., & Klima, E. S. (1998). The neural organization of language: Evidence from sign language aphasia. *Trends in Cognitive Sciences, 2,* 129–136.

Hilgard, E., & Bower, G. (1975). *Theories of learning* (4th ed.). Englewood Cliffs, NJ: Prentice Hall.

Hill, E., Nocks, E., & Gardner, L. (1987). Physical attractiveness: Manipulation by physique and status displays. *Ethology and Sociobiology, 8,* 143–154.

Hill, J. H. (1980). Apes and language. In T. A. Sebeok & J. Umiker-Sebeok (Eds.), *Speaking of apes: A critical anthology of two-way communication with man.* New York: Plenum.

Hinde, R., & Stevenson-Hinde, J. (Eds.). (1973). *Constraints on learning.* New York: Academic Press.

Hinds, P. J. (1999). The curse of expertise: The effects of expertise and debiasing methods on predictions of novice performance. *Journal of Experimental Psychology: Applied, 5,* 205–221.

Hineline, P. (1981). The several roles of stimuli in negative reinforcement. In P. Harzen & M. Zeiler (Eds.), *Advances in analysis of behaviour* (Vol. 2). Chichester, England: Wiley.

Hintzman, D. L. (1990). Human learning and memory: Connections and dissociations. *Annual Review of Psychology, 41,* 109–140.

Hirst, W., & Kalmar, K. (1987). Characterizing attentional resources. *Journal of Experimental Psychology: General, 116,* 68–81.

Hochberg, J. E. (1978). *Perception.* Englewood Cliffs, NJ: Prentice Hall.

Hoeksma, S. N. (1995, June). Emotional regulation and mental health. Paper presented at the 7th annual meeting of the American Psychological Society, New York.

Hoffman, M. (1976). Empathy, role-taking, guilt and development of altruistic motives. In T. Lickona (Ed.), *Moral development and behavior.* New York: Holt, Rinehart & Winston.

Hoffman, M. (1979). Development of moral thought, feeling and behavior. *American Psychologist, 34,* 958–966.

Hoffman, M., & Saltzstein, H. (1967). Parent discipline and the child's moral development. *Journal of Personality and Social Psychology, 5,* 45–57.

Hoffman, R. R. (Ed.). (1994). *The psychology of expertise: Cognitive research and empirical AI.* Hillsdale, NJ: Erlbaum.

Holden, C. (1980a). Identical twins reared apart. *Science, 207,* 1323–1328.

Holden, C. (1980b). Twins reunited. *Science, 80, 1*(7), 1–8, 54–59.

Holland, P. C. (1981). Acquisition of representation-mediated conditioned food aversion. *Learning and Motivation, 12,* 1–18.

Holland, P. C. (1984). Origins of behavior in Pavlovian conditioning. *Psychology of Learning and Motivation, 18,* 129–174.

Holliday, T. W. (1997). Body proportion of late Pleistocene Europe and modern hominid origins. *Journal of Human Evolution, 32,* 423–448.

Hollis, K. L. (1982). Pavlovian conditioning of signal-centered action patterns and autonomic behavior: A biological analysis of function. In J. Rosenblatt, R. Hinde, C. Beer, & M. -C. Busnel (Eds.), *Advances in the study of behavior* (Vol. 12). New York: Academic Press.

Holloway, R. L. (1976). Paleoneurological evidence for language origins. In S. R. Harnad, H. Steklis, & J. Lancaster (Eds.), *Annals of the New York Academy of Sciences* (Vol. 280). New York: New York Academy of Sciences.

Holmes, D. (1990). The evidence for repression: An examination of sixty years of research. In J. Singer (Ed.), *Repression and dissociation: Implications for personality theory, psychopathology, and health* (pp. 85–102). Chicago: University of Chicago Press.

Holyoak, K. J., Koh, K., & Nisbett, R. E. (1989). A theory of conditioning: Inductive learning within rule-based default hierarchies. *Psychological Review, 96,* 315–340.

Honig, W. K., & Thompson, R. K. R. (1982). Retrospective and prospective processing in animal working memory. *Psychology of Learning and Motivation, 16,* 239–283.

Hoosain, R. J. (1991). *Psycholinguistic implications for linguistic relativity: A case study of Chinese.* Hillsdale, NJ: Erlbaum.

Horn, L. R. (1989). *A natural history of negation.* Chicago: University of Chicago Press.

Horton, D. L., & Turnage, T. W. (1976). *Human learning.* Englewood Cliffs, NJ: Prentice Hall.

Hosch, H. M. (1980). A comparison of three studies of the influence of expert testimony on jurors. *Law and Human Behavior, 4,* 297–302.

Hosch, H. M., Beck, E. L., & McIntyre, P. (1980). Influence of expert testimony regarding eyewitness accuracy on jury decisions. *Law and Human Behavior, 4,* 287–295.

House, J., & Kaspar, G. (1981). Politeness markers in English and German. In F. Coulmas (Ed.), *Conversational routine.* The Hague: Mouton.

Hovland, C. I. (1938a). Experimental studies in rote learning. II. *Journal of Experimental Psychology, 22,* 338–353.

Hovland, C. I. (1938b). Experimental studies of rote learning. III. *Journal of Experimental Psychology, 23,* 172–190.

Howard, D. V. (1983). *Cognitive psychology: Memory, language, and thought.* New York: Macmillan.

Howard, P. J. (1994). *The owner's manual for the brain.* Austin, TX: Leornian Press.

Howe, M. L., & Courage, M. L. (1993). On resolving the enigma of infantile amnesia. *Psychological Bulletin, 113,* 305–326.

Hrdy, S. B. (1979). The evolution of human sexuality: The latest word and the last. *Quarterly Review of Biology, 54,* 309–314.

Hrdy, S. B. (1981). *The woman that never evolved.* Cambridge, MA: Harvard University Press.

Huang, Y. Y., Colino, A., Selig, D. K., & Malenka, R. C. (1992). The influence of prior synaptic activity to the induction of long-term potentiation. *Science, 255,* 730–733.

Hubel, D. H., & Wiesel, T. N. (1962). Receptive fields, binocular interaction, and functional architecture in the cat's visual cortex. *Journal of Physiology, 160,* 106–154.

Hubel, D. H., & Wiesel, T. N. (1968). Receptive fields and functional architecture of monkey striate cortex. *Journal of Physiology, 195,* 215–243.

Hudson, J. A., Fivush, R., & Kuebli, J. (1992). Scripts and episodes: The development of event memory. *Applied Cognitive Psychology, 6,* 483–505.

Hughes, H., & Cutting, A. L. (1999). Nature, nurture, and individual differences in early understanding of mind. *Psychological Science, 10,* 429–432.

Hull, C. L. (1930a). Simple trial-error learning: A study in psychological theory. *Psychological Review, 37,* 241–256.

Hull, C. L. (1930b). Knowledge and purpose as habit mechanisms. *Psychological Review, 37,* 511–525.

Hull, C. L. (1931). Goal attraction and directing ideas concerned as habit phenomena. *Psychological Review, 38,* 478–506.

Hull, C. L. (1934). The concept of the habit-family hierarchy and maze learning. *Psychological Review, 41,* 33–54, 134–152.

Hull, C. L. (1935). The conflicting psychologies of learning—A way out. *Psychological Review, 42,* 491–561.

Hull, C. L. (1937). Mind, mechanism and adaptive behavior. *Psychological Review, 44,* 1–32.

Hull, C. L. (1943). *Principles of behavior.* New York: Appleton-Century.

Hull, C. L. (1952). *A behavior system.* New Haven: Yale University Press.

Hull, C. L., & Baernstein, H. (1929). A mechanical parallel to the conditioned reflex. *Science, 70,* 14–15.

Hull, C. L., Felsinger, J., Gladstone, I., & Yamaguchi, H. (1947). A proposed quantification of habit strength. *Psychological Review, 54,* 237–254.

Humphrey, N. K. (1976). The social function of intellect. In P. P. G. Bateson & R. A. Hinde (Eds.), *Growing points in ethology.* Cambridge, England: Cambridge University Press.

Humphreys, L. G. (1939). Acquisition and extinction of verbal expectations in a situation analogous to conditioning. *Journal of Experimental Psychology, 25,* 294–301.

Hunt, E. (1983). On the nature of intelligence. *Science, 219,* 141–146.

Hunt, E. (1989). Cognitive science: Definition, status, and questions. *Annual Review of Psychology, 40,* 603–630.

Hurford, J. R. (1991). The evolution of a critical period for language acquisition. *Cognition, 40,* 159–201.

Hyde, J. S. (1981). How large are cognitive gender differences? *American Psychologist, 36,* 892–901.

Hyland, M. E. (1993). Size of human groups during the Paleolithic and the evolutionary significance of increased group size. *Behavioral and Brain Sciences, 16,* 709–710.

Hyman, I. E., Jr., Husband, T. H., & Billings, F. J. (1995). False memories of childhood experiences. *Applied Cognitive Psychology, 9,* 181–197.

Hyman, I. E., Jr., & Pentland, J. (1996). Guided imagery and the creation of false memories. *Journal of Memory and Language, 35,* 101–117.

Hyman, I. E., Jr., & Rubin, D. C. (1990). Memorabeatia: A naturalistic study of long-term memory. *Memory and Cognition, 18,* 205–214.

Imwinkelried, E. J., & Schwed, L. R. (1987). Guidelines for drafting understandable jury instruction: An introduction to the use of psycholinguistics. *Criminal Law Bulletin, 23,* 135–150.

Inhelder, B. (1972). Information processing tendencies in recent experiments in cognitive learning-empirical studies. In S. Farnham-Diggory (Ed.), *Information processing in children.* New York: Academic Press.

Inhelder, B., & Piaget, J. (1958). *The growth of logical thinking.* New York: Basic Books.

Inhelder, B., Sinclair, H., & Bovet, M. (1974). *Learning and the development of cognition.* Cambridge, MA: Harvard University Press.

Irons, W. (1982). Why lineage exogamy? In R. D. Alexander & D. Tinkle (Eds.), *Natural selection and social behavior.* New York: Chiron Press.

Isaac, G. L. (1976). Stages of cultural elaboration in the pleistocene: Possible archaeological indication of the development of language capabilities. In S. R. Harnad, H. Steklis, & J. Lancaster (Eds.), *Annals of the New York Academy of Sciences* (Vol. 280). New York: New York Academy of Sciences.

Isen, A. M. (1984). Toward understanding the role of affect in cognition. In R. S. Wyer & T. K. Krull (Eds.), *Handbook of social cognition,* Vol. 3. Hillsdale, NJ: Erlbaum.

Izard, C. E. (1989). The structure and function of emotions. In I. S. Cohen (Ed.), *The G. Stanley Hall Lecture Series* (Vol. 9, pp. 35–74). Washington, DC: American Psychological Association.

Izawa, C. (Ed) (1999). *On human memory: Evolution, progress, and reflections on the 30th anniversary of the Atkinson-Shiffrin model.* Mahwah, NJ: Erlbaum.

Jablonski, N. G., & Chaplin, G. (1993). Origin of habitual terrestrial bipedalism in the ancestor of the hominidae. *Journal of Human Evolution, 24,* 259–280.

Jackendoff, R. (1998). Possible stages in the evolution of the language capacity. *Trends in Cognitive Sciences, 3,* 272–279.

Jakobovits, L. A., & Miron, M. S. (Eds.). (1967). *Readings in the psychology of language.* Englewood Cliffs, NJ: Prentice Hall.

James, W. (1890). *Principles of psychology* (Vols. 1–2). New York: Henry Holt.

James, W. (1892). *Psychology: The briefer course.* New York: Holt.

James, W. (1904). Does "consciousness" exist? *Journal of Philosophy, 1,* 477–491.

Janis, I. L. (1984). The patient as decision maker. In W. D. Gentry (Ed.), *Handbook of behavioral medicine* (pp. 326–368). New York: Guilford.

Jaynes, J. (1976a). *The origin of consciousness in the breakdown of the bicameral mind.* Boston: Houghton Mifflin.

Jaynes, J. (1976b). The evolution of language in the late Pleistocene. In S. R. Harnad, H. Steklis, & J. Lancaster (Eds.), *Annals of the New York Academy of Sciences* (Vol. 280). New York: New York Academy of Sciences.

Jeffrey, W. E. (1980). The developing brain and child development. In M. C. Wittrock (Ed.), *The brain and psychology.* New York: Academic Press.

Jeffries, R., Turner, A. A., Polson, P. G., & Atwood, M. E. (1981). The processes involved in designing software. In J. R. Anderson (Ed.), *Cognitive skills and their acquisition.* Hillsdale, NJ: Erlbaum.

Jenkins, J. M. (1970). Sequential organization in schedules of reinforcement. In W. N. Schoenfeld (Ed.), *The theory of reinforcement schedules.* New York: Appleton-Century-Crofts.

Jenkins, J. M., & Astington, J. W. (1996). Cognitive factors and family structure associated with theory of mind development in young children. *Developmental Psychology, 12,* 70–78.

Jerison, H. J. (1973). *Evolution of the brain and intelligence.* New York: Academic Press.

Jerison, H. J. (1976). *The paleoneurology of language.* In S. R. Harnad, H. Steklis, &J. Lancaster (Eds.), *Annals of the New York Academy of Sciences* (Vol. 280). New York: New York Academy of Sciences.

Jerison, H. J. (1982). The evolution of biological intelligence. In R. J. Sternberg (Ed.), *Handbook of human intelligence.* Cambridge, England: Cambridge University Press.

Jerison, H. J. (1991). *Brain size and the evolution of mind.* New York: American Museum of Natural History.

Jerison, H. J. (1993). Number our days: Quantifying social evolution. *Behavioral and Brain Sciences, 16,* 712–713.

Johansen, D. C., & Edey, M. A. (1981). *Lucy: The beginnings of humankind.* New York: Warner Books.

Johnson, M. (1997). *Developmental cognitive neuroscience.* Oxford: Blackwell.

Johnson, M. K. (1988). Reality monitoring: An experimental phenomenological approach. *Journal of Experimental Psychology: General, 117,* 390–394.

Johnson, M. K., Bransford, J. D., & Solomon, S. K. (1973). Memory for tacit implications of sentences. *Journal of Experimental Psychology, 98,* 203–205.

Johnson, M. K., Foley, M. A., Suengas, A. G., & Rey, C. L. (1988). Phenomenal characteristics of memories for perceived and imagined autobiographical events. *Journal of Experimental Psychology: General, 117,* 371–376.

Johnson, M. K., Hashtroudi, S., & Lindsay, D. S. (1993). Source monitoring. *Psychological Bulletin, 114,* 3–28.

Johnson, M. K. J., & Raye, C. L. (1981). Reality monitoring. *Psychological Review, 88,* 67–85.

Johnson, S. (2000). The recognition of mentalistic agents in infancy. *Trends in Cognitive Sciences, 4,* 22–28.

Johnson-Laird, P. N. (1999). Deductive reasoning. *Annual Review of Psychology, 50,* 109–135.

Johnson-Laird, P. N., & Byrne, M. J. (1991). *Deduction.* Hillsdale, NJ: Erlbaum.

Johnson-Laird, P. N., Herrmann, D. J., & Chaffin, R. (1984). Only connections: A critique of semantic networks. *Psychological Bulletin, 96,* 292–315.

Johnson-Laird, P. N., & Tridgell, J. (1972). When negation is easier than affirmation. *Quarterly Journal of Experimental Psychology, 84,* 87–91.

Johnston, T. (1981). Contrasting approaches to a theory of learning. *Behavioral and Brain Sciences, 4,* 125–139; Open Peer Commentary 139–161; reply, 161–169; references 169–173.

Johnston, W. A., & Dark, V. J. (1986). Selective attention. *Annual Review of Psychology, 37,* 43–75.

Jones, S., Martin, R., & Pilbeam, D. (Eds.). (1992). *The Cambridge encyclopedia of evolution.* Cambridge, England: Cambridge University Press.

Jorgensen, J., Miller, G. A., & Sperber, D. (1984). Test of the mention theory of irony. *Journal of Experimental Psychology: General, 113,* 112–120.

Jou, J., Shanteau, J., & Harris, R. J. (1996). An information-processing view of framing effects: The role of causal schemas in decision making. *Memory and Cognition, 24,* 1–15.

Jungermann, H. (1983). The two camps on rationality. In R. W. Scholz (Ed.), *Decision making under uncertainty* (pp. 63–86). Amsterdam: Elsevier.

Just, M. A., & Carpenter, P. A. (1992). A capacity theory of comprehension: Individual differences in working memory. *Psychological Review, 99,* 122–149.

Justice, E., & Weaver-McDougall, R. (1989). Adults' knowledge about memory: Awareness and use of memory strategies across tasks. *Journal of Educational Psychology, 81,* 214–219.

Kagehiro, D. K. (1990). Defining the standard of proof in jury instructions. *Psychological Science, 1,* 194–200.

Kahneman, D. (1973). *Attention and effort.* Englewood Cliffs, NJ: Prentice Hall.

Kahneman, D., Slovic, P., & Tversky, A. (Eds.). (1982). *Judgment under uncertainty: Heuristics and biases.* Cambridge, England: Cambridge University Press.

Kahneman, D., & Tversky, A. (1973). On the psychology of prediction. *Psychological Review, 80,* 232–251.

Kahneman, D., & Tversky, A. (1982). The simulation heuristic. In D. Kahneman, P. Slovic, & A. Tversky (Eds.), *Judgment under uncertainty: Heuristics and biases.* Cambridge, England: Cambridge University Press.

Kail, R., & Bisanz, J. (1982). Information processing and cognitive development. In H. W. Reese (Ed.), *Advances in child behavior and development.* New York: Academic Press.

Kail, R. V. (1984). *The development of memory in children* (2nd ed.). San Francisco: Freeman.

Kamil, A. C., & Balda, R. P. (1990). Spatial memory in seed-catching corvids. *Psychology of Learning and Motivation, 26,* 1–25.

Kamil, A. C., & Roitblat, H. L. (1985). The ecology of foraging behavior: Implications for animal learning and memory. *Annual Review of Psychology, 36,* 141–170.

Kamin, L. (1968). Attention-like processes in classical conditioning. In M. Jones (Ed.), *Miami Symposium on the prediction of behavior: Aversive stimulation.* Miami, FL: University of Miami Press.

Kamin, L. (1969). Predictability, surprise, attention, and conditioning. In R. Church & B. Campbell (Eds.), *Punishment and aversive behaviors.* New York: Appleton-Century-Crofts.

Kant, I. (1963). *Critique of pure reason.* London: Macmillan. (Original work published 1781)

Kappelman, J. (1996). The evolution of body mass and relative brain size in fossil hominids. *Journal of Human Evolution, 30,* 243–276.

Karmiloff-Smith, A. (1991). Beyond modularity: Innate constraints on developmental change. In S. Carey & R. Gelman (Eds.), *The epigenesis of mind: Essays on biology and cognition.* Hillsdale, NJ: Erlbaum.

Karmiloff-Smith, A. (1998). Development itself is the key to understanding developmental disorders. *Trends in Cognitive Sciences, 2,* 389–398.

Kassin, S. M. (1984). Eyewitness identification: Victims vs. bystanders. *Journal of Applied Psychology, 14,* 519–529.

Kassin, S. M., Ellsworth, P. C., & Smith, V. L. (1989). The "general acceptance" of psychological research on eyewitness testimony. *American Psychologist, 44,* 1089–1098.

Kassin, S. M., & Wrightsman, L. S. (Eds.). (1985). *The Psychology of evidence and trial procedure.* Beverly Hills, CA: Sage.

Katchadourian, H. A. (Ed.). (1979). *Human sexuality: A comparative and developmental perspective.* Berkeley: University of California Press.

Katz, A. N. (1998). Figurative language and figurative thought: A review. In A. N. Katz, C. Cacciari, R. W. Gibbs, Jr., & M. Turner (Eds.), *Figurative language and thought* (pp. 3–43). New York: Oxford University Press.

Kausler, D. H. (1974). *Psychology of verbal learning and memory.* New York: Academic Press.

Keehn, J. D. (1979). *Psychopathology in animals: Research and clinical implications.* New York: Academic Press.

Keen, S. (1981). Eros and Alley Ooop: An interview with Donald Symons. *Psychology Today, 15*(2), 52–61.

Keenan, J. M., MacWhinney, B., & Mayhew, D. (1977). Pragmatics in memory: A study of natural conversation. *Journal of Verbal Learning and Verbal Behavior, 16,* 549–560.

Kehoe, E. J. (1988). A layered network model of associative learning: Learning to learn and configuration. *Psychological Review, 95,* 411–453.

Kehoe, E. J. (1989). Connectionist models of conditioning: A tutorial. *Journal of the Experimental Analysis of Behavior, 52,* 427–440.

Keil, F. (1984). Mechanisms in cognitive development and the structure of knowledge. In R. J. Sternberg (Ed.), *Mechanisms of cognitive development.* San Francisco: Freeman.

Keil, F. C. (1981). Constraints on knowledge and cognitive development. *Psychological Review, 88,* 197–227.

Kellogg, R. T. (1994). *The psychology of writing.* New York: Oxford University Press.

Kendler, H. H. (1952). What is learned?—A theoretical blind alley. *Psychological Review, 59,* 269–277.

Kendler, H., & Kendler, T. S. (1962). Vertical and horizontal processes in problem solving. *Psychological Review, 69,* 1–16. (Reprinted in R. Harper (Ed.), *The cognitive processes: Readings.* Englewood Cliffs, NJ: Prentice Hall.)

Kendon, A. (1991). Some considerations for a theory of language origins. *Man, 26,* 199–221.

Kenrick, D. T., Stringfield, D. O., Wagenhals, W. L., Dahl, R. H., & Ransdell, H. J. (1980). Sex differences, androgynyny, and approach responses to erotica: A new variation on the old volunteer problem. *Journal of Personality and Social Psychology, 38,* 317–324.

Kern, L., Mirels, H. L., & Hinshaw, V. G. (1983). Scientists' understanding of propositional logic: An experimental investigation. *Social Studies of Science, 13,* 131–146.

Kesner, R. P. (1986). Neurobiological views of learning and memory. In J. L. Martinez & R. P. Kesner (Eds.), *Learning and memory: A psychological view.* Orlando, FL: Academic Press.

Kesner, R. P. (1991). Neurobiological views of memory. In J. L. Martinez & R. P. Kesner, *Learning and memory: A biological view* (2nd ed.). San Diego: Academic Press.

Keysar, B. (1994). The illusory transparency of intention: Linguistic perspective taking in text. *Cognitive Psychology, 26,* 165–208.

Kihlstrom, J. F. (1989). On what does mood-dependent memory depend? *Journal of Social Behavior and Personality, 4,* 23–32.

Killackey, H. P. (1995). Evolution of the human brain: A neuroanatomical perspective. In M. S. Gazzinaga (Ed.), *The cognitive neurosciences* (pp. 1243–1253). Cambridge, MA: MIT Press.

Kimbel, W. H., Johanson, D. C., & Rak, Y. (1994). The first skull and other new discoveries of Australopithecus afarensis at Hadar, Ethiopia. *Nature, 368,* 449–451.

Kimura, D. (1981). Neural mechanisms in manual signing. *Language Studies, 33,* 291–312.

King, J., & Just, M. A. (1991). Individual differences in syntactic processing: The role of working memory. *Journal of Memory and Language, 30,* 580–602.

Kintsch, W. (1974). *The representation of meaning in memory.* Hillsdale, NJ: Erlbaum.

Kintsch, W. (1977). On comprehending stories. In P. Carpenter & M. Just (Eds.), *Cognitive processes in comprehension.* Hillsdale, NJ: Erlbaum.

Kintsch, W. (1992). A cognitive architecture for comprehension. In H. L. Pick, P. van den Broek, & D. C. Knill (Eds.), *The study of cognition: Conceptual and methodological issues* (pp. 143–164). Washington DC: American Psychological Association.

Kintsch, W. (1994). Text comprehension, memory, and learning. *American Psychologist, 49,* 294–303.

Kintsch, W. (1998). *Comprehension: A paradigm for cognition.* New York: Cambridge University Press.

Kintsch, W., & Bates, E. (1977). Recognition memory for statements from a classroom lecture. *Journal of Experimental Psychology: Human Learning and Memory, 3,* 150–159.

Kiraly, D. C. (1997). Think-aloud protocols and the construction of a professional translator self-concept. In J. H. Danks, G. M. Shreve, S. B. Fountain, & M. K. McBeath (Eds.), *Cognitive processes in translation and interpreting* (pp. 137–160). Thousand Oaks, CA: Sage.

Kirkpatrick, E. A. (1894). An experimental study of memory. *Psychological Review, 1,* 602–609.

Kitcher, P. (1985). *Vaulting ambition: Sociobiology and the quest for human nature.* Cambridge, MA: MIT Press.

Kitcher, P. (1987). Precis of *Vaulting Ambition:* Sociobiology and the quest for human nature. *Behavioral and Brain Sciences, 10,* 61–100.

Kjeldergaard, P. M. (1968). Transfer and mediation in verbal learning. In T. R. Dixon & D. L. Horton (Eds.), *Verbal behavior and general behavior theory.* Englewood Cliffs, NJ: Prentice Hall.

Klahr, D. (1980). Information-processing models of intellectual development. In R. H. Kluwe & H. Spada (Eds.), *Developmental models of thinking.* New York: Academic Press.

Klahr, D. (1984). Transition processes in cognitive development. In R. J. Sternberg (Ed.), *Mechanisms of cognitive development.* San Francisco: Freeman.

Klahr, D., Langley, P., & Neches, R. (Eds.). (1987). *Production system models of learning and development.* Cambridge, MA: Bradford/MIT Press.

Klahr, D., & Wallace, J. G. (1973). The role of quantification operators in the development of conservation of quantity. *Cognitive Psychology, 4,* 301–327.

Klahr, D., & Wallace, J. G. (1976). *Cognitive development: An information-processing view.* Hillsdale, NJ: Erlbaum.

Klayman, J., & Ha, Y. -W. (1989). Hypothesis testing in rule discovery: Strategy, structure, and content. *Journal of Experimental Psychology: Learning, Memory, and Cognition, 15,* 596–604.

Klein, S. B., & Mowrer, R. R. (Eds.). (1989a). *Contemporary learning theories: Pavlovian conditioning and the status of traditional learning theory.* Hillsdale, NJ: Erlbaum.

Klein, S. B., & Mowrer, R. R. (Eds.). (1989b). *Contemporary learning theories: Instrumental conditioning theory and the impact of biological constraints on learning.* Hillsdale, NJ: Erlbaum.

Klin, C. M., Guzmán, A. E., & Levine, W. H. (1999). Prevalence and persistence of predictive inferences. *Journal of Memory and Language, 40,* 593–604.

Knibb, R. C., Booth, D. A., Platts, R., Armstrong, A., Booth, I. W., & Macdonald, A. (1999). Episodic and semantic memory in accounts of food intolerance. *Applied Cognitive Psychology, 13,* 451–464.

Koch, S. (1951). Theoretical psychology, 1950: An overview. *Psychological Review, 58,* 295–301.

Koch, S. (1954). Clark L. Hull. In W. K. Estes, S. Koch, K. MacCorquodale, P. Meehl, C. G. Mueller, W. N. Schoenfeld, & W. S. Verplanck (Eds.), *Modern learning theory.* New York: Appleton-Century-Crofts.

Kohlberg, L. (1958). *The development of modes of thinking and choice in the years 10 to 16.* Unpublished doctoral dissertation, University of Chicago.

Kohlberg, L. (1971). From is to ought: How to commit the naturalistic fallacy and get away with it in the study of moral development. In T. Mischel (Ed.), *Cognitive development and epistemology.* New York: Academic Press.

Kohlberg, L. (1976). Moral stages and moralization: The cognitive-developmental approach. In T. Lickona (Ed.), *Moral development and behavior.* New York: Holt, Rinehart & Winston.

Kohlberg, L., & Kramer, R. (1976). Continuities and discontinuities in childhood and adult moral development. *Human Development, 1969, 12,* 93–120. Reprinted in *Contemporary issues in developmental psychology* (2nd ed.) by N. Endler, L. Bolter, & H. Osser (Eds.), New York: Holt, Rinehart & Winston.

Köhler, W. (1925). *The mentality of apes.* London: Routledge & Kegan Paul.

Kohnken, G., Thurer, C., & Zoberbier, D. (1994). The cognitive interview: Are the interviewers' memories enhanced, too? *Applied Cognitive Psychology, 8,* 13–24.

Kolers, P., & von Grunau, M. (1976). Shape and color in apparent motion. *Vision Research, 16,* 329–335.

Konishi, M. (1985). Birdsong: From behavior to neuron. *Annual Review of Neuroscience, 8,* 125–170.

Koriat, A. (1993). How do we know that we know? The accessibility model of the feeling of knowing. *Psychological Review, 100,* 609–639.

Koriat, A., & Goldsmith, M. (1996). Memory metaphors and the everyday-laboratory controversy: The correspondence versus the storehouse conceptions of memory. *Behavioral and Brain Sciences, 19,* 167–228.

Kosslyn, S. M. (1994). *Image and brain: The resolution of the imagery debate.* Cambridge, MA: The MIT Press.

Kosslyn, S. M., & Koenig, O. (1995). *Wet mind: The new cognitive neuroscience.* New York: Free Press.

Krafka, C., & Penrod, S. (1985). Reinstatement of context in a field experiment on eyewitness identification. *Journal of Personality and Social Psychology, 49,* 58–69.

Krantz, G. S. (1980). Sapienization and speech. *Current Anthropology, 21,* 773–779.

Krebs, J. R., Healy, S. D., & Shettleworth, S. J. (1990). Spatial memory of Paridae: Comparison of storing and nonstoring species P. ater and P. major. *Animal Behavior, 39,* 1127–1137.

Krechevsky, I. (1932). Hypotheses in rats. *Psychological Review, 49,* 516–532.

Krings, M., Stone, A., Schmitz, R. W., Krainitzki, H., Stoneking, M., & Paabo, S. (1997). Neandertal DNA seqences and the origin of modern humans. *Cell, 90,* 19–30.

Kristiansen, C. M., & Giulietti, R. (1990). Perceptions of wife abuse: Effects of gender, attitudes toward women, and just-world beliefs among college students. *Psychology of Women Quarterly, 14,* 177–189.

Kuhn, T. S. (1970). *The structure of scientific revolutions* (rev. ed.). Chicago: University of Chicago Press.

Kumon-Nakamura, S., Glucksberg, S., & Brown, M. (1995). How about another piece of pie: The allusional pretense theory of discourse irony. *Journal of Experimental Psychology: General, 124,* 3–21.

Kurtines, W., & Greif, E. (1974). The development of moral thought: Review and evaluation of Kohlberg's approach. *Psychological Bulletin, 81,* 453–470.

Kvavilashvili, L. (1998). Remembering intentions: Testing a new method of investigation. *Applied Cognitive Psychology, 12,* 533–554.

LaBerge, D. (1995). *Attentional processing: The brain's art of mindfulness.* Cambridge, MA: Harvard University Press.

Laberge, D. L. (1990). Attention. *Psychological Science, 1,* 156–162.

Lakoff, G. (1993). The contemporary theory of metaphor. In A. Ortony (Ed.), *Metaphor and thought* (2nd ed.). Cambridge, England: Cambridge University Press.

Lakoff, G., & Johnson, M. (1980). *Metaphors we live by.* Chicago: University of Chicago Press.

Lamb, M. R. (1991). Attention in human and animals: Is there a capacity limitation at the time of encoding? *Journal of Experimental Psychology: Animal Behavior Processes, 17,* 45–54.

Lamendella J. T. (1976). Relations between the ontogeny and phylogeny of language: A neorecapitulationist view. In S. R. Harnad, H. Steklis, &J. Lancaster (Eds.), *Annals of the New York Academy of Sciences* (Vol. 280). New York: New York Academy of Sciences.

Landauer, T. K. (1998). Learning and representing verbal meaning: The latent semantic analysis theory. *Current Directions in Psychological Science, 7,* 161–164.

Landauer, T. K., & Dumais, S. T. (1997). A solution to Plato's Problem: The Latent Semantic Analysis theory of acquisition, induction, and representation of knowledge. *Psychological Review, 104,* 211–240.

Landauer, T. K., Foltz, P., & Laham, R. D. (1998). An introduction to latent semantic analysis. *Discourse Processes, 25,* 259–284.

Langdon, J. H. (1985). Fossils and the origin of bipedalism. *Journal of Human Evolution, 14,* 615–635.

Langer, J. (1970). Werner's comparative organismic theory. In P. Mussen (Ed.), *Carmichael's manual of child psychology* (3rd ed., Vol. 1). New York: Wiley.

Larkin, J. (1981). Enriching formal knowledge: A model for learning to solve textbook physics problems. In J. R. Anderson (Ed.), *Cognitive skills and their acquisition.* Hillsdale, NJ: Erlbaum.

Larrick, R. P., Morgan, J. N., & Nisbett, R. E. (1990). Teaching the use of cost-benefit reasoning in everyday life. *Psychological Science, 1,* 362–370.

Larsen, S. F. (1987). Remembering and the archaeological metaphor. *Metaphor and Symbolic Activity, 2,* 187–199.

Lasch, C. (1978). *The culture of narcissism: American life in an age of diminishing expectations.* New York: Norton.

Lashley, K. S. (1923). The behavioristic interpretation of consciousness. *Psychological Review, 30*(1), 237–272; (11), 329–353.

Lashley, K. S. (1950). In search of the engram. *Symposium for the Society for Experimental Biology, 4,* 454–482.

Lazarus, R. (1977). A cognitive analysis of biofeedback control. In G. Schwartz & J. Beatty (Eds.), *Biofeedback: Theory and research.* New York: Academic Press.

Lazarus, R. S. (1991). *Emotion and adaptation.* New York: Oxford University Press.

Leahey, T. H. (1977). The development of conservation abilities: An intertask analysis of continuous quantity. *Merrill-Palmer Quarterly of Behavior and Development, 23,* 215–225.

Leahey, T. H. (1978). Adult strategies in two conservation related tasks. *Journal of General Psychology, 98,* 133–143.

Leahey, T. H. (1979). A cognitive reanalysis of anagram solution set learning. *Journal of General Psychology, 100,* 133–141.

Leahey, T. H. (1994). Is this a dagger I see before me? Four theorists in search of consciousness. *Contemporary Psychology, 39,* 575–582.

Leahey, T. H. (1996). *A history of psychology,* (4th ed.). Englewood Cliffs: Prentice Hall.

Leahey, T. H. (2000). *A history of psychology* (5th ed.). Upper Saddle River, NJ: Prentice-Hall.

Leahey, T. H., & Leahey, G. (1983). *Psychology's occult doubles: Psychology and the problem of pseudoscience.* Chicago: Nelson-Hall.

Leakey, M. G., Felbel, C. S., McDougall, I., & Walker, A. (1995). New four-million-year-old hominid species from Kanapoi and Allia Bay, Kenya. *Nature, 376,* 565–561.

Leck, K. J., Weekes, B. S., & Chen, M. J. (1995). Visual and phonological pathways to the lexicon: Evidence from Chinese readers. *Memory and Cognition, 23,* 468–476.

Le Doux, J. (1996). *The emotional brain.* New York: Simon & Schuster.

Ledoux, J. E., & Hirst, W. (Eds.). (1986). *Mind and brain: Dialogues in cognitive neuroscience.* Cambridge, England: Cambridge University Press.

Lee, L., Brittingham, A., Tourangeau, R., Willis, G., Ching, P., Jobe, J., & Black, S. (1999). Are reporting errors due to encoding limitations or retrieval failure? Surveys of child vaccination as a case study. *Applied Cognitive Psychology, 13,* 43–63.

Leithauser, B. (1987, March). A reporter at large: The space of one breath. *New Yorker,* 41–73.

Lenneberg, E. H. (1964). A biological perspective of language. In E. Lenneberg (Ed.), *New directions in the study of language.* Cambridge, MA: MIT Press.

Lenneberg, E. H. (1965). The natural history of language. In G. Miller & F. Smith (Eds.), *The genesis of language.* Cambridge, MA: MIT Press.

Lenneberg, E. H. (1967). *Biological foundations of language.* New York: Wiley.

Lenneberg, E. H. (1972). On explaining language. *Science, 1969, 164,* 635–643. Reprinted in Seligman & Hager.

Lepley, W. M. (1934). Serial reactions considered as conditioned reactions. *Psychological Monographs, 46,* 205.

Lepper, M., & Greene, D. (Eds.). (1978). *The hidden costs of reward.* Hillsdale, NJ: Erlbaum.

Leroy Ladurie, E. (1978). *Montaillou: The promised land of error.* New York: George Braziller.

Levenson, E. (1995, June). *Emotional regulation and marriage.* Paper presented at the 7th annual meeting of the American Psychological Society, New York.

Levine, C., Kohlberg, L., & Hewer, A. (1985). The current formulation of Kohlberg's theory and a response to critics. *Human Development, 28,* 94–100.

Levin, D. T., & Simons, D. J. (1997). Failure to detect changes to attended objects in motion pictures. *Psychonomic Bulletin and Review, 4,* 501–506.

Levine, F. J., & Tapp, J. L. (1973). The psychology of criminal identification: The gap from Wade to Kirby. *University of Pennsylvania Law Review, 121,* 1079–1131.

Levine, M. (1994). *Effective problem solving* (2nd ed.). Englewood Cliffs, NJ: Prentice Hall.

Levis, D. J. (1989). The case for a return to a two-factor theory of avoidance: The failur of non-fear interpretations. In S. B. Klein & R. R. Mowrer (Eds.), *Contemporary learning theories: Pavlovian conditioning and the status of traditional learning theory* (pp. 227–277). Hillsdale, NJ: Erlbaum.

Levy, C. M., & Ransdell, S. E. (Eds.). (1996). *The science of writing.* Mahwah, NJ: Erlbaum.

Levy, D. A. (1997). *Tools of critical thinking.* Boston: Allyn and Bacon.

Lewandowsky, S., Dunn, J. C., & Kirsner, K. (Eds.). (1989). *Implicit memory: Theoretical issues.* Hillsdale, NJ: Erlbaum.

Lewin, R. (1981). Do jumping genes make evolutionary leaps? *Science, 213,* 634–636.

Lewin, R. (1998). *Principles of human evolution.* Malden, MA: Blackwell.

Lewis, D. J. (1979). Psychobiology of active and inactive memory. *Psychological Review, 86,* 1054–1083.

Lewis, V. E., & Williams, R. N. (1989). Mood-congruent vs. mood-state dependent learning: Implications for a view of emotion. *Journal of Social Behavior and Personality, 4,* 23–32.

Liben, L. S. (1977). Memory from a cognitive developmental perspective: A theoretical and empirical review. In W. F. Overton & J. M. Gallagher (Eds.), *Knowledge and development. Vol. 1. Advances in research and theory.* New York: Plenum.

Liberman, A. M., Harris, K. S., Eimas, P. D., Lisicer, L., & Bastian, J. (1961). An effect of learning on speech perception: The discrimination of durations of silence with and without phonemic significance. *Language and Speech, 4,* 175–195.

Lickona, T. (Ed.). (1976). *Moral development and behavior.* New York: Holt, Rinehart & Winston.

Lie, N. (1992). Follow-ups of children with attention deficit hyperactivity disorder (ADHD): Review of literature. *Acta Psychiatrica Scandinavica, 85*(368, Suppl.).

Lieberman, P. (1975). *On the origins of language.* New York: Macmillan.

Lieberman, P. (1984). *The biology and evolution of language.* Cambridge, MA: Harvard University Press.

Lieberman, P. (1985). On the evolution of human syntactic ability. *Journal of Human Evolution, 14,* 657–668.

Lieberman, P. (1987). Some biological constraints on universal grammar. In M. L. Rice & R. L. Schiefelbusch (Eds.), *The teachability of language.* Baltimore: Paul H. Brooks.

Lieberman, P. (1992). Human speech and language. In S. Jones, R. Martin, & D. Pilbeam (Eds.), *The Cambridge encyclopedia of evolution* (pp. 134–137). Cambridge, England: Cambridge University Press.

Liebert, R., & Poulos, R. (1976). Television as a moral teacher. In T. Lickona (Ed.), *Moral development and behavior.* New York: Holt, Rinehart & Winston.

Lightfoot, D. (1989). The child's trigger experience: Degree-0 learnability. *Behavioral and Brain Sciences, 12,* 321–376.

Linde, C., & Labov, W. (1975). Spatial networks as a site for the study of language and thought. *Language, 51,* 924–939.

Linden, E. (1981). *Apes, men, and language* (rev. ed.). New York: Penguin.

Lindsay, D. S., & Read, J. D. (1994). Psychotherapy and memories of childhood sexual abuse: A cognitive perspective. *Applied Cognitive Psychology, 8,* 281–338.

Lindsay, P. H., & Norman, D. A. (1977). *Human information processing* (2nd ed.). New York: Academic Press.

Lindsay, R. C. L., Smith, S. M., & Pryke, S. (1999). Measures of lineup fairness: Do they postdict identification accuracy? *Applied Cognitive Psychology, 13,* S93–S107.

Linton, M. (1986). Ways of searching and the contents of memory. In D. C. Rubin (Ed.), *Autobiographical memory* (pp. 50–67). Cambridge, England: Cambridge University Press.

Lipton, J. P. (1977). On the psychology of eyewitness testimony. *Journal of Applied Psychology, 62,* 90–95.

Lockhart, R. S., & Craik, F. I. M. (1978). Levels of processing: A reply to Eysenck. *British Journal of Psychology, 69,* 171–175.

Lockhart, R. S., & Craik, F. I. M. (1990). Levels of processing: A retrospective commentary on a framework for memory research. *Canadian Journal of Psychology, 44,* 87–112.

Loehlin, J., Willerman, L., & Horn, J. (1988). Human behavior genetics. *Annual Review of Psychology, 39,* 101–134.

Loevinger, J., & Knoll, E. (1983). Personality: Stages, traits, and the self. *Annual Review of Psychology, 34.*

Loftus, E. (1993). Desperately seeking memories of the first few years of childhood: The reality of early memories. *Journal of Experimental Psychology: General, 121,* 274–277.

Loftus, E. F. (1974). On reading the fine print. *Quarterly Journal of Experimental Psychology, 27,* 324.

Loftus, E. F. (1980). Impact of expert testimony on the unreliability of eyewitness identification. *Journal of Applied Psychology, 65,* 9–15.

Loftus, E. F. (1993). The reality of repressed memories. *American Psychologist, 48,* 518–537.

Loftus, E. F. (1997). Memory for a past that never was. *Current Directions in Psychological Science, 6,* 60–65.

Loftus, E. F., & Coan, D. (in press). The construction of childhood memories. In D. Peters (Ed.), *The child witness in context: Cognitive, social, and legal perspectives.* New York: Kluwer.

Loftus, E. F., Donders, K., Hoffman, H. G., & Schooler, J. W. (1989). Creating new memories that are quickly accessed and confidently held. *Memory and Cognition, 17,* 607–616.

Loftus, E. F., & Hoffman, H. G. (1989). Misinformation and memory: The creation of new memories. *Journal of Experimental Psychology: General, 118,* 100–104.

Loftus, E. F., & Ketcham, K. (1991). *Witness for the defense: The accused, the eyewitness, and the expert who puts memory on trial.* New York: St. Martin's Press.

Loftus, E. F., & Ketcham, K. (1994). *The myth of repressed memory.* New York: St. Martin's Press.

Loftus, E. F., & Loftus, G. R. (1980). On the permanence of stored information in the human brain. *American Psychologist, 35,* 409–420.

Loftus, E. F., & Messo, J. (1987). Some facts about "weapon focus." *Law and Human Behavior, 11,* 55–62.

Loftus, E. F., Miller, D. G., & Burns, H. J. (1978). Semantic integration of verbal information into a visual memory. *Journal of Experimental Psychology: Human Learning and Memory, 4,* 19–31.

Loftus, E. F., & Palmer, J. C. (1974). Reconstruction of automobile destruction: An example of the interaction between language and memory. *Journal of Verbal Learning and Verbal Behavior, 13,* 585–589.

Loftus, E. F., & Pickrell, J. E. (1995). The formation of false memories. *Psychiatric Annals, 25,* 720–725.

Logie, R. H. (1995). *Visuo-spatial working memory.* Hillsdale, NJ: Erlbaum.

Logle, R. H., & Denis, M. (Eds.). (1991). *Mental images in human cognition.* Amsterdam: North-Holland.

Lolordo, V. M., & Doungas, A. (1989). Selective associations and adaptive specializations: Taste aversion and phobias. In S. B. Klein & R. R. Mowrer (Eds.), *Contemporary learning theories: Instrumental conditioning theory and the impact of biological constraints on learning* (pp. 145–179). Hillsdale, NJ: Erlbaum.

Lord, C., Ross, D., & Lepper, M. R. (1979). Biased assimilation and attitude polarization: The effects of prior theories on subsequently considered evidence. *Journal of Personality and Social Psychology, 37,* 2089–2109.

Lorenz, K. (1966). *On aggression.* New York: Harcourt Brace Jovanovich.

Lourenço, O., & Machado, A. (1996). In defense of Piaget's theory: A reply to 10 common criticisms. *Psychological Review, 103,* 143–164.

Lovejoy, C. O. (1981). The origin of man. *Science, 211,* 341–350.

Lubek, I., & Apfelbaum, E. (1981, June 10–13). *The hidden injuries of classical conditioning: An historical and psychological look at editorial taste in taste-aversion learning.* Paper presented at the Annual Meeting of the Cheiron Society, River Falls, WI.

Lubow, R. E., Weiner, I., & Schnur, P. (1981). Conditioned attention theory. *The Psychology of Learning and Motivation, 15,* 1–50.

Luckhardt, C. G. (1983). Wittgenstein and behaviorism. *Synthese, 56,* 319–338.

Lukatela, G., & Turvey, M. T. (1998). Reading in two alphabets. *American Psychologist, 53,* 1057–1072.

Lumsden, C. J., & Wilson, E. O. (1981). *Genes, mind, and culture.* Cambridge, MA: Harvard University Press.

Lumsden, C. J., & Wilson, E. O. (1983). The dawn of intelligence. *The Sciences, 23*(2), 22–31.

Lupker, S. J., Harbluk, J. L., & Patrick, A. S. (1991). Memory for things forgotten. *Journal of Experimental Psychology; Learning, Memory, and Cognition, 17,* 897–907.

Luria, A. R. (1968). *The mind of a mnemonist.* New York: Basic Books.

Lynch, G. (1985, September/October). What memories are made of. *The Sciences,* 38–43.

Lynch, G. (1986). *Synapses, circuits and the beginnings of memory.* Cambridge, MA: MIT Press.

Lynch, G., McGaugh, J. L., & Weinberger, N. M. (Eds.). (1986). *Neurobiology of learning and memory.* New York: Guilford.

Lynch, K. (1960). *The image of the city.* Cambridge, MA: MIT and Harvard University Press.

MacAuley, C. (1990, July 24–28). Assigned to Guinea-Bissau. *World Monitor.*

Maccoby, C. E., & Jacklin, C. N. (1974). *The psychology of sex differences* (Vols. 1–2). Stanford, CA: Stanford University Press.

MacCorquodale, K., & Meehl, P. (1954). Edward C. Tolman. In W. K. Estes, S. Koch, K. MacCorquodale, P. Meehl, C. G. Mueller, W. N. Schoenfeld, & W. S. Verplanck (Eds.), *Modern learning theory.* New York: Appleton-Century-Crofts.

MacDonald, K. (1984). An ethological-social learning theory of altruism: Implications for human sociobiology. *Ethology and Sociobiology, 5,* 97–109.

MacDonald, M. C., Just, M. A., & Carpenter, P. A. (1992). Working memory constraints on the processing of syntactic ambiguity. *Cognitive Psychology, 234,* 56–98.

MacEarlane, D. A. (1930). The role of kinesthesis in maze learning. *University of California Publications in Psychology, 4,* 277–305.

Mackenzie, J. (1886). The production of the so-called "rose cold" by means of an artificial rose. *American Journal of Medical Science, 91,* 45–57.

Mackintosh, N. J. (1978). Cognitive or associative theories of conditioning: Implications of an analysis of blocking. In S. Hulse, H. Fowler, & W. Honig (Eds.), *Cognitive processes in animal behavior.* Hillsdale, NJ: Erlbaum.

Mackintosh, N. J. (1985). Varieties of conditioning. In N. M. Weinberger, J. L. McGaugh, & G. Lynch (Eds.), *Memory systems of the brain: Animal and human cognitive processes.* New York: Guilford.

MacLeod, C. M. (1991). Half a century of research on the Stroop Effect: An integrative review. *Psychological Bulletin, 109,* 163–203.

Macmillan, M. (1997). *Freud evaluated: The completed arc.* Cambridge, MA: MIT Press.

MacNamara, J. (1976). Stomachs assimilate and accommodate, don't they? *Canadian Psychological Review, 17,* 167–173.

MacWhinney, B. (Ed.). (1987). The competition model. In *Mechanisms of language acquisition.* Hillsdale, NJ: Erlbaum.

MacWhinney, B., Keenan, J. M., & Reinke, P. (1982). The role of arousal in memory for conversation. *Memory and Cognition, 10,* 308–317.

MacWhinney, B., & McDonald, J. L. (1991). Levels of learning: A comparison of concept formation and language acquisition. *Journal of Memory and Language, 30,* 407–430.

Maddox, J. (1994). The age of the australopithecines. *Nature, 372,* 31–32.

Mahoney, M. J., & DeMonbreun, B. G. (1981). *Problem solving bias in scientists.* (Reprinted in *On scientific thinking* by R. D. Tweney, M. E. Doherty, & C. R. Mynatt, Eds., 1981, New York: Columbia University Press)

Maier, S. F. (1970). Failure to escape traumatic shock: Incompatible skeletal responses or learned helplessness? *Learning and Motivation, 1,* 157–170.

Maier, S. F. (1989). Learned helplessness: Event covariation and cognitive changes. In S. B. Klein & R. R. Mowrer (Eds.), *Contemporary learning theories: Instrumental conditioning theory and the impact of biological constraints on learning* (pp. 73–110). Hillsdale, NJ: Erlbaum.

Maier, S., & Seligman, M. (1976). Learned helplessness: Theory and evidence. *Journal of Experimental Psychology: General, 105,* 3–46.

Maki, R., Foley, J., Kaier, W., Thompson, R., & Willert, M. (1990). Increased processing enhances calibration of comprehension. *Journal of Experimental Psychology: Learning, Memory, and Cognition, 16,* 609–616.

Malcolm, N. (1964). Behaviorism as a philosophy of psychology. In T. W. Wann (Ed.), *Behaviorism and phenomenology.* Chicago: University of Chicago Press.

Malmi, W. A. (1976). Chimpanzees and language evolution. In S. R. Harnad, H. Steklis, &J. Lancaster (Eds.), *Annals of the New York Academy of Sciences* (Vol. 280). New York: New York Academy of Sciences.

Malpass, R. S., & Lindsay, R. C. L. (1999). Measuring lineup fairness. *Applied Cognitive Psychology, 13,* S1–S7.

Maltzman, I. (1955). Thinking: From a behavioristic point of view. *Psychological Review, 66,* 367–386.

Maltzman, I. (1977). Orienting in classical conditioning and generalization of the galvanic skin response to words: An overview. *Journal of Experimental Psychology: General, 106,* 111–119.

Maltzman, I. (1979). Orienting reflexes and significance: A reply to O'Gorman. *Psychophysiology, 16,* 274–282.

Maltzman, I. (1987). A neo-Pavlovian interpretation of the OR and classical conditioning in humans: With comments on alcoholism and the poverty of cognitive psychology. In G. C. L. Davey (Ed.), *Cognitive processes and Pavlovian conditioning in humans* (pp. 251–286). New York: Wiley.

Maltzman, I., & Morrisett, L. (1952). Different strengths of set in the solution of anagrams. *Journal of Experimental Psychology, 44,* 242–246.

Maltzman, I., & Morrisett, L. (1953a). The effects of single and compound classes of anagrams on set solutions. *Journal of Experimental Psychology, 45,* 345–350.

Maltzman, I., & Morrisett, L. (1953b). Effects of task instructions on solutions of different classes of anagrams. *Journal of Experimental Psychology, 45,* 351–354.

Maltzman, I., Raskin, D., & Wolff, C. (1979). Latent inhibition of the GSR conditioned to words. *Physiological Psychology, 7,* 193–203.

Mandler, G. (1987). Emotion. In R. L. Gregory (Ed.), *The Oxford companion to the mind* (pp. 219–220). Oxford: Oxford University Press.

Mandler, J. M., & Murphy, C. M. (1983). Subjective judgments of script structure. *Journal of Experimental Psychology: Learning, Memory, and Cognition, 9,* 534–543.

Manktelow, K. I., & Over, D. E. (1990). Deontic thought and the selection task. In K. H. Gilhooly, M. T. G. Keane, R. H. Logie, & G. Erdos (Eds.), *Lines of thinking: Reflections on the psychology of thought, Vol. I: Representation, reasoning, analogy, and decision making.* New York: Wiley.

Mantwill, M., Kohnken, G., & Aschermann, E. (1995). Effects of the cognitive interview on the recall of familiar and unfamiliar events. *Journal of Applied Psychology, 80,* 68–78.

Maratsos, M. P. (1989). Innateness and plasticity in language acquisition. In M. L. Rice & R. L. Schiefelbusch (Eds.), *The teachability of language.* Baltimore: Paul H. Brooks.

Marcel, A. J. (1983). Conscious and unconscious perception: An approach to the relations between phenomenal experience and perceptual processes. *Cognitive Psychology, 15,* 238–300.

Marcus, G. F. (1999a). Connectionism with or without rules? *Trends in Cognitive Sciences, 3,* 168–170.

Marcus, G. F. (1999b). Reply to Seidenberg and Elman. *Trends in Cognitive Sciences, 3,* 289.

Marcus, G. F. (1999c). Genes, proteins and domain-specificity. *Trends in Cognitive Sciences, 3,* 367.

Marek, G. R. (1975). *Toscanini.* London: Vision Press.

Markowitsch, H. J. (1995). The anatomical basis of memory disorders. In M. S. Gazzinaga (Ed.), *The cognitive neurosciences* (pp. 765–779). Cambridge, MA: MIT Press.

Markus, H. (1980). The self in thought and memory. In D. M. Wegner & R. R. Vallecker (Eds.), *The self in social psychology.* London: Oxford University Press.

Markus, H., Crane, M., Bernstein, S., & Saladi, M. (1982). Self-schemas and gender. *Journal of Personality and Social Psychology, 42,* 38–50.

Markus, H., & Nurlus, P. (1986). Possible selves. *American Psychologist, 41,* 954–969.

Marler, P. (1970). A comparative approach to vocal learning: Song development in white crowned sparrows. *Journal of Comparative and Physiological Psychology, 71,* 1–25.

Marler, P. (1976). An ethological theory of the origin of vocal learning. In S. R. Harnad, H. Steklis, & J. Lancaster (Eds.), *Annals of the New York Academy of Sciences* (Vol. 280). New York: New York Academy of Sciences.

Marler, P. (1991). The instinct to learn. In S. Carey & R. Gelman (Eds.), *The epigenesis of mind: Essays on biology and cognition.* Hillsdale, NJ: Erlbaum.

Marler, P., & Peters, S. (1981). Sparrows learn adult song and more from memory. *Science, 213,* 780–782.

Marr, D. (1982). *Vision.* San Francisco: Freeman.

Marschark, M., Richman, C. L., Yuille, J. C., & Hunt, R. R. (1987). The role of imagery in memory: On shared and distinctive information. *Psychological Bulletin, 102,* 28–41.

Marsh, R. L., Hicks, J. L., & Bryan, E. S. (1999). The activation of unrelated and canceled intentions. *Memory and Cognition, 27,* 320–327.

Marsh, R. L., Hicks, J. L., & Landau, J. D. (1998). An investigation of everyday prospective memory. *Memory and Cognition, 26,* 633–643.

Marshack, A. (1972). *The roots of civilization.* New York: McGraw-Hill.

Marshack, A. (1976). Some implications of the Paleolithic symbolic evidence for the origin of language. In S. R. Harnad, H. Steklis, &J. Lancaster (Eds.), *Annals of the New York Academy of Sciences* (Vol. 280). New York: New York Academy of Sciences.

Marshall, J. C. (1980). On the biology of language acquisition. In D. Caplan (Ed.), *Biological studies of mental processes.* Cambridge, MA: MIT Press.

Martin, I., & Levey, A. B. (1987). Learning what will happen next: Conditioning, evaluation, and cognitive processes. In G. C. L. Davey (Ed.), *Cognitive processes and Pavlovian conditioning in humans* (pp. 57–81). New York: Wiley.

Martin, N., Boomsma, D., & Machin, G. (1997). A twin-pronged attack on complex traits. *Nature Genetics, 17,* 387–392.

Martinez, J. L., & Kesner, R. P. (1991). *Learning and memory: A biological view* (2nd ed.). San Diego: Academic Press.

Martinez, J. L., Schulteis, G., & Weiberger, S. B. (1991). How to increase the strength of memory traces: The effects of drugs and hormones. In J. L. Martinez & R. P. Kesner (Eds.), *Learning and memory: A biological view* (2nd ed.). San Diego: Academic Press.

Martlew, M. (Ed.). (1983). *The psychology of written language: A developmental approach.* New York: Wiley.

Massaro, D. W. (1988). Some criticisms of connectionist models of human performance. *Journal of Memory and Language, 27,* 213–234.

Massaro, D. W., & Loftus, G. R. (1996). Sensory and perceptual storage: Data and theory. In E. L. Bjork & R. A. Bjork (Eds.), *Memory* (pp. 68–99). San Diego: Academic Press.

Massicotte, G., & Baudry, M. (1991). Tiggers and substrates of hippocampal synaptic plasticity. *Neuroscience and Biobehavioral Review, 15,* 415–423.

Mathews, A., Mackintosh, B., & Fulcher, E. P. (1997). Cognitive biases in anxiety and attention to threat. *Trends in Cognitive Sciences, 1,* 340–345.

Matthews, K. A., Kuller, L. H., Siegel, J. M., Thompson, M., & Varat, M. (1983). Determinants of decisions to seek medical treatment by patients with acute myocardial infarction symptoms. *Journal of Personality and Social Psychology, 44,* 1144–1156.

Mattlingly, I. G., & Studdert-Kennedy, M. (Eds.). (1990). *Modularity and the motor theory of speech perception.* Hillsdale, NJ: Erlbaum.

Maynard Smith, J. (1971). What use is sex? *Journal of Theoretical Biology, 30,* 319–335.

Maynard Smith, J. (1978). *The evolution of sex.* London: Cambridge University Press.

Maynard Smith, J. (1982a). The evolution of social behaviour: A classification of models. In King's College Sociobiology Group (Eds.), *Current problems in sociobiology*. Cambridge, England: Cambridge University Press.

Maynard Smith, J. (1982b). *Evolution and the theory of games*. Cambridge, England: Cambridge University Press.

Maynard Smith, J. (1984). Game theory and the evolution of behavior. *Behavioral and Brain Sciences, 1,* 95–126.

Mazzoni, G., Cornoldi, C., & Marchitelli, G. (1990). Do memorability ratings affect study-time allocation? *Memory and Cognition, 18,* 196–204.

Mazzoni, G. A. L., Loftus, E. F., Seitz, A., & Lynn, S. J. (1999). Changing beliefs and memories through dream interpretation. *Applied Cognitive Psychology, 13,* 125–144.

McClelland, J. L. (1988). Connectionist models and psychological evidence. *Journal of Memory and Language, 27,* 107–123.

McClelland, J. L., McNaughton, B. L., & O'Reilly, R. C. (1995). Why are there complementary learning systems in the hippocampus and neocortex: Insights from the successes and failures of connectionist models of learning and memory. *Psychological Review, 102,* 419–457.

McClelland, J. L., Rumelhart, D. E., & the PDP Research Group. (1986). *Parallel distributed processing: Explorations in the microstructure of cognition. Vol. 2. Psychological and biological models*. Cambridge, MA: Bradford Books, MIT Press.

McCloskey, M. (1983). Intuitive physics. *Scientific American, 248*(4), 122–130.

McCloskey, M. (1991). Networks and theories: The place of connectionism in cognitive science. *Psychological Science, 2,* 387–395.

McCloskey, M., & Egeth, H. E. (1983). Eyewitness identification: What can a psychologist tell a jury? *American Psychologist, 38,* 550–563.

McCloskey, M., Wible, C. G., & Cohen, N. J. (1988). Is there a special flashbulb-memory mechanisms? *Journal of Experimental Psychology: General, 117,* 171–181.

McCrone, J. (1991). *The ape that spoke: Language and the evolution of the human mind*. New York: William Morrow.

McDonald, M. A. (1995). Prospective memory: Progress and processes. In D. L. Medin (Ed.), *The psychology of learning and motivation* (Vol. 33, pp. 191–221). San Diego: Academic Press.

McGaugh, J. L., Weinberger, N. M., & Lynch, G. (1995). *Brain and memory: Modulation and Mediation of Neuroplasticity*. New York: Oxford University Press.

McGeoch, J. A., & Irion, A. L. (1952). *The psychology of human learning* (2nd ed.). New York: Longman.

McGlone, M. S. (1996). Conceptual metaphors and figurative language interpretation: Food for thought? *Journal of Memory and Language, 35,* 544–565.

McGlone, M. S. (2000). Concepts as metaphors. In S. Glucksberg & M. S. McGlone (Eds.), *Understanding figurative language comprehension: From metaphors to idioms*. Oxford, England: Oxford University Press.

McGlone, M. S., & Reed, A. B. (1998). Anchoring in the interpretation of probability expressions. *Journal of Pragmatics, 30,* 723–733.

McGlone, M. S., & Tofighbakhsh, J. (1999). The Keats heuristic: Rhyme as reason in aphorism interpretation. *Poetics, 26,* 235–244.

McHenry, H. M. (1982). The pattern of human evolution: Studies on bipedalism, mastication and encephalization. *Annual Review of Anthropology, 11,* 151–173.

McKeithen, K. B., Reitman, J. S., Reuter, H. H., & Hirtle, D. C. (1981). Knowledge organization and skill differences in computer programmers. *Cognitive Psychology, 13,* 307–325.

McKoon, G., & Ratcliff, R. (1981). The comprehension processes and memory structures involved in instrumental reference. *Journal of Verbal Learning and Verbal Behavior, 20,* 671–682.

McKoon, G., & Ratcliff, R. (1992). Inference during reading. *Psychological Review, 99,* 440–466.

McKoon, G., & Ratcliff, R. (1995). The minimalist hypothesis: Directions for research In C. A. Weaver, S. Mannes, & C. R. Fletcher (Eds.), *Discourse comprehension: Essays in honor of Walter Kintsch* (pp. 97–116). Hillsdale, NJ: Erlbaum.

McKoon, G., & Ratcliff, R. (1998). Memory-based language processing: Psycholinguistic research in the 1990s. *Annual Review of Psychology, 49,* 25–42.

McLelland, J. L., & Plaut, D. C. (1999). Does generalization in infant learning implicate abstract algebra-like rules? *Trends in Cognitive Sciences, 3,* 166–168.

McNamara, H., Long, J., & Wike, E. (1956). Learning without response under two conditions of external cues. *Journal of Comparative and Physiological Psychology, 49,* 477–480.

McNeil, D. (1970). *The acquisition of language.* New York: Harper & Row.

McShane, J. (1991). *Cognitive development: An information processing approach.* Oxford: Basil Blackwell.

Mealey, L. (1985). The relationship between social status and biological success: A case study of the Mormon religious hierarchy. *Ethology and Sociology, 6,* 249–257.

Means, B., & Loftus, E. F. (1991). When personal history repeats itself: Decomposing memories for recurring events. *Applied Cognitive Psychology, 5,* 297–318.

Medin, D., Roberts, W., & Davis, R. (Eds.). (1976). *Processes of animal memory.* Hillsdale, NJ: Erlbaum.

Medin, D. L., & Bazerman, M. H. (1999). Broadening behavioral decision research: Multiple levels of cognitive processing. *Psychonomic Bulletin and Review, 6,* 533–546.

Mednick, S. A. (1962). The associative basis of the creative process. *Psychological Review, 69,* 220–232.

Mednick, S. A., & Mednick, M. T. (1967). *Remote associates test.* Boston: Houghton Mifflin.

Mellers, B. A., Schwartz, A., & Cooke, A. D. J. (1998). Judgment and decision making. *Annual Review of Psychology, 49,* 447–477.

Merikle, P. M. (1980). Selection from visual persistence by perceptual groups and category membership. *Journal of Experimental Psychology: General, 109,* 279–295.

Metcalfe, J. (1986). Premonitions of insight predict impending error. *Journal of Experimental Psychology: Learning, Memory, and Cognition, 12,* 623–634.

Metcalfe, J., Schwartz, B. L., & Joaquim, S. G. (1993). The cue-familiarity heuristic in metacognition. *Journal of Experimental Psychology: Learning, Memory, and Cognition, 19,* 851–864.

Meyer, D. E., Schvaneveldt, R. W., & Ruddy, M. G. (1974). Loci of contextual effects on visual word recognition. In P. Rabbitt & S. Dornic (Eds.), *Attention and performance.* New York: Academic Press.

Middleton, D., & Edwards, D. (Eds.). (1990). *Collective remembering.* London: Sage.

Midgley, M. (1978). *Beast and man.* Ithaca, NY: Cornell University Press.

Milgram, S. (1974). *Obedience to authority.* New York: Harper & Row.

Millar, K. (1987). Assessment of memory for anaesthesia. In I. Hindmarch, J. G. Jones, & E. Moss (Eds.), *Aspects of recovery from anaesthesia* (pp. 75–91). Chichester, England: Wiley.

Miller, G. A. (1956). The magical number, seven, plus or minus two: Some limits on our capacity for processing information. *Psychological Review, 63,* 81–97.

Miller, G. A. (1981). *Language and speech.* San Francisco: Freeman.

Miller, G. A. (1990). The place of language in a scientific psychology. *Psychological Science, 1,* 7–14.

Miller, G. A. (1999). On knowing a word. *Annual Review of Psychology, 50,* 1–19.

Miller, G. A., & Gildea, P. M. (1987, September). How children learn words. *Scientific American,* 94–99.

Miller, J. L., & Eimas, P. D. (1983). Studies on the categorization of speech by infants. *Cognition, 13,* 135–165.

Miller, N. E., & Dollard, J. (1941). *Social learning and imitation.* New Haven: Yale University Press.

Miller, R. R., & Matzel, L. D. (1989). Contingency and relative association strength. In S. B. Klein & R. R. Mowrer (Eds.), *Contemporary learning theories: Pavlovian conditioning and the status of traditional learning theory* (pp. 61–84). Hillsdale, NJ: Erlbaum.

Milo, R. G., & Quiatt, D. (1993). Glottogenesis and anatomically modern Homo sapiens: The evidence for and implication of a late origin of vocal language. *Current Anthropology, 34,* 569–581.

Mischel, T. (1971). *Cognitive development and epistemology.* New York: Academic Press.

Mischel, W., & Mischel, H. (1976). A cognitive social learning approach to morality and self-regulation. In T. Lickona (Ed.), *Moral development and behavior.* New York: Holt, Rinehart & Winston.

Mishkin, M., & Appenzeller, T. (1987, June). The anatomy of memory. *Scientific American,* 80–89.

Mithen, S. (1996). *The prehistory of the mind: The origins of art, religion, and science.* London: Thames and Hudson.

Mitroff, I. (1974). *Scientists and confirmation bias.* Reprinted in Tweney, Doherty, & Mynatt (1981).

Minasi, M. (1990, February). Expert systems for a rainy day. *AI Expert, 5,* 13–15.

Modgil, S., & Modgil, C. (Eds.). (1982). *Jean Piaget: Consensus and controversy.* London: Holt, Rinehart & Winston.

Modgil, S., & Modgil, C. (Eds.). (1986). *Lawrence Kohlberg: Consensus and controversy.* Philadelphia: Falmer Press.

Money, J., & Erhardt, A. (1972). *Man and woman: Boy and girl.* Baltimore: The Johns Hopkins University Press.

Montague, A. (1976). Toolmaking, hunting, and the origin of language. In S. R. Harnad, H. Steklis, & J. Lancaster (Eds.), *Annals of the New York Academy of Sciences* (Vol. 280). New York: New York Academy of Sciences.

Montague, A. (Ed.). (1980). *Sociobiology examined.* New York: Oxford University Press.

Montague, M. F. A. (Ed.). (1968). *Man and aggression.* London: Oxford University Press.

Moore, J. (1984). The evolution of reciprocal sharing. *Ethology and Sociobiology, 5,* 1–14.

Morris, P. (1981). The cognitive psychology of self-reports. In C. Antaki (Ed.), *The psychology of ordinary explanations of social behavior.* London: Academic Press.

Moskowitz, B. A. (1978, November). The acquisition of language. *Scientific American, 239,* 92–108.

Mowrer, O. H. (1954). The psychologist looks at language. *American Psychologist, 9,* 660–694.

Mueller, C., & Schoenfeld, W. (1954). Edwin R. Guthrie. In W. K. Estes, S. Koch, K. Mac-Corquodale, P. Meehl, C. G. Mueller, W. N. Schoenfeld, & W. S. Verplanck (Eds.), *Modern learning theory.* New York: Appleton-Century-Crofts.

Munsterberg, H. (1908). *On the witness stand.* New York: Boardman.

Murphy, G. L. (1996). On metaphoric representation. *Cognition, 60,* 173–186.

Murphy, G. L. (1997). Reasons to doubt the present evidence for metaphoric representation. *Cognition, 62,* 99–108.

Myers, G. (1987). *William James: His life and thought.* New Haven, CT: Yale University Press.

Myers, R. E. (1976). Comparative neurology of vocalization and speech: Proof of a dichotomy. In S. R. Harnad, H. Steklis, & J. Lancaster (Eds.), *Annals of the New York Academy of Sciences* (Vol. 280). New York: New York Academy of Sciences.

Mylander, C., & Goldin-Meadow, S. (1990). Beyond the input given: The child's role in the acquisition of language. *Language, 66,* 323–355.

Mynatt, C. R., Doherty, M. E., & Tweney, R. D. (1981). A simulated research environment. In R. D. Tweney, et.al. *On scientific thinking.* New York: Columbia University Press.

Näätänen, R. (1992). *Attention and brain function.* Hillsdale, NJ: Erlbaum.

Nadel, L., & Jacobs, W. J. (1998). Traumatic memory is special. *Current Directions in Psychological Science, 7,* 154–157.

Neisser, U. (1976). *Cognition and reality.* San Francisco: Freeman.

Neisser, U. (1981). John Dean's memory: A case study. *Cognition, 9,* 1–22.

Neisser, U. (Ed.). (1982). *Memory observed.* San Francisco: Freeman.

Neisser, U., & Hyman, I. (Eds.). (1999). *Memory observed: Remembering in natural contexts* (2nd ed.). New York: W.H. Freeman.

Nelson, C. A. (1999). Neural plasticity and human development. *Current Directions in Psychological Science, 8,* 42–45.

Nelson, K. (1992). Emergence of autobiographical memory at age 4. *Human Development, 35,* 172–177.

Nelson, K. (1993). The psychological and social origins of autobiographical memory. *Psychological Science, 4,* 7–14.

Nelson, K. E. (Ed.). (1980). *Children's language* (Vol. 2). New York: Gardner Press.

Nelson, K. E. (1993). The psychological and social origins of autobiographical memory. *Psychological Science, 4,* 7–14.

Nelson, L. J., & Miller, D. T. (1995). The distinctiveness effect in social categorization: You are what makes you unusual. *Psychological Science, 6,* 246–249.

Nelson, T. O. (1988). Predictive accuracy of the feeling of knowing across different criterion tasks and across different subject populations and individuals. In M. Gruneberg, P. Morris, & R. Sykes (Eds.), *Practical aspects of memory: Current research and issues* (Vol. I, pp. 190–196). New York: Wiley.

Nelson, T. O. (Ed.). (1992). *Metacognition: Core readings.* Boston: Allyn Bacon.

Nelson, T. O., & Leonesio, R. J. (1988). Allocation of self-paced study time and the "labor-in-vain effect." *Journal of Experimental Psychology: Learning, Memory, and Cognition, 14,* 676–686.

Nelson, T. O., & Narens, L. (1990). Metamemory: A theoretical framework and new findings. In G. Bower (Ed.), *The psychology of learning and motivation* (Vol. 26, pp. 125–173). New York: Academic Press.

Newell, A. (1973). Production systems. In W. G. Chase, *Visual information processing.* New York: Academic Press.

Newell, A. (1990). Unified theories of cognition. Cambridge, MA: Harvard University Press.

Newell, A., & Simon, H. A. (1972). Human problem solving. Englewood Cliffs, NJ: Prentice Hall.

Newell, A., & Simon, H. A. (1990). Computer search as empirical enquiry: Symbols and search. *Communications of the ACM, 19.* (Original work published 1976) In M. A. Boden (Ed.), *The philosophy of artificial intelligence.* Oxford: Oxford University Press.

Newport, E. L. (1991). Contrasting concepts of the critical period for language acquisition. In S. Carey & R. Gelman (Eds.), *The epigenesis of mind: Essays on biology and cognition.* Hillsdale, NJ: Erlbaum.

Newport, E. L., Gleitman, H., & Gleitman, L. R. (1977). Mother, I'd rather do it myself: Some effects and non-effects of maternal speech style. In C. Snow & C. A. Ferguson (Eds.), *Talking to children: Language input and acquisition.* Cambridge, England: Cambridge University Press.

Newstead, S., & Evans, J. S. (Eds.). (1995). *Perspectives on thinking and reasoning: Essays in honor of Peter Wason.* Hillsdale, NJ: Erlbaum.

Nickerson, R. S., & Adams, M. J. (1979). Long-term memory for a common object. *Cognitive Psychology, 10,* 287–307.

Nisbett, R. E., & Ross, L. (1980). *Human inference: Strategies and shortcomings in social judgment.* Englewood Cliffs, NJ: Prentice Hall.

Nisbett, R. E., & Wilson, T. D. (1977). Telling more than we can know: Verbal reports on mental processes. *Psychological Review, 84,* 231–259.

Noble, W., & Davidson, I. (1991). The evolutionary emergence of modern human behaviour: Language and its archeology. *Man, 26,* 223–253.

Noble, W., & Davidson, I. (1993). From sounds to speech: A human discovery. In G. Burenhalt (Ed.), *The first humans: Human origins and history to 10,000 BC* (p. 22).

Noice, H. (1992). Elaborative memory strategies of professional actors. *Applied Cognitive Psychology, 6,* 417–427.

Noice, T., & Noice, H. (1997). *The nature of expertise in professional acting: A cognitive view.* Mahwah, NJ: Erlbaum.

Noordman, L. G. M., & Vonk, W. (1998). Memory-based processing in understanding causal information. *Discourse Processes, 26,* 191–212.

Norris, D. (1991). The constraints on connectionism. *The Psychologist, 4,* 293–296.

Novick, L. R., Hurley, S. M., & Francis, M. (1999). Evidence for abstract, schematic knowledge of three spatial diagram representations. *Memory and Cognition, 27,* 288–308.

Nussbaum, M. C. (1994). *The therapy of desire: Theory and practice in Hellenistic ethics.* Princeton, NJ: Princeton University Press.

Nyberg, L., Cabeza, R., & Tulving, E. (1996). PET studies of encoding and retrieval: The HERA model. *Psychonomic Bulletin and Review, 3,* 135–148.

Nystrand, M. (1986). *The structure of written communication.* Orlando, FL: Academic Press.

Oaksford, M., & Chater, N. (1994). A rational analysis of the selection task as optimal data selection. *Psychological Review, 101,* 608–631.

Obrist, P., Sutterer, J., & Howard, J. (1972). Preparatory cardiac changes: A psychobiological approach. In A. Black & W. Prokasy (Eds.), *Classical conditioning* (Vol. 11). New York: Appleton-Century-Crofts.

O'Connor, K., & Ison, J. R. (1991). Echoic memory in the rat: Effects of inspection time, retention interval, and the spectral composition of masking noise. *Journal of Experimental Psychology: Animal Behavior Processes, 17,* 372–385.

O'Keefe, J., & Nadel, L. (1974). Maps in the brain. *New Scientist, 62,* 749–751.

O'Keefe, J., & Nadel, L. (1978). *The hippocampus as a cognitive map.* Oxford: Clarendon Press.

O'Keefe, J., & Nadel, L. (1979). Precis of the hippocampus as a cognitive map. *Behavioral and Brain Sciences, 2,* 487–533.

Olds, J. (1960). Differentiation of reward systems in the brain by self-stimulation techniques. In E. Ramey & D. O'Doherty (Eds.), *Electrical studies on the unanesthetized brain.* New York: Paul B. Hueber.

Olds, J., & Milner, P. (1954). Positive reinforcement produced by electrical stimulation of the septal area and other regions of rat brain. *Journal of Comparative and Physiological Psychology, 47,* 419–427.

Olson, D. J. (1991). Species differences in spatial memory among Clark's nutcrackers, scrub jays, and pigeons. *Journal of Experimental Psychology: Animal Behavior Processes, 17,* 363–376.

Olson, D. R. (1994). *The world on paper: The conceptual and cognitive implications of writing and reading.* New York: Cambridge University Press.

Olton, D. S. (1991). Experimental strategies to identify the neurobiological bases of memory: Lesions. In J. L. Martinez & R. P. Kesner (Eds.), *Learning and memory: A biological view* (2nd ed.). San Diego: Academic Press.

O'Nuallain, S. (1995). *The search for mind.* Norwood, NJ: Ablex.

Orgel, L., & Crick, F. (1980). Selfish DNA: The ultimate parasite. *Nature, 284,* 600–607.

Ornstein, P. A., Merritt, K. A., Baker-Ward, L., Furtado, E., Gordon, B. N., & Principe, G. (1998). Children's knowledge, expectation, and long-term retention. *Applied Cognitive Psychology, 12,* 387–406.

Ortony, A., Clore, G., & Collins, A. (1988). *The cognitive structure of emotions.* Cambridge, England: Cambridge University Press.

Osgood, C. E. (1963). On understanding and creating sentences. *American Psychologist, 18,* 735–751. Reprinted in Jakobovits & Miron (1967).

Otto, T., Schottler, F., Staubli, V., Eichenbaum, H., & Lynch, G. (1991). Hippocampus and olfactory discrimination learning effects of entorhinal cortex lesions on olfactory learning and memory in a successive-cue, go-no-go task. *Behavioral Neuroscience, 105,* 111–119.

Owens, J., Bower, G. H., & Black, J. B. (1979). The soap opera effect in story recall. *Memory and Cognition, 7,* 185–191.

Padilla, A. M., Lindholm, K. J., Chen, A., Duran, A., Hakuta, K., Lambert, W., & Tucker, G. R. (1991). The English-only movement: Myths, reality, and implications for psychology. *American Psychologist, 46,* 120–129.

Paivio, A. (1986). *Mental representation: A dual-coding approach.* New York: Oxford University Press.

Paivio, A. (1991). Dual coding theory: Retrospect and current status. *Canadian Journal of Psychology, 45,* 255–287.

Paller, K. A., Mayes, A, R., Thompson, K. M., Young, A. W., Roberts, J., & Meudell, P. R. (1992). Priming in face matching in amnesia. *Brain and Cognition, 18,* 46–59.

Panksepp, J. (1998). Attention deficit hyperactivity disorders, psychostimulants, and intolerance of childhood playfulness: A tragedy in the making? *Current Directions in Psychological Science, 7,* 91–98.

Paquet, L. (1991). Mental rotation of compound stimuli: The effects of task demands, practice, and figural goodness. *Memory and Cognition, 19,* 558–567.

Parker, S. T. (1985). Higher intelligence as adaptation for social and technological strategies in early Homo sapiens. In G. Butterworth, J. Rutkowska, & M. Scaife (Eds.), *Evolution and developmental psychology.* New York: St. Martin's Press.

Parker, S. T., & Gibson, K. R. (1979). A developmental model for the evolution of language and intelligence. *Behavioral and Brain Sciences, 2,* 367.

Parkin, A. J., Reid, T. K., & Russo, R. (1990). On the differential nature of implicit and explicit memory. *Memory and Cognition, 18,* 507–514.

Parsons, C. (1960). Inhelder's and Piaget's the growth of logical thinking: II. A logician's view. *British Journal of Psychology, 51,* 75–84.

Pascoe, J. P., Suple, W. F., & Kapp, B. S. (1991). Learning and memory: Vertebrate models. In J. L. Martinez & R. P. Kesner, *Learning and memory: A biological view* (2nd ed.). San Diego: Academic Press.

Pashler, H. E. (1998). *The psychology of attention.* Cambridge, MA: MIT Press.

Patel, V. L., & Groen, G. J. (1991). The general and specific nature of medical expertise: A critical look. In K. A. Ericsson, & J. Smith (Eds.), *Toward a general theory of expertise: Prospects and limits* (pp. 93–125). Cambridge, England: Cambridge University Press.

Patterson, F. (1980). Innovative uses of language by a gorilla: A case study. In K. E. Nelson (Ed.), *Children's language* (Vol. 2). New York: Gardner Press.

Patterson, F., & Linden, E. (1982). *The education of Koko.* New York: Holt, Rinehart & Winston.

Pavlov, I. P. (1927). *Conditioned reflexes.* New York: Dover.

Pavlov, I. P. (1928). *Lectures on conditioned reflexes* (Vol. I). London: Lawrence and Wishart.

Payne, D. G., & Wenger, M. J. (1998). *Cognitive psychology.* Boston: Houghton Mifflin.

Payne, T. J., Connor, J. M., & Colletti, G. (1987). Gender-based schematic processing: An empirical investigation and reevaluation. *Journal of Personality and Social Psychology, 52,* 937–945.

Pearce, J. A., & Hall, G. (1980). A model for Pavlovian learning: Variations in the effectiveness of conditioned but not of unconditioned stimuli. *Psychological Review, 87,* 532–552.

Pearce, J. M. (1987). *An introduction to animal cognition.* Hillsdale, NJ: Erlbaum.

Pendery, M., & Maltzman, I. (1977). Instructions and the orienting reflex in "semantic conditioning" of the galvanic skin response in an innocuous situation. *Journal of Experimental Psychology: General, 106,* 120–140.

Penfield, W. (1969). Consciousness, memory, and man's conditioned reflexes. In K. Pribram (Ed.), *On the biology of learning.* New York: Harcourt Brace Jovanovich.

Penfield, W., & Roberts, L. (1959). *Speech and brain mechanisms.* Princeton, NJ: Princeton University Press.

Pennebaker, J. W. (1989). Confession, inhibition, and disease. *Advances in experimental social psychology, 22,* 211–244.

Pennebaker, J. W. (1995). *Emotional regulation and health*. Paper presented at the 7th annual meeting of the American Psychological Society, New York.

Penrose, R. (1989). *The emperor's new mind: Concerning computers, minds, and the laws of physics*. New York: Oxford University Press.

Penrose, R. (1990). Multiple book reviews of *The emperor's new mind: Concerning computers, minds, and the laws of physics*. *Behavioral and Brain Sciences, 13*, 643–706.

Peretz, L., Kolinsky, R., Tramo, M., Labrecque, R., Hublet, C., Demeuresse, G., & Belleville, S. (1994). Functional dissociations following bilateral lesions of auditory cortex. *Brain, 117*, 1238–1301.

Perfect, T. J., & Askew, C. (1994). Print adverts: Not remembered but memorable. *Applied Cognitive Psychology, 8*, 693–703.

Perlstein, R. (1997). Getting real: Homo economicus goes to the lab. *Lingua Franca, 7*(4), 59–65.

Perner, J., & Lang, B. (1999). Development of theory of mind and executive control. *Trends in Cognitive Sciences, 3*, 337–344.

Peters, R. (1980). *Mammalian communication*. Monterey, CA: Brooks/Cole.

Peterson, C. C., & Siegal, M. (1999). Representing inner worlds: Theory of mind in autistic, deaf, and normal hearing children. *Psychological Science, 10*, 126–129.

Peterson, L. R., & Peterson, M. (1959). Short-term retention of individual items. *Journal of Experimental Psychology, 58*, 193–198.

Petitto, L. A., & Marentette, P. F. (1991). Babbling in the manual mode: Evidence for the ontogeny of language. *Science, 251*, 1493–1496.

Pezdek, K., & Banks. (Eds). (1996). *The recovered memory/false memory debate*. San Diego: Academic Press.

Pezdek, K., Finger, K., & Hodge, D. (1997). Planting false childhood memories: The role of event plausibility. *Psychological Science, 8*, 437–441.

Pfeiffer, J. E. (1976). *The emergence of man*. New York: Harper & Row.

Pfeiffer, J. E. (1977). *The emergence of society*. New York: McGraw-Hill.

Piaget, J. (1963). *The origins of intelligence in children*. New York: Norton. (Original work published 1952)

Piaget, J. (1965). *The child's conception of number*. New York: Norton. (Original work published 1941)

Piaget, J. (1967a). Cognitions and conservations: Review of J. S. Bruner and others, studies in cognitive growth. *Contemporary Psychology, 12*, 530–533.

Piaget, J. (1967b). *Six psychological studies*. New York: Random House. (Original work published 1964)

Piaget, J. (1969). *Psychology of intelligence*. Totowa, NJ: Littlefield, Adams. (Original work published 1947)

Piaget, J. (1970a). *Genetic epistemology*. New York: Norton.

Piaget, J. (1970b). Piaget's theory. In P. H. Mussen (Ed.), *Carmichael's manual of child psychology* (3rd ed., Vol. I). New York: Wiley.

Piaget, J. (1971a). *Biology and knowledge*. Chicago: University of Chicago Press. (Original work published 1967)

Piaget, J. (1971b). *Psychology and epistemology*. New York: Viking.

Piaget, J. (1971c). *Structuralism*. London: Routledge & Kegan Paul. (Original work published 1968)

Piaget, J. (1972). *The principles of genetic epistemology.* London: Routledge & Kegan Paul. (Original work published 1970)

Piaget, J. (1973). *The child and reality.* New York: Grossman. (Original work published 1972)

Piaget, J. (1976). *The grasp of consciousness.* Cambridge, MA: Harvard University Press. (Original work published 1974)

Piaget, J. (1978). *Behavior and evolution.* New York: Pantheon. (Original work published 1976)

Piaget, J., & Inhelder, B. (1969a). Intellectual operations and their development. In P. Fraisse & J. Piaget (Eds.), *Experimental psychology: Its scope and method* (Vol. VII, Intelligence). London: Routledge. (Original work published 1963)

Piaget, J., & Inhelder, B. (1969b). Mental images. In P. Fraisse & J. Piaget (Eds.), *Experimental psychology: Its scope and method* (Vol. VII, Intelligence). London: Routledge & Kegan Paul. (Original work published 1963)

Piaget, J., & Inhelder, B. (1969c). *The psychology of the child.* New York: Basic Books. (Original work published 1966)

Piaget, J., & Inhelder, B. (1971). *Mental imagery in the child.* New York: Basic Books. (Original work published 1966)

Piaget, J., & Inhelder, B. (1973). *Memory and intelligence.* London: Routledge & Kegan Paul. (Original work published 1968)

Piatelli-Palmarini, M. (1994). *Inevitable illusions: How mistakes of reason rule our minds.* New York: Wiley.

Pichert, J. W., & Anderson, R. C. (1977). Taking different perspectives on a story. *Journal of Educational Psychology, 69,* 309–315.

Pierce, M. C., & Harris, R. J. (1993). The effect of provocation, race, and injury description on men's and women's perception of a wife-battering incident. *Journal of Applied Social Psychology, 23,* 767–790.

Pierce, W. D., & Epling, W. F. (1999). *Behavior analysis and learning,* (2nd ed.), Upper Saddle River, NJ: Prentice-Hall.

Pilbeam, D. (1984, March). The descent of hominoids and hominids. *Scientific American,* 84–96.

Pilbeam, D. (1985). Patterns of hominoid evolution. In E. Delson (Ed.), *Ancestors: The hard evidence.* New York: Alan R. Liss.

Pilbeam, D. (1986a). Distinguished lecture: Hominoid evolution and hominid evolution. *American Anthropologist, 88,* 295–312.

Pilbeam, D. (1986b). The origin of Homo sapiens: The fossil evidence. In B. Wood, L. Martin, & P. Andrews (Eds.), *Major topics in primate and human evolution.* New York: Cambridge University Press.

Pillemer, D. B. (1984). Flashbulb memories of the assassination attempt on President Reagan. *Cognition, 16,* 63–80.

Pillemer, D. B. (1998). *Momentous events, vivid memories.* Cambridge, MA: Harvard University Press.

Pinard, J., & Laurendau, M. (1969). "Stage" in Piaget's cognitive-developmental theory: Exegesis of a concept. In D. Elkind & J. H. Flavell (Eds.), *Studies in cognitive development.* New York: Oxford University Press.

Pines, M. (1979). Good samaritans at age two? *Psychology Today, 13*(1), 66–77.

Pinker, S. (1987). The bootstrapping problem in language acquisition. In B. MacWhinney (Ed.), *Mechanisms of language acquisition.* Hillsdale, NJ: Erlbaum.

Pinker, S. (1994). *The language instinct: How the mind creates language.* New York: Morrow.

Pinker, S. (1995). Language: Introduction. In M. S. Gazzaniga (Ed.), *The cognitive neurosciences* (pp. 851–853). Cambridge, MA: MIT Press.

Pinker, S. (1997). Evolutionary biology and the evolution of language. In A. B. Scheibel & J. W. Schopf (Eds.), *The origin and evolution of intelligence* (pp. 137–160). Sudbury, MA: Jones & Bartlett.

Pinker, S. (1997). *How the mind works.* New York: Norton.

Pinker, S. (1999). *How the mind works.* New York: Norton.

Pinker, S. (1999). *Words and rules: The ingredients of language.* New York: Basic Books.

Pinker, S., & Bloom, P. (1990). Natural language and natural selection. *Behavioral and Brain Sciences, 13,* 707–786.

Pinker, S., & Prince, A. (1988). On language and connectionism: Analysis of a parallel distributed processing model of language acquisition. *Cognition, 28,* 73–193.

Pisoni, D. B. (1978). Speech perception. In W. K. Estes (Ed.), *Handbook of learning and cognitive processes* (Vol. 6, pp. 167–234). Hillsdale, NJ: Erlbaum.

Plato. (1973). *Phaedrus and Letters VII and VII* (W. Hamilton. Trans.). London: Penguin.

Plomin, R., & Daniels, D. (1987). Why are children in the same family so different from one another? *Behavioral and Brain Sciences, 10,* 1–60.

Plomin, R., Owen, M. J., & McGuffin, P. (1994). The genetic basis of complex human behaviors. *Science, 264,* 1733–1739.

Plotkin, H. C., & Odling-Smee, I. J. (1979). *Learning, change, and evolution. Advances in the study of behavior* (Vol. 10). New York: Academic Press.

Plunkett, K., & Elman, J. (1997). *Exercises in rethinking innateness: A handbook for connectionist simulations.* Cambridge, MA: Bradford Books.

Plutchik, R. (1980). *Emotion, a psychoevolutionary synthesis.* New York: Harper & Row.

Pohl, R., Colonius, H., & Thuring, M. (1985). Recognition of script-based inferences. *Psychological Research, 47,* 59–67.

Posner, M. I. (1992). Attention as a cognitive and neural system. *Current Directions in Cognitive Science, 1,* 11–14.

Posner, M. I. (1995). Attention in cognitive neuroscience: An overview. In M. Gazzaniga (Ed.), *The cognitive neurosciences* (pp. 615–624). Cambridge, MA: MIT Press.

Posner, M. I., & Dehaene, S. (1994). Attentional networks. *Trends in neurosciences, 17*(2), 75–79.

Posner, M. I., & Peterson, S. E. (1990). The attention system of the human brain. *Annual Review of Neuroscience, 13,* 25–42.

Posner, M. I., & Raichle, M. E. (1994). *Images of mind.* New York: Scientific American Library.

Posner, R. A. (1992). *Sex and reason.* Cambridge, MA: Harvard University Press.

Postman, L., & Keppel, G. (1968). Conditions determining the priority of new items in free recall. *Journal of Verbal Learning and Verbal Behavior, 7,* 270–273.

Postman, L., & Sassenrath, J. (1961). The automatic action of verbal rewards and punishments. *Journal of General Psychology, 65,* 109–136.

Potts, R. (1992). The hominid way of life. In S. Jones, R. Martin, & D. Pilbeam (Eds.), *The Cambridge encyclopedia of evolution* (pp. 320–334). Cambridge, England: Cambridge University Press.

Poundstone, W. (1992). *Prisoner's dilemma: John von Neumann, game theory, and the puzzle of the bomb.* New York: Doubleday.

Povinelli, D. J. (1999). Social understanding in chimpanzees: New evidence from a longitudinal approach. In P. D. Zelazo & J. W. Astington (Eds.), *Developing theories of intention: Social understanding and self-control* (pp. 195–225). Mahwah, NJ: LEA.

Povinelli, D. J., Bierschwale, D. T., & Cech, C. G. (1999). Comprehension of seeing as a referential act in young children but not juvenile chimpanzees. *British Journal of Developmental Psychology, 17,* 37–60.

Povinelli, D. J., Povinelli, T. J., & Giambrone, S. (1998). Reaching into thought: The minds of the great apes. *Trends in Cognitive Sciences, 2,* 158–159.

Povinelli, D. J., Reaux, J. E., Bierschwale, D. T., Allain, A. D., & Simon, B. B. (1997). Exploitation of pointing as a referential gesture in young children but not adolescent chimpanzees. *Cognitive Development, 12,* 327–365.

Premack, A. J. (1976). *Why chimps can read.* New York: Harper Colophon.

Premack, D. (1959). Toward empirical behavior laws: I. Positive reinforcement. *Psychological Review, 66,* 219–233.

Premack, D. (1962). Reversibility of the reinforcement relation. *Science, 136,* 255–257.

Premack, D. (1965a). Preparations for discussing behaviorism with a chimpanzee. In F. Smith & C. Miller (Eds.), *The genesis of language.* Cambridge, MA: MIT Press.

Premack, D. (1965b). Reinforcement theory. In M. R. Jones (Ed.), *Nebraska Symposium on Motivation.* Lincoln: University of Nebraska Press.

Premack, D. (1983). Animal cognition. *Annual Review of Psychology* (Vol. 34). Palo Alto, CA: Annual Reviews, Inc.

Premack, D., & Premack, A. J. (1982). *The mind of an ape.* New York: Norton.

Premack, D., & Woodruff, G. (1978). Does the chimpanzee have a theory of mind? *Behavioral and Brain Sciences, 1,* 515–526.

Pressley, M., & Afflerbach, P. (1995). *Verbal protocols of reading: The nature of constructively responsive reading.* Hillsdale, NJ: Erlbaum.

Pressley, M., Levin, J. R., & Ghatala, E. (1984). Memory strategy monitoring in adults and children. *Journal of Verbal Learning and Verbal Behavior, 23,* 270–288.

Preston, I. L. (1975). *The great American blow-up: Puffery in advertising and selling.* Madison: University of Wisconsin Press.

Preston, I. L., & Richards, J. I. (1986). Consumer miscomprehension as a challenge to FTC prosecutions of deceptive advertising. *The John Marshall Law Review, 19,* 605–635.

Pylyshyn, Z. W. (1984). *Computation and cognition: Toward a foundation for cognitive science.* Cambridge, MA: Bradford/MIT.

Quiatt, D., & Kelso, J. (1985). Household economics and hominid origins. *Current Anthropology, 26,* 207–222.

Quinlan, P. T. (1991). *Connectionism and psychology: A psychological perspective on new connectionist research.* Chicago: University of Chicago Press.

Rachlin, H. (1989). *Judgment, decision, and choice: A cognitive/behavioral synthesis.* New York: Freeman.

Rapaport, D. (1960). Psychoanalysis as a developmental psychology. In B. Kaplan & S. Wapner (Eds.), *Perspectives in psychological theory.* New York: International Universities Press.

Rapp, B. C., & Caramazza, A. (1995). Disorders of lexical processing and the lexicon. In M. S. Gazzinaga (Ed.), *The cognitive neurosciences* (pp. 901–914). Cambridge, MA: MIT Press.

Ratliff, F. (1976). On the psychophysiological bases of universal color terms. *Proceedings of the American Philosophical Society, 120,* 311–330.

Rayner, K., & Pollatsek, A. (1989). *The psychology of reading*. Englewood Cliffs, NJ: Prentice Hall.

Reder, L. M. (1988). Strategic control of retrieval strategies. In G. Bower (Ed.), *The psychology of learning and motivation* (Vol. 22). New York: Academic Press.

Reed, P., Chih-Ta, T., Aggleton, S. P., & Rawlins, J. N. P. (1991). Primacy, recency, and the von Restorff effect in rats' nonspatial memory. *Journal of Experimental Psychology: Animal Behavior Processes, 17,* 36–44.

Reese, E., & Brown, N. (2000). Reminiscing and recounting in the preschool years. *Applied Cognitive Psychology, 14,* 1–17.

Reicher, G. M. (1969). Perceptual recognition as a function of meaningfulness of stimulus material. *Journal of Experimental Psychology, 81,* 275–286.

Reid, B. V. (1984). An anthropological reinterpretation of Kohlberg's stages of moral development. *Human Development, 27,* 57–64.

Reiser, B. J., Black, J. B., & Kalamarides, P. (1986). In D. C. Rubin (Ed.), *Autobiographical memory* (pp. 100–121). Cambridge, England: Cambridge University Press.

Rensberger, B. (1986, August 7). Getting another line on evolution. *Washington Post,* A3.

Rensberger, B. (1987, May 21). Startlingly apelike early human. *Washington Post,* A3.

Rensberger, B. (1995, April 28). Researchers find evidence of early African tools. *Washington Post,* A1 & A6.

Rescorla, R. A. (1968). Probability of shock in the presence of CS in fear conditioning. *Journal of Comparative and Physiological Psychology, 56,* 1–5.

Rescorla, R. A. (1975). Pavlovian excitatory and inhibitory conditioning. In W. K. Estes (Ed.), *Handbook of learning and cognitive processes* (Vol. 2). Hillsdale, NJ: Erlbaum.

Rescorla, R. A. (1978). Some implications of a cognitive perspective on Pavlovian conditioning. In S. Hulse, H. Fowler, & W. Honig (Eds.), *Conditioning processes in animal behavior.* Hillsdale, NJ: Erlbaum.

Rescorla, R. A. (1980). Simultaneous and successive associations in sensory preconditioning. *Journal of Experimental Psychology: Animal Behavior Processes, 6,* 207–216.

Rescorla, R. A. (1984). Comments on three Pavlovian paradigms. In D. L. Alkon & J. Farley (Eds.), *Primary neural substrates of learning and behavior change.* New York: Cambridge University Press.

Rescorla, R. A. (1985). Associative learning: Some consequences of contiguity. In N. M. Weinberger, J. L. McGaugh, & G. Lynch (Eds.), *Memory systems of the brain: Animal and human cognitive processes.* New York: Guilford.

Rescorla, R. A. (1988). Pavlovian conditioning: It's not what you think it is. *American Psychologist, 43,* 151–160.

Rescorla, R. A. (1992). Associations between an instrumental discriminative stimulus and multiple outcomes. *Journal of Experimental Psychology: Animal Behavior Processes, 18,* 95–104.

Rescorla, R. A., & Holland, P. C. (1982). Behavioral studies of associative learning in animals. *Annual Review of Psychology, 33,* 265–308.

Rescorla, R., & Wagner, A. (1972). A theory of Pavlovian conditioning: Variations in the effectiveness of reinforcement and nonreinforcement. In A. Black & W. Prokasy (Eds.), *Classical conditioning* (Vol. II). New York: Appleton-Century-Crofts.

Rest, J. R. (Ed.). (1986). *Moral development: Advances in theory and research.* New York: Praeger.

Ribback, A., & Underwood, B. J. (1950). An empirical explanation of the skewness of the bowed serial position curve. *Journal of Experimental Psychology, 40,* 329–335.

Rice, M. L., & Schiefelbusch, R. L. (Eds.). (1989). *The teachability of language.* Baltimore: Paul H. Brooks.

Rice, M. R. (1989). Children's language acquisition. *American Psychologist, 44,* 149–156.

Richards, G. (1986). Freed hands or enslaved feet? *Journal of Human Evolution, 15,* 143–150.

Richards, J. I. (1990). *Deceptive advertising.* Hillsdale, NJ: Erlbaum.

Richardson-Klavehn, A., & Bjork, R. A. (1988). Measures of memory. *Annual Review of Psychology, 39,* 475–543.

Rickheit, G., Schnotz, W., & Strohner, H. (1985). The concept of inference in discourse comprehension. In G. Rickheit & H. Strohner (Eds.), *Inferences in text processing* (pp. 3–49). Amsterdam: Elsevier (North-Holland).

Rickheit, G., & Strohner, H. (Eds.). (1985). *Inferences in text processing.* Amsterdam: Elsevier (North-Holland).

Ridley, M. H. (1996). *The origins of virtue: Human instincts and the evolution of cooperation.* New York: Viking.

Ridley, R. M., & Baker, H. F. (1991). A critical evaluation of monkey models of amnesia and dementia. *Brain Research and Brain Research Review, 16,* 15–37.

Riechmann, P. F., & Coste, E. L. (1980). Mental imagery and the comprehension of figurative language: Is there a relationship? In R. P. Honeck & R. R. Hoffman (Eds.), *Cognition and figurative language.* Hillsdale, NJ: Erlbaum.

Riley, D. A., Cook, R. G., & Lamb, M. R. (1981). A classification and analysis of short-term retention codes in pigeons. *Psychology of Learning and Motivation, 15,* 51–80.

Rindos, D. (1985). Darwinian selection, symbolic variation, and the evolution of culture. *Current Anthropology, 26,* 65–88.

Rindos, D. (1986a). The genetics of cultural anthropology: Toward a genetic model for the evolution of culture. *Journal of Anthropological Archaeology, 5,* 1–38.

Rindos, D. (1986b). The evolution of the capacity for culture: Sociobiology, structuralism, and cultural selectionism. *Current Anthropology, 27,* 315–322.

Rips, L. J. (1998). Reasoning and conversation. *Psychological Review, 105,* 411–441.

Rips, L. J. (1994). *The psychology of proof.* Cambridge, MA: MIT Press.

Ristau, C. A., & Robbins, D. (1982). Language in the great apes: A critical review. In J. S. Rosenblatt, R. A. Hinde, C. Beer, & M. C. Busnel (Eds.), *Advances in the study of behavior* (Vol. 12). New York: Academic Press.

Roazen, P. (1976). *Erik H. Erikson: The power and limits of a vision.* New York: Free Press.

Robbins, C., & Ehri, L. C. (1994). Reading storybooks to kindergartners helps them learn new vocabulary words. *Journal of Educational Psychology, 86,* 54–64.

Robbins, D. (1980). Mathematical learning theory: W. K. Estes and stimulus sampling. In G. Gazda & R. Corsini (Eds.), *Theories of learning.* Itasca, IL: F. E. Peacock.

Roberts, D., & Bache, N. C. (1981). Mass communication effects. *Annual Review of Psychology, 32,* 307–356.

Robinson, B. W. (1976). Limbic influences on human speech. In S. R. Harnad, H. Steklis, &J. Lancaster (Eds.), *Annals of the New York Academy of Sciences* (Vol. 280). New York: New York Academy of Sciences.

Roediger, H. L. (1980). Memory metaphors in cognitive psychology. *Memory and Cognition, 8,* 231–246.

Roediger, H. L. (1990). Implicit memory: Retention without remembering. *American Psychologist, 45,* 1043–1056.

Roediger, H. L., III, & Blaxton, T. A. (1987). Effects of varying modality, surface features and retention interval on priming in word-fragment completion. *Memory and Cognition, 15,* 379–388.

Roeper, T. (1987). The acquisition of implicit arguments and the distinction between theory, process, and mechanism. In B. MacWhinney (Ed.), *Mechanisms of language acquisition.* Hillsdale, NJ: Erlbaum.

Roitblat, H. L. (1987). *Introduction to comparative cognition.* New York: Freeman.

Roitblat, H. L., & Von Fersen, L. (1992). Comparative cognition: Representations and processes in learning and memory. *Annual Review of Psychology, 43,* 671–710.

Rojahn, K., & Pettigrew, T. F. (1992). Memory for schema-relevant information: A meta-analytic resolution. *British Journal of Social Psychology, 31,* 81–109.

Rolls, E. T. (1990). Theoretical and neurophysiological analysis of the functions of the primate hypocampus. *Cold Spring Harbor Symposia in Quantitative Biology, 55,* 995–1006.

Rosen, H. (1980). *The development of sociomoral knowledge.* New York: Columbia University Press.

Rosenfeld, A. (1980, September). Sociobiology stirs a controversy over the limits of science. *Smithsonian,* 73–80.

Rosenzweig, M. R. (1996). Aspects of the search for the neural mechanisms of memory. *Annual Review of Psychology, 47,* 1–32.

Ross, M., Buehler, R., & Karr, J. W. (1998). Assessing the accuracy of conflicting autobiographical memories. *Memory and Cognition, 26,* 1233–1244.

Ross, M., & Sicoly, F. (1979). Egocentric biases in availability and attribution. *Journal of Personality and Social Psychology, 37,* 322–336.

Roth, W. -M. (1999). Discourse and agency in school science laboratories. *Discourse Processes, 28,* 27–60.

Rothman, A. J., & Salovey, P. (1997). Shaping perceptions to motivate healthy behavior: The role of message framing. *Psychological Bulletin, 121,* 3–19.

Rothwell, J. D. (1982). *Telling it like it isn't: Language misuse and malpractice: What we can do about it.* Englewood Cliffs, NJ: Prentice Hall.

Rovee-Collier, C. (1999). The development of infant memory. *Current Directions in Psychological Science, 8,* 80–85.

Rozin, P. (1976). The evolution of intelligence and access to the cognitive unconscious. In J. Sprague & A. Epstein (Eds.), *Progress in psychobiology and physiological psychology* (Vol. 6). New York: Academic Press.

Rozin, P. (1977). The significance of learning mechanisms in food selection: Some biology, psychology, and sociology of science. In L. M. Barker, M. R. Best, & M. Domjan (Eds.), *Learning mechanisms in food selection.* Waco, TX: Baylor University Press.

Rozin, P. (1997). Disgust faces, basal ganglia and obsesive-compulsive disorder: Some strange bedfellows. *Trends in Cognitive Sciences, 1,* 321–322.

Rozin, P., & Kalat, J. (1971). Specific hungers and poison avoidance as adaptive specializations of learning. *Psychological Review, 78,* 459–486.

Rozin, P., & Kalat, J. (1972). Learning as a situation-specific adaptation. In M. E. P. Seligman & J. L. Hager (Eds.), *Biological boundaries of learning.* New York: Appleton-Century-Crofts.

Rubenstein, H., Lewis, S. S., & Rubenstein, M. A. (1971). Evidence for phonemic recoding in visual word recognition. *Journal of Verbal Learning and Verbal Behavior, 10,* 645–657.

Rubin, D. C. (Ed.). (1986). *Autobiographical memory.* Cambridge: Cambridge University Press.

Rubin, D. C. (1995). *Memory in oral traditions: The cognitive psychology of epic, ballads, and counting-out rhymes.* New York: Oxford University Press.

Rubin, D. C., Wetzler, S. E., & Nebes, R. D. (1986). Autobiographical memory across the lifespan. In D. C. Rubin (Ed.), *Autobiographical memory* (pp. 202–221). Cambridge, England: Cambridge University Press.

Rubin, D. L. (Ed.). (1995). *Composing social identity in written language.* Hillsdale, NJ: Erlbaum.

Ruhlen, M. (1994). *The origin of language: Tracing the evolution of the mother tongue.* New York: Wiley.

Rumbaugh, D. M. (1980). Language behavior of apes. In T. A. Sebeok & J. Umiker-Sebeok (Eds.), *Speaking of apes: A critical anthology of two-way communication with man.* New York: Plenum.

Rumbaugh, D. M. (1981). Who feeds clever Hans? In T. A. Sebeok & R. Rosenthal (Eds.), *Annals of the New York Academy of Sciences* (Vol. 364). New York: New York Academy of Sciences.

Rumelhart, D. E. (1980). Schemata: The building blocks of cognition. In R. Spiro, B. C. Bruce, & W. F. Brewer (Eds.), *Theoretical issues in reading comprehension.* Hillsdale, NJ: Erlbaum.

Rumelhart, D. E., Hinton, G. E., & Williams, R. J. (1986). Learning internal representations by error propagation. In D. E. Rumelhart, J. L. McClelland, & the PDP Research Group (Eds.), *Parallel distributed processing: Explorations in the microstructure of cognition* (Vol. 1). Cambridge, MA: MIT Press.

Rumelhart, D. E., & McClelland, J. L. (1986). On learning the past tenses of English verbs. In J. L. McClelland, D. E. Rumelhart, & the PDP Research Group (Eds.), *Parallel distributed processing: Explorations in the microstructure of cognition. Vol. 2. Psychological and biological models.* Cambridge, MA: Bradford Books, MIT Press.

Rumelhart, D. E., & McClelland, J. L. (1987). Learning the past tenses of English verbs: Implicit rules or parallel distributed processing? In B. MacWhinney (Ed.), *Mechanisms of language acquisition.* Hillsdale, NJ: Erlbaum.

Rumelhart, D. E., McClelland, J. L., & the PDP Research Group. (1986). *Parallel distributed processing: Explorations in the microstructure of cognition* (2 vols.). Cambridge, MA: MIT Press.

Ruse, M. (1979). *Sociobiology, sense or nonsense?* (Episteme, Vol. 8). Dordrecht, Holland: D. Reidel.

Rushton, J. P. (1982a). Altruism and society: A social learning perspective. *Ethics, 92,* 425–446.

Rushton, J. P. (1982b). Moral cognition, behaviorism and social learning theory. *Ethics, 92,* 459–467.

Rushton, J. P. (1985). Differential K theory: The sociobiology of individual and group differences. *Personality and Individual Differences, 6,* 441–452.

Sacks, O. (1995). *An anthropologist on Mars: Seven paradoxical tales.* New York: Knopf.

Sahlins, M. D. (1976). *The use and abuse of biology.* Ann Arbor: University of Michigan Press.

Samelson, F. (1980). Little Albert, Cyril Burt's twins, and the need for a critical science. *American Psychologist, 35,* 619–625.

Samms, M., Hari, R., Rif, J., & Knuutila, J. (1993). The human auditory sensory memory trace persists to about 10 seconds: Neuromagnetic evidence. *Journal of Cognitive Neuroscience, 5,* 363–370.

Samuelson, P. A. (1983). Complete genetic models for altruism, kin-selection and like-gene selection. *Journal of Social and Biological Structures, 6,* 3–15.

Savage-Rumbaugh, E. S. (1986). *Ape language: From conditioned responses to symbols.* New York: Columbia University Press.

Savage-Rumbaugh, E. S. (1990). Language acquisition in a nonhuman species: Implications for the innateness debate. *Developmental Psychobiology, 23,* 599–620.

Savage-Rumbaugh, E. S., Lewin, R., & Savage-Rumbaugh, S. (1996). *Kanzi: Ape at the brink of the human mind.* New York: Wiley.

Savage-Rumbaugh, E. S., McDonald, K., Sevcik, R., Hopkins, W., & Rubert, E. (1986). Spontaneous symbol acquisition and communicative use by pygmy chimpanzee. *Journal of Experimental Psychology: General, 115,* 211–235.

Savage-Rumbaugh, E. S., & Rumbaugh, D. M. (1980). Language analogue project, phase II: Theory and tactics. In K. E. Nelson (Ed.), *Children's language* (Vol. 2). New York: Gardner Press.

Savage-Rumbaugh, E. S., Rumbaugh, D. M., & Boysen, S. (1980). Linguistically mediated tool use and exchange by chimpanzees. In T. A. Sebeok & J. Umiker-Sebeok (Eds.), *Speaking of apes: A critical anthology of two-way communication with man.* New York: Plenum.

Savage-Rumbaugh, E. S., Shanker, S., Taylor, T. T., & Savage-Rumbaugh, S. (1999). *Apes, language, and the human mind.* New York: Oxford University Press.

Savage-Rumbaugh, S. (1997). Why are we afraid of apes with language? In A. B. Scheibel & J. W. Schopf (Eds), *The origin and evolution of intelligence* (pp. 43–70). Sudbury, MA: Jones & Bartlett.

Sawyer, K. (1995, November 16). Asian fossils suggest early migration. *Washington Post,* A3.

Scardamalia, M., & Bereiter, C. (1991). Literate expertise. In K. A. Ericsson & J. Smith (Eds.), *Toward a general theory of expertise: Prospects and limits* (pp. 172–194). New York: Cambridge University Press.

Scarr-Salapatek, S. (1976). An evolutionary perspective on infant intelligence. In M. Lewis (Ed.), *Origins of intelligence.* New York: Plenum.

Schab, F. R. (1990). Odors and the remembrance of things past. *Journal of Experimental Psychology: Learning, Memory, and Cognition, 16,* 648–655.

Schab, F. R., & Crowder, R. G. (Eds.). (1995). *Memory for odors.* Hillsdale, NJ: Erlbaum.

Schachter, D. L. (1985). Multiple forms of memory in humans and animals. In N. M. Weinberger, J. L. McGaugh, & G. Lynch (Eds.), *Memory systems of the brain: Animal and human cognitive processes.* New York: Guilford.

Schachter, D. L. (1986a). The psychology of memory. In J. E. LeDoux & W. Hirst (Eds.), *Mind and brain: Dialogues in cognitive neuroscience.* Cambridge, England: Cambridge University Press.

Schachter, D. L. (1986b). A psychological view of the neurobiology of memory. In J. E. LeDoux & W. Hirst (Eds.), *Mind and brain: Dialogues in cognitive neuroscience.* Cambridge, England: Cambridge University Press.

Schachter, D. L. (1987). Implicit memory: History and current status. *Journal of Experimental Psychology: Learning, Memory, and Cognition, 13,* 501–518.

Schachter, D. L. (1995). Implicit memory: A new frontier for cognitive neuroscience. In M. S. Gazzaniga (Ed.), *The cognitive neurosciences* (pp. 815–824). Cambridge, MA: MIT Press.

Schacter, D. L. (1996). *Searching for memory: The brain, the mind, and the past.* New York: Basic Books.

Schacter, D. L. (1999). The seven sins of memory: Insights from psychology and cognitive neuroscience. *American Psychologist, 54,* 182–203.

Schacter, D. L., Norman, K. A., & Koutstaal, W. (1998). The cognitive neuroscience of constructive memory. *Annual Review of Psychology, 49,* 289–318.

Schacter, S., & Singer, J. L. (1962). Cognitive, social, and physiological determinants of emotion. *Journal of Abnormal and Social Psychology, 65,* 121–128.

Schank, R. C., & Abelson, R. P. (1977). *Scripts, plans, goals, and understanding.* Hillsdale, NJ: Erlbaum.

Schank, R. C., & Abelson, R. P. (1995). Knowledge and memory: The real story. In R. S. Wyer, Jr. (Ed.), *Knowledge and memory: The real story* (pp. 1–85). Hillsdale, NJ: Erlbaum.

Schatz, C. (1954). The role of context in the perception of stops. *Language, 30,* 47–56.

Scheffler, I. (1967). *Science and subjectivity.* Indianapolis: Bobbs-Merrill.

Scheibel, A. B., & Schopf, J. W. (Eds.). (1997). *The origin and evolution of intelligence.* Sudbury, MA: Jones & Bartlett.

Schmajuk, N. A., & DiCarlo, J. J. (1992). Stimulus configuration, classical conditioning, and hippocampal function. *Psychological Review, 99,* 268–305.

Schneider, D. J. (1991). Social cognition. *Annual Review of Psychology, 42,* 527–561.

Schneider, L. F., & Taylor, H. A. (1999). How do you get there from here? Mental representations of route descriptions. *Applied Cognitive Psychology, 13,* 415–441.

Schneider, W. (1989). *Memory development between 2 and 20.* New York: Springer.

Schneider, W., Dumais, S. T., & Shiffrin, R. M. (1984). Automatic and control processing and attention. In R. Parasuraman & D. R. Davies (Eds.), *Varieties of attention* (pp. 1–27). Orlando, FL: Academic Press.

Schneider, W., & Shiffrin, R. M. (1977). Controlled and automatic human information processing: I. Detection, search, and attention. *Psychological Review, 84,* 1–66.

Schoen, L. M. (1988). Semantic flexibility and core meaning. *Journal of Psycholinguistic Research, 17,* 113–123.

Schooler, J. W., Gerhard, D., & Loftus, E. F. (1986). Qualities of the unreal. *Journal of Experimental Psychology: Learning, Memory, and Cognition, 12,* 171–181.

Schrag, D. M. (1996). *A test of the effectiveness of the mnemonic keyword method for leaning Chinese nouns and their tones.* Unpublished master's thesis, Kansas State University.

Schreiber, T. A., & Sergent, S. D. (1998). The role of commitment in producing misinformation effects in eyewitness memory. *Psychonomic Bulletin and Review, 5,* 443–448.

Schulkind, M. D., Hennis, L. K., & Rubin, D. C. (1999). Music, emotion, and autobiographical memory: They're playing your song. *Memory and Cognition, 27,* 948–955.

Schwanenflugel, P. J. (Ed.). (1991). *The psychology of word meanings.* Hillsdale, NJ: Erlbaum.

Schwartz, B. (1978). *Psychology of learning and behavior.* New York: Norton.

Schwartz, B. (1982). Reinforcement-induced behavioral stereotyping: How not to teach people to discover rules. *Journal of Experimental Psychology: General, III,* 23–59.

Schwartz, B. (1984). *Psychology of learning and behavior* (2nd ed.). New York: Norton.

Schwartz, B. (1988). The experimental synthesis of behavior: Reinforcement, behavioral stereotypy, and problem solving. *The Psychology of Learning and Motivation, 22,* 93–138.

Schwartz, B., & Reisberg, D. (1991). *Learning and memory.* New York: Norton.

Schwartz, B. L., & Metcalfe, J. (1992). Cue familiarity but not target retrievability enhances feeling-of-knowing judgments. *Journal of Experimental Psychology: Learning, Memory, and Cognition, 18,* 1074–1083.

Schwartz, J. H. (1984). Hominoid evolution: A review and a reassessment. *Current Anthropology, 25,* 655–672.

Schwarz, B. L. (1999). Sparkling at the end of the tongue: The etiology of tip-of-the-tongue phenomenology. *Psychonomic Bulletin and Review, 6,* 379–393.

Schweder, R. (1994). All emotions are basic. In P. Ekman & R. J. Davidson (Eds.) *The nature of emotion: Fundamental questions.* New York: Oxford University Press.

Scott, C. L., Harris, R. J., & Rothe, A. R. (2001). Embodied cognition through improvisation improves memory for a dramatic monologue. Discourse Processes, in press.

Scott, L. M. (1994). The bridge from text to mind: Adapting reader-response theory to consumer research. *Journal of Consumer Research, 21,* 461–480.

Searle, J. R. (1990a). Consciousness, explanatory inversion, and cognitive science. *Behavioral and Brain Sciences, 13,* 585–642.

Searle, J. R. (1990b, January). Is the brain's mind a computer program? *Scientific American, 262,* 26–31.

Searle, J. R. (1990c). Minds, brains, and programs. *Behavioral and Brain Sciences, 3,* 417–424. In M. A. Boden (Ed.), *The philosophy of artificial intelligence.* Oxford: Oxford University Press. (Original work published 1980)

Searle, J. R. (1993). *The rediscovery of the mind.* Cambridge, MA: MIT Press/Bradford Books.

Searleman, A., & Herrmann, D. (1994). *Memory from a broader perspective.* New York: McGraw-Hill.

Sebeok, T. A. (1980). Looking in the destination for what should have been sought in the source. In T. A. Sebeok & J. Umiker-Sebeok (Eds.), *Speaking of apes: A critical anthology of two-way communication with man.* New York: Plenum.

Sebeok, T. A., & Rosenthal, R. (Eds.). (1981). The clever Hans phenomenon. *Annals of the New York Academy of Sciences* (Vol. 364). New York: New York Academy of Sciences.

Sebeok, T. A., & Umiker-Sebeok, J. (1979). Performing animals: Secrets of the trade. *Psychology Today, 13*(6), 78–91.

Sebeok, T. A., & Umiker-Sebeok, J. (Eds.). (1980). *Speaking of apes: A critical anthology of two-way communication with man.* New York: Plenum.

Seidenberg, M. S., & Elman, J. L. (1999). Networks are not "hidden rules." *Trends in Cognitive Sciences, 3,* 288–289.

Seligman, M. E. P. (1975). *Helplessness.* San Francisco: Freeman.

Seligman, M. E. P., & Hager, J. L. (Eds.). (1972). *Biological boundaries of learning.* New York: Appleton-Century-Crofts.

Seligman, M. E. P., & Johnston, J. (1973). Cognitive theory of avoidance learning. In F. J. McGuigan & D. Lumsden (Eds.), *Contemporary approaches to conditioning and learning.* Washington, DC: Winston.

Sem-Jacobsen, C. (1976). Electrical stimulation and self-stimulation in man with chronic implanted electrodes. Interpretation and pitfall of results. In A. Wauquier & E. Rolls (Eds.), *Brain-stimulation reward.* Amsterdam: Elsevier (North-Holland).

Sennett, R. (1977). *The fall of public man: On the social psychology of capitalism.* New York: Vintage.

Severance, L. J., & Loftus, E. F. (1982). Improving the ability of jurors to comprehend and apply criminal jury instructions. *Law and Society Review, 17,* 153–197.

Seward, J. P., & Levy, N. (1949). Sign learning as a factor in extinction. *Journal of Experimental Psychology, 39,* 660–668.

Seward, J. P., & Seward, G. (1980). *Sex differences: Mental and temperamental.* Lexington, MA: Lexington Books.

Shanks, D. R., & St. John, M. F. (1994). Characteristics of dissociable human learning systems. *Behavioral and Brain Sciences, 17,* 367–448.

Shanteau, J. (1989). Cognitive heuristics and biases in behavioral auditing: Review, comments, and observations. *Accounting, Organizations and Society, 14,* 165–177.

Shanteau, J. (1992). The psychology of experts: An alternative view. In G. Wright & F. Bolger (Eds.), *Expertise and decision support* (pp. 11–23). New York: Plenum Press.

Shanteau, J. (1993). Discussion of "Expertise in Auditing." *Auditing: A Journal of Practice and Theory, 12,* Supplement, 51–55.

Shanteau, J., & Harris, R. J. (Eds.). (1990). *Organ donation and transplantation: Psychological and behavioral factors.* Washington, DC: American Psychological Association.

Shapiro, S., & Krishnan, H. S. (1999). Consumer memory for intentions: A prospective memory perspective. *Journal of Experimental Psychology: Applied, 5,* 169–189.

Shaywitz, S., & Shaywitz, B. (1995). Sex differences in the functional organization of the brain for language. *Nature, 373,* 607–609.

Shepard, R. N. (1978). The mental image. *American Psychologist, 33,* 125–137.

Shepard, R. N. (1984). Ecological constraints on internal representation: Resonant kinematics of perceiving, imagining, thinking, and dreaming. *Psychological Review, 91,* 417–447.

Shepard, R. N., & Feng, C. A. (1972). A chronometric study of mental paper folding. *Cognitive Psychology, 3,* 228–243.

Shepard, R. N., & Metzler, J. (1971). Mental rotation of three-dimensional objects. *Science, 171,* 701–703.

Sherman, J. W. (1996). Development and mental representation of stereotypes. *Journal of Personality and Social Psychology, 70,* 1126–1141.

Shettleworth, S. (1972). *Constraints on learning: Advances in the study of behavior* (Vol. 4). New York: Academic Press.

Shevoroshkin, V. (1990, May/June). The mother tongue. *The Sciences,* 20–27.

Shields, W. M., & Shields, L. M. (1983). Forcible rape: An evolutionary perspective. *Ethology and Sociobiology, 4,* 115–136.

Shiffrin, R. M. (1973). Information persistence in short-term memory. *Journal of Experimental Psychology, 100,* 39–49.

Shiffrin, R. M. (1985). Attention. In R. C. Atkinson, R. J. Herrnstein, G. Lindzey, & D. R. Luce (Eds.), *Stevens' handbook of experimental psychology.* New York: Wiley.

Shiffrin, R. M., & Schneider, W. (1977). Controlled and automatic human information processing: II. Perceptual learning, automatic attending, and a general theory. *Psychological Review, 84,* 127–190.

Shimamura, A. P. (1995). The neuropsychology of Metacognition. In J. Metcalfe & A. P. Shimamura (Eds.), *Metacognition: Knowing about knowing.* Cambridge, MA: MIT Press.

Shimamura, A. P., & Squire, L. R. (1989). Impaired priming of new associations in amnesia. *Journal of Experimental Psychology: Learning, Memory, and Cognition, 14,* 763–769.

Shimp, C. P. (1976). Organization in memory and behavior. *Journal of the Experimental Analysis of Behavior, 26,* 113–130.

Shimp, C. P. (1984). Cognition, behavior, and the experimental analysis of behavior. *Journal of the Experimental Analysis of Behavior, 42,* 407–420.

Shimura, A. P. (1995). Memory and frontal lobe function. In M. S. Gazzaniga (Ed.), *The cognitive neurosciences* (pp. 803–813). Cambridge, MA: Bradford.

Shuy, R. W. (1981). Toward a developmental theory of writing. In C. H. Frederiksen & J. F. Dominic (Eds.), *Writing: Process, development, and communication.* Hillsdale, NJ: Erlbaum.

Shuy, R. W., & Larkin, D. (1978). Linguistic consideration in the simplification/classification of insurance policy language. *Discourse Processes, 1,* 305–321.

Siegel, S. (1979). The role of conditioning in drug tolerance and addiction. In J. D. Keehn (Ed.), *Psychopathology in animals: Research and clinical implications.* New York: Academic Press.

Siegel, S., Krank, M. D., & Hinson, R. E. (1987). Anticipation of pharmacological and nonpharmacological events: Classical conditioning and addictive behavior. *Journal of Drug Issues, 17,* 83–110.

Siegler, R. (1999). Strategic development. *Trends in Cognitive Sciences, 3,* 430–435.

Siegler, R. S. (1983). Five generalizations about cognitive development. *American Psychologist, 38,* 263–277.

Siegler, R. S. (1986). *Children's thinking.* Englewood Cliffs, NJ: Prentice Hall.

Simon, H. (1991, June 13). *What is an "explanation" of behavior?* Keynote Address at the third annual meeting of the American Psychological Society, Washington, DC.

Simon, H. A. (1955). A behavioral model of rational choice. *Quarterly Journal of Economics, 69,* 174–183.

Simon, H. A. (1982). *Models of bounded rationality* (Vols. 1–2). Cambridge, MA: MIT Press.

Simon, H. A. (1994). The bottleneck of attention: Connecting thought with motivation. In W. D. Spaulding (Ed.), *Integrative views of motivation, cognition, and emotion* (pp. 1–22). Lincoln: University of Nebraska Press.

Simon, H. A., & Gilmartin, K. A. (1973). A simulation of memory for chess positions. *Cognitive Psychology, 5,* 29–46.

Simons, D. J., & Levin, D. T. (1997). Change blindness. *Trends in Cognitive Sciences, 1,* 261–267.

Simons, D. J., & Levin, D. T. (1998). Failure to detect changes to people during a real-world interaction. *Psychonomic Bulletin and Review, 5,* 644–649.

Singer, P. (1981). *The expanding circle.* New York: Farrar, Straus & Giroux.

Siple, P., & Fischer, S. D. (Eds.). (1991). *Theoretical issues in sign language research* (Vol. 2). Psychology. Chicago: University of Chicago Press.

Skelton, R. R., McHenry, H. M., & Drawhorn, G. M. (1986). Phylogenetic analysis of early hominids. *Current Anthropology, 27,* 21–43.

Skinner, B. F. (1938). *Behavior of organisms.* Englewood Cliffs, NJ: Prentice Hall.

Skinner, B. F. (1948a). "Superstition" in the pigeon. *Journal of Experimental Psychology, 38,* 168–172.

Skinner, B. F. (1948b). *Walden II.* New York: Macmillan.

Skinner, B. F. (1950). Are theories of learning necessary? *Psychological Review, 57,* 193–216.

Skinner, B. F. (1957). *Verbal behavior.* Englewood Cliffs, NJ: Prentice Hall.

Skinner, B. F. (1961a). *A case history in scientific method.* Englewood Cliffs, NJ: Prentice Hall. Reprinted in Cumulative Record (3rd ed.). (Original work published 1956)

Skinner, B. F. (1961b). *Pigeons in a pelican.* Englewood Cliffs, NJ: Prentice Hall. Reprinted in Cumulative Record (3rd ed.). (Original work published 1960)

Skinner, B. F. (1969). *Contingencies of reinforcement.* Englewood Cliffs, NJ: Prentice Hall.

Skinner, B. F. (1972). A critique of psychoanalytic concepts and theories. In B. F. Skinner, *Cumulative record* (3rd ed.). New York: Appleton-Century-Crofts. (Original work published 1954)

Skinner, B. F. (1972). A case history in scientific method. In B. F. Skinner, *Cumulative record* (3rd ed.). New York: Appleton-Century-Crofts. (Original work published 1959)

Skinner, B. F. (1972). Pigeons in a pelican. In B. F. Skinner, *Cumulative record* (3rd ed.). New York: Appleton-Century-Crofts. (Original work published 1960)

Skinner, B. F. (1972a). *Beyond freedom and dignity.* New York: Bantam.

Skinner, B. F. (1972b). *Cumulative record* (3rd ed.). New York: Appleton-Century-Crofts.

Skinner, B. F. (1974). *About behaviorism.* New York: Knopf.

Skinner, B. F. (1976). *Particulars of my life.* New York: Knopf.

Slobin, D. I. (1973). Cognitive prerequisites for the development of grammar. In C. A. Ferguson & D. I. Slobin (Eds.), *Studies of child language development.* New York: Holt, Rinehart & Winston.

Slovic, P. (1995). The construction of preference. *American Psychologist, 50,* 364–371.

Slovic, P., & Fischhoff, B. (1977). On the psychology of experimental surprises. *Journal of Experimental Psychology: Human Perception and Performance, 3,* 544–551.

Slovic, P., Fischhoff, B., & Lichtenstein, S. (1982). Facts versus fears: Understanding perceived risk. In D. Kahneman, P. Slovic, & A. Tversky (Eds.), *Judgment under uncertainty: Heuristics and biases.* Cambridge, England: Cambridge University Press.

Slovic, P., & Lichtenstein, S. (1971). Comparison of Bayesian and regression approaches to the study of information processing judgment. *Organizational Behavior and Human Performance, 6,* 649–744.

Smedslund, J. (1968). The acquisition of conservation of substance and weight in children, I-VI. *Scandinavian Journal of Psychology, 2,* 11–210. I, III, V, & VI. Reprinted in Sigel & Hooper. (Original work published 1961)

Smith, E. E. (1978). Theories of semantic memory. In W. K. Estes (Ed.), *Handbook of learning and cognitive processes* (Vol. 6). Hillsdale, NJ: Erlbaum.

Smith, E. E., & Jonides, J., (1997). Working memory: A view from neuroimaging. *Cognitive Psychology, 33,* 5–42.

Smith, E. E., Shoben, E. J., & Rips, L. J. (1974). Structure and process in semantic memory: A featural model for semantic decisions. *Psychological Review, 81,* 214–241.

Smith, F. (1985). A metaphor for literacy: Creating worlds or shunting information? In D. R. Olson, N. Torrance, & A. Hildyard (Eds.), *Literacy, language, and learning* (pp. 195–213). Cambridge: Cambridge University Press.

Smith, F. (1994). *Understanding reading* (5th ed.). Hillsdale, NJ: Erlbaum.

Smith, F., & Miller, C. (1965). *The genesis of language.* Cambridge, MA: MIT Press.

Smith, F. H., & Spencer, F. (Eds.). (1984). *The origins of modern humans: A world survey of the fossil evidence.* New York: Alan R. Liss.

Smith, L. J. (1986). *Behaviorism and logical positivism: A revised account of the alliance.* Stanford, CA: Stanford University Press.

Smith, P. (1974). Ethological methods. In B. Foss (Ed.), *New perspective in child development.* Baltimore: Penguin.

Smith, P. T., & Kemp-Wheeler, S. (1996). Why do we need emotions? In M. Bruce (Ed.), *Unsolved mysteries of the mind: Tutorial essays in cognition* (pp. 181–210). East Sussex, England: Erlbaum.

Smith, S. L. (1991). *Succeeding against the odds.* New York: G.P. Putnam's Sons.

Smith, S. M. (1985). Background music and context-dependent memory. *American Journal of Psychology, 6,* 591–603.

Smith, S. M. (1995). Getting into and out of mental ruts: A theory of fixation, incubation, and insight. In R. J. Sternberg & J. E. Davidson (Eds.), *The nature of insight* (pp. 229–251). Cambridge, MA: MIT Press.

Smolensky, P. (1988). On the proper treatment of connectionism. *Behavioral and Brain Sciences, 11,* 1–74.

Snow, C. E. (1978). Mother's speech to children learning language. *Child Development, 43,* 549–565. In C. P. Bloom, The roles of schemata in memory for text. *Discourse Processes, 11,* 305–318. (Original work published 1972)

Snow, C. E. (1986). Conversations with children. In P. Fletcher & M. Garman (Eds.), *Language acquisition* (2nd ed.). Cambridge, England: Cambridge University Press.

Snowden, C. T. (1983). Ethology, comparative psychology, and animal behavior. *Annual Review of Psychology* (Vol. 34). Palo Alto, CA: Annual Reviews.

Snyder, M., Tanke, E. D., & Berscheid, E. (1977). Social perception and interpersonal behavior: On the self-fulfilling nature of social stereotypes. *Journal of Personality and Social Psychology, 35,* 656–666.

Solanto, M., & Katkin, E. (1979). Classical EDR conditioning using a truly random control and subjects differing in electrodermal lability level. *Bulletin of the Psychonomic Society, 14,* 49–52.

Solomon, R. (1964). Punishment. *American Psychologist, 19,* 239–253.

Solso, R. L. (1998). Cognitive Psychology (5th ed.). Boston: Allyn and Bacon. Speech style and impression formation in a court setting: The effects of "powerful" and "powerless" speech. *Journal of Experimental Social Psychology, 14,* 266–279.

Spelke, E., Hirst, W., & Neisser, U. (1976). Skills of divided attention. *Cognition, 4,* 215–230.

Spelke, E. S. (1991). Physical knowledge in infancy: Reflections on Piaget's Theory, In S. Carey & R. Gelman (Eds.), *The epigenesis of mind: Essays on biology and cognition.* Hillsdale, NJ: Erlbaum.

Spence, H. (1897). *Principles of psychology* (3rd ed.). New York: Appleton & Co. (Original work published 1855)

Spence, K. (1944). The nature of theory construction in contemporary psychology. *Psychological Review, 51,* 47–68.

Spence, K. (1956). *Behavior theory and conditioning.* New Haven: Yale University Press.

Sperling, G. A. (1960). The information available in brief visual presentations. *Psychological Monographs, 74,* (No. 498).

Spilich, G. J., Vesonder, G. T., Chiesi, H. L., & Voss, J. F. (1979). Text processing of domain-related information for individuals with high and low domain knowledge. *Journal of Verbal Learning and Verbal Behavior, 18,* 275–290.

Squire, L. (1987). *Memory and brain.* New York: Oxford University Press.

Squire, L. (1992). Memory and the hippocampus: A synthesis from findings with rats, monkeys, and humans. *Psychological Review, 99,* 195–231.

Squire, L. R. (1994). Declarative and nondeclarative memory: Multiple brain systems supporting learning and memory. In D. L. Schachter & E. Tulving (Eds.), *Memory systems 1994* (pp. 203–232). Cambridge, MA: MIT Press.

Squire, L. R., & Knowlton, B. J. (1995). Memory, hippocampus, and brain systems. In M. S. Gazzinaga (Ed.), *The cognitive neurosciences* (pp. 825–838). Cambridge, MA: MIT Press.

Staddon, J. (1975). Learning as adaptation. In W. K. Estes (Ed.), *Handbook of learning and cognitive processes* (Vol. 2). Hillsdale, NJ: Erlbaum.

Staddon, J., & Simmerlhag, V. (1971). The "superstition" experiment: A reexamination of its implications for the principles of adaptive behavior. *Psychological Review, 78,* 3–43.

Staddon, J. E. R. (1984). *Adaptive behavior and learning.* New York: Cambridge University Press.

Staddon, J. E. R. (1985). Inference, memory, and representation. In N. M. Weinberger, J. L. McGaugh, & G. Lynch (Eds.), *Memory systems of the brain: Animal and human cognitive processes.* New York: Guilford.

Stanovich, K. E. (1998). *How to think straight about psychology* (5th ed.). New York: Longman.

Staubli, U., Thibault, O., DiLorenzo, M., & Lynch, G. (1989). Antagonism of NMDA receptors impairs acquisition but not retention of olfactory memory. *Behavioral Neuroscience, 103,* 54.

Stefik, M. (1995). *Introduction to knowledge systems.* San Francisco: Morgan Kaufman.

Steklis, H. D., & Harnad, S. R. (1976). From hand to mouth: Some critical stages in the evolution of language. In S. R. Harnad, H. Steklis, &J. Lancaster (Eds.), *Annals of the New York Academy of Sciences* (Vol. 280). New York: New York Academy of Sciences.

Sternberg, R. J. (Ed.). (1984). *Mechanisms of cognitive development.* San Francisco: Freeman.

Sternberg, R. J. (1986). *Intelligence applied: Understanding and increasing your intellectual skills.* San Diego: Harcourt Brace Jovanovich.

Sternberg, R. J. (1999). *Cognitive psychology* (2nd ed.). Fort Worth: Harcourt Brace.

Sternberg, R. J., & Lubart, T. I. (1995). *Defying the crowd.* New York: Free Press.

Sternberg, R. J., & Lubart, T. I. (1996). Investing in creativity. *American Psychologist, 51,* 677–688.

Sternberg, S. (1966). High-speed scanning in human memory. *Science, 153,* 652–654.

Sternberg, S. (1975). Memory scanning: New findings and current controversies. *Quarterly Journal of Experimental Psychology, 27,* 1–32.

Stillings, N. A., Feinstein, M. H., Garfeld, J. L., Rissland, E. L., Rosenbaum, D. A., Weisler, S. E., & Baker-Ward, L. (1995). *Cognitive science: An introduction* (3rd ed.). Cambridge, MA: Bradford/MIT Press.

Stonebreaker, T. B. (1981). *Retrospective and prospective processes in delayed matching to sample.* Unpublished doctoral dissertation, Michigan State University.

Stringer, C., & Gamble, C. (1993). *In search of the Neanderthals.* London: Thames & Hudson.

Stringer, C., & McKee, R. (1996). *African exodus: The origins of modern humanity.* New York: Henry Holt.

Stringer, C. B. (1992). Evolution of early humans. In S. Jones, R. Martin, & D. Pilbeam (Eds.), *The Cambridge encyclopedia of evolution* (pp. 241–251). Cambridge, England: Cambridge University Press.

Stroop, J. R. (1935). Studies of interference in serial verbal reactions. *Journal of Experimental Psychology, 18,* 643–662.

Suengas, A. G., & Johnson, M. K. (1988). Qualitative effects of rehearsal on memories for perceived and imagined events. *Journal of Experimental Psychology: General, 117,* 377–389.

Sulin, R. A., & Dooling, D. J. (1974). Intrusion of a thematic idea in retention of prose. *Journal of Experimental Psychology, 103,* 255–262.

Sulloway, F. J. (1979). *Freud: Biologist of the mind.* New York: Basic Books.

Suplee, C. (2000, March 9). *Key brain growth goes on into teens.* Washington Post, pp. A1, A14.

Swisher, C. C. III, Curtis, G. H., Jacob, T., Getty, A. G., Suprijo, A., & Widiasmoro. (1994). Age of the earliest known hominids in Java, Indonesia. *Science, 263,* 1118–1121.

Symons, C. S., & Johnson, B. T. (1997). The self-reference effect in memory: A meta-analysis. *Psychological Bulletin, 121,* 371–394.

Symons, D. (1979). *The evolution of human sexuality.* New York: Oxford University Press.

Symons, D. (1983). Another woman that never evolved. *Quarterly Review of Biology, 57,* 297–300.

Symons, D. (1992). On the use and misuse of Darwinism in the study of human behavior. In J. H. Barkow, L. Cosmides, & J. Tooby (Eds.), *The adapted mind: Evolutionary psychology and the direction of culture* (pp. 137–162). New York: Oxford University Press.

Taft, M. (1991). *Reading and the mental lexicon.* Hillsdale, NJ: Erlbaum.

Tager-Flusberg, H., & Calkins, S. (1990). Does imitation facilitate the acquisition of grammar? Evidence from a study of autistic, Down's syndrome, and normal children. *Journal of Child Language, 17,* 591–606.

Talbott, J. A. (1982). Development. In S. Gilman (Ed.), *Introducing psychoanalytic theory.* New York: Brunner/Mazel.

Tanford, S., Penrod, S., & Collins, R. (1985). Decision making in joined criminal trials: The influence of charge similarity, evidence similarity, and limiting instructions. *Law and Human Behavior, 9,* 319–337.

Tannen, D. (1990). *You just don't understand: Women and men in conversation.* New York: Ballantine.

Tannen, D. (1994). *Talking from 9 to 5: Women and men in the workplace. Language, sex, and power.* New York: Avon Books.

Tannen, D. (1998). *The argument culture: Stopping America's war of words.* New York: Ballantine Books.

Tart, C. (1975). *Learning to use extrasensory perception.* Chicago: University of Chicago Press.

Taylor, H. A., & Tversky, B. (1996). Perspective in spatial descriptions. *Journal of Memory and Language, 35,* 371–391.

Taylor, I., & Taylor, M. M. (1984). *The psychology of reading.* Orlando, FL: Academic Press.

Taylor, S. E. (1982). The availability bias in social perception and interaction. In D. Kahneman, P. Slovic, & A. Tversky (Eds.), *Judgment under uncertainty: Heuristics and biases.* Cambridge: Cambridge University Press.

Tennov, D. (1979). *Love and limerence: The experience of being in love.* New York: Stein and Day.

Terrace, H. (1963a). Discrimination learning with and without errors. *Journal of the Experimental Analysis of Behavior, 6,* 1–27.

Terrace, H. (1963b). Errorless transfer of a discrimination across two continua. *Journal of the Experimental Analysis of Behavior, 6,* 223–232.

Terrace, H. S. (1979a). *Nim: A chimpanzee who learned sign language.* New York: Washington Square Press.

Terrace, H. S. (1979b). How Nim Chimpsky changed my mind. *Psychology Today, 13*(6), 65–76.

Terrace, H. S. (1979c). Is problem-solving language? *Journal of the Experimental Analysis of Behavior, 31,* 161–175.

Terrace, H. S. (1982). Why Koko can't talk. *The Sciences, 22*(9), 8–10.

Terrace, H. S. (1991). Chunking during serial learning by a pigeon: I. Basic evidence. *Journal of Experimental Psychology: Animal Behavior Processes, 17,* 81–91.

Terrace, H. S., Petitto, L. A., Sanders, R. J., & Bever, T. G. (1979). Can an ape create a sentence? *Science, 206,* 891–902.

Terrace, H. S., Petitto, L. A., Sanders, R. J., & Bever, T. G. (1980). On the grammatical capacity of apes. In K. E. Nelson (Ed.), *Children's language* (Vol. 2). New York: Gardner Press.

Tetlow, P. E. (1986). Psychological advice on foreign policy. *American Psychologist, 41,* 557–567.

Teyler, T. J. (1991). Memory: Electrophysiological analogs. In J. L. Martinez & R. P. Kesner, *Learning and memory: A biological view* (2nd ed.). San Diego: Academic Press.

Thiessen, D., Young, R., & Burroughs, R. (1993). Lonely hearts advertisements reflect sexually dimorphic mating strategies. *Ethology and Sociobiology, 14,* 209–229.

Thistlethwaite, D. (1951). A critical review of latent learning and related experiments. *Psychological Bulletin, 48,* 97–129.

Thomas, M. H., & Wang, A. Y. (1996). Learning by the keyword mnemonic: Looking for long-term benefits. *Journal of Experimental Psychology: Applied, 2,* 330–342.

Thompson, C. P. (1982). Memory for unique personal events: The roommate study. *Memory and Cognition, 10,* 324–332.

Thompson, C. P. (1985a). Memory for unique personal events: Some implications of the self-schema. *Human Learning, 4,* 267–280.

Thompson, C. P. (1985b). Memory for unique personal events: Effects of pleasantness, *Motivation and Emotion, 9,* 277–289.

Thompson, C. P., Cowan, T. M., & Frieman, J. (1993). *Memory search by a memorist.* Hillsdale, NJ: Erlbaum.

Thompson, C. P., Skowronski, J. J., & Lee, D. J. (1988). Reconstructing the date of a personal event. In M. M. Gruneberg, P. E. Morris, & R. N. Sykes (Eds.), *Practical aspects of memory: Current research issues. Vol. I. Memory in everyday life* (pp. 241–246). Chichester, England: Wiley.

Thompson, R. F. (1991). Are memory traces localized or distributed? *Neuropsychologia, 29,* 571–582.

Thompson, R. F., & Donegan, N. H. (1986). The search for the engram. In J. L. Martinez & R. P. Kesner (Eds.), *Learning and memory: A psychological view.* Orlando, FL: Academic Press.

Thompson, S. C. (1999). Illusions of control: How we overestimate our personal influence. *Current Directions in Psychological Science, 8,* 187–190.

Thomson, D. M., & Tulving, E. (1970). Associative encoding and retrieval: Weak and strong cues. *Journal of Experimental Psychology, 86,* 255–262.

Thomson, R. H. (1930). An experimental study of memory as influenced by feeling tone. *Journal of Experimental Psychology, 13,* 462–467.

Thorndike, E. L. (1965). *Animal intelligence.* New York: Hafner Press. (Original work published 1911)

Thorndike, E. L. (1968). *Human learning.* New York: Johnson Reprint Corp. (Original work published 1928–1929)

Thorndike, L. (1923–1958). *History of magic and experimental science* (Vols. 1–8). New York: Columbia University Press.

Thorndyke, P. W. (1984). Applications of schema theory in cognitive research. In J. R. Anderson & S. M. Kosslyn (Eds.), *Tutorials in learning and memory* (pp. 167–191). San Francisco: Freeman.

Thorndyke, P. W., & Hayes-Roth, B. (1982). Differences in spatial knowledge acquired from maps and navigation. *Cognitive Psychology, 14,* 560–589.

Thornhill, R., & Thornhill, N. W. (1983). Human rape: An evolutionary analysis. *Ethology and Sociobiology, 4,* 137–173.

Timberlake, W., & Lucas, G. A. (1989). Behavior systems and learning: From misbehavior to general principles. In S. B. Klein & R. R. Mowrer (Eds.), *Contemporary learning theories: Instrumental conditioning theory and the impact of biological constraints on learning* (pp. 237–275). Hillsdale, NJ: Erlbaum.

Tinbergen, N. (1972). The innate disposition to learn. In M. E. P. Seligman & J. L. Hager (Eds.), *Biological boundaries of learning.* New York: Appleton-Century-Crofts. (Original work published 1951)

Tolman, E. C. (1933). Sign-gestalt or conditioned reflex? *Psychological Review, 40,* 391–411.

Tolman, E. C. (1938). The determiners of behavior at a choice point. *Psychological Review, 45,* 1–41.

Tolman, E. C. (1948). Cognitive maps in rats and men. *Psychological Review, 55,* 189–208.

Tolman, E. C. (1959). Principles of purposive behaviorism. In S. Koch (Ed.), *Psychology: A study of a science* (Vol. 2). New York: McGraw-Hill.

Tolman, E. C. (1967). *Purposive behavior in animals and men.* New York: Irvington. (Original work published 1932)

Tolman, E. C., Hall, C. S., & Bretnall, E. P. (1932). A disproof of the law of effect and a substitution of the laws of emphasis, motivation, and disruption. *Journal of Experimental Psychology, 15,* 601–614.

Tolman, E. C., & Honzik, C. H. (1930). "Insight" in rats. *University of California Publications in Psychology, 4,* 215–232.

Tomasello, M. (1999). *The cultural origins of human cognition.* Cambridge, MA: Harvard University Press.

Tomasello, M., Call, J., & Gluckman, A. (1997). Comprehension of novel communicative signs by apes and human children. *Child Development, 68,* 1067–1080.

Tomblin, J. B., & Pandich, J. (1999). Lessons from children with specific language impairment. *Trends in Cognitive Sciences, 3,* 283–285.

Tomie, A., Brooks, W., & Zito, B. (1989). Sign-tracking: The search for reward. In S. B. Klein & R. R. Mowrer (Eds.), *Contemporary learning theories: Pavlovian conditioning and the status of traditional learning theory* (pp. 191–223). Hillsdale, NJ: Erlbaum.

Tooby, J., & Cosmides, L. (1990). The past explains the present: Emotional adaptations and the structure of ancestral environments. *Ethology and Sociobiology, 11,* 375–424.

Toulmin, S. (1971). The concept of "stages" in cognitive development. In T. Mischel, *Cognitive development and epistemology.* New York: Academic Press.

Toulmin, S. (1972). *Human understanding (Vol. 1). The collective use and evolution of concepts.* Princeton, NJ: Princeton University Press.

Treisman, A. M. (1964). Monitoring and storage of irrelevant messages in selective attention. *Journal of Verbal Learning and Verbal Behavior, 3,* 449–459.

Treisman, A. M., & Gelade, G. (1980). A feature-integration theory of attention. *Cognitive Psychology, 12,* 97–136.

Trinkaus, E., & Shipman, P. (1992). *The Neanderthals: Changing the image of mankind.* New York: Knopf.

Trivers, R. L. (1971). *The evolution of reciprocal altruism.* Reprinted in Clutton-Brock & Harvey (1978); Hunt (1980); and Caplan (1980).

Trivers, R. L. (1974). *Parent-offspring conflict.* Reprinted in Clutton-Brock & Harvey (1978); and Hunt (1980).

Trivers, R. L. (1978). *Prenatal investment and sexual selection.* Reprinted in Clutton-Brock & Harvey. (Original work published 1972)

Trivers, R. L. (1983). The evolution of sex. Review of G. Bell, The masterpiece of nature: The evolution and genetics of sexuality. *Quarterly Review of Biology, 58,* 62–67.

Trivers, R. L., & Hare, H. (1976). *Haplodiploidy and the evolution of social insects.* Reprinted in Hunt (1980).

Trivers, R. L., & Willard, D. E. (1973). Natural selection of parental ability to vary the sex ratio of offspring. *Science, 179,* 90–92.

Tulving, E. (1972). Episodic and semantic memory. In E. Tulving & W. Donaldson (Eds.), *Organization and memory.* New York: Academic Press.

Tulving, E. (1983). *Elements of episodic memory.* New York: Oxford University Press.

Tulving, E. (1989). Remembering and knowing the past. *American Scientist, 77,* 361–376.

Tulving, E. (1998). Brain/mind correlates of human memory. In M. Sabourin, F. I. M. Craik, & M. Robert (Eds.), *Advances in psychological science* (Vol. 2, pp. 441–460). Hove, England: Psychology Press.

Tulving, E., & Craik, F. I. M. (Eds.). (2000). *The Oxford handbook of memory.* New York: Oxford University Press.

Tulving, E., Schacter, D. L., & Stark, H. A. (1972). Priming effects in word-fragment completion are independent of recognition memory. *Journal of Experimental Psychology: Learning, Memory, and Cognition, 8,* 336–342.

Tulving, E., & Thomson, D. M. (1973). Encoding specificity and retrieval processes in episodic memory. *Psychological Review, 80,* 352–373.

Turbon, D., Perez-Perez, A., & Stringer, C. B. (1997). A multivariate analysis of Pleistocene homonids: Testing hypotheses of European origins. *Journal of Human Evolution, 32,* 449–468.

Turiel, B. (1973). Adolescent conflict in the development of moral principles. In R. L. Solso (Ed.), *Contemporary issues in cognitive psychology.* Washington, DC: V. H. Winston.

Turkkan, J. S. (1989). Classical conditioning: The new hegemony (with commentary). *Behavioral and Brain Sciences, 12,* 1–50.

Tversky, A., & Kahneman, D. (1973). Availability: A heuristic for judging frequency and probability. *Cognitive Psychology, 5,* 207–232.

Tversky, A., & Kahneman, D. (1974). Judgment under uncertainty: Heuristics and biases. *Science, 185,* 1124–1131.

Tversky, A., & Kahneman, D. (1981). The framing of decisions and the psychology of choice. *Science, 211,* 453–458.

Tversky, A., & Kahneman, D. (1981). *The law of small numbers.* In R. D. Tweney, M. E. Doherty, & C. R. Mynatt (Eds.), *On scientific thinking.* New York: Columbia University Press. (Original work published 1971)

Tweney, R. D., Doherty, M. E., & Mynatt, C. R. (Eds.). (1981). *On scientific thinking.* New York: Columbia University Press.

Ucros, C. G. (1989). Mood state-dependent memory: A meta-analysis. *Cognition and Emotion, 3,* 139–167.

Usher, J. A., & Neisser, U. (1993). Childhood amnesia and the beginnings of memory for early life events. *Journal of Experimental Psychology: General, 122,* 155–165.

Uzgiris, I. C. (1968). Situational generality of conservation. *Child Development, 35,* 831–841. Reprinted in Sigel & Hooper.

Van Den Berghe, P. (1979). *Human family systems: An evolutionary view.* New York: Elsevier.

Van Den Berghe, P. (1983). Human inbreeding avoidance: Culture in nature. *Behavioral and Brain Sciences, 6,* 91–124.

Van Den Berghe, P., & Barash, D. (1977). Inclusive fitness and human family structure. In J. Hunt (Ed.). (1980). *Selected readings in sociobiology.* New York: McGraw-Hill.

van der Lely, H. K. J. (1999). Learning from grammatical SLI. *Trends in Cognitive Sciences, 3,* 286–288.

Vandierendonck, A., & Van Damme, R. (1988). Schema anticipation in recall: Memory process or report strategy? *Psychological Research, 50,* 116–122.

Van Dijk, T. A., & Kintsch, W. (1983). *Strategies of discourse comprehension.* New York: Academic Press.

Van Oostendorp, H., & De Mul, S. (1990). Moses beats Adam: A semantic relatedness effect on a semantic illusion. *Acta Psychologica, 74*(1), 35–46.

Velten, E. (1968). A laboratory task for the induction of mood states. *Behavioral Research in Therapy, 6,* 473–482.

Verfaellle, M., & Cermak, L. S. (1991). Neuropsychological issues in amnesia. In J. L. Martinez & R. P. Kesner (Eds.), *Learning and memory: A biological view* (2nd ed.). San Diego: Academic Press.

Verplanck, W. (1955). The control of the content of conversation: Reinforcement of statements of opinion. *Journal of Abnormal and Social Psychology, 51,* 668–676.

Vesonder, G. T., & Voss, J. F. (1985). On the ability to predict one's own responses while learning. *Journal of Memory and Language, 24,* 363–376.

Vining, D. R. (1986). Social vs. reproductive success: The central theoretical problem of human sociobiology. *Behavioral and Brain Sciences, 9,* 167–211.

Virostek, S., & Cutting, J. E. (1979). Asymmetries for Ameslan handshapes and other forms in signers and nonsigners. *Perception and Psychophysics, 26,* 505–508.

Voeks, V. (1950). Formalization and clarification of a theory of learning. *Journal of Psychology, 30,* 341–363.

Voeks, V. (1954). Acquisition of S-R connections: A test of Hull's and Guthrie's theories. *Journal of Experimental Psychology, 47,* 137–147.

Vokey, J. R., & Read, J. D. (1985). Subliminal messages: Between the devil and the media. *American Psychologist, 40,* 1231–1239.

Von Fersen, L., Wynne, C. D. L., Delius, J. D., & Staddon, J. E. R. (1991). Transitive inference formation in pigeons. *Journal of Experimental Psychology: Animal Behavior Processes, 17,* 334–341.

Vosniadou, S., & Brewer, W. F. (1987). Theories of knowledge restructuring in development. *Review of Educational Research, 57,* 51–67.

Voss, J. F., Greene, T. R., Post, T. A., & Penner, B. C. (1983). Problem solving skill in social sciences. In G. Bower (Ed.), *The psychology of learning and motivation* (Vol. 17). New York: Academic Press.

Voss, J. F., Tyler, S. W., & Yengo, L. A. (1983). Individual differences in the solving of social science problems. In R. F. Dillon & R. R. Schmeck (Eds.), *Individual differences in cognition.* New York: Academic Press.

Waddington, C. H. (1968). The theory of evolution today. In A. Koestler & J. R. Smythies (Eds.), *Beyond reductionism.* New York: Macmillan.

Waddle, D. M. (1994). Matrix correlation tests support a single origin for modern humans. *Nature, 94*(368), 432–434.

Wagenaar, W. A. (1986). A memory: A study of autobiographical memory over six years. *Cognitive Psychology, 18,* 225–252.

Wagner, A. (1978). Expectancies and the priming of STM. In S. Hulse, H. Fowler, & W. Honig (Eds.), *Cognitive processes in animal behavior.* Hillsdale, NJ: Erlbaum.

Wagner, A. R., & Brandon, S. E. (1989). Evolution of a structured connectionist model of Pavlovian conditioning (AESOP). In S. B. Klein & R. R. Mowrer (Eds.), *Contemporary learning theories: Pavlovian conditioning and the status of traditional learning theory* (pp. 149–189). Hillsdale, NJ: Erlbaum.

Wallace, A. R. (1980). On the tendency of species to depart indefinitely from the original type. Reprinted in *A delicate arrangement* by A. C. Brackman, New York: Times Books. (Original work published 1858)

Wallace, I., Klahr, D., & Bluff, K. (1987). A self-modifying production systems model of cognitive development. In D. Klahr, P. Langley, & R. Neches (Eds.), *Production system models of learning and development.* Cambridge, MA: Bradford/MIT Press.

Wallace, R. (1989). Cognitive mapping and the origin of language and mind. *Current Anthropology, 30,* 519–526.

Wallace, W. T. (1994). Memory for music: Effect of melody on recall of text. *Journal of Experimental Psychology: Learning, Memory, and Cognition, 20,* 1471–1485.

Wallace, W. T., & Rubin, D. C. (1991). Characteristics and constraints in ballads and their effect on memory. *Discourse Processes, 14,* 181–202.

Wallsten, T. S., Fillenbaum, S., & Cox, J. A. (1986). Base rate effects on the interpretation of probability and frequency expressions. *Journal of Memory and Language, 25,* 571–587.

Waltz, D., & Feldman, J. A. (1988). *Connectionist models and their implications: Readings from Cognitive Science.* Norwood, NJ: Ablex.

Warren, J. M., & Nonneman, A. J. (1976). The search in cerebral dominance in monkeys. In S. R. Harnad, H. Steklis, & J. Lancaster (Eds.), *Annals of the New York Academy of Sciences* (Vol. 280). New York: New York Academy of Sciences.

Warren, W. H., Nicholas, D. W., & Trabasso, T. (1979). Event chains and inferences in understanding narratives. In R. O. Freedle (Ed.), *New directions in discourse processing.* Norwood, NJ: Ablex.

Washburn, S. L. (1981). Language and the fossil record. *Anthropology UCLA, 7,* 231–238.

Wason, P. C., & Johnson-Laird, P. N. (1972). *Psychology of reasoning.* Cambridge, MA: Harvard University Press.

Wasserman, E., Nelson, K., & Larew, M. (1980). Memory for sequences of stimuli and responses. *Journal of the Experimental Analysis of Behavior, 34,* 49–60.

Water, T. (1989, May). Pawn to King Four. *Discover,* 28–30.

Watson, J. (1930). *Behaviorism.* New York: Norton.

Watson, J., & Rayner, R. (1920). Conditioned emotional reactions. *Journal of Experimental Psychology, 3,* 1–14.

Weaver, C. (1990). Constraining factors in calibration of comprehension. *Journal of Experimental Psychology: Learning, Memory, and Cognition, 16,* 214–222.

Weaver, C. A. (1993). Do you need a "flash" to form a flashbulb memory? *Journal of Experimental Psychology: General, 122,* 39–46.

Weaver, C. A., Mannes, S., & Fletcher, C. R. (Eds.). (1995). *Discourse comprehension: Essays in honor of Walter Kintsch.* Hillsdale, NJ: Erlbaum.

Wegner, D. M. (1994). Ironic processes of mental control. *Psychological Review, 101,* 34–52.

Wegner, D. M., & Pennebaker, J. W. (Eds.). (1993). *Handbook of mental control.* Englewood Cliffs, NJ: Prentice Hall.

Weigel, R. M. (1984). The application of evolutionary models to the study of decisions made by children during object possession conflicts. *Ethology and Sociobiology, 5,* 229–238.

Weinberger, N. M., McGaugh, J. L., & Lynch, G. (Eds.). (1985). *Memory systems of the brain: Animal and human cognitive processes.* New York: Guilford.

Weiner, H. (1970). Instructional control of human operant responding during extinction following fixed-ratio conditioning. *Journal of the Experimental Analysis of Behavior, 13,* 391–394.

Weiner, S. L., & Goodenough, D. R. (1977). A move toward a psychology of conversation. In R. O. Freedle (Eds.), *Discourse production and comprehension.* Norwood, NJ: Ablex.

Weisberg, R. W. (1986). *Creativity: Genius and other myths.* New York: Freeman.

Weldon, M. S., & Roediger, H. L., III. (1987). Altering retrieval demands reverses the picture superiority effect. *Memory and Cognition, 15,* 269–280.

Wellman, H. M., & Gelman, S. A. (1992). Cognitive development: Foundational theories of core domains. *Annual Review of Psychology, 43,* 337–376.

Wells, B. W. P. (1980). *Personality and heredity.* London: Longman.

Wells, G. L. (1993). What do we know about eyewitness identification? *American Psychologist, 48,* 553–571.

Wells, G. L., & Bradfield, A. L. (1999). Measuring the goodness of lineups: Parameter estimation, question effects, and limits to the mock witness paradigm. *Applied Cognitive Psychology, 13,* S27–S39.

Wells, G. L., Lindsay, R. C. L., & Tousignant, J. P. (1980). Effects of expert psychological advice on human performance in judging the validity of eye witness testimony. *Law and Human Behavior, 4,* 275–285.

Wells, G. L., Small, M., Penrod, S., Malpass, R. S., Fulero, S. M., & Brimacombe, C. A. E. (1998). Eyewitness identification procedures: Recommendations for lineups and photospreads. *Law and Human Behavior, 22,* 603–647.

Werner, H. (1957). The concept of development from a comparative and organismic point of view. In D. Harris (Ed.), *The concept of development.* Minneapolis: University of Minnesota Press.

Werner, H. (1978). Developmental processes. In S. S. Barten & M. B. Franklin (Vol. Eds.), *Developmental processes* (2 vols.). New York: International Universities Press.

Wexler, K., & Cullicover, P. W. (1980). *Formal principles of language acquisition.* Cambridge, MA: MIT Press.

Wharton, C. M., & Grafman, J. (1998). Deductive reasoning and the brain. *Trends in Cognitive Sciences, 2,* 54–59.

Wheeler, D. D. (1970). Processes in word recognition. *Cognitive Psychology, 1,* 59–85.

Wheeler, M. A., Stuss, D. T., & Tulving, E. (1997). Toward a theory of episodic memory: The frontal lobes and autonoetic consciousness. *Psychological Bulletin, 121,* 331–354.

White, T. D., Suwa, G., & Asfaw, B. (1994). Australopithecus ramidus, a new species of early hominid from Aramis, Ethiopia. *Nature, 94, 371,* 306–312.

Whiten, A., & Byrne, R. W. (1988). Tactical deception in primates. *Behavioral and Brain Sciences, 11,* 233–244.

Whiting, J., & Child, I. (1953). *Child training and personality.* New Haven: Yale University Press.

Whitney, P. (1998). *The psychology of language.* Boston: Houghton Mifflin.

Wickelgren, W. A. (1965). Size of rehearsal group and short-term memory. *Journal of Experimental Psychology, 68,* 413–419.

Wickens, D. (1938). The transference of conditioned excitation and conditioned inhibition from one muscle group to the antagonistic muscle group. *Journal of Experimental Psychology, 22,* 101–123.

Wickler, W. (1973). *The sexual code.* Garden City, NY: Anchor Books.

Wiegele, T. (Ed.). (1982). *Biology and the social sciences: An emerging revolution.* Boulder, CO: Westview Press.

Wiener, R. L., Habert, K., Shkodriani, G., & Staebler, C. (1991). The social psychology of jury nullification: Predicting when jurors disobey the law. *Journal of Applied Social Psychology, 21,* 1379–1401.

Wierzbicka, A. (1985). Different cultures, different languages, different speech acts. *Journal of Pragmatics, 9,* 145–178.

Wilcoxon, H., Dragoin, E., & Kral, P. (1972). Illness-induced aversion in rats and quail. In M. E. P. Seligman & J. L. Hager (Eds.), *Biological boundaries of learning.* New York: Appleton-Century-Crofts. (Original work published 1971)

Wilford, J. N. (1995, April 25). Human ancestor's earliest tools found in Africa. *New York Times,* C1 & C12.

Williams, G. C. (1980). Kin selection and the paradox of sexuality. In G. W. Barlow & J. Silverberg (Eds.), *Sociobiology: Beyond nature/nurture?* Boulder, CO: Westview Press, (AAAS Selected Symposium 35).

Williams, L. M., & Banyard, V. L. (Eds.). (1998). *Trauma and memory.* Thousand Oaks, CA: Sage.

Wilson, E. O. (1975). *Sociobiology.* Cambridge, MA: Harvard University Press.

Wilson, E. O. (1979). *On human nature.* New York: Bantam Books.

Wilson, E. O. (1980). *Sociobiology: The new synthesis* (abridged ed.). Cambridge, MA: Harvard University Press. (Original work published 1975)

Wilson, J. Q., & Hernnstein, R. J. (1985). *Crime and human nature.* New York: Simon & Schuster.

Wilson, J. R., & Wilson, S. L. R. (1998). *Mass media/mass culture* (4th ed.). New York: McGraw-Hill.

Wilson, M., & Emmorey, K. (1997). A visuospatial "phonological loop" in working memory: Evidence from American Sign Language. *Memory and Cognition, 25,* 313–320.

Wilson, M., & Emmorey, K. (1998). A "word length effect" for sign language: Further evidence for the role of language in structuring working memory. *Memory and Cognition, 26,* 584–590.

Wilson, T. D., Dunn, D. D., Kraft, D., & Lisle, D. J. (1989). Introspection, attitude change, and attitude-behavior consistence: The disruptive effects of explaining why we feel the way we do. In L. Berkowitz (Ed.), *Advances in experimental social psychology* (Vol. 22, pp. 287–343). New York: Academic Press.

Winograd, E., & Killinger, W. A., Jr. (1983). Relating age at encoding childhood to adult recall: Development of flashbulb memories. *Journal of Experimental Psychology: General, 112,* 413–422.

Winograd, E., & Neisser, U. (Eds.). (1992). *Affect and accuracy in recall: Studies of "flashbulb" memories.* New York: Cambridge University Press.

Wiseman, R., & Morris, R. L. (1995). Recalling pseudo-psychic demonstrations. *British Journal of Psychology, 86,* 113–125.

Wispe, L. G., & Thompson, J. N. (Eds.). (1976). The war between the words: Biological vs. social evolution and some related issues. *American Psychologist, 31,* 341–384.

Wittig, A. F., & Williams, G. (1984). *Psychology: An introduction.* New York: McGraw-Hill.

Woike, B., Gershkovich, I., Piorkowski, R., & Polo, M. (1999). The role of motives in the content and structure of autobiographical memory. *Journal of Personality and Social Psychology, 76,* 600–612.

Wolf, T. (1976). A cognitive model of musical sight-reading. *Journal of Psycholinguistic Research, 5,* 143–171.

Wood, B. (1996). Human evolution. *Bioessays, 18,* 945–954.

Wood, B., Martin, L., & Andrews, P. (Eds.). (1986). *Major topics in primate and human evolution.* New York: Cambridge University Press.

Wood, B. A. (1992). Evolution of the australopithecenes. In S. Jones, R. Martin, & D. Pilbeam (Eds.), *The Cambridge encyclopedia of evolution* (pp. 231–240). Cambridge, England: Cambridge University Press.

Woodruff, D. S. (1983). A review of aging and cognitive processes. *Research on Aging, 5,* 139–153.

Woods, B. T. (1980). Observations on the neurological basis for initial language acquisition. In D. Caplan (Ed.), *Biological studies of mental processes.* Cambridge, MA: MIT Press.

Woodworth, R. R., & Schlosberg, H. (1954). *Experimental psychology.* New York: Holt, Rinehart & Winston.

Woody, C. D. (1986). Understanding the cellular basis of memory and learning. *Annual Review of Psychology, 37,* 433–494.

Wrangham, R. W. (1982). Mutualism, kinship, and social evolution. In Kings College Sociobiology Group (Eds.), *Current problems in sociobiology.* Cambridge: Cambridge University Press.

Wren, T. (1982). Social learning theory, self-regulation and morality. *Ethics, 92,* 409–424.

Wright, A. M. (1989). Memory processing by pigeons, monkeys, and people. *The Psychology of Learning and Motivation, 24,* 25–70.

Wright, G., & Bolger, F. (Eds.). (1992). *Expertise and decision support.* New York: Plenum Press.

Wundt, W. (1973). *The language of gestures.* The Hague: Mouton.

Wyer, R. S., Jr. (Ed.). (1995). *Knowledge and memory: The real story.* Hillsdale, NJ: Erlbaum.

Wyer, R. S., Jr., & Radvansky, G. A. (1999). The comprehension and validation of social information. *Psychological Review, 106,* 89–118.

Yalch, R. F. (1991). Memory in a jingle jungle: Music as a mnemonic device in communicating advertising slogans. *Journal of Applied Psychology, 76,* 268–275.

Yates, A. (1980). *Biofeedback and the modification of behavior.* New York: Plenum.

Yates, F. (1966). *The art of memory.* Chicago: University of Chicago Press.

Yeni-Komshian, G. H., Kavanaugh, J. F., & Ferguson, C. A. (Eds.). (1980). *Child phonology, Vol. 2: Perception.* New York: Academic Press.

Young, A. W., Sprengelmeter, R., Philips, M., & Calder, A. R. (1999). Social cognition in the human brain. *Trends in Cognitive Sciences, 3,* 469–479.

Yuille, J. C., & Cutshall, J. L. (1986). A case study of eyewitness memory of a crime. *Journal of Applied Psychology, 71,* 291–301.

Zaragoza, M. S., & Koshmider, J. W. (1989). Misled subjects may know more than their performance implies. *Journal of Experimental Psychology: Learning, Memory, and Cognition, 15,* 246–255.

Zaragoza, M. S., & Lane, S. M. (1994). Source misattributions and the suggestibility of eyewitness memory. *Journal of Experimental Psychology: Learning, Memory, and Cognition, 20,* 934–945.

Zaragoza, M. S., & McCloskey, M. (1989). Misleading postevent information and the memory impairment hypothesis. *Journal of Experimental Psychology: General, 118,* 92–99.

Zaragoza, M. S., McCloskey, M., & Jamis, M. (1987). Misleading postevent information and recall of the original event: Further evidence against the memory impairment hypothesis. *Journal of Experimental Psychology: Learning, Memory, and Cognition, 13,* 36–44.

Zaragoza, M. S., & Mitchell, K. J. (1996). Repeated exposure to suggestion and the creation of false memories. *Psychological Science, 7,* 294–300.

Zentall, T. R., Urcuioli, P. J., Jackson-Smith, P., & Steirn, J. N. (1991). Memory strategies in pigeons. In L. Dachowski & C. F. Flaherty (Eds.), *Current topics in animal learning: Brain, emotion, and cognition.* Hillsdale, NJ: Erlbaum.

Zwaan, R. A. (1999). Situation models: The mental leap into imagined worlds. *Current Directions in Psychological Science, 8,* 15–18.

Zwaan, R. A., & Radvansky, G. A. (1998). Situation models in language comprehension and memory. *Psychological Bulletin, 123,* 162–185.

Index